W9-AIV-462

GRANT MOVES SOUTH

By Bruce Catton

THE WAR LORDS OF WASHINGTON

MR. LINCOLN'S ARMY

GLORY ROAD

A STILLNESS AT APPOMATTOX

THIS HALLOWED GROUND

AMERICA GOES TO WAR

GRANT MOVES SOUTH

In the Library of American Biography

U.S. GRANT AND THE AMERICAN MILITARY TRADITION

For Young People

BANNERS AT SHENANDOAH

Major General U. S. Grant

GRANT
MOVES SOUTH

by

Bruce Catton

WITH MAPS BY
SAMUEL H. BRYANT

LITTLE, BROWN AND COMPANY

Boston   *Toronto*

To Robert Catton

Publisher's Note

In the spring of 1950 we were privileged to publish *Captain Sam Grant*, the first volume of a three-volume biography of U. S. Grant written by the brilliant historian and biographer Lloyd Lewis. Tragically, the author died before publication and the acclaim which was accorded the book.

Mr. Lewis, however, in the course of his extensive research, amassed many notes. Therefore, with Kathryn Lewis, the author's widow, we spent years searching for a writer and historian well qualified to carry on the project. Finally, Mrs. Lewis recommended Bruce Catton, whom she had met in Chicago. She told us he was very interested in Grant and would like to continue the biography. Of course, the choice was ideal, as no living writer re-creates this great period in our history more expertly than Mr. Catton.

Thereafter Mr. Catton spent many months analyzing the Lewis notes, conducting additional research, and writing the narrative of the next volume. Now we are proud to publish *Grant Moves South*, Volume II of this important work.

Contents

Maps

GRANT MOVES SOUTH

"Tomorrow I Move South"

THE GOVERNOR of Illinois remembered that "he was plain, very plain," and men said that he usually went about camp in a short blue coat and an old slouch hat, wearing nothing that indicated his rank, nothing indeed that even proved he was in the Army. The men of his regiment spoke of him as "the quiet man," and afterward they admitted that they never exactly understood him. He was not in the least impressive, but somehow he took charge, subduing the disobedient without, apparently, using anything more than a hard look and a soft word. (It was told that one time he personally jumped a drunken private who had over-awed the guard, knocking the man down and then sitting on him while applying bonds and a gag; but this, if not exactly out of character, was at least out of the ordinary. For the most part men seemed to obey him simply because he expected them to do so.) An admiring chaplain, looking back at the end of the war, said that no stranger, seeing this man in a crowd, would ever be moved to ask who he was.[1]

There was nothing about Ulysses S. Grant that struck the eye; and this puzzled people, after it was all over, because it seemed reasonable that greatness, somewhere along the line, should look like greatness. Grant could never look like anything, and he could never make the things he did look very special; and afterward men could remember nothing more than the fact that when he came around things seemed to happen. The most they could say, usually, was that U. S. Grant had a good deal of common sense.

His experience in the early summer of 1861 with the 21st Illinois Volunteer Infantry was quite typical.

The 21st Illinois might have been set up on purpose to test a colonel. It had been formed, as the Seventh District Regiment, in the spring of 1861, made up of about one thousand farmboys from the prosperous, strongly Republican counties in the east-central part of the state, and it numbered about six hundred when it mustered for three years as the 21st Infantry. Its members were "vigorous, hardy boys," as a veteran remembered, "unused to any kind of restraint, every man much inclined to think and act for himself." There had been a colonel, but he had not lasted. He had been "literally ridiculed and badgered out of camp," and of him nothing remained but a dim memory of drunken, posturing incompetence. In mid-June the Lieutenant Colonel was despondently noting in the regimental order book that the Company Commanders had "entirely lost sight of" the rules of discipline. The Company Commanders had never known anything about these rules to begin with, and so could not have lost sight of them; but fundamentally the officer was correct: discipline did not exist. A detail of eighty men armed with clubs had been set up to patrol the fences and keep the recruits from climbing out after dark to go and see the girls, or seek some other diversion, but it was accomplishing nothing; the 21st, "a little restive under military restraint," was flitting past these guards as if they were not there. The regiment was becoming known as "Governor Yates's Hellions," and no farmer within miles of camp considered his chickens safe.[2]

The Lieutenant Colonel, conscientious John W. S. Alexander, was doing his best. (As a man, his best was good: he would die, a little more than two years later, under the Confederate guns at Chickamauga, a place that no man in Illinois had so much as heard of, in this early summer of 1861.) On June 16, which was the same day Grant wandered in on the regimental Adjutant and remarked that he "guessed he'd take command," Alexander issued a regimental order demanding stricter discipline, following it with other orders setting up a very tight routine. The men were to be turned out each morning at five o'clock, and at 7:30 — breakfast and ordinary camp chores having been disposed of — the day's work would begin, with three-and-one-half unbroken hours of drill by squad, by company and by battalion. At 2:30 in the afternoon the same would begin all over again; two hours of company drill and an hour of battalion drill, with regimental dress parade scheduled for 5:30, retreat at sundown, and tattoo sounded at 9 P.M.[3] All of this made a fairly full day for these farmboys who were so unused to restraint; further-more, it seems to have occurred to no one (except to the privates themselves, possibly) that it gets very warm on the Illinois prairie at midday in summer and that five or six hours of pack drill on the infield of a state fairgrounds may be a little more than any human being can take.

Officially, Grant took command of the 21st Illinois on June 16, at the state fairgrounds at Springfield, but his first formal order to the regiment, announcing his assumption of command, was issued on June 18. In this order Grant briefly declared himself:

> In accepting this command, your Commander will require the cooperation of all the commissioned and noncommissioned officers in instructing the command and in maintaining disci-pline, and hopes to receive also the hearty support of every enlisted man.[4]

The emphasis, then and thereafter, was on the officers, who had much to learn and who now had a colonel who was prepared to teach them. Many years afterward, writing his Memoirs, Grant confessed: "I found it very hard work for a few days to bring all the men into anything like subordination; but the great majority favored discipline, and by the application of a little regular army punishment all were reduced to as good discipline as one could ask." [5]

Actually, it was not quite that simple. Grant had the Regular Army way of doing things at his finger tips, but he was always aware that the volunteer soldier was not the Regular, and he never treated Volunteers as regular recruits were commonly treated. He would impose discipline, to be sure, but it would not be the disci-pline of the Prussian guards, and he would always act as if these raw soldiers were men who could be reasoned with, men with a sense of responsibility that would respond if anyone bothered to appeal to it. (Toward the end of the war fellow officers noticed that one of Grant's favorite remarks was that "the common soldiers are as smart as town folks.") His first major order, dated June 19, is worth a look. It is typically Grant, from its refusal to strike an attitude down to its carelessness about capitalization and spelling, and it reads as follows:

Hereafter no passes to soldiers to be out of Camp after sundown will be valid unless approved by the Commanding Officer of the Regt.

From Reveille until Retreat no passes will be required. In extending this privilege to the men of this command the Col Commanding hopes that this leniency will not be so abused as to make it necessary to retract it. All men when out of Camp should reflect that they are Gentlemen — in camp soldiers; and the Commanding Officer hopes that all of his command will sustain these two characters with fidelity.

Absence from Camp will not be received as a paliation for any absence from duty, on the contrary will be regarded as an aggrivation of the offence and will be punished accordingly.

The guards are required in all cases to arrest all men coming into Camp after retreat unless provided with a pass countersigned by the Regimental Commander.[6]

This was not the way an officer talked to recruits in the Regular Army, but it was laying it on the line, and the 21st began to respond. Long after the war a veteran said that "the effect of that order was wonderful," and went on to say that the camp guards were abolished and that there was no absenteeism thereafter.[7] As a testimonial to a remembered change, this was good enough, but it was an overstatement; no Middle Western troops at any time in the war ever displayed a pious refusal to slip out after tattoo and go a-roving, and that the guard continued to exist is clear from an order Grant himself signed two days later. The guard, indeed, was behaving no better than the guarded, and Grant's handling of the matter is another illustration of the touch he used in dealing with the Volunteers.

"The following," Grant wrote, dating the order June 21, "is published for the benefit of this command":

It is with regret that the commanding officer learns that a number of men composing the Guard of last night deserted their posts and their guard. This is an offense against all military rule and law, which no punishment can be prescribed for by a commanding officer at his discretion but must be the subject for a General Court Martial to decide upon. It cannot, in time [of] peace, be accompanied with a punishment less than the for-

feiture of 10$ from the pay of the soldier, together with cor-
poral punishment such as confinement for thirty days with ball
& chain at hard labor. In time of war the punishment of this is
death.

The Col. Commanding believing that the men of his command, now in confinement for this offence were ignorant of
the magnitude of it, is not disposed to visit them with all the
rigor of the law, provided for such cases, but would admonish
them, and the whole command against a repetition of the offence, as it will not be excused again in this Regt.[8]

Not all of this was just a matter of writing orders in the book.
There were times, in these Middle Western regiments, when the
personal force of the Colonel was all that mattered. He had it, or he
lacked it, and that was that. There was a tough private called "Mexico," rated a dangerous roughneck, who showed up on Grant's second morning with the regiment in what was officially described as a
drunk and disorderly condition, and Grant sent him to the guardhouse.

Mexico glared at the 135-pound Colonel, and growled: "For every
minute I stand here I'll have an ounce of your blood."

Grant told the guards to gag Mexico, and pursued his other duties.
Some hours later Grant came back, walked up to Mexico, undid the
gag with his own hands, and turned the man loose. Mexico took no
ounce of anybody's blood, but went quietly about his business; and
it was recorded that "all question of Grant's power to command both
himself and his men" vanished from that moment.[9]

Grant cut down the excessive amount of drill which had been prescribed by Lieutenant Colonel Alexander, stipulating that there
would be squad drill between six and seven every morning, with
company drill running from 10 to 11 A.M. and from five to six in
the evening. The wording of the order hints at previous deficiencies
in the work:

Company commanders will have their companies divided into
convenient squads and appoint suitable persons to drill them.
The officers of Companies are expected to be present and give
their personal supervision to these drills, and see that all their
men not on duty are present.

Indeed, it was the company officer rather than the enlisted man at whom Grant seemed to be aiming in his first steps toward proper military training. A week after he had taken command he was warning that at least one commissioned officer must be present at all roll calls, this officer to be responsible for making sure that all absentees not properly excused were reported. He went on to spell out the responsibilities of an officer:

> All officers not reported sick, or otherwise excused by competent authority, will attend all Drills and Parades. They will give strict attention that the men of their respective commands receive proper instruction. Officers wishing to be absent from Camp at night are required to get the countersign from the Comdg. Officer of the Camp. No one having the countersign will be permitted to communicate it to another for the purpose of enabling him to pass the Guard.[10]

In centering his attention on the company officers, Grant was approaching the great, enduring weakness of the Volunteer Armies of the Civil War. The volunteer system made it almost certain that neither platoon nor company officers would know anything about their jobs during the precise moment when such ignorance would have the worst effect — the first, formative period in training camp. Company officers were either self-appointed, or elected by vote of the recruits, and in neither case was proper qualification for the job a factor. In time many of these became good officers — like the enlisted men, they were as smart as townfolks, and most of them were almost painfully conscientious — but in the beginning, almost without exception, they knew nothing about what they were supposed to do, and, by the time they had learned, a regiment almost inevitably developed certain defects that could never be cured. Any colonel who hoped to train and discipline his men had to start with the company officers, simply because it was their deficiencies that made discipline so lax and training so imperfect; for although the volunteer system drew into the armies the most superb human material ever put into uniform, it guaranteed that this material would not be used to the best advantage. Taking command of a regiment in which riotous indiscipline had become standard, Grant would have made scant progress if he had simply invoked the brutal code of punishment which the Articles of War made available to him. He had to begin with the subalterns, to whom nobody had ever spelled out the duties and responsibilities that go with shoulder straps. Lieutenant Colonel Alexander had complained, only a few days earlier, that these officers had lost sight of the rules of discipline; Grant now was undertaking to show the officers just what these rules were.

Before June ended the 21st Illinois was formally mustered into the Federal service for three years. Almost immediately after this happened, the regiment got marching orders: Move to Quincy, Illinois, on the Mississippi River, preparatory to going into Missouri. Training camp days were over: to go into Missouri was to get into the war.

From Springfield to Quincy is about one hundred miles, and the original plan was to send the 21st there by rail. Instead the regiment went on foot, by Grant's decision. All the surviving accounts agree that the march did the regiment a great deal of good, and the only question seems to be why Grant made the decision. Governor Richard Yates remembered that he did it "for the sake of discipline"; a regimental veteran believed that it was "because we needed the drill"; and Grant himself wrote that he thought making the march on foot would be good preparation for the regiment's later experiences. A variant is that the authorities had provided railroad cars, and that a long string of these were backed into a siding at Camp Yates for the 21st to board. The cars were freight cars, they were very dirty, and the soldiers made outcry when they saw them. As free-born Americans they would ride in no filthy freight cars: if the government wanted to send them off by rail let the government bring passenger cars. Grant heard them out and remarked that if they did not want to ride in freight cars they did not have to: they could walk, and they would do so at once, with a few wagons to carry tents and other equipment.[11]

However all of this may have been, the 21st did make the hike on foot, and it learned a bit more about soldiering as it hiked. It left Springfield on July 3, 1861, and Grant as a troop commander was beginning his first cross-country movement. (He was exactly two years away from Vicksburg, and the talk with John Pemberton under a tree on a sun-baked hill; a world of marching would lie be-

tween this day and that one.) As they trudged along, the soldiers reflected that this colonel of theirs meant business, and when he was
near they had a way of breaking into a then popular gospel tune,
"Jordan Am a Hard Road to Travel," with much rolling of eyes at
the figure of the Colonel. Grant paid no attention, except that once
he was heard to say to the Adjutant: "Yes, Jordan may be a hard
road to travel. So is the road to discipline. Both have to be traveled."[12]

As it marched — toward Jordan, toward discipline, or only toward Missouri — the 21st learned to be prompt. When camp was
made for the night, there would be orders specifying the hour at
which the march would be resumed in the morning. It became clear
that a company or an individual not ready to move at that moment
would be left behind, without breakfast or even, on occasion, without pants; the military machine moved, and it was up to the soldier
to move with it. Grant continued to keep an eye on the officers.
Three days from Springfield he distributed a broadside:

> The Col. Commanding regrets that it becomes his duty to
> notice the fact, that some of the Officers of this command fell
> out of ranks yesterday, in passing through Jacksonville without
> authority to do so; and this whilst the rank & file were guarded
> most strictly. This being the first offence is overlooked, but in
> future no excuse will be received.[13]

The emphasis again was on the officers, but the colonel was not
above paying direct attention to the sins of the enlisted man. During a brief halt in one small town, many of the regiment visited the
local grocery and filled their canteens and themselves with whisky,
and when the march was resumed there was much unsteadiness and
wabbling in the ranks. Grant noticed, said nothing, called a halt after a time, and then quietly passed down the ranks on foot, making
personal inspection of every man's canteen. If it held whisky, the
fluid was immediately poured on the ground and the man was ordered to march for the rest of the day tethered behind a baggage
wagon.[14]

Somewhere near Naples, on the Illinois River, the march was
halted; orders now were to wait for steamboat transportation to St.
Louis. Grant put the regiment into camp, ordered daily squad, com-

pany and battalion drill, and called on all ranks "to give the strictest attention to all their military duties"; a matter of importance, he wrote, "when it is reflected upon how soon we may be called into actual service, and how important it is that everyone should know his duty." On this same day, July 9, Grant reflected on what had been done thus far and wrote an odd, man-to-man sort of order to the men of his regiment:

> The Col. Commanding this Regiment deems it his duty at this period of the march to return his thanks to the Officers and men composing the command on their general Obedience and Military disipline. Having for a period of years been accostomed to strict military duties and disipline he deems it not inapropriate at this time to make a most favorable comparison of this command with that of veteran troops in point of soldierly bearing, general good order, and cheerful execution of commands; making the real necessity of a Guard partially unnecessary. Although discipline has been generaly enforced, yet, the same strictness would have been unnecessary, but for a few unruly men, who have caused the Regt to be more strictly under regulation for their misdemeaniors. The Col. Comdg. trusts that a repetition of disorder on their part may never occur again; but that all may prove themselves Soldiers, fit for duty without any unnecessary means being pursued by him to make them such.[15]

The regiment waited for several days, at Naples; the expected steamboat had run on a sand bar somewhere, and by the time the vessel was clear orders were changed again. Boarding the cars at last — Grant noted with pride that it took just forty minutes to get men and baggage all ready to go — the 21st moved on to Quincy by rail, and if the men had complaint about the condition of the cars they kept quiet about it. . . . At Quincy, Grant parted with his eleven-year-old son, Frederick Dent Grant, who had been with him ever since Grant became a colonel. Mrs. Grant and the children would be campaigners, in this war, and Grant would have some or all of them with him whenever he could. He sent Fred home now, supposing that Julia would be worried if he took the lad on into Missouri — "We may have some fighting to do, and he is too young to have the exposure of a camp life," he explained — and so he put the lad on a boat, to go home to Galena by way of Dubuque. Julia Grant, as it turned out, was quite unworried; she wrote to Grant urging him to keep Fred with him, remarking that Alexander the Great was not older when he accompanied Philip of Macedon. (As a soldier's wife, she knew her military history.) The letter reached Grant too late, and Fred went home on schedule, and Mrs. Grant recalled years later Grant was rather amused by her letter.[16]

By mid-July the 21st Illinois had crossed the Mississippi and was in the war zone, if not actually in the war itself, helping to hold northeastern Missouri, especially its bridges and railroads, against Confederate molestation.

It seemed, just at first, that this assignment might bring excitement and danger. A Confederate guerilla leader named Tom Harris had been making a pest of himself in the area assigned to the 21st, and Grant got orders one day to take his regiment and break up this band of marauders. Harris and his men were supposed to be encamped in a creek bottom twenty-five miles away; Grant led his regiment out boldly enough, but along the way he discovered that command carries its own responsibilities and inflicts its own loneliness and fear. He had been in action often enough in the Mexican War, and had stood up under its dangers as well as a professional officer need do; but now, taking an infantry regiment cross-country toward an engagement which — even though it would be no more than a skirmish — would be his men's first experience of combat, Grant found himself afraid. He wanted desperately, he said, to be back in Illinois; with wry humor, he wrote long afterward that he "lacked the moral courage" even to call a halt so that he could think things over. He just kept on going, dreading the moment when he would bring his regiment over the crest of a hill and find the enemy in view.

The result was sheer anticlimax. Tom Harris had fled, and when the 21st reached the camp site in the creek bottom it was clear that the Southern raiders had cleared out hours before. And it dawned on Grant that Harris had been at least as afraid of him as he himself had been of Harris; an aspect of the situation which, he confessed, had not occurred to him before. He never forgot it, and through all the rest of the war he never again felt the cold, unreasoned sort of panic that beset him on this country road in Missouri. He always remembered that the other fellow had just as much reason to be afraid as he had.[17]

The 21st put in the rest of the month in and about a town called Mexico not far from Hannibal, in the angle between the Mississippi and the Missouri rivers. There was nothing in particular to do. Union troops here just now were actually a sort of glorified constabulary, keeping the peace and defending the loyalists as much by their presence as by any actual feats of arms, and during the next few weeks Grant had time to carry forward the "disipline" of his recruits and to reflect on the lights and shadows of a civil war. On July 15 he ordered Private Hiram Reynolds, of Company K, dismissed from the service for unspecified misdeeds. (Private Reynolds apparently was a hard case. He re-enlisted in an Indiana regiment, and in the fall of 1863 he was hanged, at Nashville, Tennessee, for killing a fellow soldier.) Before the month ended Grant had broken Corporal George A. Stevens of Company A to private "for intemperance and common street drunkenness." He had also discovered that soldiers who passed a place where liquor was sold on the line of march had a way of smuggling whisky into camp simply by filling their unloaded muskets with it, plugging the muzzles with pieces of corncob; a trick which a vigilant colonel could detect by ordering a piece cocked and then watching the whisky trickle out at the nipple.[18]

While he worked with his own men, Grant studied his fellow citizens in Missouri and tried to understand just how men's attitudes could veer and change under the pressures of a civil war. Writing to his father on August 3, Grant confessed that he found in Missouri a state of mind that he had not expected to meet anywhere in the South. Most of the people in northeast Missouri, he believed, were secessionists, as Northerners would use the word; but they were reluctant secessionists, men who "would make almost any sacrifice" to have the Union restored, and what made them secessionists seemed to be largely a conviction that the Union had in fact broken apart and that they could do nothing but go along with the Confederacy, which was bound to win anyway. (It also stuck in men's minds, said Grant, that the North's real reason for making war was to end slavery by force.)

On this frame of mind, he wrote, nothing that he could say made

any impression; "they don't believe a word I don't think." Whenever Federal troops moved from here to there, word went out that
pro-Southern state troops had waylaid them and had all but annihilated them, even though there had in actual fact been no fighting at
all; "My regt. has been reported cut to pieces once that I know of,
and I don't know but oftener, whilst a gun has not been fired at us."
These reports, he added "give confirmation to the conviction already entertained that one Southron is equal to five Northerners."[19]

Sometimes it seemed that no one quite understood this new war.
Grant was sitting in front of his headquarters tent one day when
two soldiers came up proudly leading a citizen and two horses.
They had "found this feller and brought him up," they explained, in
the course of a little expedition they had dreamed up for themselves;
out of patriotic zeal, "we thought we'd go out and look for some
'seceshers.'" Without removing his pipe from his mouth, Grant
asked them who had given them permission to leave camp. When
they confessed that they had permission from no one, he ordered
them tied to a tree for a few hours in punishment; then he questioned the captive, found the man perfectly willing to take the oath
of allegiance to the Federal government, and turned him loose.[20]

It was hard for the soldiers to realize that campaigning in a slave
state, where a large part of the inhabitants were pro-Confederate,
did not mean that every soldier could do as he liked with the persons and goods of the inhabitants. Wild stories had gone through the
countryside, in advance of the Unionists' arrival, about the pillage,
rapine and arson which were to be expected of the "Lincoln hire-
lings" and the "lop-eared Dutch." (Many stout loyalist regiments
had been recruited from the German population in St. Louis, and to
the credulous imaginations of the strictly nativist countryfolk these
"Dutch" soldiers were capable of any crime.) It happened, too, that
undisciplined soldiers in the raw Northern regiments that were entering the state often behaved so as to confirm the inhabitants' fears.

If enlisted men found it hard to understand just how the Federal
Army ought to behave in a slave state, the inhabitants also had
trouble. While Grant was at Mexico a fugitive slave came to camp,
out of breath and nervous, the exhaustion of flight still on him, demanding, "Whar's de cunnel?" The chaplain took him to Grant,
heard the fugitive beg for help, heard Grant say: "Can't help you,

sir. We're not here to look after Negroes, but after Rebels. You
must take care of yourself." Disheartened, the slave turned to leave.
The chaplain followed him, gave him fifty cents and a sack of hardtack and cold meat, told him the quickest way to the Mississippi
River, and advised him to get over into Illinois as fast as he could.
Then, having guided the man past the Union sentries, the chaplain
returned to regimental headquarters — just in time to see the slave's
indignant owner show up, demanding justice and the detention of
the fugitive. To the slaveowner Grant made the same reply he had
made to the slave: the Army was here to tend to Rebels, not to Negroes, and it had nothing to do either with freeing or with catching
the slave. . . . Neither citizens, soldiers nor black folk themselves
seemed to grasp the idea that the Army might possibly act to suppress secession without doing anything at all about slavery. As if by
instinct, everyone was assuming that this war somehow carried with
it the fate of slavery, no matter what men in Washington and Richmond might say about war aims.[21]

Grant himself saw it that way, as a matter of fact, and his point
of view had nothing to do with any feeling about slavery's rightness
or wrongness. As long ago as April, when the North was making its
first enthusiastic response to President Lincoln's call for troops to
put down rebellion, Grant spoke his mind in a letter to his father-in-
law, the devoutly Southern-minded Colonel Frederick Dent. To
Colonel Dent, Grant wrote about the Northern insistence that the
Union be preserved, adding:

> In all this I cannot but see the doom of slavery. The North
> does not want nor would they want to interfere with the insti-
> tution. They refuse for all time to give it protection unless the
> South shall return soon to their allegiance.

Slavery, as Grant saw it, could never survive of itself; in one way
or another it needed the active support of the central government,
and with that support gone — as it was gone, now that war had
come — slavery was a cut flower in a vase. Reasoning thus, he believed that the war would be very short. After "a few decisive victories in some of the southern ports" the principal Rebels would flee
the country, the price of slaves would fall so far that nobody would
want to own slaves any more, and the Federal Armies might find

themselves called on to go South in order to suppress a Negro insurrection. . . . It was easy to foresee a quick and simple end to all of the trouble, in that time before the real fighting had begun, when human affairs might still be expected to go by logic.[22]

August had come. The 21st Illinois had been in Missouri for about three weeks, and Grant had been Colonel for a little more than one month; and now, suddenly, the picture changed, and Grant was Colonel of the 21st no longer. From Washington came news that Abraham Lincoln had granted him the star of a brigadier. Now he was Brigadier General Grant.

That this happened was owing to nothing much more complicated than the innocent way in which the Republican administration was combining military business with political pleasure in this summer of 1861. A large Volunteer Army was being created, and it must have a good many generals: a handful of major generals and more than thirty brigadiers. The appointments would be made by the President and would be confirmed (or rejected) by Congress, which was now in session; and it seemed quite logical for the President to parcel out these generalships by states, just as if postmasterships or customs house appointments were to be distributed among the deserving. By this dispensation, Illinois was entitled to name four brigadiers, and the Illinois Congressional Delegation met to agree on a slate. In this delegation was the impressive Congressman from Grant's home town of Galena, the Honorable Elihu B. Washburne.

Washburne drew a good deal of water in Republican politics, both in his own state and in Washington. An admiring newspaper correspondent described him as "broad-shouldered, good-bellied, large and yet thin," a transplanted Yankee who looked like a State of Maine man, which he was, but who somehow contrived also to be wholly typical of Illinois; "the model is Yankee, but the cargo is Western." Washburne was beginning to be on Grant's side. The two were not yet intimate; indeed, they had not met before April, when the loyal folk of Galena began to hold mass meetings to let Washington and the new Confederacy know where they stood on the matter of secession; but Grant had made something of an impression on Washburne, and in any case a Galena Congressman who could bring home a brigadier's commission for a Galena resident would be bound to do so. Thus, because he had good support, Grant was one of four Illinoisans named for generalships. The others were Stephen A. Hurlbut, Benjamin M. Prentiss, and John A. McClernand; Grant was the one West Pointer in the lot. Of thirty-four new brigadiers named early in August, Grant ranked seventeenth, almost exactly in the middle; the same position, oddly enough, that he had occupied in his graduating class at West Point.[23]

The chaplain of the 21st Illinois stumbled across the news of Grant's promotion one day early in August, as he sat in the shade reading his copy of the *Daily Missouri Democrat*. He hurried over to the Colonel's tent, found Grant, and announced:

"Colonel, I have some news here that will interest you."

Grant, naturally, asked what he was talking about, and the chaplain told him. Then Grant sat down beside him, and said about all that he ever had to say about his appointment as General:

"Well, sir, I had no suspicion of it. It never came from any request of mine. That's some of Washburne's work. I knew Washburne in Galena. He was a strong Republican and I was a Democrat, and I thought from that that he never liked me very well. Hence we never had more than a business or street acquaintance. But when the war broke out I found that he had induced Governor Yates to appoint me mustering officer of the Illinois Volunteers, and after that had something to do in having me commissioned Colonel of the 21st Regiment, and I suppose this is more of his work."

Whereupon, General Grant got up, tugged his black felt hat down over his eyes, ran his hands through his whiskers — which, at that time, were quite long and luxuriant — and strolled off. To his father he wrote that he had not asked anyone to intercede for him. He had seen so much pulling and hauling for favors during his tour of duty at Springfield, he said, that he determined then never to ask for anything for himself. He permitted himself a moment of quiet pride in what he had done with the 21st Illinois: "I took it in a very disorganized, demoralized and insubordinate condition and have worked it up to a reputation equal to the best, and I believe with the good will of all the officers and men." Some rumor of his coming appointment had reached camp, he said (as a matter of fact, he had had some foreknowledge of it himself) and the regimental officers came to him and asked to be attached to his command. To easy-talking Jesse Grant, the new General added the warning: "This I don't want you to read to others for I very much dislike speaking of myself." [24]

He disliked speaking of himself; yet it seems clear that he recognized this landmark in his life and that it moved him. The last promotion he had received from his government had come in September of 1853, when he had been made Captain in the 4th Infantry. Formal papers of commission did not reach him until April, 1854; he had acknowledged them formally, in a letter to the Adjutant General, and at the same time he had written his own resignation from the Army, asking that it be made effective as of July 31, 1854. Seven years had passed, and now — having resigned in apparent disgrace — he was a brigadier general, entitled to wear a star on each shoulder, with a coat that had two parallel rows of brass buttons down the front, the buttons marching two by two in the manner prescribed by the regulations. He was entitled to wear this uniform, but he did not yet own it, and he hoped to return to Galena and buy one. To Julia he wrote that "I want very much to get back into civilization for a few days to get some things that I very much need. I am without a sword, sash or uniform of every description according to my grade and see no chance of getting them" — but he could not get back to Galena just now, and he did an odd thing: he discarded his colonel's uniform, even though he had not yet paid off the debt he had run up in order to buy it, and now he wore whatever clothing came to hand, with no insignia of rank.[25] Did the promotion mark such a turning point in his own inner life that he would wear no uniform at all until he could don the one that belonged with the new commission?

He never explained, and it does not matter much in any case. Within a very few days he was ordered to take his regiment to Ironton, seventy miles south of St. Louis, and to assume command of the district of Southeast Missouri. When the orders came he moved fast; got the regiment packed up and put on a train, took it to St. Louis, marched it through the city in the dead of night to take another train, and on August 8, 24 hours after receiving his orders, he was marching into Ironton. Here he got official notification that he was really a brigadier, with a commission dating from May 17. On August 9 the Senate confirmed the appointment. Meanwhile, Grant was taking hold of his new command.

His orders were to entrench his position well so that it could be held against any Rebel force that might appear, and to "scour the country" in his front and keep headquarters, in St. Louis, informed of what the enemy was up to. Somewhere off to the south — not too far away, according to current rumor — were some thousands of Confederates under the highly respected General William J. Hardee, famous in the Old Army as the author of a standard book on tactics. (Grant had never studied this book; he bought a copy and started to "cram" shortly after he became a colonel, then concluded that the text was "nothing more than common sense and the progress of the age" applied to the tactics West Point had taught when Grant was a cadet. After that he got along fine, without cramming.) Now Hardee was in his front; and lurking somewhere in the background there was a semi-irregular force of Confederates led by a picturesque, flamboyant and highly energetic officer, General Jeff Thompson. Essentially, Grant's job was what it had been before — to head a constabulary detachment that would protect loyal citizens, guard railroads and bridges, and secure the state against Confederate incursions.[26]

Ironton, with the adjacent settlement of Pilot Knob, was at the end of a railway line that came wandering south from St. Louis to the fringe of the Ozarks. It had been held, previously, by a detachment composed largely of ninety-day men (whose terms were now expiring) commanded by Col. B. Gratz Brown. The detachment lacked training and discipline and was badly demoralized — Grant wrote later that "a squadron of cavalry could have ridden into the valley and captured the entire force" — and worried Colonel Brown was very glad to see a professional soldier come in to take responsibility. Grant relieved Colonel Brown and his ninety-day men and sent them home; he now had four infantry regiments, including the familiar 21st, and on the day after he had taken command he wrote his first report on the situation.

From what he was able to learn, through spies "and loyally disposed citizens," he said, he believed that there was no Rebel force within thirty miles that had the least intention of attacking his own post. This struck him as very fortunate, for the Ironton contingent was not ready for a fight: "Many of the officers seem to have so little command over their men, and military duty seems to be done so loosely, that I fear at present our resistance would be in inverse ratio to the number of troops to resist with." However, he was not discouraged; as coolly as if the problem of bringing raw troops into efficient order were very simple, he promised that inside of two days "I expect to have a very different state of affairs and to improve it continuously." He did have certain needs, to be sure. Artillery and cavalry were lacking, as a result of which Confederate detachments were pillaging Union men within ten miles of camp, and the quartermaster service at Ironton was seriously deficient. There were too few teams, and many of the horses that were available lacked shoes and forage; but Grant had known the livery-and-haulage business intimately ever since his boyhood in Ohio, and "I have taken steps to remedy these latter defects." [27]

His troops were starting to make an impression. Easygoing residents of the neighborhood were amazed at the speed with which the Illinois boys, Jacks-of-all-trades and handy with tools, built their camp, made tent floors, and installed bunks, tables, writing desks and seats; "If these men stay here six months," it was said, "they could build a big city." Colored folk, watching big-eyed as the Westerners drilled and maneuvered, looked with awe at the bayonets on the muskets and were heard to mutter: "Gorry mighty! Dey got lightnin' rods on der guns. No sesesh can stand dat." And the soldiers themselves realized that there had been a big change. One man wrote afterward: "The loud laugh and bluster, the swagger of loafing squads, were hushed. Instead you heard the bugle calls, the roll of drums, the sharp commands of officers to the drilling and marching and wheeling battalions." To this man, Grant seemed to be "a man who felt that his country was beleaguered and its defenders were at the point of surrender, and it was necessary to fly to their instant relief." [28]

Grant was beginning to enjoy life. To Julia he wrote that the Ironton-Pilot Knob area "is one of the most delightful places I have ever been in," with beautiful scenery all about, plenty of good water available, and enough altitude to insure cool weather. To his superiors in St. Louis he mentioned these advantages, suggesting that

Ironton would be a healthy place to send one or two new regiments for training and discipline: "This would enable me to use the troops now here for scouting parties without calling upon the new volunteers for such service that would take them from their drill." Without cavalry, he found it impossible to keep the Confederate irregulars out of the neighborhood, but he could at least stop communication with the enemy from within his own lines. Grant was interfering with the U. S. mails, holding up letters to certain suspected persons and cutting off all letters addressed to points within the Confederate lines. This worried him a little, because "I am entirely without orders for my guidance in matters like the above" and he did not know what, if anything, Congress had enacted that might bear on the case.[29]

His need for horses he met by direct action, sending a contingent to nearby Potosi with orders to press into service as many teams as were needed, the impressment to be performed upon citizens of a secessionist tinge, "who will be pointed out by Union men of character." Provisions might also be obtained in the same way, and the officer in charge was reminded that "you have my private instructions how to conduct this pressing business so as to make it as little offensive as possible." Grant apparently had qualms about impressment, and to some regiments he prohibited it altogether. A few days after this, sending the 6th Missouri out on a scouting tour, he warned the Colonel: "Permit no pressing of horses or other property by your command. The policy meets with my decided disapproval and must be suppressed." It is possible that what worried him was the fact that this regiment came from Missouri; too many recruits in this state's service had scores of their own to settle with secessionists.

By August 13 Grant was able to report to the Assistant Adjutant General, at department headquarters in St. Louis, that some three thousand Confederates were about to move on the railroad which he was guarding, and that Hardee with five thousand more seemed to be moving directly on Ironton. He added: "I express you the facts and leave it to the general commanding whether in his judgment more troops should not be sent." Grant did not think very many more were needed; if a battery and one regiment of infantry could be sent, "I would feel that this point would be secure beyond any present contingency." [30] This unemotional report seems to have been misinterpreted in department offices at St. Louis, and the next day a telegram went from St. Louis to President Lincoln — "General Grant, commanding at Ironton, attacked yesterday by a force reported at 13,000. Railroad seized by enemy at Big River Bridge, on this side of Ironton" — as a result of which more troops and material were urgently needed in Missouri. To General Prentiss, commanding at Cairo, went orders to go at once to Ironton with four regiments and assume command. Grant, meanwhile, reported that the invading Rebels had withdrawn, started out after them with two regiments to get a clearer line on the situation, and dryly wrote to Julia:

"No doubt you will be quite astonished, after what the papers have said about the precarious position my brigade has been in for the last few days, to learn that tomorrow I move South." [31]

CHAPTER TWO

Assignment in Missouri

TO MOVE south was Grant's compelling motive, then and thereafter. He comes down in history as a stolid, stay-put sort of character, but actually he was nothing of the sort. He had the soldier's impulse to strike rather than to receive a blow; in addition (and it is a point that is easily overlooked), he was a restless person who disliked nothing more than to be obliged to remain in one place. Even as a child, driving livery rigs for his father, he had traveled about southern Ohio as extensively, probably, as any adult of his time. Then, in the Army, he had gone to Mexico City, and later he had gone to Panama and thence to California and the Northwest Coast; and many years after this, with official life left far behind him, he would go all the way around the world, for no reason except that he liked to keep moving. Now he was in southeastern Missouri, helping to hold a state of tangled emotions and divided loyalties, and while he drilled and prepared his troops he wanted to get on with the war. He believed that he could hold his position against anything Hardee might do, and his outposts tangled now and then with informal bands of roving Confederates, but there was no real action. Grant wanted to get going.

When he told Julia "tomorrow I move South," he was thinking beyond the immediate defensive problem. Ironton dangled at the terminus of the St. Louis and Iron Mountain railroad, and both town and railroad must be held if St. Louis were to be secured against Confederate attack; but what seems to have been in Grant's mind just now was nothing less than the reclamation of all of southeast Missouri. He sent his old 21st Illinois south toward Greenville, thirty-five miles away, where Hardee and five thousand Confederates were believed to be posted. He also ordered the 24th Illinois to march twenty miles east to Fredericktown, notifying a third regiment, the 17th Illinois, to be ready at any moment to follow the 24th.

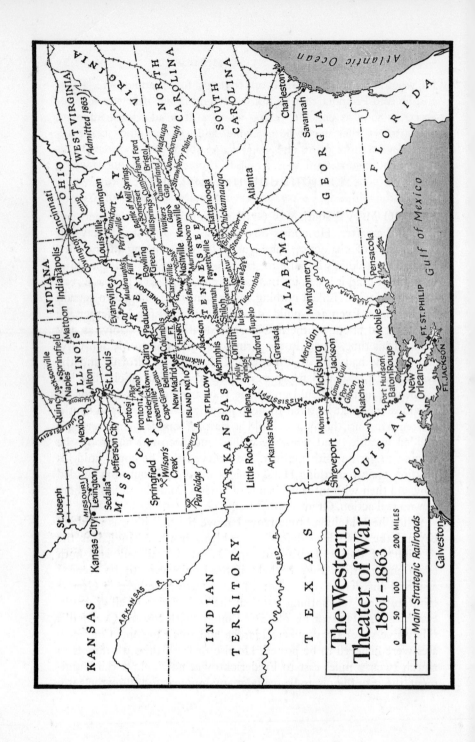

The Western Theater of War 1861–1863

He would bring all of these troops together for an attack on Hardee, and he told Frémont that he himself would move after the advance forces as soon as possible, taking along a little additional infantry, any artillery that might be available, and (if he could scrape together some more teams and wagons) a supply of provisions.[1] This movement, if successful, would help to protect Ironton, but it would also make possible an advance all the way to Cape Girardeau, which lay on the Mississippi sixty or seventy miles southeast of Ironton and a few miles upstream from Cairo.

Cairo nestled in muddy discomfort behind high levees at the point where the Ohio River joined the Mississippi. It was all-important, a gateway to and from practically everywhere, north, south east and west. It was already held by Federal troops, but Grant believed that the Federals could do more than just hold it. With Missouri safely in hand they could use it as a point of departure and carry aggressive war deep into the South. This idea was not possessed by Grant alone; Cairo's strategic importance was obvious, and Frémont had lost no time in putting reinforcements there. Its potential value as a base for an invasion of the South had occurred to Mr. Lincoln himself, and it was noted in a memorandum which the President had, at that moment, in a file in his desk;[2] but Grant's plan represented thinking which went a little beyond anything that might be expected to come from an obscure brigadier occupying a minor outpost in Missouri.

A glimpse of what was working in Grant's mind — a cloudy glimpse, put out of focus by later knowledge, but nevertheless something of genuine insight — comes out in a tale told by John Emerson, a citizen of Ironton whom Grant had known in St. Louis before the war, the man who owned the land on which Grant's headquarters tents were pitched. Emerson, who was presently to become a colonel, said that he called on Grant the day Grant reached Ironton; he wanted to show the new General some sketches of projected defense works. Grant examined them but did not seem much interested; he just put them in his pocket with a noncommittal "They look well. We shall see." When Emerson went around the next day to ask about the project, and said that refugees were coming in with alarming stories about Hardee's advance, Grant heard him out and said no more than that Hardee might need defensive works before any Unionists at Ironton needed them.

Still later, Emerson found Grant sitting at a table under a tree near headquarters, studying a map. To Emerson, Grant complained that the map was defective; could not a better one be found, one that would show all of southeastern Missouri, southern Illinois and western Kentucky? Emerson got one, and saw how Grant traced the line of the great river with a stubby forefinger, muttering that the Rebels must be driven out of the river valley. On another day, Emerson saw that Grant had made elaborate red-pencil marks on this new map, with lines running down the Mississippi and with other lines going south by the Cumberland and Tennessee rivers; and when Emerson remarked (in his capacity as innocent civilian) that this looked like business, Grant seemed flustered, said "possibilities — mere possibilities," and walked over to a little spring that went bubbling down a pebbly channel a few yards away. Emerson said that Grant drank from the spring, then looked down at the water and remarked that the little brook flowed into the Mississippi and that the Mississippi flowed into the sea, and that both brook and river must flow with complete freedom; and Emerson reported, too, that Grant said something to the effect that it was easy to make long-range plans when one was not in full control, but that the first thing to do was to drive the enemy out of southeastern Missouri. Then, he said, Grant broke off in his musing, stalked back to the table, pocketed his map and some sheets of paper on which he had been writing, and went away. A headquarters officer told Emerson that the General "spends every minute of his spare time going over maps and making plans." [3]

On the same day that Grant ordered the Illinois regiments to move east and south, he got reinforcements — two new regiments, as Western as regiments could be, 7th Iowa and 1st Nebraska. Colonel John Thayer of the Nebraska regiment called at headquarters and found Grant sitting at a table writing; he remembered that Grant wore a suit of Army blue, not unlike the suits worn many years later by graybeard members of the Grand Army of the Republic, with no shoulder straps or any other signs of rank. Grant was puffing at a clay pipe, and he asked Thayer to wait a few minutes while he finished what he was writing. Thayer was willing; an amateur soldier himself, he wanted a chance to size up this West Pointer who was to be his commander.

Studying him, Thayer thought that he saw something: firmness, self-reliance, quiet determination. (So, at any rate, it seemed to him, years afterward, when he sat down to write about it, writing in the knowledge that the unassuming little Brigadier he met in Missouri was to become the most famous soldier in the world.) When Grant at last pushed his papers aside and began to talk, Thayer liked what he heard. Grant asked a few questions about Thayer's regiment, its strength and its state of training, and he expressed satisfaction that the frontier territory of Nebraska had been able to send a thousand men to the front; he went on to say that this was a nice contrast to the course taken by older, more populous states in the South, which (as Grant saw it) had brought on a fratricidal war. "When I read of officers of the army and navy," said Grant, "educated by the government at West Point and Annapolis, and under a solemn vow to be defenders of the flag against all foes whatsoever, domestic or foreign, throwing up their commissions, going South and taking service under the banner of treason, it fills me with indignation." Later that day Grant came around to the Nebraskans' camp, riding the clay-bank horse which was to become such a familiar sight in the Army, and Thayer felt that the men were impressed, as he had been, by "his calm, composed manner, united with a soldierly bearing but entirely free from any pride or hauteur of command." [4]

More reinforcements were coming, but their arrival took Grant down a peg. Two days after the Nebraska and Iowa regiments had appeared, four more regiments came into camp, led by Brigadier General Benjamin M. Prentiss, another Illinoisan. What disconcerted Grant, who was just ready to leave Ironton and join his advanced forces, was the fact that Prentiss carried orders from Major General John C. Frémont, commanding the Western Department, putting Prentiss in command in southeastern Missouri. This relieved Grant from his command and left him without an assignment, although Frémont apparently had not quite intended it that way; he seems to have got mixed up by the intricacies of Army regulations governing seniority.

Prentiss, an amateur soldier, had been made a brigadier earlier in the year, at a time when Grant was still a civilian doing clerical work for the governor of Illinois at Springfield. When Grant became a general his commission was dated back to May 17, the same date that Prentiss's commission bore; headquarters seems to have assumed that because Prentiss had actually held the commission before Grant did he was therefore Grant's senior, and what it overlooked was the provision that when two officers whose commissions bore identical dates got together, seniority would depend on prior rank in the Army. Prentiss had fought in the Mexican War as a captain of Volunteers and then had returned to civilian life, but Grant had been a captain of Regulars; hence, by law, Grant ranked Prentiss.

What gave this mixup its cutting edge was the fact that as Army law then stood it was impossible to require an officer to serve under an officer whom he ranked. When Prentiss got off the evening train from St. Louis and displayed his orders, then, his arrival automatically put Grant out of a job. There was nothing Grant could do but report at St. Louis and see if there was another assignment for him. He turned everything over to Prentiss, explained the moves that were afoot, and then ordered a locomotive and a daycoach prepared to take him to the city.[5]

As Thayer remembered it, Grant took it rather hard. He made no official protests, and he said nothing to Prentiss about his disappointment, but he was "thoroughly cast down and disappointed" — even more so, it seemed to Thayer, than the facts really warranted. Either then or later, Thayer believed that this was not because he was mortified by being superseded but because the shift canceled Grant's own plan for occupying all of the southeastern part of the state and getting over to Cairo where he could prepare for a drive down the Mississippi and up the Tennessee.

On the night of August 18 — it was nearly midnight, and both Grant and the night were very gloomy — Grant took off for St. Louis. He asked Thayer to go along with him, and the two men had a silent ride in a nearly empty daycoach that bumped along for hours, reaching St. Louis after daybreak. In St. Louis the two men had breakfast at the Planter's House, after which Grant went to headquarters to report. He returned to the hotel later in the morning, and it seemed to Thayer that Grant was even more dejected than before. Frémont, Grant said, had told him nothing about the reason for the transfer; he had simply ordered him to go to Jefferson City, the capital of the state, on the Missouri River one hundred miles northwest of Ironton, and take charge of the Army Post which had been established at that strategic spot. Affairs at Jefferson City seemed to be in a mess, and the place looked like a side pocket, far removed from the theater of aggressive action. The prospect was not attractive.

"I do not want to go to Jefferson City," said Grant. "I do not want to go any further into Missouri. But of course I must obey orders." [6]

What happened next is hazy. Thayer said that Grant wanted very much to return to Galena for five days, which is indisputable; Grant had just written to Julia saying that he would like to get home briefly, if only to buy a proper general's outfit. But Thayer went on to say that Grant went back to Frémont, got five days leave, went to Galena, and there saw Congressman Washburne, to whom he explained his plan for an invasion of the south by way of Cairo. Washburne, said Thayer, took or sent the plan to President Lincoln, and it was discussed in cabinet meeting, as a result of which General Frémont was presently told to put Grant back in command in southeast Missouri; and all that happened thereafter in the Mississippi valley, Thayer believed, grew out of the plans Grant had made at Ironton, and out of his hurried trip to Galena in mid-August.[7]

It did not actually happen that way. Grant did apply for leave, but his application was refused. He was in St. Louis at least through the morning of August 19, and he was in Jefferson City on August 21, which leaves too little time for a visit with Washburne in Galena. In addition, the move would have been most unlike Grant. He was then a brigadier of no more than two weeks' standing, and the gap between his position and the White House was altogether too broad to be leaped by a quiet little man who had complete indoctrination about the virtue of following the proper channels of the Army hierarchy. Also, when the invasion of the South was actually under way, the following spring, and the great victory at Fort Donelson had been won, Grant wrote to Washburne saying that it was idle to give credit for the move up the Tennessee to any specific general; the strategic soundness of the plan was obvious, he said — "General

Halleck no doubt thought of this route long ago, and I am shure I did."

Yet Emerson wrote, long after the war, that some written exposition of Grant's plan had reached Washburne that summer, and he said that Washburne himself, when he asked him about it many years later, remembered presenting the plan to Mr. Lincoln; and Emerson added that Montgomery Blair, a member of Lincoln's cabinet in 1861, recalled having discussed the project at the White House. Whether all of this reflects a dim recollection of something that actually happened — a recollection dredged up after a quarter of a century, by men who would then be entirely ready to concede that General Grant had always been a military genius — is a mildly tantalizing question. The one certainty seems to be that Grant obeyed orders without making complaint to anyone except Thayer, and two days later he had assumed his new command at Jefferson City.[8]

Jefferson City was no prize package. There were plenty of Union troops there, but no Regular Army man was likely to think of them as soldiers. Many ardent patriots had obtained authority — dubious authority, for the most part, which had no particular standing in law — to recruit volunteer organizations for the Union, and had set up shop all over town, some to raise full regiments, some to raise battalions, others simply to raise companies — in tents and in huts and elsewhere, with rudely lettered signs overhead inviting all comers to join up at once. Some of these recruiters were offering six-month terms of enlistment, others were offering terms of one year; and Grant learned, when he looked into things, that most of their recruits were coming from the legal, three-year regiments which had been stationed in the place. On top of this the city was filled with fugitives — Missouri farmers and their families, who had fled from the western part of the state because it seemed likely that the Confederates would rule there. These folk came in, usually, with a team of horses hauling a farm wagon loaded with household goods; they had no means of support and no place to go, and they had come to Jefferson City not because they especially wanted to be there but simply because they wanted to get away from the Confederacy's armed forces, which had even less discipline than the Union troops Grant had been looking at and which were harrying

Union sympathizers out of every neighborhood which Federal troops did not occupy. All in all, Jefferson City was a complete madhouse.[9]

Things in Missouri were not going well for the Union just then.

Nathaniel Lyon, the red-haired, fiery little Regular Army Captain who had been made Brigadier General that spring and who had beaten down Confederate sympathizers in St. Louis by displaying a driving eagerness to strike the first blow, had moved beyond the Missouri River early that summer with an army that had neither adequate training nor proper equipment — an army, indeed, which had nothing but passionate leadership — and Lyon had planned to make Missouri secure for the Union by destroying a Confederate army which was operating in the southwestern part of the state. This army was in even worse condition, as far as training and equipment went, than the one Lyon commanded. Its armament was composed mostly of shotguns and flintlock muskets, it had a chief of ordnance who confessed that he had never set eyes on a cartridge and knew not the difference between a howitzer and a siege gun, it had no tents and no uniforms and certain of its units were officered by lawyers who knew nothing about military matters and who had their sergeants assemble their companies, when the morning's routine was about to start, by standing on the parade ground and bellowing: "Oh yes! Oh yes! All you who belong to Captain Brown's company fall in here." Commander of this motley array was a native son, General Sterling Price, a devoted man in whom Missourians had large confidence. Price's Missouri state troops were joined with Gen. Ben McCulloch's Confederates from Arkansas and some Arkansas state troops, and in one way or another Price got his outfit up to a site known as Wilson's Creek, twenty miles or so from Springfield, in the southwest corner of the state, and there on August 10 the Confederates, under the over-all command of McCulloch, had collided with Lyon's Unionists and had given them a beating. Lyon himself was killed, the remnants of his little army went streaming north and east, Price moved on to lay siege to the important Missouri River town of Lexington (which, some time later, he captured, along with its Federal garrison) and it looked as if the resurgent Confederacy might overrun the entire state.[10]

Federal affairs in Missouri were in the control — nominally, at

least — of a very famous man, an ardent patriot and a dedicated believer in freedom who was, unfortunately, neither a good executive
nor a competent soldier: Major General John C. Frémont, famous
as the Pathfinder who had helped to open the West, a man with immense political influence. He had been the first Republican candidate for President, in 1856, and he might easily be the party's next
candidate also, and he desperately wanted to rid the state of armed
Confederates but had only a foggy notion of the way to go about it.

Frémont lived in state, in St. Louis, surrounded by a colorful set
of bodyguards, glittering aides-de-camp (many of whom, as it turned
out, had been extra-legally commissioned and very few of whom
knew anything at all about the way Western troops should be officered and led) and a pervasive odor of inefficiency and corruption.
Frémont had been sent to Missouri with orders which, in effect, told
him to raise and equip an army, get the Rebels out of the state, and
win the Mississippi Valley for the Union; orders which he was most
anxious to execute, for he was a highminded man, of unquestioned
loyalty to the Union, but for whose execution he was not getting
much help from Washington. Missouri was a long way from the
Potomac, the administration's attention was largely centered on matters in Virginia, and Frémont had to play it by ear under circumstances which would have taxed even the ablest of administrators.
Professional soldiers and revolutionists-in-exile from Europe had
flocked to his standard, for he was one of the few Americans famous
in Europe when the war broke out, and Frémont had taken many
of these into the service, at fairly exalted rank, without regard for
their own capacity or for his own administrative powers. Under his
authority there had been placed orders for vast quantities of tents,
mules, uniforms, rifles, wagons and all the other things an army
needs. The pressure of time lay on the man, purchases had to be
made in an immense hurry and on credit, and many of these orders
had been placed without regard for the Army's legal forms; numerous canny traders, scenting a wide-open opportunity, had sold poor
goods at inflated prices. Things at St. Louis, in short, were in a mess,
and there would presently be a scandal about it; and through all of
it Frémont was doing his best to get more troops, hold such strategic spots as Cairo, and arrange things so that he could ultimately
take the offensive.[11]

With all of his deficiencies, Frémont had aggressive instincts. He had seen the need to possess southeast Missouri just as Grant had seen it, and even while he was desperately trying to retrieve the loss occasioned at Wilson's Creek he was dreaming exalted dreams about an offensive campaign that would cut deeply into the South, capture Memphis and Little Rock, and land Union armies in New Orleans itself. When he sent Prentiss to Ironton he seems to have had in mind the same sort of campaign Grant had been thinking of, and he ordered Grant to Jefferson City, apparently, on the theory that it would be well to have a trained soldier in this place which, in the latter part of August, was practically an outpost on the edge of Confederate territory.

Frémont was a little too aggressive for his own good, or for the good of the cause; too aggressive, or too poorly balanced, or perhaps both. He had carried the banner for the Republican party when the fight against slavery (to those who had chiefly supported him) was a high and a holy thing. Also, he commanded Union troops in a state where half of the people seemed to be dedicated to the Union and the other half were equally devoted to secession; a state, moreover, whose people had a way of burning the barns and assaulting the persons of those who disagreed with them on vital issues like slavery and disunion. Under the circumstances it was quite impossible for Frémont to consider this situation without feeling that a belief in slavery went arm-in-arm with a belief in secession, and that abolitionist principles were the stamp of a true Union man. He was very shortly to issue a proclamation which would free the slaves of all persons who were giving aid and comfort to the rebellion — a proclamation which Mr. Lincoln would make haste to disown and to rescind. Eternally beyond Frémont's comprehension would be the down-to-business attitude which led Grant to deny help both to fugitive slave and bereaved slave-pursuer. Frémont could not see that there were many slaveowners, in Missouri and all through the border states, who would willingly fight and die for the Union. Grant himself had owned a slave, his wife had owned several, his father-in-law had owned many; he hated neither the institution nor those who believed in it — and Frémont hated both.

Yet Frémont, in a way, was making progress. He was bombarding Washington with appeals for help, and the Midwestern governors were under orders to send troops to him as fast as the new regiments could be raised and mustered into Federal service. These regiments were coming in now, almost totally lacking in training, frequently lacking in arms and equipment, and Frémont's own supply arrangements, hastily improvised at St. Louis, were exceedingly inefficient, but a reserve of potential strength was being built up. Arriving at Jefferson City, Grant found himself obliged to deal with one of the centers of this reserve.

Grant found plenty of recruits, but little more. Clothing, tents, blankets, and weapons were wanting; the stock of artillery consisted of four 6-pounders (without any gunners) and one 24-pounder, too cumbersome for field service, and there was no artillery ammunition whatever. In the whole camp the supply of rifle ammunition amounted to no more than ten rounds to a man. Neither the post commissary officer nor the post quartermaster seemed to be present, and there were no rations to issue. Grant reported that "the whole country is in a state of ferment," with Rebel marauders driving Union men from their homes and appropriating their property, and he urged that companies of mounted home guards be recruited to deal with this menace.[12]

On August 23, Grant notified St. Louis: "I am not fortifying here at all. With the picket guard and other duty coming upon the men of this command there is but little time left for drilling. Drill and discipline are more necessary for the men than fortifications." Also, Grant confessed, there was no engineer officer to lay out fortifications and he himself had forgotten what little West Point had taught him about this art; and "I have no desire to gain a 'Pillow notoriety' for a branch of service that I have forgotten all about." The reference was to the Confederacy's General Gideon Pillow, who commanded something styled vaguely an "army of liberation" in the extreme southeast corner of the state; an inept, quarrelsome soldier who, in the Mexican War, had won derision by building a fortified line with the ditch on the wrong side. Grant somehow remembered Pillow with extreme distaste, and Pillow was the one Confederate officer for whom Grant consistently and openly expressed personal contempt.

Grant went to work. He tried to find some way to make use of the home guard outfits which, he had hoped, might be useful in suppressing Confederate guerilla bands, but the task was beyond him: "I have not been able to make head or tail about them, notwithstanding all my efforts." He could only find out that there were a lot of them, some mounted and some not, some with weapons and some un-armed; where they came from or how they could be used seemed insoluble problems. As an old hand with teams and wagons, Grant was disturbed by the quality of the transportation equipment that was being sent to him. The harness with which he was supplied was so weak that it broke whenever a strain was put on it, and trace chains were so light and brittle as to be worthless. He had spies out, and they were keeping him posted about Confederate movements; he was arresting Confederate spies; by orders from Department headquarters, he would send out an expedition to the towns of Lex-ington, Bonneville and Chillicothe, to seize the assets of local banks — assets which otherwise would disappear into Confederate hands. He was solving his transport problem by hiring refugees and their teams; also, he suggested to St. Louis that if adequate forces were stationed at Jefferson City it would be possible to give proper pro-tection to Unionists in all counties bordering on the Missouri.[13]

And so on; military drudgery, necessary but uninspiring, a come-down after the growing challenge of the situation around Ironton. To his father, Grant wrote that any attack on his post was highly unlikely; there seemed to be no organized body of Confederate troops anywhere near him, and although there were plenty of Southern encampments in nearby counties "the object seems to be to gather supplies, horses, transportation, etc., for a Fall & Winter campaign." The effect of this was to inflict misery on the inhabi-tants:

The Country West of here will be left in a starving condition for next Winter. Families are being driven away in great num-bers for their Union sentiments, leaving behind farms, crops, stock and all. A sad state of affairs must exist under the most favorable circumstances that can take place. There will be no money in the Country and the entire crop will be carried off to-gether with all stock of any value. . . . [Meanwhile, Grant himself was so busy that Jesse Grant must not expect to hear from him very often.] I am interrupted so often while writing that my letters must necessaryly be very meager and disconnected. . . . I think it is doubtful whether I will go home at all.[14]

The Jefferson City experience, as things worked out, lasted no more than one week. One morning, while Grant was sitting in his office, there appeared before him an undersized, pale, bearded, intense little colonel with the mildly improbable name (for a Federal officer) of Jefferson C. Davis: an old-time Regular from Indiana who had served in the Mexican War as an enlisted man, had won a commission at the war's end and had stuck to soldiering ever since. He had been in the Fort Sumter garrison, and on being exchanged after the surrender of that post he had gone to Indiana to help organize Volunteers; now, as Colonel of the 22nd Indiana infantry, he was showing up with orders relieving Grant of his command and instructing him to report at St. Louis at once for an important new assignment.

Grant spent an hour explaining the Jefferson City situation to Davis and turning the details of command over to him; then he boarded a train and left for St. Louis, to find out what new twist the military fates had applied to his career.

As to precisely what happened next there is some dispute. Emerson always believed that Grant was recalled because of representations Congressman Washburne had made at the White House, and long after the war he quoted from a letter he said Washburne had written to him, in which Washburne expressed the opinion that Secretary of War Simon Cameron had told Frémont to put Grant in a more important assignment. According to Frémont himself (also writing long after the war), the idea had been Frémont's own, and it had grown logically out of headquarters' belated realization that Grant ranked Prentiss, who had replaced him at Ironton. In any case, Grant was about to get the opportunity he had been hoping for, and it was coming to him because of a threatening new situation that was developing along the Mississippi.[15]

In this war that was tearing the country apart, Kentucky was still clinging to an improbable and tenuous neutrality. In no single state was popular sentiment so sharply divided as in Kentucky. Wholly symptomatic was the fact that of the two sons of the aging Senator

John J. Crittenden (who had worked so hard and so fruitlessly in the months just before Lincoln's inauguration to find some formula by which the argument between North and South might be harmonized) one was to be a general in the Confederate Army and the other a general in the Union Army. Governor Beriah Magoffin was strong for the Confederacy, and he had indignantly rejected Lincoln's call for troops that spring; but the state legislature was predominantly pro-Union, and with government thus divided the state was trying desperately to stay out of the war entirely. So far this effort had worked. Neither Washington nor Richmond had yet been willing to do anything that might disturb the delicate balance of forces in Kentucky, and for the time being Kentucky's neutrality was respected. Neither North nor South had troops in the state, although each side was eagerly collecting recruits there, inviting them to training camps outside of the state.

The one certainty was that Kentucky's neutrality was not likely to last very much longer. In the nature of things it could not last. If North and South were to make war in the West they would be bound to cross Kentucky sooner or later, and the only real question was who would make the first move. According to information which was reaching Frémont, the Confederacy was just about to make such a move; it was reported that General Leonidas Polk, the Episcopal bishop who had been trained at West Point and who, as an ardent Southern patriot and an intimate friend of President Jefferson Davis, had been given an important command in the Southern Army, was about to march up from western Tennessee and fortify the high bluffs at Columbus, Kentucky, the northern terminus of the Mobile and Ohio railway: a spot, which, if held, would keep Yankee gunboats and transports from descending the Mississippi River. Frémont had the notion that if this was in the cards it would be well for the Union to strike the first blow. Hence his summons to Grant.

According to Major Justus McKinstry, an Old Army Regular, who was Frémont's chief quartermaster and provost marshal, Frémont called a staff meeting to choose a commander for southeast Missouri. McKinstry got a hurry-up call to come and join in the conference. He drove to headquarters, parked his horse and buggy at the curb, and stalked through the basement hallway on his way to

Frémont's office. In the dim light of this hall he found a man sitting on a bench, an old friend from prewar Regular Army days whom he had last known as Captain Grant. Turning to him, McKinstry asked him: "Sam, what are you doing here?"

Grant told him that he had been ordered to report to Frémont and that he had been sitting in the hall for hours, trying without success to gain access to the General. (Surrounded by an officious staff, Frémont was notoriously hard to see.) McKinstry promised to let Frémont know Grant was present, and hurried up to the meeting. When he entered Frémont's room he was told that the officers present were trying to find the right man to take responsibility for meeting the anticipated Confederate thrust along the river. To this McKinstry replied that he knew just the man: Sam Grant, who was now waiting downstairs and whose gallantry and soldierly abilities he himself had observed during the Mexican War. This started an argument: the first of many similar arguments that were to be carried on during the Civil War, arguments growing out of the humiliation and failure which lay upon Grant's military record on the West Coast.

Grant, several officers objected, would not do. He drank too much and was unfit for high command. . . .

A man can get typed, justly or unjustly, and the shadow of the past, the dark stain of officers'-mess gossip, deposited over the years, can stay with him. Few of these men had actually known Sam Grant but in one way or another they had all heard of him: he was the officer who had had to resign his commission out West, six or seven years ago, because he could not leave the bottle alone. Of the exact circumstances surrounding the resignation, of the loneliness and frustration that may have led man and bottle together, of the years of struggle that came thereafter, of the man's present determination to live down the past and make fullest use of his talents, of the hard core under the surface that would make his name terrible in war — of all these things the trim men in unweathered headquarters blue knew nothing. They knew only of the gossip, of the ineradicable stain, and that was enough.

It would be enough for many others, then and thereafter, for the dark film left by gossip can never be entirely scrubbed away. In an army famous for the hard drinking done by men in shoulder straps, this was a handicap Grant would always have to carry. He began as a colonel and he became a lieutenant general; by maneuvering and hard fighting he captured three rival armies entire; in four years he won command of all the troops in the United States, making himself the completely trusted instrument of the canniest judge of men who ever sat in the White House, enforcing unconditional surrender on dedicated men who had sworn to die rather than to submit; but the stain deposited by the gossip is still there, and men still cock their eyes and leer knowingly when Grant's name is mentioned: *He drank.* For men who do not know him, that has been enough.

It was not enough for McKinstry, apparently, and he began to argue. Grant (he said) might indeed like whisky, but in a responsible command he would leave the stuff alone. The country desperately needed a fighter, Grant had a proven combat record as a fighter, the meeting had convened to find a fighter — why look further? The discussion, as McKinstry remembered it, grew heated. Some of those present urged that Grant be forgotten and that the choice light on General Franz Sigel, the German émigré who had a powerful hold on the loyalties of Missouri's numerous German recruits but who unfortunately displayed no knack for training raw soldiers or for leading them effectively in combat. In the end Frémont decided on Grant, and at last McKinstry went downstairs, dug Grant out of the obscurity of the basement hallway, and told him to come on up and join the meeting.[16]

In the main, Frémont corroborated this story. Some time after the war he told a correspondent how McKinstry had brought Grant to his office. Grant was wearing civilian clothing, but Frémont was strongly impressed by the man's soldierly qualities — "self-poise, modesty, decision, attention to details." He admitted that before Grant appeared a number of officers had strongly opposed his appointment, "for reasons that were well known," but he insisted that Grant's bearing when he came in was enough to counteract the influence of what they had said. In any case, the appointment was made, and Frémont and Grant discussed the situation for two or three hours. "I told him," Frémont said, "that the purpose was to make Cairo, and Paducah opposite, the base of important operations against Memphis and Nashville" — operations (he said) which had already been outlined in a letter Frémont had sent to the President. Frémont added that he told Grant he had better wear the proper uniform. Grant explained that he had given away his colonel's uniform and that he had not yet been able to get a brigadier's outfit; as soon as it arrived he would put it on.[17]

It may have been a little simpler than this, and indeed it is possible to suspect that the new assignment came simply because headquarters had at last realized that Grant outranked Prentiss. Grant's formal orders from Frémont are dated August 28, which is also the date on which Frémont wrote to Prentiss, explaining that Grant was taking command in southeastern Missouri. In this letter Frémont told Prentiss: "When you were ordered to go to Ironton and take the place of General Grant, who was transferred to Jefferson City, it was under the impression that his appointment was of a later date than your own. By the official list published it appears, however, that he is your senior in rank. He will, therefore, upon effecting a conjunction with your troops, take command of the whole expedition." It may be worth note, too, that on August 27 — at which time Grant was still in Jefferson City — Frémont was writing to Davis, whom he addressed as "commanding, Jefferson City," complaining that headquarters was not hearing from Davis; if the date on this letter is correct, headquarters had obviously decided on the shift before Grant ever got to St. Louis.[18]

At any rate, Grant's formal orders spelled out the movement that was contemplated. The idea back of the movement was good enough, but the information on which the idea had been built was defective; nothing concrete came of it, at the time, but in an indirect way it had a good deal to do with the way the war was going to go in the Mississippi valley.

Confederates in unknown but ominous strength (it was thought) were active in southeastern Missouri. Grant was to go to Cape Girardeau, on the Mississippi, and take command of a small Federal garrison there. The Rebels were believed to be in force at a town called Benton, fifteen or twenty miles south of Cape Girardeau and ten miles inland from the river, and there was also thought to be a Rebel detachment at the town of Commerce, which was on the river fifteen miles below Cape Girardeau. Prentiss was marching overland from Ironton with the troops Grant had once commanded, and

Col. W. H. L. Wallace, commanding at Bird's Point across the river from Cairo, was under orders to march sixteen miles west to Charleston; meanwhile, other forces from Cairo were making a reconnaissance down the river to Belmont, a steamboat landing on the Missouri side of the Mississippi, across from the commanding bluffs at Columbus, Kentucky. It would be Grant's function to tie all of these movements into one, to clear southeastern Missouri of Confederate troops, and then to move into Kentucky and occupy the potential stronghold at Columbus, as quickly as he could. Meanwhile, he was to see to it that proper defensive works were completed at Cairo, at Bird's Point, at Cape Girardeau and at Ironton.[19]

There were two noteworthy points about this order. The first was that the notion of a Confederate menace was a delusion. The Confederate General Hardee, who had been threatening Ironton from the south ten days previously, had withdrawn into Arkansas, and was now getting his slender forces over toward the Mississippi. General Pillow, who built ditches on the wrong side of earthworks, and who was displaying an unfailing ability to irritate his superiors with long, querulous, argumentative letters, had had plans for a movement toward Cape Girardeau and the area west of it, but these plans had been canceled and he was now grumpily digging in at New Madrid, in the southeastern corner of the state, on the big river. The only Confederate forces in the area where Union troops were concentrating were the informal Missouri state guards, who were sadly under strength but who enjoyed the leadership of the effervescent Jeff Thompson. These soldiers — perhaps three thousand in all, some of them mounted and some going about on foot — held forth on the fringe of a vast swamp, a score or more miles west of the Mississippi river. They were not doing very much harm to anyone, but Thompson, a minor genius, was able to make Union commanders think that they were very numerous and very aggressive, and the rumors that reached headquarters at St. Louis multiplied his raiding parties by ten.[20]

In addition, the order spelled out a radical change in Federal policy; a change which may or may not have struck Grant at the time. Kentucky was still neutral, and the decision to violate or to continue to respect the state's neutrality was technically one for Washington to make. Actually, however, the decision would inevitably be made by some commander in the field. Frémont had already warned Washington that operations along the Mississippi would eventually involve the Kentucky shore; now he was ordering Grant to move into Kentucky and take possession of the bluffs at Columbus; and the effect which this might have on public sentiment in that all-important border state was wholly problematical.

Some inkling of what Frémont had in mind seems to have reached the Confederate commander in the West, the former Bishop Polk. As well as anyone, Polk knew that the party which first put up fortifications at Columbus would be winning an important trick, and on September 1 he was writing to Governor Beriah Magoffin of Kentucky asking to be informed about the plans of "the Southern party in Kentucky" and saying frankly that he believed he "should be ahead of the enemy in occupying Columbus and Paducah." Polk believed that the Yankees were about to move, and when the Federal reconnaissance party from Cairo went down to Belmont and began planting cannon there, Polk concluded that it was time for him to do something. The egregious Pillow had been begging for orders to go to Columbus anyway, and the Federal move seems to have pulled the trigger.[21]

For the moment it did no more than that. Grant went to Cape Girardeau. Prentiss showed up on September 1, and Grant ordered him to move south, inland, to a town called Sikeston, which was roughly due west of Belmont; he himself would go to Bird's Point and lead a column inland from there; the detachment at Belmont would dig in and stay where it was; southeastern Missouri would be cleared of Jeff Thompson's raiders, and then the way would be open for the occupation of Columbus. But Prentiss threw a wrench into the scheme by refusing to admit that Grant ranked him. (Apparently the man had not yet received Frémont's explanatory order.) Prentiss hemmed and hawed and finally refused to obey Grant's order, and, when Grant insisted, Prentiss asked for a leave of absence (which was refused), tendered his resignation (which was also refused), and then put himself under arrest and took off for St. Louis, leaving Grant to put the senior Colonel in command of his column. All of this caused an abrupt halt in the projected operation. Prentiss's column remained in camp, pending the appointment of a new commander; and simultaneously the Federal naval commander on the

Mississippi sent in discouraging reports about Rebel naval strength on the river, which led Grant to recall the troops who had been occupying Belmont. So the big drive to push the Rebels out of southeastern Missouri came to a halt — and General Polk, believing correctly that Frémont planned to seize Columbus, ordered General Pillow to move into the place ahead of the Federals. Pillow marched in on September 4, Kentucky's neutrality was violated once and for all, President Jefferson Davis noted sorrowfully that he regretted the necessity for the move but approved the move itself, the necessity apparently existing; and Jeff Thompson got a copy of Frémont's proclamation, which along with its attempt to free the slaves of Confederate supporters proclaimed martial law in Missouri and threatened the death penalty to all guerillas found north of a line drawn across central Missouri.[22]

To this, General Thompson made quick reply. In a proclamation aimed at *To all whom it may concern*, Thompson (who had a perky sense of humor, as well as a stout sentiment of Southern patriotism) announced:

Therefore know ye that I, M. Jeff Thompson, brigadier general of the First Military District of Missouri, having not only the military authority of a brigadier general but certain police powers granted by Acting Governor Thomas C. Reynolds, and confirmed afterwards by Governor Jackson, do most solemly promise that for every member of the Missouri State Guard, or soldier of our allies the armies of the Confederate States, who shall be put to death in pursuance of this said order of General Frémont, I will *"hang, draw* and quarter" a minion of said Abraham Lincoln. . . . I intend to exceed General Frémont in his excesses.[23]

CHAPTER THREE

Time of Preparation

NOBODY cared very much for Cairo. General Frémont had called it "the most unhealthy post within my command," and he said that fever and dysentery were everywhere. There were mosquitoes — "awful mosquitoes," one recruit remembered — and there was a plague of rats. A sergeant of the guard used to amuse himself at night by seeing how many rats he could kill with his saber as he walked from one sentry post to another, and a doctor recalled that when a railroad train came clanking in along the tracks on top of the levee, vast numbers of rats would be crushed by the wheels. There was a great deal of malaria and an almost complete lack of hospital facilities; the Army's supply depots were deficient, and the soldiers felt that the town's inhabitants were unsympathetic and untrustworthy. A newspaper correspondent remarked that "if the Angel Gabriel should alight there the natives would steal his trumpet before he could blow it." [1]

There was also mud. A Wisconsin soldier wrote that the quarters at Cairo were worse than pigpens on the farms back home, and said that a pedestrian got completely stuck in the mud only two yards from headquarters and had to call for help. Along the water front the water was foul with the carcasses of dead mules and horses floating downstream, and an unpleasant stench filled the air. Back of the levee a good deal of the landscape seemed to be under water, and steam pumps were at work to keep this water from rising over the town's sidewalks.[2]

Yet the place was very much alive. Wet, muddy and fever-smitten it might be, but the boundless vitality of the Northwest was in it. Past its levees went the great river, and this river, because of the war, had taken on an added dimension and a fearful new significance. Blocked as an artery for commerce, it was now in the process of becoming a new trail for one of the nation's historic migrations:

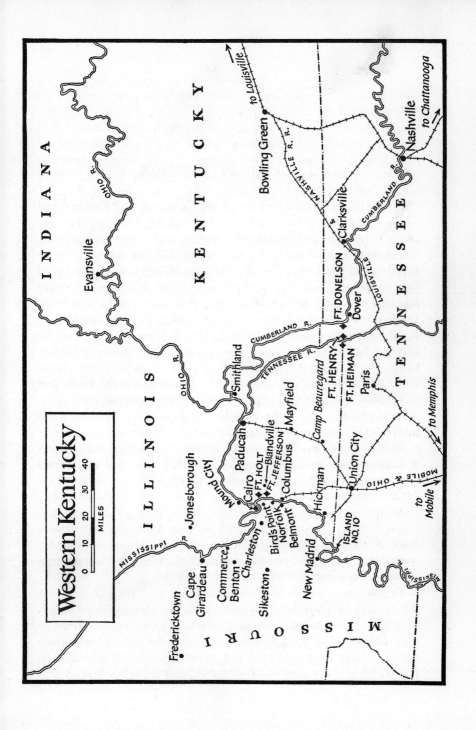

a migration that would go south rather than west, but that would finally go irresistibly, a folk movement in which armed men followed by white-topped wagons would follow river valleys toward the sea. (A movement, too, in which the nation would curl back upon itself, so that it would suffer long from wounds of its own infliction.) Cairo was the outfitting point for this new migration; no matter what the trail might lead to it would begin here, in the low land compressed between two converging rivers.

When Grant reached Cairo on September 4, to establish the command post for the District of Southeast Missouri, he was stepping into the precise place he had wanted — the precise place, as it would develop, that he was best qualified to occupy.

He had had an odd career, thus far in the war. He had been a general for less than a month, and this was his third assignment in that capacity. At Ironton he had had less than ten days to fortify an outpost, to train raw troops, to straighten out the system of supply and to organize a forward movement; at Jefferson City he had had just a week to attempt the same thing under even greater handicaps. Now he was taking hold of what could be made — what could hardly help being made — the key command in the West; and he seems to have understood the full extent of the challenge.

Before he left Cape Girardeau he had found a moment to write to his father, and to him Grant had said that his only fear now was "that too much may be expected of me." He added that he was "probably done shifting commands so much." He had also found time to get off a letter to Congressman Washburne:

> Allow me to thank you for the part you have taken in giving me my present position. I think I see your hand in it. . . . My whole heart is in the cause which we are fighting for and I pledge myself that if equal to the task before me you shall never have cause to regret the part you have taken.[3]

It would be pleasant to be able to record that someone recognized a historic moment when Grant entered Cairo, but nobody did; the man most immediately concerned, the man whom Grant relieved from command, did not even recognize Grant himself. Grant was still wearing civilian clothes, and when he strolled into

the converted bank building which housed Army headquarters nobody noticed him. (Right to the end, Grant never had the knack
of catching anyone's eye.) In temporary command here was
Colonel Richard Oglesby, another Illinoisan, a lusty politician who
would eventually become Governor of the State. Oglesby's office
was full of people. Grant introduced himself, but somehow Oglesby
did not quite catch the name and he paid no attention. Grant
waited a bit, then took a piece of paper from the table where
Oglesby was working and wrote out an order announcing his assumption of command.

Oglesby blinked at the paper in surprise, looked as if he might be
ready to arrest Grant as an impostor, concluded finally that the
man was real, and turned over the establishment to him without
demur. U. S. Grant was at last in command of troops on the Mississippi, looking south.[4]

He was also in command of warships, for the Cairo job was amphibious. At this early stage of the war Washington was playing by
ear — naturally enough, since there was no blueprint for anything it
was doing — and one of the things that came out of this informal
approach was the assignment to the Army of top responsibility for
naval affairs in the Mississippi valley. This had come about more or
less of necessity. Some sort of fleet was obviously needed on these
Western waters, and in the spring and summer of 1861 the Navy
had been obliged to direct all of its time and energy to matters
on salt water. So the War Department had moved in. At Cincinnati it had bought three river steamboats, and these had been
converted into gunboats — odd-looking creations, clumsy and
fearfully vulnerable to enemy fire, but still fighting craft: *Lexington*, *Tyler* and *Conestoga*, armed with smooth-bore 64- and 32-
pounders, given protection of a sort by extemporized bulwarks
of oak five inches thick, with boilers lowered into the hold but
with steampipes exposed to destruction by any shot. They were
officered and manned by the Navy — top man just now was Commander John Rodgers, although a replacement was on the way —
and they were under Army orders, and they would be at Grant's
disposal. In an offhand way they ranked as a division of the Army.
James B. Eads of St. Louis was hurriedly building seven gunboats
which would carry a bit of armor and would be better fitted for

combat, but these would come later. For the moment *Lexington*, *Tyler* and *Conestoga* were all the fleet there was.[5]

Grant moved into the bank building, establishing his office behind a counter, looking very much like a small-town banker, puffing at a long-shanked meerschaum pipe while he shuffled his papers;[6] and within twenty-four hours of his arrival things began to happen. There came to him, on September 5, one of Frémont's scouts, just back from a trip down the river, and this man bore news that General Polk had sent Pillow and a force of unknown but apparently respectable strength up north into Kentucky, occupying the downstream town of Hickman and moving on to the ominous bluffs at Columbus. Kentucky's neutrality was over, and Kentucky lay just across the river from Grant's office. It was time for action.

Grant sent the scout on to St. Louis, and dispatched a message to Frémont saying that unless he quickly got orders telling him not to do it he was going to occupy the Kentucky city of Paducah. He waited a few hours, got no orders, and then took off, sustained no doubt by the fact that Frémont's original orders to him had made mention of the need to seize this place.[7]

Paducah, like Cairo, was geographically important. It lay forty-five miles up the Ohio, on the Kentucky shore at the point where the mighty Tennessee River came in, and just ten miles below the place where the Cumberland joined the Ohio. Under the tree at Ironton Grant had thought about these rivers, tracing their courses on his map, examining the possibilities, making marks with red pencils. The Cumberland was a clear highway to Nashville, capital of one of the most important states in the Confederacy, and the Tennessee was a highway leading all the way to Mississippi and Alabama. Any soldier could see that it was important for the Union to hold the mouths of these rivers.

Along the waterfront at Cairo, gunboats and transports got steam up. Grant put the 9th and 12th Illinois regiments on the transports, along with a four-gun battery of field artillery, went aboard himself, and with the gunboats for escort went up the Ohio that evening. At Mound City — an embryonic naval base a short distance above Cairo — there was a delay, when one of the steamers fouled another. This did no particular harm, as Grant did not want to get to his goal before daylight, and the flotilla anchored for a while. Then it steamed on at leisure, and shortly after dawn it reached the waterfront at Paducah.

Grant believed that it did not get there very much too soon, for Confederate troops were supposed to be on their way to take possession of this place; they would have reached there, according to common report, by noon, the townsfolk (Southern sympathizers, by a large majority) were expecting them, and Confederate flags had been hoisted for welcome. When Grant's troops came ashore the flags were quickly hauled down, and the people stood about on the sidewalks looking stunned. Grant believed they were badly frightened, and he wrote that he "never saw such consternation depicted on the faces of the people." The arrival of Federal troops was clearly unwelcome, and the women set up defiant cries of "Hurrah for Jeff Davis!" but the soldiers grinned and admired the women for their spunk. One man wrote that they "fell in love with Paducah on sight," and after the war was over he still remembered: "I never saw so many pretty women in my life. . . . All fat, smooth-skinned, small-boned, high-bred looking women." Grant got his troops in position to guard the roads, took possession of telegraph office, marine hospital and railroad station, seized a quantity of rations and two tons of leather that were awaiting shipment to the Confederates, and turned the command over to Brigadier General E. A. Paine, instructing him to be sure no harm was done to inoffensive citizens, to keep the soldiers from entering private dwellings, and to "exercise the strictest discipline against any soldier who shall insult citizens or engage in plundering private property." Then he hurried back to Cairo, reaching the place less than twenty-four hours after the expedition had taken off. He found there a message from Frémont authorizing him to do what he had just done.[8]

Taking thought for the political angles of the situation, and reflecting that although the people of Paducah might favor the Confederacy the state legislature was strong for the Union, Grant got off a telegram to the speaker of the Kentucky House of Representatives:

I regret to inform you that Confederate forces in considerable number have invaded the territory of Kentucky and are occu-

pying and fortifying strong positions at Hickman and Chalk
Bluffs.⁹

Then he sent word to Cape Girardeau to ship the 8th Missouri
on to Cairo at once; getting reinforcements to Paducah was very
much on his mind. Lastly, he sent a telegram to Frémont making a
complete report on everything that had been done. Frémont up-
held the occupation of Paducah, but otherwise he was not pleased.
Grant drew a reprimand for his action in communicating with the
speaker of the Kentucky house; dealings between the military and
state officials would be carried on by the department commander,
and Grant was warned not to get out of line again. He was also
notified that "to enable you to continue personally in command
of our forces at Cairo, Bird's Point, Cape Girardeau and Ironton,"
headquarters was sending Brigadier General Charles F. Smith to
command at Paducah.¹⁰

In a way this was another snub, for this move removed Paducah
from Grant's control. (It was eventually restored, but that came
some weeks later.) But if Grant was wounded, he kept the fact to
himself, and it is probable that he welcomed the news, for there
were few officers in the Army whom Grant admired as deeply as
he admired Smith.

Smith was an old-timer, a Regular of Regulars, tall and lean and
straight, with drooping white mustachios and a parade-ground
stiffness to his manner. He had been commandant of cadets at
West Point when Grant was there, and Grant confessed that he
never felt quite right issuing orders to Smith; he still felt like a
schoolboy when Smith was around, and to the end of his days he
seems to have considered Smith the perfect soldier. William Tecumseh Sherman, who had also taken his training under Smith,
admitted that he felt the same way, and there were Regular
officers in the early part of the war who felt that it was rather
outrageous for Grant to be over Smith: Smith, they felt, had
come up through the ranks, and Grant had become a general
through the help of Congressman Washburne. Many men, writing
about Smith, said that he was the finest-looking soldier they ever
saw.¹¹

When the war began Smith was Lieutenant Colonel of the 10th

infantry, holding a colonel's commission by brevet. He was strictly business, and he never bothered to utter fine phrases about the sanctity of the Federal Union. Politicians at Washington, troubled by the number of Regular officers who did not seem to be bothered greatly about the tremendous issues at stake in this war, seem to have marked him down as a person of doubtful loyalty. He had been quietly pigeonholed, assigned to duty as recruiting officer at New York, and when George B. McClellan, given command of the Army of the Potomac following the catastrophe at Bull Run, asked for Smith he could not get him. Late in August Frémont managed to break the log jam and Smith was nominated Brigadier General (the Senate had not yet confirmed this nomination) and was sent west. He reached St. Louis just in time to take over at Paducah. This was not at all to the liking of General Paine, whom Grant had left in charge there, and Paine would presently make trouble about it, but for the moment everything was fine. When Grant sent reinforcements to Paducah — which he did, as rapidly as he could — he took pains to send the fullest, best-equipped and best-trained regiments, keeping "the raw, unarmed and ragged" at Cairo.[12]

At Cairo, everything was to be done. At the start the soldiers hardly noticed that they had a new commanding officer. Men in the 10th Illinois had never heard of Grant before; they became aware that there was a new general around the place only when the regimental Adjutant, reading Grant's first order to them on the parade ground, tripped over the unfamiliar signature and read off "U. S. Grant" as "United States Grant," and then hastily corrected himself. Chuckling at the mistake, the men looked around and saw Grant himself, sitting undemonstratively on his horse, listening. Later, an officer in this regiment said that as they saw more of Grant they found him "a firm, quiet and determined sort of man, and one wonderfully modest and retired in his manners." He never made any sort of speech to the men — orating to the troops was a common failing among officers in the early part of the war — and at reviews and parades he sat his horse quietly, saying nothing at all except that he always thanked the Colonel when the review was over. In the course of time, Grant did get a proper uniform, and one man remembered that Grant appeared before his regiment in regulation dress uniform, complete with cocked hat and ostrich feather. Across the river at Bird's Point, men of the 11th and 20th Illinois raided a farmyard and stole a quantity of honey; Grant's guards caught them, and Grant imposed fines to pay the owner, while the guards (as the soldiers believed) ate the honey. For a time thereafter, whenever an officer was within hearing the soldiers would set up a chant: "Who stole the honey? The 11th and the 20th. Who paid for the honey? The 11th and the 20th. Who ate the honey? General Grant's bodyguard." [13]

One of Grant's first concerns had to be the health of his command. He worked through an army surgeon, Dr. Joseph H. Brinton, who reached Cairo a few days after Grant's own arrival. Dr. Brinton met him behind the counter in the bank, and wrote thus about it, long afterward:

> . . . A very short, small, rather spare man with full beard and mustache. His beard was a little long, very much longer than he afterward wore it, unkempt and irregular, and of a sandy, tawny shade. His hair matched his beard, and at first glance he seemed to be a very ordinary sort of man, indeed one below the average in most respects. But as I sat and watched him then and many an hour afterward I found that his face grew upon me. His eyes were gentle, with a kind expression, and thoughtful. He did not as a rule speak a great deal . . . did nothing carelessly, but worked slowly, every now and then stopping and taking his pipe out of his mouth.[14]

Brinton found that there were many sick men. Grant selected Mound City as the best place for these; the town had been laid out a few years earlier by optimistic real estate promoters who thought it would be a thriving shipping point for river-borne freight, and it had long rows of substantial brick warehouses, empty and unused. These were turned into hospitals, but the care which the men got was rudimentary. The army at Cairo was making use of civilian doctors, holding no commissions but working under contract, and many of these were conscienceless impostors and charlatans. There seemed to be no nurses and there was a great shortage of medical supplies; for a time there was not even a chaplain, and when men died Dr. Brinton had to read the burial service. If people back home had not regularly sent money and boxes of food, the men would have been in desperate straits.

Grant told Dr. Brinton to put things right, and Brinton found that the General would always support him. The doctor would presently write that "Grant is a plain, straightforward, peremptory and prompt man. If I ask for anything it is done at once."

A big problem had to do with nurses. All over the country, women were volunteering to work in Union Army hospitals. Miss Dorothea Dix, a capable and stern-minded lady, had been given general charge of the new Army Nursing Corps. She had fixed ideas, and rigorously combed out all applicants who were either youthful or pretty; there would be no romantic passages between nurses and patients if Miss Dix could help it. In spite of her best efforts, a large number of pathetically unqualified women kept showing up, each one bearing some sort of endorsement or order from a faraway general or War Department official, all insisting that they were going to be of service. They had to be fed, housed and paid, and they were not ordinarily pleased with the accommodations that were available. "They defied all military law," Dr. Brinton asserted. "There they were and there they would stay, entrenched behind their bags and parcels, until accommodations might be found for them. . . . This female nurse business was a great trial to all the men concerned and to me at Mound City it became intolerable."

The good doctor's complaint was being echoed just at this time by Dr. John Cooper at St. Louis, who ungallantly declared that every preacher in the North "would recommend the most troublesome old maid in his congregation as an experienced nurse." Many of the women chosen by Miss Dix, said Dr. Cooper, were obtained in this way; "every day the preacher would write about his own particular ewe lamb, suggesting some post as far off as possible — the most of these ewe lambs hailed from New England and the most of them had been school marms whose only experience in nursing was of the wrath of the boys whose ears had been warmed too often because their fathers had overlooked her." Miss Dix, said Dr. Cooper, came in with many of these people in tow, "each one with spectacles on her nose and an earnest gaze in her eyes, to see the man she was to take possession of." The increase in the death rate following their arrival was heavy, Dr. Cooper added, "probably caused by the spectacles."

In one way and another, the nursing situation was got under control. Dr. Brinton improved it by sending to South Bend, in Indiana, and getting a detachment of Catholic Sisters. The change, as he recalled it, was refreshing. Each volunteer nurse, formerly, had wanted special attention. "They did not wish much, simply a room, a looking glass, someone to get their meals and do little things for them, and they would nurse the sick boys of our gallant Union army." One morning fourteen or fifteen of the Sisters arrived; apprehensively, Dr. Brinton asked what accommodation they would need, and to his pleased surprise got the answer: "One room, Doctor." [15]

There was a great deal of routine for the District Commander to handle. An exceptionally sickly regiment must be sent back to St. Louis, to be replaced by one better able to stand conditions around Cairo. It was necessary to have a mustering officer sent down, since there were many troops which had never been sworn in; necessary, too, to get the Navy to do something about paying the crews of the gunboats — as things were, the men could legally be paid only at Cincinnati, which was a long way off. Vast quantities of supplies were arriving, and since all of these would presently be shipped off by boat it was expensive and unhandy to store them on shore: Grant found and took over a big wharf boat with a storage capacity of twenty-five hundred tons, to get around that problem. Cold weather was approaching, and there must be suitable winter quarters for the troops; log huts would do nicely and would cost little, but the military chest was empty — "Credit will not do at this place any longer. I understand the credit of the Government has already been used to the extent of some hundred thousand dollars and no money ever paid out." Could department headquarters kindly send some money, along with a paymaster to pay the troops? Too many soldiers were applying for medical discharges, which the contract surgeons were recommending on trivial grounds: could Grant have the authority to approve or, more important, to disapprove these? (Studying the regulations, Grant decided that he had that authority; technically, he was commanding an army in the field, and the power he was asking for went with the job.) It was necessary for him to visit Springfield, to see whether the Governor of Illinois could send him some artillery and small arms. (The Governor could not, having none at his disposal, but he promised to send down the first that came to him.) Also, the Austrian muskets with which many troops were equipped were defective; and the troops badly needed tents, shoes, shirts, blankets, along with cavalry equipment and a good deal of field artillery. At least six telescopes were required, and if a large map of Kentucky could be provided it would be very useful.[16]

Cairo was on the frontier, and a heavy trade with the enemy was moving down the Mississippi. Packet boats plying between St. Louis and Cairo, Grant believed, were dropping off considerable amounts of freight for the armies of the Confederates, at way stations along the river; to check this, all the gunboats being busy on other assignments, Grant took a river steamer, put an armed guard aboard, and told the skipper to pick out one of the suspected packets and follow it downstream, stopping wherever the packet stopped and confiscating the freight that was sent ashore. (A fine lot of contraband was seized: unfortunately, the captain of the guard got too enthusiastic and seized the packet also, and Grant had to release it.) He also sent troops on a foray to Charleston, Missouri, some miles inland, to seize goods which he believed were en route to Jeff Thompson. He had "serious doubts whether there is any law authorizing this seizure," but he felt that his action was necessary; would the Department Commander please advise him? Grant needed eight thousand bed sacks at once; needed, as well, to make a quick trip to Cape Girardeau, where civilian property had been seized as the site for a fort, and where it was necessary to appoint a board of officers to appraise the value of the property and decide on a proper rental. At Cape Girardeau, too, a steam ferryboat had been requisitioned for Army use; the owner was demanding seventy-five dollars a day as compensation, but steamboat men said that eight dollars would be fair; the District Commander must look into things and say what would be paid. (Having looked, Grant concluded that the owner was too demanding by far, and decreed that the ferryboat would be kept in service without any rental.) [17]

With details like these Grant's time was kept occupied. Yet these, after all, were just details. The armed forces of the Confederacy were very near, and as he put his District in shape, cared for his sick, got his troops equipped and trained and dealt with all the odds and ends of military housekeeping, Grant's first responsibility was that of a commander in the field. The presence of Polk and Pillow and their men at Columbus was his biggest concern. Rumor credited them with aggressive intentions, and there must be defensive works to guard against a possible Confederate offensive; Fort Holt was built and manned, on the Kentucky side of the Ohio, and near it a second work, Fort Jefferson, came into being. On the Missouri side of the Mississippi, at Norfolk, a few miles below Bird's Point, Grant established an outpost, and he kept soldiers and gunboats busy with ceaseless reconnaissances, keeping track of what the Rebels might be doing.

As a matter of fact, the Rebels at that time were not trying to do much more than establish a good defensive line across Kentucky. Polk's invasion of the state had surprised the Confederacy fully as much as it had surprised anyone else, and in the days following his occupancy of Columbus this fact became quite apparent. If the invasion of Kentucky had been agreed on at Richmond as part of a calculated strategic move, and if the Confederacy had been ready to swarm into the state on a broad scale, with objectives selected in advance, the Union might have been caught at a sharp disadvantage; except for the area around Cairo and Paducah, the Federals were by no means ready for such a thrust. But the action had been Polk's own, forced on him by developing circumstances, and after he had made the move everything had to be improvised.

During the period of its neutrality Kentucky had maintained a state guard, commanded by an old friend of Grant's, General Simon Bolivar Buckner; the same man who, six years earlier, had met Grant in New York when Grant made his inglorious return from California, and who, finding Grant stony-broke, had loaned him money so that he could get back to Illinois. No one had been sure what Buckner would do, when and if Kentucky got into the war.

During the summer, Lincoln, believing that the man would go with the North, had made out and signed a general's commission for him, to be delivered if he should at last commit himself for the Union. But Jefferson Davis had a commission waiting, too, and after Polk made his move it was Davis's commission that Buckner accepted. By mid-September Buckner was at the strategic spot of Bowling Green, on the railroad line that angled down to Nashville from Louisville, in command of five thousand men and looking as if he meant business; his patrols had burned a bridge within thirty-three miles of Louisville, and the Federal command was most anxious. A makeshift collection of raw troops under Brigadier General William Tecumseh Sherman, who was a very nervous, uncertain man just then, advanced cautiously in Buckner's direction, establishing a camp on the high ground known as Muldraugh's Hill, thirty or forty miles from Louisville; and Sherman, reflecting on the disorganization of the Federal command and the pathetic unreadiness for combat of all the Federal troops he had seen, began to see visions of imminent disaster. Many miles to the east, at Cumberland Gap, Confederate General F. K. Zollicoffer took three unready Confederate regiments fifteen miles across the border and made ready to fortify and hold a position at Cumberland Ford.[18]

The Confederate line, then, ran roughly along the state's east-west axis, anchored solidly at Columbus in the west, held in the center at Bowling Green, and pinned down none too firmly in the eastern mountains by Zollicoffer's skimpy command. All things considered, this may have been the most vital single line in all the Confederacy, but it was not held in great strength and unless a military miracle took place it would not serve as jumping-off ground for any Southern offensive. No one knew this any better than the man Davis now put in command of the Western theater — General Albert Sidney Johnston, believed to be a man of great strategic ability; a man of whom much was expected. Just now, Johnston was laboring under the perennial handicap of all Confederate field commanders — he had too much ground to cover and not enough troops to do it with.

Polk's occupancy of Kentucky had raised a fuss, and Union adherents were trying to squeeze political advantage out of it. A

committee of the state senate sent Polk a formal resolution asserting that the good people of Kentucky were profoundly astonished that an act of invasion had been committed by the Confederate states. Having "hoped that one place at least in this
great nation might remain uninvaded by passion," they earnestly
wished that General Polk would take his troops and go back to
Tennessee. Polk replied that the Federals had already fractured
the state's neutrality, offered to withdraw if the Federals would
do the same, and stayed precisely where he was. The indignant
legislature also resolved that Governor Magoffin should order the
Confederate troops to withdraw. Magoffin vetoed the resolution, it was passed over his veto, and he dutifully issued the order,
which had no effect whatever. The Union Army's first war hero,
Major General Robert Anderson — the weary, unhappy, Ken-
tucky-born Regular who had been in command at Fort Sumter,
and who since early summer had been assigned to the Kentucky area
on an if-and-when basis — was invited by the legislature to establish himself in Louisville; he complied, found that the strain of
everything was too much for him, and in little more than a month
was compelled by failing health to resign. He would be replaced
by Sherman, to whom the assignment would bring nothing but
misery and frustration.[19]

No matter how the politicians might resolve and maneuver,
Confederate troops were in Kentucky and they would not leave
unless armed men made them leave. This fact was clear to Grant
from the start, and C. F. Smith had hardly reached Paducah before
Grant was thinking about a Federal offensive. On September 10
Grant wrote to Frémont that an amphibious reconnaissance down
the Mississippi had exchanged shots with Rebels around Columbus,
and he felt that this had been good for Federal morale. He reported: "All the forces show great alacrity in preparing for any
movement that looks as if it was to meet an enemy, and if drill and
discipline were equal to their zeal, I should feel great confidence
even against large odds." It seemed to Grant that the Confederates were playing for time, either to perfect their defenses or to
make ready for an attack on Paducah, and he added: "If it were discretionary with me, with a little addition to my present force I

would take Columbus." The next day he told Colonel Oglesby, who commanded the outpost at Norfolk, to renew the armed reconnaissance, "annoying the enemy in every way possible," and on the day after that he wrote to Frémont: "I am of opinion that if a demonstration was made from Paducah toward Union City" (a Tennessee railroad junction twenty-five miles south of Columbus) "supported by two columns on the Kentucky side from here, the gunboats, and a force moving upon Belmont, the enemy would be forced to leave Columbus, leaving behind their heavy ordnance. I submit this to your consideration, and will hold myself in readiness to execute this or any plan you may adopt." [20]

Frémont's intentions were aggressive enough. He told Grant to scout the roads toward Columbus, and if the enemy should cross the Mississippi to Belmont "be present with a force on the Missouri as well as the Kentucky shores." He promised to send more troops, and warned: "Keep me informed minutely." To President Lincoln Frémont had sent an elaborate plan for a forward movement in Kentucky and astride the Mississippi, looking toward the capture of Columbus, the occupation of Nashville, and ultimately the capture of Memphis.[21] But Frémont was beginning to have pressing problems elsewhere, and he was increasingly unable to give much attention to Kentucky. Shortly after Grant left Jefferson City his successor there, saturnine Jefferson Davis (raised now to Brigadier's rank), had sent a force under Colonel James A. Mulligan one hundred and twenty-five miles up the Missouri to occupy and hold the town of Lexington. Mulligan, gathering to himself stray detachments of cavalry as he moved, entered Lexington with between 2800 and 3500 men — the total depends on whether certain home guard units deserve to be counted as combat troops — and quickly found himself in trouble. Missouri's General Price came up from the South with a force of 10,000 or more, and Mulligan was put under siege. Federal attempts to reinforce him came to nothing, and on September 20 — overpowered, out of rations and nearly out of ammunition — Mulligan had to surrender. From Washington Frémont got a curt message saying that the President expected him "to repair the disaster at Lexington without loss of time," and he now was devoting all of his attention to the task of assembling an army that would clear western Missouri of enemy forces once and for all. Meanwhile, Washington had called on him to send troops east, and instead of reinforcing Grant Frémont had had to take two regiments away from him. The Cairo-Paducah-Columbus triangle was to get little help from the Pathfinder.[22]

Whether Grant could actually have accomplished anything if he had been told to move on Columbus is an open question. In his memoirs Grant said that Columbus could have been taken if the attempt had been made immediately after the occupation of Paducah, but he said that before November the place was so strongly held that nothing but a powerful army and a long siege would have won it. At the time, his opinion seems to have fluctuated. On October 7 he was informed that Rebel strength at Columbus had been built up to 45,000 men (a wild overestimate); yet he believed that, although there was much talk of a Confederate campaign against Paducah, General Polk's intentions were strictly defensive. Three weeks later he was more optimistic, and he told St. Louis that the Confederates had taken so many men away from Columbus for operations in other parts of Kentucky that the fortress was weak: "If Gen. Smith's and my command were prepared it might now be taken." He realized, however, as he may not have realized earlier, that his own force was not actually ready for a major offensive: "My cavalry are not armed nor my artillery equipped; the infantry is not well armed, and transportation is entirely inadequate to any forward movement." [23]

Reinforcements were delayed. In the middle of September Grant had some sixteen thousand five hundred men in the Cairo area,[24] but just after this total was recorded he lost the two regiments which Frémont had to send to Washington, and replacements were hard to get. Frémont promised to do the best he could, and he hoped that Grant and Smith between them could keep the Confederates on both sides of the Mississippi under control, but he warned Grant to be cautious: "At present I am not in favor of incurring any hazard of defeat." Grant had already confessed to Smith that his force was "scarcely more than a weak garrison," and after getting Frémont's pessimistic note he wrote to General Oglesby that, "despairing of being reinforced, I deem it the better part of valor to be prudent" — as a result of which Oglesby was to retire from the exposed post at Norfolk to Bird's Point.[25]

What all of this came to was that through September and October, despite all the reconnaissances and the projected offensives, the Cairo command was marking time. Grant expressed it accurately in his Memoirs when he wrote: "From the occupation of Paducah up to the early part of November, nothing important occurred with the troops under my command." [26] Yet something important was occurring with Grant himself. He was learning his trade. His experience as regimental quartermaster in the Mexican War had taught him a great deal about the way supplies are kept moving to an army in the field; here in Cairo he was getting a postgraduate course in this, discovering that all of the quartermasters' arrangements will break down unless the man at the top makes it his business to keep the cumbersome machinery moving. He was learning, too, the ways of the Volunteers he had in his command, discovering the means by which they could be given high morale and brought along as soldiers.

The men were not like the old Regulars. Dr. Brinton remembered that they had odd quirks. Most of them had been extremely self-sufficient and individualistic as farmboy civilians, but in the Army they seemed utterly unable to take care of themselves. Camp hygiene was likely to be atrocious unless the Commanding General kept it up to standard, for most company and regimental officers knew nothing at all about the way to care for their men, and the men themselves — the most self-reliant of individuals, in civilian life — appeared to be helpless. This, to the surgeon, was "one of the strangest peculiarities of the volunteers at the beginning of the war . . . they ceased to think for themselves and became incapable of self-protection." One veteran wrote, after the war, that much camp sickness was the fault of the men themselves: "A contented, temperate, cheerful, cleanly man will live forever in the army, but a despondent, intemperate, gluttonous, dirty soldier, let him be never so strong when he enters the service, is sure to get on the sick list, and finally into the hospital." Diseases like measles ran through the camps almost unchecked, and the level of medical knowledge at the time is reflected in a soldier's comment that "the ravages of this disease, so frequent among recruits, were largely attributed to the use of straw for beds, as the decaying straw generated the bacteria." There seemed to be no way to get either convalescents or detailed men to do any useful work in the hospitals. Scrubbing, sweeping, making beds and so on was "women's work," and these Westerners were proud in their young masculinity and would perform such chores only if someone in authority stood over them and made them do so.[27]

It was an axiom that the worst period in a Volunteer's life came about three months after he had enlisted — the stage which thousands of the soldiers around Cairo were reaching that fall. In the early days (as one veteran explained, later) patriotic excitement and the interesting strangeness of military life were a stimulus, but after a time everything seemed boring and the soldier "hated his food, his duties and his officers" with an undiscriminating passion. Men would get tired of Army fare, gorge on gingerbread and pie bought at the sutler's, suffer from digestive upsets and land in the hospital.[28]

The extent to which sickness was taken for granted at that stage of the war is shown by an innocent boast printed in a camp newspaper published by the 37th Illinois. Writing late in October, the regimental scribe asserted that this regiment was in an uncommonly healthy condition: "There will not average more than ten sick to the company throughout the regiment. In this respect they have been highly favored."[29] This, actually, meant that 10 per cent of the entire command was on the sicklist — a rate so high that a year later it would have called for an investigation by the Commanding General. In this fall of 1861 the record seemed worth crowing over.

One cure for discontent was mail from home, and Grant took pains to make sure that his armies would get good postal service. A. H. Markland, a special agent of the Postoffice Department, visited Cairo, and worked out for Grant a system whereby letters between camp and home were handled promptly and efficiently. Even when troops were on the march, mail wagons trailed after them; Grant declared that "the officers and men were in constant communication with kindred and friends at home and with as much regularity as the most favored in the large cities of the

Union." After the war, Grant remarked with pride that "the same promptness was always observed in the armies under my command up to the period of the disbandment." [30]

Another cure for discontent was work; work, together with some evidence that the work which was being done made sense. One Illinois regiment was sent across the Mississippi daily to drill in the manual of arms, firing blank cartridges, and the Colonel finally went to Grant and said that the men would not put up with this drill much longer unless they were allowed to practice with live ammunition. They had been shooting blanks at the weeds for two days, the Colonel said, and the weeds were still standing "as saucy and defiant as ever." Grant chuckled, and ordered ball cartridges issued, and the Colonel reported next day that the regiment was in the highest of spirits — "Now you can turn us loose on the southern Confederacy as quick as you please." Men in a cavalry regiment enjoyed target practice, with a life-sized human figure printed on the target; they dubbed the figure "Jeff Davis" and shot at it enthusiastically if unskillfully. Disgusted by this failure to hit the mark, some spent spare time shooting at snags in the river, then rejoiced when they shot Jeff Davis full of holes.[31]

Military red tape was a burden. The paymasters who came down periodically to pay the troops were all bound up in it, and the slightest mistake in the way a man's name appeared on the rolls — a minor misspelling, or the omission of a middle initial — caused them to refuse to make payment. Officers who listed the names of the servants for whom they were entitled to draw pay were apt to get into trouble if the listing was in any way defective. Grant himself ran into this, when one month the account which he submitted was accompanied by a list of servants written by an aide; when the papers reached Washington the Treasury Department refused to honor them, pointing out that they were made out in two different kinds of handwriting. When the paymaster was unable to explain how this had happened, the papers were sent back to Grant, with a demand for an accounting. They reached Grant in the spring of 1864, in the midst of the Wilderness campaign.[32]

John Page, officer in a Chicago militia battery, was ordered to go to Washington for assignment to a regular infantry unit, and he went to Grant's office to get an order for transportation. Grant looked at his commission, stared at it for a moment, and became lost in reverie; he looked at the officer, repeated "John Page" two or three times, and did not sign the papers until an aide nudged him. Page was the son of the first man Grant had seen killed in action — a John Page, who was standing at Grant's side in the battle of Palo Alto when a Mexican cannon ball smashed his head.[33]

As he continued to work on the details of training and housing his men — at one time Grant suggested building barracks on empty coal barges, with the idea that on subsequent expeditions down-river these floating barracks could be towed to their destination by tugboats — Grant came to see that some of his earlier ideas for the capture of Columbus had been pretty sketchy. J. N. Tyner, another special agent for the Postoffice Department, visited him that fall, and killed time after his business had been finished by chatting with Grant at headquarters while waiting for a train. He said Grant gave him a pipe and tobacco, settled back for a smoke, and with a grin suggested: "Now tell me all you know about this war — it won't take you long." Tyner did not have much to say, but presently Grant himself began to talk, and he went into a proposal which, he said, had been made "by politicians and outsiders" for getting the Confederates out of Columbus. As Tyner remembered it, this proposal involved sending men downstream to make a surprise attack, by night, on the Rebel forces at Columbus, while another column under General Smith moved across the western tip of Kentucky and assailed Columbus from the rear. This scheme may have been built on Frémont's own proposals to Lincoln, or indeed it may have grown out of the idea Grant himself had outlined to Frémont in a letter written in mid-September: Tyner got the impression that the notion had originally been Grant's own, at least in part. By now, however, Grant could see the flaws in it, and he told Tyner how risky it would be to try to co-ordinate two separate surprise attacks, at night, by forces which would be completely out of touch with each other. Grant's own hope, Tyner gathered, was to let the upper river take care of itself and strike deep into the Confederate interior, and he said vigorously that it was about time for the Union forces to make war rather than to "play war." [34]

The Grant with whom Tyner talked, it might be noted, was not quite the Grant of legend. The legend makes Grant an extremely taciturn, silent man, who weighed his words carefully and never spoke except when he had something of moment to say, but Tyner did not find him that way at all — nor did others, then or later, who found him in a relaxed mood. As a matter of fact, Grant was a chatty person who became close-mouthed only when strangers were present or when high formalities were being observed. W. S. Hillyer, who knew Grant in St. Louis before the war and served through much of the war on his staff, said Grant's friends always considered him "more than commonly talkative"; they realized, though, that he never spoke for effect, and that to be loquacious he had to be with his intimates. A Galena man who served with Grant in his Western campaigns said that "if you could get him started he was one of the most entertaining talkers I ever listened to," and John A. J. Creswell, who was to become Postmaster General in Grant's cabinet, remembered hearing Grant talk for an hour or more without a break. Once you knew him, said Creswell, Grant "would talk as much as any companion should"; but if he became suspicious of the motives of anyone who happened to be with him "he would remain cold and silent and his firm jaw would shut like a trap." A telegraph operator who handled Grant's cipher dispatches through most of the war remembered that Grant once said an odd thing to him: "I think I would always like to remain about 35 years of age for at that age one can take activity in a conversation without being considered old fogyish." [35] Despite the legend, it was perfectly in character for Grant to sit talking late into the night while the postal agent waited for his train.

Whether Grant himself realized it or not, his position at Cairo and the strategic possibilities that went with it were exerting real pressure on the Confederate command. In a military sense, the operation was running smoothly; at about this time Grant's fellow-townsman from Galena, A. C. Chetlain, now lieutenant-colonel of the 12th Illinois, was writing to Congressman Washburne that "General Grant is doing wonders in and about Cairo in his quiet way," [36] and Confederate plans had already been modified as a result. In December the Confederate Secretary of War, Judah P.

Benjamin, wrote to Braxton Bragg that when Albert Sidney Johnston was first assigned to the Western command, in the middle of September, it had been hoped that he could concern himself chiefly with affairs west of the Mississippi, leading a campaign from Arkansas up into Missouri — "the obtaining possession of the latter state is of such supreme importance that I need not say to you a word on the subject." It had never been possible for Johnston to do this, Benjamin went on, because before he even reached the river "the threatened invasion of Tennessee and the advance of the Federal forces into Kentucky rendered it necessary to detain him in this latter state." Kentucky, said Benjamin, was fully as important to the Confederacy as Missouri, and was under an even greater threat, "especially when considered in connection with the menaced attack on our lines of communication by railroad through east Tennessee." [37]

What Grant was hoping for would come soon enough. The time of preparation was just about over. Before long the Federals in the West would be making war in earnest.

CHAPTER FOUR

"You Looked Like Giants"

JOHN A. RAWLINS looked frail, but he bristled. Undersized and pale, he was almost visibly burning with an inner fire which seemed to be composed of a hatred of secession, a crusading detestation of strong drink, and a profound conviction that Ulysses S. Grant, as a man of destiny, needed just the sort of protection, help and gadfly conscience which no one but Rawlins could supply. An impressionable newspaper correspondent wrote that Rawlins's heavy black hair and beard formed a dramatic setting for the "marble pallor" of his face; a pallor that "in place of making it effeminate gave it a wondrous and melancholy beauty." The effect was heightened by "large, lustrous eyes of a deep black"; perhaps the inner fires could be glimpsed there.[1] Rawlins got to Cairo on September 14, accepted a commission as Captain of Volunteers, and took up his duties as Grant's Assistant Adjutant General — the effective head of Grant's staff, the medium through which his contacts with the rest of the military hierarchy would be carried on.

He came none too soon. Grant had been operating almost without a staff, doing much paper work which should have been delegated; Rawlins found that Grant, who was working every day from morning until midnight, was nearly worn out. Rawlins knew nothing whatever about military matters — he had never so much as set eyes on a company of Regular infantry or a squadron of cavalry — but he had driving energy, he also had administrative ability, and he possessed Grant's full confidence. The two men were already intimate, and they were to grow much more so, until finally Rawlins would come to seem almost a part of Grant, and men would assert that no one could tell the story of Grant without also telling the story of Rawlins.

Rawlins came from Galena. The son of a ne'er-do-well charcoal burner who had never quite been able either to control a taste for frontier whisky or to support his family adequately, John Rawlins had broken away from his backwoods background and had become a lawyer. A stanch Democrat, he had taken up the cause of the Union with passionate devotion once Fort Sumter was fired on, and at a mass meeting in Galena immediately after that event he had delivered a fiery save-the-Union speech which made a profound impression on Grant. ("Only one course is left for us. We will stand by the flag of our country and appeal to the God of battles!") The speech brought the two men together, and, from the moment he became a general, Grant determined that Rawlins was the one man he most wanted to have at his side. Indeed, on the day he left Galena, Grant said good-by to Rawlins with the words: "If I see anything that will suit you I will send you word"; and from Ironton he had written to him saying: "I am entitled to a captain and acting adj-gen; I guess you had better come on and take it." [2]

There had been a delay. Rawlins made a prompt reply: "Fully appreciating your kindness and friendship for me, and believing from your long experience in and knowledge of military service and its duties, you would not have offered me the position were you not satisfied it was one I could fill, gladly and with pleasure I accept it." But Rawlins's wife was dying, and it was not until after her death that Rawlins was able to join his new chief. Congressman Washburne seems to have worried about the matter, and to have feared that Grant might withdraw the offer, but Grant had no sooner reached Cairo than he was writing to Washburne that "I never had any idea of withdrawing it so long as he felt disposed to accept, no matter how long his absence." He was only sorry that Rawlins could not have been with him earlier; the experience at Ironton and Jefferson City "would have been a good shool of instruction for him in his new duties," and what lay ahead "bids fair to try the backbone of our volunteers." [3]

Rawlins took charge of staff operations at once. The situation was not entirely satisfactory, and censorious young James H. Wilson, who was later to join Grant's staff himself and who would eventually become commander of a hard-hitting corps of cavalry, wrote after the war that the staff at Cairo "contained several officers who were not only ignorant but unworthy of respect and confidence." Many of these, Wilson asserted, "were roistering, good-hearted, good-natured, hard-drinking fellows" who were not above putting temptation "in the way of those they thought would meet them halfway." Wilson, who admired Grant but who was always ready to write critically about him, believed that Grant "was more or less subject to flattery and to the kind attentions such 'jolly dogs' knew how to bestow acceptably," and he said it took Rawlins a long time to weed out those whom he considered unworthy.[4] Rawlins had no lighter side, he was the sworn enemy of all who brought liquor to headquarters, and in his stern dedication to Grant he took on the responsibility for making certain that there would never be any basis for a revival of the old rumors about Grant's weakness for whisky. He was a confidant of Congressman Washburne, and kept him posted on this matter, and on others. Washburne visited Cairo in October and either what he saw of Grant or what Rawlins told him, or both put together, satisfied him; Lieutenant Colonel Chetlain said that after the visit the Congressman's friends agreed that Washburne "has Grant on the brain." At one stage Rawlins wrote to Washburne saying that much as he loved Grant he loved his country more and if for any reason he ever felt that Grant was unfit for his position he would let the Congressman know. He showed Grant the letter before he mailed it and Grant told him: "Right; exactly right. Send it by all means." Rawlins himself said after the war that at Cairo, "beyond my friendship for Grant I felt that I was going to be attached to a man equal to the enlarging situation. And so I have remained with him ever since." [5]

The situation was beginning to enlarge itself, in that fall of 1861. Red-bearded Sherman, commanding in Kentucky, east of Paducah, could see the unreadiness of his own troops much more clearly than he could see the equal unreadiness of his Confederate opponents. He fumed, became nervous and irritable — a state of voluble irritability was never far below the surface with Sherman — and when Secretary of War Simon Cameron visited him that fall and asked him how many men the Union needed in the Kentucky sector Sherman blurted out that the total was at least two hundred thousand. The horrified Cameron retreated to Washington, newspapermen who had heard the remark proclaimed that Sherman was losing his mind, and before long Sherman was removed, to be replaced by cautious, methodical General Don Carlos Buell.

Frémont, meanwhile, was having even worse troubles. Lincoln had toned down the proclamation in which Frémont had undertaken to free the slaves of all citizens who were actively supporting secession in his bailiwick, and Frémont was under strong pressure to get an army into western Missouri and crush General Price, who had what appeared to be an army of 25,000 men and who was fresh from his victory at Lexington. Frémont had put together a force of approximately 35,000 men, and late in October he was heading west; affairs at headquarters in St. Louis were handled partly by his adjutant, Chauncey McKeever, and partly by his wife, Jessie, who had a way of acting as an extra-legal but exceedingly active vice-general when the Pathfinder was out campaigning. The orders that district commanders got under these circumstances were apt to be sketchy and impromptu.

As far as Grant was concerned these orders would have to do with General Polk and the Confederate force at Columbus; with these, and with the irrepressible Jeff Thompson, whose mobile force was a standing threat to Federal installations in the southeastern part of Missouri and who was generally credited with more strength than he really had. In the middle of October a Federal detachment had gone down from Ironton and had inflicted a defeat, of sorts, on some of Thompson's men, at Fredericktown, which led Grant to issue a rather florid, highly un-Grantlike order of congratulations,[6] but this had settled nothing and Thompson was a standing source of worry. Between Polk and Thompson, Grant's attention presently would be drawn to Belmont, Missouri, across the Mississippi from Columbus.

Belmont was a name rather than a place. Earlier that fall a Federal naval officer who had gone prospecting downstream in a gunboat (this was before the Confederates had moved into Kentucky) had reported wrathfully that he had not been able to find a town or so much as a house in Belmont;[7] it was simply a weedy, tree-grown tract of rather low farmland — it did have two or three houses which the Navy man had missed — and it was given importance only by the fact that it was just opposite the great Confederate stronghold and that roads led from the landing to the town of Charleston, a dozen miles inland, and to New Madrid, thirty miles or more down the Mississippi. If General Polk proposed to put more troops into Missouri, or to draw troops out of that state, it seemed likely that he would do it through Belmont.

Belmont had been in possession of Union troops earlier, and when Grant had been given command in southeastern Missouri at the start of September, it was taken for granted that the Federals would hold the place. But the collapse of the offensive that had then been projected — caused in part by General Prentiss's inability to agree that Grant ranked him — had led to a withdrawal, and Belmont was Confederate territory now. But the name touched a sensitive nerve at Federal headquarters, and any hint that Polk's troops were crossing the river was apt to lead to action.

Such rumors came in as October ended. On November 1 Grant received orders from St. Louis indicating that something was up: "You are hereby directed to hold your whole command ready to march at an hour's notice, until further orders, and you will take particular care to be amply supplied with transportation and ammunition. You are also directed to make demonstrations with your troops along both sides of the river towards Charleston, Norfolk, and Blandville" (this latter a hamlet on the Kentucky side, five miles or more from Fort Holt) "and to keep your columns constantly moving back and forward against these places without, however, attacking the enemy." Grant was also informed that somewhat similar instructions had been sent to General Smith at Paducah.

These orders were, to be sure, a bit confused, and might have been hard to follow, but clarification seemed to arrive the next day. Jeff Thompson, Grant was told, was posted at Greenville, forty miles south of Ironton, with three thousand men and with evil intentions; a force was being sent down from Ironton to assail him, and Grant was ordered to send troops from Bird's Point and Cape Girardeau to assist "in driving Thompson into Arkansas." Two days later the scope of the operation broadened. Polk, St.

Louis said, was sending reinforcements from Columbus to help
General Price in western Missouri, and Grant and Smith were
immediately to make a demonstration against Columbus.[8]

This could be somewhat intricate. A real campaign against
Thompson was being called for, and it had to go hand in hand with a
demonstration against Columbus, and the two were hardly com-
patible; a "demonstration," in military language, being an osten-
tatious movement which would look very threatening but which
would not lead to anything solid in the way of fighting. But
Grant was aggressive-minded, he believed that the morale of his
troops would rise if they were at last taken off the drill ground
and put into combat, and he prepared to execute his orders with
vigor. Rawlins said afterward that Grant had become convinced
that where two partially trained volunteer armies faced each
other, the one which had to take the offensive gained nothing by
waiting to get more discipline and drill; the other side would use
the delay for the same purpose, and the relative strengths of the
opposing forces would remain the same. Grant, said Rawlins, "was
always ready whenever he had what he thought a sufficient number of men, without regard to the number of days they had had
arms in their hands, to give battle." [9] He would give battle now.

On November 3 Grant ordered Colonel Oglesby to take the 8th,
18th and 29th Illinois infantry, four companies of the 11th Illinois,
three companies of cavalry and a section of artillery, head for
Sikeston, Missouri, thirty miles west of Bird's Point, and take after
Jeff Thompson in conjunction with the force that was believed to
be coming down from Ironton. Oglesby was ordered to pursue
Thompson no matter where he might go; "The object of the expedition is to destroy this force and the manner of doing it is left
largely at your discretion." (Grant had amplified his instructions
here, in a wholly characteristic manner: St. Louis had said that
Thompson's force was to be driven into Arkansas; Grant wanted it
destroyed.) Oglesby's troops moved on the evening of November 3,
and at the same time a small force was ordered to march down from
Cape Girardeau in such a way as to distract the enemy's attention.[10]

But this expedition had no sooner taken off than the word
came down to make a demonstration against Columbus, and
Grant felt that the two moves ought to be tied together. He

sent fresh orders to Oglesby, telling him to swing south toward New Madrid; and when Oglesby reached a point from which there was a handy road leading toward Columbus, "communicate with me at Belmont." He ordered Colonel W. H. L. Wallace, at Bird's Point, to get up an expedition and start out to join Oglesby, and he himself prepared to move on Belmont with all the forces he could spare.

These forces would consist of five infantry regiments and two companies of cavalry — 3114 men in all — organized in two brigades, one commanded by Brigadier General John A. McClernand — a fiery, ambitious war Democrat from Illinois, who had fought in the Mexican War, who had spoken powerfully for the Union cause earlier in the year and who now commanded the post of Cairo — and one by Colonel Henry Dougherty. Grant put them on transports, got gunboats *Tyler* and *Lexington* for convoy, and dropped down the river on the night of November 6, anchoring for the night near the Kentucky shore nine miles from Cairo to wait for daylight.

Here, at two o'clock in the morning, Grant got a message from Colonel Wallace, who was on the move: Rebel forces were crossing the river from Columbus to Belmont, apparently heading west to cut off Oglesby. It seemed to Grant that this was exactly what the Rebels were likely to be doing, and he wrote that this gave "a two-fold importance to my demonstration against the enemy — namely, the prevention of reinforcements to General Price, and the cutting off of the two small columns I had sent, in pursuance of directions, from this place and Cape Girardeau, in pursuit of Jeff Thompson." All of this, he said, convinced him that he must make a vigorous attack on Confederate forces at Belmont; if the attack failed, the gunboats would cover the retreat, which would have to be by steamer — there were no roads going north from Belmont to Bird's Point.[11]

It happened that all information the Federals had been getting was wrong. Jeff Thompson had heard about the move down from Ironton and had been getting ready to go north and offer a fight, but had changed his mind when he heard about Oglesby's sortie from Bird's Point, and he was now preparing to retreat. Polk had ordered no troops to go to Price, and had no intention of doing so;

he was having troubles of his own, and it seemed to him just now
that his command was in a bad way. Albert Sidney Johnston had
ordered him to send five thousand men east, to Clarksville on
the Cumberland River, and Polk had protested vigorously but without effect. Polk was preparing to obey — when he sent the troops
he would send Pillow with them, which would be a relief, Pillow
being a subordinate who would try any commander's spirit — but
on the day Grant left Cairo, Polk was writing to Jefferson Davis
to offer his resignation. Davis, said Polk, had finally got "a distinguished military commander, our mutual friend," for the Western area; the fortifications at Columbus were about completed;
and if Davis was willing, Polk would like to go back to civilian life
and become a bishop again. This request Davis would refuse, and
Polk would remain a general to the end of his life; but at the moment he felt none too secure — he had recently notified Johnston
that "I have my hands full with what is immediately before and
around me" — and the idea of sending troops to Price, to Thompson
or to anyone else west of the Mississippi was very far from his
mind. Price knew this as well as anyone, and while Grant's move
was beginning Price was begging the Governor of Arkansas to send
him some help so that he might stave off Frémont's advance.[12]

But Grant had to go by the news he had — by that, and by
his own instinct to hit the enemy instead of playing a waiting
game — and so he was going to Belmont. There would be a fight,
and the fight would have none of the effect Grant had hoped for,
but Belmont by now was fated. At dawn on November 7 Grant's
little flotilla got under way, dropping down the river and mooring
on the Missouri side a little above Belmont, just out of range of the
heavy Confederate guns on the bluffs at Columbus. Gunboats
Tyler and *Lexington* moved on to open fire on these batteries, and
the infantry began swarming ashore, to climb a low, steep bank
and take position in a cornfield. Ahead and all around there seemed
to be intermittent marshes, farm clearings and dense growths of
timber. Grant left a regiment to guard the transports, sent skirmishers forward, and got the men moving.

It was a fresh autumn morning, and as the march began the dull
concussion of the big guns jarred the air. The troops themselves

were full of enthusiasm. Camp life had begun to bore them, and one Illinois soldier remembered that the men had been complaining about it, indulging in "wild and vigorous criticism of the conduct of the war, foolishly threatening to desert" if they were not soon put into action. When they had been ordered, the evening before, to pack their knapsacks, take extra rations, and board the steamers for an expedition down the river, they had cheered wildly; and now as they formed line in the cornfield they frisked and capered like schoolboys beginning a holiday. Rebel shells were coming over but the range was bad and no one was being hurt; when a big shell buried itself in the mud and failed to explode, soldiers ran to the place and dug the thing up, chattering about its great size. Grant came riding up from the river bank, ordered the skirmishers forward, and then got the whole force in motion. After the 22nd Illinois had moved a matter of a hundred yards or so the Colonel halted it briefly and made a speech, reminding his men that "today the eyes of Illinois are upon us," and saying sternly, "If I should show the white feather shoot me dead in my tracks and my family will feel that I died for my country." The day began to grow warm, and some of the men took off their coats. Then the whole line moved on.[13]

Ordinarily the Confederates kept no more than a regiment of infantry, one battery and a squadron of cavalry at Belmont, but when Polk saw Grant's flotilla coming down the river he hastily sent Pillow and four more regiments over to Belmont, dispatching another regiment a few moments later. When the two forces came in contact they were of approximately equal size — twenty-seven hundred men, perhaps, in action on each side. Polk later explained that he would have sent more men, but he believed that Grant's attack on Belmont was only a feint. C. F. Smith's troops were moving south from Paducah, word of this move had reached Polk, and the Confederate believed that the real attack was to be made on Columbus itself. The business at Belmont, he thought, was meant only to divert his attention.[14]

The green Federal troops had not gone far before they ran into Confederate infantry fire. Pillow was a most distressingly eccentric general but there was nothing wrong with his personal courage, and he was sending his equally green troops forward to attack the invader with spirit. The 7th Iowa ran into a headlong Rebel charge, and Illinois soldiers who watched said that the regiment "swung back like the opening of a double gate," but the repulse was only temporary. The Iowans re-formed and went forward again, the other regiments plowed on ahead, and in a short time Grant's men were driving everything before them. Woods and cornfields were cleared and before noon the advancing Federals reached the Confederate camp, which was enclosed by low earthworks. Pillow's men were badly scattered by now, and suddenly all resistance ceased. Disorganized Confederates ran to the river and huddled behind the low banks for protection, while jubilant Northerners went romping through the captured camp, seized some cannon, began to pick up abandoned odds and ends of Rebel property — and then, cheering and dancing with joy, got completely out of hand and entered into a premature and wholly disorganized celebration of their victory.

Victory it was, to be sure; they had driven equal numbers in complete rout, taking losses but inflicting worse ones, seizing camp and flags and guns; but the day was not ended, the heavy guns on the far side of the river were beginning to drop shells into the captured camp, and Polk was preparing to send over reinforcements. Grant was riding about trying to restore order — as a soldier he knew perfectly well that the battle was not over — but for the moment there was nothing he could do. From somewhere a regimental band appeared, playing "Yankee Doodle," "The Star-Spangled Banner," and "Dixie"; an Illinois officer got astride a captured cannon and led an informal chorus in song, other officers rode madly about from one cluster of men to another, halting before each group to make speeches about the virtues of the Union cause and the extreme valor of Grant's army.[15]

Polk was keeping his wits about him. He put more regiments on steamboats and ordered them to cross the river, landing upstream so as to cut the Federals off from their own transports, and he himself was ready to go with them. (The Federal gunboats had withdrawn to their landing place, their wooden bulwarks being altogether too flimsy to stand up against the 64-pound shot the Confederates were firing.) Grant's jubilant men were about to find that victory could turn into disaster very rapidly.

Dr. Brinton, Grant's medical officer, seems to have noticed it first. He had followed Grant to the captured camp, and, while Grant was ordering officers to set fire to the Confederate tents in the hope that this would call the men to their senses, Brinton looked across the river and saw two steamboats loaded with troops leaving the Columbus side and heading upstream. He called Grant's attention to the sight, and Grant got some regimental officers in hand and began at last to succeed in bringing the Federal troops into line. He said later that there were hundreds and hundreds of beaten Confederates huddled just out of sight along the river-banks, ready to surrender if anyone had demanded it, but these rallied as reinforcements appeared and by the time the Federals had broken off their celebration and had got into military formation again there was a solid line of Confederates between them and the place where their transports were moored two miles up the river.

Senseless elation immediately gave way to equally senseless panic. Men began to cry that they were surrounded, and some of the officers concluded that there was nothing to do but surrender and get it over with. But Grant remarked that they had cut their way in and could cut their way out just as easily, and finally the Union Army turned about and began to fight its way back to the boats.[16]

It was not easy. A good many Federals had been wounded, and many of these had to be left behind. Of the six guns that had been captured, only two could be taken away; the rest had to be spiked and abandoned, and only two of the captured horses could be removed. In the hurry, Brinton lost most of his medical instruments when the orderly who was carrying them took fright and galloped away, and he noticed that even after the men had been formed in line and were moving back toward their boats there seemed to be a great deal of confusion and a disinclination to do any more fighting than was absolutely necessary. This, it seemed to him, reflected the spirit of the unmilitary Volunteers: "They had done their day's work and wanted to go home." Men remembered hearing the dry pat-pat of bullets cutting through the dead leaves overhead as they took up their march. Dr. Brinton tried to do what he could for the wounded men, but Grant came up to him and told him that when the fire was as hot as it was here a doctor had no business at the front line, and the doctor went along with the rest.

There was hard fighting that afternoon, and Federal losses were severe. In the end, the scorched column made its way to the landing, all units in hand except for the 27th Illinois, which got temporarily isolated, had to move farther up the river, and was taken off by the boats later in the evening. Earlier in the day, some Federal wounded had been put in farmhouses near the place where the transports had tied up; and, as the infantry went aboard the steamers, Grant rode out to see if these men could not be evacuated. While details carried some of them to the boats, Grant rode back to the regiment he had posted to guard the landing, fearing that the Confederates might come to close quarters and make a final attack while the embarkation was in process — but the guard had left. Returning to the boats, Grant found that the guard had already gone aboard; he prepared to bring the men back to their post, then concluded that this would take more time then he had to spare, and himself rode out again to satisfy himself that all stragglers and detached units had reached the landing.

He found nobody, except for a column of advancing Confederates who came within fifty yards of him without especially noticing him; he was riding through a cornfield where the dry stalks were still more than head high, and this apparently made him hard to see. He got back to the riverbank just as a whole line of Rebel infantry reached the fringe of the woods on the far side of the cornfield and began to open fire.

As far as personal peril goes, this was about as bad a spot as Grant got into in all the war; and as the bullets whined about his ears he gave way, suddenly, to a desperate thought of home: what would become of Julia and the children, if he should be killed here? For a moment the thought possessed him with power, and far away in their home in Galena Julia Grant, going to her bedroom to rest after some household task or other, suddenly saw a distinct but mysterious vision: Grant mounted and in the field, gazing at her with a peculiar intensity. When they met a few days later, they found that this odd experience had come to her at the moment when Grant, all alone on his horse, was the target for con-

centrated rifle fire, and was thinking of his wife and children; and
they both felt that it was the depth of his feeling that projected
this strange vision into the house in Galena.[17]

. . . All of the Federal steamers but one had cast off their moorings and were moving upstream. At the foot of the steep, muddy
bank where this last vessel was tied up, a little knot of Union soldiers
waited disconsolately, not knowing what they were supposed to do
next.

One of these men remembered that, as they stood there, a man
on horseback appeared at the top of the bank and called to them
sharply: "Get aboard the boat — they are coming." They looked
up, saw that the rider was Grant, and hastened to obey. They heard
Grant shout to the boat's captain: "Chop your lines and back out";
then, after the lines had been cut, members of the boat's crew laid
a plank from the deck to the shore, Grant's horse settled down
on its haunches and slid down the bank, and then Grant calmly
rode aboard on the swaying plank, the last Federal soldier to leave
Belmont.[18]

Grant dismounted, went to the texas deck, and entered the
captain's stateroom just behind the pilot house, lying down on a
sofa to catch his breath. After a moment he arose, to go out on
deck and see what was going on; Rebel musketry fire was getting
heavy, by now, and Grant had no more than stood up when a bullet
ripped through the bulkhead and struck the head of the sofa
where he had been lying.

All things considered, the men were in fairly good spirits. A man
in the 8th Illinois admitted that the whole retreat had been little
better than a rout, but he said that most of the soldiers were
laughing and joking as they came aboard the steamers; they felt
that they had somehow won a victory and done a great thing
even though it had been a tight squeeze at the end, and they
were proud that they had at last been through a real battle. Yet
the trip back to Cairo was pretty solemn, and once the excitement
of getting away died down the men were rather subdued. An
officer who sat at dinner in the ladies' cabin noted that all of the
officers were briskly discussing the day's events except for Grant
himself, who sat at the head of the table and said not a word except for an occasional order to the waiter. "We thought he was

hard-hearted, cold and indifferent," this officer wrote, "but it was only the difference between a real soldier and amateur soldiers." [19]

The battle of Belmont was over. It had been somewhat costly. Of the 2700 men he had put into action, Grant had lost 607, of whom 120 had been killed. Of nearly 400 wounded, many remained on the field for such care as Confederate surgeons could give them. Confederate losses had been about equal; [20] but if the Confederates had lost their camp they had unquestionably regained it, and had had the satisfaction of seeing the Yankee invader take to his heels and retreat in vast haste. Apparently nothing whatever had been accomplished. The move had not kept Polk from sending troops to Price because no such movement had been contemplated, and Oglesby had been in no real danger; learning of the outcome of the fight at Belmont he turned about and took his command back to Bird's Point without difficulty. All that had happened was that a Federal force had gone down the river, had fought a hard, pointless battle with the Confederates, and then had returned to its base. Old C. F. Smith, coming down cross-country from the northeast, had never departed from his instructions to conduct a demonstration and nothing more; when his subordinate, General Paine, hearing the sound of firing, had enthusiastically started marching his men farther than he had been told to march them, thinking to get in on the fight, Smith sternly denounced him, reporting that the action indicated on Paine's part "a fixed purpose from the start to gain notoriety without reference to the public service or his plain duty as a soldier." Smith was so angry about this that he demanded a court of inquiry to sift Paine's disobedience.[21]

Grant never felt called on to apologize for Belmont. On the contrary, to the end of his days he believed that what he did there was justified, and as soon as the steamboats got back to Cairo he issued orders congratulating his men. Later in the war, after battles whose scope made Belmont look like no more than a skirmish, Grant would be very chary about writing such orders, but on November 8 he let himself go, and the order is worth looking at if only as a sample of the kind of prose Grant was willing to offer to green troops in the early days of the war. It went as follows:

The general commanding this military district returns his thanks to the troops under his command at the battle of Belmont yesterday.

It has been his fortune to have been in all the battles fought in Mexico by Generals Scott and Taylor save Buena Vista, and he never saw one more hotly contested or where troops behaved with more gallantry.

Such courage will insure victory wherever our flag may be borne and protected by such a class of men.

To the many brave men who fell the sympathy of the country is due, and will be manifested in a manner unmistakable.[22]

As details of the battle were published in the North, Grant was criticized for getting into an expensive, meaningless fight, and the battle has never been considered a particularly bright spot on his record. The Confederates played it up as a victory, as they were fully entitled to do by all the rules of the game. Yet Grant felt that the fight had been worth all it cost. If it did nothing else, it "blooded" his raw troops, and he now had a hard nucleus of men who had been under heavy fire and who, by the standards of that day, could be considered combat veterans. Near the end of his life, looking back on it all, he wrote that "The National troops acquired a confidence in themselves at Belmont that did not desert them throughout the war." [23]

The military student A. L. Conger, who after the first World War wrote an extensive study of Grant's development as a general, concluded that in a sense Grant was correct. The battle had at least given Grant "the trust and allegiance of his men," and by the hard rules of war Conger considered that this may have been worth the six hundred casualties. What the troops sensed, Conger felt, was "the released dynamic force that swept with [Grant] into battle"; in this engagement, he wrote, "there was welded . . . that subtle bond that made them from that hour 'Grant's men.'" Conger suggested, as well, that Grant's desire to provoke a fight at Belmont may have been at least partly due to indoctrination he was getting from the naval officers at Cairo, a hard-bitten lot who were notoriously anxious to see some real fighting develop.[24]

Chief among these was the new Flag Officer in charge of the gunboats, a craggy sort of character named Captain Andrew Foote, who had been assigned to the river command in the middle of September. Foote and Grant understood one another from the start, and they made a harmonious team; in a command setup practically guaranteed to produce friction between Army and Navy commanders, Foote and Grant always got along perfectly.

Foote did not survive the war; he died in 1863, and he comes down to us, mostly, in pictures — brown solid face, looking benign and tough at the same time, with an engaging fringe of seagoing whiskers running all along the jawline from ear to ear. He was a passionate foe of slavery (he had served in the Navy's anti-slaveship patrol off the African coast, some years earlier), he disliked strong drink as no one else but John Rawlins disliked it, and he was a devout orthodox Christian, delivering sermons to his crew on the quarterdeck every Sunday morning. A few years before the war, commanding three naval vessels on the China station, he had performed the almost unimaginable feat of inducing every officer and man on each of his ships to sign the temperance pledge, and there was no grog issue on any ship he commanded — a thing which his sailors seemed to take in their stride. Foote was always ready for a fight, although he had been in St. Louis when the Belmont expedition sailed.[25]

Equally pugnacious was Commander Henry Walke, skipper of gunboat *Tyler* and ranking naval officer on this trip. Yet that either talked Grant into anything Grant was not already anxious to do seems improbable. From the day he took command at Cairo, Grant had been waiting to come to grips with Polk's men.

John Rawlins, inexpert but devoted soldier, had no doubt that the Federals had won something. In a letter written to his mother just after the battle, Rawlins jubilantly pointed out that every commanding officer in the battle save one, Colonel Jacob Lauman of the badly cut-up 7th Iowa, had been a Democrat before the war — Grant, McClernand, Dougherty, the regimental commanders, not to mention Rawlins himself. Whatever else might be true of it, this at least was no Republican war; and Belmont, Rawlins felt, had proved it to the hilt. The point seems a minor one nowadays, but at the time men like Rawlins felt that it was very important. Most Confederate officers, in the fall of 1861, mentioning Union troops or commanders in their dispatches, never referred to them as anything but "Lincolnites," the implication being that the Northern war effort was the creation and the exclusive possession of the detested Republican Party. Belmont, Rawlins felt, proved that the whole North was fighting the war.[26]

There were bits and pieces to be picked up in the wake of the battle. Under a flag of truce Grant went downstream a day or so afterward to arrange for burial of the Union dead and to work out a deal for exchange of prisoners. Union and Confederate officers chatted in friendly fashion, and Grant mentioned to one Southerner that he had been very close to a moving Confederate column just before the embarkation. The Confederate, a member of Polk's staff, replied that they had seen him, although they had not recognized him, and he said that Polk had told the soldiers near him: "There is a Yankee; you may try your marksmanship on him if you wish." Somehow, no soldier had felt moved to try a shot.

Polk and Grant met face to face on at least one of these trips. Grant left no written record of the visit, and Dr. Brinton, who seems not to have been greatly impressed, wrote that Polk was tall, thin, toothless and bland, talking a great deal and seeming somewhat flippant. Polk himself wrote to his wife about Grant in these words: "He looked rather grave, I thought, like a man who was not at his ease. We talked pleasantly and I succeeded in getting a smile out of him, and then got on well enough. I discussed the principles on which I thought the war should be conducted; denounced all barbarity, vandalism, plundering and all that, and got him to say he would join in putting it down. I was favorably impressed with him; he is undoubtedly a man of much force." (If Grant was ready to assent to an attempt to stop plundering he was probably thinking about the way his men had behaved in the captured camp at Belmont, when a passion for collecting souvenirs kept them from attending to their military duties. Nearly three weeks later he was writing to Oglesby to check on the captured property held by his troops; officers who possessed stuff seized at Belmont were to be put under arrest, and noncommissioned offenders were to be locked up.)[27]

There were several of these flag-of-truce boats, in the days that followed, and tales were told concerning them. Rival officers made a point of being very affable and courteous to one another on these occasions, and toasts were often drunk. Men said that on one trip Colonel N. B. Buford of the 27th Illinois found himself acting as a host, of sorts, to General Polk and his staff. He served drinks, and — looking for a subject both sides could drink to — raised his glass and said: "To George Washington, the Father of His Country." Polk raised his own glass, smiled, and added: "And the first Rebel." Other men reported that once Grant sailed down on the headquarters boat, *Belle of Memphis*, met Confederate General Cheatham, and got very drunk with him. After the war, a veteran wrote indignantly to the *St. Louis Republican* to deny the story. He himself had been along on that trip, he said, and the Federal officer who clinked glasses with General Cheatham was one of Grant's staff officers; Grant himself was not even on the boat at the time.[28] All in all, it seems clear that on these trips neither Grant nor Polk ever drank more than a good general should.

One effect Belmont did have: it gave Grant unbounded confidence in the fighting capacity of his Volunteers. It may even have helped get him into a frame of mind that stayed with him, at least periodically, until after Shiloh — a suspicion that the Southerner's heart was not in this war and that Northern victory would not long be delayed. In plain fact the Federals at Belmont had outfought their enemies, and the Confederates afterward gave them credit for having two or three times their actual numbers on the field. In a jubilant wire which he sent to Jefferson Davis the day after the conflict, Polk estimated Federal numbers at 8000. To Johnston he wired that he had been assailed by 7500, and in his formal report, written three weeks later, he said that "the battle was fought against great odds." An Illinois soldier, talking with a prisoner during a lull in the fighting, asked the man if he still believed in the old boast that one Southerner could whip five Yankees. "Oh," said the Confederate, "we don't mean you Westerners. We thought this morning when you were approaching that we never saw such big men in our lives before. You looked like giants." [29]

CHAPTER FIVE

General Halleck Takes Over

FROM Frémont Grant heard nothing at all about Belmont, because Frémont had lost his job. Washington had had enough. While Frémont was chasing Price across the south-western part of Missouri, at the beginning of November, a messenger caught up with him, near Springfield, bearing orders from the War Department. Frémont was to turn his command over to Major General David Hunter, return to his home, and report to the War Department by letter for further orders. (As it turned out, for some time to come the War Department would have no further orders to give him.) Furious, Frémont obeyed. He had taken elaborate pains to keep any message from Washington from reaching him on this trip — he seems to have suspected that an order of recall might be on its way — and he could not understand how this messenger had broken through the cordon of staff officers he had set up for his protection.[1]

Hunter kept command for only a few days — he had been put in simply to keep the chair warm, and when he found out about this Hunter was as angry as Frémont — and two days after the battle of Belmont was fought Hunter was replaced by an officer with whom Grant was to have many important dealings during the rest of the war, a man whose actions would have a marked effect on Grant's military career: Major General Henry Wager Halleck.

Halleck was a strange character. A West Pointer who had left the Army in California in the 1850's to practice law and to accumulate a fortune, he had translated military texts and had written largely on strategy, and he was considered a highly intellectual soldier. In the prewar Army his nickname had been "Old Brains," and except that he had a habit of rubbing both elbows, abstractedly, when lost in thought — Secretary of the Navy Welles, who never liked him, wrote acidly that he did this as if the elbows were the seat of his mental processes — Halleck at least looked like a very wise general. His book knowledge of strategy was unexcelled, he had a good understanding of the political pressures that must bear on all general officers in this war, and he was a solid, conscientious and very capable administrator.

This last was a point in his favor, for in St. Louis he had much to administer. Frémont had appointed many officers without regard to legal requirements; he had surrounded himself with an almost totally incompetent administrative staff; and, in his effort to buy the weapons and supplies his unequipped troops needed, he had been responsible for an intricate network of contracts that were nothing less than appalling to the War Department officials who had to pass on them. (They arrived finally at the conclusion that there probably had been much corruption but that none of it touched Frémont personally; the man was quite unable to run a military department but he did have integrity, and if many people made money they were not entitled to make under his administration he himself got none of it.) Halleck's immediate job was to clean up a mess, and he went to work with whole-souled industry.

But what Halleck knew about war came out of books, and when the time came for action he would make war in a bookish manner. He was, in addition, waspish, petulant, gossipy, often rather pompous, afflicted with the habit of passing the buck: an ambitious man who could lose sight of larger issues in his anxiety to keep any undischarged responsibility, embodied in copperplate script from the War Department, from coming to rest at last on his own record. Now and then he might fail to accomplish things, but he would never leave the files with anything that would prove that the lack of accomplishment was due to himself. Between Halleck and Grant there would always be a faint cloud. Grant at last would come to dislike him, and in his memoirs, written in age, Grant would give Halleck none the best of it. On balance, however, Halleck in the long run would do Grant more good than harm.

One qualification the man did have, and it worked to the country's advantage. He could see, much more clearly than most soldiers then could see, the ins and outs of politics. This war was not like previous wars. It was military only in part; the rest of it was an exercise in ward and county courthouse politics, plus an attempt to make something out of the unvoiced but dominant aspirations of millions of plain citizens, aspirations which did not always express themselves in terms a soldier could understand. Halleck sensed this, and now and again he was able to protect an officer who did not sense it, so that the man's services could be saved for the Union cause.

He was sensing it this fall in connection with Brigadier General C. F. Smith, the white-mustachioed old Regular who commanded at Paducah. Smith was in trouble, as November moved on to December, and the trouble almost drove him out of the war; and this would have been too bad, because Smith had talents which the Union badly needed, and he was prepared to exercise them.

Smith was Old Army. He ran his post the way the regulations said a post ought to be run — an Army inspector, visiting Paducah that fall, reported that this was the most soldierly and the best disciplined place he had seen in all the West — and as a result he trod on the toes of innumerable ardent Northerners. His own men had not caught on to him, yet, and his insistence on drill, on the use of spade and ax to build fortifications, and on the precise observance of what the book said enlisted men ought to do, seemed unfeeling and harsh. Once some of Smith's men descended on a house whose occupants had hoisted a Rebel flag, when some Confederate officers visited Paducah under flag of truce, and prepared to take the place apart; Smith went around in person, dispersed the rioters, and next day issued orders denouncing the whole business as a grave breach of duty, mutinous in spirit. He was believed to be too lenient with Kentucky slaveowners, and out of all this came charges that he was actually disloyal to the Union cause. Not long after the Belmont fight Halleck got an indignant if somewhat incoherent letter from a citizen of Paducah drawing up a bill of particulars:

Complain of Gen Smiths inactivity. That he permitted the rebels to murder a man — that he does not confiscate provisions bot for the rebel army — or only in part — That he protects rebels whilst union men suffer — and the soldiers almost ready to rise against his policy — with affidavit before J. P.[2]

Similar complaints seem to have gone to Washington, and late in November the War Department apparently was prepared to remove Smith from his command. But Halleck kept his balance. When the frantic Paducah letter reached him Halleck simply endorsed it *Respectfully referred to Brig. Gen. Smith for his remarks* and sent it to Paducah, in the belief that Smith ought to be allowed to get into the record any reply he cared to make. Halleck also telegraphed McClellan (who now commanded all of the Federal Armies) insisting that Smith was loyal and that he was needed where he was. The effort to get Smith out failed, but the mere fact that it had been made, and that responsible people in Washington had paid attention to it, wounded the old soldier deeply. When he wrote to Halleck's assistant adjutant general thanking Halleck for his support, Smith burst out:

> What am I to think of those in authority who, at the say-so of political tricksters, condemn one of my age, *character,* genl repu, and services without the slightest opportunity of self-defense. I ask myself who is safe. . . . Until this Civil War is over I shall to my best ability, serve in any capacity, under any commander, where chance may place me, but on its conclusion I shall certainly, from a sense of self-respect, retire from the service of a government where to be suspected merely is to be damned. I write under a strong sense of injury rec'd, both in Washington last April and here.

This was not all of it. An Indianapolis man signing himself simply "A friend of justice" wrote to Smith on December 2 saying that men in the 11th Indiana were sending home word that Smith was disloyal, and adding that these reports undoubtedly originated with one of Smith's subordinates, the brand-new Brigadier General from Indiana, Lew Wallace, who years later would write a novel called *Ben Hur.* Smith knew better — he had taken Wallace under his wing when Wallace first came to camp, and Wallace was one of his greatest admirers — and now he simply passed the letter on to Wallace, who returned it with an informal note remarking that "the peculiar manner in which the writer gives me 'fits' satisfied me that he is what the Yankees call 'a darnation smart chap.' " Smith knew well enough where the trouble lay, and a bit later he wrote to a friend that "a

poor devil as a man or as a soldier by the name of *Paine* (Brig. Genl)
hatched a base conspiracy to oust me from command on the
ground of — everything, I don't know what — disloyalty, etc., etc.
. . . Thanks to the manliness and just appreciation of me by Genl.
Halleck, who denounced the whole thing as a base conspiracy
among my subordinates, the order" (the projected War Department
order deposing Smith as commander at Paducah) "was revoked and
Paine banished to Bird's Point on the Mississippi." [3]

Halleck stood by Smith, then, and saved him for further service;
and the whole tangle is worth going into here because it represents
one of the problems that could confront any Civil War general at
any moment. Volunteer troops had Volunteer officers, many of
them men of political influence, all of them men who would be
listened to if they wrote to home-town newspapers or to Congressmen. Rigorous application of Army discipline, failure to appreciate
a subordinate's gifts as a soldier, apparent softness toward Rebel
civilians or inability to respond to the pressing demands of the antislavery people — any of these could, and often did, enmesh a soldier
in anonymous accusations of the sort which a Regular of Smith's
type might find it all but impossible to answer.

In the East, trouble of this sort had already beset Brigadier General Charles P. Stone, who was ruined despite the fact that both the
President and the Commanding General had full confidence in him.
One year later the same problem would end the career of Fitz-John
Porter, one of the ablest officers in the Army of the Potomac; it
would greatly handicap and finally help to close the military career
of McClellan himself, and in the West it would contribute much to
the ultimate downfall of Don Carlos Buell. No general officer could
consider himself safe. The war was being fought in an era of unlimited suspicion, and as Smith had so bitterly pointed out, simply
to be suspected was just about as bad as to be convicted.

All of which was deplorable but perfectly natural. War and politics were inextricably blended and the conflicting strains and pressures which resulted had to be taken into account. No lover of the
Union could fail to note that professional soldiers of long experience and high reputation were now trying to destroy the government that had nurtured them. (That these men had been moved by
the loftiest motives of inner loyalty was a point Northerners could

not at the moment recognize, nor would it have mattered to them greatly if they had recognized it.) What some men had done, it seemed, other men might do. In a civil war unquestioned loyalty to the government's cause was the one virtue that counted more than all others put together, and it was precisely the professional soldier, temperamentally unable to imagine that his loyalty could possibly come under suspicion, who was the most likely to get into trouble because of this fact.

Halleck could understand this where many abler generals could not understand it, and he could come to the rescue of a man like Smith in a way McClellan was unable to do for a man like Stone. Halleck was also, this fall, saving for the Union cause the undeniable talents of the thorny and outspoken General Sherman, whose troubles were even worse than Smith's.

Sherman had had what would now be called a nervous breakdown and had had to give up his command in Kentucky. Halleck fixed him up with a minor post in Missouri and gave him the breathing spell and the encouragement that Sherman desperately needed, but as the autumn wore away Sherman was deeply despondent. From Sedalia, Missouri, he wrote to his wife saying that Sedalia was "A bleak, desolate place without water or timber or any shelter," and predicting that "if Price does not wipe us out, winter will." The papers had asserted that Sherman was insane, and Sherman himself seems almost to have believed it. To his brother, Senator John Sherman, he wrote: "I am so sensible now of my disgrace from having exaggerated the forces of our enemy in Kentucky that I do think I should have committed suicide were it not for my children. I do not think that I can again be entrusted with a command." And, to Mrs. Sherman, he confessed frankly: "Could I live over the past year I think I could do better, but my former associations with the South have rendered me almost crazy as one by one all links of hope were parted. . . . The idea of having brought disgrace on all associated with me is so horrible to contemplate that I cannot rally under it." [4]

Once this fall Mrs. Sherman herself wrote to Halleck, reciting the dreadful things the newspapers were saying about her husband and asking his help. Halleck wrote her a soothing letter, but he himself was disturbed, and to Mrs. Halleck he wrote:

I enclose a letter just received from Mrs. Sherman. How do you suppose I answered it? I could not say her husband was *not* crazy, for certainly he has acted insane. Not wishing to hurt her feelings by telling her what I thought, and being unwilling to say what I did not believe, I treated the whole matter as a joke and wrote her that I would willingly take all the newspapers said against General Sherman if he would take all they said against me, for I was certain to gain by the exchange.[5]

Very slowly but surely, Sherman was rallying, and there would presently be work for him to do. Oddly enough, both he and Smith, who were to prove magnificent leaders of volunteer troops in action, were saying now that they simply were not qualified for such command. Sherman confessed to his brother: "I do not feel confident at all in volunteers. Their want of organization, the necessity to flatter them, is such that I cannot prosper with them." And Smith, in precisely the same vein, was writing: "Whilst my experience of human nature teaches me to know the manner in which Voln troops ought to be treated to make them soldiers with the least jar on their previous habits of life, neither my education, habits, associates nor temper fit me to command them to the best advantage. This is a frank confession for those who seek my position." [6]

Grant, meanwhile, was busy with the endless routine involved in getting his military district in order. Accusations of disloyalty were not brought against him, and in an odd way the old legend about excessive drinking seems to have been almost protective; when Grant was accused of anything — and accusers were not lacking, this fall — he was simply accused of drinking too much, and in the strange temper of that era this somehow carried less weight than the accusation of softness toward the Rebels and toward slavery. Like all other Federal commanders in or near slave territory, he was pestered by slaveowners demanding the return of fugitive slaves, and in such cases he had one answer: if the slaveowner was not a man of unquestioned loyalty to the Union, the Army would not help him regain any slave that had run away. He made his position clear in a letter one of his aides sent to a subordinate just at the end of this year:

The slave who is used to support the master who supports the Rebellion is not to be restored to the master by military authority. If such a master has a civil right to reclaim such property he must resort to the civil authority to enforce that right. The general commanding does not feel it his duty to feed the foe or in any manner contribute to their comfort.[7]

But this did not mean that Grant's troops were to hold open house for all runaways. To Colonel John Cook, commanding at Fort Holt, where stray contrabands were alleged to be in hiding, Grant sent a tart warning that departmental orders did not permit Union camps to harbor escaped slaves, and he tried to make the position clear:

I do not want the Army used as negro-catchers, but still less do I want to see it used as a cloak to cover their escape. No matter what our private views may be on this subject there are in this department positive orders on the subject and these orders must be obeyed. I direct therefore that you have a search made, and if you find these or any other fugitive slaves in camp at Fort Holt you have them expelled from Camp, and if hereafter you find any have been concealed or detained you bring the party so detaining them to punishment.[8]

Grant was quite ready to be very stern with secessionist civilians. Early in January four Union pickets were shot from ambush at Bird's Point, and to General Paine, now commanding there, Grant sent drastic orders. If, on investigation, it seemed that the men had been shot by civilians and not by Confederate soldiers, "the whole country should be cleared out for six miles around and word given that all citizens making their appearance within these limits are liable to be shot." Paine was to send out patrols to bring everyone into camp, using surplus Army tents to shelter them, and he was to be very firm about it: "The intention is not to make political prisoners of these people but to cut off a dangerous class of spies." Women and children might retire to any refuge they chose outside the six-mile limit, but at all costs the camp was to be made secure.[9]

Much more difficult was the long fight to straighten out the tangle of wasteful and frequently fraudulent supply contracts which had burgeoned here as in every Western area. Needed supplies of every sort were lacking, and when they were bought they were obtained at inflated prices; and the resulting waste and fraud came less from villainy than from desperate haste, the pressure of war, and probably also from the War Department's habit of centering its attention on affairs in Virginia and letting the West fend for itself. In his first report to Halleck, on November 21, Grant gave a picture of the situation at Cairo:

> The condition of this command is bad in every particular except discipline. In this latter I think they will compare favorably with almost any volunteers. There is great deficiency in transportation. I have no ambulances. The clothing received has been almost universally of an inferior quality and deficient in quantity. The arms in the hands of the men are mostly the old flint-lock repaired, the "Tower" musket and others of still more inferior quality.
>
> My cavalry force are none of them properly armed — the best being deficient in sword-belts and having the old pattern carbines. Eight companies are entirely without arms of any description.
>
> The quartermaster's department has been carried on with so little funds that Government credit has become exhausted. I would urgently recommend that relief in this particular be afforded at as early a day as practicable.[10]

Halleck would support anyone who was trying to set up an orderly administration. A few days after receiving Grant's letter he wrote to McClellan saying that "affairs here are in complete chaos," and to his cousin, the clergyman Henry W. Whipple, he wrote: "Affairs in this department are in a most deplorable condition — whether made so purposely or not I will not say. If I can ever get any order out of this chaos I shall be satisfied." To Mrs. Halleck he recited the long hours of work which the job entailed, saying with a touch of self-satisfaction: "I never go to bed leaving anything of the day's business undone. Nearly all back business is cleaned up, and everything is getting straightened out and put in its place. This is very encouraging and I begin to see my way through the chaos and corruption which Frémont left behind him. Of course all his satellites abuse me in the newspapers, but this does not annoy me in the least." [11]

Abuse of this kind was coming Grant's way, too. Some months later Grant described his problems in a letter to Congressman Washburne. A ring of contractors and speculators, he said, had obtained a near monopoly on Army business around Cairo. Contracts for forage were going at 30 per cent above the market rates, and there was much collusive bidding. Members of the ring would submit bids when a government contract was offered, and after the bids were opened all but the highest bidder would withdraw their offers. If some outsiders submitted a bid under the level set by the highest bidder he would be bought off, or would be cajoled into retiring; the ring boasted that it had enough influence to remove any general who did not play along, and said openly that no contractor who was not on the inside had a chance to get a contract. Grant was in position to crack down, here, partly because his quartermaster department had no funds, which meant that contractors could be paid only by voucher, and the vouchers had to have Grant's signed approval. Where prices seemed out of line, Grant would not sign. On one occasion he refused to approve a forage contract even though the Department quartermaster at St. Louis had endorsed it. When the indignant contractors displayed this officer's signature, Grant was unmoved:

My reply to them was that they had got their contract without my consent, had got it approved against my sense of duty to the Government, and they might go on and deliver the forage and get their pay in the same way. I would not approve a voucher for them under that contract if they never got a cent. Hoped they would not. This forced them to abandon the contract and to sell the forage already delivered for what it was worth.

This also brought Grant into collision with Leonard Swett of Chicago, a lawyer whose intimacy with Abraham Lincoln was widely known. Swett, said Grant, "wrote me one or more letters on the subject, rather offensive in their manner." When Swett threatened to go to President Lincoln about it, Grant told him to do so if he wished; meanwhile, Grant would continue to buy materials at what he considered fair prices, and if he had to he would seize the Illinois Central Railroad (in which Swett had an interest) in order to move the goods. He also ordered Swett out of the District of Cairo forthwith, threatening to lock him up or even to shoot him if he stayed. Long afterward, Swett himself said that he did go to Lincoln and that Lincoln remarked that Swett had better be careful: if this man Grant threatened to shoot him he was as likely as not to do it.[12]

From Swett there came no real trouble, but from the disgruntled contractors themselves there came plenty. Stories that Grant was drinking heavily began to circulate, coupled with stories that his administration of military affairs at Cairo was hopelessly inefficient. Rawlins blamed all of these stories on the disappointed contractors. In Paducah, Lew Wallace believed that some of them grew out of a visit Grant paid Smith late in October, when Grant, Smith and Wallace sat late in Smith's quarters enjoying a social glass; and some men on Grant's staff blamed Wallace himself, accusing him of political jealousy. Early in January, a fellow citizen of Galena, Lieutenant William R. Rowley, then an officer in the 45th Illinois and soon to join Grant's staff, wrote to Congressman Washburne:

> I have had an excellent opportunity of learning as to the truth or falsity of the reports which have without doubt reached you concerning Genl. Grant and I have no hesitation in saying that anyone who asserts he is becoming dissipated is either misinformed or else he lies. I think you will have no cause to be ashamed of the Brigadier you have manufactured.[13]

Washburne had indeed heard the stories, and in December he wrote to his friend Rawlins asking for a frank report. Rawlins, who was taking his self-chosen duty as guardian of Grant's morals very seriously, replied that he was "no less astounded at the contents of your note than you must have been at the information reported to you," and he answered in great detail. And because detailed, seemingly circumstantial accounts of Grant's drunkenness at Cairo are still in circulation, the letter written by this consecrated teetotaler is worth looking at in some detail.

> . . . I would say unequivocally and emphatically [wrote Rawlins] that the statement that General Grant is drinking very hard is utterly untrue and could have originated only in malice. When I came to Cairo General Grant was as he is today, a

strictly abstinence man, and I have been informed by those who knew him well that such has been his habit for the last five or six years.

Just what had Grant been drinking? Rawlins was specific.

Shortly after Rawlins's arrival someone gave Grant a case of champagne. Once or twice Grant drank a glass of this with friends, but he never took enough to show the effect. For a time he felt dyspeptic and a doctor told him to drink two glasses of beer or ale each day; he followed this advice for a week or so, found that he felt no better, and then quit. Shortly after the battle of Belmont, friends visited him for a few days and he had a few drinks with them, "but *in no instance* did he drink enough to manifest it to anyone who did not see him drink." Rawlins went with Grant to a dinner given by officials of the Illinois Central Railroad and saw the General drink half a glass of champagne; and the fact that he drank at all was remarked on "simply because of his usual total abstinence." And Rawlins stated flatly:

> No man can say that at any time since I have been with him has he drunk liquor enough to in the slightest unfit him for business or make it manifest in his words or actions. At the time I have referred to, continuing probably a week or ten days, he may have taken an occasional drink with these gentlemen and others visiting Cairo at that time, but never in a single instance to excess, and at the end of that period he voluntarily stated he should not during the continuance of the war again taste liquor of any kind, and for the past three or four weeks, though to my knowledge frequently importuned on visits of friends, he has not tasted any kind of liquor. If there is any man in the service who has discharged his duties faithfully and fearlessly, who has ever been at his post and guarded the interest confided to him with the utmost vigilance, General Grant has done it. . . . If you could look into General Grant's countenance at this moment you would want no other assurance of his sobriety. He is in perfect health, and his eye and intellect are as clear and active as can be.

This was explicit enough, but Rawlins went on:

Have no fears: General Grant by bad habits or conduct will
never disgrace himself or you. . . . But I say to you frankly,
and I pledge you my word for it, that should General Grant at
any time become an intemperate man or an habitual drunkard,
I will notify you immediately will ask to be removed from duty
on his staff (kind as he has been to me) or resign my commission. For while there are times when I would gladly throw the
mantle of charity over the faults of friends, at this time and
from a man of his position I would rather tear the mantle off and
expose the deformity.

Rawlins was prepared to give references. Specifically, he referred
the Congressman to the Navy's Captain Foote, now wearing the
slightly cumbersome title of Flag Officer — the Navy did not at that
moment have admirals — a man who had been close to Grant ever
since he reached Cairo and whose hatred of alcohol equaled Rawlins's own hatred of it. Rawlins also mentioned that Halleck had recently sent a board of officers down to Cairo to make a general inspection of the way the commanding general was handling things.
Their report must have been favorable, for shortly after they returned to St. Louis Halleck had issued an order formally designating Grant's command as the District of Cairo and adding to it the
Paducah area. Smith, an officer in whom Halleck had vast confidence, now was under Grant: Halleck would never have put him
there if he had not felt that Grant was doing his job properly.[14]

By degrees Grant was getting his supply problem ironed out.
When the *Chicago Tribune* printed a story alleging frauds in the
quartermaster department in the purchase of lumber, Grant
promptly sent Captain W. S. Hillyer of his staff to make an investigation. By the time the charges had reached Washington and St.
Louis, Grant had the facts in hand and was able to submit a satisfactory report. Early in January he got an efficient new quartermaster, Captain A. S. Baxter, placed a former assistant quartermaster and a chief clerk in the quartermaster's department under
arrest, impounded all of their books, and asked Halleck to suspend
the auditing of vouchers they had issued. "Every day," he wrote
Halleck, "develops further evidences of corruption in the quarter-

master's department." Some time later he told a friend that he believed many of the stories that were told about him at this time came
from the deposed quartermaster, who was himself something of a
sot.[15]

With Halleck Grant's relations were correct but distant, and
Grant was learning that Halleck could write acrid letters when
matters of routine went wrong. One such matter developed in the
middle of September, in connection with the exchange of prisoners.
Southern soldiers who had been captured in St. Louis when Nathaniel Lyon broke up the Camp Jackson rendezvous the previous
spring were going south, on exchange, and on December 17 Grant
got a telegram from an unknown Colonel W. H. Buel, in St. Louis,
warning him that the latest consignment, coming down by boat
from St. Louis en route to Bishop Polk's camp, was composed of
impostors; Grant was to stop them and send them back to St. Louis.
Grant did so, and got a sharp wire from Halleck:

> By what authority did you send back exchanged prisoners?
> They are not under assumed names. All were identified here
> before exchange.

Grant answered, citing Buel's message, and got another angry reply from Halleck:

> No such man as W. H. Buel, colonel, known at these head-
> quarters. It is most extraordinary that you should have obeyed
> a telegram sent by an unknown person and not even purporting
> to have been given by authority. The prisoners will be imme-
> diately returned to Cairo.

Grant replied sturdily, implying quite deftly that something was
wrong with Halleck's military housekeeping:

> In justice to myself I must reply to this telegram. In the first
> place I never thought of doubting the authority of a telegram
> received from St. Louis, supposing that in military matters the
> telegraph was under such surveillance that no military order
> could be passed over the wires that was not by authority; sec-
> ond, the signature to the telegram was made with so many flour-

ishes that I could not make it out at all and to send a copy to headquarters was obliged to send to the office here for a duplicate; third, before this telegram was received, Captain Livingston who came in charge of these prisoners reported to me that several who were to come had proven to be impostors and that he had reason to believe that two of those still with him were under assumed names; fourth, directions sufficient to detain prisoners (Camp Jackson exchanged prisoners) might come from the provost-marshal's office, from General Curtis or from headquarters, and I do not know the employees of the former nor the staff of the latter. The fact is I never dreamed of so serious a telegraphic hoax emanating through a large and responsible office like that in St. Louis.

Halleck could never back down gracefully, and his wire in reply was perfectly characteristic:

The person who sent the telegram about the prisoners has been discovered and placed in confinement. He has no authority whatever. You will hereafter be more careful about obeying telegrams from private persons countermanding orders from these headquarters.[16]

Grant would be careful. Meanwhile, he was worried about contraband trade running from the rich Illinois corn lands to Confederate territory. Steamers coming down the Mississippi from St. Louis, he was convinced, carried freight for the Rebels. This freight would be dropped at landings on the Missouri shore between Cape Girardeau and Cairo, and taken overland by wagon to Jeff Thompson's minions for transshipment south, and Grant wanted to break it up. The Missouri shore was Rebel territory. "There is not," Grant assured Halleck, "a sufficiency of Union sentiment left in this portion of the state to save Sodom." He was especially disturbed by the capture by Thompson's men of a packet steamer named the *Platte Valley*, which put in at Price's, or Pryor's, Landing, on the Missouri shore, only to be seized by Confederate raiders, who lifted the freight and captured two Federal Army officers who happened to be on board. There is a hint that this stroke had been aimed at Grant himself, who was supposed to be making a river trip at that time; Bishop Polk had sent Thompson special instructions, and Thompson had replied that he was not certain that he could catch any particular packet but that he would get one or another, and Grant complained that the officers of many of these boats were in the employ of the Confederacy. To Halleck he emphasized "the almost certain disloyalty of the entire boating interest plying between St. Louis and this place." He went on to assert: "I am informed that the owners of the packets complained of are generally enemies to the government and their acts prove conclusively that the crews employed are." [17]

Undeniably, there was a steady movement of contraband goods from Union territory to the Confederates, and Confederate spies found it easy to slip back and forth across the lines. Some of this could be corrected at department headquarters, where Halleck's subordinates often made passes easy to get, and Grant — who, as an Old Army man, knew his way about the military hierarchy — demanded tighter controls. General S. R. Curtis was, late in November, acting as commander of the military post at St. Louis, and to him Grant sent a letter bristling with independence:

> Several have come to this post with safe-conducts through, signed by yourself. I regret this, as one of the most exposed posts in the Army at this time, and would much prefer that the number sent south should be made as limited as possible or sent by some other route. Although I shall accomodate, whenever it seems to me consistent with that interest of the public service, I shall in future exercise my own judgment about passing persons through my lines, unless the authority comes from a senior and one who exercises authority over me.

A fortnight later Grant pointed out that the steamer *J. D. Perry* had landed a good deal of freight on the Missouri shore between Cape Girardeau and Cairo, under authority granted by the Provost Marshal at St. Louis, and he announced: "I have ordered the captain of the *J. D. Perry* to disregard all orders to land on the Missouri shore between Cape Girardeau and this place unless given by the commanding officer of the department or myself." Orders from Halleck himself Grant would execute without demur; orders from Halleck's underlings he would obey only if in his own opinion they were sound. The *Perry's* freight, he found, went directly from the landing point to the Confederates at Hickman, Kentucky, and at New Madrid, Missouri. Concerning this freight Grant allowed himself to be mildly facetious. "Eighty barrels of this freight," he informed Halleck, "were whiskey; a character of commerce I would have no objection to being carried on with the South, but there is a possibility that some barrels marked whiskey might contain something more objectionable." [18]

During the fall of 1861, the attempt to block trade with the South took much of Grant's time and attention. Late in November he ordered the commander of an outpost at Caledonia, Illinois, to stop all movement of people and goods between Illinois and Kentucky. "All persons known to be engaged in unlawful traffic between the two states," he ordered, "will be at once arrested and sent before the provost marshal in Cairo, with such proof as may be at hand. Whenever any property is known to be for use of the Southern Army the commanding officer may seize it, whether on the Illinois or Kentucky side of the river." [19]

On December 21 he instructed Colonel Oglesby to make a sweep of the road that ran from the inland town of Charleston to Belmont, scene of the late battle; a road by which he believed a good deal of the contraband was moving to the Confederates. Oglesby sent cavalry as close to Belmont as it was safe to go and then doubled back, seizing all loaded wagons that were met on the road and bringing them back to Bird's Point. The next day, suspecting that the hamlet of Jonesborough, Illinois — 30 miles north of Cairo, and a few miles in from the Mississippi — was a source of illegal trade, Grant ordered McClernand to descend on the place, breaking up the traffic and dispersing a band of armed desperadoes which was overawing the Unionists in that area.[20]

Meanwhile, above everything else, there was General Polk to be watched, and Grant was vigilant. A fortnight after the battle of Belmont he reported that Polk had at Columbus 47 regiments of infantry and cavalry and more than one hundred guns, with eight thousand more troops stationed at Camp Beauregard, twenty-five or thirty miles to the southeast of Columbus. The fortifications at Columbus were being extended, and although the Confederates were reported to be fearful of a Union attack Grant believed that "they may be induced to act on the offensive if more troops are not sent here soon." He found that one way to keep informed about Polk's condition was to read the Memphis newspapers. By this means, he said, he learned at the end of November that General Polk now had three gunboats — small converted river steamers, mounting only four guns apiece — and that the State of Mississippi had called for ten thousand militia for sixty days to be held in the defense of Columbus. "There seems," he wrote to Halleck, "to be a great effort making throughout the South to make Columbus impregnable."

With his new flotilla of gunboats Polk was making tentative stabs up the Mississippi. On December 1 Grant notified St. Louis that "Bishop Polk's three gunboats made a Sunday excursion up to see us this evening." Nothing came of it; a few shots were exchanged with the Union batteries at Fort Holt, without damage to either side, and when the Federal gunboats appeared the Confederate craft disappeared downstream, getting away clean because they had greater speed.[21]

The gunboat business worried Grant a little. In due time he would have a naval force that the Confederates could not match — the shipyards at Carondelet, near St. Louis, and at Mound City, just up the Ohio from Cairo, were busy, and seven brand-new warships, heavily gunned and at least partly armored, were due to go into service early in the winter — but at the moment the margin of safety did not look very wide. Grant heard that the Confederates were about to bring a number of gunboats up from New Orleans, and he warned St. Louis: "The arrival of this fleet without the floating means here of competing with them will serve materially to restore the confidence and feeling of security of the enemy, now, from best accounts, much shaken." Grant was not satisfied with the progress the Mound City yards were making, and as a matter of fact the whole construction program was somewhat behind schedule. James B. Eads had contracted to deliver seven boats at Cairo by October 10, but the designated delivery date had been set by optimists. The contract had not even been signed until August 7, and difficulties had been immense; timbers for the hulls came from trees that were still in the northern forests at the time of signing, and before the armor could be made the fabricating machinery had to be built. There were twenty-one steam engines and thirty-five boilers to build, and although Eads had four thousand workmen busy on a night-and-day basis the still incomplete hull of the first of the seven vessels was not so much as launched before the delivery date was reached.[22]

The boats would be formidable, when they did arrive. They would be squat, ugly, powerful warships, 175 feet long with a beam of 51½ feet, drawing 6 feet of water, pierced for three bow guns, four on each broadside and two at the stern, armored with 2½ inches of iron forward, and given some armor along the sides to protect boilers and machinery. They looked like nothing any naval officer had ever seen before, and they quickly acquired a descriptive nickname: "the Turtles." They would be slow, with inadequate power for proper upstream maneuvering, and their somewhat sketchy armor plating would not give very great protection, but they would be much stronger than anything the Confederates could bring against them, and in Flag Officer Foote Grant had a man who would use them with much energy. But as 1861 drew to a close they were not yet ready.

Finding crews for them was a problem. The Navy managed to send a draft of five hundred seamen from the East Coast, but the rest had to be taken where they could be found: river steamboat men, sailors from the Great Lakes, Midwestern farmboys who had never seen a body of water bigger than the nearest creek — one gunboat captain comforted himself with the reflection that there were "just enough men-o'-war's men to leaven the lump with naval discipline." The Army had to detail some men for naval service, and Army officers (including Grant himself) tended to do the obvious thing in this respect: detail the men for whom the Army had the least use. On January 6 Grant wrote to Halleck that he had a number of soldiers in the guardhouse for offenses of one kind or another, and he suggested, "in view of the difficulty of getting men for the gunboat service, that these men be transferred to that service." He had spoken to Flag Officer Foote about this, he said, and "I believe it meets with his approval." A soldier at Cape Girardeau wrote that the commanding officer there "picked out 50 to 60 of his most worthless men and put them on gunboats," and while the plan apparently met with Foote's approval — he had to get men from somewhere, and he would take what he could get — he was not enthusiastic about it.²³ The most that can be said is that the business did not cool the developing friendship between Foote and Grant. Foote doubtless consoled himself with the reflection that the Navy had had much experience in the matter of making useful sailors out of seemingly hopeless material.

In the middle of December Grant got a scare. Intelligence reports from inside the Confederate lines convinced him that some movement was about to take place from Columbus, with the probable objective a night attack on Bird's Point or Fort Holt, and he promptly sounded an alert. He told McClernand that an attack was "quite imminent" and ordered him to keep all the troops at Cairo in their camps, adding a clumsily worded but explicit instruction: "Ammunition should be issued, so as to give cartridge boxes full, and the command sleep under arms." Four regiments were to be quartered on steamboats so that they could be moved instantly to any threatened point. The commander at Fort Holt was instructed: "Be on the qui vive tonight and tomorrow. Strengthen your pickets and tell them to keep a vigilant lookout. Let every man be at his post, and have your men sleep on their arms." Similar orders went to Bird's Point. Scouting parties were to cover all the approaches against a possible attack "tonight or tomorrow," and the entire command was to be kept at its posts, with cartridge boxes filled and arms at hand. Transports were ordered to keep up steam, Foote was notified that his gunboats should be ready, word was sent to St. Louis that trouble was anticipated, and Halleck was assured that "all the troops at Bird's Point, Fort Holt and Cairo are sleeping upon their arms." These measures taken, Grant awaited developments.²⁴

No developments came, for the alarm was false and General Polk made not even a gesture of hostility. The period of alert passed, nothing happened, and all hands relaxed; and one is compelled to wonder whether the effect of this on Grant may not have been unfortunate. He had been properly vigilant only to find that the Confederates were not as enterprising as his intelligence reports had said they would be. Did a memory of this fiasco remain with him and lead him, at Shiloh, to relax his guard when he had a Confederate Army in his immediate front?

For Grant personally the latter part of the autumn went pleasantly. He was able to have his family with him, and when Julia and the children were near Grant could enjoy life. They came down, shortly after the battle of Belmont, and the commanding general at Cairo became, for the time, a family man. On the lower floor of the old bank building he had his offices, shared with Rawlins, two aides and a sergeant; on the upper floors were Mrs. Grant and the children, and before long Grant moved his own office upstairs, letting the paper-shovers take over the one-time haunt of cashiers and tellers. Men who worked with him noticed his care and affection for his family. A paymaster who spent much time in the first-floor offices often had to work on Sundays, and as he worked in the quiet office he could hear the Grant children, overhead, singing Sunday School airs. Julia's arrival caused a change in Grant's appearance. Up to now he had worn a long, flowing beard; Julia did not care much for it, and presently Grant had it trimmed to the close stubble that is familiar in the photographs. He was not, men recalled, much of a smoker at this time, and when he smoked he usually chewed on a long-stemmed pipe. He admired a gray dressing gown trimmed with red flannel which Dr. Brinton wore, and Brinton loaned it to Julia; she sent it to Chicago and had a similar gown made for Grant — somehow, one would like to have a picture of the tough little General in this robe.[25]

Family ties were always important with Grant. He had wanted Julia and the children to visit him from the moment he reached Cairo, but he had had to wait until the military situation became stable. As he wrote to his sister, Mary: "Hearing artillery within a few miles it might embarrass my movements to have them about. I am afraid they would make poor soldiers." When the visit finally became feasible, Grant urged Mary to join the party, offering to pay the expenses of her travel; meanwhile, he sent photographs of himself and his staff for Mary to distribute among his relatives — "one for Uncle Samuel, one for Aunt Margaret, one for Aunt Rachel and one for Mrs. Bailey."

With his father Jesse, Grant's relationship was affectionate — and, at times, trying. Jesse was a businessman, and he was always aware that the commanding general of an important military district could steer business acquaintances into useful jobs. Grant refused to be obliging, explaining to Mary:

I do not want to be importuned for places. I have none to give and want to be placed under no obligation to anyone. My influence no doubt would secure places with those under me, but I become directly responsible for the suitableness of the appointee, and then there is no telling what moment I may have to put my hand upon the very person who conferred the favor, or the one recommended by me. I want always to be in a condition to do my duty without partiality, favor or affection.

As a dealer in leather goods, Jesse thought he might as well be selling harness to Grant's army, and Grant had to warn him that he would do nothing to help him: ". . . it is necessary both to my efficiency for the public good and my own reputation that I should keep clear of government contracts." He also had to refuse to provide a pass through the lines for a man recommended to him by Jesse, and he found Jesse's loquacity about his soldier-son a problem. Late in November he wrote Jesse frankly about this, and in the course of his letter he set forth succinctly his own attitude on the slavery issue:

I do not write you about plans, or the necessity of what has been done or what is doing because I am opposed to publicity in these matters. Then too you are very much disposed to criticize unfavorably from information received through the public press, a portion of which I am sorry to see can look at nothing favorably that does not look to a war upon slavery. My inclination is to whip the rebellion into submission, preserving all constitutional rights. If it cannot be whipped in any other way than through a war against slavery, let it come to that legitimately. If it is necessary that slavery should fall that the Republic may continue its existence, let slavery go. But that portion of the press that advocates the beginning of such a war now, are as great enemies to their country as if they were open and avowed secessionists.[26]

Julia Grant remembered that Cairo was made no more cheerful by the fact that the muddy Ohio was swollen and angry. Yet she and the General were happy there. They had compared notes about the strange vision which she had seen at the moment when Grant was in greatest peril at Belmont; it had been vaguely like an earlier experience, in which something like second sight had been her lot. At the beginning of the war, when Grant was looking for a place where his military training might be of use to the government, he had gone to Ohio, to see if young General McClellan might have a place for him on his staff, and when he left Galena he told Julia to open any important-looking letters that arrived. During his absence she had three times dreamed of opening some mailed parcel and of seeing a sparkle of bright stars within, and she had supposed this might mean that her mother was sending her a certain ring which she owned. Then, one day, there came a letter addressed to *Colonel U. S. Grant.* Thinking nothing of the unusual title, she had opened it — to find a sheet of vellum set off by the great seal of the State of Illinois, which was spangled with shining stars. She remembered the recurring dream and looked at the document; it was the commission which made Grant Colonel of the 21st Illinois Infantry. . . .

That her husband was moving on to some place high and important, Julia Grant had no doubt in the world. She took great pride in watching him review troops in the camps around Cairo; the fresh new regiments, marching past with new flags, in uniforms whose rich blue was still unweathered, made a pageant which, as she confessed years later, moved her more deeply than any other military displays she saw in all the war . . . even though he had here but a handful of untaught regiments and she would within a few years see him, as Commanding General of all the nation's soldiers, take the salute of whole armies of hard veterans. She remembered, too, that Cairo was the only headquarters town in the war where Grant had a really comfortable mess.[27]

Dr. Brinton saw a good deal of Grant in those days. He remembered that many letters went across Grant's desk, written by loyal folk in Illinois who wanted to get in touch with relatives in the South. Grant was willing to let them write, but he was careful about the chance that military secrets might be disclosed and not all letters were passed. A Philadelphia doctor wrote to Brinton, asking that a letter he wanted to send inside the Confederate lines be passed without reading; on his word of honor, it contained nothing improper. Brinton asked Grant about it, and Grant said that "for form's sake" he would ask Brinton to take a look at the letter and assume responsibility for it — if Brinton did this, Grant said, Grant would pass the letter. Brinton looked and to his horror found the letter jammed with classified military information. He told Grant about it, and tossed the letter into the fire. Grant smiled dryly and remarked, "I expected as much."

Brinton found himself deeply drawn to Grant. Once, during Grant's temporary absence, McClernand countermanded some rule Brinton had drawn up governing the military hospitals. Brinton quietly told the hospital people to ignore McClernand's order, and on Grant's return told Grant about it.

Grant looked at the papers and said, "Doctor, this is a very serious business."

Brinton replied: "General, when you entrusted to me, as your medical director, the care of the invalids of your command, you said to me, 'Doctor, take care of my sick and wounded to the best of your ability. Don't worry over regulations.' Now, General, I have done this to the best of my ability. If I have done right you will support me; if I have done wrong you know what to do with me."

Grant looked at the papers again and then wrote an endorsement: "The object of having a medical director is that he shall be supreme in his department. The decision of Surgeon Brinton is sustained."

To Brinton this action seemed "very noble," and he wrote that "my veneration for his character and my strong personal affection for him dated from that interview." Ever afterward, he said, he was confident that Grant was the man who would finally win the war.[28]

Somewhat similar was the feeling of the paymaster who used to hear the children singing hymns on Sundays. He liked Grant's plain-as-an-old-shoe appearance, the common Army blouse he wore with no sign of rank except the starred straps tacked to the shoulders, the devotion to his family which, the paymaster felt, "won for him the respect and admiration of all with whom he came in contact." Trying to sum everything up, the officer wrote: "The one great virtue that marked General Grant's character as superior to others was that in proportion to his increased responsibility and care came increased ability to act, increased power to meet the emergency." [29]

Even the Leonard Swett who had had difficulties with Grant over supply contracts found the General a frank and friendly sort. Visiting Cairo (and battling vigorously for contracts which Grant would not approve), Swett got the General to talk about the big fight at Belmont, and he liked the way Grant admitted that at the crucial moment of the battle he had lost control over his troops. Swett thought this was a point in Grant's favor; it was refreshing, he said, to meet "one of those big men who wouldn't lie out of a scrape."

The soldiers seem to have noticed that Grant was a good family man, and to the big 64-pounder in the left flank battery at Fort Holt they gave the name "Lady Grant." [30]

CHAPTER SIX

Limited Objectives

AT THE END of 1861, what happened in eastern Tennessee might seem to be of no concern to U. S. Grant. East Tennessee was far removed both from his own military district and from the military department to which his district belonged. His responsibilities were limited, and they required him to look south, not east. But 1861 was the year of preparation, the year in which a singular tangle of conflicting strategic plans, personal rivalries and the slowly emerging imperatives of civil war would presently bring forth new opportunities and new actions. Indirectly but effectively, the fact that eastern Tennessee was putting its own pressure on events in the West would have much to do with the subsequent career of the Brigadier General commanding at Cairo.

It had begun a good deal earlier. Somewhere around October 1, Lincoln wrote out a lengthy "Memorandum for a Plan of Campaign," specifying that in the very near future — within a few weeks, if that could be managed — "I wish a movement made to seize and hold a point of the railroad connecting Virginia and Tennessee, near the Mountain pass called Cumberland Gap." There would presently be a Federal sortie down the Atlantic coast, an amphibious operation which, by November 7, would take possession of Port Royal, South Carolina, as a base for the blockading fleet and a possible take-off point for operations into the Confederate interior. It seemed to the President that this move and the drive through Cumberland Gap ought to be simultaneous, "and that, in the meantime, preparation, vigilant watching and the defensive only" should be followed elsewhere.[1]

With this view the General in Chief, George B. McClellan, agreed. McClellan was carefully getting ready for an offensive in Virginia, aimed at Richmond, and it seemed to him essential for the success of this program that the Tennessee railroad line be severed.[2] The idea also appealed strongly to the people of East Tennessee themselves, who were strongly Unionist in sentiment and who were more than willing to get into the fight if the government at Washington would provide a little help. Living in isolation south of the long rampart of the Cumberland Mountains and feeling no sympathy for the separatist aspirations of the prosperous slaveholders in the western part of the state, these East Tennesseans constituted a potential Union asset near the heart of the Confederacy. There were like-minded folk near them, in the North Carolina mountains and in northern Georgia; the railroad line that came east from Chattanooga, through Knoxville and on into Virginia, was vital to the Confederacy's existence; with a little help these mountain folk could cut the eastern tidewater off from the west and provide a rallying point for any Union sentiment there might be in the South. Lincoln may have overstated the case, a little later, when he said that once a Federal force was firmly established in East Tennessee the Confederacy would be doomed to perish "like an animal with a thorn in its vitals," but in his intense anxiety to get such a campaign started he was at least recognizing a political and military opportunity of the first magnitude.

This imperative, then, hung over Federal strategists in the west: get an army through the Cumberland Gap, destroy the Confederacy's east-west communications, and arm and sustain the tough Southern mountaineers who were prepared to die for the Union. There were just two problems. One was imposed by geography. The road to and beyond the Gap was long and very bad, leading through barren country where a moving army would have immense difficulty supporting itself. The other problem centered in the brain of the austere, methodical, intellectual soldier who commanded Federal forces in Kentucky, Brigadier General Don Carlos Buell.

Buell did not believe in the project. He did not consider himself ready to make a move of any sort this fall, and when he did move he did not want to move through those rugged mountains. The bulk of the Confederate power in the west lay along the line running from Bowling Green, in central Kentucky, over to Columbus, on the Mississippi, and by the books this was the only proper objective for a major offensive. (That the books had been prepared by men

wholly ignorant of the special problems which would be raised by
a civil war in America was unfortunately a point Buell was not willing to take into account.) To strike the main Confederate force
would bring difficulties of its own, because the Cumberland River,
rolling northwest from the great Confederate supply base at Nashville, came through the exact center of the Rebel line, and the Cumberland marked the western limit of Buell's territory. Everything to
the west, as far as Kentucky and Tennessee were concerned, was
under Halleck's control, and the offensive Buell was thinking about
could be made only through close co-operation between Buell and
Halleck.[3] That co-operation, as events were to prove, would be extremely hard to establish.

Officially, however — as far as the President and the General in
Chief could make military policy official — the Number One objective was an expedition through Cumberland Gap, and the people of
eastern Tennessee assumed (to their cost) that it was going to take
place immediately. Some two thousand of them had already filtered
across the line into southeastern Kentucky, where they had been
formed into Federal regiments by Brigadier General S. P. Carter,
a native of East Tennessee and a former naval officer. Behind them,
in the more open country below the mountains, other Tennesseans
were rising in revolt, trying to destroy the Confederacy's all-important railroad line in the belief that Union troops would presently
be on hand to protect them. Arming themselves as well as they
could, they burned bridges and they tore up track, and by November they were giving Confederate patriots much cause for alarm.
Early in the month the president of the East Tennessee and Virginia
Railroad telegraphed Confederate Secretary of War Judah Benjamin that he had evidence that these bands were ready to "destroy or
take possession of the whole line from Bristol to Chattanooga," and
he said that unless the protection of Confederate troops was quickly
provided "transportation over my road of army supplies will be an
utter impossibility." Two days later the superintendent of this road
notified President Davis that several bridges had been burned and
that the country was "in great excitement and terror"; a Confederate officer at Knoxville reported that two thousand Unionists were
under arms, five bridges were down, and there seemed to be "a
general uprising in all the counties." Governor Isham Harris of

Tennessee sadly wrote Davis on November 12 that things were really bad: "The burning of railroad bridges in east Tennessee shows a deep-seated spirit of rebellion in that section. Union men are organizing. This rebellion must be crushed out instantly." Harris would send state troops to the scene, but he begged Davis to send regulars from western Virginia. From Jonesborough, in eastern Tennessee, a correspondent told Davis that "Civil War has broken out at length," and said that the epidemic of bridge burning was "occasioned by the hope that Federal troops would be here in a few days from Kentucky." The railroad president supplemented his earlier report by saying that armed Unionists were massing to destroy the long bridges at Watauga and Strawberry Plains, and he warned: "If these two bridges are burned our road stops." [4]

Federal troops did not come; Confederate troops did; the rebellion was put down with a heavy hand; some of the leading bridge-burners were hanged, and others were imprisoned. But although order was restored, Confederate officers on the scene wrote that the whole section was incurably hostile to the Confederate government. One commander reported: "I think that we have effected something — have done some good; but whenever a foreign force enters this country be it soon or late three-fourths of the people will rise to join them." Most of the male inhabitants, he said, had fled to the mountains, and when Confederate troops appeared the women who had been left behind were "throwing themselves on the ground and wailing like savages. Indeed, the population is savage." [5]

This was the background for Lincoln's insistence that a Union Army be sent down through the Cumberland Gap. McClellan and Buell were intimate — most of their letters to each other began "Dear Friend," even when they wrote on official business — and McClellan did his best to make Buell see that the political factor might affect the military. McClellan tried to make it clear:

> Were the population among which you are to operate wholly or generally hostile it is probable that Nashville should be your first and principal objective point. It so happens that a large majority of the inhabitants of eastern Tennessee are in favor of the Union. It therefore seems proper that you should remain on the defensive on the line from Louisville to Nashville while you throw the mass of your forces by rapid marches by Cum-

berland Gap or Walker's Gap on Knoxville in order to occupy
the railroad at that point and thus enable the loyal citizens of
eastern Tennessee to rise while you at the same time cut off the
railroad communication between eastern Virginia and the Mississippi.[6]

But Buell could not be moved. In a sense, he finally had his way;
that is, the Federal blow in the west was at last directed against Confederate strength rather than against Confederate weakness. But the
war was beginning to move faster than Buell had anticipated. From
waiting at his headquarters in Louisville, studying things carefully
and making detailed and balanced long-range plans, Buell before
long would find himself making a desperate attempt to catch up
with an offensive that had slipped out from under him. The Tennessee campaign would follow the general lines he had laid down,
but he himself would have progressively less and less to do with it.
With all of his caution and his foresight, Buell was simply setting
things up for Grant.

Buell was well aware that his command was not as solid as it
looked from Washington. In a report which he sent to the Adjutant
General just before Christmas he pointed out that although he had
an aggregate of 70,000 troops in his department, only 57,000 of these
were to be reported as "present for duty, equipped," and that figure
included a number of totally untrained regiments; his efficient force
he believed was no more than 50,000. Discipline was poor. There
were 5500 officers and men absent on leave, and 1100 more absent
without leave, and Buell felt that "there is not much difference between the two classes." In a "Dear Friend" letter to McClellan he
touched on his troubles with the state governors, from whom he
was getting his troops. They tried to keep control over their regiments, the governor of Ohio "evidently looks upon all Ohio troops
as his army," and the governor of Indiana had raised a company of
cavalry to act as bodyguard to one of Buell's generals and had
shipped it off to camp without bothering to report its existence to
department headquarters. Most colonels and brigadiers seemed to
have their own personal establishments, and Buell wanted some replacements: "If you have any unoccupied brigadiers — not my seniors — send six or eight, even though they should be no better than
marked poles." [7]

For a time Buell tried to keep the East Tennessee move in mind. He assured McClellan just before the year 1861 ended that he definitely intended to send 12,000 men and three batteries down into East Tennessee, just as soon as proper preparations could be made, although he could not yet set a date for it. But he still felt that the big effort ought to be made in the western part of the state, and the center of this line, where the railroad which connected Columbus with Bowling Green crossed the Tennessee and Cumberland rivers, stuck him as "the most important strategic point in the whole field of operations." [8]

Buell's appraisal of the situation was somewhat warped by the fact that, like most generals at the time, he overestimated the strength of the forces opposing him. He lacked the emotional pessimism which had driven his predecessor, Sherman, into temporary retirement, but he did not yet realize how weak Albert Sidney Johnston really was. Aside from 4000 poorly armed and equipped soldiers who were guarding Cumberland Gap, Johnston had no more than 50,000 men of all arms at his disposal, and he was constantly begging the Richmond government (with very little success) to send him more troops. To impress the Yankees, meanwhile, he put on a bold front, circulating stories about immense levies and strong reinforcements, and these stories were believed. Not for the last time in this war, Confederate soldiers who did not exist exerted an influence on Federal strategy.

Buell believed that Johnston had at least 30,000 men at Bowling Green, and he told McClellan that this number could quickly be increased to 50,000 or 60,000 by transfers from Columbus. It seemed clear to him that he could strike no blow of his own unless Halleck, by threatening Columbus and the Confederate forts on the Tennessee and the Cumberland, could make such transfers impossible. The thrust at East Tennessee struck Buell as a move that could be made only as a supplement to a drive toward Bowling Green and Nashville, and that drive could be made only in co-operation with Halleck. East Tennessee, therefore, would have to wait and the wait might be a long one. [9]

Mr. Lincoln waited, with dwindling patience. On December 31 he sent a message to Halleck: "General McClellan is sick. Are General Buell and yourself in concert? When he moves on Bowling Green, what hinders it being reinforced from Columbus? A simultaneous movement by you on Columbus might prevent it." A copy of this message he sent to Buell.

The Generals replied promptly, but the replies did not make Mr. Lincoln happy.

Buell wired:

> There is no arrangement between General Halleck and myself. I have been informed by General McClellan that he would make suitable disposition for concerted action. There is nothing to prevent Bowling Green being reinforced from Columbus if a military force is not brought to bear on the latter place.

And from Halleck came this wire:

> I have never received a word from General Buell. I am not ready to cooperate with him. Hope to do so in a few weeks. Have written fully on this subject to Major General McClellan. Too much will ruin everything.[10]

On the following day Halleck sent word to Buell:

> I have had no instructions respecting co-operation. All my available troops are in the field except those at Cairo and Paducah, which are barely sufficient to threaten Columbus, etc. A few weeks hence I hope to be able to render you very material assistance, but now a withdrawal of my troops from this state is almost impossible. Write me fully.[11]

More correspondence followed. Slowly recuperating from an attack of typhoid fever, McClellan notified Halleck that "it is of the greatest importance" to keep the Rebels at Columbus from reinforcing those at Bowling Green, and he suggested an expedition up the Cumberland, supported by gunboats. He urged, also, a demonstration against Columbus, with strength enough to make a real attack on the place if any troops had been withdrawn, and proposed a simultaneous feint up the Tennessee. Federal success in Kentucky, he said, would depend largely on these measures, and "not a moment's time should be lost in preparing these expeditions." Buell wrote to Halleck that "the great power of the Rebellion in the west"

was arrayed from Columbus to Bowling Green, estimated that Johnston had at least 80,000 men there, and remarked that Halleck would
of course "at once see the importance of a combined attack on its
center and flanks." Whatever was done, he said, "should be done
speedily, within a few days." [12]

Lincoln's patience continued to diminish. On January 4 he asked
Buell to report on the progress and general condition of the movement toward East Tennessee, ending the telegram with the terse
word: "Answer."

Buell replied that he was planning to move a division toward the
Cumberland Gap, but that he lacked transportation and that other
preparations had not been completed. He added, frankly:

> I will confess to your excellency that I have been bound to it
> more by sympathy for the people of east Tennessee and the
> anxiety with which you and the General-in-Chief have desired it
> than by my opinion of its wisdom as an unconditional measure.
> As earnestly as I wish to accomplish it, my judgment from the
> first has been decidedly against it, if it should render at all
> doubtful the success of a movement against the great power of
> the Rebellion in the west, which is mainly arrayed on the line
> from Columbus to Bowling Green and can speedily be concen-
> trated at any point of that line which is attacked singly.

This drew a rebuke from McClellan, who wrote to Buell bluntly:

> There are few things I have more at heart than the prompt
> movement of a strong column into eastern Tennessee. The
> political consequences of the delay of this movement will be
> much more serious than you seem to anticipate. . . . I was
> extremely sorry to learn from your telegram to the President
> that you had *from the beginning attached little or no importance*
> to a movement in east Tennessee. I had not so understood your
> views, and it develops a radical difference between your views
> and my own which I deeply regret.
>
> My own general plans for the prosecution of the war made
> the speedy occupation of east Tennessee and its lines of railway
> matters of absolute necessity. Bowling Green and Nashville are
> in that connection of very secondary importance at the present
> moment. My own advance cannot, according to my present
> views, be made until your troops are soundly established in the

eastern portion of Tennessee. If that is not possible, a complete and prejudicial change in my own plans at once becomes necessary. . . . Halleck, from his own account, will not soon be in a condition to support properly a movement up the Cumberland. Why not make the movement independently of and without waiting for that? [13]

And Halleck, on January 6, wrote to President Lincoln explaining that at best he could spare only 10,000 men to help Buell, and saying: "It would be madness to attempt anything serious with such a force, and I cannot at the present time withdraw any from Missouri without risking the loss of this state." Most of the middle and northern counties of Missouri, he added, were in a state of insurrection, and the presence in them of strong Federal forces was essential. Moreover, many of Halleck's troops and officers were unreliable, and "I am in the condition of a carpenter who is required to build a bridge with a dull axe, a broken saw, and rotten timber." Halleck knew nothing about Buell's intended operations, and the idea of making simultaneous movements on the Rebel stronghold struck him as folly: "To operate on exterior lines against an enemy occupying a central position will fail, as it has always failed in ninety-nine cases out of a hundred. It is condemned by every military authority I have ever read."

At the foot of this letter President Lincoln scribbled a gloomy endorsement:

> The within is a copy of a letter just received from General Halleck. It is exceedingly discouraging. As everywhere else, nothing can be done.[14]

However, all of this prodding was beginning to have some effect, even though the effect was not at all what the President and the General in Chief had originally had in mind. On the same day that he wrote to President Lincoln, Halleck sent orders to Grant: Grant was to make an armed demonstration toward Mayfield, Kentucky, 30 miles south of Paducah, leading the Rebels, if he could, to suppose that he was going to attack either Camp Beauregard, below Columbus, or the new Confederate stronghold, Fort Donelson, which was on the west bank of the Cumberland River just south of the Tennessee-Kentucky line. Flag Officer Foote would be asked to make menacing moves with his gunboats at the same time; Grant would be reinforced as soon as possible, and he was to spread the word that twenty or thirty thousand troops would presently join him from Missouri. At all costs he was to avoid a general engagement, and he should keep the real aim of the expedition — to keep the Rebels from reinforcing Bowling Green — secret even from his own officers.[15]

Grant accepted these orders with enthusiasm. Foote would send three gunboats up the Cumberland and two more would go up the Tennessee. From Paducah, Smith would move toward Mayfield, and Grant's own force from Cairo would go down to the west to protect Smith's flank. Conditions for the move were not ideal; it had been raining for a week and the roads were excessively bad, which would mean slow marching. However, Grant wrote, this "will operate worse upon the enemy, if he should come out to meet us, than upon us." (Just why bad roads would be worse for Rebels than for Federals, Grant did not explain; obviously, he wanted to get moving, and he was going to take a hopeful view of everything.) At this time Grant had a total of just over twenty thousand men in his command, including Smith's people at Paducah; most of them would be involved in this demonstration.[16]

More letters and telegrams went back and forth between Washington, Louisville and St. Louis, including a message from Lincoln to Buell and Halleck ordering speed and remarking: "Delay is ruining us." McClellan again tried to impress on Buell the need for an advance through the Cumberland Gap: "You had no idea of the pressure brought to bear here upon the Government for a forward movement. It is so strong that it seems absolutely necessary to make the advance on eastern Tennessee at once." With Halleck, McClellan had a brief passage at arms. Halleck tried to shift responsibility by asking McClellan if he insisted on the withdrawal of troops from Missouri for the march into Kentucky, writing ominously: "If so, it will be done, but in my opinion it involves the defeat of the Union cause in this state." McClellan deftly tossed the ball back to him by replying: "If you can spare no troops it is only necessary to say so, and I must look elsewhere for the means of accomplishing the object in view. There is nothing in my letter that can reasonably be construed into an order requiring you to make detachments that will involve the defeat of the Union cause in Missouri." [17]

In spite of everything, the demonstration at last was made. On January 13 Grant issued orders to govern the conduct of the march. Straggling was not to be permitted, no one was to be allowed to leave camp in the evening, the firing of guns either in camp or on the march was prohibited unless there were armed Rebels to be shot at, and severe punishment was to be visited on all looters. On January 14 the expedition took off. At the last minute Grant had difficulties with his master of river transportation, Captain W. J. Kountz of the quartermaster department; a man who (as Grant reported to Halleck) "from his great unpopularity with river men and his wholesale denunciation of everybody connected with the Government here as thieves and cheats, was entirely unable to get crews for the necessary boats." Grant found that the civilian crews were quite willing to serve if they did not have to serve under Kountz — who, he said, "seems to have desired to be placed on duty here for no other purpose than to wreak his revenge upon some river men whom he dislikes, and to get into the service of the Government a boat in which he has an interest" — and so he put Kountz under arrest, asked St. Louis to assign him to some other field of duty, and went off without him.[18]

On the surface, Grant's expedition was a demonstration and no more, and neither he nor C. F. Smith felt that it accomplished much. The explicit orders to avoid an engagement at all costs irked Grant, and to a staff officer he remarked: "I wonder if General Halleck would object to another 'skirmish' like Belmont? I suppose, though, that it would hardly do to 'skirmish' hard enough to take Columbus." When it was suggested that if the Confederate positions on the rivers were taken General Polk would have to evacuate Columbus, Grant objected. "Better attack," he said, "and capture the entire force where they are. Why allow them to withdraw and follow and fight them in the interior of Mississippi or Alabama under greater disadvantages?" As he had shown at Belmont, Grant had no liking for simply making the enemy retreat. Nothing less than outright destruction of the enemy's main force would satisfy him.[19]

Added up, the effect of the demonstration seemed to be good. Halleck wrote McClellan that the operation would probably keep the Confederates at Columbus in check "till preparations can be made for operations on the Tennessee and Cumberland," and Grant reported that his talks with people inside the Rebel lines made him feel that "public confidence in ultimate success is fast on the wane in the South." He added that "the expedition, if it had no other effect, served as a fine reconnaissance." But he wanted to do more. One of his officers wrote that after the soldiers had returned to Cairo Grant said: "This sloshing about in mud, rain, sleet and snow for a week without striking the enemy, only exposing the men to great hardships and suffering in mid-winter, is not war." If he had been permitted to fight, he said, he could at least have taken Camp Beauregard, "and this would have been 'a demonstration' with an object and a reward." [20]

One of the deeply rooted impulses that would characterize Grant as a soldier had already become visible: the impulse to get to close quarters with his antagonist and slug it out. At Belmont he had turned a demonstration into a battle for no better reason than that he did not like to make empty gestures. As far as Grant was concerned a demonstration meant very little unless the man conducting it was free to make a real fight when the occasion offered. The January expedition left him dissatisfied because it had been designed as a feint and nothing more.

This elaborate and seemingly fruitless movement into Kentucky did, in the end, have results. It led to genuine action a short time afterward; which is to say that it disclosed — to the Army and Navy men on the spot, and apparently to Halleck himself — that a blow in this area, delivered with full weight, might be most effective. It is noteworthy, too, that when the blow was finally delivered Grant went beyond both his instructions and his own original concept of the move to make it one of the decisive strategic moves of the entire war.

In the course of this expedition old Smith had gone up the Tennessee River with the gunboats to exchange a few shots with Fort Henry. This was a fort which the Confederates had built just below the Kentucky state line, back in the days of Kentucky's neutrality, and it was not strong. Some time before the expedition took place,

Grant and Smith had sat in Smith's quarters at Paducah studying such maps of the place as they could get, and they had concluded that it was vulnerable. Built on low ground, Fort Henry was partly flooded now because the water in the Tennessee was high, and both Smith and Foote believed that it could easily be taken. At the very least, gunboats might run past it, in which case they could steam up the Tennessee all the way to northern Alabama, destroying Confederate railroad bridges and generally disrupting things, and it seemed that the effort ought to be made. Foote urged Grant, "for the good of the service," to go to St. Louis in person and propose the scheme. The worst Halleck could do, said Foote, was refuse, and even if he did "his wrath will hardly be so hot as to dry up the Mississippi before you can get back to Cairo." [21]

Meanwhile, hundreds of miles to the east, another development helped make the war in Kentucky more fluid. Johnston's troops in front of Cumberland Gap had been under the command of General Felix K. Zollicoffer, who led the skimpy little Confederate Army over the Cumberland River near Mill Springs and seemed to menace Buell's eastern outpost, a division commanded by Virginia-born General George H. Thomas. Over the inexperienced Zollicoffer the Confederate authorities then placed George B. Crittenden, son of the distinguished Kentuckian, John J. Crittenden, who had endeavored a year ago to work out a national compromise that would avert war. Crittenden recognized the exposure of his army, but was unable to rectify Zollicoffer's error. Thomas, a whole-hearted believer in the projected campaign into eastern Tennessee, gathered his troops together, and after a difficult march over muddy roads he prepared to attack Crittenden's men. But on January 19 Crittenden himself attacked, only to be beaten in what became a decisive Union victory. Zollicoffer was killed, the Confederates were driven off in disorganized retreat, Crittenden's handling of his force was so inept that men accused him of being drunk, and the eastern end of Johnston's line had come adrift. The way now was open for the advance into eastern Tennessee.

The way would not be easy. Thomas's ardor cooled perceptibly when he saw how bad the roads were in midwinter and how desolate was the country through which his army would have to march. "I have every reason," he notified Buell, "to believe that the roads leading into Tennessee are in the same condition as the one over which my division has just passed, and the enemy having passed over these roads our chances for subsistence and forage would be but poor. I would therefore again respectfully suggest that I may be permitted to move down the river" (that is, down the Cumberland, which in that part of Kentucky flows from east to west before looping down into Tennessee) "with my troops, taking our subsistence and forage in flatboats, and co-operate with the main army against Bowling Green." He added, however, that the Rebel Army in his front seemed to be entirely dispersed, "and should we go into East Tennessee now there would be no enemy to encounter." [22]

With that report, the chance for a real push into East Tennessee evaporated. General Carter would be told to move forward with his brigade and hold Cumberland Gap, but no invasion would be ordered. Inevitably, the whole weight of Federal operations would now be concentrated where Buell had always wanted it concentrated, in the general direction of Nashville; and the Tennessee and Cumberland rivers, flowing north side by side, and only a few miles apart where they descended from Tennessee into Kentucky, would loom larger and larger in the Union's strategic planning. But the hard fact remained: an offensive in western Tennessee could take place only if Halleck co-operated, and if Halleck co-operated the instrument he must use could only be the force commanded by Grant. In the most unpredictable way, the uprising of the East Tennessee loyalists and President Lincoln's insistence that the Western Armies act energetically in response was about to start Grant up the rivers that led to the Deep South.

In the latter part of January, Grant got permission to go to St. Louis and present his argument to Halleck. The experience seems not to have been a happy one. In his memoirs — written long afterward, at a time when his feelings toward Halleck were definitely hostile — Grant said that Halleck cut him short "as if my plan were preposterous." He was received, he said, with so little cordiality that "I perhaps stated the object of my business with less clearness than I might have done," and Halleck refused to hear him through. Grant returned to Cairo, he said, "very much crestfallen."

Colonel John Emerson. who was always ready to take Grant's

side in any argument presented an account of the meeting which, he said, had been given him by an officer who was present. Halleck, he said, shook hands with Grant rather stiffly, then sat at his desk, began shuffling papers, and told Grant to "state briefly the nature of the business connected with your command which brought you to headquarters." Grant took out a map, unfolded it, and began to explain the situation at Fort Henry and at Fort Donelson — which, on the Cumberland, was only a dozen miles away from Fort Henry. With a column of twenty-five thousand men aided by the gunboats, he said, he could take both forts in ten days and probably Columbus as well.

Halleck, according to the way Emerson heard it, stopped him by asking coldly:

"Is there anything connected with the good of your command you wish to discuss?"

Grant tried to trace the projected movement on the map, but Halleck stood up, waved the map aside, and said:

"All of this, General Grant, relates to the business of the General commanding the department. When he wishes to consult you on that subject he will notify you."

Having said this, Halleck stalked out, leaving Grant to pocket his map and go back to Cairo.[23]

If Grant had been humiliated it did not show on him that evening. Dr. Brinton was in St. Louis at the time, and that night the doctor went to a theater, a slightly disreputable place as he recalled it, where he was sitting "listening to wretched jabber on the stage." He felt a hand on his shoulder, and turned to see Grant looking down at him.

"Oh, Doctor, Doctor," said Grant, grinning and chewing a cigar, "if you only knew how it grieves me to find you in such a low place and in such company." Having said this, Grant sat down beside him and saw the performance. He told Brinton that he intended to have him back at Cairo with him before long. As far as the surgeon could see, Grant was in excellent spirits.

However unsatisfactory his interview with Halleck may have been, Grant found time on this St. Louis trip to attend to a few personal matters. He went to call on Harry Boggs, with whom he had had a brief, unsuccessful real estate partnership in 1858, and found that his old friends felt that he had gone up in the world. In 1858, he had occupied one room in the Boggs house; now Mrs. Boggs, vastly impressed by Grant's position as commander of the Cairo district, worried for fear her home might be too humble for him. Grant also went to a French chemist to buy some medicine for his nine-year-old son Ulysses, who was very ill with what an Army doctor had diagnosed as inflammatory rheumatism; the doctor had said that only the medicine compounded by this particular chemist was likely to effect a cure. As Mrs. Grant remembered the case, long afterward, the medicine was almost miraculously effective. When Grant returned to Cairo, little Ulysses was delirious, with a high fever. The medicine was administered, and he quickly recovered.[24]

Grant is generally given credit for bringing to Halleck's attention the desirability of an invasion of Tennessee via the Tennessee and Cumberland rivers. Actually, Halleck had already been doing a great deal of thinking about such an offensive. The long interchange of letters and telegrams around the Halleck-Buell-McClellan triangle could not have failed to impress the idea on his mind. It had been rumored for weeks that he would eventually send an expedition down the Mississippi, but as early as December 16 a newspaper correspondent had said flatly: "The movement will not go down the Mississippi but go up the Tennessee, where Gen. Halleck's forces, 75,000 strong, will leave the river and march to the rear of Columbus, Hickman and other points toward Memphis. This will compel the Rebels at Columbus and other points to fall back on Memphis, thus leaving the river clear for the gunboats and transportation vessels to pass up and down unmolested." Some time before that, Colonel Charles Whittlesey, chief of the Army Engineers at Cincinnati, had written Halleck asking:

Will you allow me to suggest the consideration of a great movement by land and water up the Cumberland and Tennessee rivers?

1st. Would it not allow of water transportation halfway to Nashville?

2nd. Would it not necessitate the evacuation of Columbus by threatening their railway communications?

3d. Would it not necessitate the retreat of General Buckner by threatening his railway lines?

4th. Is it not the most passable route into Tennessee? [25]

Colonel Emerson insisted that Whittlesey, in Washington, had heard about the river move which (as Emerson insisted) Grant had blocked out during the previous summer, and he said Whittlesey visited Grant not long after the battle of Belmont and went over the whole proposal with him, with maps on the table before them. Emerson almost certainly exaggerated. Grant himself never claimed to have originated the movement; he and Whittlesey apparently did not meet until later, and in any case the move was an obvious approach that would strike any general's eye. Several days before Grant came to see him, Halleck wrote to McClellan saying that a drive straight down the Mississippi was not quite practicable. Then he went on to set forth his own views:

A much more feasible plan is to move up the Cumberland and Tennessee, making Nashville the first objective point. This would turn Columbus and force the abandonment of Bowling Green. Columbus cannot be taken without an immense siege train and a terrible loss of life. . . . But it can be turned, paralyzed and forced to surrender. This line of the Cumberland or Tennessee is the great central line of the Western theater of war. . . . But the plan should not be attempted without a large force, not less than 60,000 men.[26]

Halleck, in other words, had been giving the Tennessee-Cumberland plan a great deal of attention, and if he was not exactly swept off his feet by the discovery that Grant had been thinking along the same lines it is not surprising. Furthermore, although Halleck had been doing nothing much more lofty than trying to keep his own record clear when he warned McClellan that a major offensive in Kentucky might mean the loss of Missouri, he did have major problems in that state and his reluctance to send troops into Kentucky is at least understandable. In many parts of Missouri Halleck was confronting exactly what the Confederates in eastern Tennessee were facing — an uprising of a dissident populace, accompanied by many annoying acts of bridge-burning, railroad-blocking and the like — and between this and the flood of Unionist-minded refugees who had been driven from their homes and were flocking into St. Louis he had his hands full.

Indeed, the whole experience was turning Halleck into a hard-war man of the most ruthless kind, and the harsh rules which other Federal commanders would enforce in the occupied South in the years to come stemmed largely from the frame of mind which Halleck developed during his tour of duty in St. Louis. Early in December he issued an extremely tough statement of policy. Thousands of loyal citizens of Missouri had been robbed and driven from their homes, he said, by the Confederates, and were reaching St. Louis "barefooted, half-clad and in a destitute and starving condition." There were in St. Louis, he continued, many well-to-do folk of secessionist sympathies, who gave encouragement and help to the marauders. Consequently, the provost-marshals in St. Louis would see to it that the refugees were quartered in the homes and at the expense of the pro-Confederates. The provost marshals were to make up lists of disloyal citizens "who are, judging by their mode of living, in good circumstances," and each person so listed would be required to contribute ten thousand dollars to the support of the refugees. In the ordinary way of things, this contribution would be made in food and living quarters; the disloyalists would have house guests, whether they wanted them or not, and their property would be seized and sold at auction if they refused to comply.[27]

Halleck was rigorous about it. Confederate sympathizers in St. Louis were greatly subdued, and Dr. Brinton noted approvingly that "It is becoming a dangerous game to be 'sassy.' " One of Halleck's orders foreshadowed the brutal rule Ben Butler was to adopt in New Orleans. Secessionist women in St. Louis took to wearing red-and-white rosettes as an emblem of their devotion to the South. Halleck did not try to stop them by direct action; he simply had a lot of the rosettes made up and given to prostitutes, who were instructed to wear them on all occasions. Then an inspired newspaper article called attention to the fact that all of the loose women in the city were coming out in red-and-white rosettes. . . .

Some of the house guests with whom women of Southern sympathies found themselves afflicted were difficult people to get along with; even Dr. Brinton referred to them as "these half-savage Union women." One secessionist woman who lived in a nice home and found herself hostess to one of these creatures thought to discourage the guest by removing her parlor furniture. The refugee, who knew that the full might of the United States government was supporting her, told her angrily: "I will tell you when I want them carpets up." [28]

Grant had no hesitation in following Halleck's lead in these matters. At the end of December he announced that the Cairo district was overrun with loyalist refugees "who have been driven from their homes and deprived of the means of subsistence by the acts of disloyal citizens of Kentucky and Missouri." These people needed food and shelter, and "justice demands that the class of persons who have caused their sufferings should bear the expense of the same"; consequently, Grant ordered that contributions be collected from disloyalists in the same manner followed by Halleck in St. Louis. He added a refinement of his own: a pro-secessionist who was liable to this assessment, and who happened to be of Northern birth and education, would be required to pay 50 per cent more than a Southerner of the same class and means.[29]

Outside of St. Louis Halleck found plenty to do. He said that at this time he had fully ten thousand soldiers guarding railroad lines, but that in a ten-day period Rebel guerillas did one hundred and fifty thousand dollars' worth of damage to rails, telegraph lines and bridges. "Nothing," he wrote, "but the severest punishment" could stop this, and he proposed to be severe "although I have no doubt there will be a newspaper howl against me as a blood-thirsty monster." He declared that "our army here is almost as much in a hostile country as it was when in Mexico," and he warned the commander of one outpost: "Missouri is and must remain in the Union, and all Rebels must be driven out or punished. There must be no more halfway measures." All persons who cut down telegraph poles or tried to damage railway lines, he ordered, were to be shot forthwith.

At the same time Halleck tried without great success to restrain the more ferocious Union adherents. In the extreme western part of the state Kansas troops under vengeful officers like General James H. Lane and Colonel C. R. Jennison were instituting a reign of terror which appalled the commander in St. Louis, and Halleck told

McClellan that they were simply creating sympathy for the Confederates. He said their excesses had "done more for the enemy in this state than could have been accomplished by 20,000 of his own army." With memories in which the lawless times of the "border ruffians" were still fresh, the Kansans were completely ruthless. Jennison announced publicly that "traitors will everywhere be treated as outlaws — enemies of God and man — too base to hold any description of property and having no rights which loyal men are bound to respect." Operating under such orders, the "Jayhawkers" in the Kansas regiments had a field day, and as they looted and burned they did not always make nice distinctions between friend and foe. One St. Louis newspaper commented editorially: "The Jayhawker bases or professes to base his operations upon the principle of never robbing or hanging one who entertains the same political creed as himself if it is possible to avoid it." [30]

It is against this background that Halleck's slowness in mounting an offensive in Kentucky must be appraised. At the same time it must in fairness be added that the impatience of his subordinates around Cairo undoubtedly spurred him on to action. In addition, no general of Halleck's intelligence could fail to see that the Federal command situation in the West, with the crucial area divided between two independent commands, was both unsatisfactory and unstable. Sooner or later, either Buell or Halleck was likely to be given the over-all command in the West, and the prize would almost certainly go to the one who bestirred himself first. The President for weeks had been demanding action, and Buell (for his own reasons) was not giving it to him. If Halleck should move first, Halleck was very likely to become top dog.

By January 22 Halleck had begun to make up his mind. He notified Grant that substantial additional forces would be sent to him, and told him to prepare a large encampment at Smithland, where the Cumberland joined the Ohio, to receive them. (This message went to Grant before Grant visited St. Louis.) An important factor in Halleck's decision undoubtedly was the fact that Washington informed him that the famous Confederate General G. T. Beauregard was being sent West to join Johnston. What gave this news, which was quite correct, added point was the totally false report that

Beauregard was taking fifteen regiments with him as reinforcements. To both McClellan and Halleck it seemed that the long-awaited blow had better be struck before these troops arrived.

Meanwhile, Grant and Foote had been making their own preparations. On January 28, Foote wired Halleck: "Commanding General Grant and myself are of opinion that Fort Henry, on the Tennessee River, can be carried with four iron-clad gun-boats and troops to permanently occupy. Have we your authority to move for that purpose when ready?" On the same day Grant supplemented this by wiring Halleck: "With permission, I will take Fort Henry, on the Tennessee, and establish and hold a large camp there." He followed this by writing to Halleck in more detail, on the following day:

> In view of the large force now concentrating in this district and the present feasibility of the plan I would respectfully suggest the propriety of subduing Fort Henry, near the Kentucky and Tennessee line, and holding the position. If this is not done soon there is but little doubt but that the defenses on both the Tennessee and Cumberland rivers will be materially strengthened. From Fort Henry it will be easy to operate either on the Cumberland, only 12 miles distant, Memphis, or Columbus. It will, besides, have a moral effect upon our troops to advance them toward the Rebel States. The advantages of this move are as perceptible to the general commanding as to myself, therefore further statements are unnecessary.[31]

It must be said that these messages do not sound quite like the offerings of a subordinate who had just been snubbed for making exactly the same proposals verbally. Halleck may have been reserved when Grant talked to him, but there is at least a hint in the wording of Grant's letter that Grant was returning to a subject on which he and his commanding general had come to some sort of understanding, and it seems quite possible that Halleck had simply wanted to be assured that Foote shared Grant's optimism.[32] In any case, Halleck now responded promptly. On January 30 he wrote certain dispatches that put the war into high gear. To McClellan he wrote:

> Your telegraph respecting Beauregard is received. General Grant and Commodore Foote will be ordered to immediately

advance and to reduce and hold Fort Henry, on the Tennessee river, and also to cut the railroad line between Dover and Paris. [Halleck meant the line that connected Johnston's stronghold at Columbus with his massed forces in the neighborhood of Bowling Green. It did not actually go within ten miles of Dover.] The roads are in such condition as to render all movements exceedingly slow and difficult.

Halleck added that he had reinforced Grant with eight regiments of infantry and that several more regiments and three batteries of field artillery were under orders to join him, and he concluded: "I will send down every man I can spare." [33]

To Buell, Halleck telegraphed: "I have ordered an advance of our troops on Fort Henry and Dover. It will be made immediately." And to Grant he wired: "Make your preparations to take and hold Fort Henry. I will send you written instructions by mail."

These instructions, dated January 30, spelled it out:

> You will immediately prepare to send forward to Fort Henry, on the Tennessee river, all your available forces from Smithland, Paducah, Fort Holt, Bird's Point, etc. Sufficient garrisons must be left to hold these places against an attack from Columbus.

Warning Grant that the roads were bad, Halleck directed that troops and supplies be moved by boat, under naval convoy. Fort Henry was to be "taken and held at all hazards"; Grant should land troops below the fort and cut the roads that led over to Fort Donelson, on the Cumberland, so as to make it impossible for the Fort Henry garrison to retreat. He should also send cavalry forward to break the railroad; the railroad bridges over the two rivers "should be rendered impassable but not destroyed." (The Union forces might need these bridges later.) Three companies of artillery were being sent down to join Grant's command.[34]

To Buell, who had been saying that he could not make an offensive move unless Halleck helped him, and to whom no promises of help had been vouchsafed, all of this was a bit surprising. He telegraphed Halleck: "Please let me know your plan and force and the time etc." Halleck replied that the movement "to take and hold Fort Henry and cut railroad" had already been ordered, that some fif-

teen thousand men would be involved, and that he would notify
Buell by telegraph of the day of investment or attack. Buell, beginning to realize that it was he, and not Halleck, who would be playing second fiddle in the coming offensive, sent back the query:

> Do you consider active cooperation essential to your success,
> because in that case it would be necessary for each to know
> what the other has to do. It would be several days before I
> could seriously engage the enemy, and your operation ought
> not to fail.

There was only a moderate amount of clarification in Halleck's
reply:

> Co-operation at present not essential. Fort Henry has been
> reinforced, but where from I have not learned. The roads are
> in such horrible condition as to render movements almost im-
> possible on land. . . . Write me your plans and I will try to
> assist you.[35]

Grant, meanwhile, got busy. On receipt of Halleck's telegram he
replied:

> I am quietly making preparations for a move, without as yet
> having created a suspicion that a movement is to be made.
> Awaiting your instructions, which we expect in the morning,
> I have not made definite plans as to my movements, but expect
> to start Sunday evening, taking 15,000 men.

The movement would be made by water as far as practicable,
and Grant would take either McClernand or Smith "to command
after my return." [36]

The last five words are significant, for they highlight the fact that
this expedition — which was soon to become one of the most con-
sequential of the entire war — was still being thought of as an
affair of strictly limited objectives. This seems to have been because none of the Federal officers involved — unless it may have
been C. F. Smith — had at this date a really clear idea of the Confederate defenses on the two rivers.

Fort Henry guarded the Tennessee: all of the Unionists knew

about that, and Foote and Smith had discerned that it was vulnerable. At Dover, on the Cumberland, twelve miles to the east, the Confederates had Fort Donelson, which was well laid out on high ground and which, if properly manned, was a much stronger place; and about Donelson the Union commanders appear to have known very little. It did not figure greatly in their planning. C. F. Smith wrote that is was "called Fort Gavock, or Fort McGavock, or something else." [37] Halleck's orders to Grant did not mention it, except to provide that Grant should block the road to Dover so as to keep the people in Fort Henry from getting away: Halleck appears to have confused Dover with Clarksville, thirty miles upstream. In his messages to Buell Halleck sometimes spoke of Fort Henry and sometimes of "Fort Henry and Dover," the clear implication being that Fort Henry was the important objective and that whatever sort of works the Confederates might have at Dover would stand or fall with the fort on the Tennessee. And now Grant was writing that he would come back to Cairo once Fort Henry was taken, leaving a subordinate to hold the place.

But all of these limitations would vanish very quickly. The important fact was that the movement had been entrusted to the one soldier in all the West to whom limited objectives were least acceptable.

CHAPTER SEVEN

Between the Rivers

ALLECK'S ORDER to go ahead and take Fort Henry hit Grant's headquarters with galvanic effect. Colonel Emerson, who had the story from Rawlins, said that staff officers stopped work at their desks "as suddenly as if a one hundred pound bomb had landed in their midst." Rawlins kicked over a couple of chairs and pounded the walls with his fists. Other officers threw their hats in the air and kicked them as they came down. Grant looked on, amused, and at last suggested that they really did not need to make so much noise that Bishop Polk would hear it, down at Columbus. Then all hands got down to work.[1]

Grant's first step was to write to Smith. He did this immediately after getting Halleck's telegram, before the receipt of the written orders, and he told Smith that "on Monday next"—that is, on February 3—he would move with fifteen thousand men to seize the Confederate fort. Smith was to take a brigade from Paducah and all of the men who were stationed at Smithland except for the 52nd Illinois and one battalion which Smith was to designate. His men were to carry two days' rations and forty rounds of ammunition; the boats from Cairo would issue a fresh supply at the place of debarkation. "Very little preparation is necessary for this move," Grant wrote. "If possible the troops and community should be kept from knowing anything of the design. I am well aware, however, that this caution is entirely unnecessary to you." [2]

On February 1, having been notified by Halleck that his requisitions for horses, mules, wagons and the like could not be filled, but that the usual supply trains could be dispensed with inasmuch as the troops would not be moving far from their steamers, Grant wrote orders for McClernand; McClernand was to hold his troops ready to move on the following evening, taking all camp and garrison equipment, issuing three days' rations and forage and limiting his transportation to four teams to a regiment. While the expedition was away General E. A. Paine — the same with whom Smith had had so much trouble at Paducah — was to be left in temporary command at Cairo, where he would have eight regiments of infantry, six companies of cavalry, two companies of artillery, and the sick of the entire command. Rawlins got off revised instructions to Smith; he was to take all the troops he had, leaving only enough to hold Paducah and Smithland in case of a sudden raid by the Confederates. Grant sent to Halleck a summary of his dispositions. Then, apparently suspecting that Beauregard (who was highly respected by the Federal commanders) might be about to replace General Polk at Columbus, Grant warned: "More troops should be here soon if a change of commander is expected at Columbus.".[3]

Grant's orders for the expedition sought to guard against the Volunteer vices of straggling and looting which had helped spoil the battle plan at Belmont. No firing of guns was to be permitted, except on order. There was to be no plundering of civilian or captured military property. Company officers were to keep their men in camp, there must be roll calls every evening and morning, and all absentees were to be reported to regimental commanders. Company commanders were to take especial pains to see that rations were not wasted. Regimental commanders would be held strictly accountable for the actions of their regiments, and commanders would be made responsible for the behavior of the individual companies.

To Buell, at Louisville, the whole business began to be disturbing. Halleck told him that "it is only proposed to take and occupy Fort Henry and Dover, and if possible cut the railroad from Columbus to Bowling Green." Then Halleck went on to make sage suggestions:

> Keep me informed of your forces and plans, and I will endeavor to assist you as much as possible. If we take Fort Henry and concentrate all available forces there, troops must be withdrawn either from Bowling Green or Columbus to protect the railroads. If the former, you can advance; if the latter, we can take New Madrid [a Missouri town on the Mississippi some miles below Columbus; the Confederates had troops there and

were building fortifications, with powerful batteries on Island Number Ten in a bend of the Mississippi a little way upstream] and cut off the river communications with Columbus. But it will take some time to get troops ready to advance far south of Fort Henry.

All of this jarred Buell into belated thought for the East Tennessee expedition, which he had so long been resisting. To George Thomas, at Somerset, a hundred miles east of Louisville, Buell on February 2 sent a slightly frantic message:

What now is the condition of roads? How soon could you march, and how long do you suppose it would take you to reach Knoxville? Are your supplies accumulating in sufficient quantity for a start? How is the road in advance likely to be affected by the passage of successive trains? What dependence can you place in supplies along it, particularly forage? Do you hear of any organization of a force there? Where is Crittenden? Are the fugitives getting together again? What progress has been made in improving the road to Somerset? Please answer at once.

It was too late now. Inexorably, the weight of effort in the West was going to move up the Tennessee and the Cumberland rivers, and, although this was what Buell had been urging, he himself was being edged toward the sidelines. Buell was a good man and he had missed the boat, and by now there was very little he could do about it. He did his best; on February 3 he wrote earnestly to Halleck, setting forth his ideas:

The destruction of bridges on the Tennessee and Cumberland by gunboats I believe to be feasible. The gunboats can at this stage of the water run past the batteries at night without great risk. This accomplished, the taking and holding Fort Henry and Dover would be comparatively easy. Without that I fear the force you name could not hold both points. It will not do to be driven away.

He warned Halleck that Confederate reinforcements to the extent of ten thousand men from Bowling Green (not to mention such troops as Beauregard might be bringing from Virginia) would probably be appearing at Fort Henry.

From Grant, on the same day, Halleck got a message: "Will be off up the Tennessee at 6 o'clock. Command, 23 regiments in all." [4]

. . . The thing had been talked about for months. President Lincoln and General McClellan had urged a drive into East Tennessee, Buell and Halleck had been discussing the possibilities of a smash at the Confederate center, a great many days had been lost. — and, at last, a job had been given to a man who was ready to move. Grant's troops were going aboard the transports at Cairo and at Paducah, Foote's gunboats were paddling heavily against the current, and the dismemberment of the Southern Confederacy was about to begin; while Halleck and Buell were sending messages to one another about co-operation, about demonstrations, about the chances that this general or that might gain especial advantages out of a victory. What nobody could quite grasp was the fact that the important decisions were going to be made in the field. The war was beginning to move and the man who could not move with it might be left behind.

Messages continued to go back and forth. On February 5 Halleck wrote to tell Buell that his column was moving up the Tennessee, and he asked plaintively: "Can't you make a diversion in our favor by threatening Bowling Green?" This jarred Buell, who had been assured a few days earlier that his co-operation was not needed, and he replied sharply:

> My position does not admit of diversion. My moves must be real ones, and I shall move at once unless I am restrained by orders concerning other plans. Progress will be slow for me. Must repair the railroad as we advance. It will probably be twelve days before we can be in front of Bowling Green.

To make Buell more unhappy, McClellan urged him to make demonstrations and told him to help Halleck if he possibly could. Buell told him what he had told Halleck — that he could not make demonstrations ("My moves must be in earnest") and he explained that Bowling Green was tough: it lay behind a river and it was strongly fortified, and the Rebels had obstructed the forty miles of roads Buell's troops would have to cover. He added piously that he hoped "General Halleck has weighed his work well," and Halleck

notified McClellan that Fort Henry was being heavily reinforced
and said: "Unless I get more forces I may fail to take it, but the attack must help General Buell to move forces forward." McClellan
asked Buell if, in view of everything, it might not be well to make
the advance up the rivers "the main line of operations," and Buell
replied that the idea was sound but that the whole venture was
hazardous; Halleck, he complained, had begun the move "without
appreciation — preparative or concert." Halleck confessed that
this was true, but pleaded that he had been under great pressure. "I
had no idea of commencing the movement before the 15th or 20th
instant till I received General McClellan's telegram about the reinforcement sent to Tennessee or Kentucky with Beauregard." Mc-
Clellan toyed with the idea of having Buell go down in person to
take charge of the move.[5]

Meanwhile, Grant's troops were moving. As Grant's headquarters boat left the wharf, Rawlins noticed that Grant seemed tense
and that he kept looking back at the wharf boat, as if he feared until the last minute that some order of recall might arrive from St.
Louis. When the steamer finally went on upstream and Cairo fell
out of sight behind, Grant "seemed a new man." He clapped Rawlins on the shoulder — a surprising act, to Rawlins, for Grant had
never behaved so before — and said: "Now we seem to be safe, beyond recall. . . . We will succeed, Rawlins; we must succeed."
Rawlins and Grant shook hands.[6]

Grant had done his best to keep the expedition a secret — Halleck had told him to keep even his own staff officers in the dark
about the destination of the force — but military security in the
Civil War was usually leaky, and it proved so in this case. Even before the transports left Cairo, the *Chicago Tribune* man sent off a
dispatch announcing that "the grand expedition up the Tennessee
and Cumberland rivers is about to start"; he estimated the force at
twenty-two thousand men, said that it would attack Forts Henry
and Donelson, and added, apparently as an afterthought, that
the military authorities were not permitting any dispatches regarding the expedition to be sent. Early on the morning of February 4 another correspondent at Paducah informed his paper's

readers that transports from Cairo loaded with troops "came straggling in here one at a time all of last night and immediately proceeded up the Tennessee." [7] The expedition went plowing on; the water in the Tennessee was high, and along the shore the soldiers could see Negroes and farm stock huddling on bits of high ground. Now and then a thinly-clad, shivering, half-starved white refugee came down to the water's edge and begged to be taken on board. Usually some boat would send a yawl ashore to rescue the fugitive; Colonel Whittlesey remembered that most of the men thus rescued told wild tales of persecution of Unionist farmers by Confederate outriders. The Negroes who watched from the banks shouted and danced and waved when they saw the Federal troops. [8]

By afternoon of February 3 the steamers nosed into the eastern bank of the river four miles below Fort Henry and started to send McClernand's men ashore. Foote and Grant with the four ironclad gunboats went on up the river to try a preliminary exchange of shots with the Confederate batteries.

The flood conditions were doing the Confederates no good. Inexpertly sited on low ground, Fort Henry was almost awash. Across the river there were hills overlooking the fort, and here, in recent weeks, the Confederates had begun to build a second work, Fort Heiman, for insurance, but the job was far from finished and Fort Heiman was useless. Torpedoes had been planted in the stream, but the rising waters had torn most of them loose from their moorings and now they were floating harmlessly down the stream, soiled white cylinders tossing on the brown current. Foote had his sailors fish some of them out and stow them on the fantail of his flagship, the *Cincinnati*, and he and Grant stood by while a gunner undertook to dismantle one and examine its mechanism. A sudden hissing of escaping air from within the container convinced everyone that it was about to explode, and Grant and Foote went swiftly up the ladder to find safety on the upper deck, while the rest of the crowd incontinently jumped overboard. Somehow, Grant beat Foote to the top of the ladder, and the two men looked at one another, somewhat sheepishly, as it became apparent that the torpedo was not going to blow up. Foote mildly asked Grant why he had been in such a hurry, and Grant calmly replied that the

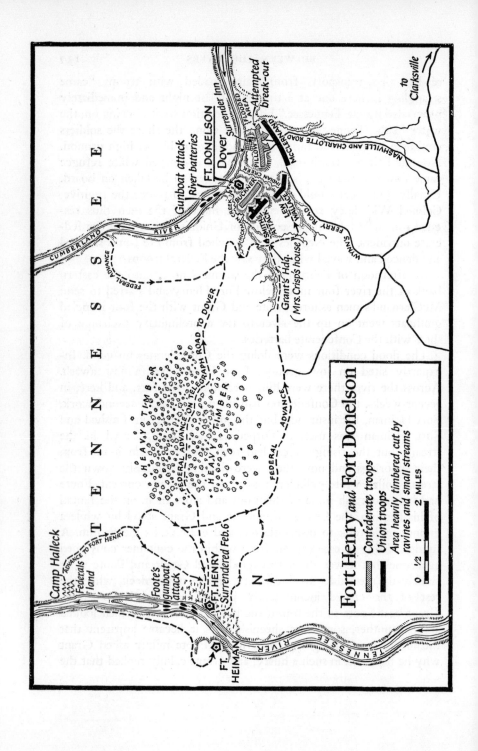

Fort Henry and Fort Donelson

Confederate troops
Union troops
Area heavily timbered, cut by ravines and small streams

0   ½   1   2 MILES

N

Army did not believe in letting the Navy get ahead of it. The examination of the mine was concluded, and the warships went on upstream to open fire.[9]

The firing was brief and inconclusive and did very little damage. A few shells were planted in the Confederate works, and one Confederate shell came aboard the gunboat *Essex*, tearing out a corner of the captain's cabin. There was no other damage, except that one of the transports, steaming too close to the bank, struck an overhanging tree, lost part of its upper-deck railing, and wrecked its barbershop, "to the great consternation of the proprietor." [10] The feeling-out process concluded, the gunboats returned to the place of disembarkation, and the transports hurried back to Paducah to get another load of soldiers.

Grant's plan reflected a little more forethought than had been evident in the head-on approach to Belmont. On the east side of the river he planted the division commanded by John McClernand. McClernand had nine regiments of infantry, two regiments of cavalry and four batteries, and except for a few of the gunners every man in the force came from Illinois. The troops Smith was bringing up from Paducah — mostly Illinoisans, with a sprinkling from Indiana and Missouri — were landed, on arrival, across the river from McClernand's division. The battle plan required McClernand to advance, cutting the road that led from Fort Henry over to Fort Donelson on the Cumberland so as to keep the garrison from escaping or from being reinforced, and standing by to assault the works if ordered. Smith, at the same time, was to move up the western bank and seize incomplete Fort Heiman, where he could plant guns to shoot into Fort Henry. The gunboats would steam straight up the river, and on signal would open a bombardment. Grant himself, instead of riding ahead in the front line as he had done at Belmont, would stay at the landing to co-ordinate the movements.[11]

With Smith's arrival Grant had some fifteen thousand troops. More were coming, for the desperate interchange of messages between St. Louis, Louisville and Washington had brought the promise of reinforcement. Halleck was sending every regiment he could spare to Cairo and Paducah, and Buell was preparing to transfer a brigade from his own army, with more to follow. Once begun, the expedition was drawing power to itself, and the Confederates were deeply worried. In Memphis, a writer for the *Memphis Appeal* had written that Fort Donelson could be held against any onslaught but that "more solicitude is felt about Fort Henry"; within the fort, he said, water had risen to within a few feet of the magazines, and the heavy guns were only six feet above the river, with the water level still going up. The Confederate commander, Brigadier General Lloyd Tilghman, watched from his battlements while the Federal force took position, and that night held a council of war at which his officers agreed that the fort must fall. Tilghman ordered that only enough men be held in Fort Henry to work the heavy guns; he himself would stay with them but everyone else must go outside the works and be ready to go over to Fort Donelson, where the real stand would be made.[12]

Below the fort something more important than anyone present could understand was taking place: an army was coming into existence. What Grant had with him was, up to this moment, simply a collection of individual regiments. Never before had all of them been brought together in one place. The habit of co-ordination had not been born; these regiments had been enlisted, organized and drilled separately, and they had seen so little of the parade ground that, as one veteran remarked afterward, they were to get their baptism of fire "before they learned that the cardinal military sin was to guide left while passing in review." They had been inadequately drilled, what their commanders knew about handling massed troops was something that would have to be learned on the battlefield, and their weapons were mixed and imperfect — "the refuse guns of Europe, with calibers as varied as the nations they came from." But as they came ashore from the steamboats and streamed out through the fields to select camping grounds and throw pickets forward they were turning themselves into what would finally become one of the great armies of American history — the informal, individualistic, occasionally unmanageable, but finally victorious Army of the Tennessee.[13]

February 5 was the day of preparation; February 6 was the day for the big attack. It rained all night, and McClernand's tentless troops had an uncomfortable time of it; at 11 o'clock in the morning they took off, floundering along muddy roads to take their assigned positions. On his flagship, Foote took note of the execrable marching conditions and warned Grant: "General, I shall have the fort in my possession before you get into your position." On the west bank, Smith got his men moving forward, and around noon Foote's gunboats raised their anchors and went steaming up the river to open fire.

Foote had four ironclads — all he could find crews for, at the moment — and he took them on in line abreast. Only their bows were well armored; they would fight head-on, using their bow guns, shielding their weakly protected sides. Foote had done his best to whip his green hands into shape. Gun crews had been warned that their fire must be accurate rather than rapid. As a good New Englander, Foote abhorred waste, and he addressed his crews just before this advance got under way, warning them that "every charge you fire from one of these guns costs the government about eight dollars." Finally, coming within range, the flagship opened fire — her first three shots, an irreverent junior noted, fell short, for a net loss of twenty-four dollars — and then the whole line opened. Bringing up the rear, out of harm's way but ready to lend a hand if needed, were the old wooden gunboats *Tyler, Lexington* and *Conestoga*.[14]

The fight was unexpectedly brief and easy. Fort Henry was all but indefensible. Tilghman had been so impressed with its vulnerable layout that he wrote that "the history of military engineering affords no parallel to this case"; and although his men did their best there could be just one outcome. The Confederate fire was accurate enough, and the gunboats had been hit fifty-nine times. Heavy shot at times broke the iron plating, and an officer who saw one shot strike the flagship said that the *Cincinnati's* side-timbers were splintered and sent flying as if the vessel had been struck by a bolt of lightning. No serious damage was done, however, except to the *Essex*. Here a bolt cracked through the armor of the casemate, decapitated a sailor, and smashed on to blow up a boiler. Scalding steam filled the gunboat, twenty-nine men were scalded, quartermaster and pilot died at the wheel, and *Essex* drifted off downstream, out of action.

Meanwhile, Foote kept on closing the range, and the gunboats' fire became increasingly effective. One of Tilghman's most powerful guns exploded, another was put out of action when spiked by an accident to its own priming wire, and Federal fire smashed a couple of 32-pounders, sending iron fragments all about and disabling every man in both gun-crews. Tilghman before long found himself with just four guns that could be fought; Foote's gunboats were within 300 yards of the fort, their projectiles were coming through the earthen embankments "as readily as a ball from a Navy Colt would pierce a pine board," and the day was obviously lost. Tilghman ordered all of his infantry to take off for Dover, and Foote's prediction was proved correct; the bad roads had delayed McClernand so much that more than two thousand of the Confederate garrison got away clean and tramped overland to the Cumberland. Six fieldpieces they were taking bogged down in the insufferable mire and had to be abandoned, but the men themselves escaped. Tilghman struck his flag, the sailors on the gunboats came out on deck to give three cheers, and a cutter from flagship *Cincinnati* went over to the fort; so high was the water that the boat simply rowed inside the enclosure. A Confederate officer gloomily admitted that if the fight had been delayed forty-eight hours no firing would have been needed: the river itself would have done the job by drowning the fort.

Tilghman came aboard Foote's flagship and made formal surrender. His garrison by now consisted of fewer than one hundred men, and his casualties had been moderate.[15]

Tilghman wrote a brief report next day, which was sent through the lines to his Confederate superiors with Grant's permission; in it, Tilghman took "great pleasure in acknowledging the courtesy and consideration shown by Brig. Gen. U. S. Grant and Commander Foote." One of his officers wrote that Grant seemed to be "a modest, amiable, kindhearted but resolute man," and said that Grant quickly rebuked an officious Federal officer who scolded a Confederate for destroying confidential papers at the time of the surrender. The Confederate officers dined with Grant and his staff on the headquarters transport, while waiting transfer to a northern prison camp, and two young Confederates got tipsy and talked too loudly and defiantly; an older Confederate remembered gratefully how Grant quietly had the men escorted to a cabin until they sobered up, explaining that he did it simply because he was afraid that some equally tipsy Union officers might make trouble for them.[16]

Foote had made his boast good. He had taken the fort before the Army had even got into position. Except for the tragedy on *Essex*, his own losses had been inconsiderable. The interior of Fort Henry looked like chaos, with wrecked guns and gun carriages strewed all about, with here and there bloody fragments of human bodies. No one took the time to realize that the river itself and the bad design and inadequate equipment with which Fort Henry had been endowed might have been largely responsible; the moral seemed to be that earthen forts simply could not stand up to a naval attack which was resolutely pushed home. Navy stock went up to dizzying heights.

Grant and Foote understood and liked one another, and a situation which might have led to a great deal of inter-service jealousy and rivalry passed off quietly. Grant came up the river promptly, once the fort surrendered, established garrisons in flooded Fort Henry and incomplete Fort Heiman, and ordered the bulk of his troops reassembled on the east side of the river. Then he got off a wire to Halleck:

"Fort Henry is ours. The gunboats silenced the batteries before the investment was completed. I think the garrison must have commenced the retreat last night. Our cavalry followed, finding two guns abandoned in the retreat."

Then — whether with or without reflecting deeply on the matter — he added a final sentence that turned out to be one of the most momentous promises in all the war:

"I shall take and destroy Fort Donelson on the 8th and return to Fort Henry." [17]

It is generally assumed that in making this statement Grant went far beyond his orders and converted what had been planned as a strictly limited blow into an offensive of unlimited potentialities and consequences. That the decision to move at once on Fort Donelson did have that effect is undeniable. Halleck and Buell and McClellan might continue to send messages back and forth to one another as long as they pleased; from this moment the major Federal effort in this theater of war was going to be an all-out offensive up the Tennessee and the Cumberland and no one could change it. Yet Grant, all things considered, was not greatly exceeding his instructions. He had been told, to be sure, simply to take Fort Henry, and this had been done; but up until now all of the Federal commanders had assumed that Fort Henry was stronger and more important than Fort Donelson, the mission had been described at various times either as a thrust at Fort Henry or as a thrust at Fort Henry "and Dover," and Donelson obviously was considered as little more than an outwork or dependency of the installation on the Tennessee. Halleck himself, who was never in the least reluctant to chide a subordinate for departing from the letter of his orders, took the news in his stride, notifying McClellan that Fort Henry had been taken and adding, more or less casually, that Grant would now go on to attack Fort Donelson "at Dover, on the Cumberland." (The fort was so little known that it had to be identified.) And Grant appears to have looked on the move as routine.

When he wrote to Halleck on February 6, not long after sending his brief wire, Grant went into some details about the fight and its results, and then spoke of Fort Donelson in the manner of one who mentions a relatively unimportant detail.

I shall take and destroy Fort Donelson on the 8th [he wrote] and return to Fort Henry with the force employed, unless it looks feasible to occupy that place with a small force that could retreat easily to the main body. I shall regard it more in the light of an advance guard than as a permanent post.

It seems clear that both he and Halleck looked upon this step as just part of the mopping-up process.[18]

Take and destroy Fort Donelson on February 8 Grant could not, as things worked out, so much as begin to do. It might be part of the mopping-up process, but there were a great many things to do before this job could be undertaken, and Grant — who was commanding a much larger army than any he had ever seen before: he had proudly written to Mary that his army was larger than the one Scott led in Mexico — was to learn that getting such an army in motion could be a laborious business. The casual way in which Grant originally regarded the venture comes out in a remark he made to a newspaper correspondent who, the day after Fort Henry surrendered, came in to headquarters to say good-by; as far as the reporter could see the mission had been accomplished and he himself was going to go back to Cairo.

"You had better wait a day or so," Grant warned him. When the newspaperman asked why, Grant said: "I am going over to attack Fort Donelson tomorrow." The newspaperman asked him if he knew how strong it was, and Grant replied: "Not exactly, but I think we can take it; at all events, we can try." [19]

It was easier to say it than to do it. To begin with, the gunboats were gone, all but ironclad *Carondelet*, which had been left as a guard ship. Foote had taken the other three ironclads back to Cairo for repairs, the three wooden vessels had gone on up the Tennessee in obedience to Halleck's original orders, and without the Navy the move against Fort Donelson would be crippled. The very fact that the victory at Fort Henry had come so easily dominated men's thinking. The gunboats had beaten the fort into helplessness without any assistance from the Army, and it seemed likely that they could do the same thing at Fort Donelson. The Army of course must be there to invest the place and round up the garrison, but the Navy could probably compel the Confederates to give up. Confederate Albert Sidney Johnston, as a matter of fact, felt much the same way about it. In his message to the War Department announcing the loss of Fort Henry, he wrote: "The slight resistance at Fort Henry indicates that the best open earthworks are not reliable to meet successfully a vigorous attack of iron-clad gunboats, and, although now supported by a considerable force, I think the gunboats of the enemy will probably take Fort Donelson without the necessity of employing their land force in cooperation." [20]

There were chores to perform at Fort Henry. There was much captured property (described by an enthusiastic newspaperman as "a vast deal of plunder") to be possessed and itemized, and the imperfectly disciplined troops were tampering with it. Grant felt compelled to issue an order remarking that "the pilfering and marauding disposition shown by some of the men of this command has determined the general commanding to make an example of some one," and harsh punishments were ordered; if individual thieves could not be identified, company or regimental commanders would themselves be punished. It was also necessary to crack down on the

numerous regimental officers who preferred the comforts of the
transports to the hardships of camp life, and colonels were ordered
to let no officer go aboard any steamboat except on specific duty.
On top of everything else the rain continued to fall, Fort Henry
was all but surrounded by water, and the nearby roads were, as
everybody had been saying, nearly impassable. The day after the
fort surrendered Grant took his staff and part of a cavalry regiment and rode forward to within a mile or so of the outworks at
Fort Donelson, just to get acquainted with the terrain. This, he
said afterward, was not as risky as it might sound. He knew that
General Pillow was in command at Fort Donelson, and Grant
"judged that with any force, no matter how small, I could march
up to within gunshot of any intrenchments he was given to
hold." (Actually, as Grant discovered, General John B. Floyd,
former Secretary of War, was in top command at Donelson, with
Pillow ranking second; but Floyd was not a trained soldier, Pillow
was the more forceful character, and Grant considered that Pillow
was the one who would be in effective control.)[21]

The three wooden gunboats that went up the Tennessee were
making a spectacular raid, underlining the importance of the victory that had been won. Immediately after the fort was surrendered the warships started up the Tennessee, under Lieutenant
Commander S. L. Phelps; the sailors seized the railroad bridge above
the fort, finding it an imposing structure twelve hundred feet
long, with several hundred feet of trestle work at either end and with
a swinging draw in the middle. A number of rails were taken up, a
considerable amount of military property was seized, three steamboats were burned, and another boat loaded with ammunition was
destroyed by shellfire. It blew up with a prodigious crash, breaking
windows and fastenings on the gunboats at a distance of half a mile
and destroying a house on the bank — a house, unfortunately, occupied by a good Union man. Phelps kept on going, took possession
of a half-finished Confederate gunboat, went all the way across
Tennessee and got at last to Florence, Alabama, at the foot of
Muscle Shoals. The people of Florence were alarmed, and a deputa-
tion came aboard Phelps's boat to beg that the wives and daughters
of honest townfolk not be molested. Phelps wrote that "I told
them that we were neither ruffians nor savages," seized three

steamboats, burned six more (all, he noted, loaded with supplies for the Rebel Army), and then leisurely came back down the river, dispersed an encampment of Confederate recruits, got the incomplete Confederate gunboat in shape to move, and triumphantly brought it back to Fort Henry, along with 250,000 feet of "the best quality of ship and building timber" and a good deal of iron plating. He reported that there seemed to be many loyal people in West Tennessee, and in northern Mississippi and Alabama; large crowds gathered at landings to cheer the United States flag, and these repeated demonstrations, he said, gave the Navy men "a higher sense of the sacred character of our present duties." There were, he admitted, many towns of a different temper, in which men, women and children unanimously took to the woods when the Union gunboats appeared, but on balance he believed that the loyalists were in the majority.[22]

While Grant was organizing the attack on Fort Donelson, things behind the lines were moving. Back in St. Louis, Halleck was continuing to funnel troops down to Paducah, and some of these were coming up to Fort Henry. By February 11, the day after Phelps and his gunboats returned from their foray up the river, four fresh regiments and a battalion of sharpshooters reached camp to be formed into a new brigade for Smith's division, and more troops were known to be on the way. Halleck sent his Chief of Staff, Brigadier General George W. Cullum, to Cairo, to superintend the forwarding of recruits and supplies; he also pulled General Sherman out of the St. Louis training camp assignment which Sherman had been filling and sent him on up to Paducah, to take command there. What would finally become the enormously effective partnership of Grant and Sherman dates from this time.[23]

Halleck had also given Grant another man who was to play a large part in the activities of the Army of the Tennessee — Lieutenant Colonel James B. McPherson, an engineer officer who was assigned to accompany the Fort Henry movement. Cullum had written to Smith that McPherson was to be "engineer of the expedition," and praised him as "a very clever young officer"; McPherson seems to have been under instructions to look things over carefully and give Halleck a confidential appraisal of Grant.[24] He and Grant fitted together harmoniously. He would become one of Grant's most trusted subordinates, a man whom Sherman finally considered the most promising soldier in the Army, commander at last of the Army of the Tennessee; he would die in battle in front of Atlanta in 1864, and hard-boiled Sherman would weep unashamedly at the news.

Foote's three ironclads reached Cairo on February 7, and people on the waterfront saw the leading gunboat come steaming in with a Confederate flag flying upside down just below the national flag. There was cheering and rejoicing, and the *Chicago Tribune* correspondent wrote that the expedition had accomplished "one of the most complete and signal victories in the annals of the world's warfare." [25] Foote prodded the shipyard to get his damaged squadron into shape. *Essex* needed extensive repairs, *Cincinnati* had been somewhat splintered, and Foote was not sure that the Navy was ready to play a major part in the attack on Fort Donelson.

But events were applying their own pressure, and what had been begun had to go on and on until it was finished.

Far off at St. Louis, in department headquarters, Halleck suddenly became very impatient. He really knew very little about the situation on the two rivers, but a glance at the map was enough to tell him that the conquest of Fort Henry could not stand by itself. With Fort Henry taken, Fort Donelson had to be attacked; it had hardly figured in the original calculations, but now it was of immediate importance — because, thirty miles up the Cumberland from Fort Donelson, there was a town named Clarksville, and at Clarksville the famous railroad line which connected the two wings of the Confederate Army crossed the Cumberland and went northeast to Bowling Green. If the Clarksville bridge that carried that railroad could be destroyed, communication between the two wings of Johnston's army would be broken, and on February 8 Halleck sent Grant word to go on to Clarksville and destroy that bridge if possible. On February 10 Halleck sent a more insistent dispatch: "If possible destroy the bridge at Clarksville. Run any risk to accomplish this."

Halleck did not often advise a subordinate to "run any risk" in order to do something, and the unwonted urgency of this message shows the importance which the railroad bridge held in his thinking. But because he had no real information about the Rebel installations and intentions at Fort Donelson, Halleck conceived of this thrust at Clarksville as a hit-and-run raid; he told Grant to entrench thoroughly at Fort Henry, shifting guns about so that he could resist any Confederate counterattack; picks and shovels were being sent up the Tennessee, and reinforcements would follow quickly. On February 11 Halleck wrote that "some of the gunboats should be sent up the Cumberland with the least possible delay," adding that "it is of vital importance that Fort Donelson be reduced immediately." He told Cullum to "push forward the Cumberland expedition with all possible dispatch. . . . Time now is everything for us. Don't delay one instant." Then Halleck sent a message to Foote:

> You have gained great distinction by your capture of Fort Henry. Everybody recognizes your services. Make your name famous in history by the capture of Fort Donelson and Clarksville. The taking of these places is a military necessity. Delay adds strength to them more than to us. Act quickly, even though only half ready.[26]

Grant had seen the importance of the Clarksville bridge as quickly as Halleck did, and since he was on the spot he realized, before the point was clear to anyone in St. Louis, that Fort Donelson would have to be reduced first. Before he got Halleck's wire he was urging Foote to get some gunboats up the Cumberland for the attack on the Fort, and when Halleck's message came he replied: "Every effort will be put forth to have Clarksville in a few days."

Foote made his arrangements quickly. He left Cairo with gunboats *St. Louis*, *Louisville* and *Pittsburgh*, planning to pick up *Carondelet* and the wooden gunboats just below Fort Donelson, in the Cumberland; steaming up the Ohio, he stopped at Smithland to pick up a covey of transports full of reinforcements — six new regiments from Ohio, Illinois and Nebraska, led by the 1st Nebraska's Colonel John Thayer, who had seen Grant's chagrin the previous August when Grant lost his command at Ironton.

Thayer had moved all the way up to Fort Henry only to be told to go back and come up the Cumberland with Foote's squadron for escort.[27]

On February 12 Grant was ready. He had kept his cavalry moving about the narrow country between the rivers, and McPherson, scouting there, found that there were two roads the army could use — very good roads, he reported, considering the excessive rains that had been falling, once the troops got past the two miles of boggy lowland immediately east of Fort Henry. The artillery and most of the infantry were sent past this intervening swamp to dry ground, bridges were built over the flooded backwaters near the fort, the cavalry kept scouring the country to keep the Rebels at Fort Donelson from sending parties out to obstruct the roads — and early on February 12 Grant notified Halleck: "We start this morning for Fort Donelson in heavy force. Four regiments from Buell's command and two from St. Louis arrived last night and were sent around by water. I hope to send you a dispatch from Fort Donelson tomorrow." [28] Then his army took off.

Smith's division took one road and McClernand's took the other. Lew Wallace was left to hold Fort Henry with some new regiments; he was to be ready to move on Fort Donelson on short notice, leaving a small garrison behind. Other reinforcements would presumably be up before long; Grant was a little worried about the safety of Fort Henry, fearing a Confederate counter-offensive from Columbus, and he suggested to Halleck that fresh troops be sent up the Tennessee. They could easily march overland to aid in the attack on Fort Donelson if they were needed; meanwhile, said Grant, "there is now appearance that that point" (Fort Henry) "is in danger." [29]

So the Army of the Tennessee (which had not yet acquired that proud title) began the first of its many marches. The roads led over hilly, broken country, thinly populated and covered with timber. There were no large plantations. Halleck had suggested that in perfecting the defenses at Fort Henry Grant might impress slaves from the surrounding countryside, and Grant had to reply that in his immediate neighborhood there seemed to be no slaves at all. The weather had turned warm and the sun was out, the troops were feeling good — they had just achieved a rather startling victory, at practically no cost to themselves — and as they marched the men airily discarded blankets and overcoats as too burdensome to carry. (Why bother with such stuff in the mild winter weather of the South?) Grant and his staff rode at the head of the column. Grant was traveling light; on this day his personal baggage consisted of a toothbrush which he had in his pocket and a fresh collar carried by one of his staff. Surgeon Brinton, who had come up from Cairo a few days earlier, rode beside him, and the surgeon's horse was a powerful black which insisted on moving ahead. Grant was a little touchy about this — one of his quirks was a strong distaste for letting anyone ride in front of him — and he turned at last to Brinton and said: "Doctor, I believe I command this army, and I think I'll go first." [30]

By evening of February 12 Smith's and McClernand's divisions came together, a little more than two miles short of Fort Donelson. The officers went to work in the dim twilight in the second-growth timber, spreading the two divisions out into line of battle, and toward nightfall the uneven lines went forward, chasing away a handful of Rebel skirmishers and making bivouac not far away from the Confederate lines. Colonel Thayer and his new brigade had not yet arrived, so word was sent back to Lew Wallace to bring his troops forward at once. Grant looked things over and concluded that as soon as the gunboats appeared the attack could begin.

The plan of attack was relatively simple, modeled on what had been done at Fort Henry. Grant's troops would form a huge semicircle, enclosing the Confederate camp, preventing all escape and taking positions on which guns could be mounted to bombard the Confederate works. The navy would pound the fort's water batteries to pieces and take control of the river, and surrender ought to follow very shortly. Grant wanted to get it finished quickly, because he believed that strong Confederate reinforcements were meant to come to Fort Donelson and he wanted to possess the works before these could arrive.

The battle plan was good enough, but it was based on a couple of misconceptions. In the first place, Fort Donelson had already been heavily reinforced; and in the second place, the fort was much stronger than Fort Henry had been. What had worked so easily in the earlier fight was not going to work at all here, which was something Grant would discover by hard experience.

News of the loss of Fort Henry had forced the Confederates to recast all of their plans. The news reached Bowling Green on February 7, and Johnston immediately went into conference with Beauregard — who was learning, to his horror, that this Western Army in which he now was second in command was very much weaker than people in Richmond had supposed — and with Hardee, who was in immediate command of the troops at Bowling Green. It was clear to all three generals that the Bowling Green-Columbus line had been fractured, once and for all, and that the only thing to do was to pull out. Johnston would stay with Hardee, and with the troops at Bowling Green they would retire south — to Nashville, perhaps all the way to northern Alabama — and Beauregard was to go to Columbus, to hold on there if he could and if not to fall back on Memphis. Eventually, the two bodies would reunite somewhere along the southern boundary of Tennessee, where they would see what could be done. Meanwhile, it seemed vitally important to make a real stand at Fort Donelson, because if Donelson fell it did not seem that there would be any chance to save Nashville. Reinforcements, therefore, would be sent to Fort Donelson, even though that would mean dividing the undersized army that was now at Bowling Green.

It is possible that Johnston made a bad decision here, although in plain fact no really good choice was open to him. Long after the war Beauregard argued that if Johnston planned to make a stand at Fort Donelson he should have taken his entire army there, to destroy Grant before Buell's army could reach the scene. This done, he said, Buell would not have dared to advance, and the line might have been held. By dividing his forces Johnston was risking more of his army than he could afford to lose and was leaving himself with too few men to hold off Buell. But whether Johnston then had enough time to get all of the Bowling Green people over to Dover ahead of Grant is open to some question — and, in any case, Johnston was badly outnumbered and dreadfully pressed, and anything that he did was likely to turn out badly. He was the man appointed to make the decision, and his decision was to send some but not all of his troops to fight Grant on the west bank of the

Cumberland. And by the morning of February 13, when Grant's men were getting up after their first night on the lines, Fort Donelson and its outlying trenches contained rather more than eighteen thousand Confederates, with an oddly matched trium-virate composed of Generals Floyd, Pillow and Buckner in com-mand. Hardee and Johnston, this morning, were evacuating Bowl-ing Green and moving south.[31]

The Cumberland River comes up to Dover from the east, and just south of the town it makes a right-angled turn to flow north to-ward the Ohio. Fort Donelson was an irregularly-shaped work on top of a high hill on the left bank, at the bend, looking north. On the steep bank of the hill, facing the river, there were two water batteries, well dug in, thirty feet or more above the level of the water; together they mounted only a dozen guns, but at least two of these were powerful, a massive 128-pounder and a rifled 64-pounder. Just north of these batteries there was a backwater, swampy, flooded and impassable, going inland from the Cumberland for a mile or more and preventing any attack on land from the north. The fort itself was not large, but it had been surrounded by an entrenched camp, whose lines, following the hills and ridges, formed a long arc that ran south from the northern backwater and then curved east to meet the flooded lowlands along the Tennessee just south of the town of Dover. These entrenchments were not especially well built, but they were on good ground and timber had been felled in front of them to make an effective abatis. They were strongly held, on February 13, and on that morning there were more Confederates than Unionists present.

Grant was not ready to make his attack, for Foote had not yet arrived. The gunboat *Carondelet,* under Commander Henry Walke, did show up while Grant was extending his lines so as to complete the investment of the fort, and Grant sent a message saying that if Walke could open a bombardment "we will be ready to take ad-vantage of every diversion in our favor."

Walke was willing, and a little after nine o'clock the ponderous gunboat went splashing forward to extreme long range and began to throw 70-pound and 64-pound shell at the fort. The fort's heav-ier guns replied, and the duel went on all the rest of the morning;

Carondelet took a massive solid shot through her side, which drove enough splinters around to put twelve seamen out of action; the fort suffered little if at all; and after Walke had withdrawn long enough to send his wounded to a hospital ship he steamed back to the firing line and the bombardment went on most of the afternoon. If it undermined Confederate ability to hold the fort and entrenched camp there was no visible evidence of the fact.[32]

On shore, part of the infantry got into action which was no more decisive than the bombardment had been. McClernand, occupying the right of the Union line, had been harassed by Confederate artillery and sharpshooter fire, and he finally sent a brigade forward to dislodge the Rebel gunners from a particularly annoying redoubt on a wooded hill. In this attack there occurred one of the odd mix-ups inevitable in a hastily-organized army. McClernand's third brigade, consisting of the 17th and 49th Illinois under command of the latter regiment's colonel, William R. Morrison, was ordered to make the assault, and the 48th Illinois, led by Colonel I. N. Haynie, was sent up in support. As the troops got ready to charge, Colonel Haynie conceived that he ranked Colonel Morrison and felt that the movement was actually under his command. Morrison — feeling that "this was no time to dispute about a question of rank" — offered to conduct the column to the take-off point and then turn command over to Haynie. As the regiments started, he turned to Haynie and said, "Colonel, let's take it together"; and the troops struggled up a steep rise through a tangle of felled timber. A bullet struck Morrison in the hip and knocked him out of his saddle, settling the command problem definitely; the attack came to a halt when the soldiers found the timber entanglements almost impassable; and after a time the men went streaming back to where they had started from, having suffered substantial losses. On Smith's front, a brigade seized a bit of high ground, found itself unable to stay, and fell back again. When evening came, progress had been nil, except that the process of enveloping the Confederate camp had been extended. Lew Wallace brought up several regiments from Fort Henry, and these men were assigned to Smith's division, taking position on Smith's right, while McClernand edged his command farther over toward the Cumberland. From the town of Dover a road led south toward Nashville, and McClernand sought to cover it so as to cut off the garrison's last chance to escape by land.[33]

As evening came on the weather abruptly turned savage. It had been mild and pleasant; now a north wind drove dark clouds across the sky and a cold rain began to fall, turning presently to sleet and snow. All along McClernand's front the men who had so incontinently thrown away blankets and overcoats found themselves making the most cheerless of bivouacs in a driving blizzard, with three inches of snow all around and sharp gusts of wind chilling them. They were within close range of the Confederate works, and fires were forbidden; the only food was hardtack and coffee, and because there could be no fires the coffee could not be prepared; tents were back on the transports somewhere, and in many commands the men stood to arms all night long simply because it was impossible to lie down. Sporadic picket firing continued in the windy darkness. Colonel Oglesby wrote that the men were subjected to "one of the most persecuting snow storms ever known in this country," and said that by morning most of them were "nearly torpid from the intense cold." [34]

To Grant, making his headquarters in a log farmhouse near the center of the lines, there finally did come welcome news. Around midnight Foote came up the river with ironclads *St. Louis*, *Louisville* and *Pittsburgh*, followed by two of the wooden gunboats, and these anchored with *Carondelet* a few miles below the fort. The naval bombardment that had been a key part of the battle plan could take place next day.

CHAPTER EIGHT

Unconditional Surrender

THE HIGH WIND put little whitecaps on the flood waters of the Cumberland on the morning of February 14, and kicked snow flurries along the surrounding hilltops, where half-frozen men beat the frost out of folds in their clothing and tried to limber their stiffened arms and legs. Three miles below the fort, on the river, Andrew Foote's gunboats lay at anchor, black and squat and menacing, working details swarming over the decks to prepare for action. Somewhere astern were numerous Union transports, puffing vast clouds of steam and smoke as they nosed into the west bank of the river to disembark reinforcements and supplies. The great military machine that reached so far — to St. Louis, to the Lakes, to Pittsburgh, to all the towns and farms of the West and beyond the mountains to the Eastern Seaboard as well — it was in full movement at last, and the weight of it was coming down on the improvised landing places along the riverbank, where muddy roads went roundabout toward the Federal camp facing Fort Donelson.

The night had been tough, and none of the men who lived through it ever forgot it; to the end of the war they remembered it as one of the worst trials they had had to endure as soldiers. As they huddled around smudgy little campfires to boil coffee — when light came, the night-time rule against campfires was discarded — they compared notes on what they had been through. Some of the men confessed that the only thing that kept them alive was the thought that the Rebels were just as cold as they were: just as cold, and, because they were used to a warmer climate, probably suffering more. Men of the 12th Iowa recalled that they spent most of the night trotting around in circles just to keep from freezing, with regimental officers improvising strange new tactical commands: "By companies, in a circle, double-quick, *march!*" Skirmishers and pickets renewed the exchange of fire that had never really ceased during the night. Little harm was done by this firing, and yet the uproar swept the ridges and the hollows with the clamor of battle to stir the pulses of men who had never before been in action.[1]

Grant was recalled as having been in an optimistic and slightly humorous mood. Two Illinois soldiers who had been wounded in McClernand's abortive assault the day before said that as they came limping out of the fight they trudged past Grant, who noticed how battered they appeared and said: "You look disfigured — been hunting bear?" They replied that they had the animal treed and would bring him down next day, and Grant chuckled and ordered a staff officer to get the men to the nearest surgeon. One of the wounded men, who nursed a shattered left arm, lingered to tell the general how he had kept on fighting even though unable to reload his musket; his comrade had loaded for two, and he himself had been able to fire so effectively that a Confederate fieldpiece which was his chosen target fell silent. Grant heard him out, then asked sharply: "You didn't hurt anyone, did you?" The soldier gaped at him, then saw a twinkle in his eye and replied: "Why, General, I dunno — I reckon I just scared 'em and they fainted." [2]

Surgeon Brinton said that Grant had been highly confident that Fort Donelson would presently be taken. He had not ordered his encircling troops to throw up breastworks, and he seemed positive that the Confederates, having been nearly surrounded, would stay meekly in their works. Late in the evening, Grant seems to have considered the notion of a sudden night attack. Brinton said Grant told him: "Doctor, if I was a little more assured of my men I would storm with every man at 12 tonight, but I am not sure of them in a night melee." Grant unquestionably was confident, although it is doubtful whether he gave any serious consideration to a night attack.

To Halleck, he set forth the situation as it looked to him on the morning of February 14: "Our troops now invest the works at Fort Donelson. The enemy have been driven into their works at every point. A heavy abatis all around prevents carrying the works by storm at present. I feel every confidence of success and the best feeling prevails among the men." To General Cullum, at Cairo, Grant wrote that it looked very much as if there would be a regular siege, and he called for more artillery ammunition. "The ground is very broken," he wrote, and "the fallen timber extending far out from the breastworks, I fear the result of an attempt to carry the place by storm with raw troops. I feel great confidence, however, of ultimately reducing the place." [3]

Clearly enough, Grant's concentration on what he was going to do to the opposing army kept him from thinking very much about what that army might do to him. Up to this point his chief worry seems to have been the possibility that Johnston might send more troops in to relieve the Confederates at Fort Donelson, and he wanted to get some of his own men all the way over to the Cumberland above the town of Dover in order to prevent this. The lay of the land, however, was against him, with high water in the Cumberland making the low ground impassable, and to Halleck he confessed that "it was impossible, in consequence of the high water and deep sloughs, to throw a force in above Dover to cut off their reinforcements. Any force sent for such a purpose would be entirely away from support from the main body." [4] Nevertheless, he remained hopeful. With the help of Foote and the gunboats it ought to be possible to force the troops in Fort Donelson to surrender before any Confederate supports could arrive.

Foote would do his part. That morning, on his four ironclads, men were busy shifting chains, lumber, bags of coal and other materials to the upper decks of the warships, as a defense against plunging shot. The ironclads would steam up to the works in line abreast, as at Fort Henry, with the two wooden gunboats hanging back to do what they could at long range. If the Confederate water batteries could be silenced the whole river front could be sealed off, and the place might come into Union possession as simply as Fort Henry had done. Preparations took most of the morning, and the noon hour was well past when the ungainly "turtles" began splashing laboriously against the current, driving on to action stations. Foote himself was in and out of the pilothouse on the flagship, *St. Louis*. He had a megaphone with him, and when one of his ships failed to keep position he would hail it with the command: "Steam up!" When the Confederate works were still about a mile away, *St. Louis* opened fire, followed by the others. Foote was a stickler for accuracy, and when *Carondelet* opened rapid fire (at the expense, thought the Flag Officer, of effective gun-laying) the megaphone came into use again, and *Carondelet* was told to fire more slowly.

Trying to fit this fight to the Fort Henry pattern turned out to be a big mistake. The Confederates had plenty of guns bearing on the river, but most of them were comparatively light, outranged and outweighed by the powerful naval ordnance; at long range Foote could hit the Confederates at very little risk to himself, but when he got closer he increased the effectiveness of the Southern guns, and as the range closed from a mile to five hundred yards and then to four hundred and less, the gunboats took a fearful pounding. Closing the range increased the naval gunners' problems, because the Fort Donelson batteries were high above the level of the river; at close range the gunboats consistently overshot their targets, and some of Foote's shell arched clear across the Confederate camp and came down in the Union lines beyond. Foote's guns did knock the earthen parapets to pieces, but the Confederate guns remained fully operational; nothing short of a direct hit would put a piece out of action, and once the inexperienced Southern gun crews saw that the heavy Union fire was not really hurting them they cheered and stuck to their work bravely.

The Confederates were pounding the gunboats hard. Decks were slippery with blood, carpenters were busy plugging shot holes along the waterlines, fire-control parties were dousing flames in the woodwork, and flagship *St. Louis* received fifty-nine hits. One of these demolished her pilothouse, killed the pilot, wounded Foote, and put the steering gear out of action, and at almost the same moment *Louisville*'s tiller ropes were shot away; the two big steamers ponderously swung about, end for end, in the current, and began to drift down out of action. *Carondelet* and *Pittsburgh* closed in to cover them, collided, three of the fleet's four pilots were down, *Carondelet* was struck along the waterline so many times she was almost in a sinking condition — and eventually all four vessels went back downstream out of range, with fifty-four casualties and a humiliating defeat to show for their pains. Jubilant Confederates capered and yelled at the sight, and it was painfully obvious that what had beaten Fort Henry was never going to beat Fort Donelson.[5]

Grant's headquarters were in a little farmhouse owned by a Mrs. Crisp, situated perhaps five hundred yards behind C. F. Smith's battle line and six miles or more, by bad roads, from the downstream landing on the Cumberland. From a point near the river, Grant witnessed the repulse of the gunboats; returning to headquarters, he ordered the new troops which had disembarked from their transports just before Foote went into action formed into a division and placed under Lew Wallace's command. This division, green soldiers under a green general they had never seen before, was put into the middle of the Union line, and McClernand moved farther to the right in an attempt to cover the half-flooded lowlands to the south of the town of Dover.

Across these lowlands ran a road which led from Dover to Clarksville and ultimately to Nashville — a possible escape route for the Confederates in the Fort Donelson lines, if the Confederate command chose to use it. If Foote had been able to knock out the water batteries and get his gunboats upstream that road would have been blocked by his guns; but since he had been beaten, the road would be open unless McClernand could seal it off with his troops. McClernand's shift to the right was designed to accomplish this, but he had much ground to cover and his lines were stretched thin, especially on his extreme right, where the Clarksville road ran. Whether Grant realized, on the night of February 14, that his weakness in this area invited a Confederate counterattack, or whether this was something he planned to attend to the next day, is not quite clear. One thing that may have influenced his thinking was the fact that the Confederate position was potentially very strong; given a few days, Floyd and Pillow might (as Grant saw it) make the place almost impregnable. Grant began to fear that he would have to bring up tents and put on a regular siege, but — as he himself confessed later — he "had no idea that there would be any engagement on land unless I brought it on myself." [6]

The night of February 14 was gloomy enough, in the Union camp. The weather remained bad, and when the newly arrived 20th Ohio reached the downstream landing, at twilight, and its Colonel Charles Whittlesey rode off to report to the Commanding General, he found the Crisp farmhouse looking almost deserted. Whittlesey hitched his horse to a peach tree in the yard and went inside, to a shadowy room where a handful of officers huddled about a fire in the hearth. A man whom Whittlesey described as "the smallest and least noticeable" of the lot was sitting at a table, dictating to an aide who wrote by the light of a tallow dip. It developed that this small officer was General Grant. Whittlesey went over and presented himself. He had recently seen Grant's father and sisters and he had messages from them, which he delivered verbally. Grant listened without comment; then, learning that Whittlesey was about to return to his regiment at the steamboat landing, he asked Whittlesey to tell Foote that a good many of his heavy-duty shells were coming over the Confederate works and exploding inside the Union lines.[7]

Whittlesey rode back to his troops. Early in the morning of February 15 a message from Foote reached headquarters. Foote's wound made it impossible for him to ride a horse or to move about with any comfort, and since it was clearly necessary for Commanding General and Flag Officer to have a conference, Foote asked that Grant come to the flagship at the downstream landing. This Grant was quite willing to do, and shortly after dawn on February 15, while the shivering troops were dragging themselves out of their uncomfortable bivouacs — and with an ominous amount of marching and grouping of troops going on inside the Confederate lines — Grant started to ride to the steamboat landing. Division commanders — McClernand, Wallace and Smith — were instructed not to bring on an engagement in his absence. The 20th Ohio was plodding up to the Union camp this morning, and its soldiers remembered meeting Grant, accompanied by a single orderly, as he rode down to consult with Foote.

From across the woods and ravines came the sound of musketry, with the heavier crash of fieldpieces now and then distinguishable. If this made any especial impression on Grant's consciousness there is no record of it. There had been a good deal of intermittent skirmishing and artillery dueling throughout each day ever since the armies came into contact; no one at a distance from the field seems to have suspected that what was going on this morning was any different from the ordinary routine.[8]

On the flagship Grant got bad news. Foote believed he should take his entire fleet back to Cairo or Mound City for repairs, and he urged Grant to entrench and prepare to hold his position until the fleet could return, which would be in ten or fifteen days. This was not at all to Grant's liking, and he asked Foote if he could not remain on the scene, damaged ships or no, while the army finished the job. In the end, something of a compromise was worked out. Foote would take the two worst-damaged boats downstream for repairs, leaving the others to give what support they could. Grant, on his part, would entrench at least a part of his position, and would wait for reinforcements before trying to fight for a decision. Orders were given to have entrenching tools unloaded from a transport at the landing and forwarded to the troops. Somewhere around noon the conference ended, and Grant got into a rowboat to get over to the landing and return to the field. As he got out of the boat Captain William S. Hillyer, one of his staff officers, came riding to the landing, white-faced; during Grant's absence the Confederates had struck a powerful surprise blow on McClernand's position, and the Union Army was close to outright disaster.[9]

The strategic motives that led the Confederates to mass troops at Fort Donelson in the first place have never been entirely clear, but by the evening of February 14 — which is to say at the conclusion of Foote's unfortunate assault with the gunboats — the Confederate commanders in the fort knew perfectly well what had to be done next. They had to save their army, which meant an immediate retreat. That they had just beaten off the gunboats made no difference; they saw the situation just as Grant saw it — Fort Donelson was a trap, and the Confederate Army would be lost if it stayed there. Somehow, the encircling Union line must be cracked; the road south must be opened at all costs so that the Confederates could get out and rejoin Albert Sidney Johnston, who had evacuated Bowling Green and was believed to be on the road to Nashville. During the evening Confederates Floyd, Pillow and Buckner laid their plans, and at dawn their troops were massed for an attack.

The Confederate plan was simple and logical. With reduced force, Buckner would hold the right and center of the line. With perhaps ten thousand men, Pillow would march out, crush the end of McClernand's line, and drive the Union right back on its center. This would open the road and the Confederate Army could get away. The fort itself would of course be lost, but men and material might be saved. If Pillow's assault succeeded, Buckner would move out to act as flank guard while the retreat proceeded. By daylight on February 15 everything was set and the move got under way.

McClernand's right was held by Dick Oglesby's brigade — five Illinois regiments, with two batteries and a handful of cavalry, and with John McArthur's three regiments, borrowed from Smith's division, somewhere in support. The chilled soldiers were preparing to fall in for breakfast when there was a sudden spatter of firing on the picket lines; then the pickets came tumbling back into camp, calling that the woods in front were all a-swarm with armed Rebels. Part of the brigade got into line just in time to receive a heavy volley from Pillow's advance. The attack was beaten off for the moment, but the Confederates reformed and came on again, and a number of extremely tough dismounted cavalry from Bedford Forrest's command struck the Unionists in flank and rear. More and more of Pillow's troops came into line, and all of McClernand's front was under pressure. Musketry fire rose to a high pitch — Lew Wallace remembered that from a distance it sounded "as if a million men were beating empty barrels with iron hammers" — and the Federals had to give ground.

McArthur's regiments had taken position the evening before, with an imperfect understanding of the lay of the land and the position of the enemy. Now they were fighting grimly with Forrest's cavalry, and heavy battle smoke streaked the hollows and clearings; the soggy snow that covered the ground was stained with red, as more and more men were shot; ammunition was running low, and soldiers went scurrying about to collect cartridge boxes from the fallen. By ten o'clock the whole right of the Union line was giving way, Oglesby's men were falling back to the west and McArthur's bewildered troops — fighting grimly, and sustaining heavy losses — were falling back with them. The Confederate plan was working. The door to the road south was swinging open wider and wider.[10]

McClernand sent a desperate message to Lew Wallace, who held the Union center, asking for help. Wallace referred the message to Grant's headquarters, but Grant was not there and in his absence his staff either lacked the power or lacked the initiative to act. Desperately pressed, McClernand repeated his plea, and Wallace finally shot a brigade cross-lots to help him, but the guide who tried to lead the brigade into position lost his way and the new troops came under heavy fire from some of Oglesby's men and, in the end, were involved in the retreat. The 20th Ohio, which had seen Grant riding to the river at dawn, came up behind the lines, noticed Colonel John A. Logan waiting with a painful shoulder wound for a surgeon's attention, and watched a demoralized colonel gallop for the rear with the cry that all of the infantry had been cut to pieces and that the Rebels were going to crush the entire army. A Chicago battery galloped furiously toward the front, upsetting one gun in a narrow woodland road, and the Ohio soldiers filed off among the trees and opened fire in what was believed to be the direction of the enemy.[11] The whole of the position McClernand had been holding was gone, and now Wallace sent Colonel Thayer's brigade into action, pushing the men forward through a cloud of disorganized fugitives. Wallace and McClernand paused in a clearing to compare notes — and just then Grant came riding up, a sheaf of papers in one hand.

From the broken country in front of the Generals a dense cloud of smoke was slowly fanning off into shreds. Grant returned the salutes which his subordinates offered, heard McClernand growl: "This army wants a head." Grant curtly replied: "It seems so," and then waited for them to tell him what had happened.[12]

What they had to say was grim enough. McClernand had lost 1500 men, and the survivors of his displaced division were desperately trying to rally behind Wallace's thin line. McArthur had been driven back with 400 casualties, and his men too were striving to regroup. Smith's division was too far to the left to come to the rescue. For whatever it might be worth the Confederates had broken the constricting Union ring and the escape route to the south was wide open; wide open, too, seemed to be the road to the Union rear, the road to final defeat of the Union cause in Tennessee. The Rebel yell was rising, jeering and triumphant, over smoky woods and littered fields where blue bodies lay helpless in the snow: and here was Sam Grant, one-time Captain of Regular Infantry, Brigadier of Volunteers now by virtue of the friendship of a prairie Congressman — stubby Sam Grant, sitting on his horse with a sheaf of documents in one fist, and what he said in answer to this tale of disaster would determine what would happen to him and to the Western war itself.

As always, he seemed unemotional, except that the flesh across his cheekbones grew red. Wallace remembered that Grant crumpled the papers in his hand convulsively, but when he spoke his voice was calm.

"Gentlemen," he said, "the position on the right must be re-taken." [13]

There was a lull in the fighting, just then. The Confederates, who had swept everything before them, had fallen back — to regroup, to mount a new attack, to retreat, to find some food or just to catch their breath. All about the Generals, Union soldiers were standing bewildered, talking to one another, trying to figure out what they were supposed to do next. A few were hunting around for dis-carded ammunition boxes, to get a fresh supply of cartridges, and they were gabbling that the dead Rebels they had seen carried full haversacks, as if they did not propose to return to their camp for food. Word of what the men were saying came to Grant, and after he had spent a moment sizing things up he turned to Colonel J. D. Webster of his staff and expressed his opinion.

"Some of our men are pretty badly demoralized," he said, "but the enemy must be more so, for he has attempted to force his way out but has fallen back; the one who attacks first now will be vic-torious, and the enemy will have to be in a hurry if he gets ahead of me."

It seemed to Grant that the Confederates had put everything they had into the assault on McClernand. If that was the case, the Con-federate right must be very lightly held; let Smith, then, make an immediate attack, breaking the network of trenches and rifle pits in his front, and compelling the Confederates to turn and protect their own rear. Wallace was to put in line all the men he could lay hands on, and when the guns had been rolled forward to prepare the way he was to counterattack; meanwhile, McClernand's broken fragments must be rallied so that they could strengthen Wallace's blow. Meanwhile, too, an aide must gallop off down the muddy, winding road to the steamboat landing; crippled or not, the gun-boats must lend a hand here, and even a show of force on the river might help the infantry in its work. On land and on the water, the Federals would immediately attack with everything they had.[14]

To everyone who saw him at this moment Grant seemed com-pletely calm and unworried, and afterward men believed that the tide of battle turned the moment he gave the order . . . "the position on the right must be retaken." Actually, Grant was far from calm. His full awareness of his peril, concealed from everyone else, is apparent in the wording of a hasty note which he scribbled and sent off to Foote:

> If all the gunboats that can will immediately make their appearance to the enemy it may secure us a victory. Otherwise all may be defeated. A terrible conflict ensued in my absence, which has demoralized a portion of my command, but I think the enemy is more so. If the gunboats do not show themselves it will reassure the enemy and still further demoralize our troops. I must order a charge to save appearances. I do not expect the gunboats to go into action, but to make an appearance and throw a few shells at long range.[15]

Never in his career as a soldier did Grant write a more completely revealing dispatch. In the confusion of its wording — unusual, with Grant, whose dispatches ordinarily are extremely clear and explicit — the note bears evidence of the haste with which it was written; bears evidence, too, that he himself had been jarred more than his intimates realized by the military catastrophe that had developed during his absence. The words "otherwise all may be defeated" sound a note which is rarely heard in anything Grant said or wrote. He had been prompt enough to reassert his control over the situation, and Wallace had marveled at his coolness, but down inside Grant clearly realized that he was elbow-to-elbow with final disaster. There is an urgency in this appeal for help that seldom appears in one of Grant's dispatches.

Beyond that, this note sums up not only Grant's immediate appraisal of the situation but the military philosophy on which his reaction to that situation was based.

He had done the obvious things, almost automatically: ordered an attack from his left on the apparent soft spot in the Rebel line, called for a counterattack in the place where ground had been lost, arranged for regrouping of the troops driven out of action, summoned the gunboats back into the fight. Back of these orders lay the lesson he had learned in Missouri: the idea that in every battle there may come a moment when each side is fought out and ready to quit, and the belief that in such a moment victory will go to the side which is able to make one final effort. It seemed to him that this moment had arrived, and it was going to be Grant's army that made the final effort. The note to Foote is supplemented by the remark to Colonel Webster: "The enemy will have to be in a hurry if he gets ahead of me."

Beyond the confusion and wreckage of the battlefield, Grant was looking to the morale of the soldiers themselves — his own soldiers, and the soldiers of the Confederacy. His men, or a substantial number of them, were indeed demoralized; that much he frankly confessed. But it was not merely native optimism that led him to add that the Confederates were no better off. The Southerners had carried full haversacks when they made their attack — certain indication that they were fighting to win a chance to get away rather than to win a battle. What was important now was what happened in men's minds. The gunboats need not bring much weight to bear, but they must "make an appearance"; Grant would order a charge "to save appearances" — and out of all of this would come tangible evidence that his army wanted to renew the engagement, that it did not own itself beaten, that the appearance of Confederate victory and Union defeat was only an appearance and nothing more. Final victory would go to the side which insisted on winning it, and the Union Army would be very insistent.

In this moment of crisis at Fort Donelson Grant met one of the supreme tests of his career as a soldier.

With McClernand, Grant galloped along the line, calling out to the beaten men that the Confederates were retreating and urging every man to refill his ammunition pouch and take his place in the line ready for an attack. Then, with the broken lines reforming, Grant rode off to the left, where the former commandant of West Point cadets, C. F. Smith, was waiting for orders.

Smith was sitting under a tree, beside one of his aides. Grant rode up to him and, without ceremony, said: "General Smith, all has failed on our right — you must take Fort Donelson." Smith unfolded his long legs, brushed his mustache as he got to his feet, said briefly, "I will do it," and sent the aide off to get the division into line. In no time the division was ready to advance — 2nd Iowa in the lead, four more regiments massed behind it. While Grant rode back to see to the right of his line, Smith rode across the Iowans' front, gestured toward the high ground where lay the Confederate works, and said: "Second Iowa, you must take that fort. Take the caps off your guns, fix bayonets, and I will support you." [16]

The Middle Westerners who made this attack remembered it as long as they lived, for the way was tough — a tangle of fallen timber, a ravine with steep banks, invisible Rebels driving in a hot fire, with double-barreled shotguns charged with buckshot reserved for close range — but even more than the fight itself, they remembered Smith. He was erect on his horse in front of them, his saber held high in the air, and when he had given the command to advance he went on in advance of everybody — turning in the saddle, now and then, to make sure that his men were following him. For faint hearts he had scornful words; seeing some of the soldiers hesitating about getting out into the thick of things, he swung about and made wrathful oration: "Damn you, gentlemen, I see skulkers. I'll have none here. Come on, you volunteers, come on. This is your chance. You volunteered to be killed for love of your country and now you can be. You are only damned volunteers. I am only a soldier and I don't want to be killed, but you came to be killed and now you can be." And so, with a mixture of oaths and sharp words, the old man led them up the wooded slope straight for the Confederate trenches. Men said he was the first man in the works, riding in so close to the Rebels that he could have put his hand on their heads, and one of his soldiers wrote that "by his presence and heroic conduct he led the green men to do things that no other man could have done." [17]

Smith's charge was a success, and the right of the Rebel line gave way. Meanwhile, McClernand's and Wallace's men were finding it unexpectedly easy to regain the ground that had been lost during the morning; and here, indeed, Grant was greatly aided by a singular paralysis which descended on the minds of the officers commanding the Confederate Army.

Gideon Pillow had done very well indeed, so far. He had smashed the Union right; as Bedford Forrest wrote, he had opened not one but three roads by which the Confederate Army could retreat. But before Grant had got his counterattack in motion, Pillow had undergone a strange change of mind. Buckner was pulling his own troops out of their trenches, preparing to join in what had been planned as a retirement to safety farther south, when he was ordered by Pillow to go back to the lines. John B. Floyd, who was technically in supreme command, at first countermanded the order, then — after conferring with Pillow — sustained it; Buckner's men were just getting back into position when Smith's assault hit them and made a fatal lodgment in their lines. Pillow, meanwhile, was ordering his own men back into the works; and at the very moment when Grant's right was reorganizing for a counterattack, the Confederates who had driven everything before them in the morning were going back to the fortifications, leaving the open road to the south to take care of itself.

Precisely what was on Pillow's mind in all of this is beyond rational explanation. It is possible that the troops which had done so well that morning were simply fought out, disorganized by their victory, worn to a frazzle by the wintry nights they had spent in the trenches; Floyd wrote afterward that some of the men were so completely exhausted that they could not keep their eyes open even when they were standing up under enemy fire, and if it was believed that the entire command needed to be pulled together and given a rest before beginning a retreat this can hardly be wondered at. Pillow himself seems to have felt that the fight to open a road for retreat was an operation entirely separate from the retreat itself; with the road opened, the army would reassemble and, after dark, the retreat would be made — the theory apparently being that the Federals would obligingly leave the escape hatch open. In any case, the Confederates left the ground they had won, and although Floyd and Pillow telegraphed Johnston that they had won a dazzling victory, they now let the victory evaporate. Meanwhile, they knew that Grant had been reinforced, and although Wallace and McClernand did not by any means reoccupy all of the ground which the Federals had held at daybreak, the Confederate commanders believed that they did. In vain did Bedford Forrest report that "there were none of the enemy in sight when dark came on." Abandoned campfires, stirred into flame by the wind, twinkled all along the line from which the Illinois soldiers had been driven, and to Pillow and Floyd it seemed clear that the encircling ring of Union troops —

stronger now than it had ever been before — had been made whole again. Forrest might write that the Confederate soldiers were "flushed with victory, and confident that they could drive the enemy back to the Tennessee river the next morning"; Pillow and Floyd thought otherwise, and what they thought was what finally mattered. Never was Grant's belief in the importance of the factor of morale so strikingly justified. The generals who faced him had accepted his own appraisal of the situation.[18]

As night came down on February 15 it was by no means clear, inside the Union lines, that the battle actually was over. The rain had stopped and a full moon floated high in a clear, wintry sky. Wagon trains came plodding up through the mud, bearing rations and tents, but only the food was distributed; for one more night, at least, the soldiers would have to get along without shelter. There were many wounded men, and every farmhouse had been turned into a hospital. Dead men were laid out in long rows by each of these, and one officer remembered how white and waxen their faces looked in the moonlight. Men of the 20th Ohio found their camp overrun with disorganized men from two Illinois regiments, worn-out men in muddy, tattered clothing who seemed not to have eaten for days and who sauntered about looking for someone to tell them what they ought to do next.

Soldiers who had not fought before were dazed by the fury of the fight they had experienced. A man in the 45th Illinois wrote a breathless letter to his parents, describing the terrible violence of cannon fire: "I have seen trees a foot and a half through cut off entirely by the cannon balls and I have had balls strike the trees at full force not more than a foot from my head and I have had shells burst within a rod of me and throw the dirt all over me but it appears that the Lord still has more work for me to do." (The Lord did: this soldier was to die in action at Shiloh, less than two months from this night.) Men who had had glimpses of Grant said that the General seemed to understand the feelings of Volunteers. One luckless German artillerist who had had to abandon his guns to the Confederates was being berated for failing to disable the weapons before leaving them. He expostulated: "What! I spike those good guns! My God, no!" Grant heard him, chuckled at this thrifty but unmilitary viewpoint, and let him off.[19]

Riding back to headquarters in the twilight, Grant passed many dead and wounded men from both armies. One scene particularly struck him: a Federal lieutenant and a Confederate private, both desperately wounded, lay side by side, and the lieutenant was trying without much success to give the Confederate a drink from his canteen. Grant reined in and looked at the two, then asked his staff officers if anyone had a flask. One officer finally produced one; Grant took it, dismounted, and walked to the two wounded men, giving each man a swallow of brandy. The Confederate murmured, "Thank you, General," and the Federal, too weak to speak, managed to flutter one hand in an attempt at a salute. Grant called to Rawlins: "Send for stretchers; send for stretchers at once for these men." As the stretcher party came up Grant got on his horse; then he noticed that the stretcher bearers, picking up the Union officer, seemed inclined to ignore the Confederate.

"Take this Confederate, too," he ordered. "Take them both together; the war is over between them."

The men were borne away, and Grant and his party rode off. There were so many dead and wounded men that the horses were constantly shying nervously, and Grant at last turned to Colonel Webster with the remark: "Let's get away from this dreadful place. I suppose this work is part of the devil that is left in us all." They got out to more open ground, and as the general watched the wounded men limping, hobbling and crawling toward the rear he was obviously depressed. One officer remembered hearing Grant — who rarely recited poetry — intoning the verse:

Man's inhumanity to man
Makes countless thousands mourn.[20]

Late that night Grant tasted the first food he had had since his early breakfast.

There was much movement and a general bustle and stir in the Union camp all night long. Troops were being reassembled, batteries were being moved to new positions, loaded wagons were creaking up from the landing, and stretcher parties were constantly bringing new loads of wounded men to the field hospitals. Far off in the darkness, men could hear the splashing and puffing of steamboats along the waterfront by the fort.

Somewhere around two in the morning, stray Confederate deserters came into the lines, reporting that the Confederate pickets had been mysteriously withdrawn. Colonel Whittlesey, worried because the way was still open for a Confederate retreat, noted that there was fully a mile of open ground between the Federal right and the banks of the Cumberland, space unoccupied except for dead and wounded men.[21]

At about three in the morning, a Confederate flag of truce came through Smith's lines, with a message for the Commanding General.

Smith and his staff had made a bivouac in the trodden snow, and an officer from the 2nd Iowa came to this bivouac to report that the Rebel officer who came in with the flag was asking if there was a Federal officer present who could negotiate terms for a Confederate surrender. Smith mounted and rode forward, and Major Thomas J. Newsham, of his staff, reported that Smith bluntly told the Confederate: "I make no terms with Rebels with arms in their hands — my terms are unconditional and immediate surrender!" Then, bearing a letter which the Confederate gave him, Smith set off the Grant's headquarters.

Grant was in the kitchen of the little farmhouse, stretched out on a mattress on the floor. Smith stalked in, stood by the open fire to get the chill out of his long legs, and as Grant drew on some clothing the onetime commandant of cadets handed the letter to him, saying: "There's something for you to read, General." While Grant was reading it, Smith inquired if anyone had a drink. Dr. Brinton owned a flask, and he handed it to Smith, who took a long pull at it, returned the flask, and then raised one foot and gazed at it ruefully.

"See how the soles of my boots burned," he said. "I slept last night with my head in the saddle and with my feet too near the fire; I've scorched my boots."

Grant finished reading the letter. It was signed by his friend from the Old Army, General Simon Bolivar Buckner, who, by an odd turn of events, was now the commanding officer in Fort Donelson, and — as the flag-of-truce officer had told Smith — it asked for an armistice and the appointment of commissioners to settle terms of surrender. Grant gave the letter to Smith, asking: "What answer shall I send to this, General?"

"No terms to the damned Rebels!" barked Smith. Grant chuckled, then sat at the kitchen table, drew up a tablet, and began to write. Presently he read aloud, to Smith and the other officers, what he had written. It would become one of the most famous dispatches in American military history. Addressed to General Buckner, it went as follows:

> Sir: Yours of this date proposing Armistice and appointment of Commissioners to settle terms of Capitulation is just received. No terms except unconditional and immediate surrender can be accepted. I propose to move immediately upon your works. I am sir, very respectfully
>
> > Your obt. svt.
> > U. S. GRANT
> > *Brig. Gen.*

Smith gave a brief grunt, and remarked, "It's the same thing in smoother words." Then, taking the letter, he stalked out of the room to deliver it to the waiting Confederate. Grant's threat to "move immediately upon your works," incidentally, was a fully loaded gun. Before the flag of truce arrived he had sent Rawlins riding off to McClernand and Wallace with orders that they attack as soon as they heard Smith's guns open, and Smith had been alerted to renew the fighting as soon as daybreak brought enough light for fighting. Buckner's message reached Smith and Grant only a short time before the all-out offensive was to have begun.[22]

General Buckner was not pleased. He had befriended Grant some years earlier, when Grant needed a friend very much, and he seems to have felt that Grant ought to remember this now. He wrote stiffly in reply:

"The distribution of the forces under my command incident to an unexpected change of commanders and the overwhelming force under your command compel me, notwithstanding the brilliant success of the Confederate arms yesterday, to accept the ungenerous and unchivalrous terms which you propose."

If this note was both grumpy and inexact — Grant was not "proposing terms" of any sort, and he was under no obligation to be chivalrous — Buckner can be forgiven. He had just been through one of the oddest farce-comedy sequences in Civil War history, and it left him with an uneven temper. During the night his two superiors, Generals Floyd and Pillow, had had a fantastic conference. Floyd, believing surrender inevitable, had no wish to be captured; he had been Secretary of War in President Buchanan's cabinet, patriotic Northerners were accusing him of having anticipated the act of secession by transferring government arms to Southern states, and it seemed likely that the Lincoln government would put him on trial if it laid hands on him. So, quite blandly, he had turned over the command to the next man in line, Pillow. Pillow entertained two conflicting opinions: that surrender was not exactly necessary, but that Floyd's decision to surrender would be binding on the new commander anyway. Also, he was as reluctant as Floyd to become the first Confederate general captured by the Unionists. So Pillow, without hesitation, had turned the command over to Buckner — who, being of stouter fiber than his two superiors, believed that an officer who surrendered his post ought to stay with his troops and take the consequences. Floyd thereupon put himself and several Virginia regiments on the transports and steamed off to Nashville; Pillow found space for himself and his staff on another transport and followed Floyd, and doughty Bedford Forrest, disgusted by the whole operation, boldly marched his cavalry off to freedom through the flooded lowlands south of the fort. That left Buckner as the residuary legatee of disaster, and he did what he had to do manfully but unhappily.[23]

When the sun came up on the morning of February 16, the area was strangely quiet. The weather had turned warm, and rivulets of melted snow trickled through the fields and clearings where many untended wounded men were still lying. In the Federal lines, soldiers looked about, bewildered, asking one another why there was no more firing; then, from Smith's division, there came a rising volume of excited cheering, and the word spread through the camp:

The Rebels have given up. Lew Wallace put his division in line to advance and occupy the Confederate works in his front, and then with his staff spurred on ahead and went into the town of Dover, where he found Buckner and his staff at breakfast in the village tavern. Half an hour later Grant joined them.

Somewhere around nine in the morning, the scarred gunboats came up the river, followed by a long file of transports. (Grant by now had twenty-seven thousand men on the scene, and reinforcements were still coming up.) A newspaper correspondent on Grant's headquarters steamer wrote that Federal regiments were massed along the shore and on the heights, each with its flag. He saw a United States flag hoisted on a flagpole and heard a tremendous cheer from the troops, and wrote that it was "a glorious moment — a Sabbath morning which will live in history." [24]

Another correspondent was present when Grant and Buckner had a talk. He described Grant, who had suddenly become so famous: "About 45 years of age, sandy complexion, reddish beard, medium height, pleasant, twinkling eyes and weighs 170 pounds. He smokes continually." Grant and Buckner settled some question of rations for the prisoners; then, said the reporter, "the Negro question came up." Grant agreed that Confederate officers might take their body servants with them, but the horde of Negro laborers in the fort would not be returned to their owners. "We want laborers," the correspondent quoted him as saying. "Let the Negroes work for us." A planter who had come to reclaim his slaves "retired silent and sullen" when he heard this verdict.

Grant's chat with Buckner was friendly. Long afterward, Buckner told how Grant drew him aside when the conference ended, remarking that Buckner, as a prisoner, separated from his own people, might have financial difficulties; if Buckner needed money, anything Grant had in his purse was available . . . and the favor which Buckner had done for Grant years earlier (which neither man mentioned) could be repaid in kind. The episode was characteristic. Up to the moment of surrender, it would not enter Grant's head that his old-time friendship with the opposing commander should in any way affect his attitude; but once the fighting had stopped and the opposing commander had laid down his arms, the old friendship could be resumed and there would be room for the chivalry whose absence in the ultimatum of surrender had struck Buckner as brusque and stern.[25]

Grant's first task was to send back word of his victory, and without delay he got off a message to Halleck at St. Louis:

> We have taken Fort Donelson and from 12,000 to 15,000 prisoners, including Generals Buckner and Bushrod Johnson; also 20,000 stand of arms, 48 pieces of artillery, 17 heavy guns, from 2,000 to 4,000 horses, and large quantities of commissary stores.[26]

It was the first of three messages which Grant would send during the war, announcing the capture of an opposing army.

CHAPTER NINE

Aftermath of Victory

NOW IT WAS a different war. The foundation of the Confederacy had suddenly cracked, and seismic vibrations ran all across the land. People began to see that something decisive had happened, and they responded quickly, with deep emotion.

At the Union Merchants Exchange in St. Louis, staid men of business forgot getting and spending in order to group themselves together and sing "The Star-Spangled Banner," and other patriotic songs, after which they went down the street to General Halleck's headquarters, where they cheered until Halleck himself appeared at a window. Responding to public acclaim was not quite in Halleck's line, but he adapted himself to it, this once, and cried out: "I promised when I came here that with your aid I would drive the enemies of our flag from your state. This has been done, and they are virtually out of Kentucky and soon will be out of Tennessee." Governor Richard Yates of Illinois, with a coterie of lesser officials, took off promptly for Dover, ostensibly to make provision for wounded Illinois soldiers, probably also to identify the state administration with the great victory. From a stopping point along the way the Governor telegraphed to Chicago: "People by thousands on the road and at the stations, with shoutings and with flags. Thank God that our Union is safe now and forever." A newspaper correspondent at Cairo wired "The backbone of the rebellion is broken," and in Chicago there was an all-day celebration. Luckless General Floyd, scuttling off to safety, was hanged in effigy in Chicago and then burned, a newspaper editorial announced that "any person found sober after nine o'clock in the evening would be arrested as a secessionist," and the *Tribune* remarked the next morning that "Chicago reeled mad with joy by that time." The *Tribune* added that the celebration had been a fine thing: "It was well that we should rejoice. Such events happen but once in a lifetime, and we who passed through the scenes of yesterday lived a generation in a day."

Illinois felt especial pride. Grant came from Illinois and so did most of his soldiers, and the state felt that Donelson was somehow an Illinois achievement. But in other places where state pride was less compelling there was equal jubilation. In Cincinnati a reporter observed: "Everybody was shaking hands with everybody else, and bewhiskered men embraced each other as if they were lovers." Business was suspended, fireworks were brought out, and "the misty atmosphere was rosy with the burning of Bengal lights and bonfires blazing at many crossings." In Washington, officers at McClellan's headquarters crowded around the General in Chief when a telegram from General Cullum, Halleck's chief of staff, announced the victory; and McClellan enjoyed a half hour of glory while his staff congratulated him "on the brilliant results of his arrangement of the plan of campaign." McClellan then set off in the rain to take the news to the War Department; in the Capitol building Senator Grimes of Iowa read Cullum's dispatch aloud on the Senate floor, and when the Senators ignored their own rule against applause and broke into cheers, Vice-President Hannibal Hamlin, presiding, condoned the outburst: "The chair rules that the Senate is neither applauding nor cheering a Senator." Guns boomed in salute all day long, and in the camps of the Army of the Potomac young men in unfaded blue uniforms who had never yet faced the enemy in battle tossed their caps and yelled until they were hoarse.[1]

The rejoicing was natural, for this was the North's first substantial victory, and it came after months of discouragement. Yet a great deal of what had been won at Fort Donelson had really been gained at Fort Henry. Taking Fort Henry, the Federals had opened the brimming highway of the Tennessee River, and with that highway open the Confederates could do nothing but retreat. Johnston and his officers had agreed to abandon the Kentucky-Tennessee defensive line before Grant had one infantryman in front of Donelson's pickets: orders for the retreat from Bowling Green had been issued, disillusioned Beauregard had gone west to pick up the pieces at Columbus, and with Fort Henry gone the Confederacy had been doomed to make its next stand at the northern border of Mississippi. But no one in the North had been able to see this, unless perhaps Grant himself had had a feeling for it; it had taken the long fight on the snowy ridges above the little town of Dover to make manifest the fact that the Confederate defensive line in the west had been shattered once and for all.

Grant found himself famous. Until now he had been one of the throng, an obscure brigadier doing a job in a remote sector; now, suddenly, he was the man who knew how to win battles, and his "immediate and unconditional surrender" note stirred men's blood. Secretary Stanton referred to it, in an announcement which was at bottom an attempt to get a little immediate action out of General McClellan, and men who had never heard of Grant before told one another that his initials stood for "Unconditional Surrender." Newspapers told how Grant had been smoking during the battle, and gifts of cigars came in from all quarters — so many that Grant largely gave up his pipe and became a confirmed cigar smoker, if for no better reason than that he had dozens of boxes of cigars lying around headquarters and it seemed a shame to let them go to waste.

He had little leisure to enjoy his fame. Conditions in Fort Donelson — where something like 14,000 men had surrendered after a trying battle, and where the victorious army contained 27,000 men, all of them eager to see the sights — were chaotic. Bodies of dead men and animals were scattered here and there, deeply mired wagons with lifeless horses still in harness were to be found in muddy streets and fields, unattached horses were munching grain from abandoned sacks of corn, and stray dogs howled dismally for their masters. There was a profusion of military supplies and equipment, much of it in bad shape. On the waterfront under the bluffs were huge piles of pork, imperfectly salted and smelling to the skies. There were also hundreds of hogsheads of sugar, piles of sacks of corn and flour, and immense stacks of sides of bacon — some of which had been tossed into the roads in an ineffectual attempt to cope with the bottomless mud. Droves of civilians were beginning to appear, and each one seemed determined to carry off some bit of captured property as a souvenir.[2]

One of Grant's first acts on the morning of the surrender was to issue an order insisting that "the utmost vigilance should be observed to guard all points captured." Lew Wallace was told to return to Fort Henry with two brigades of infantry, two batteries of artillery, and a detachment of cavalry, to hold that important staging point on the Tennessee River. McClernand and Smith were told to make up a detail of two hundred extra-duty men to preserve the stores and munitions taken in Fort Donelson. Arrangements had to be made to get the prisoners sorted out, organized, disarmed and put on transports for the trip to northern prison camps. The prisoners stacked their arms willingly enough, but insisted that they should be allowed to keep their knives, which, they said, were part of their personal property. The knives drew the attention of the Federal officers; nearly everybody seemed to have one, and most of them had been made by country blacksmiths from files and saw blades — vicious-looking weapons, some of them, with keen blades two inches wide and eighteen inches long. Baskets were placed at the gangways of the transports, and the prisoners reluctantly dropped their knives into these as they marched aboard. Federal soldiers noted that the Confederates were rather ragged, dressed mostly in gray or in butternut; for blankets, they carried square pieces of carpet, old comforters, coverlets from beds back home. Some even lugged bedraggled featherbeds. Before noon the clear sky grew dark, and a dismal rain began to fall. There were many wounded men to be put in makeshift hospitals.[3]

Dr. Brinton, taking in all of this with wide eyes, bethought himself of the formal surrender ceremonies which he had read about in accounts of past wars, and once that morning he asked Grant when the parade-ground formalities of surrender would take place, with Buckner handing over his sword, bands playing, and prisoners taking part in a solemn act of capitulation. Grant replied that there would be no ceremonies, explaining: "The surrender is a fact. We have the fort, the men and the guns. Why should we go through with vain forms and mortify and injure the spirit of brave men who, after all, are our countrymen and brothers?"

As he reflected on this surprising common sense attitude, Brinton recalled stray battle scenes that had impressed themselves on his memory. Grant had a body servant, a broken-English immigrant from France, known as French John; during the fighting on February 15, French John insisted on going to the front to see the battle at close range, saying: "I have curiosity, much curiosity, and I must go see the enemies fight." A little later a very much subdued French John was back at the safety of headquarters, murmuring: "I have no more curiosity, it is satisfied, it is all gone; the enemy did allow me to come near them, then all at once they did begin to shoot at me, but I escaped them — and behold me."

There was an Illinois chaplain, Brinton remembered, who repeatedly took his horse up to the front to carry wounded men back to safety, propping a stricken man in the saddle and stalking alongside to hold him in position. He saved a number of lives, and Brinton felt that the Confederates who saw him refrained from shooting at him. There was also a regimental surgeon in the 18th Illinois whom Brinton had found on the firing line, using a musket like the infantrymen all around him. When Brinton protested that this was unprofessional behavior, the surgeon said: "I'm all right, Doctor. I have done all the surgery of this regiment and I have fired 45 rounds, by God." [4]

On the day after the surrender, Grant issued formal orders of congratulations to his troops:

> The general commanding takes great pleasure in congratulating the troops of this command for the triumph over rebellion gained by their valor on the 13th, 14th and 15th instant.
> For four successive nights, without shelter, during the most inclement weather known in this latitude, they faced an enemy in large force in a position chosen by himself. Though strongly fortified by nature, all the safeguards suggested by science were added. Without a murmur this was borne, prepared at all times to receive an attack, and with continuous skirmishing by day, resulting ultimately in forcing the enemy to surrender without conditions.
> The victory achieved is not only great in breaking down rebellion, but has secured the greatest number of prisoners of war ever taken in one battle on this continent.
> Fort Donelson will hereafter be marked in capitals on the maps of our united country and the men who fought the battle will live in the memory of a grateful people. [5]

On this same day Grant issued another order, acknowledging a change that had taken place in his own situation. Halleck had created a new military district, the District of West Tennessee, with undefined limits, and Grant was in charge of it; his old post at Cairo was given to Sherman, who had worked so hard sending troops and supplies forward from Paducah. The significance of the shift remained to be seen. Much might depend on the way in which the limits of the new district were set. Sherman was definitely being advanced. Halleck wired him that "a still more important movement" than the Donelson campaign was impending, and promised him: "You will not be forgotten in this." [6]

If Grant permitted himself any savoring of his triumph, aside from the reference in his general order to the fact that Donelson had seen the largest bag of prisoners of war in American history, there is no record of it. He wanted to get on with the war; he realized that the sadly diminished Confederate Army under Johnston could do nothing but retreat; and he reflected that in his original orders he had been told to break the railroad bridge at Clarksville, thirty miles up the river from Dover. On February 18 Grant was ready to move. Up the river went Flag Officer Foote, carrying on in spite of his wound, with gunboats *Conestoga* and *Cairo*, accompanied by Colonel Webster of Grant's staff. The expedition found the Confederate fort at Clarksville deserted, and the mayor of the town came aboard to report that all Confederate troops had left, along with two thirds of the town's civilian population, which feared looting and pillage by the Federals. Foote assured the mayor that the Federals would take nothing but military stores, issued a proclamation to quiet the townspeople's fears, and sent back a report saying that as soon as he could bring up some more gunboats he would like to go on upstream and, in conjunction with Grant, attack Nashville itself. He added that "the Rebels have great terror of the gunboats." [7]

Grant sent Smith and his division up the river to occupy Clarksville, and on February 21 reported to Cullum that this had been done, adding that he would not do more than that without orders from Halleck, but hinting broadly: "It is my impression that by following up our success Nashville would be an easy conquest." On

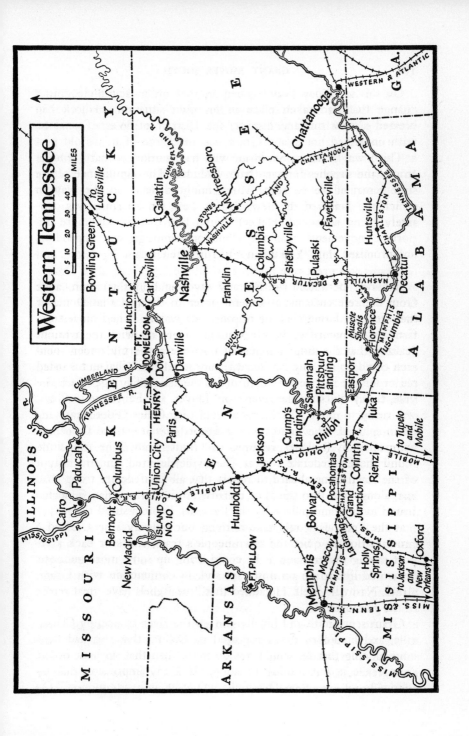

the same day Foote sent Cullum a message saying bluntly that
"General Grant and myself consider this a good time to move on
Nashville." Both of them, said Foote, felt that the city could be
taken easily.[8]

This brought no action. Grant was warned not to send gunboats
any farther upstream than Clarksville, but the rest was silence; a
strange sort of silence, actually, reflecting an even stranger situation
of which, at that time, Grant himself was almost completely unaware.

McClellan, Halleck and Buell had been interchanging letters and
telegrams at a great rate for three solid weeks — ever since Grant's
expedition left Cairo for Fort Henry — and in this interchange
Grant himself had almost been forgotten. Reading the bulky file of
these messages, one gets the impression that Grant had moved too
fast. The Generals had been upset; they were above all other things
deliberate, and although universal opinion in the Old Army held
each of the three to be brilliant, it appeared that brilliance needed
plenty of time — time to consult and confer, time to perfect the
largest and the smallest details of supply, transportation and co-
ordination, time as well to jockey and maneuver for personal advantage. Now the pressure for immediate action had become
stronger than all other pressures, and the strain was great. As the
author of this pressure — or, at the very least, the person through
whom the pressure had developed — Grant was beginning to look
like a man who had brought embarrassment rather than opportunity.

Halleck may have felt this embarrassment the most acutely, inasmuch as the new hero of the hour was a man whom he himself
— with a complete absence of personal feeling and with no thought
for anything but the good of the service — had for some time been
planning to demote. Grant himself did not know this; during the
fall he had sensed that the department contained a number of generals who were senior to him and that one or another of these
might well replace him, but he believed that this danger had
subsided. Nevertheless, on February 8 — just after the capture of
Fort Henry, the day when Grant announced that he would move
overland and take Fort Donelson — Halleck was asking Secretary

of War Stanton to make a major general out of Brigadier General Ethan Allen Hitchcock and assign him to the West, since "an experienced officer of high rank is wanted immediately on the Tennessee line." (The "Tennessee line," of course, was the line on which Grant at that moment was carrying on a campaign.)[9]

This move apparently reflected nothing more than Halleck's natural wish to get, for the number two job in his department, an officer whom he knew personally and in whom he had full confidence. Hitchcock was such a man. He was getting on in years — he had been born in 1798, and he was graduated from West Point in 1817 — but he had served on Winfield Scott's staff in the Mexican War, he was a soldier of unquestioned intellectual capacity, his standing at the War Department was good, and Stanton had approved Halleck's plan without delay. Halleck then wired to Sherman, for whom he had developed a warm regard: "Hitchcock will be appointed tomorrow morning and I am directed to assign officers accordingly. Make your preparations to take a column or division on the Tennessee or Cumberland." Sherman at this time outranked Grant; if he "took a column or division" in any area where Grant commanded, he and not Grant would be in charge.

Halleck tried to expand his plan. To McClellan, he proposed that the War Department establish a Western Division, to include three departments: Department of the Missouri, under General David Hunter, who at that time was commanding in Kansas; Department of the Mississippi, under Hitchcock (or, if Hitchcock did not want it, under Sherman), and Department of the Ohio, under Buell. Halleck would be commander of this Western Division, and his principal lieutenants thus would be Hunter, Hitchcock or Sherman, and Buell. What would happen to Grant was not mentioned, but obviously he would be down-graded.[10]

Nothing came of this; Hitchcock, who was feeling his years, declined the Western assignment.[11] But none of Halleck's proposals affecting the Western command — and he made a good many of them — held out much prospect of advancement for Grant. Halleck began, immediately after Fort Donelson had been taken, by begging Buell to "come down to the Cumberland and take command," adding: "I am terribly hard pushed. Help me and I will help you." Halleck believed that Beauregard was collecting reinforcements at

Columbus and was about to attack either Cairo or Paducah, and he assured McClellan that "it is the crisis of the war in the west." On February 17 he wired McClellan: "Make Buell, Grant and Pope major-generals of volunteers and give me command in the west. I ask this for Forts Henry and Donelson." This telegram at least acknowledged Grant's existence, although it sandwiched him in between the other two generals in clear implication that he was just one of several deserving cases; and two days later Halleck demanded a major general's commission for C. F. Smith, who "by his coolness and bravery at Fort Donelson when the battle was against us turned the tide and carried the enemy's outworks." [12]

On the heels of this, Halleck began to bid for his own advancement without permitting himself to be handicapped by modesty, false or genuine. On February 20 he wired McClellan: "I must have top command of the armies in the west. Hesitation and delay are losing us the golden opportunity. Lay this before the President and Secretary of War. May I assume the command? Answer quickly." On the following day he sent a message to Assistant Secretary of War Thomas A. Scott, who was then in Louisville, urging Scott to come to the Cumberland "and divide the responsibility with me." Plaintively, he confessed: "I am tired of waiting for action in Washington. They will not understand the case. It is as plain as daylight to me." To Secretary Stanton, Halleck wrote that "a golden opportunity" to strike the Confederates a fatal blow had been lost, "but I can't do it unless I can control Buell's army. . . . Give me authority and I will be responsible for results." [13]

For the moment this got Halleck nowhere. Both McClellan and Stanton returned abrupt refusals, and Stanton warned that the President "expects you and General Buell to co-operate fully and zealously with each other, and would be glad to know whether there has been any failure of co-operation in any particular." [14] In addition, Washington failed utterly to follow Halleck's lead in the matter of promotions. To the Senate Abraham Lincoln sent the name of just one man for promotion to major general — U. S. Grant. The Senate promptly confirmed the promotion, and now Grant outranked everyone in the Western Department except Halleck himself. If Grant and Buell — or Grant and Pope, Sherman or anyone else — came together in the same area, Grant would be in charge. Promotions for the others came a little later, but Grant's was the first, and as the first it was all-important.

While Halleck was concentrating on the problem of command, and while he and McClellan and Buell were filling the records with long, carefully-reasoned proposals regarding the next step in the campaign against the Confederacy, Grant was trying to keep moving. He was full of the idea that when Forts Henry and Donelson fell the Confederacy received a genuinely crippling blow, and it seemed to him that the Federal Armies should crowd on after the beaten foe and press their advantage to the utmost. The immediate objectives, he believed, were Nashville and Johnston's army, which army — subtracting the number lost at Fort Donelson, and not counting those in the distant stronghold of Columbus, on the Mississippi — just now numbered hardly more than seventeen thousand men, and obviously was in full retreat and must continue so for some time to come.[15] Grant had put Smith at Clarksville, in obedience to orders, and he wanted to go driving on to the south. And although headquarters refused to let Grant send his own troops to Nashville, Grant presently found troops that he could send.

While the battle at Fort Donelson was still going on, Buell had detached a division commanded by Brigadier General William Nelson, had put it on transports, and had sent it down the Ohio and up the Cumberland to reinforce Grant if Grant needed reinforcing. This division, its strength diminished to just under six thousand men by the detachment of a brigade at Paducah, reached Fort Donelson on February 24, and Grant responded immediately. Buell, when last heard from, was marching laboriously toward Nashville from Bowling Green; Nelson belonged to Buell, and there was no longer any reason to land his men at Fort Donelson, or at Clarksville either; the territorial limits of Grant's command had never been defined, and for all anyone knew they might include Nashville . . . and so, stretching his authority just a little, Grant promptly ordered Nelson to move on up to Nashville forthwith, with gunboat *Carondelet* for escort. Nelson was to report to Buell at Nashville, when Buell arrived; until he got in touch with Buell, Grant's orders were binding.[16]

What Grant had in mind comes out in a letter which Grant wrote
to Julia, immediately after he had sent Nelson on up the river. In
this letter, typically careless in matters of spelling and syntax,
Grant explained his strategic ideas:

> I have just returned from Clarksville. Yesterday some citizens
> of Nashville came down there ostensibly to bring surgeons to
> attend their wounded at that place but in reality no doubt to get
> assurance that they would not be molested. Johnson with his
> Army of rebels have fallen back about forty miles south from
> Nashville leaving the river clear to our troops. Today a Division
> of Gen. Buell's army reported to me for orders. As they were on
> steamers I ordered them immediately up to Nashville. "Secesh"
> is now about on its last legs in Tennessee. I want to push on as
> rapidly as possible to save hard fighting. These terrible battles
> are very good things to read about for persons who loose no
> friends but I am decidedly in favor of having as little of it as
> possible. The way to avoid it is to push forward as vigorously as
> possible. Gen. Halleck is clearly the same way of thinking and
> with his clear head I think the Congressional Committee for
> investigating the Conduct of the War will have nothing to en-
> quire about in the West.[17]

There would come a time when Grant would be much more reserved in his references to General Halleck's clear head, but at the
moment he had no reason to suppose that Halleck had anything but
his own impatience for delays. In a letter to Sherman he confessed
that he did not know what Halleck wanted him to do next,[18] but
his deepest instinct as a soldier was to keep a beaten foe off balance.
Unfortunately, he seemed to be the only Union officer in Tennessee who possessed that instinct.

Buell himself was greatly displeased, and there quickly developed
between him and Grant a coolness which never grew any warmer.
Nelson dutifully went on to Nashville, occupying an abandoned
fort just below the city and then moving on to take possession of
Nashville itself. (The last of Johnston's troops had left not long before.) Buell's advance guard appeared shortly afterward, on the
opposite side of the river, and Buell was indignant when he found
that a division of his own army was in Nashville ahead of him. This,

he believed, was altogether too risky; he was convinced that John-ston out-numbered him, he feared that the Confederates would come back and destroy Nelson's division before he could bring up the rest of his own men, and he hastily wired to Clarksville de-manding reinforcements.

This, in a way, was just what Grant wanted, since it gave him at least a left-handed justification for intervening at Nashville. He wrote to Cullum, telling him what had happened and saying, "I shall go to Nashville immediately after the arrival of the next mail, should there be no orders to prevent it." He sent Cullum some Memphis newspapers which his spies had brought in, to be trans-mitted to Halleck in St. Louis, and he confessed: "I am growing anxious to know what the next move is going to be." Then, having received no word telling him not to go to Nashville, he got on a steamer and set off up the Cumberland.[19]

On his way he stopped briefly at Clarksville, where he saw trans-ports — the same that had taken Nelson's troops to Nashville — lined up along the bank, with Federal troops going aboard. Grant stopped and went to see C. F. Smith, who displayed a message just received from Buell. Buell recited that Nelson had occupied Nash-ville contrary to his own wishes, and that as a result he had to hold the place whether he wanted to or not — had to hold it, as he con-ceived, with grossly inadequate forces. Johnston, Buell continued, would soon take the offensive against him, and Buell had fewer than fifteen thousand men on the scene; Smith, therefore, must bring his men to Nashville at once, and Buell had sent the transports to bring them.

This, Smith told Grant, was nonsense. Grant agreed that it was, but he remarked that Buell's request had the force of an order and that Smith would have to obey. Smith, whose whole gospel cen-tered around explicit obedience to orders from all lawful superiors, said that he knew that, and pointed out that the embarkation of his men was well under way; and then Grant hurried on up the river, full of the idea that he and Buell had better have a conference.[20]

Buell himself was not actually in Nashville — his headquarters were still on the northern side of the river — and that evening, the evening of February 27, Grant wrote Buell a letter:

I have been in the city since an early hour this morning, anxious and expecting to see you. When I first arrived I understood that you were to be over today, but it is now growing too late for me to remain longer. If I could see the necessity of more troops here I would be most happy to supply them. My own impression is, however, that the enemy are not far north of the Tennessee line. [In other words, Johnston was altogether too far away to threaten any Union troops in Nashville.] I am anxious to know what information you might have on the subject.

He notified Buell that Smith was bringing two thousand soldiers, and asked: "If not needed, please send him back." [21]

This note, it must be confessed, is just a little starchy. Writing as a senior to a junior (he signed himself, U. S. GRANT, *major general*) Grant was making it clear that he had been kept waiting and that he was slightly surprised to find that the General commanding the forces of occupation was not actually present with his troops; he was also making it clear that he did not quite agree with his junior about the urgency of the situation, the need for more troops, or the complete reliability of the junior's information — and, altogether, it was quite a letter, considering that its author had been just an ex-captain of infantry, of shadowed fame, less than ten months earlier. One gathers that Grant rather enjoyed writing it and that Buell got very little pleasure out of reading it. Having written, Grant set off for his own steamboat. On his way to the wharf he met Buell in person.

The meeting appears to have been icy. Grant noted that the only Federals in Nashville were men of Nelson's division, sent there by himself, and that the others in Buell's command were still on the other side of the Cumberland. He mentioned that the Confederates, from all he could learn, were retreating as fast as they could, and Buell retorted that fighting was going on no more than ten or twelve miles away. This, said Grant, might be true, but it could be no more than a rear-guard action; Nashville had been full of munitions, foodstuffs and Army equipment, and the Confederates were undoubtedly trying to carry off all they could. (They had entrusted the job to Bedford Forrest, as good a man for such a job as could have been found anywhere.) Buell insisted that Nashville was in danger of a Confederate attack, Grant said that he did not believe it, and Buell insisted that he knew he was correct. Grant let it go at that, replying merely that Smith's troops were at that moment disembarking in Nashville. Writing about it long afterward, Grant commented that on that evening "the enemy were trying to get away from Nashville and not to return to it." [22]

It took Halleck a long time to find out what was going on, an unexpected complication having arisen to disturb the operation of high strategy. The communications system by which Halleck and Grant were supposed to be keeping in touch had lapsed, and for the moment neither man knew it. Originally, messages between headquarters at St. Louis and the advanced force in the Fort Henry-Fort Donelson area had been relayed by steamer to Paducah or Cairo. The telegraph line had been extended to Fort Henry, but it was not working well. Years later, Grant learned that the operator at the Fort Henry end of the line was a Rebel sympathizer, indulging in sabotage by failing to deliver telegrams; but the basic trouble was a queer organizational setup which had been devised by Secretary Stanton, who had a strange mania for keeping administrative controls in his own hands. The military telegraph system was run by civilian operators who were entirely out from under the jurisdiction of Army and departmental commanders; they were answerable only to the Superintendent of Military Telegraphs, Colonel Anson Stager, who had his office in Washington and was himself answerable only to the Secretary of War. If the Fort Henry man had been under either Grant or Halleck, his failure presumably would have been noted and corrected, but he was independent of both officers; messages simply vanished and no one realized that they were vanishing, and as a result Halleck and Grant were out of touch without knowing that they were out of touch.[23]

This was to have consequences. Halleck had concluded (his attempt to get Buell under his command having failed) that he should leave the Cumberland to Buell and make his own advance up the Tennessee, and he had ordered that Grant bring Smith back from Clarksville, establish stand-by garrisons at Fort Donelson and Fort Henry, and concentrate the bulk of his forces near Danville, on the Tennessee thirty-five miles upstream from Fort Henry, ready for a movement well to the west of Nashville. Of all of this, Grant at the moment knew nothing, and of Grant's recent moves Halleck knew nothing. The measure of the mutual misunderstanding is in a telegram Halleck sent to McClellan at the moment Buell and Grant were meeting in Nashville — a telegram which said that Buell, by now, was probably in Nashville, that Nelson's division had relieved Smith at Clarksville, that reports about Confederate dispositions were obscure and that it seemed unwise to order any further movements until the situation became a bit clearer.[24]

By the end of the month, indirect news began to reach Halleck. On March 1 he got off an angry wire to Cullum, demanding to know: "Who sent Smith's division to Nashville? I ordered them across to the Tennessee, where they are wanted immediately. Order them back. What is the reason that no one down there can obey my orders? Send all spare transports to Grant up the Tennessee." On the same day he wrote a message to Grant, addressing it to Fort Henry, where Grant had not been for a number of days. Grant, he said, was to take a column up the Tennessee River, to destroy Rebel railroad bridges near Eastport, Mississippi, and railroad connections at Corinth, Mississippi, and at Jackson and Humboldt, in Tennessee. This, he pointed out, was to be a raid, pure and simple; at all costs Grant must avoid an engagement with superior forces, and it would be better to retreat than to risk a general battle. Having broken the railroads, Grant was to re-concentrate at Danville and was to move off toward the town of Paris, Tennessee, which lay west of the river on the line of the railroad running up from Memphis to the Tennessee River crossing.[25]

While Halleck was writing this, Grant was sending a report of his own to St. Louis. In it, he innocently remarked that he had made daily reports ever since he left Cairo — a point that would presently be in dispute — and said that his troops were suffering badly from camp dysentery, that transportation was lacking, and that if he should have to move he would move with less strength than Halleck probably anticipated, sickness and battle losses having weakened him. He was mentioning this, he said, "not to make suggestions but that my true condition may be known." On this same day Buell wired Halleck that he now felt safe in Nashville and that he was sending Smith and Smith's troops back to Clarksville.[26]

Upon General Halleck, as a result, it abruptly dawned that

nothing on the upper rivers had been going on as he had planned, and his waspish temper got entirely out of control. His irritability is at least understandable, because he was an extremely busy man and at the beginning of March, 1862, most of the hot spots in the war seemed to be in his own territory. In the far southwestern corner of Missouri, he had troops under Brigadier General Samuel Curtis chasing Price and his Confederates into Arkansas. Along the Mississippi, the General Pope whom he had recommended for promotion was assembling an army that was to occupy Columbus, break the Confederates loose from their river strongholds at New Madrid, Island Number Ten and Fort Pillow, and bring about the capture of Memphis. On the Tennessee, Grant was supposed to be cutting Confederate railroad connections, which would isolate the Confederate forces that were facing Pope, and on the Cumberland Buell was sending daily messages offering and demanding co-operation and proposing a top-level conference to work out grand strategy.

In addition, Halleck's relations with Washington were not happy. The additional powers he had been demanding so eagerly had been flatly refused him. McClellan, himself a badly harassed man this spring, was complaining that Halleck was not sending adequate reports, and was acidly suggesting that he himself could hardly make proper decisions touching on matters in Tennessee when he did not even know how many troops Halleck had and what he was doing with them. And now, on top of everything else, Halleck was discovering that Grant was not at all where Halleck had supposed him to be, and that movements on the Cumberland had been determined, not at St. Louis or at Washington but in the headquarters tent at Fort Donelson — at which place, Army gossip said, the Federal troops were getting badly out of hand, looting captured supplies, oppressing Tennessee civilians and in general behaving with a great lack of discipline.[27]

Halleck digested this, and on March 3 he sent a furious report to McClellan:

I have had no communication with General Grant for more than a week. He left his command without my authority and went to Nashville. His army seems to be as much demoralized by the victory of Fort Donelson as was that of the Potomac by the defeat of Bull Run. It is hard to censure a successful general immediately after a victory, but I think he richly deserves it. I can get no returns, no reports, no information of any kind from him. Satisfied with his victory, he sits down and enjoys it without any regard to the future. I am worn out and tired with this neglect and inefficiency. C. F. Smith is almost the only officer equal to the emergency.[28]

To a man carrying the load Halleck then was carrying, much can be forgiven; but this dispatch, even after all allowances are made, is fundamentally unforgivable, and when Grant found out about it (as he did, long afterward) he was stonily unforgiving to the end of his days. Of all the commanders in western Tennessee, he had been the one who tried to keep driving on at the moment when the foe was reeling from a decisive defeat, and to say that he was sitting down complacently to bask in his victory without regard for the future was to make a woeful misstatement of fact — a misstatement, furthermore, for which no information in Halleck's position provided the slightest justification. Grant had done what an energetic district commander might be expected to do, in the way of clearing his visit to Nashville with headquarters; also, the limits of his command not having been spelled out, it simply was not correct to say that he had "left his command" when he went to Nashville to see Buell.

McClellan responded to this message as a very busy general in chief might be expected to respond to a subordinate complaining about his troubles; that is, he offered Halleck full support in any disciplinary program which Halleck might consider necessary. He wired in prompt reply:

The future success of our cause demands that proceedings such as Grant's should at once be checked. Generals must observe discipline as well as private soldiers. Do not hesitate to arrest him at once if the good of the service requires it, and place C. F. Smith in command. You are at liberty to regard this as a positive order if it will smooth your way. I appreciate the difficulties you have to encounter, and will be glad to relieve you from trouble as far as possible.

To show that Halleck had backing at the very top for anything he might do in this matter, the telegram was countersigned as approved by Stanton himself.

Halleck was not yet finished. On March 4 he sent McClellan a message which read:

A rumor has just reached me that since the taking of Fort Donelson General Grant has resumed his former bad habits. If so, it will account for his neglect of my often-repeated orders. I do not deem it advisable to arrest him at present, but have placed General Smith in command of the expedition up the Tennessee. I think Smith will restore order and discipline.

Then, on the same day, he gave Grant the first news that Grant was in trouble. To him he sent this telegram:

You will place Major General C. F. Smith in command of expedition and remain yourself at Fort Henry. Why do you not obey my orders to report strength and positions of your command? [29]

This telegram arrived just sixteen days after the unconditional surrender of Fort Donelson.

CHAPTER TEN

"What Command Have I Now?"

GENERAL HALLECK probably meant nothing in particular by his sudden attack on Grant. He himself had been chided by McClellan for failure to keep Washington informed about troop numbers and dispositions, and a major general who is reprimanded is quite likely to do two things almost automatically — to pass the reprimand along to an underling, and to show that whatever fault existed was not his own. Grant was ideally situated to take both reprimand and blame, and Halleck gave them to him — his attitude sharpened, possibly, by his recent disappointments. He certainly had no intention of driving Grant out of the Army, even though he almost succeeded in doing it.

Nor was Grant himself actually harmed very greatly. He went under a cloud, but only briefly; and if, much later, he came to see that Halleck had played a double game with him, and grew to dislike the man intensely, his discovery did not come until the war had ended, by which time the relations between Grant and Halleck were no longer matters of especial public concern. It may even be that the experience was a useful step in Grant's military education.

In the beginning, at least, the trouble did not seem especially serious. Grant replied to Halleck's wire promptly, saying that he had put Smith in charge of the upriver expedition, as directed, and asking whether he was to abandon Clarksville altogether; there were Army stores and heavy ordnance items there that would have to be disposed of before the post was given up. Then Grant went on, temperately enough, to state his defense:

> I am not aware of ever having disobeyed any order from headquarters — certainly never intended such a thing. I have reported almost daily the condition of my command and reported every position occupied. I have not, however, been able to get returns from all the troops, from which to consolidate a

return for departmental headquarters. All have come in except from General Smith's command at Clarksville — five small regiments of infantry and two companies of artillery. The general has probably been unable to get his in consequence of being ordered to Nashville by General Buell. General Smith has been relieved by General Buell and was ordered immediately to the Tennessee by me.

As soon as I was notified that General Smith had been ordered to Nashville I reported the fact and sent a copy of Buell's order. My reports have nearly all been made to General Cullum, chief of staff, and it may be that many of them were not thought of sufficient importance to forward more than a telegraphic synopsis of.

Grant gave Halleck an outline report of his own forces. He had in his command forty-six infantry regiments with an average strength of five hundred men, three cavalry regiments and eight independent companies, and ten batteries of light artillery. He proposed to leave four small regiments at Fort Donelson and, until further notice, two at Clarksville. Fort Henry itself was badly flooded, with six feet of water inside the walls, and the Tennessee River was so high that there were few places where troops could be embarked; continuous rains had made it almost impossible to go across-country from Fort Donelson to Fort Henry. And, finally:

In conclusion I will say that you may rely on my carrying out your instructions in every particular to the very best of my ability.[1]

The matter might have ended there, if Halleck had been willing, and although Grant much later wrote that he was "virtually in arrest" at this time it is clear that this was not the case; he was tied to Fort Henry, but otherwise he was under no restriction whatever. But Halleck was the sort that must repeat, explain and underline a scolding, to make certain that the person scolded is properly impressed, and in this case he lit a fire that almost got away from him. Also — and this was much more important than any incidental damage to either man's self-esteem — the whole process unquestionably served as a brake on action; Federal movements in the Tennessee Valley thereafter went more slowly than would otherwise have been the case, and this was too bad because speedy movement was of very great importance.

Ever since the capture of Fort Donelson, the high command's contribution to the campaign had been negative, and what had been gained had come from sheer on-the-spot energy acting in the absence of orders from above. Halleck had been out of touch, contributing an occasional "Not so fast!" when the erratic telegraph let his voice be heard; Buell had occupied Nashville in spite of himself, had had the vapors as a result and was calling for top-level conferences; and McClellan had been too far off, too poorly informed and too busy with other matters to exert much influence. What had been done had been done by subordinates who would take advantage of any leeway provided by a system of defective communications and loose controls. Now the system was being tightened and the leeway was vanishing. In consequence, nobody would be moving very rapidly.

Halleck's plan was for a raid on Confederate railroad connections. Grant had planned to interpret his orders rather liberally, and just before Halleck's disciplinary blast struck him he had written to Smith explaining that he himself would immediately start upstream with part of the troops and that Smith was to assume command at Forts Henry and Donelson and lead an expedition to the town of Paris, twenty-five miles west of the Tennessee, on the railroad to Memphis. Grant was thinking beyond the immediate tactical problem, when he wrote this. Governor Isham Harris of Tennessee, a loyal Confederate and an all-out war man, was pushing the Confederate conscription act, and had ordered all Tennesseeans to register for the draft. Certain Confederate troops were in Paris to help enforce this order, and Grant believed that if his soldiers could disperse these troops, break up the conscription and in general weaken Confederate control over western Tennessee they would be inflicting lasting damage on the Confederacy's ability to make war.[2]

However, this now was impossible. Grant sent Smith a copy of Halleck's plan of campaign, copying out for him the telegram of March 4: "You will place Major General C. F. Smith in command of expedition and remain yourself at Fort Henry." Significantly, Grant did not add the final sentence which conveyed Halleck's reprimand. Was he, in dealing with his former commandant at West Point, reluctant to put that humiliating note in the record?[3]

On the first of March, Lieutenant William Gwin of the Navy had taken gunboats *Lexington* and *Tyler* far up the Tennessee to disperse a Rebel outpost at a place called Pittsburg Landing. This was a spot of no apparent consequence; there was a landing place at the water's edge, with a road climbing to high ground and meandering off through half-settled country (passing a log meetinghouse known as Shiloh Church, on the way) and going at last to the important railroad junction town of Corinth, which was a little more then twenty miles from the river. Lieutenant Gwin drove the Confederates away, picked up such news as he could get, and came back downstream to report; and from that moment Pittsburg Landing, Shiloh Church, and the fields and woods and orchards and ravines between and around them were invisibly touched with a power that would draw two great armies together.

Gwin brought back word that the Confederates were in considerable strength in the vicinity of Corinth — a thing which was not true then, but which very soon would be — and Grant, passing it along, warned Smith that he might find as many as twenty thousand enemy troops there. He went on:

> If this should prove true I can hardly say what course should be pursued to carry out the instructions. A general engagement is to be avoided while the bridges are to be destroyed, if possible. The idea probably is there must be no defeat and rather than risk one it would be better to retreat.

Whether a battle could actually be avoided was an open question; a few days later Smith himself, writing to a friend, commented dryly:

> My orders are to accomplish a certain purpose without bringing on a general engagement, to retire rather than to do so. Now if my men were soldiers in the proper acceptation of the term, this piece of strategy might do very well, but as they are not soldiers I mean to fight my way through if necessary. And when I get them into a fight it shall be no child's play. They begin to understand me about that.[4]

Grant gave Smith his final orders on March 5, and on the same day Halleck sent Grant a telegram amplifying the original orders:

It is exceedingly important that there should be no delay in destroying the bridge at Corinth or Bear Creek. Don't delay the matter a moment. If successful, the expedition will not return to Paris but will encamp at Savannah [a town on the eastern bank of the river, about nine miles downstream from Pittsburg Landing] unless threatened by superior numbers. Prepare everything to reinforce him [Smith] there. Dismount the water batteries at Henry and Donelson, and remove all stores, except for a small garrison at Donelson. Travelers can pass to Nashville, but no one will be permitted to land at the forts except in extreme cases. None must be allowed to go up the Tennessee. See to this. What we do there must not be communicated to the public.[5]

This, clearly, was not the sort of dispatch a department commander would send to a general who was "in virtual arrest." Grant acknowledged it, saying that the transports would be loaded and sent upstream as soon as the gunboats arrived. Then Halleck returned to the question of the reprimand, sending Grant this telegram, dated March 6:

General McClellan directs that you report to me daily the number and positions of the forces under your command. Your neglect of repeated orders to report the strength of your command has created great dissatisfaction and seriously interfered with military plans. Your going to Nashville without authority, and when your presence with your troops was of the utmost importance, was a matter of very serious complaint at Washington, so much so that I was advised to arrest you on your return.

There were times when Grant seemed very modest, almost self-effacing, but there was not really anything meek about him. He promptly sent back a reply which conceded nothing whatever and which invited a showdown:

I did all I could to get you returns of the strength of my command. Every move I made was reported daily to your chief of staff, who must have failed to keep you properly posted. I have done my very best to obey orders and to carry out the interests of the service. If my course is not satisfactory, remove me at once. I do not wish to impede in any way the success of our arms. I have averaged writing more than once a day since leaving Cairo to keep you informed of my position, and it is no fault of mine if you have not received my letters. My going to Nashville was strictly intended for the good of the service, and not to gratify any desire of my own.

Believing sincerely that I must have enemies between you and myself, who are trying to impair my usefulness, I respectfully ask to be relieved from further duty in the department.[6]

Halleck picked this up without delay, and telegraphed in retort:

Y ou are mistaken. There is no enemy between you and me. There is no letter of yours stating the number and position of your command since capture of Fort Donelson. General McClellan has asked for it repeatedly with reference to ulterior movements, but I could not give him the information. He is out of all patience waiting for it. Answer by telegraph in general terms.

Dutifully enough, Grant made his report. Of infantry, present for duty, he had 35,147; of cavalry, 3169; of artillery, 54 pieces and 1231 men. Approximately 25,000 were embarked on the expedition, and 5700 more were at the landing above Fort Henry awaiting transportation. The rest of the men were at Clarksville, Fort Donelson and Fort Henry. In the grand total, he noted, were 7829 men in a new division commanded by Sherman.

Grant also returned to the argument, still without discernible meekness:

Y our dispatch of yesterday just received. I will do all in my power to advance the expedition now started. You had better chance of knowing my strength whilst surrounding Fort Donelson than I had. Troops were reporting daily, by your orders, and immediately assigned to brigades. There were no orders received from you until the 28th February to make out returns, and I made every effort to get them in as early as possible. I have always been ready to move anywhere, regardless of consequences to myself, but with a disposition to take the best care of the troops under my command. I renew my application to be relieved from further duty.[7]

Halleck seems to have been inclined to let the matter rest here. He replied that McClellan had repeatedly asked for information which he could not give, saying: "This certainly indicated a great want of order and system in your command, the blame of which was partially thrown on me, and perhaps justly, as it is the duty of every commander to compel those under him to obey orders and enforce discipline. Don't let such neglect occur again, for it is equally discreditable to you and me." Then Halleck dropped the argument, beginning a new paragraph, "But to business . . ." Guns and stores at Clarksville should be sent down to Paducah, skeleton garrisons should be planted at Fort Henry and Fort Donelson and all other troops should be rushed up the Tennessee as rapidly as possible. And, finally:

> As soon as these things are arranged you will hold yourself in readiness to take the command. There will probably be some desperate fighting in that vicinity and we must be prepared. . . . I shall organize and send you reinforcements as rapidly as possible, and when I get them under way I shall join you myself.[8]

This probably would have ended it, except that on March 11 Grant got a letter which Halleck had mailed on March 6, enclosing an unsigned letter which had been passed on by the eminent Judge David Davis and which alleged extensive disorders at Fort Donelson and much defalcation of captured Confederate stores and equipment. In a covering note, Halleck remarked:

> The want of order and discipline and the numerous irregularities in your command since the capture of Fort Donelson are matters of general notoriety, and have attracted the serious attention of the authorities at Washington. Unless these things are immediately corrected I am directed to relieve you of the command.

The anonymous letter rambled slightly. It asserted that a good deal of captured food had been taken over by a regimental quartermaster and by him delivered to sutlers, who repackaged the goods and sent them to Illinois for private sale. A Colonel John Cook — an Illinois officer, acting as brigadier in C. F. Smith's division — was alleged to be assisting in all of this, in conjunction with one G. W. Graham, a civilian who frequented Grant's headquarters. Rather confusingly, the writer added that he did not think that either Cook or Graham was profiting by the deals; Cook, he believed, was just accommodating his friends. He went on to say that a good many captured dirks, pistols, muskets and the like had been carried off by individuals; if all could be taken care of and sold by the government, the Treasury would receive several thousands of dollars.

Grant's reply displays about as much unvarnished anger as anything he ever wrote. He sent back this telegram:

Yours of the 6th instant, inclosing an anonymous letter to the Hon. David Davis, speaking of frauds committed against the government, is just received. I refer you to my orders to suppress marauding as the only reply necessary. There is such a disposition to find fault with me that I again ask to be relieved from further duty until I can be placed right in the estimation of those higher in authority.

In plain English, Grant would demand a court of inquiry, which would involve an official ventilation of the entire situation. Halleck did not want this to happen. He replied, in a vein much more soothing than anything in his earlier messages:

You cannot be relieved from your command. There is no good reason for it. I am certain that all which the authorities at Washington ask is that you enforce discipline and punish the disorderly. The power is in your hands; use it, and you will be sustained by all above you. Instead of relieving you I wish you as soon as your new army is in the field to assume the immediate command and lead it on to new victories.[9]

What Grant did not know when he got this reply was that the entire situation had suddenly changed. Washington at last had lost patience with McClellan, had removed him from the over-all command of the Union Army, and had limited him to the command of the Army of the Potomac. On top of that, Halleck had finally been given what he had been demanding so long — full control in the West. The eastern limit of his department was extended to a north-and-south line drawn through Nashville, which brought Buell and his field army under Halleck's control. If earlier refusals had put him badly out of humor, this was calculated to make him feel much better.

In addition, President Lincoln had quietly intervened in Grant's favor. Some of the details of Halleck's complaints had reached the White House, and the White House was in no mood to see the victor at Fort Donelson dropped without a fair hearing. To Halleck, on March 10, had come a formal wire from Lorenzo Thomas, Adjutant General of the Army:

It has been reported that soon after the battle of Fort Donelson Brigadier General Grant left his command without leave. By direction of the President the Secretary of War desires you to ascertain and report whether General Grant left his command at any time without proper authority, and, if so, for how long; whether he has made to you proper reports and returns of his force; whether he has committed any acts which were unauthorized or not in accordance with military subordination or propriety, and, if so, what.

The significance of this was clear enough. In effect, the White House was telling Halleck: either file formal charges against Grant and make them stick, or drop the whole subject.

Halleck was quite ready to drop it. He had exculpated himself and passed a reprimand on to the lower echelon, McClellan was no longer his superior, and in any case it would be quite impossible to make out a case against Grant. Halleck sent word to Washington that Grant had, after all, behaved properly; that any irregularities in his command had taken place in his absence, in violation of his orders, and (all things considered) unavoidably; that Grant had explained everything satisfactorily, that "he acted from a praise-worthy although mistaken zeal for the public service" when he made that trip to Nashville . . . and that the whole unpleasantness had been a regrettable misunderstanding which might as well be forgotten.[10]

Before he found out about this, Grant had written to Halleck that although the handling of the anonymous letter led him to want a court of inquiry, Halleck's succeeding telegram made him feel much better; "I will again assume command, and give every effort to the success of our cause." Grant seems to have felt that this made him sound like a touchy character who would not play when his feelings were hurt, for he added the sentence: "Under the worst circumstances I would do the same." Then Halleck sent him copies of the messages he had just exchanged with Lorenzo Thomas, and Grant felt quite grateful. He wrote a word of thanks: "I must fully appreciate your justness, General, in the part you have taken, and you may rely upon me to the utmost of my capacity for carrying out all your orders." When he came to write his Memoirs, Grant noted bitterly that Halleck "did not inform me that it was his own reports that had created all the trouble," and said that at the time "I supposed it was his interposition that had set me right with the government." [11]

Grant's intimates appear to have felt that the trouble was chiefly due to Buell. Dr. Brinton remembered that he understood Buell's complaints were responsible. Captain Rowley, the fellow townsman who had just been confirmed in his appointment to Grant's staff, wrote to Congressman Washburne: "We are now lying at Fort Henry, owing I think to the petty jealousies of some interested parties," and another Galena resident, Colonel Chetlain of the 12th Illinois, made a glancing reference to it by writing the Congressman: "I know but few of the facts connected with the difficulty between him" (Grant) "and Gen. Buell." Grant's friends felt strongly that someone was maneuvering, offstage, to destroy Grant, and most of them blamed Buell. [12]

Even though the difficulty was at last ironed out, it unquestionably left a scar on Grant, injuring him emotionally more than anything else that happened in all the war. When he got Halleck's first telegram, ordering him to give the upriver command to Smith, he showed it to a friend, and (as the friend remembered it) "with tears in his eyes," asked miserably: "I don't know what they mean to do with me. . . . What command have I now?" [13] He always spoke of Halleck's order as one which virtually put him under arrest — al-

though actually it did nothing of the kind — and after he had left
the White House and was making a round-the-world tour he told
his friend John Russell Young that "after Donelson I was in disgrace and under arrest, and practically without a command." The
loneliness and failure of the pre-war years were still too close to
Grant, in the spring of 1862, to let him rest quietly under a public
rebuke from his superior, and he was almost pathetically grateful
when Halleck at last dropped the whole business, restored him to
his old command, and soothed him with friendly words.[14] If any
Civil War soldier had a tough inner core, Grant was the man; but
with it, in the early days, there was a sensitivity, a remembrance
of past difficulties, that made him vulnerable.

A few days after the matter had been settled, Grant wrote about
it to Congressman Washburne:

> After getting into Donelson Gen. Halleck did not hear from
> me for near two weeks. It was about the same time before I
> heard from him. I was writing every day and sometimes as often
> as three times a day. Reported every move and change, the con-
> dition of my troops, &c. Not getting these Gen. Halleck very
> justly became dissatisfied and was, as I have since learned, send-
> ing me daily reprimands. Not receiving them they lost their
> sting. When one did reach me not seeing the justice of it I
> retorted and asked to be relieved. Three telegrams passed in this
> way each time ending by my requesting to be relieved. All is
> now understood however and I feel assured that Gen. Halleck is
> fully satisfied. In fact he wrote me a letter saying that I could
> not be relieved and otherwise quite complimentary. I will not
> tire you with a longer letter but assure you again that you shall
> not be disappointed in me if it is in my power to prevent it.[15]

Just before Halleck put an end to Grant's period of disgrace,
there was a significant little ceremony in the ladies' cabin of the
steamboat *Tigress*, which, anchored in the stream abreast of Fort
Henry, was serving as Grant's headquarters boat. Surrounded by
brigadiers and staff officers, Grant was called on to receive a presentation sword. The speech of presentation was made by Colonel
C. C. Marsh, of the 20th Illinois, who remarked that the sword had
been ordered a long time ago but that fortunately its delivery had

been delayed: "Fortunately, we say, because at this moment when the jealousy caused by your brilliant success has raised up hidden enemies who are endeavoring to strike you in the dark it affords us an opportunity to express our renewed confidence in your ability as a commander."

The sword was handsome — ivory-handled and mounted in gold, as a newspaper correspondent saw it — and when he accepted it Grant choked up and was unable to stammer out a speech of thanks. He hurried out on deck, and Dr. Brinton found him there with tears in his eyes. After a while Grant took the doctor by the arm and led him back to the cabin, where the sword in its open case lay on a table. Pushing the case toward him, Grant said: "Doctor, send it to my wife. I will never wear a sword again."

The presentation ceremony is worth dwelling on a moment. The sword was inscribed: *Presented to Gen. U. S. Grant by G. W. Graham, C. R. Lagow, C. C. Marsh and Jno. Cook,* and the date under these names was 1861: the Cairo period, when Grant was just setting up his military household, grappling to himself some, like Rawlins, who would do much good for him, and others who would do him harm. Captain Rowley, in the fall of 1862, would write to Washburne angrily denouncing four officers on Grant's staff, saying "I doubt if either of them have gone to bed sober for a week," and remarking that with such men around him it was small wonder if Grant occasionally kicked over the traces; and Lagow was one of the four Rowley named. Jno. Cook was the colonel whom the anonymous correspondent had blamed for the disappearance of captured foodstuffs at Fort Donelson, and G. W. Graham was the civilian whom this correspondent had named. A former Cairo business man who had tied his fortunes to Grant's, Graham acted as headquarters sutler, kept a supply of cigars and liquor on hand and became, as an Illinois observer believed, "the power behind the throne" and a trusted member of the headquarters mess. Men like these were remembered by General Sherman, and long after the war he would write that Grant "did not have about him, near his person, officers of refinement and culture." [16] Rumors about free-and-easy ways at district headquarters had reached St. Louis — Colonel McPherson, who came down from Halleck's office just after Fort Donelson was taken, told Dr. Brinton that many of these were

in circulation — and there were, close to Grant, men whose habits
would create such rumors and make others believe the rumors
true. . . .

In spite of wrangling, place hunting and staff talk about the cor-
rosive jealousy of rivals, a substantial Federal Army was slowly
inching its way up the river in this spring of 1862. The town of
Savannah had been occupied on March 5 by part of the 40th
Illinois, with the 46th Ohio coming in the next day; then more than
eighty transports, with escorting gunboats, began moving upstream,
a long cloud of smoke billowing up from the river valley, and by
March 11 the steamers were tying up on both sides of the river at
Savannah. There were five divisions in Grant's army, with more to
come. McClernand led the men he had commanded at Fort Donelson, and Lew Wallace had his own Donelson division. C. F. Smith
had his, too, but when he assumed command of the expedition as a
whole he assigned divisional command to a new brigadier, W. H. L.
Wallace. There was a new division led by Brigadier General S. A.
Hurlbut, and a fifth under Sherman; and Smith gave Sherman the
advance and sent him on ahead to cut the railroad near Eastport,
Mississippi. Nothing went right; unending rains flooded all the little
creeks and turned the roads into mud, and after some ineffective
floundering about Sherman brought his men back to the high
ground around Pittsburg Landing. Hurlbut's division was there,
too, sent forward by Smith, and while his own men went ashore
Sherman hurried back to Savannah to report. Smith told him to
assume command of all hands at Pittsburg Landing and to post the
men well back from the river; the rest of Grant's army would be
sent there in due course; Smith himself would come on up, and
then they would see about Halleck's orders for a seizure of the
railroad.[17]

Buell, meanwhile, was bringing his army overland from Nashville, aiming for Savannah, his movements slow because the Rebels
in retreat had destroyed bridges, and because the rain made bad
roads worse. Grant would get reinforcements from Missouri, as
well; General Curtis had beaten Confederates under Earl Van Dorn
in a sharp two-day battle at Pea Ridge, Arkansas, and troops which
had been ear-marked for his support could now be used on the

Tennessee. Grant passed on to Smith the news that these troops were coming, and said that when they arrived he himself was expected to take immediate charge of the upriver activities. He added: "I think it exceedingly doubtful whether I shall accept; certainly not until the object of the expedition is accomplished." [18] Smith had begun the expedition and was entitled to any glory that might be won. Grant would not get in his way; his former commandant was entitled to his fame.

From Halleck, through all of this, came repeated orders that there must not be a substantial fight just yet. Grant was still planning to send troops over to Paris, to break up the Confederate conscription, and Halleck warned him: "Don't bring on any general engagement at Paris. If enemy appears in force, our troops must fall back. It is not the proper point to attack." And as far as the Rebels at or near Corinth were concerned, the same rule applied: "My instructions not to advance so as to bring on an engagement must be strictly obeyed." Reinforcements of 10,000 or 15,000 would be forwarded soon, but "we must strike no blow until we are strong enough to admit no doubt of the results." [19]

Once it looked as if orders from department headquarters offered an opening which an energetic general could exploit. Grant had moved up from Fort Henry to Savannah, and here, on March 18, he got a wire from Halleck which read: "It is reported that the enemy has moved from Corinth to cut off our transports below Savannah. If so, General Smith should immediately destroy railroad connection at Corinth."

The Confederates were not trying to do this and Grant knew that they were not, but the injunction to destroy the rail connection at Corinth sounded like a signal for battle and Grant pounced on it. He ordered Smith and Lew Wallace to keep their commands ready to march at a moment's notice, with three days' rations in haversacks and seven more in wagons; he told McClernand, whose division was at Savannah, to prepare to send at least two brigades up to Pittsburg Landing, and he telegraphed Halleck with enthusiasm: "Immediate preparations will be made to execute your perfectly feasible order. I will go in person, leaving General McClernand in command here." [20]

This puzzled Halleck slightly, and he sent back the warning:

"Don't let the enemy draw you into an engagement now. Wait until you are properly fortified and receive orders." This clearly narrowed the scope of the projected movement, and Grant, obediently promising that he would take no risks, suggested that he might at least strike some part of the railroad where the Rebels were not prepared to fight and so "at least seem to fill the object of the expedition without a battle and thus save the demoralizing effect of a retreat upon the troops." Although he could not stir up a fight in flat disobedience to his orders Grant could at least behave aggressively and hope that the orders might be liberalized. On March 21, he warned Halleck frankly that Corinth could not be taken without a fight; the Confederates, he believed, had fully thirty thousand men there, with more coming, and if Grant's army moved over there a general engagement would be inevitable; "Therefore, I will wait a few days for further instructions."

Grant went on to provide an estimate which, he no doubt hoped, might affect the formulation of orders:

The temper of the Rebel troops is such that there is little doubt but that Corinth will fall much more easily than Donelson did when we do move. All accounts agree in saying that the great mass of the rank and file are heartily tired.

This would eventually be exposed as a major misconception, but at the moment Grant honestly believed it. It had no effect at St. Louis, however, and Grant began to get increasingly restless. To General Smith he confided: "I am clearly of the opinion that the enemy are gathering strength at Corinth quite as rapidly as we are here, and the sooner we attack the easier will be the task of taking the place." [21]

Grant was unable to do as he had planned and let Smith have sole charge of the advance, because Smith, as March drew toward its end, went out of action, the victim of what looked like a wholly unimportant little accident. A few days after Grant had established his own headquarters at Savannah, Smith had to go on the sicklist, and in a letter to a friend the old man described his trouble: "In jumping into a yawl I raked the whole of right leg — the shin and calf — with the seat. The doctor fears injury to the bone. Although it is greatly better I still limp about the cabin of the steamer and cannot put on a boot. Super-added and immediately after I was prostrated by sickness, against which I had been fighting ever since Ft. Donelson. But I had no time to be sick. At length I had to go to bed. Now I am well tho' weak."

Laid up by this infection, Smith complained about the Army's delay:

> Our force here is very large and daily increasing. We are chafing like hounds in the leash to move at the enemy just in front but are forbidden by Halleck until the force is about doubled. . . . The troops are encamped between Lick and Snake creeks, the different divisions in nearly parallel lines. The advance division is about four miles off. I occasionally send out a few thousand men to look at the enemy in the direction of Corinth and wake them up.[22]

Smith shared Grant's impatience, and each man saw an opportunity which needed to be grasped at once — saw it all the more clearly simply because it had gone unexploited for so long. Straining against Halleck's leash, they had come to believe that the only problem was the problem of getting permission to strike a blow; had reached the point, indeed, where they thought about this almost to the exclusion of everything else. Neither man seems to have reflected that Johnston and Beauregard might be most wakeful, preparing to strike a blow of their own. Grant was looking at the missed opportunity so intently that it was hard for him to see anything else — an extremely dangerous mood for an Army commander deep in the enemy's country.

That much valuable time had in fact been wasted is undeniable. The victory at Fort Donelson had left the Confederate armies between the Mississippi River and the Alleghenies hopelessly fragmented and badly outnumbered, with powerful Federal forces standing squarely between the fragments. To make any sort of contest for what was left of their western front the Confederates needed, in the third week of February, time that could have been denied them. Yet a free gift of the time had been made, the fragments had been brought together and strengthened to make a new army, and a battle which aggressive Federal strategy might have prevented altogether was now inevitable.

When Fort Donelson fell, on February 16, Johnston's position was desperate. He had perhaps seventeen thousand men in and around Bowling Green, and he took them south as fast as he could, pausing only briefly at Nashville and moving on, by way of Murfreesboro, Fayetteville, and Decatur, Alabama, to Corinth, the junction town which had been chosen as a rallying point. In the Columbus area — to which Beauregard had been sent as soon as Bowling Green was abandoned — there were something like twenty-three thousand more troops, under Polk. Half of these, or more, had to be left on the river to hold such points as Island Number Ten, New Madrid and Fort Pillow; the rest must be brought down to the neighborhood of Corinth to unite with the force that was coming down from Bowling Green and Nashville. Even should this reunion take place, Johnston would have fewer men than either Grant or Buell had; and, to complete the tale of his predicament, at the end of February both Grant and Buell were closer to Corinth than either Johnston or Beauregard.

When March began, as a result, the Confederacy was facing nothing less than destruction of its power in the West. It reacted with great vigor — Richmond could see, as clearly as anyone else, that the loss of the Mississippi must ultimately be fatal — and reinforcements were summoned, even at the cost of stripping the sea coast of defenders who were badly needed where they were. Five thousand troops were sent to Corinth from New Orleans, and Braxton Bragg was rushed up with ten thousand more from the Gulf Coast; but it took time to move these troops, just as it took time for Beauregard and Polk to come down from Columbus and for Johnston and Hardee to move down from Murfreesboro, and by any logical appraisal of the situation the Confederacy did not have time enough. But in the end it was given forty-nine days — seven weeks, from the fall of Fort Donelson to the opening day of Shiloh — and this was just time enough.[23]

There were understandable reasons for the Federal delay, of course. Halleck had had many problems. He had to prepare and develop Pope's advance down the Mississippi, and he had to provide supports for Curtis's offensive in the far southwestern corner of Missouri, and the combined maneuver of angling for his own advancement and standing Grant in a corner had called for a good deal of attention and energy. Buell, in his turn, had been in a trying position. Naturally cautious, unwilling to move until every preparation had been made, he had been pulled into Nashville against his will, had been unable to arrange the needed conference with Halleck, and had never been given a clear directive from Washington; and McClellan, general in chief during the first weeks of the campaign, had been under such pressure in connection with his handling of the Army of the Potomac that the situation in Tennessee had received only a minor part of his attention. The whole command situation had made swift, decisive movement highly improbable if not actually impossible.

But the excuses are not good enough. From first to last the triumvirate had seen the map rather than the battlefield — the map, and "strategic points" which must be occupied, and not the broken Confederate Armies which were hurrying off in retreat, three hundred miles apart, inviting destruction. Early in March Halleck had complained: "I cannot make Buell understand the importance of strategic points till it is too late." [24] Buell actually understood this just as well as Halleck did, and their only real difference of opinion had to do with the precise location of these points and the way in which they should be seized. These generals believed in positional warfare. A careful study of the map would disclose certain places whose retention was vital to the enemy; take those points and the enemy would then become helpless. This was clear enough; but men like Grant and Foote and Smith felt that a surer way to make the enemy helpless was to push on without delay and destroy his armies in the field. After Donelson fell and Nashville was taken, Halleck had ordered a raid up the Tennessee to break the Memphis and Charleston railroad. While the raid was under way he had broadened his plan to allow for the occupation of Corinth, where he would concentrate a vast army which Johnston must face with the odds against him. This strategic plan was limited, and it had assumed that time was on the side of the Federals. As a result, one of the brightest chances of the war had been missed.

One thing in all of this figuring had been correct. Johnston would indeed fight for Corinth. But he would not wait until the place was held by an army twice the size of his own. He would fight before that army had been put together; and when March came to an end Johnston was about to regain the initiative. Six weeks earlier his position had been all but hopeless; now he was going to call the signals, and if his luck was in he might with one blow undo most of the damage that had been done in February along the Tennessee-Kentucky border.

As April began, Johnston had between forty and forty-five thousand men at Corinth, with able lieutenants to lead them — Beauregard, Bragg, Polk and Hardee. Twenty-five miles away was Grant, with a slightly smaller army; coming down from Nashville was Buell, with an army about the size of Grant's. Johnston's only chance was to beat Grant before Buell arrived, and when April began he undertook to do this. His army had been hastily put together, most of his soldiers had never been under fire before and were imperfectly trained, and staff organization was so poor that, when the advance began, the different divisions got into one another's way, straggled all over the landscape, and made such bad progress that Beauregard, in despair, wanted to cancel the whole operation, on the logical ground that such a stumbling, disorganized offensive could not possibly succeed. But Johnston's mind was made up. He muttered grimly, "I would fight them if they were a million," and he drove his men on toward Pittsburg Landing.[25]

So a Confederate army, which had been considered too weak and dispirited to do anything better than await destruction, was about to launch a sudden, shattering offensive; and in the ironic chance of war the offensive was to strike the one Union Army commander in Tennessee who, in the campaign now approaching its surprising climax, had been trying without success to bring on a fight. Striking him, it would find him unready — as if the hoped-for battle were inconceivable unless it were imposed by him on his opponent. Grant had learned much in war's brutal school, but his military education was still incomplete. Now he was about to learn a great deal more — at prodigious cost to himself and to some thousands of young men who, without quite realizing it, had joined the Union Army in order to pay for his education. (The peach trees near Shiloh meetinghouse were in pink blossom, the clear streams ran down the ravines to the flooded river, and between Snake Creek and Lick Creek the high ground was waiting to absorb the blood that would flow so soon and so copiously; and farmboys who were proud of their new blue uniforms, and never had been taught which end of a rifled musket is which, were lolling innocently in their camps, enjoying the spring sunshine and writing letters home about the power and the glory of male youth in time of war.) [26]

Grant was developing as a military realist. The war had taught him a few good lessons: that when untrained armies face each other, neither general gains by deferring a fight until the training of his own men is perfected; that in any hard battle there comes a time when both armies are ready to quit, and that the one which can nerve itself for one more attack at such a time is very likely to win; that troop morale is better in an active campaign than in training camp; that war means fighting, so that feints and demonstrations accomplish little, and the real object of a campaign is not to make the enemy retreat but to destroy him root and branch.

These were good things to learn, and in learning them Grant had done little more than sharpen his naturally aggressive instincts. But he had the defects of his qualities, and experience had not yet applied a corrective. He underestimated both the fighting heart and the initiative of his enemy, believing that a Confederate army in his front was likely to be very passive, and in his devotion to the offensive he was likely to overlook defense. He was still an optimist — a week ahead of time he had promised to take Fort Donelson "tomorrow," and when he was warned about muddy roads he had blithely remarked that they would be worse for the enemy than for him — and now he had spent a month and a half trying in vain to win permission to strike the enemy. Apparently he was only slightly impressed by the possibility that the enemy might strike first.

A newspaper correspondent assayed the headquarters feeling correctly when, at the end of March, he wrote that there would be a big fight just as soon as Buell's army arrived: "Within two weeks, measures will have been accomplished that will render retreat by the Rebel army at Corinth impossible." Writing to Julia, Grant said that "a big fight may be looked for some place before a great while," and adding that he believed this would be the last big battle in the West.

Like a great many of his soldiers, Grant had been unwell. Whether, as the men believed, the water supply around Shiloh was contaminated, or whether the standard diet of fried pork and hard-tack was having its natural effect, there was a great deal of camp diarrhea, which Grant in a letter referred to as "Dioreah" and which the rank and file commonly mentioned derisively as "the Tennessee quickstep." [27] Grant recovered from this malady, but shortly thereafter he received a painful injury to his leg. On the evening of April 4, Confederate cavalry jumped a picket post on the Corinth road a few miles from the landing, and Grant rode out to see about it. Returning with W. H. L. Wallace and Colonel McPherson, he found the night so impenetrably dark (a heavy rain was coming down) that there was nothing any rider could do but trust to his horse to stay in the road. Grant's horse lost its footing and fell in the mud, pinning Grant's leg and wrenching his ankle severely. Grant's boot had to be cut off, and for the next day or two he needed crutches when he walked. Fortunately, the sort of infection that still kept C. F. Smith off duty did not set in.

On the day after this injury was received, April 5, Grant believed that as soon as Buell's men arrived the advance could begin. His own army now contained six divisions, the newest of which had been made up from six green regiments that had just reached camp; its command went to the same Brigadier General Prentiss who had disputed Grant's seniority the summer before, in Missouri. Five divisions, with a total of possibly thirty-seven thousand men, were camped on high ground between the creeks near Pittsburg Landing. The sixth, Lew Wallace's division of seventy-five hundred, was stationed on the western bank of the Tennessee at Crump's Landing, half a dozen miles downstream. There had been increasing contacts with aggressive Confederate patrols in the last few days, and these aroused a suspicion that some sort of attack on Wallace's men might be brewing. Sherman had been alerted to be ready to send help if necessary, but the general assumption was that the

Rebels meant no particular harm along the main Federal front. One Federal explained, long afterward, that "the almost absolute necessity that no battle should be fought before the arrival of Buell's army seemed to forbid scouting or anything that might appear aggressive," and Sherman said much the same thing when an officer on outpost duty told him he had seen Rebel infantry not far beyond the Union lines. "I have got positive orders," Sherman told him, "to do nothing that will have a tendency to bring on a general engagement until Buell arrives." To Colonel Appler of the 53rd Ohio, Sherman was more snappish. Appler formed his regiment in line and sent word to Sherman that the enemy was in sight; for his pains he got the reply — "Take your damn regiment back to Ohio. There is no enemy nearer than Corinth." [28]

It took diverse elements to make Shiloh what it was. The Federal Army's position had been chosen by C. F. Smith, who did not think green soldiers should be ordered to entrench — Smith, whose opinion Grant respected, probably, more than he respected any other man's. Another element was the fact that Sherman commanded the advance. Sherman's nervousness in the face of a Confederate advance in Kentucky, six months earlier, had cost him his command and had led the newspapers to deride him as insane; recovering his confidence, he had unquestionably overcompensated, and by now he was probably the last man in the Army to take alarm because Confederates were skirmishing on his front.

Sherman did notify headquarters that there was plenty of contact with Rebels on his front, and on the afternoon of April 5 Grant went to the front to see for himself. Everything seemed to be fairly quiet — undeniably there was a good deal of Confederate activity not far off, but it seemed to be mostly reconnaissance parties — and Grant accepted Sherman's appraisal. When he returned to Savannah, Grant wired to Halleck: "I have scarcely the faintest idea of an attack (general one) being made upon us, but will be prepared should such a thing take place." After the battle had taken place, Grant admitted that his outposts had been skirmishing freely with Confederate patrols for two days: "I did not believe, however, that they intended to make a determined attack but were simply making reconnaissances in force." [29]

The head of Buell's column reached Savannah around noon on April 5. Colonel Jacob Ammen, an old acquaintance of Grant, commanded a brigade in the leading division, which was under the same General Nelson whom Grant had sent off to Nashville more than a month earlier; and at some time during the afternoon Grant and Nelson stopped at Ammen's tent to discuss plans. Ammen said his men were not tired and could easily march down to Pittsburg Landing that afternoon, if need be. Grant told him to take it easy, and in his diary Ammen recorded Grant's words this way: "You cannot march through the swamps; make the troops comfortable; I will send boats for you Monday or Tuesday, or some time early in the week. There will be no fight at Pittsburg Landing; we will have to go to Corinth, where the Rebels are fortified. If they come to attack us we can whip them, as I have more than twice as many troops as I had at Fort Donelson." Then Grant rode off, saying he had an engagement that evening.[30]

The Union Army's position at Pittsburg seemed strong, even though the five divisions were arrayed rather loosely. The ground was high, the deep creeks protected both flanks, and if the Confederates did attack they would have to come in head-on in a straight frontal assault. Proper field entrenchments would have made the position invulnerable, but no trenches had been dug — partly because everybody was thinking about offense rather than defense, and partly because professional soldiers just then believed that an army which dug itself in would lose its aggressive touch. Buell and the head of his column were supposed to reach Savannah on Sunday, April 6. Once they arrived things could begin to happen.

The soldiers waited in the Tennessee springtime and admired the budding leaves and the peach-tree blossoms, and bathed in the little streams that ran down to the Tennessee. An Iowa soldier, looking at the innumerable tents scattered through "the delightful Tennessee forest," felt that this vast camp had the appearance of "a gigantic picnic." There was a noisy, holiday air over the place. Untrained soldiers kept discharging their muskets in the woods, moved by nothing more than a simple desire to see if the things would go off after a rain, and regimental bands were playing; on the river, a steam calliope on one of the transports brayed out patriotic tunes. That evening, quite unnoticed, Johnston arrayed his men in order of battle, remarking grimly: "I intend to hammer 'em. I think we will hammer them beyond doubt." His army was so near that his pickets stood at ease in the dark and enjoyed the music of the Union bands.[31]

The Guns on the Bluff

JOHN RAWLINS was awakened early on the morning of Sunday, April 6. The mail steamer from Cairo reached Savannah at 3 o'clock, disembarking a passenger who came up the hill from the landing to headquarters — Captain W. S. Hillyer, the onetime St. Louis real estate agent who was now a member of Grant's staff and who had just returned from a trip down-river. Hillyer's arrival aroused Rawlins, who found himself unable thereafter to go back to sleep, and — since a good deal of activity was scheduled for this day — Rawlins got up and dressed with the first light of dawn and went down to Grant's office to look at the mail.

Army headquarters was in a fine mansion overlooking the Tennessee, the home of William Harrell Cherry. Cherry was a man of substance, owner of a store and a ferryboat, several thousand acres of farmland, and a good-sized collection of slaves. He was stoutly Unionist in his sympathies (although Mrs. Cherry was inclined to be on the side of the Confederacy), and he was known as a Unionist to President Lincoln himself; Grant, it was said, had made his headquarters in the Cherry mansion because Washington had told him the owner was a loyalist. The fact that the house was roomy enough to accommodate the General and his staff was doubtless a factor, as well; Grant slept here, and his aides; and in an upstairs bedroom was General C. F. Smith, bedridden now with the infected leg that stubbornly refused to heal.

While Rawlins sorted the mail, Grant himself came into the headquarters office on the first floor. Headquarters today was to be moved from Savannah to Pittsburg Landing, and orders had been issued the evening before to prepare an early breakfast and to have the horses saddled and ready to be put aboard Grant's steamer, *Tigress,* which lay at the landing with steam up. Ordinarily, Grant would probably have stayed on at Savannah a few days longer; it was the point of contact for Buell's divisions and for reinforcements coming up the Tennessee from Cairo, and Grant hoped to confer with Buell before going on to Pittsburg Landing. (Actually Buell had arrived the night before, but through some lapse in staff work Grant did not yet know about it.) The afternoon before, Grant had received disturbing news. Major generals' commissions, Halleck notified him, had been issued to two of Grant's division command-ers, John A. McClernand and Lew Wallace — neither man a profes-sional soldier, each a man with excellent political connections. As a result, these two officers now outranked everybody in Grant's army except Grant himself (and, of course, Smith, who was on the sick-list), and as long as Grant stayed in Savannah one or the other of them would be in effective command around Shiloh. Grant felt that Wallace was too inexperienced and McClernand too erratic to be entrusted with such authority; consequently, he himself must move on upstream, and today was the day for it.

Grant went through his mail in the office and chatted casually with an Illinois officer who had just returned from leave, and at six o'clock, or a little later, breakfast was announced. Grant and his officers had just begun the meal when the quiet of the spring morn-ing was unexpectedly broken by the sound of dull concussions from far upstream — cannon firing, somewhere in the vicinity of Pittsburg Landing.

Grant sat motionless for a moment, an untasted cup of coffee in his hand. A private soldier detailed for headquarters duty came in from outside to confirm what everyone had sensed: judging by the sound, this was a real fight and not just a skirmish. Grant set his cup down, stood up, and said: "Gentlemen, the ball is in motion. Let's be off." Within fifteen minutes General, staff, clerks, orderlies and horses were aboard the *Tigress,* and the steamer was moving up-stream.[1] Before the boat left, Grant wrote two hasty notes. One, to General Nelson, said simply: "An attack having been made on our forces, you will move your entire command to the river opposite Pittsburg. You can obtain a guide easily in the village." The other, addressed to Buell — who, as Grant supposed, would be reaching Savannah a little later — was slightly more detailed. It read:

Heavy firing is heard up the river, indicating plainly that an attack has been made upon our most advanced positions. I have been looking for this, but did not believe the attack could be made before Monday or Tuesday. This necessitates my joining the forces up the river instead of meeting you today, as I had contemplated. I have directed General Nelson to move up the river with his division. He can march to opposite Pittsburg.[2]

The note is interesting for its bearing on the puzzling question: Precisely what had Grant been expecting in the way of enemy action? This morning he was writing, "I have been looking for this"; the afternoon before he had assured Halleck that he anticipated nothing like a general attack on his position. Apparently he did feel that Lew Wallace's force might be attacked, and he may have taken this morning's gunfire for confirmation of that suspicion. He had warned both Sherman and W. H. L. Wallace that an attack at Crump's Landing seemed quite likely and that both men should be prepared to reinforce that spot at a moment's notice. Saturday night he had had Colonel McPherson — who had become one of his most trusted staff members — stay with W. H. L. Wallace at Pittsburg Landing, the significance of this being that this division was the reserve, held ready to reinforce any trouble-spot in case of need. Both Sherman and Prentiss, who had the forward line, sent out patrols very early Sunday morning, to see what might lie in front of them. McPherson wrote that "it was well known that the enemy was approaching our lines," and on Saturday Grant had notified Halleck that the Confederates in and around Corinth were present in great strength. He believed that Johnston had eighty thousand men with him, and he suspected that some of these were arrayed along the line of the Mobile and Ohio Railroad, which ran from Corinth up to the recently-evacuated Confederate stronghold at Columbus — ideally situated, if his suspicion were correct, to strike the Union flank at Crump's Landing.[3] Clearly enough, Grant had believed that some sort of fight might soon be thrust upon him; the one thing he had not anticipated was what was actually happening this morning — a massive drive on the front of his position by the entire Confederate Army.

The *Tigress* went on up the river, the sound of cannon and musket fire coming in more and more clearly, and somewhere between

seven and 7:30 the steamer closed in by the bank at Crump's Landing, next to Lew Wallace's headquarters boat. Wallace was on deck,
waiting, and Grant leaned over the railing of his own boat and
called out his orders: Wallace was to hold his division ready to
march on receipt of orders, and he was also to send patrols out to
the west to see whether the Confederates were moving toward him
as well as toward the troops around Shiloh church. Wallace agreed.
He was an ambitious man, deeply wanting to win fame as a soldier.
What would happen in the next twenty-four hours would put military fame out of his reach, although fame at last would be his: *Ben
Hur* would come out of the brain that could not quite create victory
in battle. To the end of his days he would try to explain the baffling
things that went wrong on this sixth of April. So far, none of them
had gone wrong, and Wallace faced the day with confidence. *Tigress* swung away from the bank and went on upstream, and at
eight o'clock or a little later nosed into the bank at Pittsburg Landing.[4] Grant got on his horse and went ashore, to ride straight into
the middle of the great Battle of Shiloh.

At the moment of going ashore, it was evident that an enormous
fight was going on and that it was not going well for the Union
Army.

Off to the southwest — not two miles away, and obviously drawing closer — there was a tremendous noise of battle, continuous
racket of rifle fire, heavy thud of artillery, the sound of thousands
of men shouting. Smoke was drifting up from the woods, and a dis-
maying crowd of stragglers, weaponless and winded, was knotting
up on the hillside that went from the river to the high ground;
panicky men, disorganized and unmanned, who had been shoved
unready into their first battle and who had gone for the rear in wild
desperation, officers of rank among them. There were hordes of
stragglers in the rear of every army in every battle in the Civil War,
but Shiloh was the one battle that put them on display: a man running from the battle area here was in effect a man running down a
funnel, for even the dullest fugitive could see that the only road to
safety was the road to the steamboat landing, and men who in any
other fight would be drifting across square miles of open country
were packed in a solid mass, cowering under the lee of the bluff

above the river. They were beginning to assemble, now, with the day hardly more than begun, and they would continue to assemble all day long, pathetic evidence that troops with inadequate training and no battle experience whatever had been called on to stand up to one of the worst combats of the entire war.

There was a great deal for the Commanding General to do, and Grant promptly set about it. The volume of firing warned that the men up front would need ammunition, and Grant put his staff to work to organize an ammunition train so that there might be a steady supply of cartridges. The job was intricate: the Union Army's weapons had not yet been standardized, and in Sherman's division alone cartridges of six different calibers must be supplied. Another staff officer was sent downstream on the *Tigress*, with orders for Lew Wallace to bring up his division as fast as possible.[5] Something had to be done about the stragglers, and Grant seized two Iowa regiments which, having disembarked a few minutes earlier, were lined up on the bluff awaiting orders; as soon as they had been given ammunition they were to form across the roads a little way from the landing and halt all fugitives, holding themselves ready at the same time to obey further orders. The Colonel of one of these regiments, James T. Reid of the 15th Iowa, looked blank when Grant gave him these instructions, and Grant had to identify himself with the remark: "I am General Grant." Then, having sent most of his staff off on various tasks, Grant set out for the front to see for himself what was happening.[6]

What was happening was both simple and complex, confusing in its innumerable details but appallingly clear in its general drift. This was not one battle but a vast number of intense and bewildering small battles, each one overlapping with its neighbors and yet strangely isolated, the only true pattern coming from the inexorable application of overwhelming force on a loose battle line which had come into being without any central direction but solely in response to immense pressure. Of the five Federal divisional commanders involved, only one had been a professional soldier. The two divisions which had been hit first and hardest and which, on Grant's arrival, had been fighting the longest, contained few regiments that had ever fought before. Reinforcements had gone forward, not in response to any general plan, but simply because officers at the front were calling desperately for help. Fugitives from the combat area were coming to the rear almost as fast as the new troops were going forward; as the two tides flowed past and through each other, Grant lost forever the belief that he had held thus far — that the ordinary soldiers of the Confederacy were halfheartedly serving a cause that never fired their inmost loyalties. The one unmistakable fact, now, was that these ordinary soldiers of the Confederacy — no better trained and no more experienced than Grant's own men — were fighting with a sustained fury and were giving his army the worst of it. His immediate and most pressing task was to stave off unredeemed disaster.

Grant went first to W. H. L. Wallace, commanding what was supposed to be the reserve division, and got from him a sketchy picture of what had happened so far.

At dawn, the Union Army had been grouped loosely in preparation for a march on Corinth. Up in front, nearest the Confederates, were the divisions of Sherman and Prentiss, with McClernand's and Hurlbut's divisions lined up back of them and Wallace's division in the rear. At three in the morning, Prentiss — no professional, but a stout fighter with combat experience in the Mexican War — had sent three companies from the 25th Missouri out on a long reconnaissance. These soldiers, groping past the Federal picket line, and drifting to the right, in front of Sherman's division, had bumped into Confederate skirmishers at five o'clock, or thereabouts. They had attacked at once, and before long Prentiss had sent other Missourians forward to support them. Meanwhile, Sherman's 77th Ohio had also gone forward on the prowl, and it too had kicked up a fight with unidentified Rebels in the murky woodlands.[7] (One of the many oddities about this battle was that it began with Federals attacking Confederates.) The advance elements had fought hard for a short time, and then the Confederate offensive had begun to roll, and ever since then the men in blue had tried desperately to hold on to what they had.

Sherman was on the right. Prentiss was to his left, not in immediate contact, and isolated on Prentiss's left was a lone brigade from Sherman's division, three Midwestern regiments under Colonel David Stuart. Albert Sidney Johnston was attacking with his entire army, less three brigades held back as reserve, an army massed in three consecutive battle lines, each line following closely behind the one ahead; a defective tactical arrangement, because it meant that Confederate troops would be hopelessly scrambled, once the fighting became intimate, but a powerhouse nonetheless, because it put more than thirty thousand men in a broad mass to attack little more than a third of their own number.

Sherman's men got it first. Unluckiest of all the new regiments, on a day when everybody's luck was bad, was the 53rd Ohio. It got into line, fired two volleys, then heard its colonel howl: "Fall back and save yourselves!" The Colonel ran for the rear and cowered behind a log, white-faced; two companies of the 53rd stayed and fought and the rest lit out for the steamboat landing. By the end of the day, scattered portions of this regiment were fighting in three separate Union regiments. The 71st Ohio also lost its colonel, who spurred his horse for the rear the moment the fighting began. In the confusion that followed, the 71st was hit hard by an Alabama regiment and fled in a wild, disorganized stampede. The 6th Iowa, doing its best in its first fight, found that its colonel was drunk. He tried to put the regiment through pointless, impossible maneuvers in the face of a Confederate attack, and was placed under arrest by the brigade commander. (Growing sober a bit later, he took a musket and fought in the ranks of some other regiment as a private soldier.)[8] Sherman's division was driven back and so was Prentiss's, and when McClernand and Hurlbut got their men in beside them the Confederate attack seemed to increase in intensity. One of McClernand's brigadiers said later that his troops lost more men in their first five minutes of action than in all the rest of the day.[9] Now Wallace's troops were going into action, and by 10 in the morning practically all of Grant's army was strung out in a loose, uneven front, fighting desperately.

Grant went on to see the other divisional commanders. Iowa soldiers in Hurlbut's division saw him riding up, attended by two or three staff officers. He was wearing a sword, today, and a buff sash; one officer said Grant's face "wore an anxious look, yet bore no evidence of excitement or trepidation," and he trotted forward with a leisurely air. Another soldier said Grant was smoking a cigar, seemingly as cool as if he were making a routine inspection, and he believed that the sight reassured the men, who felt that the worst must be over.[10] Grant visited Sherman briefly. Sherman's horse had been shot, he had a minor wound in one hand, he was covered with dust, and his tie had worked around to the side so that it stuck out under one ear; but this man who had been so nervous in the early days at Kentucky that he lost his command and was called insane was cool and at his ease in the heat of actual battle, and when Grant asked how things were going Sherman said the situation was not too bad, except that he did need more ammunition. Grant told him arrangements for ammunition had already been made, and cantered off to see Prentiss. When he wrote of the battle, long afterward, Grant remarked that on this first day at Shiloh "I never deemed it important to stay long with Sherman." [11] The intimacy that would bind these two men together all the rest of the war was born this day at Shiloh.

Prentiss had been driven back into an eroded lane that ran parallel with the Confederate front, with a stretch of woodland behind it and a nondescript field overgrown with brambles out in front, and here his raw troops were making a determined stand. W. H. L. Wallace and most of his division joined them here, now or a little later, and the resistance these soldiers put up was so effective that the Confederates were held at bay for five or six hours; they referred to this section, ever after, as the hornets' nest. Grant told Prentiss to hold his ground at all hazards — an order which Prentiss would obey with dogged fidelity — and cantered off. As Grant and his escort rode past the 5th Ohio battery, the captain of the battery saw his own father riding along as a member of Grant's cavalry escort.[12]

Off to the right and rear there was an important bridge, where a road that passed the rear of the Federal position crossed Owl Creek and went north to Crump's Landing. Here Grant found a cavalry detachment and two regiments of infantry. He posted the infantry to hold the bridge, and sent a cavalry officer with a company of cavalry to ride to Crump's Landing and guide Lew Wallace's division to the field.[13] Then he wrote a note to Buell and gave it to a staff officer to take to Savannah. It was an anxious appeal not unlike the one he had sent to Foote during the crisis at Fort Donelson:

The attack on my forces has been very spirited from early this morning. The appearance of fresh troops on the field now would have a powerful effect both by inspiring our men and disheartening the enemy. If you can get upon the field, leaving all your baggage on the east bank of the river, it will be a move to our advantage and possibly save the day to us. The rebel force is estimated at over 100,000 men. [The fury and effectiveness of the Confederate attack apparently had made a great impression on Grant; not often did he so greatly overestimate the forces against him.] My headquarters will be in the log building on top of the hill, where you will be furnished a staff officer to guide you to your place on the field.

Still uncertain whether Buell was actually at Savannah, Grant addressed the dispatch to *Comdg Officer Advance Forces Near Pittsburg, Tenn.*[14]

At some time in the middle of the morning, Rawlins and a lieutenant colonel in the paymaster's department rode up from the landing to find Grant. They did not know exactly where he was, but Rawlins confidently told his comrade, "We'll find him where the firing is heaviest." The firing, as the paymaster remembered it, was extremely heavy. As they trotted up a forest lane he heard a steady pattering in the leaves overhead, and asked Rawlins if it was raining. Rawlins replied: "Those are bullets, Douglas." (An Iowa soldier wrote that at one time this morning he saw what he never saw before or afterward — swarms of musket bullets in flight, overhead, visible like buzzing insects.) They found Grant, as Rawlins had predicted, in the thick of things, and both Rawlins and McPherson urged Grant not to expose himself so much; Grant replied that he had to see and know what was going on.[15]

Once Grant and his staff drew up in an open space, while Grant studied the situation. The fire was heavy, and Captain Hillyer, who never pretended to be the stoical military type, confessed that he and most of the others were in an agony of apprehension. Grant seemed almost to enjoy it, as a man might enjoy being out in the rain on a hot day. One staff officer nudged Hillyer and begged: "Go tell the Old Man to leave here, for God's sake!" Hillyer shook his head: "Tell him yourself. He'll think me afraid, and so I am, but he shan't think so." At last someone mustered the nerve to ride up and

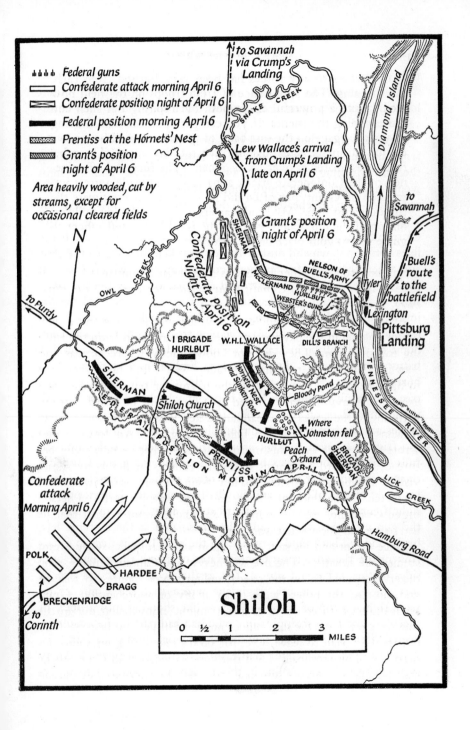

Federal guns
Confederate attack morning April 6
Confederate position night of April 6
Federal position morning April 6
Prentiss at the Hornets' Nest
Grant's position night of April 6

Area heavily wooded, cut by streams, except for occasional cleared fields

N

to Savannah via Crump's Landing

SNAKE CREEK

Lew Wallace's arrival from Crump's Landing late on April 6

Diamond Island

Grant's position night of April 6

to Savannah

Buell's route to the battlefield

OWL CREEK

Confederate Position Night of April 6

SHERMAN

McCLERNAND

NELSON OF BUELL'S ARMY

HURLBUT

WEBSTER'S GUNS

Tyler

Lexington

Pittsburg Landing

to Purdy

SHERMAN

FEDERAL POSITION

Shiloh Church

I BRIGADE HURLBUT

W.H.L. WALLACE

Hornets' Nest and Sunken Road

DILL'S BRANCH

Bloody Pond

TENNESSEE RIVER

HURLBUT

Where Johnston fell

Peach Orchard APRIL 6

PRENTISS MORNING

I BRIGADE SHERMAN

Confederate attack Morning April 6

LICK CREEK

POLK

HARDEE

BRAGG

BRECKENRIDGE

to Corinth

Hamburg Road

Shiloh

0   ½   1   2   3   MILES

tell Grant: "General, we must leave this place. It isn't necessary to stay here. If we do we shall all be dead in five minutes." Grant looked about him, muttered, "I guess that's so," and led the cavalcade away.[16]

Now and then there would be a brief lull somewhere along the front, but these breathing spells never lasted long or spread all along the line. Morning wore away, and afternoon came, and the fight went on unabated. The tough knot of resistance at the hornets' nest remained, despite repeated Confederate attacks, but elsewhere the Union lines were crowded back steadily; by the day's end, McClernand noted that his division had occupied eight separate battle lines between dawn and dusk.[17] Beaten men kept drifting to the rear, and when they met fresh troops coming up they would cry that their regiments had been destroyed and that this was the Bull Run story all over again. One regiment that was moving toward the firing line passed the 41st Illinois, which had been badly shot up, and the Illinois colonel called out to the new troops: "Fill your canteens. Some of you will be in hell before night and you'll need water." A battery in Sherman's division had to limber up and retreat in a hurry, and one gun, swinging around, locked itself around a green tree, the trunk jammed in hard between wheel and gunbarrel. All the gunners fled, on foot, except for the drivers who rode the six horses attached to the gun; these, lying flat on the animals' necks, too frightened even to look around, flogged their steeds unmercifully, and the poor beasts bucked and pawed the ground and did their unavailing best to gallop; and other soldiers, themselves beset by panic fear, looked on and howled with sudden laughter at the sight. Cannoneers from some other battery at last came over and got the gun clear. Stuart's brigade, almost isolated at the extreme left, broke and fell back, and as men from the 55th Illinois fled up a narrow ravine the advancing Confederates overtook them, lined both sides of the ravine and shot as fast as they could load and fire. A survivor of this unhappy regiment wrote that the Confederates were right on top of them — "It was like shooting into a flock of sheep" — and a Mississippi major who had had part in the assault reflected afterward: "I never saw such cruel work during the war." [18]

In the mad violence of battle, bizarre things happened. Many men ran from Prentiss's line in the hornets' nest; some of them, regaining a little nerve, crept back to the fight, and the boldest took place behind a stout tree on the firing line. Others followed him, and in no time a grotesque tail of thirty or forty men, each clutching the waist of the man in the front of him, swayed out behind that tree, while a distracted company officer, unable to control either himself or his men, paced insanely back and forth from end to end of this line. In W. H. L. Wallace's division, six men were lined up in single file behind one six-inch sapling, each one firing past the ones in front of him, the blast from their muskets scorching and almost deafening the man at the head of the line.[19] A sixty-year-old private in the 9th Illinois refused to retreat when his regiment went to the rear, falling in with another unit and fighting there, doing the same when this regiment fell back; that evening, rejoining his comrades, he displayed notes signed by several captains and one colonel, certifying that he had been fighting and not straggling. A six-gun Ohio battery galloped bravely to the front in Hurlbut's division, and halted abruptly when a Rebel shell blew up a caisson; in the next few seconds every man in the battery ran for the rear, leaving guns, limbers and plunging horses quite unattended. Amid heavy fighting, an Iowa private, told that his brother had been killed, asked: "Where is he?" A comrade pointed to the body, which lay not far away. The Iowan, who had been in the act of loading, walked over, musket-muzzle in one hand, ramrod in the other. He bent, saw that his brother was dead, then put the butt of the musket beside the dead man's head, finished loading, and fired. He stayed there as long as his regiment held its position, loading and firing beside his brother's body. One soldier saw a comrade, hit by a bullet that did not even break his skin, fall to the ground and writhe in wild agony, grasping at leaves and sticks with frantic hands; and he realized that a thing he had been told by a veteran was true — that a spent bullet could cause more immediate pain than a serious wound.[20]

It went on for hour after hour, and the Union Army was driven back, closer and closer to the high ground above the steamboat landing — all except the hard core in the hornets' nest, which seemed immovable. Grant visited Prentiss here, late in the afternoon, when the hornets' nest was a blunt salient jutting far out in front of the rest of the line; again he told Prentiss to hold his ground, and rode off to patch up the sagging remainder of the battle line as best he could. He saw Colonel Chetlain, dismounted and pale from a recent illness, with his badly battered 12th Illinois, coming back out of action; placed the regiment in support of a battery, told Chetlain to go back to the landing and lie down — "You ought not to have come out today" — and then dropped a word of encouragement. "I think they have done all they are going to do," he said. "We have fresh troops coming, and tomorrow we'll finish them." [21] Yet the fresh troops did not arrive, neither Lew Wallace's division — both Rawlins and McPherson had been sent to hurry it along — nor Buell's men from Savannah, and they were needed desperately. Between heavy casualties, straggling, and the general disorganization, many units had virtually ceased to exist. Colonel Jesse Hildebrand, commanding Sherman's third brigade, found that his brigade had gone almost entirely to pieces; he himself, with no one to command, was serving on McClernand's staff. Colonel Stuart, who commanded Sherman's isolated brigade on the extreme left, had only eight hundred men left from his three regiments — one of these, 54th Ohio, boasting an average age of eighteen, had lost more than 50 per cent — and he led the remnant back toward the landing. Grant rode up, and sent the little brigade off to a new place in the line.[22]

Grant was placing many troops personally that afternoon. It may be that his biggest single contribution to what was finally classed as a victory was the encouragement he gave to badly beaten troops, simply by his presence and his obstinate refusal to act as if things were going badly.[23] The 15th Illinois, driven from its position, badly mauled when a Union battery took it under fire, minus its field officers and able to muster no more than a hundred men, was led by Grant to a new fighting position. The 81st Ohio, driven from the area around the hornets' nest, met Grant and was sent back into the fight; driven back again, the regiment encountered Grant once more and was directed to another place on the firing line. The 11th Iowa, broken and in retreat, managed to reform; as it did so, Grant rode up and ordered it to counterattack. Later, retiring once more, it again met Grant, and was again ordered forward. Grant put Birge's Missouri sharpshooters in line, late in the day, and sent the 15th Iowa up to a weak spot in the line after that regiment had been forced to retreat. He found time to chat with Major Belknap, of this regiment; he asked for his name, and recalled that the Major's father had been "Colonel Belknap, of the old army," and added that they had served together in Mexico.[24]

Briefly, in midafternoon, Grant saw Buell, who had come down from Savannah on a steamboat. The two men talked, and accounts of their conversation conflict, which makes little difference — there was not much for them to say, since the general situation spoke eloquently for itself. Grant wanted Buell's troops at the earliest possible moment, and Buell would get them to the scene as quickly as he could. Rawlins insisted that Buell asked Grant what preparations he had made for retreat, and said that Grant replied he still thought he was going to win; Grant added, according to another account, that if necessary they could make a bridge of boats to the far side of the river and protect it with artillery. The bank above the landing was jammed with stragglers when Buell arrived — five thousand of them, at the least, and possibly more — and Grant believed that the spectacle made Buell feel that the situation was worse than it really was. Buell, for his part, wrote that Grant seemed dull, and he insisted that "there was none of that masterly confidence which has since been assumed with reference to the occasion." The two men came ashore, mounted, and then went their separate ways. Buell believed that the number of disorganized stragglers may have been as high as fifteen thousand, and said that at the top of the bluff all was confusion.[25]

The confusion was genuine enough. Most of the men who huddled in the lee of the bank seemed totally demoralized. Wild rumors were in circulation: the whole army had been surrendered, a Rebel officer had been seen paroling a lot of dismounted Federal cavalry, fugitives were going to build rafts and float down the river all the way to Paducah and safety. Here and there officers made earnest but completely fruitless efforts to rally the men. A member of Grant's staff, returning to the landing, saw a mounted officer riding back and forth in the crowd, waving a flag and urging the men to come back and fight; the men heard him, unmoved, and one was heard to remark, casually: "That man talks well, doesn't he?" [26]

Late in the afternoon there came a lull, right on the heels of disaster.

The men in the hornets' nest were still fighting, but by now they were isolated. They had killed General Johnston himself, when that energetic leader exposed himself too bravely in their front, but they had lost contact with the troops to their right and left, and now they were all but surrounded. W. H. L. Wallace undertook to pull his men out, and was mortally wounded; most of his soldiers got away, and went off toward the landing badly disorganized. At one open place, a disorganized crowd of soldiers heading for the rear was overtaken by a single gun galloping toward the landing; they assumed it was one of their own pieces joining in the retreat. Suddenly the gun wheeled, the gun crew dismounted and unlimbered it, and it began to fire rapidly into the backs of the fugitives: this was part of a Confederate battery, spear-heading a new attack. One Federal in the crowd said that the Confederates coolly went on loading and firing, while fugitives continued to scamper past. There were enough Union soldiers present, he said, "to pick up gun, carriage, caisson and horses and hurl them into the Tennessee," but no one made any effort to capture the gun or silence the gunners.[27]

The hornets' nest finally caved in. Prentiss had done precisely what he had been told to do — hold on at all hazards — and so had his men, but now the end came. After Wallace's men left, the little division was surrounded. A long line of Confederate guns plastered the front at close range, and infantry swept past the flanks and got into the rear. Survivors dimly recalled a scene of complete confusion. A Texas colonel recalled that when Prentiss's lines finally cracked, a Federal officer galloped forward to meet the Confederate line of battle, crying: "Boys, for God's sake stop firing, you are killing your friends!" He and his horse were shot dead, and the line came sweeping on. Another Federal officer was killed as he rode toward the rear in, of all things, a buggy; then, while the Southerners regrouped for a new assault, there was a general cry of "White flag!" and "Cease firing!" and the uproar of battle died. Prentiss had surrendered, with approximately twenty-two hundred men. With the surrender, a half hour of comparative silence came down on the field.[28]

The Federals did not realize it, but conditions in the Confederate Army — it was Beauregard's army, now that Johnston was dead — were just about as disorganized as in their own. During much of the battle, effective control of the Confederate attack had been exercised by a group of staff officers from the three Confederate corps, the corps commanders having been thrown out of effective touch with most of their troops. At the time Johnston lost his life, Beauregard had Hardee and a handful of staff officers rounding up stragglers to form improvised battalions to renew the attack on the Federal right — just as Grant, at about the same moment, had men creating similar formations out of disorganized men in his own rear. After Prentiss's surrender, crowds of Confederates wandered through the hornets' nest, gaping at the prisoners, picking up souvenirs, and acting as if the battle had ended. At this particular stage, it is probable that neither army had more than half of its men on the firing line. Dour Braxton Bragg, commenting on the lack of discipline in the Gray ranks, wrote bitterly: "This is one of the evils of raw troops, imperfectly organized and badly commanded; a tribute, it seems, we must continue to pay to universal suffrage, the bane of our military organization." [29]

The lull came just in time. Grant had Colonel Webster assembling all the siege guns and field artillery he could find in a compact line, a quarter of a mile inland from the landing, overlooking a ravine formed by a backwater that came in from the Tennessee; and Webster was working hard at his job — he had fifty guns, or more, arranged in a great shallow crescent, and if Beauregard's troops were going to reach the river they would have to overrun this powerful battery. Off in the woods, Confederate artillery was still firing, and shells were striking around the landing — so many that the ammunition-supply steamer *Rocket* cast off its lines and steamed down-river to get out of range. Webster's guns began firing in reply, and gunboats *Tyler* and *Lexington* moved in near the mouth of the backwater and opened fire with their heavy naval guns; the whole, said a staff officer, making "a noise not exceeded by anything I ever heard afterward." A staff officer at Grant's side was killed by one of the Confederate missiles.[30]

A newspaper correspondent saw Grant sitting his horse in the midst of all of this, apparently unruffled. News of Prentiss's surrender had spread, and most of the men around the landing were very gloomy, and someone found the nerve to ask Grant if he did not think the situation extremely dark.

"Oh no," said Grant. "They can't break our lines tonight — it is too late. Tomorrow we shall attack them with fresh troops and drive them, of course."

The correspondent, describing this incident, said long afterward that "from that moment I never doubted Grant would be recognized not only as a great soldier but a great man." [31]

And now, with the fragmented Union Army backed up almost to the river's edge, the long-awaited help arrived. Nelson's division appeared on the far side of the Tennessee, and steamboats began to bring the men to the landing.

Nelson's men had had a time of it. The original march down from Nashville to Savannah had been rather leisurely, since, as one officer wrote, "It was considered that there was no occasion for haste." Several days had been spent getting across the Duck River, at Columbia; pontoons were not at hand, and the Army had not yet learned the art of building improvised bridges in a hurry. Most of the men waded, carrying their pants on their bayonets, their knapsacks loaded in wagons: one wrote after the war that by 1864 this business of the Duck River would hardly have caused a halt. Reaching Savannah, the men had gone into camp Saturday afternoon, and, although on Sunday morning they could hear firing up the river, no one had seemed in a great hurry. An Indiana soldier wrote that Buell seemed quite unconcerned, and said that men in his regiment paced impatiently up and down the bank "like so many caged animals." One captain shouted that Buell was a Rebel; Buell, sitting his horse not forty yards away, seems to have heard the remark, but he ignored it. During the wait Colonel Ammen, commanding one of Nelson's brigades, went to the sickroom in the Cherry mansion to visit with old C. F. Smith. Smith was jovial, and laughed at Ammen for thinking that there was a great battle going on; it was only a picket-line skirmish, Smith insisted, but Buell's soldiers were accustomed to small affairs. As the racket went on, swelling and thundering all morning long, Smith changed his tune a bit, Ammen remembered, and admitted finally that "a part of the army" might be engaged. [32]

In any case, the march down the eastern bank of the Tennessee began around 1:30 in the afternoon. It had been hard to find good guides, and the roads were atrocious, but once the column got moving Nelson did his best to drive the men along fast. Ammen reflected that of the three regiments in his brigade, one had been in action before and the other two had not; and the two regiments which had never fought were full of enthusiasm, crowding along impatiently and expressing the hope that the fight would not end before they got there. The veteran regiment was less impetuous, and seemed quite willing to let events take their natural course.[33]

Now, at last, Nelson's division was on the scene, and the men came ashore proudly, with bands playing, through the depressing backwash of stragglers, teamsters, dismounted cavalry and men whose fighting instincts had evaporated. Some of these seemed to be quite unmoved by the arrival of the fresh troops. Leading his brigade ashore, Ammen had to crowd through a huge mass of listless soldiers; an earnest chaplain was exhorting these men, "in whangdoodle style," repeating in frantic voice: "Rally, men, rally and we may yet be saved! O rally, for God and your country's sake, rally . . ." No one was paying the least attention, and Ammen broke in: "Shut up, you Goddamned old fool, or I'll break your head. Get out of the way." Some of the rear guard took new heart when they saw Nelson's men marching in. One of Grant's soldiers wrote that he could never forget the new hope that came to him when he heard Nelson's bands playing "Hail Columbia," and he said the men all around him cheered " 'till the whole woods on either bank fairly shook for joy." [34]

The moment of crisis was over. Nelson's men were assigned to support Webster's immense battery, General Hurlbut was put to work organizing temporary units of stragglers, the still unbroken parts of Grant's army were drawn up to the right, and the artillery opened a stupendous cannonade. The Confederate attack, as a matter of fact, was about over for the day; a brigade or two had got into the ravine in front of the heavy guns and was trying in vain to renew the fight, but Beauregard could see that for the time being his army was utterly fought out, and he was ordering a halt and a general regrouping in preparation for another fight in the morning.[35]

Grant seems to have sensed that the Confederates were through for the day. While Webster was getting his guns into position, worried John Rawlins asked Grant: "Do you think they are pressing us, General?" Grant replied, casually: "They have been pressing us

all day, John, but I think we will stop them here." It was at about
this time that Grant detached an Ohio regiment from Ammen's brigade and sent it forward in the twilight woods to try to learn where
the Rebels might be. The regiment marched forward half a mile,
found no Confederates, halted, and at midnight was recalled to the
main line.[36]

Once Webster's bombardment got into full voice it was stupendous. The 81st Ohio was in position a little in front, and men said
the thunderous discharges behind them knocked their hats off. One
soldier wrote that the concussion almost broke his neck, and inflicted the sharpest pains he felt in all the war. . . . "Guns pounded
away all night long. The sensation at every shot was that of being
lifted two feet and slammed down with a good healthy whack."
Two weeks later, he said, his ears still "played me all sorts of pranks
and tricks," and the ordinary creaking and clicking of wagon wheels
sounded like volleys of musketry. In the 6th Iowa, also drawn up
close to the guns, the violent concussion drew blood from men's
noses and ears, and gave permanent injury to some soldiers' hearing.
Out in the river, *Lexington* and *Tyler* continued to slam in their
eight-inch shells, firing down the length of the supposed location of
the Confederate battle line. Since this line was withdrawn, they did
little actual damage, but they were ordered to keep on firing at intervals throughout the night so as to keep the exhausted Southerners from sleeping. After dark a heavy rain began to fall, with intermittent thunder and lightning, rolling crash of thunder mingling
with explosions from the guns, red flames from the massed batteries
streaking out in the wet darkness; one Federal veteran probably
spoke for everyone in both armies when he wrote of it as "a weird,
wearisome and wrathful night." [37]

The danger had passed, but not everyone was ready to recognize
the fact. A surgeon in the 55th Illinois, which had been drawn up in
support of the line of guns, found Grant nearby and ventured to remark: "General, things are going decidedly against us today." Grant
told him: "Not at all, sir. We are whipping them there now." The
doctor, with some reason, felt that not another man in the army
would have said that just then. In the midst of the rain, a staff officer found Grant and others grouped around a smoldering fire of

straw. McPherson rode up, after inspecting the lines, and Grant
greeted him with a cheerful: "Well, Mac, how is it?" McPherson
was not encouraging; at least a third of the army was out of action,
he said, and all the rest were disheartened. Grant said nothing, and
McPherson sought to prompt him by asking: "General Grant, under this condition of affairs, what do you propose to do, sir? Shall I
make preparations for retreat?" Grant snapped back: "Retreat? No.
I propose to attack at daylight and whip them." [38]

Nelson's division was over the river now, and more of Buell's
troops were coming up on the other side, waiting to be ferried
across; and, finally, the lost division of Lew Wallace came marching
up, to take position on the right. Wallace had had a miserable day.
Some of Grant's impatient staff officers felt that he had been inert
and slothful, but apparently the man had simply been misled by a
complete misunderstanding about the roads he was supposed to take.
He had marched his division off on a wrong road, under this misunderstanding, had had to make a laborious countermarch, and was
now reaching the scene many hours too late, his great day of opportunity gone forever — if his division could have come in early in
the afternoon, on the Confederate flank, it would almost certainly
have brought about a smashing Union victory. Not until near the
end of his own life would Grant come to see that Wallace had been
much more sinned against than sinning on this stormy Sunday at
Shiloh.[39]

It was a horrible night for everyone — a night of black darkness,
insistent rain, jarring noise and acute physical discomfort. Thousands upon thousands of men had been wounded, and the ones who
had not been hurt were completely exhausted and had no chance to
get a decent rest. (The Colonel of a Missouri regiment told how his
men bivouacked in the downpour without fires, and recorded: "The
men, lying in the water and mud, were as weary in the morning as
they had been the evening before.") Grant tried to make a go of it
lying under a tree on the bluff near the landing, but the pain in his
injured ankle kept him awake and along toward midnight he hob-
bled off to the log house that was supposed to be his headquarters. It
had been put into service as a hospital, it was full of moaning
wounded men with many more lying outside awaiting attention, and
after one look at all of this Grant went back into the rain. Years la-

ter, recalling all of it, he wrote: "The sight was more unendurable than encountering the enemy's fire, and I returned to my tree in the rain." [40]

Late that night tough Sherman came to see him. Sherman had found himself, in the heat of the enemy's fire that day, but now he was licked; as far as he could see, the important next step was "to put the river between us and the enemy, and recuperate," and he hunted up Grant to see when and how the retreat could be arranged. He came on Grant, at last, at midnight or later, standing under the tree in the heavy rain, hat slouched down over his face, coat-collar up around his ears, a dimly-glowing lantern in his hand, cigar clenched between his teeth. Sherman looked at him; then, "moved," as he put it later, "by some wise and sudden instinct" not to talk about retreat, he said: "Well, Grant, we've had the devil's own day, haven't we?"

Grant said "Yes," and his cigar glowed in the darkness as he gave a quick, hard puff at it. "Yes. Lick 'em tomorrow, though." [41]

So ended Sunday, April 6, at Pittsburg Landing.

CHAPTER TWELVE

The Question of Surprise

TWO EXHAUSTED ARMIES pulled themselves out of the mud at daylight on Monday, April 7, stumbled into line, and made ready to go on with the battle. There really was no need for any more fighting, because the ultimate decision had already been reached. Johnston and Beauregard had had one slim chance to cancel all that the Federals had won at Fort Henry and Fort Donelson, one desperate hope to restore the balance that had been upset during the winter, and they had come within a hand's grasp of seizing it. But when the night and the storm came down on April 6, with Webster's great row of guns pounding the thickets and ravines, with Buell's soldiers shouldering their way through the fugitives on the riverbank and with Lew Wallace's men marching across the Owl Creek bridge, the business was settled. There might be more killing, with much bloodshed and agony to be drawn from young men not yet hurt, but the moment when the main current of the war could be reversed had passed.

The opposing armies had paid a dreadful price for what had been done on the first day. General Johnston was dead, W. H. L. Wallace was dying, Prentiss was a prisoner, and fully 17,000 of other ranks had been killed, wounded or captured. There had been immense losses from straggling, and probably no more than half of the men who had taken up their muskets Sunday morning were in line ready to fight on Monday. The concentrated fury of the fighting had been appalling, and it left its mark for all the rest of the war. The Southern novelist George W. Cable was to write sadly that New Orleans "had never really been glad again after the awful day of Shiloh," and a Union veteran said that the most any Union soldier could say of any later fight was: "I was worse scared than I was at Shiloh." In all the story of the Civil War, nothing is much more amazing than the fact that these two armies were able to fight at all on Monday.[1]

The Federal Army had all of the advantage today. Beauregard was able to muster no more than twenty thousand infantry, and every man had fought hard the day before, nor had any man had a decent sleep on Sunday night. Grant's veterans were no better off, but reinforcements were on hand. On his left, Grant had Buell's men; Nelson's division, and that of Brigadier General Alexander McD. McCook, and two brigades from the division of Brigadier General Thomas L. Crittenden. These soldiers were bone-tired from a forced march. McCook's division had hiked thirty miles on Sunday, had been ferried across the river at midnight, and had stood in the mud in pelting rain most of the rest of the night, so miserably uncomfortable that one veteran remembered that night as the worst of his entire three years' service. But they had not fought, their organization was complete, and they considered themselves the saviors of Grant's army and accordingly were somewhat cocky. On the right of Buell's troops were three battered divisions from Grant's army — Hurlbut's, McClernand's and Sherman's — and on the right flank was Lew Wallace's unfought division. Grant's orders were to attack at dawn, and as the gray light streaked the sodden fields and thickets the big line began to roll forward.[2]

Grant rode over to see Wallace just before the attack began. He looked fresh and unworried, and when he said "Good morning" he did not sound like a man who had been within inches of a disastrous defeat twelve hours earlier; looking back long afterward, Wallace put into words a thought that struck many men, at various times: "If he had studied to be undramatic, he could not have succeeded better." Grant asked Wallace if his division was ready, and when Wallace said that it was Grant led him to a little field, indicated the location of the Confederates, and told him to get moving, promising to send supports if they were needed. Then he cantered off, leaving Wallace feeling that Grant had been just a little too laconic; after all, there were several things Wallace wanted to know about the general situation. Wallace got his division in motion, and the second day's fight was on.[3]

Overpowered they might be, but the Confederates were very stubborn about giving up the ground they had won. In the main, it was like Sunday's battle, a soldiers' fight, a tangled series of desperate small combats all going on at once; as Lew Wallace said, before the battle ended "the two armies as a general thing degenerated into mere fighting swarms," tactical formations and maneuvers were forgotten, and in advance or retreat only one rule prevailed — "to watch the flag and stay with it." [4] The Confederates slowly gave ground, but until the middle of the day things were fairly even. Then the Federal advantage in numbers began to tell, by 2 in the afternoon the Confederate front was ready to cave in, and when one of Beauregard's staff came to the General, in the rear of Shiloh church, and suggested that it was time to retreat, Beauregard said that he had the same idea: "I intend to withdraw in a few moments." Rear-guard lines were set up, the Confederates began to pull away, and Grant, sensing the change, picked up two regiments, formed them in line of battle, and led them forward for one final blow. Reaching a proper vantage point he ordered the men to charge, and it seemed to him that this broke the last enemy resistance. [5]

But the Confederates were leaving anyway, and after the most perfunctory of pursuits the Federals let them go with blessings on them. No one in Grant's army wanted to keep in touch with these foes any longer than the law required, Buell was not the man to crowd anybody, and Beauregard got his shattered army off on the muddy roads toward Corinth.

He should have been pressed, but Grant had nothing much with which to make an effective chase. His own army was disorganized and ready to drop in its tracks, and Buell's army was not precisely under Grant's full control. Before the battle began, Halleck had notified Grant that he and Buell were to act in concert; Buell would exercise his separate command "unless the enemy should attack you," and although the enemy had indeed attacked on Sunday this was another day, Buell was stiff and touchy, and by this time the relationship between Buell and Grant was very delicate. On Monday evening Grant sent Buell a note which betrays his own uncertainty about the command situation:

When I left the field this evening my intention was to occupy the most advanced position possible for the night with the infantry engaged throughout the day, and to follow up our success with cavalry and fresh troops expected to arrive during my last absence on the field.

The great fatigue of our men, they having been engaged in two days' fight and subject to a march yesterday and fight today, would preclude the idea of making any advance tonight without the arrival of the expected reinforcements. My plan, therefore, will be to feel in on the morning with all the troops on the outer lines until our cavalry force can be organized (one regiment of your army will finish crossing soon) and a sufficient artillery and infantry support to follow them are ready for a move.

Under the instructions which I have previously received, and a dispatch also of today from Major-General Halleck, it will not then do to advance beyond Pea Ridge, or some point which we can reach and return in a day. General Halleck will probably be here himself tomorrow. Instructions have been sent to the different division commanders not included in your command to be ready in the morning either to find if an enemy was in front or to advance.[6]

The writing is slightly confused, but the basic idea is clear enough: the Confederates were retiring, Grant's army was incapable of pressing them, if Buell could keep moving on it would be fine, but if he felt that he could not Grant was not going to make him do so. Grant was not treating Buell as a subordinate; he was dealing with him as an equal, a point which becomes even clearer in a note which he sent to him on the following day: "If the enemy are retreating, and can be made to hasten across the low lands between here and Pea Ridge, they will probably be forced to abandon their artillery and baggage. Will you be good enough to order your cavalry to follow on the Corinth road, and give two or three of your fresh brigades to follow in support."[7]

More than this, under the circumstances, Grant probably could not have done. Yet from this distance it seems clear that the great missed opportunity at Shiloh was the failure to press the retiring Confederates pitilessly during the twenty-four hours following Beauregard's withdrawal. The Union Army was worn out, and its command arrangements were very imperfect; but the Confederates' plight was desperate. They were, in short, ready to be had, and a driving chase down the muddy roads to Corinth might have knocked them out of the war for good. Braxton Bragg, who was one of the most dour pessimists in either army but who nevertheless had a clear military eye, wrote to Beauregard on the morning after the battle: "Our condition is horrible. Troops utterly disorganized and demoralized. Road almost impassable. No provisions and no forage; consequently everything is feeble. . . . Our artillery is being left all along the road by its officers; indeed, I find but few officers with their men." A few hours later he sent in another gloomy report: "If we are pursued by a vigorous force we will lose all in our rear. The whole road presents the scene of a rout, and no mortal power could restrain it." [8]

One solid blow on April 8 could have shattered the Confederate Army beyond repair, but the Federal Army was not up to it. The Federals followed their foes just long enough to make sure that they had actually left the premises and then stopped, and although Grant exhorted both Sherman and McClernand to jam the Rebel rear guard with cavalry and infantry in hot pursuit,[9] nothing much came of it. The Unionists went into the camps they had occupied before the battle began, the Confederates loitered just out of gunshot range, and the terrible battle of Shiloh was over. Between them, Grant and Buell had lost more than 13,000 men, Beauregard had lost more than 10,000, and the greatest battle ever fought on the North American Continent up to that date had come to a conclusion.

It had been a very near thing indeed, and the most that could be said for the Northerners was that they had beaten off an unexpected attack; and yet one of the decisive struggles of the Civil War had been won. The end of the war was a long way off, in April of 1862, yet when the exhausted Confederates drifted southwest from Pittsburg Landing a faint foreknowledge of what that end would be went down the road with them. The Northern victory had been purely negative, but it was of far-reaching consequence.[10] For this was one battle which the Confederacy had had to win in order to survive, and the Confederacy had not quite been able to win it. In the long run many things killed the dream of Southern independence; one of them, compacted in the wilderness above the Tennessee River, was made up of the desperate fighting of many Middle Western soldiers, the power of the row of guns on the bluff in the twilight . . . and, with these, the unbreakable stubbornness of Ulysses S. Grant.

Beauregard had a stubbornness of his own, and he was in no haste to get back to Corinth. On Tuesday he was still close enough to the battlefield to send a note to Grant, under flag of truce, proposing that a Confederate burial detail be allowed to go back to the Shiloh area to bury the Confederate dead. Grant sent a reply the following morning, remarking that because of the warmth of the weather he had promptly assigned heavy details to such duty and that the dead of both armies were already under the sod.[11] The work was not done quite as rapidly as Grant may have imagined. An Iowa soldier said that his regiment was kept busy on this assignment for most of the week, wrote that "it is an awful sight to see the dead lying all about," and remembered that seven hundred dead Confederates were put in one enormous grave. An Indiana cavalry colonel wrote home in mid-April saying that "men who were killed a week ago are still unburied," and he added that many wounded had not yet been given medical attention.[12]

There was a great deal to be done, for the formless battle of Sunday had revealed gross imperfections in Federal drill and discipline. The thousands who had strayed from their commands had to be brought back into camp and kept there. Officers who had fled incontinently had to be sent home, and the dismayingly large number of wounded had to be cared for. Hospital boats were coming upstream, and Halleck wired that arrangements had been made to care for 10,000 casualties in hospitals at Cincinnati; in addition to the wounded, the army had many men down with illness, and volunteer Samaritans of high and low degree from the Middle Western states were hurrying to the scene to help them. Once the pursuit had been halted, Grant issued orders prohibiting soldiers or citizens from passing picket lines, stationing cavalry details on all approaches to the camps, tightening the regulations about sanitation, and cracking down on one of the oddest habits of this poorly trained army — the custom of promiscuously firing muskets on any and all occasions. In wet weather, a whole regiment might discharge its muskets in the air just to see whether the powder charges had dampened; a newspaper correspondent referred to "this abominable habit," and said there had been such a continual pop-popping of firearms before the battle that men in camp paid no attention to a skirmish-line clash, so that when the battle began on Sunday many soldiers assumed that it was nothing more than the casual routine of firing muskets at nothing. Grant's order specified:

> All firing by the troops is positively prohibited in camp. Where it is necessary to discharge fire-arms it will be done under proper regulations, made by division commanders, and such men as are to discharge their pieces will be marched in an orderly manner to the front of the outguards for that purpose and back to their camps.[13]

The mere fact that such an order was necessary tells a good deal about the carefree, happy-go-lucky atmosphere that had prevailed before the battle.

Shortly after this, Grant followed with another order: each division commander was to detail ten mounted men, under a commissioned officer, to patrol the camp and arrest all officers and men who fired their weapons in disregard of this regulation. All enlisted men found outside their proper camps were to be arrested, as were all civilians who could not display passes signed either by the Departmental Commander or by a general commanding an army corps. There was to be more work, too, and Grant's order frankly admitted the need for it: "Most of the command being deficient in drill and discipline, division commanders will see that as many hours per day as is consistent with the health of the men be devoted to drill and that company commanders excuse no soldier from any part of his duties." [14]

With all of this, Grant was considering the next move. On April 9, forty-eight hours after the battle ended, he sent this dispatch to Halleck:

> There is but little doubt but that the enemy intend concentrating upon the railroad at and near Corinth all the force possible leaving many points heretofore guarded entirely without troops. I learn this through Southern papers and from a spy who was in Corinth after the rebel Army left.
>
> They have sent steamers up White river to bring down Van Dorn's and Price's commands. They are also bringing forces from the East — Prisoners also confirm this information.
>
> I do not like to suggest but it appears to me that it would be

demoralizing upon our troops here to be forced to retire upon the opposite bank of the river and unsafe to remain on this, many weeks, without large reinforcements.

The attack on Sunday was made, according to the best evidence I have, by one hundred & sixty-two regiments. Of these many were lost by killed, wounded and desertions.

They are at present very badly crippled and cannot recover under two or three weeks. Of this matter you may be better able to judge than I am.[15]

Halleck, meanwhile, was on his way to Pittsburg Landing, to exercise active command in the field. Powerful reinforcements would be available. John Pope had finally taken New Madrid and Island Number 10, and his strong army could be used; for a time Halleck was uncertain whether to send it straight down the Mississippi toward Memphis or to bring it around and up the Tennessee to join Grant and Buell, and he told Secretary of War Stanton that he could not decide until he learned more about Rebel strength at Corinth. He concluded presently that Pittsburg Landing was the place, and Pope was ordered to bring his army to the scene without delay, leaving enough men with Commodore Foote, on the Mississippi, to enable that officer to land troops and occupy Fort Pillow if the Confederates should evacuate that post.[16] On April 9, Halleck notified Grant that he was leaving St. Louis, and that substantial reinforcements were coming. He added the warning: "Avoid another battle, if you can, till all arrive. We then shall be able to beat them without fail." [17]

Halleck arrived without much delay, and on April 13 he issued General Orders Number 16, officially thanking Grant and Buell and their soldiers for the victory. His order remarked that "The soldiers of the great West have added new laurels to those which they had already won on numerous fields," emphasized the need for greater discipline and order, and stated that Grant and Buell would retain the immediate command of their respective armies in the field. On the heels of this Halleck sent Grant a stiff but not unfriendly note demanding that he get his troops into better shape:

Immediate and active measures must be taken to put your command in condition to resist another attack by the enemy.

Fractions of batteries will be united temporarily under competent officers, supplied with ammunition, and placed in position for service. Divisions and brigades should, where necessary, be reorganized and put in position, and all stragglers returned to their companies and regiments. Your army is not now in condition to resist an attack. It must be made so without delay. Staff officers must be sent out to obtain returns from division commanders and assist in supplying all deficiencies.[18]

The interesting thing about this note — in view of Halleck's readiness to cast blame on a subordinate — is the fact that it was not a great deal sharper; for Grant was coming under heavy criticism by newspapers and by politicians for his handling of the first day's fight at Shiloh. At no time in the war was he more bitterly attacked, publicly, than now, and the accusations ranged all the way from the old charge of drunkenness to the allegation that through blind incompetence he had allowed his army to be caught completely by surprise.

The country got its first news about the battle from a dispatch which the *New York Herald* published on April 10 — a clean "beat," scored apparently by an enterprising character named W. C. Carroll who got downstream to the telegraph station at Fort Henry ahead of all the other correspondents and sent the *Herald* an enthusiastic and inaccurate account of a massive victory which reflected unsullied glory on the national arms. Carroll had been serving briefly as a volunteer aide on Grant's staff — it was not uncommon then for a correspondent to wangle such a position with some general — and he was frankly out to present the General and his accomplishments in a favorable light. Months afterward, he wrote that at the close of the battle he had appraised "the bitterness of feeling and jealousy of Gen. Buell and his officers toward General Grant and the Illinois troops," and had concluded that they would try to bring General and Illinoisans "into disrepute by a series of false and slanderous reports"; as a result, he raced for the telegraph office determined to get a properly oriented account before the public.[19]

His story made a huge splash. It began by asserting that "one of the greatest and bloodiest battles of modern times" had just ended in complete rout of the enemy; it contained a fantastic overestimate of the number of casualties (from 18 to 20 thousands of Federals,

and between 35 and 40 thousands of Confederates) and it contained
no hint that the Confederate attack had not been fully expected and
prepared for. It also included the completely false assertion that
Grant in person had turned the tide, on the second day, by himself
leading a desperate charge on the Rebel position, brandishing his
sword "while cannon balls were falling like hail around him."

Carroll's story was not very long, and there was not actually a
great deal of meat in it, but the *Herald* played it as a magnificent
scoop and fleshed it out by printing, with the runover, nearly a
solid page of secondary material — biographical sketches of the
leading generals, an account of the strategic significance of the Corinth area, and so on. Its Washington bureau got busy, a copy of the
dispatch was sent to the White House, and the document was read
aloud to an enthusiastic House of Representatives. Secretary Stanton
issued a statement congratulating generals and troops for this and
other victories, and ordering every regiment in the nation's armies
to convene on the following Sunday and listen to prayers of thanks-
giving. Other newspapers all around the country reprinted the
Herald's dispatch, after the fashion of that day, New York City was
bedecked with flags and bunting, and reporters who came north
from Shiloh a day or so later found victory celebrations going on in
towns in southern Indiana and Ohio.[20]

This did not last very long. One correspondent at Shiloh was
young Whitelaw Reid, who wrote dispatches for the *Cincinnati
Gazette* under the pen name AGATE. Reid was with Lew Wallace at
Crump's Landing when Grant's steamer came up the river on the
morning of April 6, and he slipped on board while Grant was talking over the railing with Wallace, rode on upstream, and got off at
Pittsburg Landing at the same time Grant did. He spent two days
in the battle area, doing a good reporter's best to get a comprehensive account of everything, and what he learned appalled him. (Sherman bitterly declared, later, that Reid got a highly slanted version
of the battle from Buell and Nelson.) Reid lost the race to the telegraph station, and went on all the way to Cincinnati, where, almost
exhausted, he worked at prodigious speed to write out a complete
story. The *Gazette* promptly put it into type, the *Herald* reprinted
it on April 14, and the gloss permanently vanished from Carroll's
jubilant and sketchy story.

Reid's story was a shocker. The man was convinced that the army had been miserably taken by surprise, that its generalship had been all but nonexistent, that a ruinous defeat had been averted by the narrowest of margins, and that nothing about the whole affair could be considered with pride except for the bravery of some of the common soldiers and a few subordinate generals. He began in the breathless, involved manner of the times: "Fresh from the field of the great battle, with its pounding and roaring of artillery, and its keener voiced rattle of musketry still sounding in my wearied ears; with all its visions of horror still seeming seared upon my eyeballs, while scenes of panic-stricken rout and brilliant charges, and obstinate defences, and succor, and intoxicating success are burned alike confusedly and indelibly upon the brain, I essay to write what I know of the battle of Pittsburg Landing." Then, after plowing his way through a few more paragraphs of similar tenor, he got down to cases and presented a workmanlike account of what had really been going on at Shiloh. He had infinitely more detail than the *Herald* man had bothered to collect, and in column after column he presented to the country a convincing picture of a military debacle as humiliating and as disgraceful, in all but its final scenes, as the disaster of Bull Run itself. In the end it was his story that the country took to heart.

The army, he said flatly, had been surprised in its camps. Many officers and men were not out of bed when the Confederate attack struck, others were washing or getting dressed, some were at breakfast, and organized musket and artillery fire swept through the camps before the men even fell into line. Some men were shot dead in their tents, others were bayoneted while still in bed; everybody retreated in haste, and although a new line was patched up many of the fugitives continued all the way to the river and refused to return to the fight. Prentiss's division was swept away and was captured by ten o'clock in the morning. Heroic resistance was described here and there, but in the main the narrative was one of unrelieved bungling and retreat.

The story made little mention of Grant himself; when he was mentioned, the reference was highly critical, and the entire article was searing in its implications. Grant did not even arrive on the field "until after nearly all these disasters had crowded upon us" — Sherman and McClernand routed, most of Prentiss's division captured, most of the camps taken — and there had been shameful neglect in regard to Lew Wallace: his division, drawn up and ready to march all morning, "was not ordered to Pittsburg Landing until nearly if not quite twelve o'clock." There was no evidence that any general control was exercised over any part of the battle; a council of war was held Sunday night, "but if the Major General commanding developed any plans there beyond the simple arrangement of our line of battle, I am very certain that some of the division commanders didn't find it out." Reid gave his readers the impression that Buell's troops and the guidance of Buell himself won most of whatever was won on Monday.[21]

Others joined in the chorus. Many men had run away at the first shock of battle; some of these were officers, men of prominence in their Middle Western home towns, and they tried to prove their innocence by showing that the army had been surprised because of lack of leadership. The Governor of Ohio — two of whose regiments had practically dissolved once the shooting started — said that these men were not cowards: they had been surprised because of the "criminal negligence" of the top command, and the lieutenant governor of the same state cried that most of the soldiers felt that "Grant and Prentiss ought to be courtmartialed or shot." The *Chicago Times* announced solemnly that "the neglect of one man, intrusted with high responsibilities, has left fearful, heartrending testimonials on the savage battlefield of Pittsburg Landing," and the *Cincinnati Commercial* editorialized: "There was something in the management of that great, destructive and indecisive battle that has caused apprehensions to be felt as to the competency of the then commanding general, and while several ugly-looking points have been explained away, public opinion demands something more than even General Halleck's endorsement to reconcile it to the retention of Gen. Grant in command." A *New York Herald* correspondent at Pittsburg Landing wrote shortly after the battle about the "universality of sentiment that Grant was accountable for the reverse of Sunday," and went on to assert: "Probably 60 officers, brigade and regimental, have expressed themselves to that effect, while a word in his defense is scarcely to be heard in any quarter. What the Gen-

eral's defense may be is therefore not public, but if he is not amen-
able to the charges so freely promulgated and discussed he is the
best abused man in the country." The 35th Ohio, which reached
Shiloh shortly after the battle, found that the camps were full of
stories of bad generalship, and a veteran remembered: "These rumors were generally accepted as fact by us. . . . We were in a humor to believe any kind of a report that reflected on our regular
army officers. Volunteer troops at that stage of the contest were
impressed with the idea that regular army officers were tyrannical
and devoted more time to good drinks than to required military
duty." [22] The Middle West was in a somber mood; the steamboats
were bringing north thousands upon thousands of wounded men,
and in Indiana and Ohio and Illinois people began to feel the tragic
impact of what had in truth been the bloodiest battle yet fought in
the New World.

Shiloh casts a long shadow, in whose dusk it is hard to see the
precise truth. Of all the complaints about folly and fumbling
leadership, the one which is the clearest, and which has lived the
longest, is the dispatch which Reid wrote out of his fury and his
disillusionment — a dispatch which is a singular blend of great reporting and abysmally bad reporting. It gave the nation the truth
about this battle, but it also gave it certain untruths, which have
lived to this day; and in what they said when they tried to reply to
the untruths, both Grant and Sherman now seem to have been trying to disown the truth itself. Their statements appear either willfully false or wildly incomprehensible to anyone who has not examined Reid's story and compared it with the record.

Reid was wrong on several counts. He had the bulk of Prentiss's
division captured by 10 in the morning, although it held out until 5
in the evening and by its heroic resistance kept the army from complete ruin. He said that Grant did not reach the field until after the
worst had happened, although — since he himself reached the landing on Grant's own steamboat — Reid was fully aware that Grant
got to the scene promptly and went immediately to the front. He
said that there was unconscionable delay in ordering Lew Wallace
to the battlefield, although the orders were sent as soon as Grant arrived at Pittsburg Landing and were repeated, with much urgency,

several times thereafter. Altogether, there was enough bias in Reid's dispatch to give a hot-tempered man like Sherman some reason to suspect that the jealousy of the Buell faction had been at work.

But it was in what he said about the surprise that Reid did the most damage — and, doing it, led Grant and Sherman into a defense which a later generation has found quite unacceptable.

Reid said flatly that the men in their camps, especially the men in Sherman's and Prentiss's divisions, were taken wholly by surprise, with Confederate battle lines charging in on them before they were up and dressed, and he wrote scathingly about mismanagement which caused men to be shot in their tents and bayoneted while still in bed. In substance, his story said that the forward portion of the army had been overwhelmed and routed before the men could even get their muskets and face the enemy; the damage was done, according to Reid, before the army had so much as got ready to fight.

Now all of this, quite simply and demonstrably, is not true. The battle began in the very earliest light, with Prentiss's forward elements — and, soon afterward, Sherman's — pitching into the Confederate advance. No Federal camp was overrun before battle lines had been formed, and some of the sharpest fighting of the entire day took place before any camp had been taken. No one was bayoneted while in bed or shot while in his tent. Both Union and Confederate records make this clear.[23] In collecting his facts here, Reid obviously had absorbed the wild tales told by panicky fugitives at the landing.

It was this part of Reid's dispatch which Grant and his defenders — including above all others Sherman, who would be Grant's man forever from now on — were most anxious to knock down. In their desperate attempt to show that there had been no surprise as Reid used the word, in which they were entirely correct, they seemed to be saying that there had been no surprise at all at Shiloh, and beyond all argument there had been one. None of their statements about what happened at Shiloh makes any sense unless it is remembered that they were trying to reply to one particular segment of the Reid dispatch.

That the criticism stung Grant painfully is obvious. Not long after the battle he did something which he did rarely, if ever, at any other time in his military career: he wrote a letter to an editor in reply to newspaper criticism. On May 3 the *Chicago Times* and other papers reprinted a letter which Grant had sent to the *Cincinnati Commercial*. In it, after asserting that he would continue to do his best to bring the war to a speedy close and that he himself was "not an aspirant for anything at the close of the war" — this was a point on which he seems to have been especially touchy — Grant wrote:

> There is one thing I feel assured of; that is the confidence of every brave man of my command, and those who showed the white feather will do all in their power to attract attention from themselves. I had perhaps a dozen officers arrested for cowardice in the first day's fight. These men are necessarily my enemies. As to the talk about a surprise here, nothing could be more false. If the enemy had sent word when and how they would attack we could not have been better prepared. Skirmishing had been going on for two days between our reconnoitering parties and the enemy's advance. I did not believe, however, that they intended to make a determined attack, but were simply making reconnoissances in force. My headquarters were at Savannah, though usually I spent the day at Pittsburg. Troops were constantly arriving to be assigned brigades and divisions, all ordered to report at Savannah, making it necessary to keep an office and someone there. I was also looking for Buell to arrive, and it was important that I should have every arrangement complete for his speedy transit to this side of the river.[24]

Grant's writing usually is very clear, but in this case it is uncommonly opaque and it obviously reflects confused thinking. In one breath Grant says that he could not have been better prepared if he had known precisely when and how Johnston was going to hit him; in the next he confesses that he had misinterpreted all of the omens and that Johnston had deceived him. He had anticipated an attack, but he had not anticipated the kind of attack that was actually made. That the attack failed and that the Union army was able to win a victory the next day apparently was all that mattered; but the talk about "surprise" obviously rubbed him where he was raw.

His reaction was mild compared to that of Sherman. Sherman's case was a good deal tougher. He had been in immediate command at the front and had refused to admit that a Confederate offensive was impending, and his contemptuous "Take your damn regiment back to Ohio. There is no enemy nearer than Corinth" was a reveal-ing remark that could not be explained away. In his fury at the Reid dispatch Sherman hit back with a vigor that put his own costly mis-appraisal of enemy intentions entirely out of his mind.

To his brother, Senator John Sherman, Sherman wrote that the worst complaints were "made by people who ran away and had to excuse their cowardice by charging bad management on the part of leaders," and he noted that the two runaway Ohio regiments which were being so stoutly defended by homestate officials had done almost no fighting; one had lost seven men, the other, nine. A few days later he wrote furiously:

> The scoundrels who fled their ranks and left about half of their number to do their work have succeeded in establishing their story of surprise, stuck with bayonets and swords in their tents, and all that stuff. *They* were surprised, astonished and disgusted at the utter want of respect for life on the part of the Confederates, whom they have been taught to regard as inferior to them, and were surprised to see them approach with banners fluttering, bayonets glistening and lines dressed on the center. It was a beautiful and dreadful sight and I was prepared for and freely overlooked the fact that many wilted and fled, but gradually recovering rejoined our ranks. But those who did not recover, their astonishment has to cast about for a legitimate excuse; and the cheapest one was to accuse their officers, and strange to say this story is believed before ours who fought two whole days.
>
> For two days they hung about the river bank filling the ears of newspaper reporters with their tales of horrid surprise, regi-ments all cut up, *they* the only survivors and to our utter amaze-ment we find it settling down as history.

More soberly, he wrote shortly after this:

> All I know is we had our entire front covered by pickets, intermediate guards & grand guards and I had my command in line of battle well situated long before we had seen an infantry soldier of the enemy. . . . Nor was Prentiss surprised . . . all his men were drawn up in line of battle before the enemy was seen in columns of attack.[25]

Inevitably, times being as they were, the attack on Grant moved no more than a few millimeters before it picked up, embroidered and disseminated the charge that Grant had been drunk. To this charge, the officers who had been with Grant during the battle reacted with immediate fury.

Captain Rowley wrote to a friend in Chicago: "As to the story that he (Grant) was intoxicated at the battle of Pittsburg. I have only to say that the man who fabricated that story is an infamous *liar*. And you are at liberty to say to that man that I say so." To Congressman Washburne, Rowley went into a little more detail:

> . . . A word with reference to the Thousand and one stories that are afloat with reference to Gen. Grant. suffice it to say they have the same foundation as did those that were circulated after the Battle of Donelson and no more. It is sufficient to say that Gen. Halleck is now here and the conduct of the battle and all the *details* meet *his entire* approbation. And the stories in circulation have their origin in the efforts of Cowardly hounds who "stampeded" and now would be glad to turn public attention from themselves, and direct it elsewhere. Together with the eagerness of Newspaper Correspondents to get "items." I who was on the field know that had it not been for the almost superhuman efforts of the Gen. added to the assistance he had from his officers we would have been forced to Record a defeat instead of one of the most *Brilliant* victories that was ever won on any field.

Colonel J. E. Smith of the 45th Illinois, another of the Galena men serving with this army, wrote Washburne that the army had undoubtedly been surprised — "it was worse, we were astonished" — but he believed that this was more the fault of the division commanders than of Grant. He added: "I see also that Grant is severely censured by the public for drunkenness got up no doubt by those who are jealous of him. There is no foundation for the report." Colonel Jacob Ammen of Buell's army, who had seen Grant at Savannah on the afternoon before the battle and at Pittsburg Landing late on the afternoon of the first day's fighting, recorded in his diary on April 8: "Note — I am satisfied General Grant was not under the influence of liquor, either of the times I saw him." [26]

Congressman Washburne was convinced. He was hearing from friends and fellow-townsmen in whom he had faith, and he presently rose in the House of Representatives to uphold Grant's record. He spoke, he said, to defend "the general who has recently fought the bloodiest and hardest battle ever fought on this continent, and won one of the most brilliant victories. . . . Though but 40 years old, he has been oftener under fire, and been in more battles, than any other man living on this continent excepting Scott." Grant had not been surprised, Washburne insisted, and while complaint was made that he was downstream at Savannah, ten miles from his army, when the battle began, that was his proper place, given the situation as it existed that weekend. He had started for the field within five minutes of the moment the first firing was heard, reached it promptly, and immediately assumed active and effective command, "evincing, in his dispositions, the genius of the greatest commanders." And as to the other question: "There is no more temperate man in the army than General Grant. He never indulges in the use of intoxicating liquors at all. He is an example of courage, honor, fortitude, activity, temperance and modesty, for he is as modest as he is brave and incorruptible. . . . It has well been said, that 'Falsehood will travel from Maine to Georgia while Truth is putting on its boots.' " [27]

When Washburne rose to speak for a protégé he pulled out all of the stops, and the speech unquestionably helped Grant's cause. Shortly after it was delivered, Washburne got a letter of thanks:

Hon. E. B. WASHBURNE
DEAR SIR
    It is with a feeling of deep interest and pleasure that I have just perused a document from you in defence of my husband — It is indeed gratifying to know that he finds in you so true a friend and one who manifests such a ready willingness to exonerate him from the malicious and unfounded slanders of the press.
    Your noble and generous remarks in behalf of Mr. Grant were timely made and bearing as they do the impress of truth cannot fail of having a salutary influence.
    It is evident that you appreciate the motive that prompted him to challenge the dangers and horrors of the battle field

when first our glorious government was assailed by domestic foes.

In conclusion permit me to thank you for your bold and gallant effort to right the public mind in regard to a matter in which I feel so great a personal interest.

Yours truly and respectfully,

Your friend,

JULIA D. GRANT.[28]

Grant rode out the storm, but for a time the waters were rough. As good an appraiser of public opinion as Joseph Medill of the *Chicago Tribune* would warn Washburne, six weeks after the battle:

> There is no whistling fornenst the wind. The army are fornenst you in relation to Grant. It was a most reprehensible surprise followed by an awful slaughter. Our cause was put in terrible peril. Want of foresight, circumspection, prudence and generalship are all charged upon the wretched man. But we need not dispute about it. I admire your pertinacity and steadfastness in behalf of your friend, but I fear he is played out. The soldiers are down on him.[29]

Medill overstated the case. It is always hard to say just what an army had on its mind at any given moment, especially when that army has been out of existence for the better part of a century, but a careful study of the available indicators of army morale does not show any especial feeling against Grant, on the part of the soldiers, in the period immediately after Shiloh. After all, Shiloh had been a victory — damnably expensive, but nevertheless a victory — and as they buckled down to camp routine in the days following the battle the men came to feel that they had done a great thing. Before, they had been a conglomeration of separate regiments; now they were an army, and an army that was beginning to be very proud of itself. This army would never feel that it owed a great deal to any general. It would not develop, for anyone, the kind of rapturous adoration which the Army of the Potomac would bestow on General McClellan; nor would it ever feel the intense, bitter dislike and distrust which the Potomac Army would feel for McDowell and Burnside. Here, taking its characteristic shape in the camps above Pittsburg Landing, was the Army of the Tennessee, which would presently come to believe that it could never be beaten. It did not acquire that belief under a general in whom it had no confidence.

Certainly Grant's standing with his superiors was not greatly impaired by Shiloh, the best barometer in this being the attitude of Halleck himself. One of this officer's distinguishing traits was his everlasting readiness to place blame upon a subordinate in a case wherein much heat had been developed; but to the War Department he gave Grant full exoneration, as far as Reid's story of shameful surprise was concerned. Halleck being what he was, his verdict can be taken as final on this point. Writing to Secretary Stanton on June 15, more than two months after the battle, Halleck asserted that "the impression which at one time seems to have been received by the Department that our forces were surprised in the morning of the 6th is erroneous. I am satisfied from a patient and careful inquiry and investigation that all our troops were notified of the enemy's approach some time before the battle commenced." [30]

Grant himself believed that the army had been properly placed west of the river and that he had been right in maintaining his headquarters at Savannah; he felt that the charge of panicky surprise was unjustified, and he was bitter about the accusations of personal misconduct; and he summed up his case in a letter which he wrote to Washburne on May 14. This letter reads as follows:

> The great number of attacks made upon me by the press of the Country is my apology for not writing to you oftener, not desiring to give any contradiction to them myself. — You have interested yourself so much as my friend that should I say anything it would probably be made use of in my behalf. I would scorn being my own defender against such attacks except through the record which has been kept of all my official acts and which can be examined at Washington at any time.
>
> To say that I have not been distressed at these attacks upon me would be false, for I have a father, mother, wife & children who read them and are distressed by them and I necessarily share with them in it. Then too all subject to my orders read these charges and it is calculated to weaken their confidence in me and weaken my ability to render efficient service in our present cause. One thing I will assure you of however: I can not be driven from rendering the best service within my ability to sup-

press the present rebellion, and when it is over retiring to the same quiet it, the rebellion, found me enjoying.

Notoriety has no charms for me and could I render the same services that I hope it has been my fortune to render our just cause, without being known in the matter, it would be infinately prefferable to me.

Those people who expect a field of battle to be maintained, for a whole day, with about 30,000 troops, most of them entirely raw, against 70,000, as was the case at Pittsburg Landing, whilst waiting for reinforcements to come up, without loss of life, know little of War. To have left the field of Pittsburg for the enemy to occupy until our force was sufficient to have gained a bloodless victory would have been to left the Tennessee to become a second Potomac. — There was nothing left for me but to occupy the West bank of the Tennessee and to hold it at all hazards. It would have set this war back six months to have failed and would have caused the necessity of raising, as it were, a new Army.

Looking back at the past I cannot see for the life of me any important point that could be corrected. — Many persons who have visited the different fields of battle may have gone away displeased because they were not permitted to carry off horses, fire arms, or other valuables as trophies. But they are no patriots who would base their enmity on such grounds. Such I assure you are the grounds of many bitter words that have been said against me by persons who at this day would not know me by sight yet profess to speak from a personal acquaintance.

I am sorry to write such a letter, infinately sorry that there should be grounds for it. My own justification does not demand it, but you, a friend, are entitled to know my feelings. As a friend I would be pleased to give you a record, weekly at furthest, of all that transpires in that portion of the army that I am, or may be, connected with, but not to make public use of.[31]

When he wrote this letter Grant was still laboring under the delusion that Johnston and Beauregard had brought a much larger army than his own to the field. He had had time, however, to go over the battle and the campaign in his mind, to reflect on all of the might-have-beens, and to review his own actions in the light of knowledge he did not have when the actions were taken; and his considered judgment was expressed in the flat statement: "I cannot

see for the life of me any important point that could be corrected."
This, of course, was simply a firmer way of saying what he had already written to the Cincinnati editor — that "we could not have
been better prepared" if the enemy had given advance notice of the
time and place of the attack. Years later, when he wrote his Memoirs, Grant did not repeat this assertion, but he did not retreat from
it either. Military critics might make of it what they would: he had
said his say and he would let it ride.[32]

This was supremely characteristic. Shiloh had been fought, it had
been won, and then and always Grant's idea was to get on with the
war without wasting time on the backward glance or on a long
counting of the cost. What had been gained might have been gained
more cheaply, but it was what had been gained that really mattered.

CHAPTER THIRTEEN

The Unpronounceable Man

A FTER SHILOH the war moved very slowly. Halleck was on hand and in full control, and men who looked at him had different opinions. To an irreverent newspaper correspondent, he seemed like some "oleaginous Methodist parson dressed in regimentals with a wide, stiff-brimmed, black felt hat sticking on the back of his head at an acute angle from the ground"; the reporter felt that the man neither looked like a soldier nor rode like one, and considered that the General's face was "large, tabular and Teutonic." A young staff officer who had just reached Pittsburg Landing gave a more favorable picture: "His green eyes made you feel as he talks along that there is something strong behind them. He is a handsome man in face and form. His mouth is small but very determined in looks. . . . As he sits talking you fancy that he is one of those who thinks all the while." [1] The nickname, "Old Brains," sent its shadow in front of him, given added point by the impressive victories which had been won by armies in his department. With Halleck on the spot, there would be no repetition of the errors that had preceded Shiloh.

Halleck was extremely cautious, and it appeared that he would at all costs avoid mistakes. This army which was beginning a new offensive would think constantly about its own defense, and every camp would be deeply entrenched, down to the position of the last platoon. The army would go south with gelatinous majesty, as if it were conducting a moving siege, burrowing its way with a ripple of earthworks always going on ahead. Beauregard's Confederate Army, badly mangled and far under strength (although swollen by incompetent intelligence reporting to several times its actual size) would be distrusted and feared but would not be regarded as the true objective of the campaign.[2] That objective would be the Mississippi town of Corinth, the "strategic site" which had obsessed high command thinking ever since the capture of Fort Donelson, and the enemy to be conquered would be the Southern landscape itself, with its railroad lines, its bridges and its towns and its roads, rather than the Confederate Army. Whatever happened, Corinth was going to be taken, and if the taking of it took a long time — well, there was a great deal of time to spare, because the Federal Government, rich in men and equipment and the munitions of war, was rich also in hours and days and weeks and could spend them to the limit.

It took time to get the offensive started, because army organization had to be perfected. Grant's troops undeniably needed pulling together and much additional drill, the shattering impact of Shiloh having descended on a force that was still in its formative stage. There were many new troops on hand, too, Buell's and John Pope's beside Grant's, and Halleck must make one army out of three separate ones. All in all, he commanded more than one hundred thousand soldiers in the wooded camp-sites above the river. Not even McClellan had more men to maneuver in the field.

Getting everything in order called for a change in the general command situation, and on April 28 Halleck announced a tentative new organization. His army would consist of a right wing, Grant's Army of the Tennessee; a center, Buell's Army of the Ohio, and a left wing, Pope's Army of the Mississippi, with a general reserve to be formed by detachments from the several corps. Nomenclature was slightly confused; the different forces, or wings, were sometimes referred to as armies, sometimes as army corps. Two days after he had announced this setup, Halleck amplified it with a new order which made a substantial change. George H. Thomas and his division were shifted from Buell's army to Grant's and Thomas was named commander of the right wing — under Grant, technically, yet somehow not really under him in actual practice. McClernand, the ambitious Illinois political general, was given charge of the reserve, which was to be composed of his own and two other divisions, one of them taken from Buell. Pope and Buell retained their old places, although Buell's force was sadly diminished; and Grant, remaining in general command of the District of West Tennessee, would act as second in command to Halleck himself.[3]

The first officer to be grieved by this order was Buell. A few weeks ago he had been commander of an independent army, and now he had only eighteen thousand men, in three divisions, and he promptly sent Halleck a dignified protest, calling attention to the slight that had been laid upon him and remarking: "You must excuse me for saying that, as it seems to me, you have saved the feelings of others very much to my injury." [4] But the real injury had been suffered by Grant. His announced position as second in command meant nothing, and carried no more real responsibilities than the ones normally borne by a Vice-President of the United States. The right wing and the reserve were technically under his command, but in actual practice they were under Halleck; in an order dated May 1, announcing his assumption of command of "the Army of the Tennessee, including the reserve," Grant specified that reports would be forwarded "to these headquarters," but it did not work out that way and Grant was effectively by-passed. One unfortunate result of this new command situation was that it created a coolness between Grant and Thomas. A newspaper correspondent recalled that Grant's position "was really none at all . . . and was felt by him to be an insult put upon him (he imagined at the time) at the instigation of General Thomas," and although Grant got over this feeling he and Thomas never grew really cordial.[5]

Grant waited for a time, and then sent Halleck a letter of protest:

> . . . As I believe it is generally understood through this army that my position differs but little from that of one in arrest and as this opinion may be much strengthened from the fact that orders to the Right Wing and Reserve, both nominally under my command, are transmitted direct from headquarters, without going through me, I deem it due myself to ask either full restoration to duty, according to rank, or to be relieved entirely from further duty with this Department. I cannot, do not, believe that there is a disposition on the part of yourself to do me any injustice but my suspicions have been aroused that you may be acting under instructions, from higher authority, that I know nothing of. That there has been a studied, persistent opposition to me by persons outside of the army, and it may be by some in

it, I am fully aware. This I care nothing for further than it is calculated to weaken confidence in me with those whom it is necessary for me to command.

In conclusion then General, I respectfully ask either to be relieved from duty entirely or to have my position defined so that there can be no mistaking it. I address you direct instead of through the Adjt. Genl. because this is more of a private matter, and one in which I may possibly be wrong, than public.[6]

Halleck was unresponsive. On the following day he wrote Grant insisting that orders from headquarters would, if headquarters thought it necessary, go direct to commanders of "army corps, divisions, brigades or even regiments," and expressing surprise that Grant should find any ground for complaint: "You have precisely the position to which your rank entitles you." He went on to say that his own feelings toward Grant were friendly, adding: "For the last three months I have done everything in my power to ward off the attacks which were made upon you. If you believe me your friend you will not require explanations; if not, explanations on my part would be of little avail."[7]

With this Grant had to be content. The army slowly moved south, digging innumerable entrenchments, corduroying miles of road, fighting small front-line skirmish actions (which, Grant observed caustically, later, "ought to have served to encourage the enemy")[8] and covering itself against any possible counterblow from Beauregard. Headquarters got fantastic reports about Beauregard's strength. Assistant Secretary of War Thomas A. Scott, who was with Halleck at this time, wrote to Stanton early in May that Beauregard would presently have an increase in strength of at least 60,000 men and that the Confederate government, in addition, would probably detach men from in front of Richmond to add further strength, and he urged that "it becomes a grave question for you to consider as to whether a column of 40,000 or 50,000 men should not be sent from the East." McClernand notified Grant that an Illinois army surgeon, captured at Belmont and just released, had learned during his captivity that the Rebels had 140,-000 men at Corinth; a little earlier, Halleck was informed that there were at least 100,000 men in Beauregard's army, with additional reinforcements coming in every day.[9] Actually, although

Beauregard was reinforced after Shiloh, he was never able to muster more than 52,000 effectives at Corinth, and in the early part of the campaign his strength was much weaker than that. In April he sent an impassioned appeal to Richmond, pointing out that he had but 35,000 men and that he would be badly outnumbered even when the 15,000 fresh troops which had been promised should reach him. "If defeated here," he wrote, "we lose the Mississippi Valley and probably our cause." The Federals got and deciphered this message, it was printed in the *New York Herald* on April 21, and it was in Buell's hands before the end of the month, but it seems to have been ignored; its only effect was to bring Beauregard a sharp warning from Lee to change his cipher.[10]

The soldiers themselves found the slow advance laborious, but conditions in the camps around Pittsburg Landing were so unpleasant they were glad to be moving. Camp diarrhea was extremely prevalent, brought on by bad water and by the indigestible messes which untrained cooks concocted from flour, rice and beans. Many sutlers had come on the scene, selling whisky at a dollar a pint — they were supposed to sell this only to officers, but in this informal army most privates could easily find a lieutenant to buy for them — and charging fifteen cents each for lemons and forty cents a pound for cheese. (The 41st Ohio remembered how one man borrowed an officer's coat, collected an armful of bottles at one sutler's tent, and told the sutler to charge it to the brigade commander.) Camps were overrun by sight-seers, looking for souvenirs; roving merchants opened restaurants and bakeries, and there was an influx of professional gamblers who played at long wooden tables with stacks of silver dollars in front of them, each gambler armed with navy revolvers. With the gamblers came prostitutes, who were presently rounded up by army authorities and unceremoniously shipped off down the river.

The march at least provided movement in a new and rather strange country. Men tried to kill squirrels and wild turkeys for camp messes; forbidden to shoot them, they went on forays armed with sticks and stones. In the swamps, they said, there were frogs so big that they bleated like lambs. The rich lushness of Southern spring was on the land, and Midwestern boys goggled at blossoming magnolias, at evergreen hedges formally trimmed in the yards of town houses, at crepe myrtle and mimosa and more familiar flowers like dahlias and verbena. Colored folk in the fields seemed overjoyed to see the Federal soldiers, but the whites were sullen and unmistakably hostile, and an Illinois officer noted darkly: "As for the Union sentiment that was to be developed by the presence of our army it is all nonsense." Corduroying roads through the endless swamps was hard work, with parties of six or eight men lugging ten-foot logs, hour after hour; the roads that were built in this way were bumpy and slippery, and loaded wagons often slid off and were hopelessly mired, the horses sometimes sinking entirely out of sight. Imperfectly disciplined soldiers looted houses on the march, and some regiments became notorious for this habit; one planter who complained that he had been robbed of "everything except my hope of eternal salvation," was told, "Just wait until the 8th Missouri comes along." Most soldiers suffered from an infestation of chiggers, and men in an Ohio brigade complained that for twenty-eight days they were not able to get their clothes off.[11]

Without especially noticing it at the time the army had acquired one new member who would occupy a large place in the story of the war: a swarthy, undersized, irritable little captain of infantry, who came up to Pittsburg Landing as a quartermaster officer on Halleck's staff and who was promoted, at about this time, to a colonelcy commanding the 2nd Michigan Cavalry — Phil Sheridan, who wrote that this advance to Corinth was uncommonly leisurely and spiritless. "The desultory affairs between rear and advance guards," he recorded, "seemed as a general thing to have no purpose in view beyond finding out where the enemy was, and when he was found, since no supporting columns were at hand and no one in supreme command was present to give directions, our skirmishing was of little avail and brought but small reward." [12] So dilatory was the movement that a modern historian of Beauregard's army contemptuously referred to the Federal move as "doubtless the very slowest uncontested advance ever recorded of any army"; he added that if Halleck had been as fast and as confident as his superior force justified he might have surrounded and captured Beauregard's entire force.[13]

Once, as the army drew close to Corinth, Grant believed he saw an opening. The right wing was within four miles of the Rebel entrenchments, Sherman had carried an advanced position, and Grant suggested to Halleck that Pope's force, which was off on the left, be brought around behind the army and sent in past Sherman's right in a dawn attack; the advance would be along dry, elevated ground, and a network of streams and swamps would make it easy for the Federals to hold the rest of the line with a reduced force while the attack was made, and Grant believed that the offensive could move straight into Corinth. He recalled ruefully, later, that "I was silenced so quickly that I felt that possibly I had suggested an unmilitary movement," and Colonel Webster said that Halleck pooh-poohed the proposal "in the most insulting and indignant manner." Webster added that this was one of the very few times he ever saw Grant have to struggle to keep his temper; afterward, he said, Grant "was depressed for hours." [14]

One duty Grant did have to perform, during this period. Just before the army moved away from Pittsburg Landing he had to make formal announcement of the death of General C. F. Smith. The infection that had set in when the old soldier scraped his leg getting into a rowboat a fortnight before the battle had been beyond remedy, and on April 25 he died. In a letter to Mrs. Smith, Grant wrote that the nation had lost "one of its most gallant and most able defenders," and he added a few words to express his own sense of loss: "It was my fortune to have gone through West Point with the general (then captain and commander of cadets) and to have served with him in all his battles in Mexico and in this rebellion, and I can bear honest testimony to his great worth as a soldier and a friend. Where an entire nation condoles with you in your bereavement no one can do so with more heartfelt grief than myself." Old Smith would in truth be missed. Long after the war, Sherman wrote: "Had C. F. Smith lived, Grant would have disappeared to history after Fort Donelson." It was only because Smith's injury incapacitated him, Sherman said, that Halleck consented to let Grant have have charge of the army in the period leading up to Shiloh.[15]

Grant made the rounds of his troops, issued occasional orders and tried to keep busy, but in truth there was little of importance to occupy his time. A newspaperman who was with the army said that Grant spent much time by his own campfire, silently smoking, pacing restlessly back and forth, or looking on while others played cards — breaking in, once in a while, in the manner of card-table onlookers everywhere, to make some suggestion about the play. Newspaper attacks on him were still being printed, but he rarely complained about them; it was remembered that he did say, to a correspondent whose paper had been especially venomous in its criticism: "Your paper is very unjust to me, but time will make it all right. I want to be judged only by my acts." [16] Major Belknap of the 15th Iowa, to whom Grant had addressed words of reminiscence during the heat of the first day's action at Shiloh, felt that Grant at this time had no real position — he "was apparently neither private nor general." One evening, after several days of rain, Belknap saw Grant riding up, water streaming from his clothing; when Grant greeted him, Belknap burst out that the army was in a very bad situation. Grant asked why he thought so, and Belknap replied that the rain had turned fields and roads into bottomless mud; movement was impossible, the enemy was only a short distance away, and if the Rebels should attack the army would be helpless.

"Young man," said Grant, "don't you know that the enemy is stuck in the mud, too?"

To this the abashed major could only reply: "No, I did not, General, but I do now." [17]

A *New York World* correspondent found Grant something of a puzzle, and in his attempt to describe him stumbled upon a fortunate phrase. Grant, he wrote, "has none of the soldier's bearing about him, but is a man whom one would take for a country merchant or a village lawyer. He has no distinctive feature; there are a thousand like him in personal appearance in the ranks. . . . A plain, unpretending face, with a comely, brownish-red beard and square forehead, of short stature and thick-set. He is we would say a good liver, and altogether an unpronounceable man; he is so like hundreds of others as to be only described in general terms." [18]

Grant wanted to get away. Halleck had turned down his request for a transfer, but toward the end of May the attempt to get duty in some other field was renewed through other channels. Major General David Hunter, who had had charge of things in St. Louis in the brief interim between Frémont and Halleck, and who later had served in Kansas, was this spring in charge of Federal troops along the Carolina coast. Camp rumor said that Hunter was about to be sent somewhere else, and Grant's staff angled to get the coastal command for Grant.

On May 24, Captain Rowley wrote to Washburne about it: "There is a matter which has just suggested itself to us. From certain articles in the few newspapers we get hold of it seems probable that Gen. Hunter may be superseded by some one. If such is to be the case I am *certain* that Gen. Grant would like *extremely* well to be assigned to the command that he now holds. And all things considered I think it would also be for the good of the service. We have now quite a number of their eastern generals in this department and have given them a fair start. Now let us do something for the Coast. Let us hear from you." In a brief note mailed the same day, Rowley added: "Gen. Grant would be very much pleased to be transferred to a command on the coast as I have just heard him conversing upon the subject."

On the same day Colonel Clark Lagow of Grant's staff wrote to Washburne on the same topic. He reported the general impression that Hunter was about to be relieved and urged that Hunter's position be given to Grant: "I am satisfied that the command would please him. I have heard him say as much (although he knows nothing of my writing this)." [19]

Nothing came of this, and a few weeks later Rowley wrote to Washburne saying: "I am sorry there is no chance to get Genl. Grant into a wider field but am pleased to observe that public opinion is again beginning to set strongly in his favor." Grant himself seems to have had no part in the wire pulling. On May 24 he wrote to a friend in the North, the Rev. J. M. Vincent of Galena, remarking that he was "quite unwell," was presently confined to his bed, and feared that he might be in for a spell of sickness. He then went on to sum up his position at that moment:

> I never asked for any position or any rank but entered with
> my whole soul in the cause of the Union, willing to sacrifice

everything in the cause, even my life if needs be, for its preservation. It has been my good fortune to render some service to the cause and my very bad luck to have attracted the attention of newspaper scriblers. It certainly never was my desire to attract public attention but has been my desire to do my whole duty in this just cause.[20]

Nevertheless, by the end of May Grant was about ready to leave. Sherman one morning rode over to visit with him, and found trunks and boxes packed and stacked up as if for some movement. Grant was sitting in his tent, at a rough table made of boards fastened to planks that had been driven into the ground, sorting letters and tying them into bundles with red tape. As Sherman recalled the matter, long afterward, Grant explained that he had leave to go home and was going to take advantage of it; he was simply in the way, here in Halleck's army, and he could not endure it any longer. Sherman argued with him, pointing out that he himself had almost left the Army, a few months earlier, when all the newspapers were proclaiming him a lunatic; he finally made up his mind to stick it out, he won advancement, and "now I am in high feather." As Sherman told it later, Grant thanked him for this and agreed to stay for a while; and Sherman always believed that it was his own argument that kept Grant from dropping out of the Army altogether.[21]

When he wrote his Memoirs Grant gave this account a rather casual confirmation, saying that he had obtained permission to leave the department and that Sherman, calling on him just as he was about to leave, had talked him out of it. What he wrote at the time, however, provides a substantially different version. According to Sherman's story, the leave of absence which Grant had been about to take would, in effect, have taken him out of the Army and out of the war; Grant's contemporary letters make it look much more like a routine matter, and — surprisingly enough — indicate that it was Halleck himself who persuaded him to stay with the Army. Sherman may have been influential in the case, but Grant failed to mention him when he described the episode to Congressman Washburne.

On June 1, Grant wrote to Washburne asking him to intercede with the Secretary of War to win promotion for a young Lieutenant Dickey, son of the colonel of the 4th Illinois cavalry and brother-in-law of the late General W. H. L. Wallace. He then remarked: "I leave here in a day or two for Covington, Ky., on a short leave of absence. I may write you again from there if I do not visit Washington in person." [22] The projected Washington visit may conceivably have been in connection with the attempt to get a transfer to some other department, but the trip to Covington — where Jesse Grant lived, and where Julia and the children spent a good deal of time during the war — does not sound like a momentous step that would have brought Grant's military career to a close. In any case, a little more than a fortnight after writing this letter Grant sent Washburne another one, which tells how he came to abandon the trip north.

Your letter of the 8th inst. addressed to me at Covington Ky. has just reached. — At the time the one was written to which it is an answer I had leave to go home, or to Covington [here Grant added "for a few days," then crossed the phrase out] but Gen Halleck requested me to remain for a few days. Afterwards when I spoke of going he asked that I should remain a little longer if my business was not of pressing importance. As I really had no business, and had not asked leave on such grounds, I told him so and that if my services were required I would not go atal. This settled my leave for the present, and for the war, so long as my services are required I do not wish to leave.

He added that he would presently be going to Memphis, where his headquarters were to be for the immediate future.[23]

It is possible to read more strain into the Grant-Halleck relationship in the spring of 1862 than really existed. Grant's feeling toward Halleck became extremely bitter after the war, but there was no bitterness in evidence during the war, and Grant apparently did not then feel that Halleck had seriously mistreated him. He undoubtedly described his emotional condition accurately when, a month after the letter just cited, he told Washburne that Halleck "is a man of gigantic intellect and well studied in the profession of arms. He and I have had several little spats but I like him and respect him nevertheless." [24] Halleck, for his part, seems to have had nothing in particular against Grant: he simply was, and for a long time remained, very lukewarm in respect to this subordinate, not so much because Grant had got into his black books as because he himself was a dismally bad judge of men. The only proof that is needed, as far as this point is concerned, is the fact that in the summer of 1862 Halleck could write: "It is the strangest thing in the world to me that this war has developed so little talent in our generals. There is not a single one in the west fit for a great command." [25] When he wrote that, Halleck was fresh from a command that included, among others, Grant, Sherman, Thomas and Sheridan!

Halleck underrated Grant, but so did almost everyone else. There was a rather general impression, through most of 1862, that Grant was nothing more than an earnest, uninspired plodder who had blundered his way into certain victories. Halleck had planned to replace him early in the winter, had been reluctant to keep him in command in the pre-Shiloh period, and indeed was to make one more effort to put another man in his place; but it seems likely that all of this reflects nothing much more than acceptance of the common opinion regarding the unimpressive-looking soldier who could never manage to appear like a great strategist.[26]

Meanwhile, the military picture took a sudden turn. Beauregard had been sparring and running a long bluff, in his effort to keep the Federals away from Corinth; he adopted various devices, including the trick of running empty trains into the town, after dark, with much whistling and chuff-chuffing, with the garrison cheering each arrival, which led Federal scouts to report the steady arrival of heavy reinforcements; but he was hopelessly overmatched, and at the end of May he got his army and most of his supplies out, headed south, and let the Federals have the strategic spot which they wanted so badly. To the last moment, the invaders were misled. At 1:20 A.M. on May 30, John Pope sent Halleck word that Beauregard was being heavily reinforced, and warned: "I have no doubt, from all appearances, that I shall be attacked in heavy force at daylight"; five hours later Pope realized that he had been cruelly deceived and he ordered his skirmishers forward, while the explosion of ammunition dumps which Beauregard had been unable to salvage sent huge clouds of smoke into the morning air. Before 9 o'clock Pope held Corinth, the United States flag was hoisted over the courthouse, and Pope informed Halleck that the Confederates "evacuated yesterday and last night. They marched down the Mobile railroad." [27] An officer in the 3rd Iowa wrote that he and his comrades had "an undescribable feeling of mortification that the enemy with all his stores and ordnance had escaped," and Colonel John Smith from Galena wrote angrily that he hoped "all that twaddle about Grant" would stop, because "this biggest of all blunders the Commanding Genl. is responsible for." Years later, Grant recalled that officers and men were disappointed, since "they could not see how the mere occupation of places was to close the war while large and effective Rebel armies existed." He himself believed that a two-day campaign could have turned the trick.[28]

In Richmond, Jefferson Davis was indignant because Beauregard had not put up a fight, and he called him sharply to account for it, replacing him in command shortly afterward with Braxton Bragg; but Beauregard's position had been hopeless from the start, and he had done all anyone could have expected of him in getting his army away uncaptured. At his peak strength he had had no more than 52,000 effectives, of all arms; when Corinth was occupied Halleck commanded 128,315 in the Corinth area, not to mention 22,000 more at Nashville, Cumberland Gap and in northern Alabama,[29] and the whole Confederate position in the West was rapidly crumbling. Far to the south the Navy had opened the mouth of the Mississippi, smashing its way past Forts Jackson and St. Philip and occupying New Orleans, which was now held by Federal troops under Major General Ben Butler. The Navy had had similar success in the upper river, destroying a Confederate fleet in a pitched battle near Memphis and occupying both that city and Fort Pillow. Federal troops under General J. M. Schofield held all of Missouri, and another Federal army led by General Samuel R. Curtis, which had beaten the Confederates in the battle of Pea Ridge early in the spring, was moving eastward across Arkansas toward the city of Helena, eighty miles below Memphis. The Confederates still occupied Vicksburg, and controlled the river from there down to Baton Rouge, but Rear Admiral David Farragut was bringing his salt-water fleet up the river and he seemed likely to repeat at Vicksburg the triumph he had won below New Orleans.

When Halleck reported the occupation of Corinth, Secretary Stanton telegraphed: "I suppose you contemplate the occupation of Vicksburg and clearing out the Mississippi to New Orleans," and Halleck replied that if the Navy did not take Vicksburg unaided "I shall send an expedition for that purpose as soon as I can re-enforce General Curtis." This message Halleck sent on June 12; two weeks later he still hoped that the Navy could take Vicksburg, but "if not it will probably be necessary to fit out an expedition from the army." Apparently Halleck really did have some such expedition in mind — for a time, at least — and Grant hoped that he himself would be ordered to lead it, but the expedition never materialized.[30]

The expedition never materialized because Federal strategy in the West began to sag just when the opportunity was greatest. It sagged because the old desire to occupy territory of strategic importance kept the high command from realizing that if enemy armies were pulverized the strategic importance of cities, railroad lines and the like would take care of itself.

Pope was ordered to pursue the retreating Confederates, and he reported that the woods were full of Rebel stragglers and that the enemy force seemed to be disintegrating, but he was not allowed to keep up the pressure. Halleck said frankly that if the Confederates would just go as far as Okolona — a town on the Mobile and Ohio railroad, sixty miles south of Corinth — he would be satisfied, because "the repair of the railroads is now the great object to be attended to." [31] Halleck had a number of weighty problems on his mind, and the books from which he had gained his strategic wisdom had somehow failed to teach him that the destruction of the last sizable Confederate army in the West would solve all of those problems for him.

He did have an extensive railroad network to maintain. There was the Mobile and Ohio, coming down to Corinth and the deep south from Columbus, Kentucky; and there was the Memphis and Ohio, running northeast from Memphis to Kentucky, crossing the Mobile and Ohio at Humboldt, Tennessee. There was also the

all-important Memphis and Charleston, which came east from
Memphis to Corinth and ran thence to Chattanooga, where it connected the western Confederacy with a line running on to Virginia. There was, finally, the Mississippi Central, which left the
Mobile and Ohio at Jackson, Tennessee, came south to cross the
Memphis and Charleston at Grand Junction, halfway between Corinth and Memphis, and then struck south through Mississippi all
the way to New Orleans. If the Federals proposed to occupy
Tennessee and northern Mississippi and Alabama it was vital to get
and keep these lines in shape, especially so since the approach of
summer meant that the Tennessee River would be at low-water
stage, with reduction of steamboat traffic.

But the railroads were only part of it. Corinth had to be fortified and garrisoned. As Halleck said, there must be reinforcements
for Curtis, in Arkansas. Troops were needed to occupy Memphis
— Sherman and his division were sent there as soon as Corinth
was taken, and they took possession of the city by June 14 [32] —
and, weighing more than all else, there was East Tennessee: East
Tennessee, where Union adherents had been begging for Federal
troops for six months and more, and to which President Lincoln
now was firmly directing General Halleck's attention. A small
force under General G. W. Morgan was about to occupy Cumberland Gap, but it could go no farther unaided; what was called for
now was a march on Chattanooga itself, and this march Halleck
ordered Buell to make. As it happened, a division from Buell's army
had gone into northern Alabama while the Shiloh-Corinth campaign was in progress, and this division, commanded by a former
astronomer named Ormsby Mitchel, held a segment of the Memphis and Charleston between Tuscumbia, fifty miles east of Corinth, and Stevenson, forty miles west of Chattanooga. It seemed
to Halleck and Buell that Buell's army might well follow this line
in its move. Bridges had been burned, and these must be repaired;
the line was exposed to Rebel guerillas, and regulars operating
from Alabama and Mississippi, and troops would be needed to guard
the repair parties and to give continuing protection to the things
repaired; and, all in all, the movement to Chattanooga — to which
Washington had assigned a priority second only to that held by

McClellan's march on Richmond itself — looked like an extended and intricate operation.[33] Clearly, more than enough was going on to engage all of a department commander's attention.

But the fact did remain that the only really sizable Confederate Army in all the West was the one which, passing from Beauregard to Bragg, was now being permitted to reorganize and refit at Tupelo, Mississippi, a place not far from the Okolona which Halleck had specified as the point to which he hoped it would be willing to retire.[34] Everything the Confederacy had west of the Alleghenies depended on that army, because if it ceased to exist Halleck's troops could go anywhere they chose to go — to East Tennessee, to Vicksburg, to the Gulf, or around-about all the way to Richmond if necessary. A whole map full of strategic lines and places could not be as important as this.

The old pattern was being repeated. After Fort Donelson there had been delay and a regrouping, after Shiloh there had been more of it, and it was the same story now; to consolidate its "conquest" of empty land, the high command ignored the final victory that might be won by relentlessly hounding a beaten army into the last ditch. Holding an enormous advantage in man power and equipment, the Federal commanders both in the East and in the West — for McClellan was moving on Richmond with time-killing deliberation — persisted in acting as if the Federal government and its opponent were evenly matched. Its greatest single military asset, the power to set and follow its own course, compelling the enemy to one desperate expedient after another to avoid outright annihilation, was forgotten.

All of this, at bottom, was probably little more than a simple and understandable reflection of the Army's peacetime experience. Ever since there had been a United States Army, it had been operated on a constabulary basis, with many isolated posts and forts grouped together into departments under localized control. When campaign time arrived, the Army would be assembled from these posts and made into a mobile force; when the campaign ended, it would be redistributed all over the country, not to be reassembled until there was to be another campaign. This was the system that was being followed now. As a result, each victory was followed by a long breathing spell. There was no real continuity to any program; a campaign would break up into isolated segments, and no advantage was ever followed up properly.[35] In a real sense the story of Grant's development as a soldier is the story of his attempt to break out of this crippling tradition and apply the country's strength in a remorseless, continuing pressure.

Halleck's first act, once pursuit of the retreating Confederates had been given up, was to revoke the order which had divided his army into right wing, left wing, center and reserve.[36] Grant, Buell and Pope resumed their original commands; Thomas returned to his infantry division; and Grant asked and got permission to establish his district headquarters in Memphis. (A rather odd request, this, since it would put him on the western edge of what would clearly be an active district. It is just possible that Grant preferred to operate at a little distance from Halleck, whose headquarters would remain in Corinth.) He set out for Memphis on July 20, riding with a small cavalry escort through a country that was by no means safe for small parties of Federals; narrowly escaped capture by armed Confederates, reached Memphis after three days, and told Halleck no more than that the weather had been warm and the roads excellent. Memphis he found wholly unreconstructed, and he reported: "Affairs in this city seem to be in rather bad order, secessionists governing much in their own way." However, he had set up a post-command system and provost marshals, and — just as he had written in the early days in Missouri — he confidently asserted that "in a few days I expect to have everything in good order."

Local clergymen insisted on offering prayers for the President of the Confederate States, and refused to pray for the President of the United States, and some of Grant's subordinates felt that their prayers needed editing, but Grant was not prepared to go very far in this direction. On the day after his arrival, his headquarters sent a warning note to General Hurlbut, who apparently was eager to take steps: "I am directed by Major General Grant to say that you can compel all clergymen within your lines to omit from their church services any portion you may deem treasonable, but you will not compel the insertion or substitution of anything."

More important was the business of preparing to get reinforcements over to General Curtis, in Arkansas. These would have to go by steamboat, up the White River, through country full of Confederate guerillas, and after consultation with the Navy's Captain Phelps Grant felt this could be done by preparing light-draft river steamers, with some protection for the boilers, howitzers for armament, and an infantry escort to rout sharpshooters out of hiding places.[37]

During his time of comparative idleness in the Corinth campaign Grant had been doing a good deal of thinking about the way the war was developing and the principles that should govern a Federal commander, and he was beginning to arrive at certain conclusions. Earlier, he had believed that the Confederacy would collapse once it had lost a few battles; now he was coming to see that nothing but complete conquest would do, and although he still felt that many Southerners were compelled to support the Confederacy by their own fears of what would happen to them if they did not, he was beginning to believe in hard war pursued to the limit. Just before leaving for Memphis he had given Washburne a glimpse of his appraisal of the situation in his own territory:

> Fast Western Tennessee is being reduced to working order and I think with the introduction of the Mails, trade, and the assurance that we can hold it, it will become loyal, or at least law abiding. It will not do however for our arms to meet with any great reverse and still expect this result. The masses this day are more disloyal in the south, from fear of what might befall them, in case of defeat to the Union cause than from any dislike to the Government. One week to them (after giving in their adhesion to our laws) would be worse under the so-called Confederate Government than a year of Martial Law administered by this army.

He went on, then, to spell out the duty of a soldier as he saw it:

> It is hard to say what would be the most wise policy to pursue toward this people, but for a soldier his duty is plain. He is to obey the orders of all those placed over him and whip the enemy wherever he meets him. "If he can" should only be thought of after an unavoidable defeat.[38]

When he wrote his Memoirs, twenty years later, he elaborated on the change that came over his thinking at this time. Until Shiloh, he said, he had supposed that one decisive victory would defeat the Confederacy. Afterward, however, "I gave up the idea of saving the Union except by complete conquest." This affected not only his attitude toward enemy armies in the field but also his conduct in respect to the civilian population and the Southland's material resources:

I regarded it as humane to both sides to protect the persons of those found at their homes, but to consume everything that could be used to support or supply armies. Protection was still continued over such supplies as were within lines held by us and which we expected to continue to hold; but such supplies within the reach of Confederate armies I regarded as much contraband as arms or ordnance stores. Their destruction was accomplished without bloodshed and tended to the same result as the destruction of armies. I continued this policy to the close of the war. . . . This policy I believe exercised a material influence in hastening the end.[39]

His stay in Memphis would not be long. Far off in Virginia, events were taking place that would profoundly change the conditions under which the war in the West would be fought. Grant's period of development was about over. From now on he would enter a different phase of his career.

CHAPTER FOURTEEN

"To Be Terrible on the Enemy"

T
HE FEDERAL armies in Virginia were having trouble, and
their troubles affected the armies in Tennessee and Mississippi. All of the plans that had been made would be forgotten, and new ones would have to be made by different people.
For the moment, what men did in the West would be determined
by what General Lee did in front of Richmond. (The initiative,
once surrendered, may be picked up in very faraway places.)

During the spring General McClellan had moved up the Virginia Peninsula with a methodical caution fully as great as Halleck's
own. He considered himself heavily outnumbered, and shortly after
he fought the hard, inconclusive action at Seven Pines and Fair
Oaks he suggested to the War Department that some of General Halleck's troops might properly be sent to him.[1] Nothing had
come of this, but the complete inability of the fragmented Federal
forces in upper Virginia to cope with Stonewall Jackson led the
War Department eventually to create a new army — the short-
lived, grotesquely unlucky Army of Virginia — and to command
this army Secretary Stanton reached West and selected Major
General John Pope. Halleck did not like this, and said so, but it
did no good, and Pope went East, to brief eminence and then inglorious exit.[2] On his departure his old Army of the Mississippi went
under red-faced, energetic Brigadier General W. S. Rosecrans.

This was only part of it. Like Halleck, McClellan had planned
on the unspoken assumption that there was unlimited time, and
in the last week of June Lee showed him his error. Mechanics-
ville was followed by Gaines's Mill, the Army of the Potomac
began its risky retreat to the James River, and on June 28 Stanton
sent Halleck a telegram that canceled any scheme of conquest
Halleck might have had:

The enemy have concentrated in such force at Richmond as to render it absolutely necessary, in the opinion of the President, for you immediately to detach 25,000 of your force and forward it by the nearest and quickest route by way of Baltimore and Washington to Richmond. . . . in detaching your force the President directs that it be done in such way as to enable you to hold your ground and not interfere with the movement against Chattanooga and East Tennessee. . . . The direction to send these forces immediately is rendered imperative by a serious reverse suffered by General McClellan before Richmond yesterday, the full extent of which is not yet known.[3]

Halleck protested that Washington was asking the impossible: he could not hold his ground, continue the advance on Chattanooga and East Tennessee, and also send twenty-five thousand troops East, and he suggested that the Chattanooga move be canceled. Having filed his protest, he then set about getting the troops ready to move. Grant was told to report immediately on the number of men he had at Memphis and to describe the river transportation available to get them up to Cairo; he had better fortify the land side of Memphis at once, because the divisions of Sherman and Hurlbut might have to leave — "The defeat of McClellan at Richmond has created a stampede in Washington." Buell was notified that his whole railroad-repair scheme might be halted, and McClernand was ordered to prepare to move east with his entire command. Halleck glumly told him, "The entire campaign in the west is broken up by these orders and we shall very probably lose all we have gained."[4]

As it turned out, things were not quite that bad. Now as always, President Lincoln was profoundly interested in anything that affected eastern Tennessee, and Stanton immediately notified Halleck that "the Chattanooga expedition must not on any account be given up" — instructions which Lincoln supplemented with a personal wire to Halleck:

Would be very glad of 25,000 infantry — no artillery or cavalry; but please do not send a man if it endangers any place you deem important to hold or if it forces you to give up or weaken or delay the expedition against Chattanooga. To take and hold the railroad at or east of Cleveland, in East Tennessee, I think fully as important as the taking and holding of Richmond.[5]

During the next few days Washington's fear diminished, as it became clear that the Army of the Potomac had suffered a repulse but not a disaster, and Halleck presently was notified that he need send no troops after all. But if Halleck's troops were not to be moved, Halleck himself might be: he was increasingly on the mind of the President, who had already suggested that he would be glad if the General could make "a flying visit for consultation," and on July 10 there appeared at Halleck's headquarters Governor William Sprague of Rhode Island, armed with a letter from Lincoln. Sprague, at the moment, looked like a rising star; he was young, wealthy, about to become a member of the U. S. Senate, about to become son-in-law of Secretary of the Treasury Salmon P. Chase, and the Presidential letter which he carried said that although his mission was unofficial it bore full White House approval.

Sprague wanted Halleck to go to Washington, presumably to advise the President on military matters. Halleck demurred, and he wrote Lincoln: "If I were to go to Washington I could advise but one thing: to place all forces in North Carolina, Virginia and Washington under one head and hold that head responsible for the result." [6] The oracular vagueness of this was about all Sprague got out of the interview, but Lincoln and Stanton had made their decision, and on July 11 Halleck was notified that he had been appointed General in Chief of the Armies of the United States, and that he was to move at once to Washington.

Much later, when Halleck's inability to function as General in Chief had become painfully obvious, people would wonder why Lincoln and Stanton had ever chosen him; yet, at the time, the selection was eminently logical. In the light of what men then knew, it must have seemed almost inevitable. The country had no General in Chief and it obviously needed one very badly, and as the record then stood it could be argued that Halleck was the only possible choice. He commanded the military department in which the war's chief successes had been won. Kentucky and Missouri had been saved for the Union (neither state was held as firmly as seemed to be the case in July, 1862, but that would not be apparent until later), West Tennessee had been taken, Arkansas was in the process of being conquered, and it seemed likely that the Mississippi would soon be opened from headwaters to Gulf. Halleck had just told Admiral Farragut that he could not give him any help at Vicksburg just now, but he felt that although "this may delay the clearing of the river . . . its accomplishment will be certain in a few weeks." [7] On form, Halleck was the man to pick, and the government picked him.

All of this, of course, made a vast difference in the status and prospects of U. S. Grant.

Grant learned of the impending change on July 11, when he got an abrupt wire from Halleck ordering him to come to Corinth at once. The wire contained no hint of what was up, and Grant, slightly bewildered, asked if he was to bring his staff with him. Halleck replied that he could decide that for himself, but that Corinth was to be his headquarters hereafter. Grant took off, and did not learn what was in the wind until he arrived. Then, on July 16, Halleck signed Special Field Orders No. 161, which enlarged Grant's old District of West Tennessee to include the Districts of Cairo and Mississippi; which meant that Grant now controlled everything between the Tennessee and Mississippi rivers all the way up to and including his old base of Cairo, and that he also commanded Pope's old force, now Rosecrans's, "heretofore known as the Army of the Mississippi." There would be no over-all Department Commander. Grant and Buell would be independent of one another, each answerable only to Washington.[8]

It appears that Halleck had not been certain whether to hand this job to Grant or not. In accepting his new command, Halleck asked Stanton whether he should turn his old headquarters over to the next in rank — who, he pointed out, was Grant — or whether the President wished to designate a successor. Privately, he seems to have wanted to give the place to a member of his own staff, Colonel Robert Allen, his chief quartermaster. Much later, Allen told Adam Badeau that Halleck came into his tent, informed him that he himself had been called to Washington, and asked: "Now, what can I do for you?" Allen replied that he was not sure Halleck could do anything for him, and Halleck replied: "Yes, I can give you command of this army." When Allen remarked that he did not have enough rank, Halleck said that could easily be fixed; but Allen pointed out that he was up to his neck in the huge expenditures and complicated administration of a large and active supply organization which would make it inexpedient for him to leave his present position, and the subject finally was dropped.[9] Grant formally assumed command of his enlarged district on July 17, Halleck left for Washington, and Grant was on his own.

On his own, geographically, and to a limited extent: no officer who served under Halleck was very often on his own, no matter how far away Halleck's headquarters might be. But Halleck in Washington would operate a little differently than Halleck in Corinth. In Corinth, he had displayed a penchant for reaching over the head of a district commander and issuing orders direct to the district commander's subordinates, and Grant had had two or three vigorous passages of arms with him about this. It had come up immediately after Grant's removal to Memphis, in June, and there had been a flare-up a week or two later, when Halleck misunderstood the wording of a telegram Grant had sent him about reported Confederate movements and commented that the message "looks very much like a mere stampede." Grant replied stoutly that "stampeding is not my weakness," and went on to assert: "Your orders have countermanded mine . . . all the dispositions of the forces of the Army of the Tennessee have been made without my orders, and in most cases without my being informed of the changes." Halleck, in return, insisted that he would, whenever he thought proper, issue orders to any parts of Grant's command he chose, and contributed a final stinger: "I must confess that I was very much surprised at the tone of your dispatch and the ill-feeling manifested in it, so contrary to your usual style, and especially toward one who has so often befriended you when you were attacked by others." [10] There would be no more of this, with Halleck in Washington, engrossed with problems far weightier than the proper placement of a brigade or a division along a railroad line in southwestern Tennessee. Within limits, Grant would be lord of his new domain.

For the time being these limits would be restrictive. The great opportunity that had been visible after the occupation of Corinth was gone, now, and the Army of the Tennessee would have to go strictly on the defensive. Indeed, the whole Federal position between the Mississippi and the Alleghenies had changed. The initiative was held by the Confederates, both in the East and in the West. In the East, Lee had simply taken it out of the hands of an overcautious McClellan: in the West, Halleck had given the Confederacy just enough leeway to let it regain the offensive, and the great Union host which had looked so irresistible at the end of May was widely scattered, reduced to the inglorious task of rebuilding and guarding a network of railway lines, occupying cities and country garrisons, worrying about supply depots, and in general waiting to see what the Rebels were going to do next. Looking back in his old age, Grant was to remember the summer and fall of 1862 as his most anxious period in all the war.[11]

At an undetermined distance to the south, in Mississippi and Alabama, there were substantial bodies of Rebel troops, obviously preparing for some new blow at the invaders. Braxton Bragg had Beauregard's old army of 50,000 men or more, Kirby Smith was gathering forces in eastern Tennessee, and Earl Van Dorn and Sterling Price had 15,000 men brought from the trans-Mississippi area. Lumped together, the armies of Grant and Buell outnumbered them; but the Federal armies were spraddled out along a front running from Memphis to Bridgeport, Alabama, in no shape to engage in anything but strictly defensive operations. As far as the Federals were concerned, this had suddenly become a railroad war, and Grant had more than 360 miles of track to maintain and protect. The youthful engineer officer who had come down to join him in the Donelson period, James B. McPherson — promoted now to brigadier general — was acting as a highly efficient superintendent of railroads, and track and bridge gangs which he had selected from the ranks were doing great things, but they were not fighting Rebels. The Mobile and Ohio line was open all 143 miles from Corinth to Columbus, Kentucky; and although the Memphis and Charleston road between Corinth and Memphis had not been reopened, a roundabout connection was available by way of Grand

Junction and Jackson. Yet these lines, running through hostile territory, where almost every civilian was both willing and able to contribute to the interruption of Yankee communications, were more liability than asset. Sherman had glumly noted that "along and on the road our every movement is known and reported, while we can hear nothing," and Confederate cavalry raiders of uncommon talent, John Hunt Morgan and Nathan Bedford Forrest, were showing an exasperating ability to sift past the Federal outposts and smash up installations far behind the lines.[12]

It had been optimistically supposed, early in the spring, that the people of western Tennessee were good Unionists at heart, waiting only for "liberation" by Federal troops. When Memphis was first occupied a correspondent for the *Chicago Times* had sent back a glowing dispatch about deep-seated loyalty to the Union, asserting that the good people of Memphis had firmly resisted "the encroachments of Jeff Davis' government," and declaring that "joy at deliverance is overwhelming," [13] but this picture was obviously false. Before he moved from Memphis Grant had reported to Halleck that the city was full of "many families of officers in the Rebel army . . . who are very violent," and had obtained permission to send them all south of the Federal lines. It was his first experience in the occupation of a hostile city, and he was left in no doubt about the way the inhabitants felt. Much of his time, he remembered after the war, was spent listening to protests and complaints from citizens who seemed to feel that even a Yankee general would admit the justice of the Confederate cause if he could just be induced to take a reasoned view of the situation.[14] It was becoming more and more apparent that Grant's army was precariously established in a land where the civilian was as devout an enemy as the soldier in gray.

The enmity was active as well as devout. Guerilla warfare was developing, and it was giving the war a new cast. A war in which the only foes were organized bodies of regular troops was one thing, but a war in which every farmer might be a night-raider who would shoot a courier, or band with other farmers to capture a wagon train or tear up railroad track, was something very different, and it would provoke a grim harshness. On July 3 Grant issued an order:

> The system of guerilla warfare now being prosecuted by some troops organized under the authority of the so-called Southern Confederacy, and others without such authority, being so pernicious to the welfare of the community where it is carried on, and it being within the power of communities to suppress this system, it is ordered that wherever loss is sustained by the Government collections shall be made by seizure of a sufficient amount of personal property from persons in the immediate neighborhood sympathizing with the rebellion to remunerate the Government for all loss and expense of collection. Persons acting as guerillas without organization and without uniform to distinguish them from private citizens are not entitled to the treatment of prisoners of war when caught and will not receive such treatment.[15]

Writing thus, Grant was simply going by the book of traditional warfare, which said that armies of occupation must respect the persons and property of civilians in occupied territory but that the civilians themselves must abide by the rules: that is, that armies which did not make war on civilians must not themselves be warred on by civilians. Any community (said the tradition) was responsible for the actions of its members; if its members behaved like peaceful farmers by day and resistance fighters by night the community was supposed to restrain them, and it was proper for the occupying army to inflict punishment on the community to stimulate it in this respect. When Halleck told Secretary Stanton that he was going to stamp out guerilla warfare in occupied territory and that "I shall probably be obliged to use hemp pretty freely for that purpose," [16] he was saying no more than the ordinary rules of warfare entitled him to say. So far, the Federal commanders had at least tried to keep the invasion from crushing the rights of enemy civilians.

But it was a losing effort even at best, and as the soldiers began to get the idea that every man's hand was against them, here in the Confederacy, it would become utterly hopeless. Federal

troops were forbidden to rob barns or hen-roosts, to enter in-
habited houses or to remove fence rails in order to make campfires,
and armed guards were often stationed at plantations to enforce
these orders. But there was no way to keep the poorly disciplined
individualists in blue from acting on their own initiative; they had
the drill and training which enabled them to parade and maneuver
and fight, but the ingrained habit of obedience which would compel them to respect the property of their enemies they did not
have and they would never get it. In certain important respects
they were almost wholly undisciplined. Their indiscipline grew out
of the society which produced them. This society had given
them a great lack of respect for constituted authority, and then
it had created an army organized in such a way that this lack of
respect could not be corrected. In the end, this army would decide
how the war was to go.

Whatever might happen later in the war in other states, Federal
armies in Tennessee at this time were not marauding, pilfering and
devastating under orders. The mischief invariably was done by
soldiers who had wandered away from their regiments and were
acting on their own. It was not possible for the high command to
stop this, because the high command was utterly unable to prevent straggling. One of Buell's officers stated the case very simply
when he testified that "it has been impossible to get the subaltern
officers to either report or punish the straggling of soldiers,"
adding that this was a practice which "would ruin any army in the
world." The captains and lieutenants, he said, were brave enough
and intelligent enough; they just would not try to enforce the
kind of discipline which would protect civilian property in enemy
territory.[17] And an army of this kind, faced with guerilla warfare
which would provoke even a tightly-held force on the European
model into harsh reprisals, was likely to behave in a very heavy-
handed manner.

Once this took place, slavery was doomed. What happened in
western Tennessee in the middle of 1862 was important, not
just because it meant unlimited woe for plantation owners and
ordinary farmers, but because the Western soldiers had, in effect,
ratified the Emancipation Proclamation before it was even written. They did this by instinct rather than by thought. Back of

Grant, Sherman and the others was the vast, still shapeless body of enlisted men, whose emotions were beginning to be dominant for the entire war. The steps by which this happened are worth reciting.

More and more, the Northern soldiers this summer were coming to feel that they were in a foreign land, whose people were not merely hostile but were deserving of rough treatment, their very foreignness being, somehow, just cause for blame. The Southland was set apart, not by the fact that it was in rebellion, but by its strangeness; its fields and houses were not like the fields and houses of the Middle West, its habits of speech and action were different — outlandishly different, to Western eyes — and the strangeness and irritating differences all seemed to center around the existence of human slavery. An officer would write to his wife: "If slavery existed in every state in the Union, we would as a nation be miserably sluggish and stupid." An enlisted man felt that the countryside and the people "all bore the impress of another life," and said that it was almost a surprise to find that Southerners spoke the same language as Northerners spoke. Marching boys jeered at the tumble-down quality of occasional country schoolhouses, and marveled that there were so few of them; they began to talk, as the slaves themselves talked, about poor white trash, "a poor, degraded, ignorant, thriftless people," scoffed at the primitive equipment they saw on eroded farms, and commented that hardly any of the towns seemed to have sidewalks.

Grant's fellow townsman, Dr. Edward Kittoe, wrote that the only friends of the Union in Tennessee were the slaves. "The darkies seemed joyous at our presence," he wrote, when he entered the railroad junction town of Jackson, "but the whites are sullen and look spitefully and with an evident attempt to appear disdainfully indifferent. The women, I cannot say ladies, are peculiarly vindictive." The looked-for Union sentiment had not appeared; the doctor was convinced that it did not exist, and he asked plaintively: "Why is it that we are to submit to open insult and secret injury, and yet our tired and poorly-fed soldiery are to guard the property of these scoundrels?" All in all, he confessed that he was "at a loss to understand how this very remarkable war is to be finished, if the government continues to pursue a course so well calculated to foster the views of these rebels, the iron gauntlet must be used more than the silken glove to crush this serpent." [18]

If all of this had represented nothing more than the arrogant provincialism of young men who had never before been fifty miles away from home it would not have meant much, but it went a great deal deeper than that; it marked the beginning of a profound shift in Army opinion. Not only were the soldiers beginning to believe in hard war; they were seeing slavery as the justification for this belief, were blaming it for the war itself, and were coming to feel that slavery must be stamped out along with rebellion, as if the two were indeed different aspects of the same thing. As the generals grew more ruthless, the enlisted men (not to mention the company officers who reflected their viewpoint so completely) ran on ahead of them and turned the war into a conflict which was certain to destroy the peculiar institution.

Not long after he got to Washington, Halleck sent Grant specific instructions about the need for a harder attitude: "It is very desirable that you should clear out West Tennessee and North Mississippi of all organized enemies. If necessary, take up all active sympathizers, and either hold them as prisoners or put them beyond our lines. Handle that class without gloves, and take their property for public use. As soon as the corn gets fit for forage get all the supplies you can from the rebels in Mississippi. It is time that they should begin to feel the presence of war on our side." [19]

The key to all of this lay in the admonition to "take their property for public use." Slaves were property, and because they were property they were to be taken from their owners. When Grant undertook to fortify Memphis, he rounded up a small army of contrabands to do the spadework, and the soldiers suddenly realized that the orders under which they had been operating before — that fugitive Negroes were not to be allowed within their lines — had been suspended. At Trenton, Tennessee, Grenville Dodge took the cue, writing, in mid-July: "The policy is to be terrible on the enemy. I am using Negroes all the time for all my work as teamsters, and have 1,000 employed. I do it quietly and no fuss is made about it." One of Sherman's soldiers remembered that the old policy of exclusion lapsed at this time, and that the thousands of roving Negroes who tried to follow the army were no longer driven off: "All that came within our lines were received and put to work and supplied with clothing and subsistence. This policy was viewed by the soldiers with very general approbation." In the middle of June, Sherman had warned his troops that "the well-settled policy of the whole army now is to have nothing to do with the Negro," but the policy was collapsing. Brigadier General James A. Garfield, who served in the Corinth area that spring, said later that "the Army soon found, do what it would, the black phantom would meet it everywhere, in the camp, in the bivouac, in the battlefield and at all times"; from this, he said, grew the conviction in the mind of every soldier that "behind the Rebel army of soldiers, the black army of laborers was feeding and sustained the rebellion and there could be no victory until its main support was taken away." [20] It was no longer possible to fight the war on the old basis.

The soldiers who helped to create the new policy were not reflecting any reasoned change in sentiment about the rights or wrongs of slavery. Most of them came from areas which detested abolitionists, and sentiment back home had not changed appreciably. At the very time when the Army was beginning to emancipate the Negro, Abolitionist Wendell Phillips was mobbed in Cincinnati; speaking from the stage of the Opera House, he was met by a shower of eggs and stones, while "whisky-faced, blatant wretches roared in the galleries and lobbies," with the mayor of the city sitting by unmoved. Crowds on the sidewalk outside brandished knives and muttered threats of a lynching, and a reporter said that the most furious outburst was provoked by Phillips's assertion that no one could any longer doubt that "the war is between the real democracy of the country and the sectional aristocracy that wields the power of African slavery in one hand and that of the ignorance of the whites in the other." Sentiment in regard to the Negro himself had not changed; what was rising was a cold fury with secession and secessionists, a back-home attitude which, as one of Buell's officers said, "led the men to think they were justified by their friends at home in indiscriminate plunder when operating in the seat of war." A chaplain in an

Ohio regiment noted that the men in his regiment expressed satisfaction when they marched past a fine plantation house which had been set on fire, and wrote: "This thing of guarding rebel property when the owner is in the field fighting us is played out. That is the sentiment of every private soldier in the army." [21] Beauregard himself noted the new attitude, reflected that it did not mirror a genuine change in Western notions about slavery, and wrote a word of advice to Bragg: "By the bye, I think we ought hereafter in our official papers to call the Yankees 'Abolitionists' instead of 'Federals,' for they now proclaim not only the abolition of slavery but of all our constitutional rights and that name will have a stinging effect on our western enemies." [22]

But the word "abolitionist" was losing its sting. In the middle of this July the Congress in Washington passed a Confiscation Act, decreeing freedom for the slaves of all persons who supported the rebellion. President Lincoln was not yet ready to issue his great Proclamation, but the lines had been drawn. The North was becoming emancipationist in spite of itself, driven to it by the conviction that the war had to be hard and merciless. Men who would cheer the burning of a Southern manor house were bound to do something about the slaves who supported that manor. They might continue to despise the Negro as a man, they might throw eggs at those who said that he ought to be a free citizen, but they would set him free simply because his bondage propped up the power of the Confederacy.

Grant himself found no difficulty in adjusting to the new situation. He was a complete realist in regard to slavery and the war, and while he was still in Cairo, in November of 1861, he had set forth to Jesse the views we have quoted: "My inclination is to whip the rebellion into submission, preserving all constitutional rights. If it cannot be whipped in any other way than through a war against slavery, let it come to that legitimately. If it is necessary that slavery should fall that the Republic may continue its existence, let slavery go." Shortly before Shiloh, he had been denounced by antislavery people at home for returning to their owners certain slaves captured at Fort Donelson, but the antislavery people had their facts mixed. Grant had sent cavalry to recover slaves which had been used to build the Donelson fortifications — under the rules, at that time, these chattels were legal contraband — and the cavalry, instead of rounding up the working gangs, had swept up a miscellaneous handful of Negro women and children, burning various cabins and looting farmhouses along the way. Grant had put the cavalry commander under arrest and had returned the Negroes and the inanimate loot, and he had made his position clear in a letter to Washburne: "I have studiously tried to prevent the running off of Negroes from all outside places, as I have tried to prevent all other marauding and plundering. So long as I hold a commission in the army I have no views of my own to carry out. Whatever may be the orders of my superiors and the law I will execute. . . . When Congress enacts anything too odious for me to execute, I will resign." [23]

Now, with Halleck's new orders about the confiscation of property in effect, and with the new act of Congress before him, he wrote to Jesse Grant: "I am sure that I have but one desire in this war, and that is to put down the rebellion. I have no hobby of my own with regard to the Negro, either to effect his freedom or to continue his bondage. If Congress pass any law and the President approves, I am willing to execute it." A little later, he mused more at length about the subject in a letter to his sister Mary:

The war is evidently growing oppressive to the Southern people. Their *institution* are beginning to have ideas of their own; every time an expedition goes out many of them follow in the wake of the army and come into camp. I am using them as teamsters, hospital attendants, company cooks and so forth, thus saving soldiers to carry the musket. I don't know what is to become of these poor people in the end, but it weakens the enemy to take them from them.[24]

Once established at Corinth, Grant had Julia and the children come down for a visit. After the war, men said that Julia Grant hurried to the General's side as soon as each battle was finished; when a reporter asked her about this, in 1880, she replied, simply: "That was not true at all. The General would not have put up with it." But Grant always wanted to have his family with him when active campaigning was not in progress, and during the early part of this August he was able to gratify his wish. On the edge of Corinth there was a pleasant house owned by a thick-and-thin Confederate sympathizer, one of the few Southern civilians whom Grant ordered to a northern prison camp for inflexibly rebellious actions, and this house became Grant's headquarters. (When he wrote his Memoirs, Grant said that he did not remember having arrested one civilian during all of the war. His memory apparently failed him; he had caused the arrest of at least this one Mississippian in the summer of 1862, and in a note to his father early in August he remarked that "we are keeping house on the property of a truly loyal secessionist, who has been furnished free lodging and board at Alton, Illinois.") [25] The surroundings were pleasant, and Grant hastened to quiet Jesse's fear that an Army camp might not be a wholesome place for small children; the house was far enough from camp to be homelike, and there was room for the children to play just as they would have done back in Galena. A company of Ohio cavalry acted as headquarters guard.

A surgeon in the 11th Iowa was called to headquarters one day, and he supposed that he was to prescribe for one of the headquarters servants and so came, informally, in his shirt sleeves. When he got there, however, Rawlins introduced him to Grant, whose manner and looks struck the surgeon as a pleasant surprise — he was prejudiced against the General, he admitted, because the only picture he had ever seen of him was an absurd woodcut made at Cairo, more caricature than portrait, which showed Grant with a high felt hat and a beard reaching nearly to his waist. What he saw, now, was a neat, well-shaven officer, with the sort of hat anybody could wear, a grave but affable man who asked him to come upstairs and see his son. Ulysses Grant, Jr. — "Buck," to the family — was ten, and he had just been kicked by a horse. The surgeon attended to him, came back next day for a final visit, and went away feeling that both the General and Mrs. Grant were gracious and unassuming folk.[26]

In moments of relaxation, Grant liked to leave off his uniform and dress like a civilian. Mrs. William H. Cherry of Savannah, Tennessee, whose house Grant had used as headquarters before the battle of Shiloh, remembered that Grant once asked her to present him to her mother; knowing that the mother had firm

Southern loyalties, he wore civilian clothing, and when he was introduced he touched himself on the shoulder — where his insignia of rank would have appeared, if he had been in uniform — and remarked, "I thought you would like this best." A reporter noticed that Grant was in mufti at an Independence Day celebration in Memphis, and felt that he gave "a fair representation, to all outward appearance, of a well-to-do Southern planter." [27] Men remembered that headquarters was always cheerful when the Grant family was together. Grant spent much time with the children, who "used to play about and over and around the general by the hour," with neither General nor children saying a word.[28]

This was too good to last, and after little more than a fortnight Julia and the children left for St. Louis, to visit Mrs. Grant's father, old Colonel Dent. It was necessary to go to some place where the children could attend school during the fall and winter months; also, there were ominous signs of renewed Confederate activity in Mississippi, and Grant felt that it was time his family returned to a place of safety. He was feeling the strain, he frankly confessed, and he wished that he could go North too and get some rest, but it was not possible. Meanwhile, he had to admit that the responsibility of command had perhaps been good for him; since he left Cairo, at the end of January, he had gained fifteen pounds! [29]

By the end of July it was clear that Braxton Bragg was up to something. Colonel Phil Sheridan, now commanding a two-regiment brigade of cavalry, went roving south of Corinth, and he came back with disturbing news. Bragg's army had been based at Tupelo; now, Sheridan learned, he was moving up through northern Georgia in the direction of Chattanooga — moving roundabout, by way of Mobile, to take advantage of railroad transportation and avoid a long hike cross-country — and fresh troops under Price were active in northern Mississippi, spread out over the territory from Tupelo to Holly Springs. Sheridan raided a Confederate camp and seized a quantity of soldiers' letters, which expressed a new confidence: the Yankees were about to be attacked on the right and on the left, and would soon have to "skedaddle." Sheridan's activities impressed Rosecrans so much that he and some of his subordinates got off a telegram to Halleck urging that Sheridan be made a brigadier general: "He is worth his weight in gold." [30]

Observing the Federals' inaction, Bragg had formed a bold resolve. He would put the bulk of his forces around Chattanooga and would drive straight north for Kentucky and the Ohio river, gambling that the luckless Buell, wholly engrossed in railroad building operations, could be outmaneuvered. Price and Van Dorn would keep Grant busy, and with luck might be able to knock his scattered forces out of the way and go north to help Bragg. In any case, the Confederacy would be on the offensive, and if all went well everything that had been lost at Donelson, Shiloh and Corinth might presently be regained.

Grant's strength was not adequate for a decisive countermove. All told, he commanded 63,000 effectives, but most of the men were tied down on garrison duty. Two divisions, Sherman's and Hurlbut's, were at Memphis. General E. O. C. Ord was at Corinth with another division and McClernand was at Jackson, Tennessee, fifty-five miles to the north on the Mobile and Ohio Railroad. Several thousand men were posted in small detachments at various places in Tennessee and northern Mississippi. Brigadier General Isaac F. Quinby had nearly five thousand at Columbus, and Rosecrans with twenty-five thousand men occupied the line of the Memphis and Charleston in the general neighborhood of Iuka, east of Corinth. That was the lot, and there was very little flexibility. Buell had already called George Thomas's division away, and it seemed likely that he would need reinforcements in the near future. When Grant wired Halleck for permission to move forward and attack the Confederates in the area below Corinth, Halleck replied he could maneuver his forces as he saw fit, but that he must not scatter them because he might at any time be called on to send troops to Buell.[31]

For the moment, nothing could be done but mark time and maintain a vigilant watch. At one point Grant felt that the thing Washington had been dreading might actually be happening — the Confederates might be detaching troops from Mississippi for use in front of Richmond — and on August 7 he warned Halleck about it, remarking that the Price-Van Dorn contingents might be trying to do no more than "hold the Western army in check," but this delusion did not last long. Halleck himself believed that it would be possible for the Federals to open a new western campaign in the fall, but the fall was still some time away; "All we can hope to do for the next month is to hold our positions and prepare for an onward movement." [32] He added that the administration was very unhappy about Buell's "want of energy," and said frankly that Buell would soon be removed unless he accomplished something.

Meanwhile, there was the task of administering occupied territory. The people of Memphis continued to detest the Yankee invader, and they took no pains to hide their feeling. A newspaper correspondent said that the Memphis women were especially bitter, ostentatiously drawing their skirts aside whenever they had to pass a Union soldier on the street; employing a delicate euphemism, he wrote that the women of the town, "with a breadth of misapplied maternal attractions," would parade haughtily in the evening "in the fleeciest and scantiest of magnificence," each one usually accompanied by a little Negro girl carrying parasol and other minor impedimenta. But Sherman believed that he was getting things under control, and with his usual brutal frankness he wrote Grant about it in the middle of August:

> I find them [the people of Memphis] much more resigned and less presumptuous than at first. Your orders about property and mine about "niggers" make them feel that they can be hurt, and they are about as sensitive about their property as Yankees. I believe in universal confiscation and colonization. Some Union people have been expelled from Raleigh. I have taken some of the richest Rebels and will compel them to buy and pay for all of the land, horses, cattle and effects, as well as damages, and let the Union owner deed the property to one or more of them. This they don't like at all. [33]

Grant was supposed to be a man without nerves, but the strain of this summer was beginning to tell on him. He was moved, presently, to do something out of character: he arrested and imprisoned a newspaper reporter, and the incident tells something about the tense atmosphere which surrounded the camps of the occupying army.

The *Chicago Times* was notorious as a Copperhead paper, and its Memphis correspondent was one W. P. Isham, brother-in-law to Wilbur Storey, the paper's proprietor. Isham's reputation was bad. His room in the Gayoso Hotel at Memphis was considered a resort for local secessionists, and he was described by a hostile newspaper as "one of the still sort: has a mild blue eye, a pleasant face, his mouth always wears a secret, crafty smile." He had been sending North stories calculated to dishearten loyal Unionists, depicting Memphis as a city full of drunkenness and disease, cursed by a bad climate and an infected water supply, inadequately garrisoned in the face of rising Rebel strength. The story which moved Grant to hostile action was one which Isham filed late in July, describing the wholly imaginary arrival at Mobile of a fleet of ten English-built ironclad gunboats — impregnable vessels mounting from 10 to 30 guns apiece and sheathed in six-inch armor, whose appearance (according to Isham) broke the blockade and gave the Confederacy a naval force "of superior strength and weight of metal" to anything the Union possessed. Grant sent a clipping of the story to Sherman, with a note remarking that the story was "both false in fact and mischievous in character," and directing Sherman to "have the author arrested and sent to the Alton Penitentiary, under proper escort, for confinement until the close of the war, unless sooner discharged by competent authority."

Sherman complied willingly enough — he hated newspaper correspondents of all descriptions, and unquestionably would have been happy to arrest every reporter in Tennessee, loyal or otherwise — and the *Chicago Tribune* mentioned the action with approval. Isham's story, said the *Tribune*, was made up out of whole cloth; "There was design in it — to induce discouragement into the North at a critical time." So Isham went to Alton, under guard, and the *Times* sent down a reporter of a very different stripe to take his place, a former Milwaukee newspaperman named Sylvanus Cadwallader. Cadwallader ultimately persuaded Grant to order Isham's release; meanwhile, he established his own integrity as a reporter and in time became one of Grant's chosen intimates, winning for himself a place at headquarters that no other correspondent could match.[34]

But the significance of the incident remains. The North was rapidly approaching the most chancy period of the entire war. There was reason for despondency back home, and if the imperturbable little General in Tennessee was growing jumpy there was plenty in the war situation to make him so. As the summer of 1862 drew on toward autumn the Confederacy was reaching its high tide, and everything that the Union had won down to date seemed in a fair way to be lost forever.

CHAPTER FIFTEEN

Victory, and a New Plan

WHAT made Corinth important was the railroads. The great Memphis and Charleston line, the Confederacy's vital East-West axis, ran through here on its way to Chattanooga, and at Corinth it crossed the Mobile and Ohio, which linked Kentucky with the Gulf. With these roads securely held and with Corinth itself properly fortified, the mighty Union Army could digest its conquest of West Tennessee and, at its leisure, could gather strength for an irresistible new advance into a half-paralyzed South. Everything that had been done since Shiloh had been based on the belief that this would be so. Now, in the middle of the summer of 1862, this belief was being exposed as a massive error in judgment.

One trouble was that holding the railroads did not paralyze the Confederates in the least. On the contrary, it inspired them to a new activity, for it offered a wealth of targets which could be hit by small bands of guerillas (whose name was legion) or by detachments of roving cavalry. Simply to get the roads into operating condition kept thousands of Union soldiers so busy they had no time for anything else, and whatever they did could be undone, overnight, by a handful of Southerners. The army of occupation became half constabulary and half track-repair gang, and the main current of the war simply flowed out from under it.

Buell, moving east to take Chattanooga, was tied to the rail road, and two months after Corinth was occupied he still had not reached his goal, although his men had performed prodigies of road-building. (This did little good, because the road ran squarely across the Confederate front and it could be cut anywhere at a minor expenditure of Southern effort.) Grant was no better off; the line from Corinth to Memphis still was not open, the connecting lines farther to the rear were in little better shape, and the handiest way to get from Memphis to Corinth was to go up to Columbus, Kentucky, by steamboat and then to come down from Columbus by rail.

The guerillas were an expensive nuisance. Lacking cavalry, Grant had to shift whole infantry divisions about to meet them, an expedient that never worked because the swiftly moving Confederates refused to wait for the ponderous columns to arrive. Grant tried to extemporize a mounted force — his appeal for cavalry reinforcements having been turned down — by putting foot-soldiers on horses seized from Tennessee plantations, but this did little good.[1] His army's rear seemed no more secure than its front lines.

A painful illustration of this fact came on August 22, when Grant was obliged to report to Halleck that a guerilla detachment had captured one of his posts far back at Clarksville, on the Cumberland. This loss was especially irritating because of the way in which it came about. Clarksville had been garrisoned by six companies of the 71st Ohio, under Colonel Rodney Mason, and Mason had been one of the fainthearts who led his regiment off the field at Shiloh in the first shock of battle. He had come to Grant afterward, with tears in his eyes, begging for a chance to redeem himself, and Grant had put him at Clarksville. Now it developed that when a Rebel band surrounded this detachment and sent in a demand for surrender, Colonel Mason had taken counsel of his fears and his junior officers. He sent a subordinate out, under flag of truce, to count the Rebels who had surrounded him, and this man came back with the report that there were at least eight hundred of them, one company being horrendously "armed with volcanic rifles," by which it appears that the man meant repeaters. The juniors argued that the case was hopeless, Mason agreed, and the whole place was ingloriously surrendered. Mason and twelve of his juniors were promptly cashiered, by order of the President, but this did not help very much.[2]

Guerilla warfare in the rear was not only unsettling; it distracted attention from the front, and by the middle of August the Confederates were obviously up to something extensive. Their target was Buell's army rather than Grant's, but whatever happened to Buell would have an immediate effect on Grant — Halleck had already warned Grant that he must be prepared to give Buell some reinforcements — and by this time the Confederates had brought more soldiers east of the Mississippi and seemed inclined to strike at both armies. A Southern offensive of large dimensions was in fact getting under way, and for the moment there was nothing the Federals could do but wait for the blow to fall. Grant's army and Buell's were all but completely immobilized, and Braxton Bragg had worked out a plan to take advantage of this.

At Knoxville there were nearly twenty thousand Confederate troops led by Major General Edmund Kirby Smith, and in the middle of August these started north, outflanking the small Union force which held Cumberland Gap and forcing it to retreat, and driving on for the heart of Kentucky. Shortly after this, Bragg with nearly thirty thousand left Chattanooga — which he had reached long ahead of Buell's fumbling advance — and moved North, aiming to get into Buell's rear, to recapture Nashville if possible, and perhaps to move on into Kentucky and join forces there with Kirby Smith.[3] He had had strong cavalry detachments under John Morgan and Bedford Forrest raiding Buell's supply lines, and Buell's unhappy railroad-building activities came to a complete halt. Buell was in many ways the stuffiest of all Union generals, but he was also one of the unluckiest, and he was caught now in a pitiless vise. He had to keep step with Bragg, and for the moment Bragg was moving to a very lively tune. Not the least of the Federals' problems was the fact that Price and Van Dorn, in Mississippi, had between them nearly thirty thousand men. Some of these had to be retained for the defense of Vicksburg, but since most of Grant's men were tied down to fixed positions it would be quite possible for the Confederates in Mississippi to launch a mobile field army that would give Grant a great deal of trouble.

Bragg's and Kirby Smith's Confederates moved north with speed, and as they moved the whole Confederate war effort approached its high tide. In Virginia, Lee was pulverizing Pope and his makeshift Army of Virginia, and was going on into Maryland, meditating a slashing invasion of Pennsylvania. Bragg was hopeful that the Western contingents "may all unite in Ohio," and Halleck was frankly warning Grant that a junction of Price and Bragg in Tennessee or Kentucky "would be most disastrous." Buell demanded reinforcements, and Grant sent two divisions from Rosecrans, and realized that he might at any time have to send more. He was confident that he could hold Corinth, and he did not believe that the Price-Van Dorn combination could get past him into Tennessee, but he had nothing whatever to spare.[4]

The first result of all of this was that it completely wrecked Buell's railroad-building activities. He had gone toward Chattanooga with painful deliberation, partly because he was deliberate by nature and partly because Halleck considered that the Memphis and Charleston railroad, having been captured, ought to be used, and everything Buell's army had done since Corinth was taken had been keyed to the notion that the Union must at all costs keep, use and protect the long lines of track. Now, with Bragg swirling past him toward Kentucky, all of the summer's work was abandoned. The Confederacy was providing Union strategists with abundant proof that conquests made on the map mean nothing as long as enemy armies themselves are undefeated. The fact that Chattanooga was connected by railroad with both Corinth and Nashville amounted to very little, if the Federal armies at Corinth and Nashville should be defeated.

When the campaign began Confederate strategy was somewhat formless; Bragg, Van Dorn and Price were all independent, answerable only to Richmond, and in the beginning Bragg could do no more than urge Van Dorn and Price to keep active in Mississippi in order to help his own invasion. Price obediently moved up into northeastern Mississippi and occupied the town of Iuka, capturing Federal stores there, and Grant notified Halleck that although he believed this was only a feint intended to pin his own forces down, "sending so many troops away, may it not be turned into an attack?" What Grant feared was about to come true. President Davis put Price under Van Dorn's orders, and Van Dorn promptly began to plan a real attack.[5]

Grant's problem thickened. Buell was moving all the way up to Louisville — Bragg having outmarched him — and he needed more help. Raw troops from Ohio, Indiana and Illinois were being rushed down to his aid, but he needed veterans, and Grant had to send a third division, Gordon Granger's, from Rosecrans's force. With it, much to Grant's displeasure, went Phil Sheridan, who was about to be made a brigadier general. Granger was assigning Sheridan to the command of an infantry brigade, and Sheridan, eager for combat service, was delighted with the assignment; Grant met him at the railroad station where Granger's troops were getting on the cars for the move north and tried to persuade him to remain at Corinth. Sheridan angrily refused, and bystanders saw the two generals, who later were to become so intimate, arguing hotly. Grant lost the argument and Sheridan went north.[6] He had already shown himself to be a highly capable cavalry leader; in Kentucky he would win distinction leading an infantry division for Buell in the battle of Perryville.

By now Buell was living on borrowed time. Washington was profoundly displeased at his inability to keep Bragg out of Kentucky, and Halleck told Major General Horatio Wright, who was in command along the Ohio River, that "unless he [Buell] does something very soon I think he will be relieved." He added a comment describing the new pressures which would hereafter rest on all Federal commanders: "The Government seems determined to apply the guillotine to all unsuccessful generals. It seems rather hard to do this where the general is not in fault, but perhaps with us now, as in the French revolution, some harsh measures are required." The true harshness of these measures became visible to Buell late in September, when a War Department messenger gave him orders removing him from command and ordering him to turn his army over to Thomas. These orders were suspended, at Thomas's request: Thomas pointed out that Buell had laid plans to bring the invaders to battle, that he himself had not become familiar with those plans, and that a change in commanders right now might be ruinous. For the time being the orders were suspended and Buell retained his position, but it was clear that one more mistake would end his career.[7]

Grant, meanwhile, had lost three divisions from his army, and Price and Van Dorn were beginning to crowd him. When he sent Granger's troops to Kentucky he won Halleck's permission to abandon the railroad east of Corinth — the whole railroad from Corinth to Chattanooga, object of an entire summer's work, was thus given up — and Grant had to regroup his remaining troops to protect his own communications and the few places which it seemed essential to hold. In effect, he divided his troops into three principal detachments. At Memphis there was Sherman, holding that important river port and the immediately adjacent territory; in the center, guarding the north-south railroad line, there was Ord, a solid soldier who was rising in Grant's estimation; and in the Corinth area there was Rosecrans, with three infantry divisions, two brigades of a fourth, and a quota of cavalry and artillery. Grant established his own headquarters at Jackson, on the Mobile and Ohio fifty-five miles north of Corinth. At this time he had, all told, something like forty-five thousand men in his command. Slightly more than half of these were available in the forward areas to meet Van Dorn and Price.[8]

By the middle of September the Federal cause looked shaky. In Maryland, Lee had captured the Harpers Ferry garrison from the Union and was about to fight the great battle of Antietam. Of the other Confederate generals, Bragg was in mid-Kentucky, Kirby Smith seemed to be menacing Cincinnati, and Price, at Iuka, might be on the verge of slipping past Grant's flank and moving on toward the Ohio River; Van Dorn, meanwhile, was fifty miles west of Corinth, meditating an attack on either that town or Memphis. Even more than during the week of Gettysburg ten months later, the agonizing crisis of the war was at hand.

While Lee and McClellan were fighting along Antietam Creek, Grant made plans to defeat Price. Rosecrans, with 9000 men, was to swing out and come in on Iuka from the south; Ord, meanwhile, with about 8000, was to attack Iuka from the west, and Grant confidently wrote Halleck "I think it will be impossible for Price to get into Tennessee." Actually, Grant was hopeful that this two-pronged attack might destroy Price's entire command. He himself moved with Ord. At the same time he ordered Hurlbut to make a demonstration south and east from the Memphis area and to create the impression that a strong Federal column was going to march down into the Yazoo Delta country. It was hoped that this would impress Van Dorn and keep him from coming to Price's rescue.

Grant's plan to bag Price's little army at Iuka was good, on paper, but it was a little too ambitious. It involved bringing two separated bodies of troops together on the field of battle, which is always a risky operation, and the maneuver was to be done in a rough, broken country whose inadequate roads made communication between the columns almost impossible. Ord's troops had a hard march, groping along a narrow road in a swamp, where heavy bushes and a tangle of decayed logs constricted all movement. They remembered, once, how Grant tried to ride past the marching column, found that his horse was spattering the soldiers with mud, and left the road to pick his way through the underbrush, not returning to the road until he had reached the head of the column. An Ohio private recalled that the men were ready to cheer him for this considerate act, and wrote that the little incident "shows the kind of man on whose shoulders the greatest responsibilities were to be placed." [9] Grant and Ord finally got their men in position a short distance west of town, and Price marshaled his own troops to give battle.

The plan was for Ord to attack on the morning of September 19, with Rosecrans coming up from the south and west and taking Price's troops in the flank, and if it had gone according to schedule Price might well have been annihilated. As usually happens with plans of this kind, however, things did not go according to schedule. Grant got word that Rosecrans had been delayed, and told Ord to wait; they would attack when they heard the sound of Rosecrans's guns, and not before. Rosecrans, meanwhile, gained position a mile or two southwest of Iuka during the afternoon and began to form line of battle; and Price, realizing the trap that was about to be sprung, pulled away from Ord's front and moved down just before evening to break his way through Rosecrans's line.

An uncommonly sharp little battle developed, and some freak of atmospheric conditions perverted the acoustics. Not a sound reached Grant and Ord; and while Rosecrans's troops were fighting desperately, the column that was to have co-operated with them rested on its arms a few miles away, with Grant and Ord wondering why Rosecrans was not getting into position and opening the battle. Rosecrans had sent a courier with word that he was on the edge of Iuka, but the message did not reach Grant until after night-fall.

Rosecrans had not actually reached his chosen battle position when Price struck him, and the bulk of the Confederate attack was borne by the Union advance, a brigade of Brigadier General C. S. Hamilton's division. General Hamilton wrote afterward that he never saw "a hotter or more destructive engagement," and said that Price's unaccountable hesitancy in opening the action was all that saved the Federals from defeat, since the delay gave just time enough to get the Federal regiments out of march-ing column and into line. Men in the 11th Ohio battery, drawn up to repel the anticipated Confederate charge, found the waiting hard to bear. They could see their enemy massed for the attack, and the gunners muttered: "Why in hell can't we let them have it?" A sergeant complained: "My God, they're coming right here in the bush and are going to gobble the whole damned caboodle and shooting match of us, and damned quick if we don't mind, before we strike a damned lick." Then the shooting started, Hamilton sent frantic messengers back to Rosecrans for reinforcements, and the 11th Ohio battery lost forty-eight men, ending the day with no more than one cannoneer to a gun. Colonel Joe Mower, a giant of a man who was beginning to develop into one of the army's most gifted combat soldiers, led a brigade for-ward in a bayonet attack, and when darkness came the line was just held. Rosecrans called a midnight council of his brigade and division commanders, feeling that a fresh Rebel attack at dawn might over-whelm him; he cried bitterly "Where in the name of God is Grant?" and concluded that his only salvation was to make a bayonet charge at the moment of dawn. David Stanley, commanding the first division, remarked glumly: "I feel that I shall be killed to-morrow, but your order shall be obeyed," and then retired to his blanket for a brief sleep.[10]

But with dawn the menace was gone. In his advance on Iuka, Rosecrans had left uncovered one road to the south, and during the night Price used it, getting his army away and then moving west in a forced march to rejoin Van Dorn. The Federals had Iuka, the battle went into the books as a victory, it was no longer possible for Price to get around Grant's flank and go north toward Kentucky — but his army had not been destroyed, and Grant's elaborate enveloping movement had failed. It was clear that Price and Van Dorn together would make a new assault, sooner or later, and during the following ten days it became equally obvious that when this attack came it would strike Corinth.

A fight for Corinth would be Rosecrans's fight, mostly, and the Army figured that the fight would be in good hands. Rosecrans was big, burly, a devout Roman Catholic who nevertheless had a good command of profane idiom in the heat of battle, a tireless excitable officer who, in the jargon of the time, "looked after his men." It was recalled fondly that at a regimental inspection held not long after he took command, "Old Rosy" came upon one private soldier whose shoes were badly worn. He demanded why the soldier let himself wear such trashy equipment, and the soldier replied that he had asked for new shoes but had not received them. Raising his voice for all to hear, Rosecrans announced that the man should demand shoes of his first sergeant, go on from there to his company commander and thence, if need be, to regimental, brigade and divisional command; and if he still did not get shoes he was to come to Rosecrans himself. There were plenty of shoes in the warehouse, Rosecrans declaimed, and all hands ought to raise a fuss until the shoes were properly issued. It was told, too, how the new shelter tents, popularly called "pup tents," had been issued early that fall, and how the men did not like them; in one brigade the men put up derisive signs over their cramped new homes — PUPS FOR SALE . . . RAT TERRIERS . . . DOG HOLE No. 1 . . . SONS OF BITCHES WITHIN and so on. Rosecrans and his staff came riding through the camp and saw all of this, and the general threw back his head and roared with red-faced laughter. It was known, too, that Rosecrans was certain to appear on the front lines when there was fighting. General Hamilton had complained that the commanding general was hard to find when the battle opened at Iuka, but the men insisted that he always got up where there was shooting and said that the sight of him there, fearless amid flying bullets, steadied them and helped them behave as good soldiers should. An Illinois soldier said that Grant was well-liked and "could get more votes than any other man for commander of the army — always excepting Rosey." [11]

Grant had welcomed Rosecrans's appointment, and although he was somewhat disillusioned with him for the performance at Iuka — the Rebel army had got away, and for Grant that made the battle very imperfect — he trusted him as a solid fighting man, and when it became clear that the Rebels were going to try to take Corinth Grant was content to leave the defense in Rosecrans's hands.[12]

Corinth was ringed by massive fortifications built during the spring, fieldworks extensive enough to accommodate a large army; these were far too big for the numbers now available, and Grant had had new works built, close to town, far inside of the old works. When October began, Old Rosy was planted here, with something more than twenty thousand men, and when Van Dorn and Price led an army of approximately equal size down from the northwest the Federals were ready.

They needed to be ready, because defeat at Corinth would in all probability cost the Union all of West Tennessee; and Grant's army might find itself hastening back to Kentucky, where Buell was painfully maneuvering in the hope of bringing Bragg's army to battle. Lee's invasion of Maryland had, by this time, ended in defeat; President Lincoln, taking heart from it, was issuing his preliminary proclamation of emancipation, but to lose West Tennessee while Bragg and Kirby Smith still were on the loose near the Ohio River would be as heavy a blow as the Union cause could easily absorb.

Grant remained back in the vicinity of Jackson, where he was in relatively close communication with all three segments of his army, and Rosecrans prepared to give battle. He had three divisions in line north and west of the town, with a fourth held in reserve, and his advance skirmish line occupied the old works which Beauregard had built, two miles or more from the inner line. The Confederates showed up on the morning of October 3, Van Dorn's battle line collided with the Federal skirmishers, and the battle was on.

It was a hot fight, from the moment it began. The skirmish line put up a stiff resistance, and two of Rosecrans's four divisions moved up in support. Going forward, they lost contact with each other, and the advancing Confederates got in between them and broke them, inflicting heavy losses and driving the Federals back to the inner line of defense. Rosecrans tried to swing his right around — Hamilton's division, which had been so heavily engaged at Iuka — to strike the advancing Rebels in the flank, but his orders were poorly worded, Hamilton had to ask for a clarification, and by the time the misunderstanding was straightened out darkness had come and any further fighting would have to wait until the next day. Rosecrans held council with his division commanders, drew his force into a compact semicircle with strong redoubts for anchors, and rode the whole length of his front to make sure that all of his troops were where they were supposed to be.

The day had been hot, and water was scarce. Federal wagons loaded with water barrels went lumbering along the lines during the night, giving drink to exhausted soldiers; fires were not allowed, so no one could cook anything to eat, and the men were too weary to dig entrenchments. Rosecrans himself did not reach his cot at headquarters until after three in the morning, and his sleep was short. At 4:30 the Confederate batteries opened, Union batteries fired in reply, and the battle was renewed. Van Dorn was not able to get his infantry forward as promptly as he had hoped, but by ten o'clock or thereabouts he got things moving and his Confederate brigades came on in a charge which, for a time, looked as if it would drive the Federals all the way to the Tennessee River. One of the stout Union battery positions was lost, recaptured, and then lost again, and the dazed cannoneers who lost their guns said that before they were driven away they had been firing in three different directions at once. Cheering Confederates swept on past the captured battery and got all the way into Corinth, and there was sharp, confused fighting in the streets of the little town. At one time it was rumored that the army's reserve artillery had been captured, and baggage and commissary trains were hastily driven out of reach. Then some of the beaten Federal regiments rallied; a brigade from Hamilton's division made a hot counterattack; the Confederates were driven back out of the town and the lost battery was recaptured.

Bitterest fighting of the day centered around a Federal redoubt known as Battery Robinette, over on the left of the inner defense line. Before the battle the Federals had cut down all of the trees for several hundred yards in front of this place, to give the guns a field of fire, and across the stumps and logs which littered this clearing came a solid mass of Confederates, making an attack which drew postwar tribute from Rosecrans himself: "It was as good fighting on the part of the Confederates as I ever saw." Rocked back by heavy musket fire, the Southerners huddled in the down timber, keeping up a hot fire of their own; then they sprang up and renewed the advance, and a Union officer watched, fascinated, as a Texas colonel led his men straight up to the battery — "He looked neither right nor left, neither at his own men nor at mine, but with eyes partly closed, like one in a hail storm, was marching slowly and steadily upon us." This Texas colonel got clear into the battery, and died amidst the guns. Five Confederate color bearers were shot down, and men who could not get over the parapet stayed in the ditch just outside and tried to keep up the fight.

But the Union fire was too intense. One of the Confederates who tried to hold his ground in the ditch wrote afterward that "it seemed that by holding out my hand I could have caught a dozen bullets." He and the others got up to run for it, most of them being shot down as they ran — and suddenly the climax of the battle was over, and the men who had charged so furiously were in full retreat. Van Dorn drew his mangled army away, and the Federals, too exhausted to pursue, let them get away unmolested. The battle of Corinth was over.[13]

Considering the relatively small size of the armies engaged, it had been one of the sharpest battles of the war. Rosecrans had lost 2500 men, and Confederate losses ran close to 5000, including a substantial number of prisoners. Rosecrans himself had been all over the place, and at the end of the action he had bullet holes in his clothing and blood on his gauntlets, a mounted aide having been shot at his side. Ohio soldiers who defended Battery Robinette said that immediately after the final Confederate repulse

Rosecrans rode up to them, took off his hat, and announced that he was baring his head in tribute to brave men. His reputation as a general who liked to get up into the fighting zone had been abundantly justified, and his care for his men was illustrated by the order he issued as soon as the Confederates began their retreat: his troops were to return to their camps, get some sleep, stock up with five days' rations, and prepare to take up the pursuit the next morning, October 5.[14]

It was this last act which displeased General Grant, and which led to a permanent coolness between himself and Rosecrans. Grant was never interested in simply making an enemy army retreat; he always wanted it destroyed, and he had done what he could to make sure that Van Dorn could never use his army again. While the battle was going on Grant had ordered General McPherson, then at Jackson, to pick up four regiments of infantry guarding the railroad line near Jackson and hurry down to Corinth, and McPherson and his improvised brigade reached the town just after the fighting ended on October 4. Meanwhile, Grant had taken steps to cut off Van Dorn's retreat. To reach his base at Holly Springs, which is sixty-five air-line miles west of Corinth, Van Dorn had to follow poor roads and make several difficult river crossings. Grant had Hurlbut's division posted at Bolivar, a railroad town some forty-five miles northwest of Corinth, and on the morning of October 4, before the battle at Corinth had been decided, Grant ordered Hurlbut to march cross-country to the town of Pocahontas, on the Memphis and Charleston railroad, and sent Ord down to assume command. By evening of October 4, therefore, it seemed to Grant that with good management Van Dorn and his army should be captured; Ord was in front of him and Rosecrans was close behind, and it should be very hard for him to escape. Grant sent Halleck a confident dispatch: "At this distance everything looks favorable, and I cannot see how the enemy are to escape without losing everything but their small arms." [15]

But nothing went right. Van Dorn had halted for the night at Chewalla, no more than ten miles from Corinth, and Rosecrans moved after him on the morning of October 5, with McPherson in the lead; but the march was poorly handled, there was some mixup about the roads, and the Federals got into a traffic jam at a crossroads which delayed them so badly that by evening they had got no farther than Chewalla, which of course Van Dorn had left early that morning. Ord, meanwhile, had planted himself on the banks of the Hatchie river, squarely across Van Dorn's line of march, and there he fought a brisk little action with Van Dorn's advance guard, believing that Rosecrans would at any moment be pitching into the Confederate rear. Rosecrans was too far away, however; Ord was severely wounded in the fighting, and Van Dorn was eventually able to break off the action, march upstream six miles, and make a crossing unopposed. In the end he got away clean, and Rosecrans, picking up Hurlbut's division, plodded after him. Van Dorn reached Holly Springs in safety, and Grant ordered Rosecrans, who was thirty miles east of Holly Springs, to break off the pursuit and come back to Corinth.

Rosecrans protested vigorously — so much so that Grant referred the question to Halleck, by telegraph. Halleck told Grant to use his own judgment, but expressed surprise at Grant's order, suggesting that the chase might well be continued, with the Federal army living off the country, requisitioning supplies as it went along. Grant stuck to his decision, Rosecrans grumpily brought his troops back to Corinth, and the campaign was over.

Grant's reasoning was clear, even though the decision he made may not have been one he would have made six months later.

His original belief had been that Rosecrans and Ord, between them, could catch Van Dorn's army while it was still in flight and either capture it or scatter it so effectively that it would be practically destroyed. Once Van Dorn got to Holly Springs the case would be very different; there were reinforcements there, and fieldworks, and the Union Army would be compelled to fight a regular battle, on ground of its enemy's choosing, a long way from its own base. The thing might possibly work, but Grant thought it would be more likely to lead to disaster. It is possible to suspect that the lesson of the Shiloh campaign was on Grant's mind. Beauregard had not been effectively pressed, when he retreated after that battle; when, at last, he was followed down to Corinth, an entirely new campaign was involved, and the opportunity offered by a disorganized retreat had vanished.

"An army," Grant told Halleck, "cannot subsist itself on the country except in forage." This was an idea which Grant himself would abandon, some months later, but he had not yet learned what could be done by an army that boldly cut loose from its base in an area as full of foodstuffs as northern Mississippi. In his wire to Halleck, Grant did make one further point: "If you say so, however, it is not too late yet to go on, and I will join the moving column and go to the farthest extent possible. Rosecrans has been reinforced with everything at hand, even at the risk of this road [the Mobile and Ohio] against raids." [16] In other words, his considered judgment was against the move, but if Halleck wanted it made he would take on the job himself and fight it to a finish.

However much soreness the incident may have created between Grant and Rosecrans, the administration and the country were satisfied. President Lincoln sent congratulations to Grant, and no one but Grant seems to have been bothered very much by the fact that the Confederates, twice beaten, had been able to get their troops away safely. The Union cause, which had been in such a dire situation in September, was beginning to look much better. Lee's invasion of Maryland had been defeated, the Confederate blow at Western Tennessee had failed, and now Bragg's invasion of Kentucky was coming to nothing. On October 8, Bragg and Buell fought a bloody, indecisive battle at Perryville, forty miles southwest of Lexington, and after this fight all of Bragg's driving energy left him. He had missed his big chance, the Kentuckians had not given him the warm support which he had expected — he commented bitterly that "The people have too many fat cattle and are too well off to fight" [17] — and now he abandoned his campaign and marched back into Tennessee. Kirby Smith withdrew likewise, and the great Confederate counteroffensive was over.

If Bragg had woefully disappointed Confederate expectations, Buell had done no better with Northern hopes. The administration believed that Bragg should be followed and roundly beaten and that the old dream of Federal occupation of East Tennessee could at last be realized; and when the methodical Buell showed that he was quite unlikely to fulfill either of these hopes he was finished. On October 24, the War Department relieved him of his command, and Rosecrans — made major general in reward for his victory at Corinth — was named to succeed him.

This pleased both Grant and Rosecrans, who were finding it increasingly hard to work together. Rosecrans blamed Grant's staff, believing that "the mousing politicians" there were working successfully to make Grant jealous of his subordinate. Not long after the battle of Corinth, Grant had chided Rosecrans for letting his own staff plant newspaper stories implying that Rosecrans's army was independent of Grant; Rosecrans had denied this with some heat, ending with the assertion: "If you do not meet me with the frank avowal that you are satisfied, I shall consider that my ability to be useful in this department has ended." To Halleck, Rosecrans confided: "I am sure those politicians will manage matters with the sole view of preventing Grant from being in the background of military operations. This will make him sour and reticent. I shall become uncommunicative, and that, added to a conviction that he lacks administrative ability, will complete other reasons why I should be relieved from duty here." [18]

To Grenville Dodge, Grant said that Rosecrans's promotion was a good thing. Grant believed that Rosecrans was insubordinate, Dodge recalled, saying that the man had some fundamental reluctance to respond to the orders of a superior; as an independent army commander, however, Grant thought Rosecrans ought to do very well. One of Grant's aides told Sherman that Rosecrans's transfer was "greatly to the relief of the general, who was very much disappointed in him," and such generals as McPherson and Hurlbut had made bitter complaints about the handling of the pursuit of Van Dorn. Julia Grant was at the Jackson headquarters for a time, late in October, and she received a number of these complaints. Long afterward, Dodge said Mrs. Grant told him that Grant had made up his mind to relieve Rosecrans from duty, and that when the telegram announcing the new assignment was received Grant brought it to her with the remark that his greatest trouble was over. Dodge believed that one thing that set Grant against Rosecrans was Rosecrans's public criticism of Brigadier General Thomas Davies's division, whose line had been broken in the first day's fighting at Corinth. The core of this unit was the division

C. F. Smith had led at Fort Donelson, and it was a pet outfit of Grant's; assigning Dodge to the command of it, shortly after Corinth, Grant told him, "I want you to understand that you are not commanding a division of cowards." [19]

If Rosecrans's assignment pleased both Rosecrans and Grant, it was not quite so pleasing to George H. Thomas. Although Thomas had refused to take Buell's place when it was offered to him a month earlier, he did not consider that he had permanently declined it, and when the job went to Rosecrans his feelings were hurt. With great dignity, Thomas stated his case in a letter to Halleck. Early in the fall of 1861, he pointed out, he had promised to occupy East Tennessee if given twenty thousand men. The twenty thousand had not been given him, East Tennessee had not been occupied, and Thomas still believed he could have done what he had promised to do; and, in any case, during the year "I performed my duty patriotically and faithfully and with a reasonable amount of credit to myself," and now he was "deeply mortified and aggrieved." He made it clear that he was not demanding the army command; what wounded him was the fact that an officer junior to him in rank should be placed over him.

Halleck assuaged him with a friendly letter, in which he pointed out that Rosecrans's new rank of major general had been dated back in such a way that he was now in fact Thomas's senior. Thomas immediately withdrew his protest. He was no self-seeker, and once it was made clear that the government was not going out of its way to slight him he had no complaint: "I have no objection whatever to serving under General Rosecrans now that I know his commission dates prior to mine." [20]

Meanwhile it was time to get on with the war. The Federals had regained the initiative which had been lost early in the summer, and each Northern army was planning to take the offensive. Grant was evolving plans of his own — at the moment, they involved nothing much more concrete than a determination to get to grips with his enemies to the southward — but he could not do much unless he could get more men. If the Corinth affair had done nothing else it had clearly shown that the Union forces in West Tennessee were badly under strength.

Halleck would be helpful if he could. In the middle of October Grant's district was designated a full-fledged military department; it would include Cairo, Forts Henry and Donelson, western Kentucky and Tennessee, and as much of northern Mississippi as Grant could get, and Grant was named as its commander.[21] Halleck in far-off Washington seemed to be a more understanding superior than Halleck in Tennessee; the day of the petty pin-prickings seemed to be over — one reason, perhaps, being that Grant himself had learned a little more about his own job. In any case, if Grant could take the offensive Washington would support him.

In the middle of September, Halleck had notified Grant that the Rebels were believed to be building ironclad gunboats somewhere on the Yazoo river, and he had suggested that Grant consult with the Navy people and with General Frederick Steele, who commanded Union forces in Arkansas, and see whether there might not be an expedition that would thwart this project. Grant worked out a scheme for an advance by his own army down the Mississippi Central Railroad, which ran south from Memphis just east of the rich Yazoo delta country. If Steele, with the Navy's help, could get some men across the river, while Grant seized the town of Grenada, one hundred miles below Memphis, the thing might work. But before he could do anything Grant would have to be reinforced.[22]

All of this was being planned at the very height of the scare raised in the north by Bragg's presence in Kentucky, when Middle Western governors were being urged to send all the recruits they could get to Louisville to help defeat the invader. Even so, Grant's appeal was approved, and Halleck told Wright, commanding along the Ohio, to ear-mark some of the new regiments at Cairo for Grant's department. Between the battles of Iuka and Corinth Grant made a quick trip to St. Louis to arrange for co-operation from west of the Mississippi.

For the moment, nothing came of this Yazoo expedition, but it helped to set a pattern. The idea of a two-pronged advance down the Mississippi took root; also, both Sherman and Grant began to wonder whether holding all of the Tennessee railroads might not be costing a good deal more than it was worth. While the battle of Corinth was in progress, Sherman wrote to Grant about it:

. . . I am daily more and more convinced that we should hold the river absolutely and leave the interior alone. Detachments inland can always be overcome or are at great hazard, and they do not convert the people. They cannot be made to love us, but may be made to fear us, and dread the passage of troops through their country. With the Mississippi safe we could land troops at any point and by a quick march break the railroad, where we could make ourselves so busy that our descent would be dreaded the whole length of the river, and by the loss of Negroes and other property they would in time discover that war is not the remedy for the political evils of which they complained. . . . We cannot change the hearts of those people of the South, but we can make war so terrible that they will realize the fact that however brave and gallant and devoted to their country, still they are mortal and should exhaust all peaceful remedies before they fly to war.[23]

Grant was never addicted to reading lectures on changing Southerners' hearts, making war terrible and teaching an enduring lesson, but his ideas about the way to penetrate the deep South were changing. It seems likely that the war did not look quite as simple to him now as it had looked earlier. He had believed, originally, that the Confederacy would collapse after one or two defeats, and that most Southerners were not really committed to the fight. Then he had thought that a quick, slashing follow-up after the victory at Fort Donelson would settle things. By the books, this should have been so, but this war was being fought by no book anyone had ever seen before, and Grant was not quite ready to desert military orthodoxy entirely. He was beginning to see, however, that to occupy western Tennessee and try to make use of all of its railroads was to devote most of his muscle to purely defensive duties, and this he wanted to stop; and on October 26 he tried to put his thoughts on paper in a dispatch to Halleck.

No plan of operations, he pointed out, had yet been suggested from Washington, and Grant had no way of knowing what the other Federal armies were going to do. At the moment he could do little more than defend his position, and he did not feel at liberty to abandon any occupied place without Halleck's consent. Still, he would suggest:

Destruction of the railroads to all points of the compass from Corinth . . . and the opening of the road from Humboldt to Memphis. The Corinth forces I would move to Grand Junction, and add to them the Bolivar forces except a small garrison there. With small re-enforcements at Memphis I think I would be able to move down the Mississippi Central road and cause the evacuation of Vicksburg and to be able to capture or destroy all the boats in the Yazoo river.

This, clearly, was a proposal to reverse all of the strategic planning that had gone on since the Federals first occupied Corinth. To hold the railroad network was to immobilize most of the Army: give it up, then, occupy the railroad junction of Humboldt so as to give Memphis a railway connection with Columbus and the interior, base the main army just north of the Mississippi border halfway between Memphis and Corinth, and then drive south along one railway line, using it for supplies. Vicksburg and the Yazoo Delta area could be cut off and could be occupied at leisure. This, three weeks after Van Dorn's defeat, was Grant's suggestion.[24]

Grant got no answer to this proposal, but his concept of the job before him was taking form. In the weeks ahead he would amplify it, and then he would try to act on it. The one complication which was still to be revealed centered around a seemingly insignificant little fact: Major General John McClernand, the doughty Illinois politician, had taken leave of absence in the middle of August and had gone to Washington to consult with Mr. Lincoln. What Grant finally would do in the Mississippi Valley would have to be adjusted to fit that fact.

CHAPTER SIXTEEN

Forrest, Van Dorn and McClernand

J OHN A. McCLERNAND, formerly a Democratic Congressman from Illinois and currently Major General of Volunteers with a good combat record, was ambitious, cantankerous and energetic, and he thoroughly understood Middle Western politics. He realized that a serious political crisis was building up in the great farm belt north of the Ohio River, and although this crisis demanded a military solution he doubted that the professional soldiers would ever provide it. In a year and a half of war the professionals had not managed to break the Confederate grip on the lower Mississippi River, and McClernand believed that this grip was inexorably strangling the life out of the Middle West's willingness to go on with the war for Union. Getting leave of absence in the late summer of 1862, McClernand went to Washington to present his views to President Lincoln and Secretary Stanton. As a result, the war in the West was about to undergo a far-reaching change.

McClernand's argument was simple. The great outlet for the huge surplus of grain and meat raised in the Middle West had always been the Mississippi. This outlet was closed, and the West now had to rely on the East-West railroad lines, supplemented by steamboats and schooners on the Great Lakes. The railroad men, monopolists devoid of conscience, had raised freight rates to an extortionate degree, which was fine for Eastern financiers and industrialists but ruinous to the Middle West. Resenting this, Westerners were beginning to elect anti-war men to Congress; before long they might even produce a new political party, which would consent to Southern independence if the Southerners would agree to reopen the river, and which might eventually work for secession of the Western states themselves. Therefore, said McClernand, unless the government wanted to lose the war it had better do something drastic to clear the river.[1]

McClernand was not the only man who was thinking along these lines. The cabinet had discussed the matter as early as August 3, and Acting Secretary of the Interior John P. Usher, of Indiana, had suggested the advisability of raising a special force to open the Mississippi. Secretary of the Treasury Salmon P. Chase, another Westerner, had warmly supported the proposal, and the cabinet had asked General Halleck about it. Halleck thought the river ought to be opened but did not like the notion of trying to do it with brand-new troops, and for the time being the project was dropped; but when McClernand got to Washington it was revived, and both President Lincoln and Secretary Stanton developed a strong enthusiasm for it.

A key feature of McClernand's proposal, of course, was the suggestion that the expedition be entrusted to McClernand himself. He was an all-out-war man and he was also a Western Democrat, and it seemed probable that in an area where there were many Democrats he could bring many new recruits into the Army; also, the President and the Secretary of War were in a mood just then to welcome any suggestion which involved direct action. It had begun to seem that the West Pointers were excessively deliberate men who did not like to fight, and the very word "strategy" had come to sound like an excuse for avoiding combat. Discouraged by the apparent lack of fighting spirit, Lincoln that fall wrote that "the army, like the nation, had become demoralized by the idea that the war is to be ended, the nation united and peace restored, by *strategy*, and not by hard desperate fighting." McClernand wanted to fight, he knew where to fight, and since he could also help to provide a new army the administration was ready to give his proposal substantial backing.[2]

There were reservations, to be sure. Secretary Chase consulted both Lincoln and Halleck about McClernand's fitness for the job, and Lincoln admitted that although the man was brave and capable he was very anxious to be independent of everybody else. Halleck agreed; McClernand had courage and ability, he said, but he was no disciplinarian, his chief trouble being that all of his officers and men were his political constituents. Colonel John E. Smith of the 45th Illinois wrote that McClernand was a politician rather than a soldier: "He has gerrymandered his division so as to give commands to his particular friends against not only the expressed wishes of officers but of all military precedent." Halleck himself bluntly told McClernand that he would not support the new scheme.

Grant did not want McClernand in his command, he told Halleck shortly after this time, because he was "unmanageable and incompetent," and when he wrote his Memoirs Grant stiffly said that he did not think McClernand had "either the experience or the qualifications" to fit him for an important job. But the administration was desperate. There were times when it seemed impossible to get the professional soldiers to do anything at all; Buell's record of inaction in the West seemed remarkably similar to the exasperating inactivity of McClellan in the East, and even Halleck was discouraged. To Governor Gamble of Missouri he was confessing that "I am sick, tired and disgusted with the condition of military affairs here in the East. . . . There is an immobility here that exceeds all that any man can conceive of. It requires the lever of Archimedes to move this inert mass." [3] McClernand at least proposed to do something, and he proposed to do it quickly, and the administration was prepared to go along with him.

Nevertheless, both Lincoln and Stanton hedged just a little. On October 20 Stanton gave McClernand a top-secret order, on which Lincoln wrote his own endorsement saying that he approved of McClernand's expedition and wanted it "pushed forward with all possible despatch"; but the order was curiously worded. It specified that McClernand was to visit Indiana, Illinois and Iowa, "to organize the troops remaining in those states and to be raised by volunteering or draft, and forward them with all dispatch to Memphis, Cairo or such other points as may hereafter be designated by the general-in-chief, to the end that, when a sufficient force not required by the operations of General Grant's command shall be raised, an expedition may be organized under General McClernand's command against Vicksburg, and to clear the Mississippi river and open navigation to New Orleans." A final paragraph stipulated that "the forces so organized will remain subject to the designation of the general-in-chief, and be employed according to such exigencies as the service in his judgment may require." [4]

There was a big loophole in all of this. McClernand was to have an independent command — if Grant did not need his men, and if Halleck finally approved. This compound qualification escaped McClernand's notice at the time, but it did not escape Halleck's; nor is there any reason to think that it was supposed to, since both Lincoln and Stanton were competent lawyers who knew how to write airtight documents when they chose to do so. The administration was definitely giving the Mississippi campaign top priority, but it was not really committed to McClernand.

The ultimate effect of this order would be to throw Halleck and Grant much closer together. Halleck had had reservations about Grant for a long time, but these would disappear altogether under the weight of the heavier reservations which he had in respect to McClernand. The idea of the campaign itself Halleck liked. Shortly after McClernand got his orders, Halleck wrote to Major General Nathaniel P. Banks saying that "our prospect for an early movement down the Mississippi is improving," and adding: "at the west, everything begins to look well again." [5]

For the moment, however, a situation had been created which would make Grant's task extremely confusing. McClernand's orders were secret, and Halleck was unable to give Grant any explanation of what was happening. Grant knew that something very odd was going on behind his back, but he had no way of finding out just what it was. Grant began what would become one of the most important campaigns of his life under conditions guaranteed to bewilder him.

There were plenty of rumors about McClernand's new assignment, but they were rumors and nothing more. All that Grant knew was that he himself was expected to plan and execute a new offensive, with the capture of Vicksburg and the final opening of the river as the objective, and he modeled his campaign on the formula that had been so successful down to date. During the past ten months the Mississippi had been opened from Cairo to a point below Memphis, and this had been done chiefly by an advance inland, parallel to the river but well removed from it. Grant had taken Forts Henry and Donelson, Buell had occupied Nashville, Grant and Buell together had defeated the Confederates at Shiloh, and then Halleck's combined host had gone on to Corinth, and this had flanked all of the river defenses. Columbus had fallen without a blow, Pope's success at New Madrid and Island Number Ten had been a clean-up operation rather than a full-fledged campaign, and although there had been a sharp naval battle in the river just above Memphis that city had really fallen because a large Federal army was in its rear. The way to take Vicksburg and open the remainder of the river seemed to call for a continuation of this sort of approach, and so as November began Grant prepared to move south along the line of the Mississippi Central Railroad, sixty or seventy miles east of the Mississippi River itself.

On November 2, Grant notified Halleck that he was beginning to mass his troops at Grand Junction, halfway between Memphis and Corinth. He would move on to Holly Springs, Mississippi, twenty-five miles to the south, and after that he would push for Grenada, eighty-four miles below Holly Springs. Sherman, at Memphis, was ordered to make a demonstration toward the southeast, to confuse the Rebels. Halleck endorsed the plan, saying "I hope for an active campaign on the Mississippi this fall," and promising reinforcements; on November 5 Halleck said that twenty thousand new troops would shortly be coming down to join Grant's command, and he suggested that they might as well go direct to Memphis. On learning this, Grant told Sherman to forget about the planned demonstration; the campaign had not yet got off the ground but it was obviously growing, since Federal troops at New Orleans were planning to make an advance upstream, and it seemed likely now that a contingent from Curtis's command in Arkansas would cross the river to co-operate with the southward drive from western Tennessee. Sherman had better stay at Memphis for a while, Grant said, and when he was able to assemble two full divisions he could then march down and join Grant's column. Grant estimated that the Confederates had approximately thirty thousand men somewhere in the neighborhood of Holly Springs, and Grant was not quite ready to tackle so large a group: "I cannot move from here with a force sufficient to handle that number without gloves." He would wait, therefore, until the picture got a little clearer, and when he moved Sherman would move with him.[6]

Grant was assembling a field army of considerable strength. Massed along the railroad he had McPherson, with two divisions, and Hamilton, with three, and for the first time he had a fair allotment of cavalry, which was driving Confederate patrols southward and clearing the way for an advance. The Confederate command picture, meanwhile, had changed. Van Dorn had been blamed for the defeat at Corinth, had been relieved of his command, and had demanded a court of inquiry, which presently would clear him of charges that he had handled his troops incompetently; the Confederate forces in Mississippi now were under Lieutenant General John C. Pemberton; Van Dorn would serve as Pemberton's chief of cavalry, and no less imposing a figure than General Joseph E. Johnston would soon be coming down with instructions to coordinate Pemberton's movements with those of Bragg, whose unhappy army was stationed in central Tennessee. Grant believed that as soon as he could bring Sherman and the reinforcements down from Memphis he could push south along the railroad to good effect.

There were, however, two very serious problems. One of these grew out of the rumors about McClernand. It was an open secret now that he was organizing a large new force north of the Ohio, and although Halleck saw to it that as fast as his fresh regiments were organized they were sent to places in Grant's department, while McClernand himself stayed in Springfield, it was beginning to be plain that some sort of amphibious movement of major proportions was going to go down the river from Memphis. Grant had planned nothing of the kind. Vicksburg was his objective, and Memphis was in his command, and he had to find out what McClernand was up to. On November 10 Grant sent a message to Halleck: "Am I to understand that I lie still here while an expedition is fitted out from Memphis, or do you want me to push as far south as possible? Am I to have Sherman move subject to my order, or is he and his forces reserved for some special service? Will not more forces be sent here?"

To this Halleck sent the cryptic but reassuring reply: "You have command of all troops sent to your department and have permission to fight the enemy where you please." [7] Halleck could not tell Grant what was up, but he obviously wanted him to get his campaign developed well enough so that it would take precedence over anything McClernand might be contemplating. As far as Grant was

concerned the picture still was very shadowy, but what he could
see looked encouraging. On November 14, after he had been given
a little additional information, he tried to explain the situation to
Sherman.

Halleck had told him, he said, that in addition to the troops already promised more would come down from Ohio and Kentucky,
all to be collected at Memphis. It seemed definite that some sort of
combined military and naval expedition would eventually move
from Memphis toward Vicksburg, and this, "taken in connection
with the mysterious rumors of McClernand's command, left me in
doubt as to what I should do." But Halleck had told him to keep
going — "fight the enemy my own way" — and Grant would act
on this direction. Sherman, accordingly, was to assemble his troops
and march overland to join Grant's army somewhere along the
Tallahatchie River, which crossed the railroad a little distance south
of Holly Springs. If Sherman could move with three divisions, that
would be fine; future plans would be developed once all the troops
were assembled.[8] By the end of November Sherman had made
the move, and Grant had his army south of Holly Springs, the
troops massed in three wings — Sherman, McPherson and Hamilton. Back home, news of the advance aroused enthusiasm, and the
Chicago Tribune, unaware of the behind-the-scenes maneuverings,
rejoiced that Grant was no longer tied to Halleck's leading string:
"Gen. Grant is invested with large discretionary powers and we
are sure that he will use it wisely. His forward movement is an
indication that he means work, and with him work is not bloodless
strategy but strategy that leads to hard fighting and decisive results. He is looking for the enemy and when he finds him there will
be bloodshed." [9]

Much more tangible than the problem raised by McClernand's
venture was the problem of supplying the advancing army. This
at bottom was a matter of the railroads. There still was no direct
connection between Grant's army in northern Mississippi and
Memphis, even though Memphis was no more than fifty miles
away. Food, ammunition and equipment for the army had to come
by boat to far-off Columbus, Kentucky, and from Columbus these
supplies had to come to Holly Springs by railroad — a two-hundred-
mile haul over a single-tracked line through hostile territory. When

he moved south along the line of the Mississippi Central, Grant's ultimate goal — if he wanted to capture Vicksburg and break the Confederates' blockade of the river — would be the Mississippi capital, Jackson, two hundred miles to the south, a scant forty-five miles due east of Vicksburg. His army was already dangling at the end of an extremely vulnerable supply line, and its position would get progressively worse as it advanced.

Chief quartermaster for the army at St. Louis was Robert Allen — the same whom Halleck had once thought of for Grant's own job; the same, also, who had helped Grant return from California to New York in 1854, when Grant badly needed help — and to Allen, in the middle of November, Grant sent word that he needed at least two hundred freight cars and six locomotives as soon as possible. He had nearly 30,000 men at Holly Springs and he would have from 10,000 to 15,000 more when Sherman reached him; he was keeping a reserve of 100,000 rations on hand, he proposed to double this as soon as possible, he had 800,000 rations in stock near Grand Junction; and he wanted two solid trainloads of grain brought down for his horses. All in all, the railroad was his lifeline, and Holly Springs was to be his advance base, and it was vital to keep it in good operating condition. Grant supplemented his wire to General Allen by revising his figures upward, notifying Halleck that he wanted twelve locomotives.

Back from Halleck came a surprising reply. The locomotives could not be had, because "it is not advisable to put railroads in operation south of Memphis. Operations in north Mississippi must be limited to rapid marches upon any collected forces of the enemy, feeding as far as possible upon the country. The enemy must be turned by a movement down the river from Memphis as soon as a sufficient force can be collected." To Allen, Halleck wrote to the same effect, saying that no cars or engines should be purchased except those needed for the roads already in operation.[10]

Considered in the light of what Grant knew at the time, this was nothing less than astounding. All spring and summer, Halleck's emphasis had always been on repairing and using the railroads. When Grant suggested that the network near the Mississippi border be abandoned Halleck had failed to approve, and Grant had set out, with Halleck's blessing, on an offensive which was directly dependent on railway transportation. Now he was being told that the railroads were not to be relied on, and his plan of campaign was being turned inside-out. Yet it was hard to get things explained. Grant wrote that he planned to attack Pemberton, that Sherman would be in his force, and that Steele with troops from beyond the Mississippi would cross the river so as to threaten Pemberton's flank: must this plan be countermanded? Halleck replied simply: "Proposed movements approved. Do not go too far." [11]

Grant moved. The anticipated Confederate resistance along the Tallahatchie River failed to materialize, and Grant got his army to the town of Oxford, thirty miles south of Holly Springs. Pemberton, as far as Grant could learn, had his troops grouped below the Yalobusha River, at Grenada, fifty miles farther on; Grant believed that he himself could go that far, pinning Pemberton in position there, and sending his cavalry under Colonel T. Lyle Dickey off on a swing to the east, to cut the state's other north-south railroad line at Tupelo and, if possible, to destroy the Confederate munitions plants at the Mississippi industrial city of Columbus. Meanwhile, if there was to be a move down the river from Memphis, he wanted the soldier he most relied on, Sherman, to lead it. Sherman, accordingly, taking one division with him and leaving his other two divisions with Grant, must return to Memphis, assemble the new troops that were gathering there, add to them if possible part of Steele's force from Arkansas, and (with the Navy's gunboats for escort) steam down the river to the mouth of the Yazoo, just north of Vicksburg. Then, if Grant kept Pemberton busy at Grenada, Sherman ought to be able to dislodge the Rebel garrison at Vicksburg, and in the end Pemberton and all his troops could be driven off into eastern Mississippi and then brought to battle.[12] Grant informed Halleck that heavy rains and flooded rivers had made Mississippi's roads almost impassable, and that he would be tied pretty closely to the railroad.

Halleck was dubious, and on December 5 he warned Grant that he probably ought not to try to hold the country south of the Tallahatchie; the troops that were to go down the river from Memphis must be ready to leave by December 20, and Grant's main purpose now must be to hold the line from Memphis to Corinth as economically as possibly and put all possible weight into the river expedition. Two days later, however, Halleck had a second thought. If Grenada could be taken, the prospect would be different; after all, Grant was to "move your troops as you may deem best to accomplish the great object in view."

Hidden beneath all of this there was a challenge to Grant's capacity for generalship, a challenge as searching as any which the war was to bring him. He had planned and begun a major campaign, Washington had suddenly changed the conditions under which the campaign was to be made; and now, with all of his plans needing revision because of deep political pressures painfully clear in Washington but utterly invisible along the line of the Mississippi Central, Washington was brightly telling him to do as he thought best and to go ahead and win. Six months earlier the same thing had happened to McClellan, in front of Richmond. Protesting bitterly against injustice, McClellan had stressed the military soundness of his own program . . . and had lost. Now it was Grant's turn, and he could either butt his head against the wall or adapt his plan to necessity. The real challenge was that he make the best of a bad situation instead of building up a record showing that its badness was not of his making. On December 8, Grant sent Halleck a summary of his plans, dating his dispatch from Oxford, Mississippi:

> General Sherman will command the expedition down the Mississippi. He will have a force of about 40,000 men. Will land above Vicksburg, up the Yazoo, if practicable, and cut the Mississippi Central railroad and the railroad running east from Vicksburg where they cross Black river. I will co-operate from here, my movements depending on those of the enemy. With the large cavalry force now at my command I will be able to have them show themselves at different points on the Tallahatchie and Yalobusha, and where an opportunity occurs make a real attack. After cutting the two railroads General Sherman's movements to secure the ends desired will necessarily be left to his own judgment. I will occupy this railroad to Coffeeville [a point seventeen miles short of Grenada].

Back from Halleck came a word of caution, with a veiled warning that the White House might upset Grant's command arrangements:

Do not make the Mississippi expedition so large as to endanger West Tennessee. I think 25,000 men, in addition to the forces to be added from Helena, sufficient; but send more if you can spare them. The President may insist upon designating a separate commander; if not, assign such officers as you deem best. Sherman would be my choice as the chief under you.[13]

McClernand's shadow was growing larger. On December 1 he had written to Stanton, explaining that the job he was doing in Illinois was about finished and suggesting that it was nearly time he himself went to Memphis to take command. On December 12, he told Lincoln that he had sent forward fully forty thousand men, forty-nine regiments of infantry and two batteries. There was little to be done at Springfield that could not be left to a good staff man, and it was time to get the Vicksburg expedition moving; "May I not ask therefore to be sent forward immediately?" Halleck, meanwhile, was dragging his feet. His official position was that he knew nothing definite about the President's plans and that in the absence of specific orders he would let things follow their normal course. General Curtis, in St. Louis, seeing some of his own troops detached for the Vicksburg move, had written to Halleck saying that he would rather like to take charge of this movement himself, and Halleck wrote a smooth answer: "In regard to the proposed expedition down the Mississippi and its commander I can give you no reply. I have been informed that the President has selected a special commander and that instructions have been or will be given to him by the War Department. If so they have not been communicated to me, and until I receive them I shall consider the officer of the highest rank as the commander, whoever he may be." [14] The officer of the highest rank, of course, was Grant.

McClernand, in fact, was by now on the end of a limb, and Halleck was getting ready to saw it off. Sherman was in Memphis, pulling his troops together. He had brought 7000 men back from the Tallahatchie, and two divisions under A. J. Smith and G. W. Morgan, half of whose men had been sent down by McClernand, were on hand, totaling 14,000 more; as soon as he got the troops from Arkansas — he hoped there would be at least 10,000 of these — he would be ready to move. Grant had his cavalry in motion, striking east to destroy the Mobile and Ohio railroad, and Dodge at Corinth was sending a small force of infantry down to co-operate.[15] Unless McClernand reached Memphis very quickly, the big offensive which he had helped to make possible would be moving without him.

Amid all of this Grant had time to take a meditative look at his own situation. On December 15, he wrote to his sister a letter breathing quiet confidence; a strangely revealing letter, indicating that the newspaper criticism that had descended on him earlier in the year still hurt him, so that even at the crucial moment of a great campaign he had to think about it and voice a protest. The letter read:

> We are now having wet weather. I have a big army in front of me as well as bad roads. I shall probably give a good account of myself however notwithstanding all obstacles. My plans are all complete for weeks to come and I hope to have them work out just as planned.
>
> For a conscientious person, and I profess to be one, this is a most slavish life. I may be envied by ambitious persons, but I in turn envy the person who can transact his daily business and retire to a quiet home without a feeling of responsibility for the morrow. Taking my whole department, there are an immense number of lives staked upon my judgment and acts. I am extended now like a peninsula into the enemy's country, with a large army depending for their daily bread upon keeping open a line of railroad running one hundred and ninety miles through an enemy's country, or, at least, through territory occupied by a people terribly embittered and hostile to us. With all this I suffer the mortification of seeing myself attacked right and left by people at home professing patriotism and love of country, who never heard the whistle of a hostile bullet. I pity them and a nation dependent upon such for its existence. I am thankful however that, although such people make a great noise, the masses are not like them.[16]

If the people of the South were "terribly embittered and hostile," part of it was due to the way in which the Army of the Tennessee had been behaving. A soldier was writing that all the country along the Tennessee-Mississippi border had been laid waste and made desolate, and said that every vacant house had been burned. Men who marched past the smoking ruins would look at the gaunt, smoke-blackened chimneys and jeer: "There's another Mississippi headstone." Foragers would butcher a farmer's hogs in the owner's presence, threatening him with bayonets if he protested, and the movement south had hardly begun before Grant found it necessary to rebuke his men for "gross acts of vandalism." On three successive evenings, he had a notice read to each regiment in his command, warning that the legal penalty for straggling and looting was death and announcing that company and regimental officers would be held accountable for the misdeeds of their men. When parties from the 20th Illinois looted a store in La Grange, Tennessee, Grant figured the damage at more than twelve hundred dollars and ordered the sum deducted from the pay of the regiment's officers, pro rata; he also had two captains, who had tried to shield the culprits and hide the loot, mustered out of service. Yet all of this did little good. One veteran remarked that "such orders soon got to be a joke with the men, they in a quiet way giving the commanding officers to understand that they did not go down South to protect Confederate property." [17]

By mid-December, McClernand was anxious to leave Springfield, Sherman was anxious to leave Memphis, and Grant was anxious to fight Pemberton so that Sherman's thrust might succeed; and now, unexpectedly, there came drastic intervention on the part of the Confederates, to compel a revision of everybody's plans.

The intervention came chiefly from a rough-hewn Confederate officer who did not at all share in the cavalier tradition but who was one of the most striking military geniuses developed in the war: Nathan Bedford Forrest, whose activities would finally wring from Sherman a grim tribute — there could be no peace in western Tennessee, Sherman would cry bitterly, until Forrest was dead. Forrest was taking off just now on a raid. He had very little in the way of an army, and less in the way of equipment, but he figured that he would get horses and weapons from Yankee supply bases and that he would enroll new recruits from western Tennesseans in Yankee-held territory — an estimate which proved entirely correct. He was moving up now on the far side of the Tennessee River, and Rosecrans at Nashville got wind of it and sent Grant a warning telegram: "Tell the authorities along the road to look out for

Forrest." Grant passed the word along, alerted Dodge at Corinth, and sent word to Admiral David Porter, at Cairo, that there was ominous Rebel activity along the Tennessee: could some light-draft gunboats be sent up to keep Confederate cavalry from crossing into West Tennessee? On December 15 one of Grant's outposts notified him that Forrest was crossing the river, and Grant wired Porter that Forrest was over the river bent on mischief. He believed that the raid could be broken up; he told McPherson that he was concentrating troops in the threatened area, and that he did not think many of Forrest's men would ever get back into their own territory, although they might be able to break the Mobile and Ohio for a day or two. To Dodge he sent word that his own forces would make no further advance until Forrest was disposed of. To one subordinate he sent a wholly characteristic wire. After specifying movements that should be made to bring Forrest to bay, Grant added: "Don't fail to get up a force and attack the enemy. Never wait to have them attack you." [18]

If any man but Forrest had been leading the raid, Grant's dispositions would probably have been effective. The raiders were heavily outnumbered, with Federal detachments closing in on them from every direction, and dependable Grenville Dodge was moving up from Corinth to take charge of the operation. But Forrest was something special. As the Federal columns converged on him he dodged, fought when he had to, outguessed and outmarched his foes, and got back to safety east of the Tennessee, at last, with a prodigious achievement purchased by insignificant losses. He had broken the all-important Mobile and Ohio at various places over a sixty-mile stretch, running nearly to the Kentucky line, had completely cut off Grant's telegraphic communications with the outside world, had put at least twenty-five hundred Federal troops out of action, and had left Grant's army isolated, its supply line broken so badly that it would be many weeks before it could be restored. For nearly a fortnight Grant would not even be able to get or send telegrams.

By an odd coincidence, this interruption of communications came just when it would be most damaging to the aspirations of General McClernand.

Earlier in the fall Grant had been left in the dark about the backstage manipulating that was going on; now it was McClernand who was bewildered. Like Grant, he was hearing plenty of rumors, and the rumors were disquieting. Most of his troops had gone down the river but he had not gone with them, and he suspected that some very fast footwork was being performed by somebody. On December 16 he wired Halleck, asking to be sent downstream "in accordance with the order of the Secretary of War of the 21st of October giving me command of the Mississippi expedition." On the following day he telegraphed Lincoln: "I believe I am superseded. Please advise me," and he wired in similar vein to Stanton. Stanton's reply was only moderately soothing:

> There has been, as I am informed by General Halleck, no order superseding you. It was designed, as you know, to organize the troops for your expedition after they should reach Memphis or the place designated as their rendezvous. The troops having been sent forward, they are now to be organized. The operations being in General Grant's department, it is designed to organize all the troops of that department in three army corps, the First Army Corps to be commanded by you, and assigned to the operations on the Mississippi under the general supervision of the general commanding the Department. General Halleck is to issue the order immediately.[19]

This was bad news. McClernand had supposed that he would be an independent army commander, answerable to Washington; now he was being told that he would simply command an army corps under Grant. Even worse, however, was the prospect that the corps he was supposed to command might leave Memphis before he himself could join it. McClernand needed to get orders from Grant — and it was precisely now that Forrest's raid prevented anything Grant might say from reaching McClernand in time to do any good.

On December 18, the War Department notified Grant that, by order of the President, he was to divide his forces into four army corps — the 13th, to be commanded by McClernand; the 15th, to be commanded by Sherman; the 16th, to be commanded by Hurlbut, and the 17th, to be commanded by McPherson. Dutifully enough, Grant immediately wrote a long dispatch for McClernand:

I have been directed this moment by telegraph from the General-in-chief of the Army to divide the forces of this department into four army corps, one of which is to be commanded by yourself, and that to form a part of the expedition on Vicksburg.

I have draughted the order and will forward it to you as soon as printed. The divisions now commanded by Brig. Gen. George W. Morgan and Brig. Gen. A. J. Smith will compose all of it that will accompany you on the expedition, and the divisions of Brig. Gen. F. Steele and Brig. Gen. M. L. Smith will accompany you and will be commanded directly by Maj. Gen. W. T. Sherman, who will command the army corps of which they are a part. Written and verbal instructions have been given General Sherman, which will be turned over to you on your arrival at Memphis.

I hope you will find all the preliminary preparations completed on your arrival and the expedition ready to move.

I will co-operate with the river expedition from here, commanding this portion of the army in person.

On the same day Grant sent a wire to Sherman, notifying him about the formation of the new army corps and specifying that McClernand was to have command of the expedition to Vicksburg.[20]

All of this was fine. On paper, the administration's plan was being carried out just about as ordered. The trouble was that Grant's messages did not get through. Both of them had to go from Grant's headquarters at Oxford, by telegraph, to Columbus, Kentucky, to be relayed thence to Springfield and to Memphis, and because of what Forrest had done they could not be delivered. McClernand still had no orders telling him to go to Memphis; Sherman had no orders saying that he had to wait for McClernand. Growing more and more restless, McClernand waited until December 23 and then wrote to Stanton: "I am not relieved from duty here so that I may go forward and receive orders from General Grant. Please order me forward." Stanton promptly replied: "It has not been my understanding that you should remain at Springfield a single hour beyond your own pleasure and judgment of the necessity of collecting and forwarding the troops. You are relieved of duty at Springfield and will report to General Grant for the purpose specified in the order of the General-in-Chief." [21]

McClernand at last was ready to leave, but by now it was too late. He took off from Cairo by steamboat, accompanied by his bride — this energetic widower had recently been remarried, at Jacksonville, Illinois, to the sister of his former wife — and on December 28 he was in Memphis, only to find that Sherman and the two army corps had gone on down to Vicksburg. Consumed with fury, McClernand could do no more than start belatedly after his missing army. Quite clearly, he had been had, and he would blame the West Pointers for it to the end of his days, but he would never quite be able to prove that anyone had willfully disobeyed the President's orders. Beyond any question, Halleck had done his utmost to circumvent him, and Grant had been a party to it, but the record was straight enough. Halleck had stayed precisely within the limits of legality, and it is hard to escape the impression that neither Lincoln nor Stanton had expected him to do anything else. McClernand's troops had gone into Grant's department and had thereby come under Grant's control; Stanton had pointedly refrained from upsetting Halleck's program, and had indirectly but effectively endorsed the scheme whereby McClernand had become a mere corps commander instead of an independent operator; Grant had done exactly what Washington had told him to do, and if Bedford Forrest had kept Grant's orders from getting to Sherman and McClernand on time, Grant was blameless enough. Nevertheless, McClernand had been given the works. In his Memoirs, Grant dryly remarked: "I had good reason to believe that in forestalling him I was by no means giving offense to those whose authority to command was above both him and me." [22]

Meanwhile, the Confederates had visited Grant's campaign with a second disaster. Earl Van Dorn, leading thirty-five hundred Confederate cavalry, had gone north to strike at Grant's immediate rear while Forrest was raiding in western Tennessee. Grant's own cavalry, moving east on the raid Grant had ordered earlier, just failed to intercept Van Dorn, and on December 20 the Confederate cavalry struck the big Federal supply depot at Holly Springs. There were enough Federal troops in the place to hold it, and Grant gave the Post Commander, Colonel R. C. Murphy, warning that the blow was coming, but Murphy was a weakling; on Van

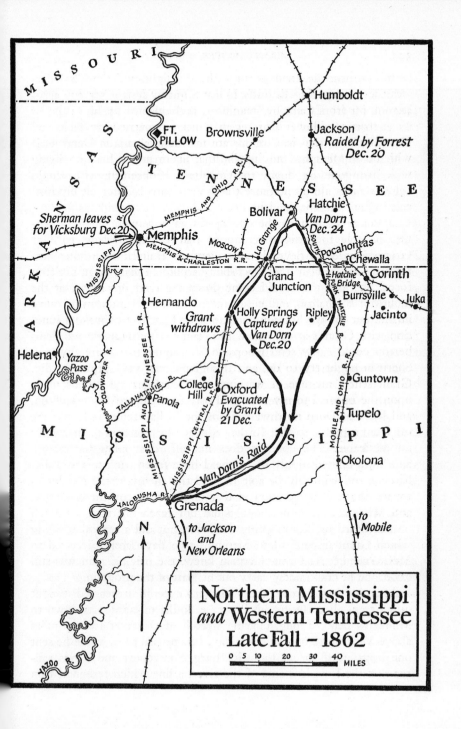

MISSOURI

Humboldt

FT. PILLOW

Brownsville

Jackson
Raided by Forrest Dec. 20

TENNESSEE

Hatchie
Van Dorn
Dec. 24

Bolivar

Sherman leaves for Vicksburg Dec. 20

MEMPHIS AND OHIO R.R.

Moscow

La Grange

Pocahontas

Chewalla

Corinth

Memphis

MEMPHIS & CHARLESTON R.R.

Grand Junction

Hatchie Bridge

Burrsville

Iuka

Hernando

Holly Springs
Captured by Van Dorn Dec. 20

Ripley

Jacinto

ARKANSAS

MISSISSIPPI

Grant withdraws

Helena

Yazoo Pass

COLDWATER R.

TALLAHATCHIE R.

TENNESSEE R.

Panola

College Hill

Oxford
Evacuated by Grant 21 Dec.

Guntown

MOBILE AND OHIO R.R.

Tupelo

MISSISSIPPI AND

MISSISSIPPI CENTRAL R.R.

Okolona

Van Dorn's Raid

YALOBUSHA R.

Grenada

to Jackson and New Orleans

to Mobile

N

Northern Mississippi *and* Western Tennessee Late Fall – 1862

0 5 10   20   30   40
MILES

Dorn's demand he surrendered without a fight, and the Confederates went rampaging through Holly Springs, destroying or carrying off foodstuffs, forage, munitions and other material valued at
more than a million dollars. Van Dorn got away unharmed, and
Grant's army, deep in Confederate territory, abruptly found itself
with no supplies and no supply line, in an area where no living
white man would give any assistance to a Yankee army if he could
help it. Taken together, Forrest and Van Dorn had completely canceled Grant's campaign plans.

Sherman and the Vicksburg expedition now were in great danger. The idea all along had been that Grant, pushing hard at
Grenada and below, would keep Pemberton and most of Pemberton's troops so busy that Vicksburg would be held by a skeleton
force. Sherman thus could come down the river, go ashore at the
mouth of the Yazoo, and either take Vicksburg by storm or move
inland, cut the city's communications, and prepare to make a junction with Grant's army. But with Grant's army immobilized, Pemberton could easily send troops to Vicksburg to thwart anything
Sherman might try to do, and this Pemberton very promptly did.
Grant sent a message of warning, on December 23: "Raids made
upon the railroad to my rear by Forrest northward from Jackson,
and by Van Dorn northward from the Tallahatchie, have cut me
off from supplies, so that further advance by this route is perfectly
impracticable. The country does not afford supplies for troops,
and but a limited supply of forage. I have fallen back to the Tallahatchie, and will only be able to hold the enemy at the Yalobusha
by making a demonstration in that direction or toward Columbus
and Meridian." But the message did not reach Sherman, although
he had heard of Holly Springs' capture, nor did a second warning
which Grant dispatched to Memphis two days later, addressed to
McClernand.[23] As far as Sherman knew, the original plan was still
good, and he could safely carry out his part of the program.

As an inevitable result, the Vicksburg expedition steamed straight
into a trap. Sherman got his immense flotilla of transports down to
Milliken's Bend, a long, curving stretch of the river twenty miles
above Vicksburg, on Christmas day, and paused there while he sent
one brigade off to cut the Vicksburg, Shreveport and Texas railroad on the Louisiana side of the river, a line which terminated on

the tongue of land just across from Vicksburg. Then he moved on, and on December 26 he was at the mouth of the Yazoo River.

The Yazoo is a tangled stream which comes down from northern Mississippi through rich bottom lands, meandering lazily and communicating, by way of bayous, backwaters and flood channels, with almost every other stream in the neighborhood, and it entered the Mississippi river five or six miles above Vicksburg. By following it a short distance upstream, Sherman believed that he could find ground from which his troops could assault the Walnut Hills, a stretch of high ground which goes off north and a little east from the city's bluffs, and during the next two days he got his men ashore on the soggy bottom land along a backwater called Chickasaw Bayou, a land cut up by creeks and swamps and dismal little ponds, ten miles up the Yazoo from the big river.

The prospects were not encouraging. The ground itself was forbidding, there were Confederate rifle pits along the base and slopes of the hills, and there were guns and infantry on the higher ground. Grimly outspoken as always, Sherman looked at the terrain, remarked that it would cost five thousand men to take Vicksburg eventually, and that the five thousand might as well be lost here as elsewhere, and on December 29 he launched the assault. His men tried hard enough, but the Rebel position was impregnable and it was held in strength; the assault was a dismal failure, the Federals never got past the swamps. Sherman lost more than 1700 men — if it was any comfort, he was at least well under the stated minimum of 5000 — and the Confederates lost no more than 200.[24] Sherman pulled his men back out of range, projected and then abandoned a plan for another assault farther up the Yazoo, and at last loaded the troops on the transports and steamed back to Milliken's Bend. If he could do nothing else he could at least wait here for Grant.

And then, on January 2, the river steamer *Tigress* came down from Memphis, bearing General McClernand and his staff.

McClernand exhibited his orders and took charge. Clinging to the idea that he was to command an independent army, he denominated the expeditionary force "The Army of the Mississippi"; Sherman was to command one corps (which in fact was already the case) while the other would be directed by Brigadier General

G. W. Morgan. McClernand himself would command the whole.

McClernand also brought news. He had left Memphis on December 30, so he knew about what Forrest and Van Dorn had done; knew, also, that Grant's army was withdrawing from its position near Grenada, and that any sort of advance in the near future was out of the question. When McClernand and Sherman consulted about what they should do next, McClernand talked broadly about opening the navigation of the Mississippi and cutting their way to the sea, but he seemed to have no specific plan. In a letter to Secretary Stanton — in which he complained that "the authority of the President and yourself . . . has been set at naught" — he proposed that Grant might base himself on Memphis, repair the railroads down to Grenada, and resume his march south to Jackson, while McClernand co-operated from the river.[25] Sherman, however, had a more immediate suggestion. The Arkansas river entered the Mississippi about halfway between Memphis and Vicksburg, and forty miles up the Arkansas the Rebels had a fort, Fort Hindman, more commonly known as the Post of Arkansas, which posed a threat to the supply route of any Federal force operating down-river. Sherman proposed that the Army of the Mississippi, with the Navy's help, go up the Arkansas and capture this fort. This would at least provide a victory to counterbalance the defeat that had just been suffered. McClernand agreed — he had given thought to such a venture before he left Memphis — and the army took off for Fort Hindman.[26]

Grant, meanwhile, was in a fog. He had put his army on three-quarters rations, and he had ordered out foraging parties to sweep the country for food; but he could not find out what was happening on the Mississippi, and although he knew that his own inability to advance had left Sherman in a bad spot he kept getting rumors that Vicksburg had been captured. The hope that Sherman might have taken the place vanished when he got a dispatch from that general telling what had happened at Chickasaw Bayou, but the rumors of a Federal victory continued, and Grant began to suppose that the expedition from New Orleans was making itself felt.

General Nathaniel P. Banks had reached New Orleans in the middle of December, to replace Ben Butler and to lead up the river an army to co-operate with the troops that were coming down. He was not, as a matter of fact, making any especial progress, but as far as Grant could tell the man was on his way, and it would be essential for the McClernand-Sherman force to be ready to co-operate with him if he drew near.

Halleck emphasized this, in a message sent January 7. Richmond newspapers left no doubt that Sherman had been defeated, and "every possible effort must be made to re-enforce him." No one knew where Banks was, but he was under orders to move upstream as fast as he could; Grant must take everything he could spare from Tennessee and Mississippi and strengthen the column on the river. Halleck's dispatch emphasized the urgency of the situation: "We must not fail in this if within human power to accomplish it." [27]

On the heels of this, Grant got a dispatch from McClernand, in which that general announced that the army was off for the Post of Arkansas. McClernand recited the obvious reasons for making the move, remarked that it was impossible to do anything against Vicksburg without a co-operative movement along the inland route, and spoke airily of the need to make a diversion against the Rebels in Arkansas and to co-operate with General Curtis's movements. The column would return to the Mississippi, McClernand said, "after completing any operations undertaken in Arkansas."

This was too much for Grant. Just when Banks might be approaching Vicksburg, ambitious McClernand was plunging into Arkansas on a mission that might end no one knew where or how. Grant sent Halleck an angry wire: "General McClernand has fallen back to White River and gone on a wild-goose chase to the Post of Arkansas. I am ready to re-enforce but must await further information before knowing what to do." Then he wrote a curt letter to McClernand, announcing that he disapproved of the Arkansas movement and telling the General: "Unless you are acting under authority not derived from me keep your command where it can soonest be assembled for the renewal of the attack on Vicksburg." Since no steamer was ready to go down the river, this letter could not be forwarded, and Grant supplemented it on January 13 with a calmer note. In this he told McClernand that he could not tell just what was best to do immediately, but he warned him that "unless there is some object not visible at this distance your forces should return to Milliken's Bend, or some point convenient for operating on Vicksburg, and where they can co-operate with Banks should he come up the river." [28]

One thing had become clear. Grant could not hope to make sense out of the operation against Vicksburg as long as he himself was isolated in western Tennessee, and it was futile to try to co-ordinate the movements of widely-separated armies. He would have to give up the overland move, arrange troops so as to hold the line between Memphis and Corinth, and go down the river himself with every regiment he could spare. He ordered his advance withdrawn to Holly Springs, took off for Memphis, and on January 13 wrote to McPherson that "it is my present intention to command the expedition down the river in person." He was doubtless strengthened in this resolve by a brief message from Halleck:

"You are hereby authorized to relieve General McClernand from command of the expedition against Vicksburg, giving it to the next in rank or taking it yourself." [29]

CHAPTER SEVENTEEN

A Noun Is the Name of a Thing

I T IS easy to get a distorted picture. A general is maneuvering an army deep in enemy country, hoping to strike a blow that may win the war. To him come rumors of enemy movements, reports about things done by his own troops, accounts of clashes and skirmishes on the front or on the flanks, veiled warnings of policy decisions far away in Washington. He studies these, reaches the best conclusions he can, issues his orders, and then goes on to victory or to defeat; and when we look back long afterward we suppose that all of his attention was taken up by purely military problems.

Yet really it was not that way at all when Grant made his drive down the shaky railroad line at the end of 1862. No matter what might happen with McClernand and Sherman, with Pemberton and Forrest and Van Dorn, or with the advancing brigades of his own army, Grant had to give much the greater part of his time and energy to matters that had nothing to do with the progress of the invasion. Before everything else he was an administrator of occupied territory. This territory was generating problems of incredible intensity, for whose solution nothing in his training offered any guidance at all. He had to deal with these problems every hour of every day, and each one was loaded with extraordinary pressures. Even if his front had been totally inactive Grant would still have been occupying one of the most difficult spots held by any Federal commander. Since his front, instead of being inactive, was the key strategic location of the entire war, Grant was carrying a staggering load.

To begin with, there was cotton.

Grant's armies were entering some of the richest farming land in America — the "cotton garden of the world," as it was called, the heart and center of the South's great cotton empire. All about him, on vast plantations and on tiny farms, were immense quantities of this staple, which a powerful industry in the North wanted more than it wanted anything else on earth. Until Grant's army came there was no legitimate market for this cotton. Many planters, strong in their Confederate patriotism, simply burned theirs; others, less steadfast, held onto their bales and waited to see what would happen. What happened was a miraculous continuing boom in the cotton market, with an immense number of Northern traders, fixers and schemers swarming in from everywhere to get as much cotton as they could in any way and at any price possible. The market was made livelier by the fact that the area which produced all of this cotton was desperately short of items like coffee, medicines, whisky, flour and salt, not to mention an endless list of manufactured goods, so that the Southern planter had an almost overwhelming incentive to let the detested Yankee have some of the cotton. (The prices being offered were the highest in sixty years; also, the traders were prepared to pay in U. S. Treasury notes, or even in gold, so that the man who wanted to sell did not have to take depreciated Confederate currency.) To intensify the pressure still further, the Confederate Armies could not survive without salt, with which the beef and pork which the soldiers ate could be preserved; if the Confederate authorities winked at letting cotton go North they could get salt, as well as gunpowder, revolvers and other munitions of war; and Pemberton was warned by the Confederate War Department that certain "irregular modes of supply" had to be countenanced if his army was to be fed and maintained.

At the exact storm center of this pressure was Grant, who did not want to think about anything except the best way to whip the opposing armies but who possessed the power of life or death over a trade as insistent, and as charged with the chance for immense profits, as anything a California or a Klondike gold rush ever saw. Commerce, the administration had decided, would follow the flag; there would be no trade with the enemy, but in a region held by the Union Armies trade would be encouraged, and although cotton in theory would be bought only from loyal citizens, the Treasury agents who were on hand to give out permits were very often men who could be corrupted — and, in any case, who was to say that a Southern farmer who took the oath of loyalty was willfully perjuring himself in order to sell a couple of bales of cotton? A trader who could establish contacts outside of the Union lines could make utterly fantastic profits, provided the Army would enable him to transport his cotton back to a market. One man operating out of Oxford, Mississippi, while Grant had his headquarters there, paid 12,000 dollars for 1500 bales of cotton, contingent on his ability to move it to Columbus, Kentucky — where it would be worth 500,000 dollars to him. This trader told Grant that he himself would find the transportation; all he wanted from Grant was a permit. Grant refused to give it to him, and warned him that if the cotton came within his lines he would confiscate every bale of it for the government; whereupon the trader offered to cut the General in on the profits. There was no deal; and it was about this time that Grant wrote to his sister, remarking: "To all the other trials that I have to contend against, is added that of speculators whose patriotism is measured by dollars and cents. Country has no value to them compared with money." [1]

Most generals made no deals, but there were rumors of deals all over the place, and they poisoned the atmosphere in which Grant's army lived. If that army sent troops out to seize any place, there was certain to be talk that the real reason for the expedition was to help some speculator buy cotton, and a Northern newspaper would ask: "Is it just that our soldiers should peril their lives for the pecuniary benefit of a few speculators?" The *New York Times*, wondering why Grant drew his supplies all the way from Columbus, asked why the long railroad line should be kept open and offered its own answer: "We venture the assertion that cotton-speculating influences have controlled the policy and kept the road open. The profit of individuals and not the prosperity of the campaign has ordered it." [2]

Early in the summer Grant tried to keep things in hand by ruling that no gold or silver could be paid for cotton. U. S. Treasury notes might be offered, and if a man who offered cotton for sale refused to accept such money he could be arrested and his cotton could be seized and sold by the Army, the money to be held in trust for settlement later. Washington disapproved of this, however, and Grant was ordered to encourage the cotton trade and to permit the use of hard money in its purchase. He complied, much against his will, and Sherman protested bitterly that "the cotton order is worse to us than a defeat," pointing out that gold which entered the Confederacy would immediately be used to buy munitions of war. "If we provide our enemies with money we enable them to buy all they stand in need of," he wrote Grant. "Money is as much contraband of war as powder." To Secretary of the Treasury Chase, Sherman declared that Memphis now would be more valuable to the Confederacy under Union rule than it was when the Confederates held it.[3] This did no good. The new orders had to stand, and shortly after he began his march to the south Grant tried to restrict the trade as much as possible with a new set of regulations.

Under these rules, a man who wanted to buy cotton and send it North must have, in addition to a Treasury Department permit, a permit from the nearest Army provost marshal. No one could go beyond Army lines to buy cotton or anything else; railroad freight agents were required to make daily reports on all cotton shipments, and cotton shipped by persons lacking the proper permits was to be confiscated. Recognizing that civilians in occupied territory greatly needed manufactured goods from the North, Grant permitted licensed dealers to carry such goods in stock and allowed their sale to citizens who would take the oath of allegiance and who would specify that the items bought were for their own use and not for resale. Government teams were forbidden to haul any private property, and any cotton found in Army wagons was to be confiscated by the quartermaster for the benefit of the government.[4]

Enforcing such rules, however, was something else again. As Sherman pointed out, payment in gold provided an irresistible stimulus. Both inside and outside of Federally-held territory, Southerners who previously had hidden their cotton were having a change of heart, the gold that flowed south was creating an immense traffic in munitions, and Sherman angrily asserted that the great Northern merchandising center of Cincinnati "furnishes more contraband goods than Charleston, and has done more to prolong the war than the state of South Carolina."[5] There were times when it seemed that cotton and gold were corrupting both sides. A Confederate cavalry officer patrolling northwestern Mississippi complained that he found "the whole community engaged in trading cotton with the enemy," in river towns cotton smuggling was widespread and open, and one Confederate officer wrote to Braxton Bragg that "Yankee gold is fast accomplishing what Yankee arms could never achieve — the subjugation of this people." Newspaperman Charles A. Dana, who had left the *New York Tribune* in order to indulge in a little cotton trading on his own hook, wrote that parts of the Union Army were becoming demoralized; "Every colonel, captain or quartermaster is in secret partnership with some operator in cotton; every soldier dreams of adding a bale of cotton to his monthly pay." Grant agreed with him that the net effect was very bad, although he insisted that Dana had overstated the extent of corruption in the army. Six months later Grant wrote to Secretary Chase saying that trade with the rebellious states "is weakening us of at least 33 percent of our force. . . . I will venture that no honest man has made money in West Tennessee in the last year, whilst many fortunes have been made there during that time." Soldiers noticed with grim amusement that when Van Dorn captured Holly Springs his troopers rounded up a number of cotton traders, took their gold away from them, and marched them through the street at the point of the bayonet.[6]

All of this was a heavy distraction for a general conducting a delicate military operation in a hostile land. It was all the heavier because the cotton fever had infected members of Grant's own intimate circle. Traveling with him at this time was another Galena crony, one J. Russell Jones, a close friend of Congressman Washburne, and a United States marshal at Chicago; and while Jones was on hand ostensibly just to visit with an old friend he was extremely anxious to buy a little cotton if the price was right. He wrote to Washburne that he would be moderate; if he could buy cotton at 25 to 40 cents a pound he would spend what money he had with him and go home content; but the gold rush atmosphere got into his blood, and he told Washburne later that he "could have made an eternal, hell-roaring fortune" if, when he got to Memphis, he could have seen how cotton prices were going to rise. If he could just get down into Arkansas below Helena, he said, "I can make all the money any one man ought to have in ten days." As it was, he reported rather unhappily on his return to Chicago, he had made no more than twenty-five thousand dollars.[7] There is no hint in any of his letters that Grant was in any way a party to his deals; still, there it was — an acquaintance of the General, and a close friend of the Congressman who had been the General's stanchest supporter, moving with the army, was himself on the make.

Even worse was the nasty tangle created by Grant's father, canny little Jesse Grant.

Between Grant and his father there had always been a strange, tragic lack of understanding. Long ago, in southern Ohio, Jesse had sent Grant to West Point when an Army career was the last thing on earth the son wanted. Later, when the peacetime Army had been too much for him, Grant had not been able to get the help which Jesse could easily have given him; finally, apparently without enthusiasm, Jesse had given his son a little job in the Galena harness shop, muttering to his acquaintances that the Army had spoiled his son for business. More recently, Jesse had taken great pride in the new fame which his son had won, and had made so much noise about it that Grant had felt called on to rebuke him, in a letter which, for Grant, was amazingly cold and sharp. Now, with the cotton problem lying heavily on his stooped shoulders, Grant was to find Jesse making book with the very traders who were Grant's worst trial — coming in, sly and insinuating, to help the men whose patriotism, as Grant believed, was to be measured by dollars and cents.

The whole business is a little less than crystal clear, but what happened apparently went like this: Jesse Grant, in Cincinnati, formed some sort of partnership with three brothers, Henry, Harmon and Simon Mack, merchants who traded as Mack and Brothers. Under this deal, Jesse and the Macks would go South to buy cotton in the military department controlled by Jesse's son, the General; the Macks would furnish the capital, Jesse would furnish the son — who was in a position to say whether any trader in West Tennessee or northern Mississippi could buy and ship cotton at all — and the profits would be split. And so, early in December, while Grant was trying to get his army down to the Tallahatchie, and while Sherman was hurriedly getting his own expedition on transports at Memphis, with Porter's gunboats puffing in the stream, Jesse and the Macks came down to northern Mississippi to see General Grant.[8]

At first, Grant was cordial enough — glad, as any son might be, to meet businessmen who were good friends of his father. Then the truth of the matter dawned on him. What Jesse and the Macks wanted was permits to buy and ship cotton, and Grant's own authority was being put up for sale. By the next train, under orders, the Cincinnati merchants went back North, lacking permits. The Chicago newspaperman, Sylvanus Cadwallader, wrote that Grant was bitter, indignant and mortified; and on December 17, at Holly Springs, Grant put his fury into an order which would leave a queer enduring stain on his own name. This order, published for the guidance of the whole department, read as follows:

> The Jews, as a class violating every regulation of trade established by the Treasury Department and also department orders, are hereby expelled from the department within twenty-four hours from the receipt of this order.
>
> Post commanders will see that all of this class of people be furnished passes and required to leave, and any one returning after such notification will be arrested and held in confinement until an opportunity occurs of sending them out as prisoners, unless furnished with permit from headquarters.
>
> No passes will be given these people to visit headquarters for the purpose of making personal application for trade permits.[9]

Concerning all of which there is much to be said.

The first thing to say is that the brothers Mack, unfortunately, were Jewish. The second is that the Army officers of that time and place, infuriated by the activities of the traders who were infesting western Tennessee and northern Mississippi, had long since concluded that most traders were Jews (which was not at all the case) and were using the word "Jew" much as superheated Southerners at the same time were using the word "Yankee" — as a catch-all epithet which epitomized everything that was mean, grasping and without conscience. The third is that there did exist then, in the United States, latent for years, but now suddenly blooming under forced draft, a violent Ku Klux spirit, hang-over perhaps from the recent Know-Nothing era, a spirit which could rise to what now seem incredible heights of misunderstanding and hatred for all people who were not Northern Americans of English descent. All of these, taken together, were reflected in Grant's famous General Orders Number 11.

On November 9, Grant had told General Hurlbut, at Jackson, to let no civilians go south of Jackson, adding the injunction: "The Israelites especially should be kept out." The next day he told General Webster, in charge of his railroad supply line: "Give orders to all the conductors on the road that no Jews are to be permitted to travel on the railroad south from any point. They may go north and be encouraged in it; but they are such an intolerable nuisance that the department must be purged of them." And on the day he issued General Orders Number 11 he wrote to C. P. Wolcott, Assistant Secretary of War, a detailed explanation of his action:

> I have long since believed that in spite of all the vigilance that can be infused into post commanders, the specie regulations of the Treasury Department have been violated, and that mostly by Jews and other unprincipled traders. So well satisfied have I been of this that I instructed the commanding officers at Columbus to refuse all permits to Jews to come south, and I have frequently had them expelled from the department, but they come in with their carpet-sacks in spite of all that can be done to prevent it. The Jews seem to be a privileged class that can travel anywhere. They will land at any wood-yard on the river and make their way through the country. If not permitted to buy cotton themselves they will act as agents for someone else, who will be at a military post with a Treasury agent to receive cotton and pay for it in Treasury notes which the Jew will buy up at an agreed rate, paying gold. There is but one way that I know of to reach this case; that is, for Government to buy all the cotton at a fixed rate and send it to Cairo, St. Louis or some other point to be sold. Then all traders (they are a curse to the army) might be expelled.[10]

Grant's emotions are clear enough, and his idea about the best way to handle the cotton traffic was excellent, but his language was confused. He wanted to get the traffic under decent control so that he could get on with the war, and like many other officers at that time and place he was using the words "Jews" and "cotton traders" interchangeably. In the same way, Dana had been warning Stanton about the get-rich-quick mania that had infected "a vast population of Jews and Yankees," and Brigadier General Alvin P. Hovey, complaining about the bargain-hunting that was going on, was denouncing unprincipled sharpers, Yankees, bloodhounds of commerce, and Jews all in one sentence, making all of the words mean the same thing.[11] Grant himself, later on, seemed honestly puzzled by the furore his order had raised. Talking with a rabbi after the war, he tried to explain what he had done: "You know, during war times these nice distinctions were disregarded. We had no time to handle things with kid gloves. But it was no ill-feeling or a want of good-feeling towards the Jews. If such complaints" — that is, complaints about extortionate practices in the cotton trade — "would have been lodged against a dozen men each of whom wore a white cravat, a black broadcloth suit, beaver, or gold spectacles, I should probably have issued a similar order against men so dressed." [12]

There were some odd aspects to the whole business. A week before Grant issued his order, the Commanding Officer at Holly Springs, Colonel John V. Dubois, announced that "all cotton speculators, Jews and other vagrants having no honest means of support except trading on the miseries of their country" must leave town within twenty-four hours or be conscripted into the Army; Grant revoked this order and Dubois was transferred to other duty — an unfortunate shift, perhaps, since he was replaced by the Colonel Murphy who would surrender so meekly when Van Dorn demanded it. There was also persistent gossip to the effect that Grant himself did not devise General Orders Number 11. Old Jesse told Congressman Washburne that the order was issued on instructions from Washington; several newspaper stories said the same thing; and one witness asserted that one of Grant's subordinates prepared and issued the order without Grant's knowledge.[13] But, however all of this may have been, the order did come out — to stand as a melancholy example of the kind of prejudice which was taken for granted in the 1860's.

It remains to be said that it did not stand very long. Within two weeks Grant received instructions to revoke the offending order, which he promptly did. Shortly afterward, Halleck sent an oddly worded note of explanation: "The President has no objection to your expelling traitors and Jew peddlers, which, I suppose, was the object of your order; but, as it is in terms proscribed an entire religious class, some of whom are fighting in our ranks, the President deemed it necessary to revoke it." [14] As a footnote, there is the fact that Congressman Washburne sent a hurried letter to President Lincoln, saying he believed Grant's original order "the wisest order yet made by a military commander," and urging: "As the friend of that distinguished soldier Gen. Grant I want to be heard before the final order of revocation goes out if it be contemplated to issue such an order. There are two sides to this question." [15] If Washburne was heard he changed nobody's mind. General Orders Number 11 died, and no more was heard about it. The whole affair created much more of a stir in later years than it did at the time. Examination of contemporary newspapers indicates that neither the order nor the act of revocation drew very extensive newspaper headlines or coverage.

Cotton was one distraction. Curiously allied was another distraction — Negro slavery. What was happening to Grant in this respect was much like what was happening to the government in Washington. The attempt to fight the war without taking a positive stand on slavery was collapsing, for the peculiar institution was central to the whole military problem. No matter where the Union Armies went and no matter what they did, they met the Negro slave, and they had to do something about him simply because he was there. He represented a problem that could not possibly be postponed, and the inner sympathies of the men on whom the problem was being thrust made no difference at all. Generals might hopefully announce that the Army would have nothing to do with the Negro, but that was like saying that it would have nothing to do with the weather. An invading army that did not work out some policy for dealing with the Negro would inevitably be swamped in a rising sea of black folk.

Grant's army was operating in an area where a good many plantations had been hastily abandoned, and the slaves who remained — people who had been left to their own resources, and who had none — were clogging the roads and the lanes, and overflowing into the Army camps, joined in even greater numbers by slaves who had drifted away from bondage in unoccupied areas and were wandering the countryside, pulled by an ignorant, formless hope for they did not quite know what — a people utterly rootless and helpless. The Army might not want to do anything for them, but if it did not do something about them it would quickly be smothered. The sheer weight of the slave population compelled attention.

Whenever a body of troops was on the march, slaves would line the road to watch, idly expectant. Some of these would be grabbed by officers, to act as servants. A newspaper correspondent believed that even more were pressed into temporary service by weary soldiers, who, "seeing a stout nigger by the roadside, cannot well resist the temptation of loading their knapsacks and guns upon him and trotting him along as a pack horse"; the correspondent said that at the end of the day's march none of the slaves thus put to work would try to get back to their homes. A soldier in northern Alabama wrote that every camp was surrounded by Negroes who were delighted to be given something to do; all of them, he said, were anxious to "go wid yer and wait on you folks," and he asserted that there were not fifty Negroes in the South who were not ready to risk their lives to get away from the plantation. Chaplain John Eaton of the 27th Ohio said that the flood of colored people brimming about each camp "was like the oncoming of cities," and he wrote that the tide was irresistible and frightening: "There was no plan in this exodus, no Moses to lead it. Unlettered reason or the more inarticulate decision of instinct brought them to us. Often the slaves met prejudices against their own color more bitter than any they had left behind. But their own interests were identical, they felt, with the objects of our armies; a blind terror stung them, an equally blind hope allured them, and to us they came."

The condition of these refugees, said Eaton, was appalling:

> There were men, women and children in every stage of disease or decrepitude, often nearly naked, with flesh torn by the terrible experiences of their escapes. Sometimes they were intelligent and eager to help themselves; often they were bewildered or stupid or possessed by the wildest notions of what liberty might mean — expecting to exchange labor, and obedience to the will of another, for idleness and freedom from restraint. Such ignorance and perverted notions produced a veritable moral chaos. Cringing deceit, theft, licentiousness — all the vices which slavery inevitably fosters — were the hideous companions of nakedness, famine and disease. A few had profited

by the misfortunes of the master and were jubilant in their unwonted ease and luxury, but these stood in lurid contrast to the grimmer aspects of the tragedy — the women in travail, the helplessness of childhood and of old age, the horrors of sickness and of frequent death. Small wonder that men paused in bewilderment and panic, foreseeing the demoralization and infection of the Union soldier and the downfall of the Union cause.[16]

This problem had been on Grant's mind all fall, and at first he tried to cope with it by getting the most helpless cases sent North for attention. In September he started sending groups of Negro women and children to the base at Cairo, Illinois, with the understanding that charitable committees of Northerners would make arrangements for their care, and later on he wired from Holly Springs to Halleck: "Contraband question becoming a serious one. What will I do with surplus Negroes? I authorized an Ohio philanthropist a few days ago to take all that were at Columbus" — Columbus, Kentucky, that is: the northern terminus of the Mobile and Ohio — "to his state at government expense. Would like to dispose of more the same way." Halleck wired that this expedient would have to be abandoned.[17] Whatever was to be done with the frightening crowd of displaced Negroes, the Army Commander on the spot would have to do it.

In the end, Grant handed the problem to Chaplain Eaton, who turned out to be a good man for the job.

In giving the job to Eaton, Grant was doing what he usually did — meeting a complicated problem by taking the first, most obvious step, and letting future developments grow out of that. All about his army were abandoned farms and plantations, full of cotton waiting to be picked; everywhere there were idle slaves with whom something simply had to be done; the North wanted cotton very badly, the supply and the labor force were at hand — why not get the cotton, use the labor, and as a by-product relieve the chaotic destitution of the immense mob of fugitives? On November 11, Eaton received an order from Rawlins:

Chaplain Eaton, of the 27th Ohio Infantry Volunteers, is hereby appointed to take charge of the contrabands that come into camp in the vicinity of the post, organizing them into suitable companies for working, see that they are properly cared for, and set them to work picking, ginning and baling all cotton now out and ungathered in the field.

Eaton was dumbfounded. He had no idea what this job would involve, except that on the surface it looked impossible. He had never set eyes on Grant himself, but what he had heard about him was disturbing; as far as Eaton could see, "the order required me to report to an incompetent and disagreeable man . . . to fulfil a most arduous and unpleasant duty." He hastened off to Grant's headquarters, next day, to see if he could not talk the General out of it.[18]

Headquarters, then, were at LaGrange, Tennessee. Eaton found the house Grant was occupying, and was told by an aide to go down a passage and knock on a closed door. He did so, was invited to enter, and found Grant in the middle of a conference with other generals. Grant told him to sit down, and when Eaton gave his name Grant remarked: "Oh — you are the man who has all these darkies on his shoulders."

Eaton sat there while the conference continued, and took his first look at the Major General commanding. He had heard tall tales about Grant's dissipation, and he studied his face carefully and, to his relief, saw no signs to indicate that these tales were true — "Everything about him betokened moderation and simplicity" — and the generals at the conference clearly respected him. The meeting broke up at last, and as the officers left Grant asked Eaton to pull his chair over to the table: "Sit up and we'll talk." Eaton at once began to ask that he be excused from the unwelcome new assignment. He pointed out that he was usefully employed where he was, that he had no military rank to speak of, that to pull the Negroes out of camp would bring him into conflict with all of the officers who were now using escaped slaves as servants, and that all in all he just did not feel up to the job. Grant listened attentively without being in the least impressed, and said finally: "Mr. Eaton, I have ordered you to report to me in person, and I will take care of you." Then he began to explain just what Eaton was to do.

It was necessary to set up a special camp for the fugitive slaves, Grant explained, for two reasons — sheer military necessity, to protect the troops against disease and demoralization, and common humanity, to keep the Negroes themselves from misery and death. The contrabands would not be a dead weight on the army, because there were many things they could do. About the army camps they could relieve soldiers of fatigue duties for the surgeon general, the quartermaster and the commissary, and they could work for the engineers on the building of roads and bridges and fortifications. Some women could help in camp kitchens and in hospitals, and a great many could help to pick, bale and ship the waiting cotton. Those who picked cotton would be paid for their work, and the baled cotton would be sent North and sold for government account. Citizens who had not left their plantations could use the contraband labor to gather their crops if they paid for it.

As Grant went on, Eaton began to see that this General had given the problem a great deal of thought. The Negro at the moment had a peculiar status, somewhere between slavery and freedom; Grant believed that if the Negro could show his worth as an independent laborer he could later be given a musket and could be used as a soldier, and eventually, if this worked out well, he could even become a citizen and have the right to vote. "Never before," wrote Eaton, "had I heard the problem of the future of the Negro attacked so vigorously and with such humanity combined with practical good sense." Reconciled to the task which he had been given, and greatly encouraged as to the capacity of Grant himself, Eaton went off to tackle the new job.

It was not easy. The first contraband camp was set up near Grand Junction, Tennessee, several miles from the nearest army camp, and the bewildered contrabands from all around were brought to it. An improvised hospital, with an Army surgeon in charge, was set up for the innumerable sick, and an abandoned house was taken over for a pesthouse — the first combing-out of the Army camps brought in eight Negroes suffering from smallpox. Grant ordered the quartermaster corps to meet Eaton's requisitions for condemned tents and surplus clothing, as well as for axes, spades and other tools, ordered the commissary department to honor requisitions for rations, and detailed a regiment to act as camp guards. He did this, as a matter of fact, without authority, and if Washington had overruled him he might eventually have been personally liable for enormous sums; long afterward, talking to Eaton, Grant touched on this point, asking lightly: "I wonder if you ever realized how easily they could have had our heads?" However, authorization of a sort was presently received from Halleck, and the work went forward.

Problems were immense. Among the refugees, "want and destitution were appalling," and although Grant consistently gave Eaton full support the means to deal with the suffering never seemed quite adequate. It was nearly impossible for Eaton to get assistants; almost to a man, the soldiers of this army hated to do anything which seemed to resemble serving Negroes, and just about the only helpers Eaton could get were reluctant enlisted men formally detailed for the job. (He got these, he recalled, in the ratio of one helper for each thousand of contrabands.) Provost marshals objected when Eaton tried to take fugitives away from them — they did not especially want the Negroes, but they did not like to see their own authority cut down — and on at least one occasion Eaton had to go to Grant himself to make a refractory provost understand who was boss. The citizens of the neighborhood were bitterly opposed to anything the Yankees might do, especially to anything which involved turning slaves into free men, and their antagonism was a constant pressure — particularly so when Eaton began to send out foraging details to impress foodstuffs for his charges. After a few weeks of it, Eaton had to take an intricate bundle of problems off to Grant for settlement. Grant then was far down the railroad, at Oxford, and so to Oxford Eaton went. He got there just as the campaign of invasion was reaching its worst moment.

Grant gave him plenty of time, shelving for the moment the heavy problems arising from Forrest's raid, McClernand's anticipated arrival at Memphis and the down-river movement of Sherman's troops, and Eaton was able to explain his difficulties. He had just finished doing this, and was sitting beside Grant in front of headquarters, when a courier gave Grant the message which signified the final collapse of Grant's campaign: the news that Colonel Murphy had surrendered the vast Holly Springs base to Van Dorn's cavalry.

Grant read it impassively. Eaton said that the General did not change expression, except that his mustache twitched a little. Then

Grant told Eaton what the message said and what it meant: he would have to withdraw his army and work out a completely new plan of campaign. He explained that he had given plenty of warning of Van Dorn's approach, and that with ordinary diligence Murphy should have been able to save the depot, and he added: "People will believe that I was taken unawares and did nothing to protect my supplies, whereas I did all that was possible."

Then Grant returned to Eaton's problems and wrote out the comprehensive order which Eaton had requested. He also told Eaton that it would probably be necessary, in view of what Van Dorn had done, to move the whole Grand Junction camp bodily off to Memphis.

Returning to Grand Junction, Eaton rode on the train with Jesse Grant and with Julia. Jesse, he remembered, kept calling his attention to the enormous waste of hides at the slaughterhouses where the Army butchered its beef cattle. As an old tanner, Jesse could see that these would be very valuable, if he could just get them North, but he confessed that his son would not let him do anything at all about them. General Grant would not permit a profit to be made for anyone connected with the Grant family.

Moving the contrabands off to Memphis was something. The camp near Grand Junction had hardly got into operation; now every man, woman and child — most of them completely helpless, and all of them scared and bewildered — had to be taken cross-country to a city that did not want them, and the railroad which was to take them, the war-wracked line of the Memphis and Charleston, was swamped with the movement of troops. Such trains as were made available were hopelessly crowded, but the frantic Negroes refused to be left behind. They jammed passenger and freight cars, clinging to platforms and roofs, so that the trains had to go very slowly to keep from dislodging the refugees. At Memphis, accommodations were inadequate, and all over the city for a night or two little groups of hopeless people built bonfires on street corners and huddled around them while an early snowfall came down. Somehow, the first few nights and days were survived — by most of the Negroes, at any rate — and Eaton set up a new camp for his charges. Except in his capacity as a willing unpaid servant who would do anything at all which his new masters asked of him, the Negro was wanted by nobody. The townspeople disliked him, and so did the army, and merely to keep him from starving, freezing or dying of disease or of plain, unvarnished discouragement was the most anyone could hope for.

Yet amid all of the confusion and unavoidable harshness, one thing was happening: the homeless Negro was slowly beginning to be recognized as a human being. Eaton was insisting that families — where they existed in any sort of understandable form — should be kept together, and he found that many of his people wanted to be married. Most marriages, he learned, merely solemnized unions which had existed for years on a sort of stock-farm basis, and he did his best to make such unions permanent and legal; he recalled that one day a chaplain who worked for him performed 119 marriages in one hour, and the morale of the contrabands began to rise. Eaton was able to use the services of a number of plantation-trained Negro preachers, whose qualifications sometimes were tenuous. One of these had deserted his own wife, and insisted on living with another woman, and an army chaplain tried to get this man to see the error of his ways, which scandalized the righteous. The Negro could not be moved; he had prayed and prayed about it, he said, but the Lord had sent him no clear call to make a change and so he thought he would go on as he had been doing. Soldiers finally had to get him out of the camp, whereupon he and his light o'love caught smallpox and died — a retribution which deeply impressed his former congregation.[19]

All of this was more than just another problem for General Grant, to whom nearly all of Eaton's problems sooner or later came for final disposal. Grant was not merely working out the most important military campaign of the war; he was also cutting out the path along which a race would move toward freedom and manhood, and he had little to go on beyond his own instincts. The new policy toward the Negro was only technically being made in Washington. President and cabinet and Congress might make any plans they chose, but in the long run what would happen to the colored man was pretty much up to the Army commander in the field, and a good part of the underlying meaning of the war was bound up in what the field commander might do.

Different commanders had tried different things. Away back in 1861 at Fort Monroe, Ben Butler had ruled that fugitive slaves entering the Union lines were, as property owned by Rebels, mere contraband of war, and since this ruling enabled the Army to meet the problem on an *ad hoc* basis it was welcomed. But the fugitive slave was a source of ferment. Nothing that was done about him was ever final; in the last analysis he was what the war was mostly about, and he grew as the war grew. He had been a thing and the war was revealing him as a man, and every soldier in one way or another had to adjust himself to that fact.

David Hunter, along the South Carolina coast — the General whose place Grant had thought he himself might fill, when his own unhappy role in the army that was advancing on Corinth that spring had seemed unendurable — had tried to make the adjustment by enlisting Negroes as soldiers; but the effort was just one jump ahead of anything Washington was then prepared to recognize, and Hunter had first been overruled and then displaced. Ben Butler, in New Orleans, had begun to crack the problem by enlisting free Negroes as soldiers; then Hunter's successor, Brigadier General Rufus Saxon, had won permission to recruit fugitive slaves, and the dark regiment of First South Carolina Volunteers had come into being as a result. But Washington had not quite made up its mind, and all anyone could say was that a recent Act of Congress authorized the President to receive into the service, for any useful labor which they might perform, such contrabands as local commanders might care to enroll. People in the North, happy enough to see slaves deserting their Confederate owners, were still frightened of what the Negro might mean if he came into their own midst as a free man, seeking a job and some recognition, and James Gordon Bennett had jeered in his *New York Herald:* "The Irish and German immigrants, to say nothing of native laborers of the white race, must feel enraptured at the prospect of hordes of darkeys over-running the Northern states and working for half wages, and thus ousting them from employment." [20] Within a year the workers of New York City whom Bennett was thus exhorting would put on a hideous race riot to prove that the hordes of darkeys frightened them beyond endurance.

In the middle of a trying military campaign Grant had this prob-

lem along with that of the Jewish traders who wanted to buy cotton at a bargain, and the problems were strangely related; related, not merely because cotton was common to both of them, but because Grant and most other men were children of their time and, without thinking, used derisive words denying human dignity to whole groups of people whose right to claim human dignity was what was chiefly at stake in this war. Like nearly everyone else, Grant could thoughtlessly say "Jews" when he meant scheming fixers who would have sold their own mothers for gain, and he could say "Darkeys" — as James Gordon Bennett said it — when he meant pathetically displaced men and women who were struggling upward to the point where people might recognize their decency as human beings. He could say "Jews" when he struck angrily at the sharpers, and he could say "Darkeys" when he devoted priceless time and effort that should have gone to a military campaign to an attempt to help people who were climbing a hard ladder.
. . . When he wrote his Memoirs, Grant chuckled mildly about the frontier schoolrooms in which, as a child, he had been taught over and over again that "a noun is the name of a thing." He was grappling with the names of things now, and the grapple was like Jacob's, wrestling with the angel, for the names were important. Far ahead of him, not visible but perhaps dimly sensed, dependent in a strange way on the very campaign which he now was trying to repair, there might be a day when people of good will, like himself, would use no abraded epithets but would simply talk about human beings.

CHAPTER EIGHTEEN

Winter of Discontent

WHEN SHERMAN first started downstream from Memphis for the attack at Chickasaw Bayou the soldiers were full of confidence. This movement, they felt, could not miss; they spoke of it as "the castor oil expedition," meaning that it would go straight through and bring speedy results, and for a few days they suspected that they were about to win the war. Then came the let-down. The attack was not simply repulsed; it was beaten back so easily that Sherman himself had to admit that it had no chance to succeed — if he had had two hundred thousand men, he muttered, the result would have been the same.[1] The minor success at the Post of Arkansas raised the men's spirits temporarily, but when McClernand took over and the soldiers found themselves camped in discomfort on the muddy levee west of the river, upstream from Vicksburg, disillusionment became acute. There was much sickness, the new regiments were deeply homesick, and nothing that anyone was doing seemed likely to cause Vicksburg to fall.

The veterans were ragged even before the expedition took off, and an Illinois soldier complained that the seats of their pants were so tattered that the girls laughed when the troops marched through the streets of Memphis. One of the newer regiments reported 352 sick out of a total strength of 842, and an Indiana recruit said that half of his outfit was sick and the other half contained hardly anyone who was really healthy; it was "the worst times the 15th corps ever saw, for the sickness was general and the soldiers continued to die off by hundreds." It rained steadily, the country beyond the levee was mostly under water, and the tents were pitched in malodorous mud. In the new regiments organized by McClernand, camp diseases such as measles were running their course, and a hospital steward noted that many sick men grew listless and seemed to lose

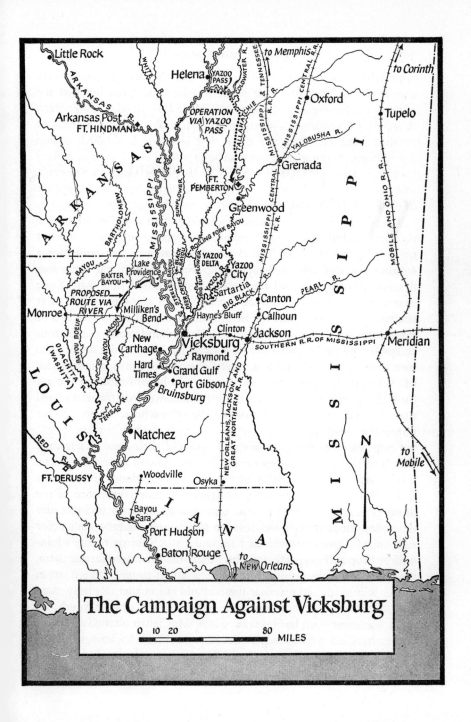

The Campaign Against Vicksburg

0 10 20   80   MILES

their will to live. Mails were delayed, and disturbing rumors were about: one of these said that peace had been declared but that the authorities, for reasons of their own, were keeping the news secret. A steamer fitted up as a floating hospital took aboard hundreds of invalids from McClernand's corps, but someone had failed to ship any rations. A regimental surgeon who visited the boat a few days later found twenty-two men from his regiment dead on the deck, and he asserted: "I believe before God some of them died for want of proper nourishment." [2]

There were many desertions. An Ohio recruit commented, "Now the hour of darkness began," and enlarged on the problem in a letter to his parents: "Go any day down the levee and you could see a squad or two of soldiers burying a companion, until the levee was nearly full of graves and the hospitals still full of sick. And those that were not down sick were not well by a considerable. Men at the north, who were not to be trusted, were taking advantage of the occasion by writing discouraging letters and sending traitorous scraps of printed matter to their sons and friends in the army. The men became discouraged in a great degree. There was common talk of deserting, for they felt sure they would be protected in the act by their friends at home." A soldier from the 103rd Illinois asserted that the sick actually out-numbered the men who were present for duty.[3]

Copperhead newspapers in the North did their best to persuade everyone that the Vicksburg campaign was bound to end in failure. The New York World, in particular, spread gloom in its news dispatches and in its editorials, asserting that "the confidence of the army is greatly shaken in Gen. Grant, who hitherto undoubtedly depended more upon good fortune than upon military ability for success." It stated gravely that Sherman was subject to fits of insanity: "He hates reporters, foams at the mouth when he sees them, snaps at them, sure symptoms of a deep-seated mania." The trouble, as the World saw it, was that the administration was too busy warring on its own generals to make effective war on the South; its only successes had been made when McClellan was General in Chief: McClellan had been replaced by Halleck "whose ways are notoriously past finding out," and Grant's record was dismal — his only victory, Fort Donelson, had been won for him by C. F. Smith,

Belmont had been a failure, Shiloh "a surprise and a disgrace" and the campaign in Mississippi had been a blunder from the start. The *World's* editorial writer summed him up: "His famous Jew order proves him to be wanting in tact and judgment and without these no man can be great though accident can make him a successful general." Even the stoutly loyal *New York Times* denounced mismanagement of the Army hospitals near Vicksburg, and wrote bitterly of one general who took over an airy mansion for his own headquarters but ordered his sick soldiers quartered in the slave cabins; as a result, said the *Times*, his men were dying at the rate of from fifteen to thirty every day. Getting decent rations for the sick, the *Times* complained, was just too much trouble, and it quoted an unnamed general as saying that it was easier to dig two graves than to sign one set of requisitions.[4]

What men said privately was worse than what was printed for the public to read. The Middle West contained no more thoroughgoing Northern patriot than Joseph Medill, editor of the *Chicago Tribune*, but Medill this winter was about ready to quit. In a letter to Congressman Washburne, Medill confessed that "the rebs can't be conquered by the present machinery," and admitted that the war was bound to end in an armistice sometime during 1863. "We have to fight for a boundary — that is all now left to us," he wrote, and his only hope was that the North could somehow capture Vicksburg before the armistice was made. If Vicksburg could not be taken, then the South had won the war — "they will have a ring in our nose and the string in their hands." The administration ought to withdraw at least sixty thousand men from the Army of the Potomac and send them to Banks, in New Orleans. The Vicksburg campaign probably should remain in Grant's hands; Medill was not very enthusiastic about Grant, "but he can plan and fight — the others can't." The editor then went on to hymn his despair in plain words:

> I can understand the awful reluctance with which you can be brought to contemplate a divided nation. But there is no help for it. The war has assumed such proportions — the resistance is desperate and stubborn. Our finances are so deranged and exhausted. The democratic party is so hostile and threatening that complete success has become a moral impossibility. The war

has been conducted so long by "central imbecility," Seward intrigue, and McClellan, Buell, Porter, Halleck, Steele, Franklin, Nelson, McCook and other pro-slavery half-secesh generals, that the day of grace is past. It is now "save what we can." If there is to be reform it comes too late. But I see no prospect of reform with anything. Halleck and his gang are firmly retained. Lincoln is only half awake, and will never do much better than he has done. He will do the right thing always too late and just when it does no good.[5]

Unquestionably the general war picture was bad. In the East, General Ambrose E. Burnside had taken over the Army of the Potomac after the administration had finally sent McClellan back to private life, and Burnside had blundered into fearful defeat at Fredericksburg, Virginia, on December 13. Morale in his unlucky army had gone far down, sickness and discouragement were even worse along the Rappahannock than along the Mississippi, and the administration was nerving itself to remove Burnside and put handsome Joseph Hooker in his place. In central Tennessee at a bend in Stones River near Murfreesboro, Rosecrans, with the army that been Buell's, had fought a desperate, inconclusive battle with Bragg at the beginning of the new year. Bragg, unpredictable as always, had retreated after apparently having won one of the bloodiest fights of the war, and so the battle was recorded as a Union victory, but Rosecrans's army had been so mangled that it would be immobilized until summer. The autumn elections had gone against the administration, the peace party in the North was riding high, and Medill's profound pessimism was a reflection of the general temper. Even tough Medill, ready to consent to a division of the Union, was staking what hope remained to him on the faith that Vicksburg could be taken; but the most he could say for Grant — who must take the place, if anyone did — was that he was the best of a poor lot. The principal hope of the North rested on the shaky belief Medill had voiced — that Grant at least was a fighter.

It was a legend, a true tale that would be remembered a long time, that in the dark days after Shiloh the canny Pennsylvania politician A. K. McClure had gone to President Lincoln to say that Grant must be discarded; he was a fumbler and a drunkard, and he represented a political liability heavier than the administration could carry. And McClure told how Lincoln heard him out, thought it over in silence, and then returned his verdict: "I can't spare this man: he fights."

Grant would fight; that statement, in this gloomy winter, represented the best hope of the Union cause. But right now Grant could not fight, because the enemy was hopelessly out of his reach.

Grant was so near the great Confederate citadel that a brief walk and the use of a pair of field glasses would bring Vicksburg river fortifications into clear view,[6] but Pemberton's army was where he could not get at it. Adapting himself to the new campaign forced upon him by Washington, Grant had to start all over again. He was west of the river and the Confederate Army was east of it, and until he found some way to get his troops over the river to a place where Pemberton could be forced to give battle he could do nothing. If Grant was in fact no more than a heads-down slugger, this campaign was over before it could even begin.

East of the Mississippi there was high ground, more or less continuously, from the mouth of the Ohio down to Memphis. All of this high ground the Union now owned; but below Memphis there was a 200-mile stretch of delta country, half-overflowed now because the river was abnormally high, and the high ground was fifty miles or more inland. It did not return to the river until after the Yazoo River emptied into the Mississippi a few miles above Vicksburg; then it came in on a long slant, the Walnut Hills, looking down into the half-drowned valley of the Yazoo. Sherman had tried to fight his way out of this valley with no success at all, and there was no sense in repeating that effort. A dozen miles up the Yazoo the Confederate line was anchored at a height known as Snyder's Bluff; gunboats and transports coming up the Yazoo could not hope to pass these fortifications. Unless the Union Army could somehow get around to the east and approach this bluff from the rear, that end of Pemberton's line was secure.

Reaching the Mississippi just below the Yazoo, the high ground ran south close to the water's edge, and Vicksburg was built on the bluffs, its wharves and docks down by the water's edge, streets climbing to the plateau above. There were many guns planted here, at water level and above, and the one certainty in an uncertain world was that the place could not be taken from the river. Gunboats and mortar boats could bombard it, to be sure, and a stout fleet under a determined admiral could always run past it, if the admiral cared to stand the hammering; tough old Farragut had already proved that, and Porter would prove it again, but it meant very little. The finest army in the world could not land along the waterfront and take the city by storm. From the west Vicksburg was completely impregnable.

Downstream things looked no better. The left end of Vicksburg's immediate defenses was solidly posted at Warrenton, a few miles south of town. Twenty-five miles farther downstream the Confederates had guns in position on the bluffs at Grand Gulf; it seemed unlikely that the Yankee army at Milliken's Bend could get around these defenses, because the ground west of the river was half-flooded, virtually impassable to marching columns with wheeled vehicles, and there were no transports at all below Vicksburg. Banks, to be sure, might some day come up from the river's mouth, but he would have to pass the Rebel works at Port Hudson first and this might be beyond his means.

As far as anyone could see, in this unhappy January of 1863, Grant's army was in a blind alley.

Grant knew this as well as anyone. To get at Pemberton's army he had to approach Vicksburg from the land side, the east. In the light of what he knew now, he could see that from a strictly military point of view it had been a mistake to give up the move down the Mississippi Central Railroad. To be sure, Van Dorn had captured his base of supplies and Forrest had destroyed his communications; but during the fortnight in which his army had collected food and forage from the surrounding countryside Grant had learned something about the possibility of operating in this rich southland without any supply line at all. He confessed later that his army could have lived off the country for two months instead of two weeks and that it might have been possible simply to drive ahead, letting Rebel cavalry do anything that it cared to do in his rear, and force Pemberton to fight east of Vicksburg. His troops had lived high after the supply lines were broken. Plantations provided plenty of meat, poultry and corn; local mills had been put to work grinding meal, Western farmboys had raided plantation corn cribs and made quantities of hominy, and on Christmas Day General Mc-Pherson had found himself treated to an elaborate feast by his pioneer corps — roast turkey, chicken, meat pies, corn bread, wheaten cakes, stewed fruit. All in all, the old rule that an army of invasion must retain a firm connection with its own base looked like a rule that might be discarded, in a land that produced a surplus of food. The lesson would stick in Grant's mind.[7]

But it had not been possible, at the end of December and the first of January, for Grant to make the decision which, later, he believed should have been made. Washington had decided that there was going to be an expedition on the river, and that was that. Halleck had warned Grant sharply to do everything possible to reinforce the Mississippi Army: "Take everything you can dispense with in Tennessee and Mississippi. We must not fail in this if within human power to accomplish it." [8] So Grant had come to the river, and now that he was here he could not turn back. To uproot the whole expeditionary force, return to Memphis, and plan a new campaign east of the delta would be to confess a failure and to perform what North and South alike would consider an ignominious retreat. Militarily the move might be wise, but politically it was out of the question. There was nothing to do but go ahead with the river expedition and somehow make it work.

At the end of January, Grant had in his department approximately 103,000 officers and men, present for duty, equipped. About half of these would have to stay in Tennessee, even though Grant was ordering much of the railroad network and the rear-area installations abandoned in order to make as many men as possible available for duty at the front. On hand, in the general vicinity of Vicksburg, he had nearly 40,000 men, with perhaps 15,000 more waiting at Memphis to join him.[9] He might be reinforced, later, and he might not. As far as he could learn, Pemberton's numbers — in Vicksburg, at Port Hudson, and at various inland points — were about equal to the numbers he himself could use.

Grant's troops were spraddled out over a wide area, for this Mississippi country was not hospitable. On the eastern shore, above Vicksburg, it offered no place at all for an army to camp. The troops had to pitch their tents on the western side, which was bad

enough in all conscience — muddy levee, with limitless acres of
swamps, swollen backwaters, stumpy bayous and drowned lakes
sprawling out on the Louisiana side for miles. The army made its
camp mostly at Milliken's Bend, a lazy crescent edging the river
twenty miles upstream from Vicksburg; at the lower end of this
crescent there was Young's Point, where Grant's headquarters
steamer, the *Magnolia,* was tied up; and below Young's Point there
was low, muddy ground directly across the river from Vicksburg,
terminus for a railroad that came in from Monroe, Louisiana. At all
of these places, and at isolated spots farther up the river, there were
Federal troops, sharing the ground, as a newspaper correspondent
remarked, with frogs and crawfish. The latter were being eaten,
in quantities; a soldier could dig a shallow hole near his tent, let it
fill with water — which it would do, in no time — and then, after a
short wait, dangle in it a piece of meat on a string. He could quickly
obtain a peck of crawfish, "of good flavor and easily digested." [10]

Grant took up his new job with tempered optimism. On his way
down the river he stopped at Helena, Arkansas, and talked briefly
with Congressman Washburne's brother, Brigadier General Cadwallader C. Washburn. (The Congressman retained a final "e" on
the family name and the younger brother dropped it; writing to
either of them, Grant was likely to spell the name both ways, im-
partially, in the same letter.) To the Congressman, General Washburn sent a brief report on Grant: "He looks well and feels pretty
well, but feels that he has got a heavy job on his hands. The high
water and overflowed country render it very difficult to operate now
on land, and Vicksburg can only be taken by a great sacrifice, except
by a land force in the rear." Sherman gave Grant a gloomy appraisal;
troops aided by gunboats might perhaps land along the city's waterfront, or an assault might possibly be made at Snyder's Bluff, but
the only real hope seemed to be to find some way of getting a large
force on the high ground east of Vicksburg. Meanwhile, Sherman
feared that impetuous McClernand "may attempt impossibilities."
To Halleck, as he went downstream, Grant sent a brief wire: "What
may be necessary to reduce the place I do not yet know, but since
the late rains think our troops must get below the city to be used
effectively." [11]

Before he could begin to operate properly Grant had to show

McClernand who was boss. When Grant reached Young's Point, he found that McClernand considered the river force a separate army under his own command; McClernand was writing letters and orders under the heading, "Headquarters, Army of the Mississippi," and he did not propose to give up any part of his authority. On January 30, shortly after Grant's arrival, McClernand sent Grant a letter bristling with independence and inviting a showdown:

> I understand that orders are being issued directly from your headquarters directly to army corps commands, and not through me. As I am invested, by order of the Secretary of War, indorsed by the President, and by order of the President communicated to you by the General-in-Chief, with the command of all the forces operating on the Mississippi river, I claim that all orders affecting the condition or operation of those forces should pass through these headquarters; otherwise I must lose a knowledge of current business and dangerous confusion ensue.
>
> If different views are entertained by you, then the question should be immediately referred to Washington, and one or the other, or both of us, relieved. One thing is certain, two generals cannot command this army, issuing independent and direct orders to subordinate officers, and the public service be promoted.

Grant did not need McClernand to tell him about the necessity for a unified command. Looking far beyond his immediate surroundings, he had previously written to Halleck to say that all of the Western departments really ought to be combined under one head; then, lest it seem that he himself was angling to get the top job, he added: "As I am the ranking department commander in the west, I will state that I have no desire whatever for such combined command, but would prefer the command I now have to any other that can be given." Halleck made no change in the chain of command, and Grant proceeded now to put McClernand in his proper place. On the same day he got McClernand's letter, he issued orders announcing that he was assuming command of the Vicksburg expedition and that Department headquarters would thenceforth be on the Mississippi. Army corps commanders were formally directed to resume the immediate command of their respective corps and to report to and get orders from Grant's headquarters — an unmistaka-

ble way to let McClernand know that he was now a corps commander and nothing more. The order added that McClernand's 13th
Corps would be responsible for garrisoning the post at Helena and
any other point on the west bank south of Helena which it might
be necessary for the army to hold.

McClernand responded at once. He drew Grant's attention to the
fact that, "having projected the Mississippi river expedition, and
having been by a series of orders assigned to the command of it, I
may be entirely withdrawn from it" if this order of Grant's meant
what it seemed to mean. Just what, he asked, did Grant have in
mind?

Grant's reply, sent the following day, was blunt. The order, he
wrote, meant that "I will take direct command of the Mississippi
river expedition, which necessarily limits your command to the
Thirteenth Army Corps." Also, as a clincher: "I have seen no order
to prevent my taking immediate command in the field, and since
the dispatch referred to in your note I have received another from
the General-in-Chief of the Army, authorizing me directly to take
command of this army." Stiffly, McClernand replied that he would
submit "for the purpose of avoiding a conflict of authority in the
presence of the enemy," but he asked that the whole business be
referred to Halleck and, through Halleck, to Stanton and Lincoln.
Grant by this time must have been fairly confident that he held the
winning hand, and he quickly sent the papers to Halleck. In a
covering note, he remarked that he had no confidence in Mc-
Clernand's ability to conduct a major campaign; still, if President
and Secretary of War ruled in McClernand's favor, "I will cheer-
fully submit . . . and give a hearty support." [12]

Washington refused to interfere; the army was all Grant's. The
question now was what he would do with it.

For the immediate future the problem seemed to be one for the
engineers. Three opportunities apparently existed. All of them
would be tried.

The first involved an attempt to induce the Mississippi river to
by-pass Vicksburg entirely.

Directly across the river from Vicksburg, the Louisiana shore in
the 1860's formed a long, narrow peninsula, a muddy finger point-

ing northeast into the hollow of a hairpin curve which the Mississippi then made just above the city. Anyone who looked at the map could see that if the river could somehow be induced to cut through the base of the peninsula, instead of flowing around its tip, Vicksburg would be left high and dry, an inland town instead of a river stronghold, a problem for Federal armies no longer. The river's current could do strange things with a fissure in the lowland banks, and it seemed likely that if a modest ditch were cut across the peninsula the river would quickly scour it out and create a new channel. The line such a ditch might follow had even been traced, before the war, during some long-forgotten dispute between Mississippi and Louisiana, and when Farragut brought his salt-water fleet up the river in June, 1862, the idea came to life. With Farragut was Brigadier General Thomas Williams, leading a brigade of Federal infantry, and for several weeks Williams's men toiled in the summer heat, digging away at this ditch until the abandonment of the expedition called them all back to Baton Rouge.

Now the notion was revived once more. It particularly struck the fancy of President Lincoln, who knew something about the Mississippi at first hand and who had a frontiersman's pragmatic interest in projects of this kind. Halleck gave Grant warning that the President wanted this canal dug, and Grant took it up where Williams had left it.

Grant had no great hope that anything very valuable would come of this work. The canal had been planned wrong. On the upstream side of the long point, the canal struck the river in a backwater; the current hugged the opposite bank here, and it was not probable that it would ever come into the ditch with enough force to create a new channel. Downstream, the canal would touch the river below Vicksburg, but still above Warrenton, and when the Confederates perceived what the Yankees were up to they simply put new guns in position at Warrenton and waited, quite unconcerned; even if the whole affair worked just as planned, Confederate batteries would still control the river.

Still, it had to be tried. Washington had ordered it, and anyway it would give a few thousand of the soldiers in this immobilized army something to do. Grant put Sherman and the 15th Corps to work, bringing in dredges to rush the job along, while his engineers tried to re-design the layout so that the river would actually flow through the canal when the job was done.[13]

Much more promising was a project which involved making use of a crescent-shaped body of water called Lake Providence, which lay just west of the river fifty miles or more above Vicksburg. Grant learned about this as soon as he reached Young's Point.

All of the Louisiana country west of the river seemed to be half-drowned, the land being low and the river being high, and Lake Providence apparently offered a way into a two-hundred-mile waterway by which the army could float past Vicksburg undisturbed. Lake Providence was near the Mississippi, separated from it by a levee. From the lake, a sluggish stream known as Bayou Baxter meandered through a cypress swamp for half a dozen miles, connecting beyond the swamp with a more open bit of water, and running thereafter into a series of streams which finally came out into the Red River, which in turn reached the Mississippi a little above Port Hudson. If Grant wanted to get below Vicksburg without bloodshed, this might be the way: very roundabout, to be sure, but feasible, if the levee were cut and if a way could be opened through the trees and mud of Bayou Baxter. Slightly skeptical but anxious to try everything, Grant sent an engineer officer up to look the situation over, and on January 30 he got off a note to Admiral Porter:

> By inquiry I learn that Lake Providence, which connects with Red river through Tensas Bayou, Washita and Black rivers, is a wide and navigable way through. As some advantage may be gained by opening this, I have ordered a brigade of troops to be detailed for this purpose, and to be embarked as soon as possible. I would respectfully request that one of your light-draught gunboats accompany this expedition, if it can be spared.[14]

A few days later he went up the Mississippi to see for himself, grew more enthusiastic, and sent a quick message to McPherson asking him to bring a division and come down at once.

> This bids fair to be the most practicable route for turning Vicksburg [he wrote]. You will note from the map that Lake Providence empties through the Tensas, Washita, Black and

Red rivers into the Mississippi. All these are now navigable to within a few miles of this place, and by a little digging, less than one-quarter that has been done across the point before Vicksburg, will connect the Mississippi and Lake, and in all probability will wash a channel in a short time.

Sherman saw the reports and concluded that Lake Providence offered a much better chance than the ditch his own soldiers were digging. He wrote to Grant:

It is admirable and most worthy of a determined prosecution. Cover up the design all you can, and it will fulfill all the conditions of the great problem. This little affair of ours here on Vicksburg Point is labor lost.[15]

The third possibility seemed for a while to be the best of the lot. It involved another job of levee-cutting, this one far up the Mississippi a few miles below Helena, Arkansas. In olden times there had been an opening in the Mississippi's eastern bank here, giving access to a bayou known as Yazoo Pass. This offered a connection with the Coldwater River, which soon entered the Tallahatchie, and farther downstream the Tallahatchie joined the Yalobusha to form the Yazoo. This chain of rivers had once provided a route for light-draft steamboats serving the back country in the Yazoo delta; but because the delta land was so low that a moderate rise in the Mississippi would cause floods, a levee had been built across the mouth of Yazoo Pass, blocking the passageway. Cut this levee, now, let the Mississippi's flooded waters enlarge the channel, and it should be possible to get gunboats and transports over into the Yazoo — in which case, with moderate luck, the expedition could steam far inland, reach the high ground many miles above the Confederate strongpoint at Snyder's Bluff, and get in behind all of Vicksburg's fortifications east of the city, the same area that could have been reached if the movement down the line of the Mississippi Central Railroad had gone according to plan. When he first came to the river Grant took note of this route, and he wrote to McClernand that "it is barely possible that Yazoo Pass might be turned to good account." As soon as he had established himself at Young's Point, he sent a staff member, Lieutenant Colonel James H. Wilson, up the river to do something about it.

Wilson was a young man, not long out of West Point. A member of the corps of Topographical Engineers, he had served with distinction in General Quincy Gillmore's successful expedition against Fort Pulaski on the Georgia coast a year earlier, and he possessed boundless energy and self-confidence. He came to Grant in the fall of 1862, and fitted in quickly. McPherson had served with him in California, and liked him, and McClernand had known him in Illinois before the war and wanted to get him on his own staff. Rawlins, discovering that Wilson neither used nor approved of whisky, quickly formed an offensive-defensive alliance with him to serve and protect Grant; and in his old age Wilson came to feel that he had been the mainspring of the whole Vicksburg campaign and that Grant would have been helpless without him, which was a slight exaggeration. Wilson plunged into the Yazoo Pass job with much vigor; reached the scene on February 2, blew up the levee next day, and on February 7 had the first steamboat careening through the pass to explore the new channel. His reports were optimistic, and Grant presently came to feel that this Yazoo route offered the only really feasible way to get at Vicksburg from the east.[16]

Three projects, then, all being pushed hard as February went by, each one meaning much toil for the soldiers. The high water in the Mississippi was an eternal problem, and there were times when it seemed likely that floods would put an end to all canal-digging; the work had hardly begun when Sherman was glumly writing that "if the river rises 8 feet more — we would have to take to the trees," and in the middle of February he confessed: "The river is about full and threatens to drown us out, the ground is wet, almost water, and it is impossible for wagons to haul stores from the river to camp, or even horses to wallow through." In the end, indeed, the canal across the point came to nothing. Rising waters broke through the dam at the upper end, and instead of gouging out a deep channel the river simply spread all over the peninsula, submerging camps and forcing the troops to flee for their lives and causing the loss of many horses and much equipment. By the beginning of the second week in March it was clear that this canal was not going to be the answer.[17]

The Lake Providence scheme seemed more promising, and, although in the end it accomplished nothing, some of the people who

worked on it at least got a little fun out of the job. Early in February, the soldiers spent ten days hauling a river tugboat a mile and a
half overland from the Mississippi into Lake Providence. The idea
back of this was to find a navigable passage through the connecting
swamps into navigable river channels, but various generals and their
staffs managed to make some use of the boat for festive cruising.
One soldier who was assigned to duty on this vessel wrote that Mc-
Pherson liked to get friends aboard of an evening, with a regimental
band, and go cruising up the lake to a landing at a back-country
plantation which had an excellent wine cellar. The boat would
come puffing back long after midnight, whistle blowing, band playing, moonlight shining on the black water, mysterious shadows lying under the half-submerged trees on either hand. Men who could
not join in these cruises found Lake Providence pretty, and discovered that it was full of fish. The swamps, unfortunately, were
full of trees and submerged stumps which had to be removed, and
up-rooting a stump whose base was eight feet under water took
some doing. In addition, it began to be clear that even if a passage
could be opened Grant could not get enough light-draft steamers to
carry his army down to the Red River anyway, and the Lake Providence venture slowed down to a halt about the time Sherman's
canal had to be abandoned.[18]

That left Yazoo Pass, which was both the most promising and, in
the end, the most exasperating venture of the lot.

Like all of these attempts to create a new channel for steamboats,
this called for a great deal of very hard work, all of it performed by
enlisted men who had come down here with the notion that they
were going to fight Rebels. The pass itself, which led from the cut
levee into the Coldwater, was deep enough for ocean liners, but it
was very narrow, and there were lush forests on each bank. Rebel
working parties had come in and had felled scores of trees, some of
them four feet through the trunk, dropping them so that they lay
completely across the river. Wilson, who had the working details
in hand, found that the best way to get these out was to haul them
out by hand, and he borrowed hawsers from the Navy and put
whole regiments to work, five hundred men tailing onto one cable
to drag a tree up on the bank. It worked, he said, better than one
would expect. After watching it, he never wondered how the an-

cient Egyptians had moved the ponderous stones they put into the pyramids; put enough men on a rope and you could move anything. In a short time he was telling Grant that "no one here entertains a doubt of our being able to work through," and Galena's Russ Jones, still trying to turn an honest dollar by a cotton deal (and balked by Grant's refusal to permit any trade whatever below Helena), wrote enthusiastically about the work to Congressman Washburne, predicting that "Grant will get Vicksburg before he quits." [19]

By the end of February the way into the Coldwater was open, and an imposing flotilla moved in — two ironclad gunboats and divers lighter naval craft, under the Navy's Lieutenant Commander Watson Smith, and twenty-two light transports carrying forty-five hundred soldiers under Brigadier General Leonard F. Ross. As this expedition moved forward, Grant's hopes rose, and his ideas of what could be accomplished grew larger. He had hoped, originally, at least to clean out certain Confederate warships which were supposed to be lurking, or under construction, somewhere in the Yazoo, and to break the railroad bridges over the Yalobusha River at Coffeeville — the town that had marked the southern limit of his advance when he came down the Mississippi Central in December. The Confederates were repairing that much-abused railroad, and seemed likely to strike north along that route into Tennessee, to compel Grant to send troops back from before Vicksburg; and Grant notified Admiral Porter that if the bridges could be destroyed "it would be a heavy blow to the enemy and of much service to us." Now it seemed likely that the whole campaign could be based on this Yazoo River move, with the entire army getting in to the high ground northeast of Snyder's Bluff; Grant ordered a second division moved up to support Ross, and told McPherson to be prepared to follow with his entire corps.[20]

However, there were problems. The Mississippi was much higher than the connecting streams, and when the levee was cut a powerful current came through; gunboats and transports spun end for end, often being swept into the banks where trees wrecked their upper works. Floating trees came down with the current to batter the boats' hulls, and now and then the flotilla would run into a tangle of driftwood, uprooted trees and old logs which two days' labor would hardly clear. Commander Smith found the business a nightmare, and Admiral Porter wrote later that this officer — understandably, perhaps — was showing "symptoms of aberration of mind." Smith was a deep-water sailor, used to handling a vessel off soundings in the open ocean; here he was in a narrow, twisting river, where overhanging trees knocked down smokestacks and stumps punctured hulls, cruising in what looked like an unbroken wilderness. Even after the flotilla got into the Coldwater it took six days to go thirty miles, and by the time the Tallahatchie was reached all of the vessels were more or less battered. One of the ironclads had hit a snag and had a hole in her bottom, with a patch held in place by beams shored in from the deck above; one of the lighter gunboats was wholly disabled with a wrecked paddle wheel, and the commander was wishing he had never heard of the State of Mississippi. And finally, when the expedition approached the Yazoo itself, the Confederates were waiting, prepared to fight in a constricted spot where proper naval maneuvering was quite impossible.

Some two hundred miles in from Yazoo Pass the Tallahatchie makes a wide horseshoe loop to the east, with a little town named Greenwood lying at the eastern end of the loop, just where the Yalobusha river joins the Tallahatchie. The two rivers together form the Yazoo, and it swings back west to complete the loop, leaving a neck of land no more than a quarter of a mile wide; and on this neck the Confederates had built Fort Pemberton out of cotton bales and heaped-up earth, with several fieldpieces, one heavy rifle and a few lighter rifles in position. The Tallahatchie flowed down to this fort in a straight reach. The gunboats had to come in head-on, and there was just room for two boats to fight abreast; and on March 11 Commander Smith took a last doubtful look at the layout and brought in his ironclads, *De Kalb* and *Chillicothe*, to begin the fight.

Fort Pemberton had been hastily built, completed just before the warships appeared, and it was of no great strength. But Smith could bring only a fraction of his strength to bear, the Rebel gunners were firing straight down the alley at him, and in a short time both gunboats were put out of action. Patchwork repairs were made, and the warships renewed the action two days later, but the results were no better; the fort was knocked about but her guns remained in service, the gunboats were badly hammered, and by March 17 the bombardment was called off. The gunboats could not silence Fort Pemberton so that the transports could run by, and it was impossible to land troops and take the place by storm because all of the land thereabouts was under water; and when the supporting division came down the river it found the whole expedition steaming back up the Tallahatchie en route to Helena. Commander Smith, who had been in bad health to begin with, collapsed and had to go back to a hospital — in which, a little later, he died — and by the end of March the movement was an obvious failure.

Young Colonel Wilson fumed angrily, and wrote furious letters to Rawlins, back at Young's Point. "To let one 6½-inch rifle stop our Navy. Bah!" he sputtered. Commander Smith, he insisted, was not quite the equal of Lord Nelson: he was responsible for the failure of the expedition, "for no other reason than his timid and slow movements." The thing would not work unless the Navy cleared the way; the Army could always get through, in time, but "if the land forces are required to stop at every point of importance and reduce it by a siege, how long do you think it will require them to reach Yazoo City?" He grew darkly pessimistic: if this move failed — and its failure was apparent — the whole Vicksburg operation would become of secondary importance, Rosecrans and his Army of the Cumberland would get the play, and Grant might find himself compelled to send fifty or sixty thousand men to help some other general win a reputation.[21]

To Grant came the discouraging word that the expedition was hung up. Along with it came reports that Pemberton was sending troops to the Tallahatchie, hoping to block the river upstream and trap gunboats, transports, soldiers and all in a net from which they could not escape. Grant took counsel with Admiral Porter, who set about it to see if there might not be some other way into that unattainable stream, the Yazoo River.

Porter was a salty character, of the bluff-seadog persuasion; a stocky, bearded man with a rough sense of humor and an innocent fondness for spinning tall tales, a man with enough drive and force to satisfy even the impatient young Colonel Wilson. He had originally had a profound distrust of West Pointers, and hoped to work with generals who had been appointed from civilian life, but Sherman and McClernand between them had cured him of this; Sherman he liked and could work with, but McClernand he considered utterly impossible, and he now was developing a great liking for Grant. He went to work energetically, and he presently found a way into the Yazoo — a tangled, roundabout but possibly feasible route which led up through a backwater called Steele's Bayou.

Steele's Bayou entered the Yazoo five miles up from the place where the Yazoo flowed into the Mississippi. Gunboats and transports could ascend the Yazoo to that point without difficulty; the frowning Confederate works that barred passage up the Yazoo were at Snyder's Bluff, six or eight miles farther upstream. Steele's Bayou was nothing much, but — like all other waterways in this half-flooded delta country — it had important connections. Forty miles from the place where it emptied into the Yazoo it led into a chain of sloughs and forgotten streams — Black Bayou, Deer Creek and something called Rolling Fork — and these, after a time, led to the Sunflower River, a substantial stream which flowed leisurely south for fifty miles and then joined the Yazoo, well above Snyder's Bluff. The waterway was excessively complicated, and the connecting creeks and bayous were narrow, inordinately crooked, and full of trees, and all in all it was a good two hundred miles by this channel from Young's Point to Snyder's Bluff, although these places were not twenty miles apart in an air line; but if the high ground along the Yazoo was the objective, and if the Yazoo Pass outfit could not get by Fort Pemberton — which was obviously the case — then this was the only chance. Grant and Porter spent a day looking at the lower reaches of this waterway from the deck of a gunboat, and then Grant gave the orders: Porter would force his way through, and Sherman and a division of his army corps would follow.

If the lamented Commander Smith had found the Yazoo Pass route nightmarish, he would have been utterly unable to find words to describe this Steele's Bayou business: it was so impossible it made the northern approach look simple. Porter went ahead, hammering his way through channels where his ironclads had to act like modern-day tanks, butting trees out of the way, in channels so crooked that at times five warships, steaming along nose to tail, would be headed in five different directions. Half a mile an hour was good progress. Rebel sharpshooters infested the surrounding forest and sniped at all sailors who showed themselves, and the trees grew so close to the channel that a plague of squirrels, raccoons, fledgling birds and lesser wildlife dropped from the branches onto the boats' decks and had to be swept overside with brooms. In all his years of going to sea Porter had never met anything quite like this. In one intricate little stream, he found his flagship, which had a 42-foot beam, moving in a channel no more than 46 feet wide. Bridges spanned the watercourse here and there, and had to be butted down by main strength; now and then a gunboat would get hung up, wedged firmly between two trees, immobilized until the crew could get axes and cut through the thick trunks.

Things got worse. Porter at last reached a spot where hundreds of limber saplings grew out of the bed of the stream, bringing his already slow progress down to the merest crawl; and as the steamer puffed away, making a few feet in an hour's time, he began to hear, far behind him, the sound of many men chopping away with axes — Confederate working parties in the rear, felling trees across the river so that the Yankee flotilla, unable to advance any farther, could never get back by the way it had come. It seemed quite likely that the whole fleet would be lost in the middle of a forest.

In the end Sherman came to the rescue, marching troops up along the banks, driving the Confederate working parties away, and enabling Porter to extricate his luckless little fleet. Rudders were unshipped and the ironclads were hauled out stern-to, all of them more or less damaged, everyone aboard from Porter down to the most humble powder-monkey worn out and disillusioned. The Steele's Bayou venture had been the worst failure of the lot. Army and Navy by mutual consent abandoned all further attempts to get into the Yazoo. If Vicksburg were ever taken, it would be taken by some other approach than this one.[22]

Now it was past mid-March, and the entire Vicksburg operation had come to a dead end. Grant had had high hopes — a week earlier he had written to Washburne that "the Yazoo pass expedition is going to prove a perfect success," and he had proudly assured the Congressman that "we are going through a campaign here such as has not been heard of on this continent before." The men were in good health and good spirits: "The health of this command is a subject that has been very much exagerated by the press. I will venture the assertion that there is no army now in the field showing so large a proportion of those present with their command being for duty. Really our troops are more healthy than could possibly have been expected with all their trials." But Pemberton's army was still out of reach, and Grant confessed in a letter to the distant General Banks, far downstream, that "there is nothing left for me but to collect all my strength and attack Snyder's Bluff. This will necessarily be attended with much loss, but I think it can be done." To Congressman Washburne came a doleful letter from his brother, General Cadwallader Washburn:

> This campaign is being badly managed. I am sure of it. I fear a calamity before Vicksburgh. All Grant's schemes have failed. He knows that he has got to do something or off goes his head. My impression is that he intends to attack in front. . . . As one after another of the schemes fail, I hear that he says he has a plan of his own which is yet to be tried in which he has great confidence.[23]

If Grant had a new plan it was time to try it. He had been on the river for two months, and Vicksburg was no nearer falling now than when he came.

CHAPTER NINETEEN

The Man on the River

CHARLES A. DANA had been around. New Hampshire-born and Harvard-educated, he had spent five years in the famous Brook Farm colony, where he wrote essays, sang in the choir, gave lectures, taught various classes and displayed a bump of practical common sense so uncommon among the precious colonists that he was made one of the managing trustees. After Brook Farm evaporated he went into journalism and in 1847 started to work for the *New York Tribune*, where he developed powerful talents as an editor and soon was second in command to Horace Greeley. Meanwhile, he traveled in Europe, compiled a best-selling volume of poetry, and began work on the very successful American Cyclopaedia. He resigned from the *Tribune* in the spring of 1862 when he found the convolutions of the Greeley line in respect to the conduct of the war too hard to follow.

In this varied experience Dana had seen all sorts and conditions of men and had shown the ability to render judgments on them, and now he was supposed to tell Secretary Stanton and President Lincoln all about U. S. Grant. The world had not yet shown him anyone quite like Grant, and Dana was about to have a broadening experience — which, in the end, would be of service to himself, to the administration, and to Grant as well.

Dana was coming out to the Mississippi this spring as a sort of high-class spy for the Secretary of War. He carried a letter of appointment specifying that, as a special commissioner of the War Department, he was to investigate and report on the condition of the pay service in the Western Armies, but in actual fact he was supposed to report on Grant. Both the President and the Secretary of War had their doubts, they were getting many complaints, they wanted a man on the spot who could tell them just what Grant was like and what he was up to, and in the latter part of March Dana reached

Memphis prepared to enlighten them. General Hurlbut, commanding at Memphis, gave him a quick fill-in on Grant's progress, or
lack of progress, down to date; but what could be learned at
Memphis was secondhand and fragmentary, and Stanton presently
directed Dana to go to Grant's headquarters, stay there as long as
he wished, and get the facts at first hand. Dana appeared at Milliken's Bend on April 6, took up quarters on a steamboat that was
moored by the levee, noted that the countryside was lush with
roses, magnolias, Osage orange and stately trees, but desolate because all of the slaves had vanished and the fields were untilled, and
got down to work.

The exact nature of his mission was one of the most poorly kept
secrets of the Civil War. Grant and his staff knew all about it before
Dana arrived, and some of the staff members argued that this War
Department emissary ought to be thrown into the river on arrival.
Rawlins took a different line, however, insisting that Dana be
received and treated with proper hospitality, and Grant himself
seemed to be glad Dana was present. If Dana was going to be sending daily progress reports to the Secretary of War Grant himself
would not have to write nearly so many letters; also, Grant had
nothing to hide, and in no time Dana found himself a member of
the family, with access to all of the top-secret plans.[1]

Dana was about to have an experience — the experience of seeing
Grant as a plain, seemingly unremarkable man who somehow, in a
wholly indefinable way, conveyed an impression of solidity and
capacity. He did not really seem a *great* man; like most people who
saw him at close range, Dana felt compelled to make that point; and
it is clear that this polished Easterner who had traveled so widely
and known so many men was just a little baffled by what he was
looking at now. Years afterward, Dana tried to sum up his impres-
sions of Grant, and his words are obviously the words of a man who
has rubbed elbows with someone profoundly out of the ordinary
but who cannot quite say just how or why he was so impressed.

Grant was an uncommon fellow — the most modest, the most
disinterested and the most honest man I ever knew, with a
temper that nothing could disturb and a judgment that was
judicial in its comprehensiveness and wisdom. Not a great man
except morally; not an original or brilliant man, but sincere,

thoughtful, deep and gifted with courage that never faltered; when the time came to risk all, he went in like a simple-hearted, unaffected, unpretending hero, whom no ill omens could deject and no triumph unduly exalt. A social, friendly man, too, fond of a pleasant joke and also ready with one; but liking above all a long chat of an evening, and ready to sit up all night talking in the cool breeze in front of his tent. Not a man of sentimentality, not demonstrative in friendship, but always holding to his friends and just even to the enemies he hated.[2]

Other men were coming to the same sort of conclusion. Even the *New York World*, which had attacked Grant so bitterly a little earlier, was beginning to see him in a different light. Its correspondent wrote, almost as if he were saying it against his will:

> Gen. Grant still retains his hold upon the affections of his men. His energy and disposition to do something is what they admire in him and he has the remarkable tact of never spoiling any mysterious and vague notions which may be entertained in the minds of the privates as to the qualities of a commander-in-chief. He confines himself to saying and doing as little as possible before his men. No Napoleonic displays, no ostentation, no speech, no superfluous flummery. Thus distance lends enchantment to the view of the man.

Another newspaperman summed him up in more cordial terms. Writing for the *New York Times*, the correspondent who signed himself "Galway" said that Grant "moves with his shoulders thrown a little forward of the perpendicular, his left hand in the pocket of his pantaloons, an unlighted cigar in his mouth, his eyes thrown straight forward, which, from the haze of abstraction that veils them, and a countenance drawn into furrows of thought, would seem to indicate that he was intensely preoccupied." Galway agreed that the soldiers trusted him. He went on:

> The soldiers observe him coming and rising to their feet gather on each side of the way to see him pass — they do not salute him, they only watch him . . . with a certain sort of familiar reverence. His abstract air is not so great while he thus moves along as to prevent his seeing everything without apparently looking at it; you will see this in the fact that how-

ever dense the crowd in which you stand, if you are an acquaintance his eye will for an instant rest on yours with a glance of recollection, and with it a grave nod of recognition. A plain blue suit, without scarf, sword or trappings of any sort, save the double-starred shoulder straps — an indifferently good "Kossuth" hat, with the top battered in close to his head; full beard of a cross between "light" and "sandy"; a square-cut face whose lines and contour indicate extreme endurance and determination, complete the external appearance of this small man, as one sees him passing along, turning and chewing restlessly the end of his unlighted cigar.[3]

A doctor on McPherson's staff wrote that Grant was "plain as an old shoe," and said that it was hard to make new troops believe that this man in a common soldier's blouse with a battered felt hat, and with cavalry pants stuffed in muddy boots, was actually the Commanding General. A private soldier said that the army believed Grant never made mistakes: "Everything that Grant directs is right. His soldiers believe in him. In our private talk among ourselves I have never heard a single soldier speak in doubt of Grant." The men liked Grant's unassuming ways. Most generals, when they rode the lines, went attended by swanky staffs, usually with a cavalry escort; Grant was customarily attended by no one save a couple of orderlies, to carry messages if need arose. "The soldiers seem to look upon him as a friendly partner of theirs, not as an arbitrary commander. As he passes by, the private soldiers feel as free to greet him as they would to address one of their neighbors when meeting him at home. 'Good morning, General,' 'Pleasant day, General,' and like expressions are the greetings he meets everywhere. The soldiers when meeting him are never embarrassed by the thought that they are talking to a great general." Yet they rarely cheered him, and when he rode the lines they did not throw their hats in the air and yell. "A pleasant salute to, and a good-natured nod from him in return, seems more appropriate." [4]

The simple fact is that Grant was not quite the same person in the early spring of 1863 that he had been before. He had been growing, developing, finding himself, in the months since Halleck left for Washington. The change is evident through a study of his dispatches, reports and official correspondence. They become crisper, more solid, straight to the point, business-like; the impression gained by studying them is that of a man who has at last mastered the job of running an army, who no longer doubts either his own status or his own powers and who is moving ahead with full confidence.

Sherman commented, years later, on the way in which Grant liked to write his own orders and dispatches. He was jealous, said Sherman, of any secretary's attempt to write anything for him: "He would sit down and scribble off an order easier than he could tell another what he wanted. If anyone came along and remarked to him, 'That was a clever order Rawlins put out for you today,' Grant would say right out, 'I wrote that myself.' I presume I have 150 orders and memoranda all in his own hand. Some of them read about like this: 'Take plenty of shovels and picks up to Rye Bend to clear the way.' I think that is just how one of them reads. He had been over the ground I was to go on . . . He knew what was wanted and so sent me word. He may have spoken to me about it before. He was a great man for details. He remembered the most minute details and watched every point." On a very different level, a private soldier got the same impression, saying: "He will ride along the long line of the army, apparently an indifferent observer, yet he sees and notices everything. He seems to know and remember every regiment, and in fact every cannon in his large army." 5

Grant owed something, undoubtedly, to the change in his relationship with Halleck. The nagging faultfinding of the Donelson-Shiloh-Corinth period was gone. Halleck was treating him now as a tested, fully competent officer, writing gossipy letters to him, giving him friendly advice, offering him the support which a general-in-chief would give to a trusted subordinate. In part, this may have been because none of the other army commanders with whom Halleck was dealing was measuring up: more and more, the tone of Halleck's letters shows that he was relying on Grant as he never could rely on Burnside, Hooker or Rosecrans — to say nothing of McClellan and Buell. The McClernand tangle had unquestionably brought Grant and Halleck closer together, and it had left Grant with a fuller awareness of his own authority.

The winter had been difficult. None of the schemes to bring the

army into a good fighting position had worked. Yet Grant was confident, as the last of the Yazoo ventures faded out, and he proudly
told Washburne "we are going through a campaign here such as has
not been heard of on this continent before." At Donelson and Shiloh, Grant could cry out that he did not know what Washington
wanted of him: now that note is gone, he knows what he wants and
he knows, deep within himself, that what he wants will be what
Washington wants. The Grant of April, 1863, is at last the Grant
who knows precisely what he is about.[6]

Nobody was quite ready to say that Grant was a great man: nobody, at the same time, failed to realize that when you touched this
stoop-shouldered, unassuming little man you touched somebody
very special. The reputation that had been built up around Grant —
hard-drinker, butcher, blundering man who knew nothing much
except killing — still existed, and people were forever being pleasantly surprised to find that when they got at the man himself nothing of this nature was visible. Some devoted women came down the
river this winter, dreading what they were going to see when at last
they met this slouchy little general: they met him, and found that
nothing that they had heard about him came close to the truth, and
their hearts beat faster when they realized that this soldier was the
kind of person they had doubted but dreamed about. Mary Livermore led this delegation from the Sanitary Commission down to
Milliken's Bend, as the winter of 1863 ended, and she and the
others who came with her had heard all of the stories — Grant
boasted that he would take Vicksburg if it cost him three quarters
of his army, Grant would turn the Mississippi out of its course and
leave Vicksburg high and dry, Grant was a conscienceless drunkard who had to be put to bed at night by sorrowing juniors — and
here, in a cramped room on a steamboat, they were talking with the
man. They looked at him, these women who ahead of their generation knew men and their frailties and the bad things that could happen in a womanless army, and Mrs. Livermore wrote down what
they saw:

"Grant was not a drunkard — that was immediately apparent to
us. This conviction gave us such a joy that had we been younger
we should all, men and women alike, have tossed our hats in the
air and hurrahed. As it was, we looked each other in the face and

said heartily, 'Thank God!' . . . The clear eye, clean skin, firm flesh and steady nerves of General Grant gave the lie to the universal calumnies then current concerning his intemperate habits and those of the officers of his staff. Our eyes had become practiced in reading the diagnosis of drunkenness."

There were several things Mrs. Livermore wanted from the General, beside the chief thing — confidence, and an understanding — but when she saw him alone she realized that he was pressed for time, so she asked for only one favor. There were twenty-one desperately sick soldiers, whose names she had on a bit of paper, who needed to be discharged from the Army but who could not be discharged because somehow their papers had been lost so there was nothing on which Army routine could act. Twenty-one lives, which would very soon be lost unless something was done, and the doctors and officers she had talked with had raised difficulties . . . Lady, you don't know the Army, we can't do things this way, if the man's papers aren't straight he is out of luck. . . .

So Mary Livermore got into the cabin on the steamboat where Grant was working. The place was wreathed in heavy cigar smoke, and the table where Grant sat was stacked high with papers. Grant, when this woman came in, "seemed the most bashful man I ever encountered." He got up in a hurry, tried to shove half a dozen chairs forward for her to sit in, took his cigar out of his mouth and his hat off of his head and then replaced both without knowing that he was doing it, and asked what he could do. She explained the matter of the 21 soldiers who were going to die. Grant mumbled something to the effect that this was a case for the medical director; she blurted out that it was time to cut a little red tape; Grant muttered that he would let her know about it . . . and the next day a staff officer came to Mary Livermore from Grant with the signed papers that sent the soldiers home with discharges, men who now had a chance to live again. From that moment, as far as this woman was concerned, Grant was a great man.[7]

The old attacks continued, to be sure. In the middle of the winter Murat Halstead, editor of the *Cincinnati Gazette*, forwarded to Secretary Chase a despairing letter from a correspondent at Vicksburg: "There never was a more thoroughly disgusted, disheartened, demoralized army than this is, and all because it is under such men as Grant and Sherman." The letter repeated all of the old allegations about sickness, about inefficiency of the medical department, about sick men who lacked care "while drunken doctors ride from barrooms to whore houses in government ambulances," and Halstead inquired: "How is it that Grant who was behind at Ft. Henry, drunk at Donelson, surprised and whipped at Shiloh and driven back from Oxford, Miss., is still in command? Gov. Chase, these things are true. Our noble army of the Mississippi is being *wasted* by the foolish, drunken, stupid Grant. He can't organize or control or fight an army. I have no personal feeling about it, but I know he is an ass." [8]

Even worse was an attack which came from a former friend of Grant's, Brigadier General C. S. Hamilton. Hamilton and Grant had known one another in the Old Army, Hamilton had fought well at Iuka and Corinth, and when Grant went down the Mississippi he left Hamilton in charge of the district of West Tennessee. Hamilton wrote Grant cordially, wishing him well and adding: "I hope you will be entirely successful in your undertaking. The taking of Vicksburg is *your* right, and I hope it may be added to the laurels which belong to you as the most successful general of the war." But although he wrote in this friendly fashion, Hamilton was growing bitter. Others were being promoted past him — McPherson, among them — and Hamilton suspected that it was because of favoritism. He had been brooding for a long time, and on February 11 — two days after writing that friendly letter to Grant — he wrote to his friend, Senator Doolittle of Wisconsin, in quite a different vein:

> You have asked me to write you confidentially. I will now say what I have never breathed. *Grant is a drunkard.* His wife has been with him for months only to use her influence in keeping him sober. He tries to let liquor alone but he cannot resist the temptation always. When he came to Memphis he left his wife at LaGrange & for several days after getting here was beastly drunk, utterly incapable of doing anything. Quimby and I took him in charge, watching him day & night & keeping liquor away from him & we telegraphed to his wife & brought her on to take care of him.

Hamilton was full of bitterness. He asserted that General Hurlbut, who commanded at Memphis, was another drunkard; that Mc-

Pherson had done nothing to deserve his recent elevation to Major General; and that McClernand was not to be trusted. (In an earlier letter, Hamilton had explained that Gordon Granger, a major general in the Army of the Cumberland, was "an ignorant, drinking, blatant, obscene loafer" and that Rosecrans was probably mixed up in cotton deals and, despite his reputation as a devout Catholic, was a very profane man and a hard drinker to boot.) [9]

There is nothing to show that Grant knew anything about what Hamilton was saying, either then or later. He did know, however, that Hamilton was scheming to replace McPherson in command of the 17th corps, and Grant wrote to Halleck to protest about it; and a little later, when Hamilton found himself unable to get along with Hurlbut and offered his resignation, Grant promptly sent the resignation along with the recommendation that it be accepted. The War Department agreed, and Hamilton ceased to be a problem.

The point is that things were a little different now. Washington had been told, over and over again, that Grant was a drunkard. The fact that these stories — the detailed, seemingly circumstantial ones, at any rate — nearly always came from men who had been having a fight with Grant, or who found some order of his oppressive, may have taken a little of the sparkle off of the charges; in any case, they were beginning to collapse of their own weight, they were no longer raising a sensation. Washington was beginning to see that this general was an entirely different sort of man. The one quality in Grant which was becoming more evident than any other was a quiet, unshakable strength of purpose which made him wholly reliable, a man who could be counted on, a man who had a sort of inevitability about him — and this, of all human qualities imaginable, is the last thing to be found in an alcoholic.

It was just a little later this spring that Chaplain Eaton, who had "all of those darkies on his shoulders," went to Washington to report to the President on the work he was doing. He found that Lincoln had come to his own conclusion. Lincoln told him how a delegation of Congressmen had come to the White House to urge Grant's removal on the ground that he drank too much. As Eaton remembered the conversation, Lincoln said: "I then began to ask them if they knew what he drank, what brand of whiskey he used, telling them most seriously that I wished they would find out. They conferred with each other and concluded they could not tell what brand he used. I urged them to ascertain and let me know, for if it made fighting generals like Grant I should like to get some of it for distribution." Eaton recalled that when he went to see Grant at the beginning of the spring he had been warned that the man was showing the signs of hard work, "looking like half a dozen men condensed into one"; he found it so, seeing Grant clad in an old brown linen duster and a battered slouch hat, with his trousers worn through by constant rubbing against saddle leather — "His very clothes, as well as the crows' feet on his brow, bore testimony to the strenuousness of the life he was leading." [10]

If the Vicksburg campaign was getting a bad press in the North, much of the blame undoubtedly belonged to Sherman. No American soldier ever disliked reporters more than Sherman did. The going-over he had received while commanding in Kentucky in the fall of 1861 had permanently embittered him; he considered newspapermen liars at best and Confederate agents at worst, and, quite literally, he would have been delighted to hang some of them if he could have found a proper excuse. This winter Sherman had been having a bitter passage at arms with Tom Knox of the *New York Herald*. Knox had written highly critical articles about the fight at Chickasaw Bayou and had recited the old charges that Sherman was insane, or on the edge of insanity. Sherman ranted that Knox was "a spy and an infamous dog," asserted that his dispatch had given the Confederates information about Union strength and tactics before Vicksburg, and had the reporter court-martialed as a spy. The courtmartial dragged on for days, refused to convict Knox of espionage, but did order him sent outside the army's lines, under penalty of imprisonment if he returned. In Washington, the press rallied in Knox's support, a delegation called on President Lincoln, and on March 20 Lincoln issued orders revoking the sentence of the courtmartial; Knox could return to the Vicksburg area, said the President, and could stay there, "if General Grant shall give his express assent."

Back to Milliken's Bend came Knox, seeking Grant's express assent. He did not get it. Grant told him bluntly that he was not going to overrule Sherman on this point. If Knox could make his peace with Sherman, so that Sherman would agree that he should remain in this military area, then Grant would agree likewise; otherwise, Knox would have to leave. Grant suggested that Knox write Sherman a letter.

Knox would not apologize or beg. He wrote Sherman a stiff note which did no more than express regret at "the want of harmony between portions of the Army and the Press," with a rider voicing hope that this want of harmony might presently diminish. This was not good enough for Sherman, and he refused to let Knox come back as a correspondent. "Come with a sword or musket in your hand, prepared to share with us our fate in sunshine or storm, in prosperity and adversity, in plenty and scarcity, and I will welcome you as a brother and associate," he wrote to Knox. "But as a representative of the Press which you yourself say makes so slight a difference between truth and falsehood, and my answer is Never!" Grant sustained Sherman, Knox went elsewhere, and the *Herald* sent a new man down to cover the army's doings.[11] The whole business unquestionably hurt the army's press relations, since Knox clearly had done nothing worse than to write a badly biased news story — no uncommon failing in those days. But the affair had a certain significance. Anyone could have guessed that Grant would not overrule Sherman — but here, in a case which had generated much heat, Lincoln was refusing to overrule Grant. Slowly but increasingly, the President was beginning to understand this far-off general.

Grant himself lacked Sherman's high-pressure temper, and had fewer personal problems with the press. Sylvanus Cadwallader remembered that during the advance down the Mississippi Central in the fall he had sent home a story commenting bitterly on the marauding and pillaging which Grant's soldiers inflicted on the people along the Tennessee-Mississippi border. When copies of the *Times* reached camp, Grant called Cadwallader to his tent. Cadwallader went, expecting to be sent home, perhaps even to be imprisoned as his predecessor had been. But Grant was calm enough; he asked whether the story in the *Times* was Cadwallader's, and when told that it was he went on to admit that the troops had indeed behaved very badly. They could not well be restrained, he said, without the cooperation of the regimental officers; invading the enemy's country, he could not stop everything in order to hold courts of inquiry and courts-martial; if he himself caught a soldier engaged in acts of vandalism he would probably have him shot at once — and, all in all, if Cadwallader never wrote anything more untruthful than this particular story he would never be in any trouble at headquarters. Then Grant went on to sum up his own policy in regard to war correspondents. He would not try to censor letters or dispatches in advance of publication; newspapers and their reporters must determine what to publish, and he would make the reporters personally responsible by ordering them home if they sent off improper dispatches. All correspondents in his department, he added, were at liberty to give all of the facts about an army move that had already taken place; all he would insist was that they must not publish predictions about future movements.[12] Sherman might, and did, storm that unless the press could be muzzled "we are defeated to the end of time"; Grant simply said that the press must not reveal his military plans to the enemy, and let it go at that.

As winter turned to spring, a faint change in the tone of press comment on affairs at Vicksburg was evident. The *New York World* continued to complain that muddleheaded management had let affairs slip into a stalemate, and it proposed that General McClellan be sent West to take hold of things and work out a campaign that would mean something, but even this paper was moderate in its discussion of Grant; the worst it had to say, just now, was that the Steele's Bayou expedition had failed because the "ever-sanguine Grant" had entrusted it to Sherman the incompetent. The *Chicago Journal* reported that the health of the army, which never had been as bad as the North had been led to believe, was steadily improving, and the *New York Times* agreed that this was so. The real trouble, the *Times* explained, came from the utter indiscipline of the new regiments, the inevitable result of a defective system of organization. The *Times* correspondent went on to explain: "Each colonel comes into the field expecting to run for Congress, each captain has his eye upon a seat in the state legislature, each lieutenant and noncommissioned officer is looking forward to the hour when he can appeal to the patriotism of the public for the position of justice of the peace, constable, pound master or something; and in consequence not one of these dare say a peremptory word. . . . Not all

are like this, but the sick, the arsonites, robbers and criminals come
from these regiments." The *Times* man added that he had been told
by one colonel, in a tone obviously meant for the lounging soldiers
to hear, that discipline degraded men and made mere machines out
of them.

The press no longer predicted gloomily that the army would
sicken and die in the mud before it could get into action, but it was
not able to forecast a quick end to the campaign. Rather plaintively,
the *Times* this spring was asking, "what man of genius, in this fer-
tile land of genius" would suggest to "our bedevilled country and
baffled generals, some possible mode of taking Vicksburg — and
take it?" The eternally gloomy *World* remarked sagely that "we
have the best reasons for believing that neither the generals in command of our land forces there nor their superiors at Washington
expect or hope to take Vicksburg this year." [13]

In all the Mississippi Valley, apparently, only one man believed
that Vicksburg would presently be taken, and that man was Grant
himself. But the plan on which the successful campaign would
finally be based seems to have been worked out slowly, over many
weeks. Much later, Grant wrote that he had had this plan in his
head all along, and had brought it out only after trying all of the
expedients which others had suggested, but it seems likely that his
memory betrayed him on this point. Judging by what he said and
wrote at the time, one is forced to believe that if this plan did indeed exist in the General's mind it was lodged in his subconscious,
revealing itself slowly, emerging piece by piece from the haze
of cigar smoke in the cabin of the headquarters steamer. This
smoky haze, indeed, was quite literally present, and there is at least
one shadowy glimpse of Grant sitting in the middle of it, bent over
a table of maps and reports in what had been the "ladies' cabin" of
his boat while other generals and lesser officers listened to the military band play, passed the bottle, and relaxed. Up to Grant's table,
at last, came McPherson, glass in hand, to say: "General, this won't
do, you are injuring yourself; join us in a few toasts and throw this
burden off your mind." Grant, it is told, looked up, smiled at Mc-
Pherson, said that whisky would not help — and suggested that if
McPherson would give him a dozen cigars and then go away and
let him alone, he could probably get his plans in order.[14] So he

smoked and brooded, and the basic elements of the great Vicksburg campaign began to fall into place in his head.

As Grant smoked and reflected and made ready for the spring campaign he was compelled to see that the war itself was changing profoundly. It was becoming very grim, and in the steps he took to check guerilla warfare Grant was showing a grimness of his own. At the beginning of the winter he had notified Hurlbut, at Memphis, that the Memphis and Charleston railroad must be kept open as far as Corinth in spite of all opposition . . . "if necessary I will remove every family and every species of personal property between the Hatchie and Coldwater rivers. I will also move south every family in Memphis of doubtful loyalty . . . if it is necessary for our security." He explained the basis for such actions: "If the enemy, with his regularly organized forces, attack us I do not propose to punish non-combatant citizens for it; but these guerillas receive support and countenance from this class of citizens, and by their acts will bring punishment upon them." [15] In addition, Halleck was warning him that the war now must be fought without gloves, and there was a new emphasis on the problem of fugitive slaves. Grant had put Chaplain Eaton in charge of the camps for lost contrabands, and he had found that this problem was growing larger and larger; the question of the slave was central to the whole war effort, and it could be handled only if those who handled it adopted a new attitude toward the attempt to beat down the rebellion.

It had been decreed that slaves who wanted to leave their masters were to be welcomed into the Union lines, and were to be cared for; but there were so many of them that the mere act of receiving and caring for them got in the way of the war effort, and Grant had tried this winter to whittle the problem down to size. In mid-February he had issued orders, setting forth the fact that the army had enough to do without making itself responsible for this mass of helpless fugitives and specifying that "the enticing of Negroes to leave their homes to come within the lines of our army is positively forbidden." Negroes now within the Union lines would not be turned out, but no more would be permitted to come in. To McPherson, Grant wrote a note of explanation: "In regard to the con-

trabands, the question is a troublesome one. I am not permitted to
send them out of the department, and such numbers as we have
it is hard to keep them in." But Halleck wrote that this exclusion
policy was wrong. Escaped slaves must not only be harbored; they
must be positively encouraged to leave their masters, because the
Army's attitude toward them could become a powerful instrument
toward the winning of the war.

> This is not only bad policy in itself [wrote Halleck in refer-
> ence to the exclusion order] but is directly opposed to the
> policy adopted by the government. . . . It is expected that you
> will use your official and personal influence to remove prejudices
> on this subject and to fully and thoroughly carry out the policy
> now adopted and ordered by the government. That policy is to
> withdraw from the use of the enemy all the slaves you can, and
> to employ those so withdrawn to the best possible advantage
> against the enemy.

Then Halleck went on to explain the new situation.

> The character of the war has very much changed within the
> last year. There is now no possible hope of reconciliation with
> the rebels. The Union party in the South is virtually destroyed.
> There can be no peace but that which is forced by the sword.
> We must conquer the rebels or be conquered by them. The
> North must conquer the slave oligarchy or become slaves them-
> selves — the manufacturers mere "hewers of wood and drawers
> of water" to Southern aristocrats.
> This is the phase which the rebellion has now assumed. We
> must take things as they are. The Government, looking at the
> subject in all its aspects, has adopted a policy, and we must
> cheerfully and faithfully carry out that policy.[16]

Grant adapted himself without delay. Shortly after hearing from
Halleck he passed the word along in a letter to Major General Fred
Steele:

> Rebellion has assumed that shape now that it can only termi-
> nate by the complete subjugation of the South or the overthrow
> of the Government. It is our duty, therefore, to use every means

to weaken the enemy, by destroying their means of subsistence, withdrawing their means of cultivating their fields, and in every other way possible. All the Negroes you have you will provide for where they are, issuing to them necessary rations until other disposition is made of them. You will also encourage all Negroes, particularly middle-aged males, to come within our lines. General L. Thomas is now here, with authority to make ample provision for the Negro.[17]

The reference was to the lean, dusty Adjutant General of the Army, Major General Lorenzo Thomas, who was visiting Grant's army now on a vaguely defined mission which apparently had a faint overtone of the job assigned to Dana — that is, to give the War Department a report on Grant — but who also had something more concrete to do: to organize combat regiments out of the able-bodied males in the mass of contrabands in the Army's camps. Thomas was making speeches to the troops, explaining the new program, pointing out that the colored regiments would be officered by white men chosen from the Army — cunningly picked bait, this, since it meant that some hundreds of enlisted men might aspire to commissions — and he was warning that the full weight of government authority lay back of this. . . . "All of you will some day be on picket duty, and I charge you all if any of this unfortunate race come within your lines that you do not turn them away but receive them kindly and cordially. They are to be encouraged to come to us. They are to be received with open arms; they are to be fed and clothed; they are to be armed." Not only, continued the General, was he authorized to commission men for these Negro regiments; he was also authorized to dismiss from the Army any man, regardless of rank, who resisted the new policy; and "this part of my duty I will most assuredly perform if any case comes before me." [18]

This program was not popular with all of the troops, and there was a good deal of grumbling. An Ohio soldier wrote that there was so much opposition to the formation of Negro regiments that it "at times assumed the character of anarchy"; many officers and enlisted men, he said, muttered that "they would lay down their arms and unbuckle their swords." An Illinois soldier complained that the Negroes he had seen could no more take care of themselves than so many eight-year-old children, and said: "If we have to keep those Negroes in the country, I say keep them as slaves. Take them from secesh and turn them over to Unionists, but don't free them in America. They can't stand it." But the grumbling did not last long, and the threatened mutinies did not take place. The business of the commissions was attractive; so, too, was the dawning notion that the colored soldiers who stopped a Confederate bullet was simply intercepting a missile that otherwise might strike a white soldier. The Illinoisan who had held forth so bitterly about the Negro's lack of capacity for a free man's status wrote a few weeks later that he had been visiting the Negroes' camps and that "an honest confession is good for the soul."

"I never thought I would," he went on, "but I am getting strongly in favor of arming them, and am becoming so blind that I can't see why they will not make soldiers. A year ago last January I didn't like to hear anything of emancipation. Last fall, accepted confiscation of rebels' Negroes quietly. In January took to emancipation readily, and now believe in arming the Negroes. The only objection I have to it is a matter of pride. I almost begin to think of applying for a position in a regiment myself." [19]

Grant threw the weight of his authority back of the program, ordering all corps, division and post commanders to help complete the Negro regiments that were being organized and to see that supplies, stores and the like were issued just as for other troops. "It is expected," he wrote, "that all commanders will especially exert themselves in carrying out the policy of the administration, not only in organizing colored regiments and rendering them efficient, but also in removing prejudice against them." [20]

This was not a one-way proposition. The North had been bumbling its way through a connected chain of inevitabilities, and from fighting to put down rebellion it was now prepared to fight for a new status for the Negro, although not very many of those who were doing the fighting could work up much enthusiasm for the change; but of all the things which the North might have done, nothing could have been better designed to touch off a last-ditch resistance among the leaders of the Confederacy. The tip-off had come much earlier — in August of 1862, to be precise, when Major General David Hunter (he whose place Grant's staff had thought

Grant might well take, if the difficulties with Halleck became unendurable), commanding Union troops along the South Carolina
coast, had organized a regiment of Negro troops. When Secretary
Stanton asked him what he thought he was doing, Hunter had
blandly replied that he was not enlisting fugitive slaves: he was
simply making up a regiment of Negroes who had belonged to fugitive Rebels, Negroes who were "working with remarkable industry to place themselves in a position to go in full and effective pursuit of their fugacious and traitorous proprietors." This had gone
down well with the abolitionists, but it had stirred fury in Richmond. From the Confederate Adjutant General, Samuel Cooper,
there came an order stating that Hunter, or any other Federal,
"employed in drilling, organizing or instructing slaves with a view
to their armed service in this war," would not, if captured by
Confederates, be treated as a prisoner of war; he would be held for
execution as a felon, at such time and place as the President of the
Confederacy might order. As professionally-minded a soldier as
Beauregard was moved, in the fall of 1862, to write to his good
friend, Congressman W. Porcher Miles, in Richmond: "Has bill
for execution of abolition prisoners after 1st of January next
passed? Do it and England will be stirred into action. It is high time
to proclaim the black flag for that period. Let the execution be with
the garrote." Addressing the Confederate Congress at the beginning of 1863, Jefferson Davis had referred bitterly to the Emancipation Proclamation, speaking of "our own detestation of those
who have attempted the most execrable measure recorded in the
history of guilty man." [21] The South would assuredly meet grimness with grimness.

There was more to all of this than a mere business of tightening
up on the guerillas and trying to turn contrabands into useful soldiers. Unexpressed but implicit, there was a final departure from
the original notion that a permanent political settlement could be
obtained by a purely military victory. The war was taking on its
final character: it was no longer a mere matter of armies, but of
two nations putting every resource into a struggle for survival. All
of the capacities which the country possessed were to be used re-
morselessly, to the hilt, until the enemy's ability to fight had been

destroyed. And as it changed, the war was becoming more and more the kind of struggle which Grant, more than any other Union officer, was fitted to conduct. His distinguishing characteristic from the start had been an uncomplicated determination to make direct and complete use of the North's obvious advantages. He had never had any of McClellan's or Buell's feeling that the end in view was to outmaneuver an opposing army, so that its general might be induced to confess defeat, and he had never shared in Halleck's belief that the war might be won by the simple occupation of Confederate territory. His deepest instinct was not to beat the army that opposed him, but to annihilate it. Halleck's current warning that there could be no peace but by the sword was, in effect, a charter of authority. From now on, increasingly, the war would go Grant's way.

But first of all there was Vicksburg. Grant wanted it, not so much because it was a fortress that closed the Mississippi as because it contained a powerful army which had to be eliminated. He would take Vicksburg, and he would eliminate Pemberton's army . . . but first, he had to get across the river; and, as the early Southern spring came to the great valley, Grant meditated, chewed his cigars, and stared into the hazy smoke in the headquarters cabin, evolving the plan that would get his army into a position where it could fight.

CHAPTER TWENTY

An End to Worry

EVERYTHING else had failed. Grant's area of choice was so narrow that it seemed to offer little more than the chance to select one of two routes to probable disaster. He could go back to Memphis and start all over again, which was out of the question for political reasons, or he could risk everything (and lose everything too, more likely than not) in a massed assault on the works at Snyder's Bluff. By military logic these were the only options that remained.

It was time, therefore, to go beyond military logic. As Grant reflected on the situation, one fact began to be clear: an army which lay west of a fortified river and wanted to fight an enemy east of that river might conceivably reach that enemy in the simplest way imaginable — by walking downstream until it was past the fortifications, crossing the river in boats, and then walking upstream on the eastern side. If nothing else would work perhaps this would be the solution.

It was the solution which Grant at last found, but it was not nearly as simple as it may look now. West of the river the ground was swampy, cut up with innumerable pesky watercourses — too wet to march across, not quite wet enough for steamboats. If it did march, the army could not cross the river without transports, and the Federals had none of these below Vicksburg. Once across, it would have intricate problems of supply; and, finally, the Confederates would be bound to see what was going on, and presumably they would have the time, the means and the strategic intelligence to take effective countermeasures. The last point was important: over-all command of Confederate forces in Mississippi and Tennessee was held now by General Joseph E. Johnston, a strategist for whom Grant had immense respect.

Nevertheless, there was no other solution which offered any hope at all; and, indeed, it appears that this notion of getting into the rear of Vicksburg by moving downstream had been in the back of Grant's mind all winter. It appears, also, that he owed something to the presence in Louisiana, somewhere below the Confederate stronghold of Port Hudson, of the Federal army commanded by General Banks.[1] Grant and Banks were supposed to co-operate in the opening of the Mississippi River, and Banks apparently was about to move against Port Hudson. If Grant could get downstream and join hands with him, his supply line could run upstream from New Orleans and everything would be a good deal simpler. On March 22, just as the Steele's Bayou fiasco was approaching its melancholy conclusion, Grant sent Banks a letter.

The letter is interesting because it shows Grant thinking out loud. His plans were still in the process of formulation; he was almost (but not quite) ready to abandon the approach he had been following through the winter, but he had not yet settled on the program he would finally follow. It is as if, writing to Banks, he was groping toward the final solution, being led toward it by Banks's mere existence in the lower Mississippi valley.

He would not, he explained, be able to put his army on the eastern shore of the river above Vicksburg; he could see, by now, that nothing was going to come of the move through the Yazoo country. He had not, however, quite given up on the notion of a direct assault: indeed, when he wrote to Banks he felt that this might be his only recourse. The Yazoo move failing, he wrote, "there is nothing left for me but to collect all my strength and attack Haynes' [Snyder's] Bluff. This will necessarily be attended with much loss, but I think it can be done." (In this last remark Grant was expressing an optimism that quickly died: he did not continue to think it could be done or he would have tried it.) But, Grant wrote, if Banks could take Port Hudson, Grant could send troops down to meet him, Banks could bring up his own transports — he had Admiral Farragut on the lower river — and the united forces could go anywhere they chose. If Banks could not take Port Hudson, he could at least pin down a good many Confederate troops there. Grant would bring part or all of his army down, and between them they could pinch off Port Hudson and open the lower river.

The day after he wrote to Banks, Grant wrote to Farragut, offering a slight elaboration of the plan. If he could assemble enough light-draft steamers from the Ohio River, he told the admiral, he could move at least twenty thousand men down to the Red River by the Lake Providence route. (He had not quite given up on this plan, at this moment.) From the Red River it would be easy to get in touch with Banks, and for the united armies the progression from Port Hudson to Vicksburg would be comparatively simple.

But Grant had no sooner written to Farragut about the Lake Providence route than he was compelled to cancel this plan. The light-draft steamers he needed simply could not be had: he would need from forty to fifty of them to carry twenty thousand men, without counting the freighters needed to move ammunition, rations and ordnance; and the quartermaster's people at St. Louis could not get their hands on a third of the required number.[2] If Grant was to go down the river and meet Banks, his army would have to take the deceptively simple, potentially disastrous overland route down from Milliken's Bend.

Below Milliken's Bend, Louisiana is full of crescent-shaped bits of lost river bed brimming with stagnant water, all tied together by little watercourses which do not seem to lead anywhere in particular. Not far inland from Milliken's Bend, a complicated chain of these began — Roundaway Bayou, Bayou Vidal, Lake St. Joseph, and the like, rimmed by muddy levees meant to keep the bottom land from ruinous floods, dotted here and there with plantations and, once in a great while, by a little town. This chain of bayous, lakes and swamps could with a little work be turned into a continuous, if shallow, waterway; if water from the Mississippi were then admitted, somewhere in the vicinity of Milliken's Bend, the waterway should become deep enough to float tugboats, scows and perhaps some undersized steamboats; in which case the whole army could float down to a point on the Mississippi known as New Carthage, twenty miles below Vicksburg in a straight line, thirty-five miles downstream as the winding Mississippi flowed.

New Carthage might be exactly the spot Grant was looking for. It was safely below the Rebel batteries at Warrenton, and it was fifteen or twenty miles upstream from the other batteries at Grand Gulf. A Federal army at New Carthage (if it had transports, and some gunboats to guard the river crossing) could either move up and strike Warrenton or move down and strike Grand Gulf — or, for all anyone could tell, it might land on the eastern bank of the Mississippi somewhere between the two points, blotting out these riverside garrisons at its leisure.

The army would go to New Carthage, then — if it could get there. As March came to an end, McClernand was instructed to send out a detachment to explore the route, to clear it of any Confederate military elements that might be on hand, and to make possible the movement of the rest of the army.

Spearhead of the movement was the 69th Indiana infantry, accompanied by two companies of cavalry, a field battery and a detachment of engineers with a pontoon train: perhaps a thousand men, all told. The men started out on a clear spring morning, with a warm wind drifting north under a bright sun, and they remembered afterward that the fields were green, with flowers in bloom on occasional hilly slopes, and that it was good to be on the move after the tedious winter. What they did not know at the time — what nobody knew, unless Grant himself had a prevision of it — was that as their advance files moved away from the river and went tramping south in the end-of-March sunshine, the final doom of Vicksburg and of the Confederate cause in the West was beginning to take shape.

The movement went on at first without great difficulty. In the afternoon the soldiers drove Rebel patrols out of the village of Richmond, and the next day they went on, following the watercourse. The engineers commandeered a scow on some plantation, turned it into a gunboat of sorts by erecting plank bulwarks and mounting a couple of howitzers, and with this odd craft (christened, for some reason no one could remember, *Oppossum*) and a flotilla of skiffs as its naval arm, the expedition moved on, and it pulled up at last on Smith's plantation on the Bayou Vidal, two miles from the objective point, New Carthage.

Prospects here looked poor. There were breaks in the levee, and the surrounding country was badly flooded, so that New Carthage appeared to be an island. Still, if further reconnaissance must be made by boat, these soldiers had plenty of boats, and they had demonstrated that the route down from Milliken's Bend, if difficult, was perfectly feasible. They went on to New Carthage, and they found that the foraging on the Louisiana plantations was excellent; when McClernand came down to join the advance the soldiers gave him a notable dinner of sweet potatoes, stewed chicken, and coffee laced with real cream. McClernand got more troops in motion, some guns were emplaced on the Mississippi levee, and Grant was given a progress report.[3]

Most of McClernand's troops were still at Milliken's Bend, but he had various regiments spread out over the whole thirty-mile route. As far as Smith's plantation, he reported, the road was in fairly good shape, but beyond that point everything seemed to be mud and water, and there would be much work for the engineers. Grant digested all of this and notified Admiral Porter that he was going to need some gunboats. He believed that the inland waterway could be made passable for flatboats and tugs, and with these he should be able to cross the Mississippi; but to insure a safe landing on the eastern side he had to have the help of the Navy, since "without the aid of gunboats it will hardly be worth while to send troops to New Carthage, or to open the passage from here to there." [4]

Porter was willing to do anything that was asked of him, but he wanted one thing made perfectly clear: once the gunboats ran downstream by the Vicksburg batteries, Grant would have passed the point of no return. Porter's ironclads were those squat, ugly creations universally known as "Turtles," and although they were exceedingly useful they had been sadly underengined. Going downstream they could run the batteries without much difficulty, but if they tried to come back upstream their progress against the current would be so very slow that the batteries might pound them to pieces.

You must recollect [Porter wrote] that when these gunboats once go below we give up all hopes of ever getting them up again. If it is your intention to occupy Grand Gulf in force, it will be necessary to have vessels there to protect the troops or quiet the fortifications now there. If I do send vessels below, it will be the best vessels I have, and there will be nothing left to attack Haynes' Bluff, in case it should be deemed necessary to try it. It will require some little preparation to send these vessels below. Coal and provisions are wanted; they cannot well do without.

Grant's mind was made up. He explained his reasons to Porter in a letter written on April 2:

I am satisfied that an attack upon Haynes' Bluff would be attended with immense sacrifice of life, if not with defeat. This, then, closes out the last hope of turning the enemy by the right. I have sent troops through from Milliken's Bend to New Carthage, to garrison and hold the whole route and make the wagon road good. At Richmond a number of boats were secured, which can aid in carrying subsistence from that point to New Carthage, and will also answer for ferrying any intermediate bayous. In addition to this, I have a large force working on a canal from the river to Willow [Walnut] Bayou, and in clearing this latter out. With this done, there will be good water communication from here to Carthage for barges and tugs. I have sent to St. Louis and Chicago for barges and tugs, and ordered all empty barges here to be fitted up for the transportation of troops and artillery. With these appliances I intend to be able to move 20,000 men at one time.

A final paragraph gave Porter a fuller insight into Grant's plan:

Having then fully determined upon operating from New Carthage either by way of Grand Gulf or Warrenton, I am of the same opinion as when I addressed you a few days since, that is, that it is important to prevent the enemy from further fortifying either of these places. I am satisfied that one army corps with the aid of two gunboats can take and hold Grand Gulf until such time as I might be able to get my whole army there and make provision for supplying them. If necessary, therefore, I would send this number of troops as soon as the necessity for them was demonstrated. I would, admiral, therefore renew my request to prepare for running the blockade at as early a day as possible.[5]

At this moment, hardly any of the Federal commanders aside from Grant himself really believed in the new movement. Frank Blair recalled after the war that Grant had explained the operation to a conference of his generals and his staff just before the move began, and that all of them were opposed to it. Sherman, in particular, was disturbed; the whole thing was most unmilitary, he told Grant, and he did not think it could possibly succeed. Grant replied that he knew as well as anyone that the move was unmilitary, but that as far as he could see it was the only movement that had any chance at all; he then dismissed the council, and issued the formal orders that put McClernand's troops on the road.

Some of the opposition unquestionably arose from the fact that it was McClernand who would be in the lead, carrying the heaviest share of responsibility. Nobody believed McClernand was quite up to it, and both Sherman and Porter warned Grant that he was taking a long chance in giving him the assignment. (Dana added his own remonstrance, and wrote to Stanton about it. For reply, he got a curt reminder from the Secretary that he was there strictly as an observer, not as a shaper of high policy: "Allow me to suggest that you carefully avoid giving any advice in respect to commands that may be assigned, as it may lead to misunderstandings and troublesome complications.") In any case, the protests accomplished nothing. Grant pointed out that McClernand after all was the senior corps commander, that his corps was placed where it would logically take the advance, that McClernand was an especial favorite of the President, and that McClernand himself was highly in favor of the new campaign and could be counted on to do his best. Sherman remained unconvinced, and he sent Grant a long letter, urging him to cancel all of his plans, go back to Memphis, and start a new advance along the old line of the railroad, but Grant's mind was fixed.[6] He relied on Sherman more than on any other man, but this decision was his and his alone and he would stick to it. This new move was going to work . . . or else.

McClernand's corps kept moving on, McPherson's troops got ready to follow, and Porter prepared to take his gunboats down the river to help reduce Grand Gulf and guard the river crossing. It took time to assemble the flotilla and get it in proper shape, after the Steele's Bayou expedition, and just as Porter had things ready a violent storm swept down the river, breaking steamers loose from their moorings and threatening to send warships, transports and supply vessels drifting down under the guns of the Vicksburg batteries; one officer remembered seeing Grant on the hurricane deck of a steamer, shouting orders as Army and Navy together fought to get the boats under control. In the end no great harm was done, but "the excitement while it lasted was equivalent to that of a first-class battle."[7]

Porter made his preparations with care. He was using eight warships — seven regular gunboats and a ram which had been captured from the Confederates at Memphis the summer before — plus three ordinary river steamers loaded with stores. Each vessel had lashed to its starboard side a barge full of coal, leaving the port-side guns of the warships free to respond to the fire of the batteries. Water-soaked bales of hay and cotton were stacked around the otherwise unprotected boilers of the transports, and were banked up across the fragile sterns of the gunboats, to guard against raking shots. To ensure quiet, all steam exhaust pipes were led into the paddle boxes, and captains were ordered to proceed at low speed, letting the current do most of the work, until the Rebels discovered them and opened fire. Porter was so anxious to avoid noise that he even ordered all poultry and pets to be sent ashore. There were to be no lights, except for dim signals carried astern, hooded so as to be invisible to the Confederates. Boats were to proceed in single file, at fifty-yard intervals, and each captain was to steer a little to one side of the boat ahead, so that if that boat should be wrecked he could go past it without changing course. Men were stationed at intervals in the holds of the steamers, ready to cram wadded cotton into shot holes in the hull.

The flotilla ran the batteries on the night of April 16; a clear night, with bright stars in a cloudless sky, but very dark down by the surface of the water. Nothing could be seen except the lights of Vicksburg itself, banked up on the bluff, visible over the top of the low point of land. It grew late, and one by one most of these lights blinked out, and the officers and men who waited felt that there was something theatrical about it all — the stage was black, but it would be brilliantly and violently lighted before long. Grant's family was visiting him at this time, and Julia and the children were with him on the upper deck of the headquarters steamer, which had steamed down to a vantage point just safely beyond the range of the Vicksburg guns; and on this night when everything had a dramatic tinge, one observer, seeing the Grants behind the white railing, with staff officers standing near, thought at once of an oversized party in the proscenium box of a huge theater. Young Colonel Wilson sat in a chair near Mrs. Grant, with one of the smaller Grant children on his lap.

For a long time there was nothing to see, except the deeper patches of blackness by the invisible shores. Then, upstream, a massive shadow seemed to detach itself from the edge of the night and to come drifting slowly down the river; and behind it there was another shadow, similarly adrift, with another behind that — all noiseless, mysterious, seemingly utterly lifeless . . . and the people on the headquarters boat, and all of the other watchers on other boats and on the levees, became silent, so quiet and so tense that a newspaper correspondent noticed that when a man let the breath out of his lungs it sounded like a sob. The shadows drifted on; now the gunboats were rounding the point and drifting straight past the Vicksburg waterfront — and then, suddenly, there was a quick flash of light, and then another, from the Vicksburg hillside, as watchful Rebel gunners opened fire. Confederate pickets on the point set fire to some wrecked houses there, the flames threw a revealing red glare over the river, all of the batteries opened, and black smoke drifted down on the water, throbbing with enormous blows of sound. The child in Colonel Wilson's lap whimpered, and clung closer to him, an arm about his neck. Mr. Dana, taking a detached interest in the drama, counted the reports of the cannon and said afterward he made note of 525. Grant chewed the end of a cigar and said nothing; downstream, Sherman came out on the river in a yawl to greet the survivors of this bombardment; and Admiral Porter stood on the open deck of his flagship and saw such a blaze of illumination along the Vicksburg batteries that he thought for a moment the city was on fire.[8]

Some time after midnight, the firing died down. The fleet had got through without major damage. One transport had caught fire and sunk, another one had been put out of commission with a shot through her steam chest, one of the Turtles was leaking badly from a waterline shot in the bows, and several of the coal barges had been lost. But casualties to personnel had been light, and by dawn of April 17 the fleet was at anchor above New Carthage, fully operational. Grant was too impatient to wait for reports by courier; he had his horse saddled and rode off to New Carthage to see for himself.

Porter had warned him: once the fleet got below Vicksburg there could be no turning back. But now that the fleet had moved, the great river itself was complicating things afresh. All winter long it had been too high; now, when Grant wanted it to remain high, its level was perversely falling, and as a result it was becoming impossible to make a useful waterway out of the interlinked lakes and streams that came down from Milliken's Bend to New Carthage. The whole campaign rested on the assumption that certain essential supplies — to say nothing of the soldiers themselves — could come down by this route. Gunboats might run past the batteries, but a transport full of men or explosives could not. McClernand was already estimating that his corps ought to take with it, when it crossed the river, six million rounds of musket ammunition. If all of this had to come down by road, it would take three days and 300 wagons — with 90 additional wagons needed to move the necessary 300 rounds per gun for his 10 six-gun batteries. In addition, it was clear that the whole army could never be rationed by wagon train over the narrow, winding, muddy roadway.[9]

Grant hurried back to Milliken's Bend to make arrangements. Porter had got his ironclads past the batteries without trouble; now Grant would try sending a squadron of ordinary transports down the same route — regular river steamers, with civilian officers and crews, under government charter. They could carry forage and rations; once downstream they could ferry the army across the Mississippi; and, although the river men might pull their chins and mutter about the hazard of exposing unarmored vessels to concentrated gunfire, Grant had reason to suspect that the danger was less than was supposed. During the winter the unarmored ram *Queen of the West* had run the gantlet in broad daylight. Under fire for fifty minutes, she had been struck twelve times but had received no major injury. That the Confederates later captured her in the Red River did not alter the case; and the whole army was still chuckling about the way the impish Porter had made an imitation gunboat out of an old coal barge, some tar barrels, and odds and ends of scantling, to send it drifting downstream one night while the Confederate gunners, taking it for a regular warship, flailed away with everything they had. The flimsy, unmanned craft had gone as far as Warrenton without damage, and its appearance there had scared a Confederate salvage crew into destroying a wrecked Yankee gunboat which they had been trying to restore to serviceable condition. Late in March the ram *Switzerland* ran the batteries successfully.

Even transports, then, might come down past the batteries, if officers and crew had enough nerve; but they could not carry troops or ammunition as they made the trip, and bad as the twisting road south from Milliken's Bend might be, the army was going to have to use it — building bridges, filling in ditches and corduroying swamps as it went. Grant was committed, now, and there could be no turning back. On April 20 he issued Special Orders No. 110, setting forth the details.

The purpose of the move, the orders stated, was "to obtain a foothold on the east bank of the Mississippi river, from which Vicksburg can be approached by practicable roads." McClernand's corps would have the advance, McPherson's would follow, and Sherman's would bring up the rear. No camp equipage would be carried: each company might take one tent, to protect rations from rain, and each regimental, brigade and division headquarters could have one wall tent. Corps commanders might take more, since they had books and papers to protect, but the army would travel light and the troops would bivouac without shelter. Each corps was to detail two regiments to guard the route from Richmond south; sick and disabled soldiers would remain at Milliken's Bend, and suitable drill officers would stay with them to organize the convalescents into camp guards. McClernand was notified that it was important to take Grand Gulf at the earliest possible moment. Once the army was concentrated there, McClernand was to be prepared to move on downstream and work with Banks.

Porter seemed optimistic. He wrote Grant that he thought his gunboats could suppress the Grand Gulf batteries but that they might get so knocked about doing it that they could not protect the troop crossings, and so he believed they ought to wait until a joint Army-Navy attack could be made. He distrusted McClernand, who was moving slowly, and he told Grant bluntly: "I wish 20 times a day that Sherman was here, or yourself, but I suppose we cannot have all we wish. . . . We can, with the steamers and barges, land 6,000 men, if you think that enough; if we can get more transports it will be better." Privately, Porter had more serious misgivings, and he confessed in a letter to Assistant Secretary of the Navy Gustavus Fox: "I am quite depressed with this adventure, which as you know never met with my approval." McClernand, he complained, was very slow, and his corps was encumbered with too much equipment: "Sherman, the moving spirit, is left behind, where he should have been in the advance. With his corps we might ere this have landed on the Miss. side of the river, for he scorns tents and eatables and pushes his men ahead when there is an object in view." Sherman himself continued to have doubts, and he wrote to Fred Steele: "I confess I don't like this roundabout project, but we must support Grant in whatever he undertakes." [10]

The transports came down the river on the night of April 22. Six boats made the dash. They were manned largely by Volunteers from the army; the civilian crews balked at the job, and soldiers took their places, so many men offering themselves that they had to be chosen by lot. From one regiment, 116 men presented themselves as qualified by experience to act as pilots, engineers, firemen and deck-hands, and competition for places was so keen that soldiers who were not chosen offered cash money for the chance to replace those who had been selected. Loaded with rations and forage, the steamers got through; only one — unfortunately, the one which carried medical supplies and hospital equipment — was lost.[11] Now the army could cross the river whenever it chose.

During all of this, the infantry columns kept moving. The roadway was bad, and it rapidly grew worse. One brigadier asserted: "a worse march no army ever made in the history of military operations," remarking that it took from twelve to eighteen horses to move a single gun, and that the infantry floundered along kneedeep in mud. There was a good deal of rain, the march went on day and night, with innumerable halts during which men lifted guns and wagons bodily out of the mire and boosted them on toward drier ground. Everything except the road itself seemed to be under water, and Midwestern boys listened apprehensively to the sound of alligators bellowing in the bayous. An Iowa soldier reported that for three weeks nobody in his regiment had a chance to take his clothes off, and reported bleakly: "We are all as dirty as hogs . . . we are all lousy." The days were hot, and men threw away blankets and overcoats, only to find that spring nights could be cold even in Louisiana. A gunner reflected that a hike which took a fortnight could have been made in two days if there had been good roads, dry ground and a few bridges.[12]

Yet morale was high. The army was moving at last, and there was a general feeling that the campaign was beginning to make sense. Even the incessant labor of creating the road on which they marched seemed to give the soldiers a sense of accomplishment. Colonel Wilson marveled at the army's capacity. Without a pontoon train, and with no bridging materials except the lumber that could be obtained by tearing down barns and houses, these troops could make a highway across swamps and bayous without appreciable delay. In a few days, he said, one division built two floating bridges, each one more than 300 feet long, creating a practicable road in a flooded country that might have stumped trained engineers, and he paid his tribute: "Those bridges were built by green volunteers who had never seen a bridge train nor had an hour's drill or instruction in bridge-building." The men in this army had pioneer backgrounds, and they brought to this work all of the pioneer's ingenuity and adaptiveness. One private noted with pride that his division had bridged 1000 feet of water and cut two miles of road through dense woods. Grant was as impressed as Colonel Wilson: he began to see that these Volunteers could do almost anything — build roads, erect bridges, operate steamboats, march day and night in mud and water, fight like veterans — and his confidence in the enlisted men of his command became almost limitless. When he reported on the Vicksburg campaign he recalled this overland march and wrote: "It is a striking feature, as far as my observation goes, of the present volunteer army of the United States, that there is nothing which men are called upon to do, mechanical or professional, that accomplished adepts cannot be found for the duty required in almost every regiment."

New troops coming down the river to Milliken's Bend to take part in the campaign caught the spirit and felt that there was something romantic and inspiring in this movement. A Wisconsin regiment, floating down the Mississippi under a full moon, remem-

bered "the great calm river, more like a long winding lake than a
stream; the fleet of boats moving forward with that light puff-
puff of the river steamer, and leaving the long triangular wake in
the rear of each; the long, low banks stretching away on either side;
the music now and then from some regimental band filling all the
air above the water with melody, and then floating away over the
dark woodlands of both Mississippi and Arkansas; the cheers, laughter and song of the men — the scene was indeed both an enlivening
one and a quieting one."13

Grant drove himself as hard as he drove anyone, and he seemed to
appear at every point where a traffic jam developed, riding up,
dismounting, and getting things straightened out, telling the men
to keep moving on. The soldiers turned to look at him, recognized
him, but indulged in no cheers. An officer who watched Grant getting a column across an improvised bridge reflected that Grant somehow made a profound impression by his very lack of dramatics:
"There was no McClellan, begging the boys to allow him to light
his cigar by theirs, or inquiring to what regiment that exceedingly
fine-marching company belonged. There was no Pope, bullying the
men for not marching faster, or officers for some trivial detail remembered only by martinets. There was no Bonaparte, posturing for
effect. . . . There was no nonsense, no sentiment; only a plain business man of the republic, there for the one single purpose of getting
that command across the river in the shortest time possible." 14
Another officer, who had seen much of Grant during the long winter, said that a new sense of energy and movement was evident in
everything the General did, so that he seemed almost like a different
person. "None who had known him the previous years could recognize him as being the same man. . . . From this time his genius and
his energies seemed to burst forth with new life." In all of the previous campaign, this officer said, he had never seen Grant ride at a
gallop, or even at a fast trot: no matter what was going on Grant had
never seemed to be in a hurry. But now everything was different:
Grant was riding at top speed all the time, and "he seemed wrought
up to the last pitch of determination and energy." Yet Dana could
see no cracks in the man's control. He recalled one night riding beside Grant in black darkness; Grant's horse stumbled and nearly
pitched the General into the mud, and Dana found himself thinking,

"Now he will swear." Grant disappointed him. He regained control of his horse and went on with his ride without giving any sign of impatience or irritation, and Dana reflected afterward that from one end of the campaign to the other he never heard Grant use an oath.[15]

Getting possession of Grand Gulf was a little harder than had been anticipated. It developed that the New Carthage area was not a suitable place from which to make the crossing; there was no good spot on the Mississippi side, between Warrenton and Grand Gulf, to put the troops ashore, the works at Grand Gulf itself were more formidable than had been supposed, and in the end the troops had to keep on moving downstream, fetching up at last at Hard Times plantation, twenty-odd miles farther south; and from there, finally, they had to move on another half-dozen miles until they reached the western bank of the river a little distance below Grand Gulf. The transports ran the Grand Gulf batteries successfully, and soldiers on the bank cheered mightily as the steamers swung in to make a landing, while a band at headquarters played "The Red, White and Blue." Grant had moments of doubt, and he expressed these in a letter to Sherman on April 24:

> I foresee great difficulties in our present position, but it will not do to let these retard any movements. In the first place, if a battle should take place we are necessarily very destitute of all preparations for taking care of wounded men. All the little extras for this purpose were put on board the *Tigress*, the only boat that was lost. The line from here to Milliken's Bend is a long one for the transportation of supplies and to defend, and an impossible one for the transportation of wounded men. The water in the bayous is falling very rapidly, out of all proportion to the fall in the river, so that it is exceedingly doubtful whether they can be made use of for the purposes of navigation.

Sherman, still encamped above Vicksburg, was to watch things closely; if Pemberton should weaken his forces there Snyder's Bluff might become vulnerable, and if so Sherman must be ready to pounce on it.[16]

One thing that could not be overlooked was the obvious fact that if Pemberton caught on to what was being attempted he

could easily move plenty of troops down to Grand Gulf to meet
the Federal thrust. It was necessary to deceive him, and Grant had
been giving thought to this. As early as the middle of February
Grant had felt that a fast cavalry raid down the interior of Mississippi would give the Confederates something to think about,
and among the troops in Tennessee he had an officer who looked
capable of leading such a raid — an unlikely character named Benjamin Grierson, who had been a small-town music teacher and band-
master in Illinois before the war and who now was colonel commanding a cavalry brigade in the area of La Grange, Tennessee.
Grierson marched south with three regiments, about seventeen
hundred men, on April 17, the day after Porter's ironclads ran the
Vicksburg batteries, and went driving south twenty-five miles
west of the line of the Mobile and Ohio Railroad, one hundred
miles east of the river. His orders were simple: he was to destroy
railroad track and supply dumps, stir up all the alarm he could,
creating if possible the impression that a big move was in preparation, and he was to keep going until he reached Banks's lines at
Baton Rouge, four hundred miles to the south. Grierson handled
the assignment smartly. Pemberton was short of cavalry just then
— most of his mounted troops had been sent away to help Bragg,
in central Tennessee — and he was never able to catch up with
Grierson or to find out precisely what the raid meant. By May 2
Grierson had his men safe at Baton Rouge; he had done substantial
damage to Pemberton's communications, he had compelled various
Confederate units to wear themselves out chasing him, and he had
stirred up precisely the sort of confused alarm which Grant had
intended.[17]

Meanwhile, there was another diversion. McClernand's corps was
downstream, and McPherson's was on its heels, but Sherman's men
were still in camp by the river above Vicksburg, and to Sherman,
on April 27, Grant sent word that a convincing feint in the direction of Snyder's Bluff might deceive Pemberton as to the real
direction of the Federal offensive. Grant did not give Sherman
positive orders; the move might easily deceive the soldiers themselves and the people back home as well as the Confederates in
Vicksburg, and the newspapers would probably be happy enough

to accuse Sherman of having led the army into another defeat. Grant worded his letter carefully:

> The effect of a heavy demonstration in that direction would be good as far as the enemy are concerned, but I am loth to order it, because it would be hard to make our own troops understand that only a demonstration was intended and our people at home would characterize it as a repulse. I therefore leave it to you whether to make such a demonstration. . . . I shall probably move on Grand Gulf tomorrow.

Sherman remained skeptical about the Grand Gulf maneuver, but he was indignant at the notion that he might need protection against criticism. To a staff officer he remarked: "Does General Grant think I care what the newspapers say?" He promptly wrote to Grant, pledging full co-operation and bristling with angry contempt for public opinion:

> We will make as strong a demonstration as possible. The troops will all understand the purpose and will not be hurt by the repulse. The people of the country must find out the truth as best they can; it is none of their business. You are engaged in a hazardous enterprise, and, for good reasons, wish to divert attention; that is sufficient for me, and it shall be done.

He outlined his plans in detail, and then took a final side-swipe at the newspapers:

> I will use troops that I know will trust us and not be humbugged by a repulse. The men have sense, and will trust us. As to the reports in newspapers, we must scorn them, else they will ruin us and our country. They are as much enemies to good government as the secesh, and between the two I like the secesh best, because they are a brave, open enemy and not a set of sneaking, croaking scoundrels.[18]

Sherman's troops put on a good show. Light gunboats and transports went puffing up the Yazoo, troops were landed and put to maneuvering as if unlimited numbers were about to make a frontal attack on the bluffs, and the Confederate commander there called for reinforcements. Troops that were to move south to meet

Grant were delayed, there was a deal of frenzied countermarching and preparation — and far down the river Porter's ironclads steamed in and opened a five-hour bombardment of the Grand Gulf batteries, while the transports waited on the western shore to bring the troops across.

The Grand Gulf batteries were tough: with powerful guns well emplaced forty feet above the water, served by good gunners; they could not be beaten down, and it became clear that troops could not land in front of them to take the bluffs by storm. At the end of April 29 the fleet drew away, somewhat battered, and it was time to make another revision in the plan.

Grant made it promptly. He would put his army across the river below Grand Gulf, move inland, and then march north, cutting off Grand Gulf and taking it from its unprotected rear. His maps were inadequate, and no one in the army knew much about the country east of the river. It was known, however, that an army approaching Grand Gulf from the east or south would have to cross a stream known as Bayou Pierre, which came in from the east, and this stream could best be crossed, apparently, at or near the town of Port Gibson, which was ten miles southeast of Grand Gulf. The immediate objective thus seemed to be Port Gibson, but simply to land troops on the eastern bank of the Mississippi and send them floundering off through the trackless bottom lands was to invite disaster. To get to Port Gibson a guide was needed.

After dark a detachment of Illinois soldiers rowed across the river, scouted about among the farms, and at last seized a Negro slave who had lived in that vicinity all of his life, knew how the roads went, and seemed to be a cut or two above the illiterate, Bress-de-Lawd plantation hand of tradition. He did not especially want to be carried off by the Union soldiers but he was over-powered and put in a rowboat, and after a time the men brought him to Grant's tent. Grant satisfied himself that the Negro was familiar with the country back of Grand Gulf, explained briefly where he wanted to go, and then led him to a table where there was a map.

"Look here," said Grant. "Tell me where this road leads to — starting where you see my finger here on the map and running down that way."

"Dat road fetches up at Bayou Pierre, but you can't go that way, 'kase it's plum full of backwater."

Grant put it up to him.

"Which road would you take if you were going to lead me, followed by a great army and trains of loaded wagons and artillery — which road would you take to reach Bayou Pierre?"

"Dar is only one way, General, and dat is by Bruinsburg, eight miles furder down. Dar you can leave de boats and the men can walk on high ground all the way. De best houses and plantations in all de country are dar, sah, all along dat road." [19]

Promptly on the morning of April 30 the transports went puffing out into the river, drifting downstream and coming in to the eastern shore at Bruinsburg, ten miles below Grand Gulf. The troops took to the road for Port Gibson — all of McClernand's corps, and a division of McPherson's — and many years afterward Grant told how the crossing struck him at the time:

> When this was effected I felt a degree of relief scarcely ever equalled since. . . . I was now in the enemy's country, with a vast river and the stronghold of Vicksburg between me and my base of supplies. But I was on dry ground on the same side of the river with the enemy. All the campaigns, labors, hardships and exposures from the month of December previous to this time that had been made and endured were for the accomplishment of this one object.[20]

In the course of the war Grant wrote a number of memorable sentences: "My only terms are immediate and unconditional surrender"; "I propose to fight it out on this line if it takes all summer" — and so on. But he never wrote anything that expressed the essential nature of the born soldier, the relentless and unpretentious army-killer, better than that simple expression of his release from tension — "I was on dry ground on the same side of the river with the enemy." Everything remained to be done, the desperate battles were still ahead, the key decision itself had not yet been made, but that mattered little: at last Grant had got to a place where he could fight. From that moment he could stop worrying.

CHAPTER TWENTY-ONE

"Hardtack! Hardtack!"

G RANT had twenty-three thousand troops east of the river, and for the moment the Confederate command was confused. The long weeks that had been wasted on the Yazoo Pass and Steele's Bayou expeditions had had one valuable result — they had led the defenders to believe that the big attack on Vicksburg would come from above. When Grant crossed below Grand Gulf, Pemberton was in Jackson, Mississippi's capital, forty-five miles east of Vicksburg, and Pemberton ordered the Vicksburg people to hurry reinforcements down to Port Gibson, where Brigadier General J. S. Bowen had 6000 men ready to resist this Federal thrust. But the Confederate commander at Vicksburg felt that the Yankees could not possibly be intending a real offensive so far downstream: this must be a feint, and if the Vicksburg garrison went off to help Bowen the main attack would probably be made at Snyder's Bluff.[1] For a short time Grant had the advantage — the bulge, as tough Bedford Forrest used to say — and the whole campaign would depend on the way he used it.

No time would be lost. As fast as the troops could be put ashore they set off on the road for Port Gibson, tramping through the evening and the night, and before dawn on May 1 McClernand's advance ran into Bowen's outposts a few miles west of the town. There was a good deal of ineffective skirmishing in the darkness, and in the morning as soon as there was light enough for fighting the battle lines formed and began shooting.

It was a bad place for a fight. As Grant put it, "the country in this part of Mississippi stands on edge." The roads ran mostly along the ridges, and between the ridges there were ravines clogged with woods, vines and canebrakes. McClernand's troops went into action along two roads and it was hard to co-ordinate their movements;

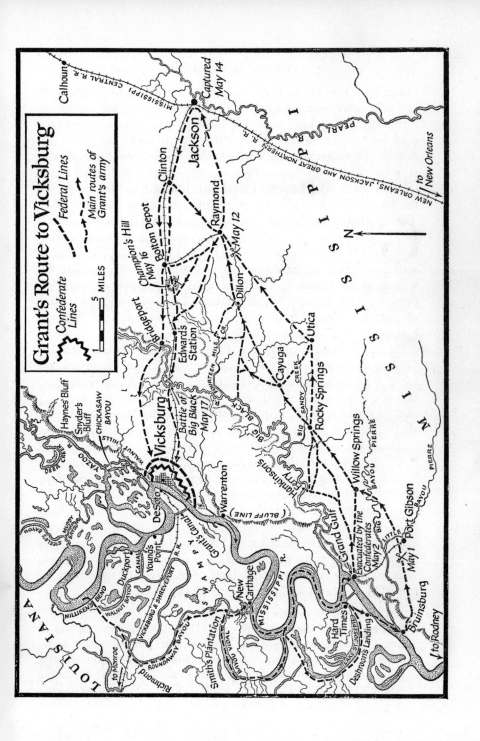

Grant was not satisfied with the way McClernand handled the operation and rode forward to expedite matters. One soldier remembered seeing him, mounted, looking very careworn and covered with dust; another recalled that as his outfit went into action it was Grant himself who prodded the soldiers forward with repeated orders to "push right along — close up fast." Logan's division from McPherson's corps was brought to the front, and the heavy Union superiority in numbers began to have its effect. The Confederates put up a stout fight, and Grant confessed that Bowen handled them capably; but, as Grant proudly wrote to Halleck, "My force, however, was too heavy for him, and composed of well-disciplined and hardy men who know no defeat and are not willing to learn what it is." By nightfall Bowen was compelled to draw off to the north in full retreat. Grant ordered McClernand to push the enemy "until it gets too dark to see him," and told him to renew the advance at earliest dawn.[2]

Promptly next morning the Federals hurried in pursuit. Port Gibson was empty, and the bridges across Bayou Pierre and the Little Bayou Pierre had been destroyed. The bridge-building details went to work, the damage was made good, and the army pushed on eight miles to the north fork of the little river, where another bridge had been burned. All night long the repair gangs worked, and by dawn of May 3 McPherson's advance crossed the river, scattered a Confederate rear guard, and moved on to a place known as Willow Springs. Four or five miles due north of this hamlet, the road to Vicksburg crossed the Big Black River; running off northeast at an angle was the road to Jackson, where the Confederates were reputed to be gathering reinforcements. McPherson arranged one division to hold the road to the Big Black, McClernand brought his corps up in close support, and Grant himself went hurrying over to Grand Gulf, with twenty cavalrymen for escort. Here he sent a jubilant message to Halleck:

This army is in the finest health and spirits. Since leaving Milliken's Bend they have marched as much by night as by day, through mud and rain, without tents or much other baggage, and on irregular rations, without a complaint, and with less straggling than I have ever before witnessed. [He added that he would not bother to bring his army to Grand Gulf; instead he would immediately follow the enemy, and] if all promises as favorable hereafter as it does now, not stop until Vicksburg is in our possession.[3]

Pemberton himself was beginning to suspect that he was in trouble. He had hurried from Jackson to Vicksburg, and he quickly realized that Grant was not feinting. While Bowen was making his fight at Port Gibson, Pemberton wired Jefferson Davis that "enemy's movement threatens Jackson and if successful cuts off Vicksburg and Port Hudson from the east." He called for reinforcements, pointing out that "enemy's success in passing our batteries has completely changed character of defense." On the following day he warned the governor of Mississippi to move the state archives away from Jackson, and on May 3 he notified Davis that he would concentrate his own forces behind the Big Black River. Here he would interpose between Grant and Vicksburg, and if Grant did move on Jackson Pemberton would potentially be on his flank and rear.[4]

Grant found plenty to do. He began by going aboard the flagship at Grand Gulf for a bath and a change of clothing — he had not had his clothing off for a week, and his entire baggage kit thus far had consisted of a toothbrush — and then he started to call on the rear echelons for more speed. Before he crossed the river he had told Sherman to bring two divisions down, overland, as fast as he could, and he had ordered the quartermaster at Milliken's Bend to send down two towboats and barges full of rations and forage. Every order stressed the importance of speed; the quartermaster was to man the supply boats with volunteers from the army if the civilian crews refused to serve, and he was instructed: "Do this with all expedition, in 48 hours from receipt of orders if possible. Time is of immense importance." On May 3, at Grand Gulf, Grant notified the Commanding Officer at Milliken's Bend to get working parties busy on the roadway down to New Carthage — "Everything depends upon the promptitude with which our supplies are forwarded." On the same day Sherman was told to send down one hundred and twenty wagons with rations; Sherman's men were to draw five days' rations, and Grant warned: "See that they last five days," underlining it with the remark: "It is unnecessary for me to remind you of the overwhelming importance of celerity in your movements," and he explained in a few brief sentences:

> The enemy is badly beaten, greatly demoralized, and exhausted of ammunition. The road to Vicksburg is open. All we want now are men, ammunition and hard bread. We can subsist our horses on the country and obtain considerable supplies for our troops.[5]

The final sentence was the key to what followed. All winter, Grant had reflected on the abundance of food that was to be found in Mississippi; now, operating at the end of a difficult and insecure supply line, he was preparing to act on the knowledge he had gained following Van Dorn's capture of his base at Holly Springs in December. He would not limit himself by dependence on any base. As much hard bread, salt and coffee as could be moved would be brought down from Milliken's Bend, and the State of Mississippi itself would be called on for whatever else was needed. Dana explained this in a wire to Secretary Stanton on May 4. Grant, he said, would move at once toward the Big Black River and toward Jackson: "As soon as Sherman comes up and the rations on the way arrive, he will disregard his base and depend on the country for meat and even for bread. Beef cattle and corn are both abundant everywhere." [6]

The attempt to float towboats and barges past the Vicksburg batteries came to grief; a towboat and barges were sunk by gunfire, and Grant sent back word: "We will risk no more actions to run the Vicksburg batteries." Four newspaper correspondents had daringly boarded the towboat to make the trip downstream, and these men were captured by the Rebels. First reports said that the four had been drowned, and Sherman permitted himself a wicked chuckle. To Frank Blair he wrote that the reporters "were so deeply laden with weighty matter that they must have sunk," and he added: "In our affliction we can console ourselves with the pious reflection that there are plenty more of the same sort."

Convinced that running unprotected transports past the batteries no longer paid, Grant rode his subordinates mercilessly to get as much material as possible brought down overland. To a supply officer whom he had made responsible for this operation, Grant wrote that "every day's delay is worth two thousand men to the enemy," and expressed his impatience in a series of staccato questions: "How many teams have been loaded with rations and sent forward? I want to know as near as possible how we stand in every particular for supplies. How many wagons have you ferried over the river? How many are still to bring over? What teams have gone back for rations?" To General Hurlbut, back in Memphis, Grant sent orders to make cavalry demonstrations so as to distract the Rebels' attention, to get reinforcements down the river as fast as possible, and to lay in a sixty days' surplus of rations and forage. Hurlbut loyally did his best; like Sherman, he found this daring campaign a bit frightening, and he sent Grant a brief warning: "I hope you will sweep out the rabble, especially as I learn that mischief-makers are looking after you, with hopes based upon your downfall." [7]

To the soldiers, Mississippi looked good, and the expedition began to seem exciting. A *New York Times* correspondent noted that the men were tough and brown, thoroughly acclimated by now to Southern weather, and he said that Port Gibson was one of the most beautiful places he had ever seen; with some provincialism, he wrote that it had many houses "of a character equal to some of the finest villas on the Hudson," and he grew positively lyrical about the beauty of Mississippi's young women. He found them "plump, rosy, engaging and delicious," with dark eyes radiating "starry splendor" and lips that seemed "a fit resting place for kisses." The Deep South, he added, was not starving, no matter what Northern patriots liked to think; he had just dined at a plantation, eating roast turkey and duck, wheat bread, biscuits, ham and an abundance of vegetables. An officer wrote to his sister that the country looked prosperous as well as beautiful, and found many of the plantations "magnificent in the extreme." Believing that most Northern boys had no enthusiasm for invasion, Mississippi girls grew deceptively friendly and passed around newspapers which urged the men to demand that their officers take them home. (The papers struck the men as just plain funny, and they read them with amused interest. When a worried staff officer told Grant that the circulation of these papers ought to be suppressed, Grant retorted that if necessary he would appoint a special news agent to make sure that every man in the army got his share.) One officer remarked that all ordinary Army red tape procedures connected with the issuance of rations had been discarded. The troops now were simply marched past long piles of bacon, open barrels of salt pork and boxes of hardtack, and from major general to private each man helped himself. The colonel of the 20th Ohio, impressed by the need for constant movement, had details seize mules from plantations and saw to it that soldiers too footsore to walk could have a ride.[8]

Constant movement was the imperative. Deep in enemy country and a long way from its base, this army could do almost any imaginable thing but sit still. The very terms on which Grant had got it east of the river placed on him a necessity for rapid and unceasing movement — rapid if possible, unceasing at any cost whatever.[9] This dictated what Grant would do during the crucial days just ahead.

To the best of Grant's knowledge, Pemberton had perhaps 25,000 maneuverable troops in and around Vicksburg. There was a small detachment at Jackson, and all the intelligence Grant could get said that this would be strongly reinforced in the immediate future. At Port Hudson the Confederates had 10,000 men under Major General Frank Gardner, and Pemberton (as Grant soon learned) was ordering Gardner to bring most of his infantry north to help drive the Federals into the river.[10] Grant had to smash these encircling foes before they could form a compact mass too strong for him to handle.

But to do this he would have to abandon the plan which, in a somewhat unfinished form, had been in his mind ever since he started down the river — the plan by which he would join forces with Banks and reduce Port Hudson before attempting the main attack on Pemberton and Vicksburg.

He had told both Banks and Halleck that his army would establish itself at Grand Gulf and then would send at least an army corps downstream to help Banks take Port Hudson. After that, he and Banks together could move on Vicksburg. This suited Halleck, who was insisting that the one great object in the West was to open the river, and who also felt that Banks and Grant should pool their resources in order to do it. It also suited Banks, who would get the top command (and, no doubt, the glory) out of any such venture; he was senior to Grant, and Washington definitely contemplated that he would be in charge of any combined operation in the valley.[11] Yet Banks, as Grant learned at Grand Gulf, had somehow managed to go off on such a tangent that a combined operation in the immediate future was completely out of the question.

Banks, as a matter of fact, had taken his army up the Red River, directly away from the Port Hudson-Vicksburg area; and when Grant entered Grand Gulf, Banks and his army were near Alexandria, Louisiana, one hundred miles away in a straight line, probably twice that far away as the rivers went. It appears that Banks feared that Confederate forces in northwestern Louisiana might slice down at New Orleans, which was his base, if he did not attend to them before he moved up the Mississippi. Whatever the reason, Banks had moved eccentrically up the Red River instead of up the Mississippi; and at the moment when Grant was prepared to join hands with him at Port Hudson, Banks was enmeshed in a campaign that was likely to keep him busy for some time to come. Grant got the news at this time in a letter Banks had written three weeks earlier — communication between the two armies was very roundabout — and found that the best Banks could promise was that he would have fifteen thousand men near Port Hudson by May 10. The letter was clearly out of date, and it seemed likely to Grant that the May 10 estimate was exceedingly optimistic.[12]

It was at this moment that the plan for a combined push at Port Hudson went out of Grant's mind forever. He would go for Pemberton and Vicksburg alone; if Banks could come along sometime and help, that would be fine, but Grant was going to send no army corps down the river, nor was he going to spend one day waiting at Grand Gulf for Banks to join him. After May 3, 1863, the Vicksburg campaign would be Grant's and Grant's alone.

As a matter of fact, the plan for a joint move against Port Hudson had always been more the expression of a pious hope than the precise formulation of a working military program. Even Halleck

himself apparently did not count too greatly on it; when Grant
started down from Milliken's Bend, the most Halleck had said to
Banks was that Grant was going to attack Grand Gulf "and perhaps co-operate with you against Port Hudson," and he had
warned Banks that Grant's primary object must be "to concentrate his forces so as to strike the enemy an important blow." [13]
The Port Hudson plan contemplated one of the most delicate of
all military operations — the bringing together of two widely separated armies, far down in hostile territory, in the presence of an
active, vigilant enemy — and with communications between
Grant and Banks as imperfect as they necessarily were it is doubtful that either Halleck or Grant had ever felt deeply bound to the
Port Hudson idea. The notion that Grant was breathing defiance
in the face of the General in Chief by abandoning the Port Hudson
venture is, quite simply, a fiction. The one person who was deeply
offended by Grant's change in plan was Banks himself, and Banks's
displeasure was something Grant could easily live with.

Forgetting about Banks, Grant for several days did not even
bother to let that general know that he had forgotten. (His dispatch telling Banks that the Port Hudson date was broken was
not written until May 10.) He did, however, take pains to keep
Halleck posted; and, indeed, throughout the Vicksburg campaign Grant was extremely careful to keep a steady flow of dispatches going to Washington, although it took several days for
messages he sent from this part of the country to reach the War
Department. (From Grand Gulf they had to go overland to Milliken's Bend and then by steamer via Memphis to Cairo, where
they could be put on the telegraph wire.) He had already told Halleck that he was going to follow up the advantage gained at Port
Gibson, Dana had given Stanton equally clear notice — and now
Grant waited only for Sherman and for the wagons from upriver
before plunging into action.

Even though the luckless farmers of Mississippi were going to
have to provide most of the army's food, some sort of wagon train
was necessary. The number of army wagons that could be brought
down from Milliken's Bend was limited; a staff officer reported that
there would be only two wagons to a regiment, in which all ammunition, rations and equipment must be carried, and he soberly

noted that "it will be impossible to keep the army from suffering." It was necessary to improvise — for, as Grant noted, even if the soldiers could get food and forage from the plantations, they had to bring all of their ammunition, and the quantity a foot soldier could carry on his back was limited. And so even before the fighting around Port Gibson had ended Grant had detachments swarming all over the countryside, collecting every four-wheeled vehicle, and every draft animal capable of pulling such vehicles, to make up a fantastic, unmilitary wagon train: fine carriages, long-coupled wagons made to carry cotton bales, farm carts, anything at all on wheels, pulled indiscriminately by horses, mules and oxen, many of them wearing makeshift harness put together from whatever was at hand. With these, and with such Army wagons as could be brought down the river and ferried over to the Mississippi shore, his army could carry the things it had to have in order to live and fight.[14]

While Grant prepared to move, his advance guard kept up a ceaseless movement of reconnaissances and skirmishing thrusts to give Pemberton the notion that a direct advance on Vicksburg was in preparation. Grant's attention, however, was primarily centered on the railroad which ran from Vicksburg to Jackson. This town was, in effect, Vicksburg's connection with the rest of the Confederacy. At Jackson the railroad from Vicksburg crossed the north-and-south line that came down to New Orleans from West Tennessee; through this place, troops and supplies meant for Pemberton would move; to Jackson, as Grant would presently learn, Joe Johnston in person was coming, to arrange for the formation of a relieving army. A hard blow to break the railroad connections, destroy military supplies and disperse the gathering reinforcements would isolate Pemberton and doom both his army and Vicksburg itself.

At the end of the first week in May, Grant's troops were placed to threaten both Jackson and Vicksburg. The left was at Hankinson's Ferry, on the Big Black, and the right, under McClernand, lay half a dozen miles to the east, behind Big Sandy creek. McPherson could move eastward toward Jackson while McClernand and Sherman moved to break the railroad at Edwards Station and guarded the Big Black crossings against a sudden thrust by Pemberton.

For Sherman was on the scene by now, and Grant had thirty-five thousand men, with eight thousand more marching down to join him. Sherman reached Grand Gulf on May 6, spent the next day bringing his troops across — except for Frank Blair's division, which was still on the march from Milliken's Bend — and promptly moved up to Hankinson's Ferry. Sherman was still uneasy about this campaign, and he reflected now that the entire army would have to be supplied by one inadequate road running north from Grand Gulf. Eighteen months later, he would be world-famous as the general who marched unconcernedly off into the unknown with no supply line at all, but he had not reached that point yet; he could be the most unorthodox of soldiers, but in the spring of 1863 the textbook formula still held him, and he sent a quick warning to Grant: "Stop all troops till your army is partially supplied with wagons, and then act as quickly as possible, for this road will be jammed as sure as life if you attempt to supply 50,000 men by one single road." Back from Grant, who had his headquarters five miles east, at Rocky Springs, came the reply: "I do not calculate upon the possibility of supplying the army with full rations from Grand Gulf. I know it will be impossible without constructing additional roads. What I do expect, however, it to get up what rations of hard bread, coffee and salt we can and make the country furnish the balance. . . . A delay would give the enemy time to re-enforce and fortify. If Blair were up now I believe we could be in Vicksburg in seven days." [15] As he read that dispatch, Sherman advanced a long stride in his military education.

The army moved, slipping to the northeast, with the Big Black River winding down across its left flank: a shield for Pemberton's army, as that general supposed, but also a curtain, blotting out knowledge of what the invader was up to. About fifteen miles to the north, the Southern Railroad of Mississippi, going due east from Vicksburg, crossed the river near Edwards Station and then went on thirty miles east to Jackson, and as Grant's marching columns drew closer to this railroad, General Pemberton's perplexity increased. He had supposed, after Bowen was driven out of Port Gibson, that Grant would move straight up the Mississippi to Warrenton; then he guessed that a raid on Jackson was being attempted; then it struck him that what Grant really was intending might be a blow at the railroad bridge over the Big Black River near Edwards Station; and from Vicksburg, on May 12, he sent an unhappy dispatch to Jefferson Davis:

"I am obliged to hold back large forces at the ferries on Big Black, lest he cross and take this place. I am also compelled to keep a considerable force on either flank of Vicksburg, out of supporting distance of Edwards, to prevent his approach in those directions." 16

Pemberton, as a matter of fact, had four problems, and taken all together they were far too much for him. The first problem was Grant himself. The second problem was President Davis, who believed that both Vicksburg and Port Hudson must be held at all costs and who kept sending Pemberton orders based on that belief. The third problem was Joe Johnston, Pemberton's immediate superior, who felt that Pemberton ought to abandon all fixed positions, concentrate his forces so as to beat Grant in the open field, and then regain the places he had given up. And the final problem was the great imponderable that bore on every Confederate commander in this war — the fact that the Federal government, with its vast advantage in man power, economic strength, and the materials of war, was bound to win whenever it found a general who would relentlessly and steadfastly put all of those advantages to the fullest use. The Confederacy had few generals unluckier than John Pemberton.

Grant was traveling light, in this campaign, but he did have his oldest son with him — Frederick Dent Grant, the bouncy twelve-year-old who had been allowed to make the overland trip down from Milliken's Bend and who had no intention of missing any of the fun. When the army made the crossing at Bruinsburg, Fred had been left in bed on the headquarters boat, but he roused himself and followed on foot — joining forces, as he trudged after the

Commanding General, with the War Department's Mr. Dana, who also wanted a front-row seat. Fred wore the sash and sword which his father never bothered to use, and he and Dana followed the sound of the guns. Somewhere along the way some staff officers presented the pair with a couple of somnolent plantation horses, and Grant remembered meeting them, "mounted on two enormous horses, grown white with age," just after the close of the battle of Port Gibson. They stuck with headquarters for the rest of the campaign, and Grant loyally recorded that Fred's presence "caused no anxiety to me or to his mother, who was at home." [17]

There was plenty for a small boy to see. Forty years later Frederick Dent Grant remembered riding into Willow Springs and joining his father and other officers on the porch of a little house just as an indignant plantation owner, mounted on a mule, rode up to complain that marauding Federals had robbed him of everything he owned. The troops, he said, belonged to the command of Brigadier General A. J. Smith, who had a division in McClernand's corps; Smith, a blunt and salty character, happened to be present, and he was told to talk to the man. He listened to the planter's complaint, then asked: "Whose mule is that you rode up on?" His own, said the planter. "Well," said Smith, turning away, "those men didn't belong to my division at all, because if they were my men they wouldn't even have left you that mule." [18]

Now the army was picking up speed; and as it moved Grant kept spurring his subordinates to forget about rations and supplies and keep crowding forward. When McClernand sent him a note, protesting that he had so few wagons that his corps could not carry all the foodstuffs and cooking utensils it needed, Grant curtly replied that he had seen McClernand's corps on the march, and that it was accompanied by plenty of horses and mules to carry a full five days' rations "if relieved of the knapsacks, officers, soldiers and Negroes now riding." To McPherson, Grant sent word to move for the town of Raymond, fourteen miles west of Jackson: there was reported to be a Confederate brigade there and Grant wanted it driven out —"We must fight the enemy before our rations fail, and we are equally bound to make our rations last as long as possible." And finally, on May 10, Grant found time to send a letter to Banks explaining the new campaign plan:

It was my intention on gaining a foothold at Grand Gulf, to have sent a sufficient force to Port Hudson to have insured the fall of that place with your co-operation, or rather to have co-operated with you to that end. Meeting the enemy, however, as I did, south [west] of Port Gibson, I followed him to the Big Black and could not afford to retrace my steps. I also learned, and believe the information to be reliable, that Port Hudson is almost entirely evacuated. This may not be true, but it is the concurrent testimony of deserters and contrabands.

Many days cannot elapse before the battle will begin which is to decide the fate of Vicksburg, but it is impossible to predict how long it may last. I would urgently request, therefore, that you join me or send all the force you can spare to co-operate in the great struggle for opening the Mississippi river. My means of gaining information from Port Hudson are not good, but I shall hope, even before this reaches Baton Rouge, to hear of your forces being on the way here.[19]

On May 12, two days after he sent this letter to Banks, Grant began to cut the regular communication with Grand Gulf. McPherson got his advance up to Raymond, and McPherson's men had a brisk fight there, driving the badly outnumbered Confederates out of the town. When the news reached Grant — who was some miles away, with Sherman's corps — it brought him to his final decision. So far he had carefully guarded the lower crossings of the Big Black, to keep Pemberton from getting in his rear and breaking his sketchy communications with Grand Gulf. Now he would use everything in a drive straight at Jackson, maneuvering in the hope of destroying Pemberton's army in the open field, and letting the lower crossings of the Big Black go unguarded — if Pemberton wanted to get in his rear and cut his communications he was welcome to try, since there would be no rear, and no communications. Grant got off a quick dispatch to Halleck, warning him that he would be out of touch for a while: "As I shall communicate with Grand Gulf no more, except it becomes necessary to send a train with heavy escort, you may not hear from me again for several days." Then he sent word to McPherson to push on for Jackson, and ordered Sherman to follow. McClernand was to take position along a stream known as Fourteen-Mile Creek, with his outposts near Edwards Station.[20]

McPherson put on the pressure. Men of the 20th Ohio remembered that they had halted just west of Raymond, to stack their guns and light fires to cook supper; the order to move on reached them just as the meal was cooked, but before anyone had had a chance to eat it, and the men went tramping through Raymond, coffeepots and frying pans in hand, trailing a tantalizing odor of fried bacon. They went on through Raymond, Sherman moved east on parallel roads, and McClernand disengaged his pickets from the Edwards Station line and followed after. It began to rain early in the morning, and on May 14 McPherson's and Sherman's men went splashing across the fields through ankle-deep water to attack the capital of Mississippi.

Joe Johnston, weak from a spell in sickbed, had reached Jackson the day before. He found 6000 soldiers in town, and since Grant had fully 25,000 men moving in to the assault Johnston could not hope to do anything but fight a delaying action. His men held Grant off for most of the day, but more than that they could not do; and what Johnston wanted was a delay of a week or more — that, and some chance to bring his own troops and Pemberton's together in one solid mass. Reinforcements were on the way, from the east; Johnston would have 15,000 men in a few days, and 9000 more a little after that, and he sent word to Pemberton to meet him on or near the railroad line so that they could put up a real fight. But Pemberton, who conceived that he was not allowed to evacuate either Vicksburg or Port Hudson even for the sake of victory in the field, was unable to concentrate his own troops. With some 23,000 men he was now prowling forward in the Edwards Station area, hoping to compel Grant to retreat by striking his rear and his line of supply.[21] Johnston moved his troops off to the north, and the Federals marched triumphantly into Jackson.

Among those who entered in triumph was Master Fred Grant, presumably still girt with sash and sword. He had been with his father and Sherman during the fight, and when the Confederates retreated Fred broke away and went trotting into the capital on his own hook, heading straight for the Statehouse. In the town he ran into a column of infantry in butternut — Confederate troops, marching out to the North — and he huddled in a side street until they had passed. Then he saw one of McPherson's staff officers, riding hard for the Statehouse, carrying a United States flag. Sensing what the officer was going to do, Fred rode after him, but the officer was not cordial; he hurried on ahead, got into the Statehouse, and hoisted the flag. Fred saw a cavalcade of Federals approaching, and galloped to meet it — his father, with a cavalry escort, leading the infantry advanced into town.[22]

The soldiers were whooping with joy. They jeered mightily as they picked up copies of a local newspaper boasting that Yankee vandals would never pollute the streets of Jackson with their presence, and a gunner wrote: "If there ever was a jubilant army, Grant's army in Jackson was that night." The men began to realize that this campaign was something special and that they were being led with cold audacity. Seizing Jackson, they had left a strong army in their rear and had cut it off from reinforcements; if things went on as they had begun, the Rebels would have to retire into Vicksburg, but if anything went wrong Grant's whole army would probably be destroyed. Proudly, these Middle Western soldiers told one another how captured Confederates, who had fought heretofore in the Eastern theater, admitted that when the fighting in the Jackson works began the Confederates had quickly realized "they were not fighting New York troops." [23]

There would be no lingering in Jackson. Grant knew as well as Johnston that strong Confederate reinforcements would show up before long and that it was up to him to settle the campaign before these could arrive. (He also enjoyed a stroke of luck, just here. A Union agent in Confederate uniform, riding as courier for Johnston's troops, brought to Grant Johnston's order telling Pemberton to meet him somewhere near the railroad line.) McPherson, accordingly, was sent doubling back to the town of Clinton, eight miles west of Jackson, and McClernand was told to move his corps to Bolton, another half-dozen miles to the west of Clinton.

Above everything else, Grant now wanted to keep Johnston from joining Pemberton, and his orders to McClernand set forth his anxiety: "It is evidently the design of the enemy to get north of us and cross the Black river and beat us into Vicksburg. We must not allow them to do this. Turn all your forces toward Bolton station and make all dispatch in getting there. Move troops by the most direct road from wherever they may be on receipt of this order." Grant also took the time to write a wire to Halleck, telling him what had happened and explaining his refusal to try to meet Banks at Port Hudson with the all-sufficient remark: "I could not take the time." [24]

Sherman was to remain in Jackson, destroying railroads, bridges, factories and military supplies — a task his soldiers performed with an uninhibited vigor that foreshadowed some of the things that would happen later on, in Georgia. Grant stayed in Jackson overnight, sleeping (as he was told) in the hotel room Johnston had occupied the night before. On the morning of May 15, Grant rode west to join McPherson.

Things were breaking for him. He knew where his enemies were and what they were planning, and his own army was posted where it could intervene effectively. The roads were muddy from the heavy rains, but the troops were in high spirits and went tramping along with enthusiasm. Reinforcements were near at hand: Frank Blair, with Sherman's missing division, had crossed the Mississippi and was not a dozen miles away from Bolton. Also, while at Jackson Grant got final and significant assurance that he and he alone was boss of this army. Dana showed him a telegram just received from Secretary Stanton:

> General Grant has full and absolute authority to enforce his own commands, and to remove any person who, by ignorance, inaction, or any other cause, interferes with or delays his operations. He has the full confidence of the Government, is expected to enforce his authority, and will be firmly and heartily supported; but he will be responsible for any failure to exert his powers. You may communicate this to him. [25]

Whatever might lie ahead, Grant knew that he no longer needed to handle McClernand with gloves on.

Pemberton, belatedly, was moving east to make a fight of it. With some 23,000 men he crossed the Big Black, proposing to go somewhere south of the railroad line to strike Grant's rear. He moved reluctantly, and only after a council of war had considered the matter, for he believed that to cross the river was to invite defeat; and when he moved he left ten thousand men or more in the vicinity of Vicksburg, disregarding the fact that if he did fight Grant he would need to have his entire force on hand. When the move was well under way, Pemberton received a second order from Johnston to come north of the railroad so that his and Johnston's forces could be united, and he was in the middle of this countermove when Grant's troops began hurrying west.[26] McClernand's advance made contact with Pemberton's forces southeast of Edwards Station on the morning of May 16, and the severest battle of the campaign soon began.

McClernand's leading division was led by Brigadier General Alvin P. Hovey, a former Indiana lawyer who, as Dana remarked, devoted himself to soldiering "as if he expected to spend his life in it." Hovey was marching directly west from Bolton, and when he found armed Confederates in his front he sent his mounted escort forward to see what was up. The Confederates were in position on a rugged plateau known as Champion Hill; Hovey shook out a skirmish line, sent it forward, and followed it with a regular line of battle.

Champion Hill rises one hundred and forty feet above the surrounding country, and has steep sides, cut up with ravines and little gullies, overgrown with dense woods. The fields which the approaching Federals had to cross were under sharp fire, and the country was so broken that it was almost impossible for Hovey or anyone else to tell just how the terrain lay or where the enemy was posted. Hovey's infantry plowed straight ahead, moved six hundred yards up the slope and through the woods, seized some guns and a good bag of prisoners, and then met a furious Confederate counterattack which drove it back in some confusion. The 24th Iowa, which had seized a battery in a wild bayonet charge, promptly lost the guns and had to retreat; one of Hovey's brigadiers described this part of the fight as "one of the most obstinate and murderous conflicts of the war," another testified that it was an "unequal, terrible and most sanguinary" struggle, and Hovey sent back a desperate plea for reinforcements.[27]

The rest of McClernand's corps was not on hand, but McPherson's advance was coming up. John Logan's division had gone into action on low ground off to Hovey's right, at an angle; as a matter of fact it was out on the Confederate flank, posted so that a direct advance would have cut off Pemberton's line of retreat, but nobody was quite aware of the fact. Grant, who had reached the scene, did not see it himself, and he sent one of Logan's brigades over to help Hovey, following it a little later by telling Logan to bring over the rest of his men. Other reinforcements came up from McPherson's second division, led today by Brigadier General Marcellus M. Crocker — a frail, tubercular man, whom Grant considered one of the best division commanders in the Army; a man who was often on the sicklist but never, as Grant testified, when a battle was developing.

The reinforcements went up the hill, picked up Hovey's men just as they were about to be driven down the slopes, and moved on into action. For a time the battle was a formless melee in which, as one of Hovey's officers said, Federals and Confederates took turns in driving one another. A colonel in one of Logan's brigades wrote that the rifle fire was so intense that a staff officer who came forward to give him an order kept shading his eyes with his hand, precisely like a man who is facing into a driving rain. The Iowa regiment which had been driven away from the captured battery rallied, charged and retook the guns — and suddenly, by the middle of the afternoon, Pemberton's army broke and moved off in rapid retreat. It was obviously half-demoralized; a division selected to act as rear guard got completely separated from the rest of the army, lost guns and men when it tried to move back along inadequate plantation roads, and finally went drifting off to the south and east, its baggage train and even its cooking utensils lost in the rout. It wound up, after an all-night march through the fringes of the Union camps, somewhere south of Jackson, and Pemberton saw it no more.[28]

Grant pushed his men on as long as the light lasted, and Pemberton got west of the Big Black, leaving a detachment to make a fight for the crossings. Pemberton was gloomy; as he had foreseen, he had run into a shattering defeat, and as he headed back for the Vicksburg lines he reflected that his career was in ruins. (Grant noted that even in defeat Pemberton played the wrong card: he could, said Grant, have made a night march, swung around to the north, and moved east to join Johnston. This would have given up Vicksburg but, said Grant, "It would have been his proper move. . . and the one Johnston would have made if he had been in Pemberton's place.") Grant was not satisfied with his own handling of the battle, for that matter. If he had been able to bring the rest of McClernand's corps into action, he said, or if he had realized just how the land lay and so had used Logan's division to the best advantage, he might have obliterated Pemberton's whole army.[29] As always, anything short of complete destruction of the enemy struck Grant as an imperfect victory.

But if the victory had been incomplete it was nevertheless decisive. Pemberton had lost 3800 men and 27 guns, his army was on the verge of demoralization, and, once and for all, he had been isolated and driven back into the fortress from which the rest of the Confederacy would be unable to extricate him. From now on, Johnston could do no more than hover on the perimeter of things. He wrote Pemberton that if the Yankees moved on and occupied the works at Snyder's Bluff Vicksburg could not be held, and he added: "If, therefore, you are invested in Vicksburg you must ultimately surrender. Under such circumstances, instead of losing both troops and place, we must, if possible, save the troops. If it is not too late, evacuate Vicksburg and its dependences and march to the northeast." [30]

The victory had not been cheap. Federal casualties came to upwards of 2400 men. Hovey had lost a third of his entire division, and when he wrote his report he testified to the unleashed fury of the fighting his men had been through: "I cannot think of this bloody hill without sadness and pride. . . . It was, after the conflict, literally the hill of death." Totaling his losses, he added: "I never saw fighting like this." [31]

Next day was May 17, and Grant's advance hurried up to the crossings of the Big Black. The Rebel rear guard was waiting, and the position was a tough one. A muddy bayou half filled with down timber ran from swamp to river directly across the front. The Confederates were entrenched behind it, the position could not be flanked, and to reach it the Federals would have to cross open fields devoid of cover and swept by rifle and artillery fire. But the defenders were hopelessly outnumbered, and the disaster at Champion Hill had left them in low spirits, while the Federal soldiers by now had the notion that they themselves were irresistible; they crowded forward in line of battle, two divisions from McClernand's corps, and a brigade led by Brigadier General Michael Lawler went forward on the extreme right to see if this Confederate position was really as strong as it looked.

Lawler was one of the picturesque characters in this army; an enormous jovial man, in peacetime an Illinois farmer, so stout that he could not make a swordbelt go properly about his waist and so wore his sword suspended by a strap from one shoulder. A devout Catholic, he always said his prayers before going into battle, and then whooped his men forward so vigorously that Grant was moved to remark: "When it comes to just plain hard fighting I would rather trust old Mike Lawler than any of them." Lawler was coatless today; he got impatient under the hot sun and the blistering rifle fire the Confederates were sending across the plain, and he decided to attack without waiting for orders. Swinging his sword and yelling mightily, he led his men across a cotton field into the muddy, shoulder-deep bayou, floundering up to the Rebel line in what a watching newspaper correspondent called "at the same time the most perilous and ludicrous charge I witnessed during the war." Lawler's men broke in the end of the Confederate line, and the other Federals who were waiting in support took fire from Lawler's example and began to charge on their own account. Quite typical was the case of the 99th Illinois, which had been crouching under an annoying fire, whose colonel suddenly stood up and shouted: "Boys, it's getting too damned hot here. Let's go for the cussed Rebels!" Presently the entire Union line was advancing, and resistance ceased abruptly as the defenders set fire to their bridges and lit out for Vicksburg. Casualties in this unusual battle were comparatively light, but in their hasty retreat the Confederates lost fully 1700 men as prisoners, to say nothing of 18 guns. Mike Lawler proudly reported that his brigade captured 1120 Confederates — more men, he said, than the whole brigade took into action.[32]

While the soldiers began to improvise new bridges — out of cotton bales, old logs, and lumber gained by tearing down every building in the vicinity — Grant sent a hasty, exultant note to Sherman: "The enemy have been so terribly beaten yesterday and today that I cannot believe that a stand still will be made unless the troops are relying on Johnston's arrival with large re-enforcements, nor that Johnston would attempt to re-enforce with anything at his command if he was at all aware of the present condition of things." Sherman hurried to the front, and when darkness came the bridges were finished. Huge fires of pitch pine were built on each side of the river to give light, and Grant and Sherman sat together on a log and watched the army go west over the Big Black. In his old age Sherman recalled the endless moving lines of troops, smoke piling up from the bonfires to intensify the shadows of the night, firelight gleaming from the black water and touching red flecks of light from polished gun barrels, and he remarked that the whole made "a fine war picture." [33]

During this battle of the Big Black there was an odd incident. Up to Grant came an officer from Banks's command, bearing what Grant always remembered as a letter from Halleck, ordering Grant to drop everything, go back to Grand Gulf, and join forces with Banks. The officer who brought this message appears to have been Brigadier General William Dwight, and he was insistent that Grant return to the Mississippi at once. Grant remarked that the order came too late and that no one, in view of what had happened in the last few days, could expect him to retrace his steps now. Just then Mike Lawler's charge began to move, and Grant galloped on to watch it, leaving the sputtering officer behind. Writing about it years later Grant remarked: "I saw no more of the officer who delivered the dispatch; I think not even to this day." [34]

It makes a good story, and the only trouble is that the message which Dwight gave to Grant almost certainly was not an order from Halleck telling Grant to go back to Grand Gulf. Halleck very probably would have disapproved of Grant's march inland if the plan had been submitted to him in advance, but when it actually took place Halleck seems to have adjusted himself to it with remarkably little fuss. The only message in the records that even remotely resembles the order Grant refers to is a mild dispatch which Halleck wrote on May 11, telling Grant that "if possible, the forces of yourself and of General Banks should be united between Vicksburg and Port Hudson so as to attack these places separately with combined forces." It seems likely that General Dwight came up with a strong complaint from Banks himself; Banks was furious when he learned that Grant was not going to help him take Port Hudson, and he protested to Grant, to Halleck and to the unrelenting Heavens. The traditional picture of Grant on the field of victory defying the General in Chief can hardly be classed as anything much better than legend.[35]

In any case, the triumphant Federals pressed ahead, on May 18, and they came up at last to the fortifications that covered the land side of Vicksburg. These ran for miles, touching the hairpin bend of the great river just above the city and following the high ground to the east and south for eight or nine miles until they reached the muddy bottom lands below. Riding west on the road from Jackson, McPherson and his staff came out on a wooded ridge late in the afternoon and looked at the fortress they had marched so far to see; and the infantry moved on to take position in front of the trenches, while regimental bands jubilantly played "The Girl I Left Behind Me."

Grant himself rode straight for the Yazoo river. It was the high ground on the left bank of this river that had been the objective of all of his maneuvering and marching and fighting — the Walnut Hills, that rose back of Chickasaw Bayou where Sherman's men had made their unhappy fight five months ago and that went on all the way to Snyder's Bluff. If Grant could win this high ground, gunboats and transports from the north could come up the Yazoo and unload men and supplies without limit; he would have a secure, permanent base and Vicksburg would be doomed. Johnston had just warned Pemberton that the city could not be held unless these hills were held. They were empty now, unguarded except for a few retreating Confederate skirmishers, and with Sherman at his side Grant rode to the top of the bluffs on May 19, and looked down at the looped course of the Yazoo; and Sherman, who had been skeptical from the moment this campaign was suggested, turned to him impulsively and blurted out his apology:

"Until this moment, I never thought your expedition a success. I never could see the end clearly, until now. But this is a campaign; this is a success if we never take the town."

The sentimental outburst might come from Sherman; the rank and file would respond in its own way a couple of days later, and in the response there would be something everlastingly characteristic of this matter-of-fact aggregation of fighting men . . . who had somehow patterned themselves, just a little, on the man who commanded them. Grant got his troops posted where he wanted them, sent word to Admiral Porter that the transports and store ships could find good landing places along the Yazoo, got off a quick message to Halleck, and then went riding down just in the rear of the fighting lines. The soldiers, drawn up facing the powerful Confederate works, were quite impressed with themselves and with what they had done, but they were also hungry: living off the country was all very well, but during the last few days rations had been skimpy and uneven, many soldiers had been on a straight meat diet, and it seemed to the men that what mattered most was that they were at last in contact with the army's line of supplies . . . and as Grant rode along a private soldier looked up, saw him, and, in a conversational tone, said: "Hardtack." Other soldiers looked up, recognized Grant, and took up the call; and very soon everyone in the vicinity was yelling "Hardtack! Hardtack!" at the top of his lungs . . . the Army of the Tennessee, saluting its general at the supreme moment of his greatest campaign.

Grant reined in and explained: a road was being built just back of the Union lines, steamboats were at the landing, and everything anybody needed would be issued directly. The men laughed and cheered, and that night the army wagons trundled past with hardtack and coffee for everybody. As Grant wrote, "The bread and coffee were highly appreciated." [36]

CHAPTER TWENTY-TWO

The Core of Iron

THE CONFEDERATE DEFENSES covering Vicksburg were powerful. One of McPherson's staff officers remembered how they looked when he rode in along the Jackson road: "A long line of high, rugged, irregular bluffs, clearly cut against the sky, crowned with cannon which peered ominously from embrasures to the right and left as far as the eye could see. Lines of heavy rifle-pits, surmounted with head logs, ran along the bluffs, connecting fort with fort, and filled with veteran infantry." In front, on the slopes, was a tangle of fallen timber, tree-tops interlaced to make an almost impenetrable abatis. The officer confessed: "The approaches to this position were frightful — enough to appal the stoutest heart." [1]

But the Federal Army was cocky, from Commanding General down to the men in the ranks. At Champion Hill they had seen Pemberton's army streaming off in disorganized retreat, and the business at the crossings of the Big Black had been a stampede rather than a battle; these works might be strong, but the army that held them looked weak, and one quick, hard smash might settle matters. On May 19, after brief preliminary skirmishing, Grant ordered an assault — only to discover that even badly demoralized troops can recover their fighting edge quickly enough if they are put into solid fortifications and allowed to fight on the defensive. The assault failed — five stands of Federal colors were left lying on the slopes — and Grant spent the next two days perfecting his lines and making ready for a new, more comprehensive attack. He still believed that the Confederates were badly dispirited; he knew that Johnston was off to his rear somewhere, gathering strength for an attempt to come to Pemberton's relief; and he did not propose to settle down to the long, wearing business of a siege if there was any chance to take the place by storm. He knew, too, that his own men

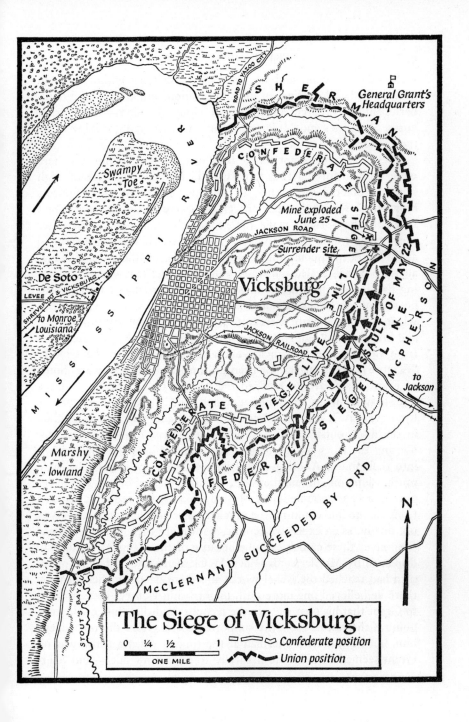

General Grant's
Headquarters

SHERMAN

CONFEDERATE

Mine exploded
June 25
JACKSON ROAD

Surrender site

CONFEDERATE SIEGE LINE

Vicksburg

De Soto
LEVEE
SHREVEPORT & VICKSBURG
to Monroe
Louisiana

JACKSON
RAILROAD

FEDERAL SIEGE LINE

ASSAULT OF MAY 22

McPHERSON

to
Jackson

MISSISSIPPI RIVER

Swampy
Toe

ROAD TO YAZOO CITY

CONFEDERATE SIEGE LINE

FEDERAL SIEGE LINE

Marshy
lowland

N

McCLERNAND SUCCEEDED BY ORD

STOUT'S BAYOU

The Siege of Vicksburg

0   ¼   ½   1   ⌐‾⌐‾⌐‾⌐ Confederate position
ONE MILE   ᴧᴧᴧᴧᴧ Union position

were still confident, and he wanted to use their enthusiasm. On May 22 he had long lines of guns in position, and after a hard bombardment he ordered an attack all along the line — three army corps, Sherman's and McPherson's and McClernand's, driving in on the Confederate works.

These works were not simple lines of trenches. At intervals there were regular forts with steep walls, posted on the crest of high slopes, protected by ditches. In McPherson's corps, the engineers built forty scaling ladders, fifteen or twenty feet in length, and when the first assault wave ran forward men dragged these after them with ropes. Two Iowa regiments, an Illinois regiment and another from Wisconsin, headed for a fort beside the railroad. Their advance patrols scaled the walls and got inside, triumphantly planting flags on the parapets; they stayed there for two or three hours, beating off determined counterattacks, and then were overwhelmed when a Texas contingent came in with bayonets, capturing flags and invaders and plugging the gap for good. The Texans' feat won from Confederate Brigadier General Stephen D. Lee the tribute: "A more daring feat has not been performed during the war." Some of Frank Blair's troops reached the parapet on another part of the line, braving what an Illinois colonel called "the most murderous fire I ever saw": they could not enter the Rebel works, and huddled in the ditch outside until the defenders at last dislodged them by lighting the fuses of 12-pounder shells and rolling the shells down into their midst. Another party managed to plant its flags halfway up the slope on still another fort, and one of McPherson's brigades got four flags mounted just outside of a strong redoubt, but the Confederate line could not be cracked. The whole attack was given up, finally, as an expensive repulse, with more then 3000 casualties.[2]

Some of these casualties came because of the excess of enthusiasm displayed by McClernand. When McClernand saw that some of his men had reached the Rebel works and were flaunting their banners there he believed one more push might bring victory; he sent word to Grant that his men were in the trenches and that they could keep going if the rest of the army supported them. Grant did not believe him, but he was with Sherman at the time — when a battle was on Grant seemed to gravitate naturally to Sherman's side — and Sherman told him that the message from McClernand was an official communication which could not be ignored. Grant sent McClernand reinforcements and ordered Sherman and McPherson to renew their assaults. The battle flared up again, but McClernand had appraised the situation wrong, and the new attacks accomplished nothing. Grant commented on all of this, two days later, in words much more bitter than he ordinarily used:

> General McClernand's dispatches misled me as to the real state of the facts, and caused much of this loss. He is entirely unfit for the position of corps commander, both on the march and on the battlefield. Looking after his corps gives me more labor and infinitely more uneasiness than all the remainder of my department.

Grant did not, however, remove McClernand from command. Probably he realized that the real trouble on this day lay in the fact that he and his entire army had been overconfident. One of his engineer officers summed it up in his report. Everyone, he said, had underestimated the strength of the Confederate Army, and "Our own troops, buoyant with success, were eager for an assault and would not work well if the slow process of a siege were undertaken."

When night came the troops were pulled back to form a trench system of their own on a range of loosely connected hills a few hundred yards away from the Confederate lines. Grant got off a dispatch to Halleck, a curious mixture of justified confidence and a jaunty optimism which may in part have come from imperfect knowledge of just how little the day's fighting had actually gained:

> Vicksburg is now completely invested. I have possession of Haynes' [Snyder's] Bluff and the Yazoo; consequently have supplies. Today an attempt was made to carry the city by assault, but was not entirely successful. We hold possession, however, of two of the enemy's forts and have skirmishers close under all of them. The nature of the ground about Vicksburg is such that it can only be taken by a siege. It is entirely safe to us in time, I would say one week if the enemy do not send a large army upon my rear.

Two days later he gave Halleck further reassurance: "The enemy are now undoubtedly in our grasp. The fall of Vicksburg and the capture of most of the garrison can only be a question of time." [3]

Aside from his airy guess that the job could be done in a week, Grant was giving an accurate appreciation. Pemberton and his army were locked up, and Johnston was off on the rim, trying without success to build up a force strong enough to fight his way through to perform a rescue. Grant's army was as securely based now as it would have been at Memphis; its access to supplies was clear, and reinforcements were on the way. The processes of siege warfare were slow, laborious and painful, but ultimately certain; the Federal lines would be made impregnable to any possible sally by the beleaguered garrison, approach trenches would be brought nearer and nearer to the Confederate lines, and in the end — if sheer hunger did not compel them to surrender — the Confederates could be overwhelmed. From this moment, given competent management, the Federal Army was bound to win.

Siege warfare was a job for engineers, and of regular military engineer officers Grant's army had very few — during most of the operation, it could put no more than three on duty at one time. Yet the engineer officers were discovering anew, as they had seen during the march downstream from Milliken's Bend, that these soldiers were handy jacks-of-all-trades who could do almost anything they set their hands to. One engineer confessed after it was all over that in the immense task of constructing trenches, saps, batteries and covered ways he could safely rely on the "native good sense and ingenuity" of the men in the ranks. "Whether a battery was to be constructed by men who had never built one before," he wrote, "a sap-roller made by those who had never heard the name, or a ship's gun carriage to be built, it was done, and after a few trials well done. . . . Officers and men had to learn to be engineers while the siege was going on." [4]

Watching pessimistically from afar, Confederate Joe Johnston paid his own tribute to the uncommon qualities of Grant's army. Not long after this date he sent a letter to Secretary of War Seddon, saying that he hoped soon to have about 23,000 effective men. He did not think these would be enough, for he pointed out: "Grant's army is estimated at 60,000 or 80,000 men, and his troops are worth double the number of northeastern troops. We cannot relieve General Pemberton except by defeating Grant, who is believed to be fortifying." [5]

Far downstream, Banks was at last getting his troops over to Port Hudson. The strength of this place had been reduced, but Grant's earlier guess that the garrison was too weak to hold out in face of a determined attack was wrong; Confederate General Gardner was well dug in, Banks's force was not quite large enough, and Banks asked Grant for the loan of ten thousand men. Grant explained that he did not propose to spare a man, and in a letter, which one of his staff officers took to Banks, Grant described his own situation:

> Concentration is essential to the success of the general campaign in the west, but Vicksburg is the vital point. Our situation is for the first time, during the entire western campaign, what it should be. We have, after great labor and extraordinary risk, secured a position which should not be jeopardized by any detachments whatever. On the contrary, I am now and shall continue to exert myself to the utmost to concentrate. The enemy clearly see the importance of dislodging me at all hazards. General Joe Johnston is now at Canton [a Mississippi town 25 or 30 miles north of Jackson] and making his dispositions to attack me. His present strength is estimated at 40,000 and is known to be at least 20,000.

Grant believed that he could hold his position and could reduce Vicksburg by the latter part of June, but he could not and would not send away any troops.[6]

It would take time to make Vicksburg cave in, but men who were paid to comment on all of this began to see that what had already been done was prodigious. The *New York Times* man, looking back at the recent past, spread himself in an enthusiastic dispatch just after the May 22 assault had failed: "A more audacious plan than that devised by the Commander has scarcely ever been conceived. It was, in brief, nothing else than to gain firm ground on one of the enemy's flanks, which to be done involved a march of about 150 miles through the enemy's country and in which communication with the base of supplies was liable at any moment to be permanently interrupted." Grant's army, said this correspondent, had fought the Rebels five times, winning every fight, had captured more than fifty guns and six thousand prisoners, and had done all of this "in a foreign climate, under a tropical sun ablaze with the white heat of summer, with only such supplies as could be gleaned from the country." He added that "it must be admitted that whether ultimate success crowns our efforts, our gallant army has done sufficient within the last month to entitle it at once to the esteemed gratitude and admiration of the people at home." Even the correspondent of the *New York World*, a paper which was dedicated to the belief that anything a Federal commander did was probably wrong, confessed handsomely that "Vicksburg is ours beyond a reasonable doubt," and added that Grant could take the Confederate fortifications whenever he was ready to spend from six to ten thousand men in the attempt. The fate of Vicksburg was settled, this writer felt, when the Rebels were beaten at Champion Hill.[7]

As the lines were drawn more tightly, McClernand smoldered. His own bright dream of glory had faded badly. He had put together a fair number of the troops which would presently capture Vicksburg and he had been allowed to see himself as the hero of the war, but Grant had relentlessly whittled him down to size, and when the great day came it was not going to be McClernand who had opened the Mississippi Valley and won the great war in the West. He believed that the West Pointers had ganged up on him, and with some reason he felt that the clear intent of the President and the Secretary of War had been nullified; he was a man with a grievance, and it burst out, one day, when young Colonel Wilson came to him with an order from Grant directing McClernand to strengthen a force which he had sent back to watch the crossings of the Big Black River.

McClernand read the order and then snapped: "I'll be God-damned if I'll do it. I'm tired of being dictated to — I won't stand it any longer, and you can go back and tell General Grant." He added some more remarks in the same vein, and Colonel Wilson dropped his own West Point formality, pointed out that McClernand was insulting not only the Commanding General of the army but Wilson himself, and offered to get off his horse and use his fists if the offensive expressions were not promptly withdrawn. McClernand withdrew them, and, by way of apology, went on to say: "I was simply expressing my intense vehemence on the subject matter, sir, and I beg your pardon." When Wilson reported on this to Grant, Grant found the apology most amusing. All through the rest of the campaign, when Grant heard anyone use profanity — it was usually hotheaded Rawlins, who was profane when in a temper — Grant would explain: "He's not swearing — he's just expressing his intense vehemence on the subject matter." [8]

McClernand continued to smolder, and he sat down to write an order congratulating his corps on its achievements and implying broadly that if the rest of the army had supported it properly Vicksburg would have fallen on May 22. In the end this order would create a storm that would blow McClernand all the way out of the Army, but for the moment the routine of the siege went on smoothly.

The routine was inexorable. Grant's lines ran from the Yazoo River, above the town, to the lowlands along the Mississippi to the south — fifteen miles of camps, trenches and gun emplacements on the hills and ridges, so tightly held that a Confederate defender wrote despairingly: "When the real investment began a cat could not have crept out of Vicksburg without being discovered." Pemberton was woefully outnumbered. He had more than 30,000 soldiers, but they were plagued by illness and malnutrition, and by no means all of them were fit for duty in the trenches.[9] His supply of food and ammunition was strictly limited, and he had no way to get any more. Unless Johnston could break the Federal lines, Pemberton could do nothing but hold his ground and watch the remorseless construction of Federal approaches: a day-and-night process which brought the Union outworks closer and closer to his own defenses, getting the Federals constantly nearer to places from which they could mine the Confederate trenches, making inevitable the day when the assault troops would be close enough to swarm in over the Southern lines in unbeatable strength.

A strange apathy seemed to descend on the defenders. Their abundant artillery was seldom used; for the most part, the Federal working parties which kept pushing their trenches closer were harassed by nothing more than musketry fire. Federal engineers reported afterward that although the Confederate artillery had been badly battered by the Union siege guns, it could have been used more effectively — could, indeed, have made the progress of the investment much more costly.

Odd things happened on the picket lines. One night Northern troops who were bringing two approach trenches forward at an angle found that the place where the two new trenches were supposed to join lay inside the Rebel picket line. Northerners and Southerners held informal consultation, while the firing died down; a Federal engineer came forward and indicated the place where the two trenches were to meet, and suggested that if necessary his men would fight to gain the necessary ground. In the end the Confederates pulled their guards back so that the construction could go forward without a fight. As a Northern soldier remarked, "It certainly was a strange war scene for the opposing men . . . to meet and talk over the disputed ground just as though it was adjoining neighbors who had met in a friendly way to establish their line fence." At one stage, indeed, one Northerner suggested that the approaches be redesigned so that the Confederate guards need not be disturbed; and a Confederate replied, "Oh, that don't make any difference. You Yanks will soon have the place anyway." In front of one corps, rival officers met between the lines to make a harmonious arrangement of picket lines, and a Federal engineer officer confessed: "As the enemy could have stopped our work by remaining in his lines and firing an occasional volley, the advantage of this arrangement, novel in the art of war, was entirely on our side, and was not interfered with." This officer characterized the Confederate defense as "far from being vigorous," and said that the whole object of the defenders seemed to be "to wait for another assault, losing in the meantime as few men as possible." [10]

Yet although an engineer might say that the defense lacked vigor, none of Grant's men considered the siege of Vicksburg a picnic. Infantry firing usually died down at night — there was an unspoken agreement along the picket lines not to do any shooting after dark except under orders from higher up — but the Federal artillery was apt to break out with a heavy barrage at any moment, and shell fuses were so defective that many Federal shells burst over Federal trenches; some soldiers insisted that these caused more casualties than Rebel bullets. Daybreak usually brought a hard bombardment from the siege lines, and from dawn to dusk the musket fire was heavy. It was common for a man in the trench lines to use from fifty to one hundred cartridges in one day, at a time when no attack was being made or threatened. After darkness, the Confederates liked to jeer at their Yankee opponents, asking them how they liked the sunny South, and inquiring — with pointed reference to the large number of rifles the Federals had lost in the unsuccessful assaults of May 22 — whether the Yankees wanted to get rid of any more Enfields. The heat and the constant labor of trench building were a burden, and men complained that they were "as dirty as hogs," with no chance to change clothing and no water to wash face or hands. One boy who wrote to his sister said the Confederates had not fired a cannon for seven days, but that at least fifty rifle bullets had whizzed over his head in the last ten minutes. Many men were wounded simply because they got too used to trench warfare and exposed themselves unnecessarily; one man insisted that "as long as a man uses proper caution he is not in much danger." [11]

Grant was out on the firing line often enough, and at times he was rebuked for making a target of himself. When he climbed a timber observation tower which often came under enemy fire, a Minnesota private, not recognizing him, yelled up angrily: "You old — — ——, you'd better keep down off of there or you'll be shot." A comrade tugged at the man's sleeve and told him: "That's Grant!" and the man quickly lost himself. One day Grant rode a mule behind an exposed section of line, and was greeted with a shout from the trenches: "See here, you damned old fool, if you don't get off that mule you'll get shot." When the man who had shouted was told who this mule-rider was, he stoutly replied: "I don't care who he is, what's he fooling around here for anyway? We're shot at enough without taking any chances with him." A newspaper correspondent visiting the trenches one day saw two men walking without haste toward a gun emplacement, while Confederate bullets kicked up spurts of dust about their feet, and he stuck his own head above the parapet long enough to call: "Stoop down, *down,* damn you, down!" The pedestrians walked in among the guns, and the reporter saw that they were Grant and Hovey. Grant, he said, stood on the parapet to examine the Rebel works through his field glasses, motioning Hovey to get down under cover, and Hovey protested that it was Grant who should take shelter — "I'm only a general of division and it's easy to fill my place, but with you, sir, it's different." [12]

Strong reinforcements were coming down from the north, and before long Grant had more than enough men to keep Pemberton's force under complete control. Hurlbut at Memphis combed out the western Tennessee garrison to send new troops, a full division came from Missouri, and two divisions of the Ninth Army Corps were brought down from Kentucky. Admiral Porter with his gunboats guarded the Mississippi, sealing the western approaches. Frank Blair took a division on an expedition up the Yazoo, to clear out lurking Confederates and despoil the rich delta land of food and forage, and more than thirty thousand men, with Sherman in command, were sent to hold the open country between the Yazoo and the Big Black — the territory across which Joe Johnston would have to march if he came in to break the siege.

With more than seventy thousand soldiers now on hand, Grant felt a new confidence. When a staff officer remarked that he feared Johnston might fight his way in to Vicksburg, Grant disagreed: "No, we are the only fellows who want to get in there. The Rebels who are in now want to get out, and those who are out want to stay out. If Johnston tries to cut his way in we will let him do it, and then see that he don't get out. You say he has thirty thousand men with him? That will give us thirty thousand more prisoners than we now have." Men in an Illinois regiment said that one evening Grant strolled out, sat down by a campfire, and "talked with the boys with less reserve than many a little puppy of a lieutenant." Grant told the soldiers that everything was under control, said that "Pemberton was a northern man who had got into bad company," and insisted that the Union position could be held even if the Confederates sent in a relieving column of fifty thousand men.[13]

Off to the rear, Sherman kept a sharp eye on the crossings of the Big Black. At one crossing, where Rebel cavalry patrolled the eastern bank, Sherman detected a security leak, and he wrote to Rawlins about it; a plantation house on his side of the river was full of women, he said, wives and daughters of Confederate soldiers, and these were in constant communication with the cavalrymen across the river. "So," said Sherman, "I moved them all by force, leaving a fine house filled with elegant furniture and costly paintings to the chances of war." It occurred to Sherman that Grant might not approve of this ruthless deportation of civilians, and he gave Rawlins a note of warning: "These may appeal to the tender heart of our commanding general, but he will not reverse my decision when he knows a family accessible to the enemy — keen scouts — can collect and impart more information than the most expert spies. Our volunteer pickets and patrols reveal names and facts in their innocence which, if repeated by these women, give the key to our points."

Sherman need not have worried. Rawlins showed the letter to Grant, who promptly wrote to Sherman: "You need not fear, general, my tender heart getting the better of me, so as to send the secession ladies to your front; on the contrary, I rather think it advisable to send out every living being from your lines, and arrest all persons found within who are not connected with the army." [14]

The exchange of notes illustrates a profound difference between Grant and Sherman.

Sherman was and remains famous as a hard man who believed in hard war. In his complex nature there apparently was some strain that vibrated to this note — something that led him to talk brutally about the brutal things which war obliged him to do. Over and over, from this moment to the time, years after the war, when he wrote his Memoirs, Sherman would dwell on the waste and destruction which his army inflicted on the people of the South; would dwell on it so enthusiastically that at times he actually exaggerated the harsh deeds done by the men in his command. Sherman was in most ways a tough realist, and yet far underneath he retained a touch of the romantic viewpoint in regard to war. He could talk about the grand and glorious game of war, could retain in his memory vignettes of light and shadow as fine war pictures, could see and appreciate the figure which he and his men were cutting; and in some way his habit of tough talk reflects this trait, as if his very sensitivity to the changing nature of war had brought it forth — as if, indeed, in an oddly inverted way he were a Middle Western Jeb Stuart who wore toughness instead of the horseman's plume and scarlet-lined cape in order to cut a flourish.

Grant's nature was much simpler, and deeper. He had no liking at all for the cruel weight which modern warfare puts on the civilian, on all who are helpless and luckless enough to stand in its path, and he never wasted any words talking about it; but he could order the weight applied without the slightest hesitation when it seemed to him to be necessary. His concept of his role in the Civil War had become mature, in this campaign. Superior force had been put in his hands, and it was to be used not so much to win strategic victories as to destroy a nation. The richness of the Mississippi land had been taken to feed his army, during the march away from Grand Gulf, but it would have been well to take it even if his army had not been hungry, because this richness was a military target in itself: it helped to support the fabric of a nationhood which the North was sworn to obliterate. Sherman could, and did, write graphically about the cruelty of driving helpless women out of a good home which must be left to the prankish destructiveness of hard-handed soldiers; Grant was the one who calmly suggested that instead of removing one family the army ought to drive every family out of whole counties. Of the two men, the one who had the direct vision and the real core of iron was Grant.

Early in June there was one little incident to interrupt the even course of Grant's way. Just what happened is obscure, and the matter is of no importance anyway, since whatever actually happened did not prolong the resistance of the Vicksburg garrison by as much as five minutes, or cost the life of one Union soldier, or give to either Pemberton or Johnston an opening that could be used. But because it fits into the deathless legend of Grant as a hard drinker it survives. . . .

Grant went up the Yazoo to see how operations there were coming on, and according to the newspaper correspondent Sylvanus Cadwallader he had much too much to drink on a headquarters steamer, took a wild, breakneck ride across country, and was at last, by Cadwallader, with much difficulty, got under control and brought back to headquarters in an army ambulance. At headquarters, said Cadwallader, a thin-lipped, censorious Rawlins met the ambulance, saw Grant safely to bed, and then turned on Cadwallader in a fury and demanded: "I want you to tell me the exact facts — all of them — without any concealment. I have a right to know them, and I will know them." So Cadwallader told Rawlins the facts, which — as the reporter put them down later — involved a horrendous two-day binge which narrowly missed being a scandal for the whole army.

It makes a gaudy tale. The difficulty with it is that it does not jibe with a letter which was written at the time by Rawlins himself; differs with it so much, indeed, that it is not possible to accept both Cadwallader and Rawlins as witnesses in the matter.

At one o'clock in the morning on June 6, Rawlins wrote Grant a subsequently famous letter, beginning: "The great solicitude I feel for the safety of this army leads me to mention, what I had hoped never again to do, the subject of your drinking." Rawlins then went on to say that he might possibly be "doing you an injustice by unfounded suspicion"; still, he had been informed that Grant had recently had a glass of wine at Sherman's headquarters, he himself had that very day discovered a box of wine in Grant's tent and had been told, by Grant, that it was being saved to celebrate the eventual capture of Vicksburg; and, finally, on this very evening "I find you where the wine bottle has just been emptied, in company with those who drink and urge you to do likewise." This was bad; and, Rawlins continued, "the lack of your usual promptness and decision, and clearness in expressing yourself in writing conduces to confirm my suspicion." More in sorrow than in anger, Rawlins recalled that Grant had promised two months earlier to drink no more during the present campaign, and he wrote sadly: "If my suspicions are unfounded, let my friendship for you and my zeal for my country be my excuse for this letter."

Years after the war Captain John M. Shaw of the 25th Wisconsin

Infantry, a Galena man who had known Rawlins well before the war, read the text of this letter in a public address. The copy which he had, he said, bore an endorsement in Rawlins's hand:

> This is an exact copy of a letter given to the person to whom it is addressed at its date, about four miles from our headquarters in the rear of Vicksburg. Its admonitions were heeded and all went well.—JOHN A. RAWLINS.[15]

The Rawlins letter is moving, and it seems clear enough that somebody around headquarters had been doing some drinking; but Rawlins's letter makes no sense at all if the Cadwallader story is true. Rawlins speaks of his possibly "unfounded suspicions," of finding Grant in the company of men who had been tipping the bottle, and so on; but according to Cadwallader, Rawlins had direct, immediate knowledge of a colossal drunk that could not conceivably be referred to in the terms Rawlins used. The spree could not have taken place after delivery of the letter, either: Rawlins's endorsement is explicit. In his dealings with Grant, Rawlins was never at any time mealy-mouthed. That letter and its endorsement simply could not have been written if Rawlins himself had seen Grant brought back from a forty-eight-hour drunk in an ambulance and had immediately thereafter been given a detailed, first-hand description of the whole business. It is extremely hard to see how the Cadwallader story can be classed as anything but one more in the dreary Grant-was-drunk garland of myths.

It is not necessary, in writing this story off, to try to portray Grant as a steadfast teetotaler. The simple truth apparently is that, like most other officers of that generation, he occasionally wanted, and took, a drink, and then went on about his business. After the war an officer on George Thomas's staff said that at about this time he was visiting briefly at Grant's headquarters. The day was hot and dry, and the visitor had a certain thirst, but there did not seem to be any whisky about the place; people explained quietly that the stuff was outlawed because "Rawlins is death on liquor." Finally, however, after dark, the visitor found himself in a tent with a surgeon, who produced a bottle of rye, poured some into a tin cup, and put the cup on a cracker box for the guest. Just then there were footsteps outside, someone fumbled with the tent flap, and the surgeon muttered "It's Rawlins!" Then the flaps opened and Grant appeared. Without a word he reached for the cup, drained it, replaced it and went away. Years later, the officer said, he met Grant on a train, and Grant asked him if he remembered that little occasion. When the officer replied, "Perfectly," Grant said: "I don't think I ever wanted a drink so much, before or after." [16]

It makes a great stir and it means very little. All that matters is the fact that the Commanding General of this army continued to draw an increasingly tight line around Vicksburg and its defenders. From Porter's gunboats and mortar boats and from the land batteries, intermittent bombardments struck the city and its defenses. Lacking coehorn mortars to toss shells into the enemy trenches, Grant's infantrymen made usable imitations out of wood, boring short logs to take 6- or 12-pound shells and binding the logs with stout iron bands. Once, the Confederates approached the river on the Louisiana side and made a spirited attack on the troops around Milliken's Bend; they were driven off, after a sharp fight, in which the fire of a couple of gunboats proved decisive, and Grant noted that some of his new Negro soldiers fought here and, for raw troops, behaved very well.[17]

Pemberton grew increasingly despondent. He sent Johnston a message expressing doubt that he could cut his way out, as Johnston had been hoping he could do, and saying that even if he succeeded Vicksburg itself and many men would be lost; in his despair, he suggested a fantastic expedient. Grant, he said, did not know how many men Johnston had or what his plans were; he might, if approached properly, agree to let the whole Vicksburg army march out with its guns and equipment, taking the city and fortifications as a gift and, in return, letting the defenders go scot free. Pemberton did not see how he himself could send such a proposal to Grant, but he thought Johnston could. Johnston contented himself by replying coldly that if there were to be any negotiations with Grant, they must be made by Pemberton.[18] It is hardly necessary to remark that Grant would have listened to no such proposition. From first to last it was the army he wanted rather than the city.

Grant's confidence was running high. On June 15 he wrote to a friend that "all is going on here now just right," and he went on to specify:

We have our trenches pushed up so close to the enemy that we can throw hand grenades over into their forts. The enemy do not dare show their heads above the parapets at any point, so close and so watchful are our sharpshooters. The town is completely invested. My position is so strong that I feel myself abundantly able to leave it so and go out twenty or thirty miles with force enough to whip two such garrisons.

Johnston, said Grant, could not force his way in unless he could muster "a larger army than the Confederacy have now at any one place."

Having written all of this, Grant apparently felt that he may have sounded vainglorious, for he added: "This is what I think but do not say it boastingly, nor do I want it repeated or shown." [19]

An even surer sign of Grant's confidence was the fact that he finally relieved McClernand of his command and sent him back to Illinois. He had come close to doing this when the May 22 attacks ended so badly, but had concluded it would be better to let McClernand stay until Vicksburg fell and then quietly ease him out;[20] but McClernand's injudicious order of congratulation to the 13th Corps got into the papers in mid-June — not without some assistance from McClernand's headquarters — and that was the end. The order infuriated both Sherman and McPherson, who felt that McClernand was reaching out for glory at the expense of their commands, and they immediately sent Grant vigorous letters of protest. Sherman wrote bitterly that the order was really addressed, not to the soldiers, "but to a constituency in Illinois," and McPherson agreed that it was designed "to impress the public mind with the magnificent strategy, superior tactics and brilliant deeds" of McClernand. Unfortunately for McClernand, in getting his order into the papers he had violated a standing War Department regulation which stipulated that such papers must be submitted to army headquarters before publication. This congratulatory order had not been submitted. Grant sent McClernand a note, asking if the order as published was genuine, and when McClernand replied that it was and that he was prepared to stand by it, Grant had Rawlins draw up an order of dismissal. This order, dated June 18, read as follows:

Major General John A. McClernand is hereby relieved from the command of the Thirteenth Army Corps. He will proceed to any point he may select in the state of Illinois and report by Letter to Headquarters of the Army for orders.

The order added that Major General E. O. C. Ord would replace McClernand as corps commander.

Rawlins drafted the order and got it signed after working hours, and Grant supposed that it would be given to McClernand the next morning. But Colonel Wilson returned to headquarters sometime after midnight, and when Rawlins told him about it the two staff men agreed that the order ought to be served without any delay whatever. Headquarters expected the Vicksburg garrison to attempt a sortie at any time. The sortie would very probably hit the lines held by McClernand; McClernand would fight, and he had a good, fighting corps; and once the fighting began Grant would probably suspend or even cancel the order of removal. It had better be delivered while it was hot.

So Wilson got the Provost Marshal, a sergeant and four enlisted men, donned his own best uniform, and rode off to McClernand's headquarters, arriving about two in the morning and demanding that the General be aroused. McClernand received him, after some delay; he could be punctilious about the formalities, too, and Wilson found him in full uniform, seated behind a table in his tent, two candles burning, general's sword lying on the table in front. With the Provost Marshal and his squad drawn up outside, Wilson handed the letter across the table, remarking that he was instructed to see that the General read it and understood it. McClernand adjusted his glasses, scanned the paper, and burst out: "Well sir! I am relieved!" He paused, and added: "By God sir, we are both relieved!" [21]

McClernand went back to Illinois, remarking that since he had been appointed by the President he did not think a mere major general could dismiss him, but that with the army in the immediate presence of the enemy he would not linger to make a point of it.

From Illinois he wrote vigorously — to Halleck, to Stanton and to Lincoln himself — demanding a reversal, an accounting, a court of inquiry, any official action that would restore the bright promise of the last autumn. He could get nowhere, and in the following September, with the Vicksburg campaign long since ended and the participants gone on to other things, he sent Halleck a letter complaining that Grant's report of the campaign did him grave injustice. He showed his fangs over this, writing:

> How far General Grant is indebted to the forbearance of officers under his command for his retention in the public service so long, I will not undertake to state unless he should challenge it. None know better than himself how much he is indebted to that forbearance. Neither will I undertake to show that he is indebted to the good conduct of officers and men of his command at different times for the series of successes that have gained him applause rather than to his own merit as a commander, unless he should challenge it, too.[22]

It did no good. Grant challenged nothing, and Washington — holding perhaps the view that a general who had twice captured entire armies might have some asset besides the forbearance of his officers and the good conduct of his men — buried the protests deep in the War Department files. Ord took over the 13th Corps, McClernand simmered the summer away in Illinois, and the Army of the Tennessee got on with the siege.

Summer was coming, the hot sun blistered the long lines of trenches, water was scarce and hard to get, and between Confederate sharpshooters and the nightly pick-and-shovel details the soldiers were having hard enough times. From the North came well-intentioned visitors, bringing parcels of food — poultry, usually, a drug on the market in this army which had lived on Mississippi chickens so long that it actually preferred ordinary salt pork and hard bread.[23] On the picket lines, Yank and Reb discussed the progress of the siege, traded coffee and hardtack for tobacco, and now and then sent personal messages back and forth: the brother-against-brother legend would grow hackneyed, with the passage of years, but it was a literal reality here. Each army contained regiments from Missouri, and one day the men on one part of the front stopped firing so that a Missourian in one of the Union regiments could walk across and see his brother, who served Missouri in a Confederate regiment . . . the Northern brother wanted to hand over some greenbacks for the Southern brother to send home to the old folks.[24]

Federal trenches grew wide and deep, designed so that a column of fours could march through in safety. The approaches crept closer and closer to the Rebel lines, and the Federals' amateur engineers busily dug tunnels and planted mines. On June 25 a mine was exploded under a Confederate strongpoint near the Jackson road; it blew off the top of a hill, but did no serious harm. Another mine was exploded on July 1. Inexplicably, it tossed a Negro cook all the way into the Union lines (he landed more or less unhurt, and wound up with a job in John Logan's headquarters) and created a dusty hollow which Union soldiers occupied for twenty-four hours and then abandoned.[25]

This mine warfare accomplished little but symbolized much. It meant that the Union lines were being brought so close to the defensive works that before long the Union advantage in numbers would become decisively effective. Pemberton's lines would simply be swamped. What could not be done on May 22, when assault troops had to run forward for a quarter of a mile under heavy fire, could certainly be done at moderate cost once the attackers were close enough to blow the defensive works apart and then charge in through the dust cloud. In front of Sherman's corps, the engineers began a new tunnel, working day and night to put a mine under a Confederate salient. The heat was oppressive, especially in the cramped, unventilated mine shaft, and the soldiers toiled in six-hour shifts; twenty-eight feet below the Rebel trench, they would plant twenty-two hundred pounds of gunpowder, tamped in with sandbags, ready to explode whenever Grant ordered a final attack.[26]

This attack would come, according to headquarters planning, on July 6. Johnston, meanwhile, had plans of his own. He had thirty-two thousand men by now, and as June ended he began to move toward the Federal lines, maneuvering toward the south in the hope of flanking the formidable fieldworks which ran cross-country from the Big Black to the Yazoo. He proposed to make an attack on July 7. He did not think this would drive the Federals away, but it might create enough of a diversion so that Pemberton could cut his way out of Vicksburg and save most of his army.

Pemberton was trying to find out whether such a thing was physically possible, and he circularized his generals to ask if their men could stand a fight and a long hard march. The replies he got were not encouraging. Duty had been hard, rations had been poor, there had been much sickness and men had had to remain in the trenches when they should have been on the sicklist; they could probably hold the lines a while longer, but a field campaign was just about out of the question. The Federal rifled artillery spoke with power; only the most massive earthworks offered any protection — rifled shell could drive through parapets sixteen feet thick — and the periodic Federal cannonades brought the Confederate Army nearer and nearer to exhaustion. Water was so scarce that sentinels were posted around wells, so that "none might be wasted for purposes of cleanliness." Brigadier General Louis Hebert probably spoke for most of Pemberton's subordinates when, in his final report, he summed up the things that had ground his men down until they were incapable of field service:

"Forty-eight days and nights passed in the trenches, exposed to the burning sun during the day, the chilly air of night; subject to a murderous storm of balls, shells and war missiles of all kinds; cramped up in pits and holes not large enough to allow them to extend their limbs; laboring day and night; fed on reduced rations of the poorest kinds of food, yet always cheerful . . ." [27]

In plain terms, the men had had it. They could not possibly break out; they could not even stay where they were very much longer; and the next step was up to the Lieutenant General commanding.

At ten o'clock on the morning of July 3, white flags blossomed out along a portion of the Confederate works. As the firing died down, two horsemen rode forward toward the Union lines — the General Bowen who had fought so hard and so well at Port Gibson, and a colonel on Pemberton's staff. They had a letter from General Pemberton to General Grant, proposing an armistice and the appointment of commissioners to determine the formula under which Vicksburg should be surrendered. [28]

CHAPTER TWENTY-THREE

Sling the Knapsack for New Fields

G ENERAL PEMBERTON felt that he was in a position to bargain. He warned that he could hold his position for a long time, and he said that his proposal sought to avert "the further effusion of blood," which must "be shed to a frightful extent" if the siege continued. General Bowen handed the note to salty General A. J. Smith, and said that he himself would like to talk to General Grant, whom he had known in Missouri before the war. Grant would not see him. He liked Bowen and respected him, but he would be friendly after the surrender, not before. He sent word that he would be glad to talk to Pemberton that afternoon, and he wrote a note for Bowen to take to the Confederate commander. The note was pithy:

> . . . the useless effusion of blood you propose stopping by this course can be ended at any time you may choose, by the unconditional surrender of the city and garrison. Men who have shown so much endurance and courage as those now in Vicksburg will always challenge the respect of an adversary, and I can assure you will be treated with all the respect due to prisoners of war. I do not favor the proposition of appointing commissioners to arrange the terms of capitulation, because I have no other terms other than those indicated above.

Bowen took the message back inside the Confederate lines, while the soldiers lounged in the trenches and an unaccustomed quiet settled down along the scarred range of sun-baked hills. At three that afternoon Pemberton, Bowen and a staff officer came out, and Grant and a handful of his own officers rode forward to meet them. Dismounting, Grant and Pemberton walked aside, near a stunted oak tree, and had a stiff, unsatisfactory conference. Pemberton asked what terms Grant would give if the Confederate Army surrendered, and Grant replied that his letter said everything he had to say.

Pemberton was irritable: a man under great pressure, to whom a touch of temper might be forgiven. He was a Northerner, trusted by Jefferson Davis, distrusted by many Confederate soldiers and civilians. He knew that he would be blamed, bitterly, for giving up his army and his citadel, and that blame would also go to Davis who had promoted and supported him; and he clung to a notion that his opponent would grant lenient terms in order to win his victory on July 4, Independence Day. Now he was being offered nothing more than had been offered to Buckner at Fort Donelson. Dana, watching from a place not far off, said that Pemberton seemed excited and impatient, and Grant recalled that Pemberton said, "rather snappishly," that if Grant had no other terms the conference might as well end then and there. Grant thought so too; Pemberton turned away, and it appeared for a moment that there would be no deal. But either Bowen or Grant himself kept the conference alive by suggesting that the subordinate officers discuss terms for a while. They did so, while Pemberton and Grant had a few more fruitless words together; and at last it was agreed that at ten that night Grant would send another letter through the lines, giving his final terms.[1]

So the conference ended. The cease-fire arrangement continued, and as dusk came Grant called a meeting of all corps and division commanders who were in the immediate vicinity — the nearest thing to a regular council of war, he said, that he ever had. Northern and Southern soldiers wandered out between the lines by hundreds for a chat. One Federal private wrote that "several brothers met, and any quantity of cousins. It was a strange scene."[2] Meanwhile, Grant and his generals considered what ought to be done.

There was a good deal to discuss. Every man present knew, as the leading Confederates also knew, that Vicksburg was doomed. If it did not give up now it would almost certainly be taken by storm once the July 6 assault took place, and in any case there simply was not enough food in the city to enable the defense to be prolonged indefinitely. But Pemberton was flatly refusing to accept the unconditional surrender proposition. (It developed later that his intelligence service had been intercepting and decoding messages

wigwagged back and forth between Grant and Porter, and knew
that to ship thirty thousand prisoners up the river to Northern prison camps would put an excessive strain on the available river transportation.) The question, then, was whether it would be better to
offer no terms and pay in time and bloodshed for a delayed victory,
or to recede from the famous formula and give the beaten General
something he would immediately accept.

It came down, at last, to a question of whether Grant should
agree to parole for Pemberton's army. Paroled soldiers were in a
class apart. They belonged to the Army, they were supposed to
stay in camp, subject to full military discipline, but they could not
be used; they were uniformed ghosts, idling their lives away until
the intricate machinery of exchange permitted them to be put back
in the ranks of the fighting men. In an era wherein warring govern-
ments could still find a narrow area of mutual trust and confidence,
they were men placed on the shelf; out of the war, but still liable to
be drawn back into it whenever the infinite mathematics of two
warring high commands put them where the chances of war would
bear on them again without restriction.

In theory, Confederate soldiers paroled at Vicksburg were just as
much prisoners of war as Confederates who had been shipped
North to the squalid camps in Illinois and Ohio. But nobody trusted
his foes beyond endurance, in this war. To put thirty thousand soldiers on parole was to take a certain chance. It was to gamble that
no one on the other side would cut any corners or pull any fast
ones; it was to suppose that men fighting for self-preservation
would honor a pledge written bloodlessly on flimsy paper, keeping
a whole army out of the fight until such time as some other army,
similarly held inactive, could be permitted to go back into action.
The whole arrangement rested on the assumption, still valid but
getting paler day by day, that men who were at each other's
throats would continue to abide by the rules.

A gamble: but examined very closely, a gamble that should win.
Paroled soldiers were an immense problem to their own authorities. Civil War armies were badly disciplined and loosely indoc-
trinated. Paroled men were very hard to handle, because the soldiers assumed that when they had been captured and paroled they
were out of the war. The officer in charge of Northern parolees

had written, less than three months before the surrender at Vicksburg, that "there are no troops more difficult to control, officers and men, than those on parole," and had complained that the difficulty of the problem increased in direct ratio to the number on parole. Lew Wallace, who was presiding over camps full of such people back in Indiana, remarked that men on parole "become lousy, ragged, despairing and totally demoralized," and a citizen of Columbus, Ohio, observing the habits of paroled Unionists in that Northern capital, had told Secretary Stanton that "unless the paroling system is abandoned we will be beaten by the number of paroled prisoners we shall have." Another Federal officer who had to deal with this problem had remarked that paroled men felt themselves out from under every sort of discipline, and said that "a spirit of insubordination, bordering on mutiny" was their chief characteristic.[3] All things considered, dropping a large lump of paroled soldiers in the heart of the Confederacy might do the Confederates more harm than good.

Long afterward, Grant wrote that he himself had favored paroling Pemberton's soldiers but that most of his officers had opposed him. This, apparently, was rationalization after the fact. At the time he seems to have hoped that he could force Pemberton to make an unconditional surrender, in which case the Vicksburg garrison would have gone north as prisoners or been paroled on the spot at the Federal commander's option. As evidence, there is the message Grant sent to Porter some time late on this third of July:

I have given the rebels a few hours to consider the proposition of surrendering; all to be paroled here, the officers to take only side-arms. My own feelings are against this, but all my officers think the advantage gained by having our forces and transports for immediate purposes more than counterbalance the effect of sending them north.

Dana wrote that the paroling plan was proposed by McPherson and that all of Grant's officers but Steele favored it; Grant, he said, "reluctantly gave way" to the arguments, and finally sent off a letter to Pemberton proposing that the Confederates stack their arms outside of their lines, give their paroles, and then go off weaponless to such Southern internment camps as the Confederate authorities might suggest. In any event, this was the program that was at last adopted. Grant was canny enough to have Rawlins send a note to Ord and McPherson:

> Permit some discreet men on picket tonight to communicate to the enemy's pickets the fact that General Grant has offered, in case Pemberton surrenders, to parole all the officers and men and to permit them to go home from here.[4]

Grant, as a matter of fact, made a virtue out of necessity. Judging by Northern experience, the paroled men would be out of control. They would fade away, drifting off to their homes as fast as their legs would take them, and the Confederacy would be able to get very few of them back on the firing lines, exchange or no exchange. The Federals would be spared the labor and expense of sending their thirty thousand prisoners to Illinois and Ohio; the Vicksburg captives would be a problem for the Confederacy, not for the North, and in the long run their presence in the South would help to show that the Confederate government could not control its own people. . . . So Grant sent his revised terms off to Pemberton shortly before midnight:

> In conformity with the agreement of this afternoon I will submit the following proposition for the surrender of Vicksburg, public stores, etc. On your accepting the terms proposed I will march in one division as guard, and take possession at 8 A.M. tomorrow. As soon as rolls can be made out and paroles be signed by officers and men, you will be allowed to march out of our lines, the officers taking with them their side-arms and clothing; and the field, staff and cavalry officers one horse each. The rank and file will be allowed all their clothing, but no other property. If these conditions are accepted, any amount of rations you may deem necessary can be taken from the stores you now have [a pointed reference to Pemberton's boast that his supplies would enable him to hold out indefinitely] and also the necessary cooking utensils for preparing them. Thirty wagons also, counting two-horse or mule teams as one, will be allowed to transport such articles as cannot be carried along. The same conditions will be allowed to all sick and wounded

officers and soldiers as fast as they become able to travel. The paroles for these latter must be signed, however, whilst officers present are authorized to sign the roll of prisoners.[5]

Whether Grant imposed this plan on his own reluctant generals or was persuaded by them to accept it, he quickly concluded that it made a great deal of sense. Many of Pemberton's men came from the southwestern part of the Confederacy, and, said Grant, "I knew many of them were tired of the war and would get home just as soon as they could." Taken to a parole camp, most of them would simply desert; to have sent them North "would have used all the transportation we had for a month." There was also another consideration: "The men had behaved so well that I did not want to humiliate them. I believed that consideration for their feelings would make them less dangerous foes during the continuance of hostilities, and better citizens after the war was over." [6]

Pemberton's reply came back during the small hours. He accepted the terms, but proposed minor amendments: his army would march out, stack arms in front of the trenches and then go away, officers would retain their personal property, and all rights and property of citizens would be respected. These amendments Grant refused to accept. Each brigade, he said, might move out and stack arms in front of its own trenches, but thereafter all must go back in the city and stay there as prisoners until the long process of parole should be completed. Officers' rights in respect to their own property would be as originally stated — side arms, baggage, and, for mounted officers, one horse apiece; and although Grant would protect citizens against "undue annoyance or loss," he would make no stipulation regarding treatment of their private property — which, among other items, would include large numbers of slaves. Pemberton could have until nine o'clock in the morning to accept these terms. If he did not accept, the Federal Army would start to fight again.

And so at last it was arranged. On the morning of July 4, white flags fluttered over the Confederate works. The cease-fire became permanent, and John Logan was ordered to march his division into the city, post guards to keep unauthorized persons from entering or leaving, and take charge of captured people and property.

Meanwhile, Sherman was to move at once to drive Johnston off and relieve the captured town of any threat from the east.

Grant had had Sherman's move in mind from the moment the surrender negotiations began. On July 3 he notified Sherman that surrender was imminent, and told him to strike the moment it became a fact: "I want Johnston broken up as effectually as possible, and roads destroyed. I cannot say where you will find the most effective place to strike; I would say move so as to strike Canton and Jackson, whichever might seem most desirable." A little later he amplified this: "When we go in I want you to drive Johnston from the Mississippi Central railroad; destroy bridges as far as Grenada with your cavalry, and do the enemy all the harm possible. You can make your own arrangements and have all the troops of my command except one corps — McPherson's, say. I must have some troops to send to Banks, to use against Port Hudson." On July 4 a telegram went to Sherman as soon as Pemberton's acceptance of terms reached Grant's headquarters. Sherman replied in a characteristic note that was pure rhapsody:

> I can hardly contain myself. Surely I will not punish any soldier for being "unco happy" this most glorious anniversary of the birth of a nation whose sire and father was a Washington. Did I not know the honesty, modesty and purity of your nature, I would be tempted to follow the example of my standard enemies of the press in indulging in wanton flattery; but as a man and soldier and ardent friend of yours, I warn you against the incense of flattery that will fill our land from one extreme to the other. Be natural and yourself, and this glittering flattery will be as the passing breeze of the sea on a warm summer day. To me the delicacy with which you have treated a brave but deluded enemy is more eloquent than the most gorgeous oratory of an Everett.
>
> This is a day of jubilee, a day of rejoicing to the faithful, and I would like to hear the shout of my old and patient troops; but I must be a Gradgrind — I must have facts, knocks and must go on. Already my orders are out to give one big huzza and sling the knapsack for new fields. . . . I did want rest, but I ask nothing until the Mississippi is ours, and Sunday and July 4 are nothing to Americans until the river of our greatness is free as God made it.[7]

In every army there is always somebody who does not get the word. So it was here; a blameless engineer officer and a sweating work detail toiled vigorously all through the night of July 3, completing the 175-foot tunnel that had been dug under a Confederate salient in preparation for the big assault of July 6. On the morning of July 4 this officer was busy, far underground, getting a ton of powder tamped down in the magazine — until, at last, somebody remembered him, and a headquarters courier reached him with verbal orders to stop everything: the Rebels had surrendered, the shooting had stopped, this mine would never be used.[8]

Grant and his staff rode into the captured city shortly after the final terms had been accepted. They met Pemberton in a house on the Jackson road, and — according to Colonel Wilson — their reception was glacial. No one offered Grant a seat, and when he remarked that he would like a drink of water someone ungraciously remarked that he could go where the water was and help himself. Wilson angrily recorded that the behavior of Pemberton and his officers "was unhandsome and disagreeable in the extreme," but he noted that three young West Pointers on Pemberton's staff did their best to be courteous, "in recognition of which their haversacks and canteens were well filled with provisions and whisky when they bade us goodby." If all of this bothered Grant he gave no sign of it; he rode on, presently, and went down to the river to see Admiral Porter, from whom he had just received a reassuring note:

> I congratulate you on getting Vicksburg on any honorable terms. You would find it a troublesome task to transport so many men, and I think you will be left so free to act it will counterbalance any little concession you may seem to make to the garrison.[9]

The "little concession" that had been made looked larger to some of the men on the scene than it looked to men at a distance. Colonel Wilson, indeed, complained that Grant had in effect given Pemberton all Pemberton asked for, and considered that the General had made a serious mistake, and Halleck chided Grant mildly for letting the captured army go home on parole; but the nation as a whole, then and thereafter, recognized the achievement for what it was — a sweeping victory that fatally limited the Confederacy and pointed unmistakably toward final triumph, a victory which was the enduring capstone to one of the most daring and brilliant campaigns of the entire war. The Confederacy had lost a citadel which had to be held; losing it, it had lost the Mississippi River, and all the country to the west. (Port Hudson, hopelessly cut off, surrendered to Banks as soon as authentic news of the fall of Vicksburg came down; Grant sent Banks a division, as soon as he could get the men on steamboats, but the reinforcements were not needed.) Even more important, the Confederacy had lost an irreplaceable army. All in all, Grant had taken more than 40,000 Southern soldiers out of circulation. Nearly 31,000 became prisoners when Vicksburg fell, 6000 had been captured in the campaign before the siege began, and an equal number had been battle casualties. (Five or six thousand more would be lost in the surrender of Port Hudson.) Neither then nor later could the hard-pressed Southland afford a loss of that magnitude. Much war material had also been lost: 172 cannon and 60,000 rifles came into Grant's possession when his troops entered Vicksburg, and many of the rifles were better than the ones Grant's own men were carrying — so much so that he re-equipped many regiments with captured arms.

All of this Grant had won at moderate cost. From the moment he crossed the river to the day Pemberton surrendered, he had lost fewer than 10,000 men. (The legend of Grant as the heedless, conscienceless butcher finds nothing to feed on in the story of the Vicksburg campaign.) He had taken long chances — a newspaper correspondent had correctly reported: "A single mistake or disaster might have overwhelmed his army . . . but the mistake was not made, the disaster did not come." Pemberton had been confused from beginning to end; with inferior numbers, Grant had driven him into Vicksburg and fended off the relieving army until reinforcements put him beyond danger. Johnston's cry that Grant's Western troops were twice as good as the Easterners he fought in Virginia was, in the end, a simple testimonial to the unerring skill with which Grant had handled them.

Grant's first act, after he reached Porter, was to send a message to Halleck:

> The enemy surrendered this morning. The only terms allowed is their parole as prisoners of war. This I regard as a great advantage to us at this moment. It saves, probably, several days in the capture, and leaves troops and transports ready for immediate service. Sherman, with a large force, moves immediately on Johnston, to drive him from the state. I will send troops to the relief of Banks, and return the Ninth Army Corps to Burnside.[10]

There were annoying details in connection with the business of parole. Pemberton wanted the victors to compel all prisoners to sign paroles; some of the men, vowing they would fight no more, hoped to be sent North, out of their own Army's reach forever. Pemberton also wanted Grant to let him have enough weapons to arm a battalion to act as guards, so that men who gave their paroles could be kept from deserting. Grant turned down both requests; if paroles meant trouble for the Southern authorities he had no intention of doing anything to ease the situation.

There was also the matter of slaves. The terms of surrender did not allow Confederate officers to take their body servants with them when they left, but one of Pemberton's staff came to Grant saying that in most cases the body servants actually wanted to go; they had been brought up in the family, and it would be cruel to enforce a separation. Might not those loyal, faithful servitors who could not bear to be parted from Old Massa go along with the officers whom they worshiped? Grant laid down the rule in a note to McPherson:

> I want the Negroes to understand that they are free men. If they are then anxious to go with their masters I do not see the necessity of preventing it. Some going might benefit our cause by telling that the Yankees set them all free. It is not necessary that you should give yourself any trouble about Negroes being enticed away from officers. Everyone that loses a Negro will insist that he has been enticed off, because otherwise his Negro would not leave.

    . . . because otherwise there was something very wrong indeed with the whole legend which the white man had built up about the benefits, to those who were owned, of the institution of slavery; and while McPherson did his best to be guided by this order, he could hear the death rattle of the ancient institution which both he and Grant were trying to destroy. The first warning came from General John Logan, the stout Illinois Democrat who had never had any abolitionist tradition in his blood and who, when war started, was thought to be a man who was as likely to go with the South as with the North. Two days after Vicksburg had surrendered, Logan wrote to Rawlins to voice a hard protest "against the manner in which Confederate officers are permitted to intimidate their servants." The Negro who was asked if he wanted to go with his master, said Logan, was asked in the presence of the man who had always owned him; knowing that the men in blue uniforms would probably take the master's word over his own. This struck Logan as wrong, and he complained that "the manner in which this is done is conniving at furnishing Negroes to every officer who is a prisoner in Vicksburg." Grant told McPherson to "give instruction that no passes are to be given to Negroes to accompany their masters in leaving the city," and on July 7 McPherson sent a note to Pemberton:

I am constrained, in consequence of the abuse of the privilege which was granted to officers to take out one private servant (colored) each, to withdraw it altogether, except in cases of families and sick and disabled officers. The abuses which I speak of are: 1. Officers coming here with their servants and intimidating them, instead of sending them by themselves to be questioned. 2. Citizens have been seen and heard in the streets urging Negroes who were evidently not servants to go with the officers. 3. Negroes have also been brought here who have been at work on the fortifications.[11]

Much died when Vicksburg died; meanwhile, Sherman was dogging the heels of General Joseph E. Johnston. Johnston learned on July 5 that Vicksburg had been lost, and he retreated at once to Jackson, where he dug in and waited to see what Sherman would do. Sherman followed, flung a semicircle of men and guns around the city, had everybody open fire, and began pounding.

Johnston fended him off, and found time to write to Richmond protesting that the paroling of Pemberton's men had given the Confederacy a very tough problem: "What shall be done with the men? They cannot remain in this Department without great injury to us from deficiency of supplying them. Shall they go to their homes until discharged, or be distributed in regiments in their respective states? Can they be exchanged immediately for prisoners taken in the recent great Confederate victory?" (At that moment it was believed in the Deep South that Lee had won a smashing triumph at Gettysburg.)

Pemberton was equally unhappy. Two weeks after the surrender, he wrote to President Davis to say that his paroled men insisted on going home and that he had no way to stop them, because they just wanted to see their families. Most of the men from Mississippi and the trans-Mississippi, he said, had already left, and the men from Georgia, Alabama and Tennessee would go as soon as they were near their homes. Of the 31,600 men who had been paroled, he had about 1600 — men from Missouri — who could be counted on for immediate service. Nothing but a universal grant of furloughs, he said, would give any prospect of getting the rest of the men back.

Grant's own intelligence service was saying the same thing, and Grant assured Halleck that Pemberton's army had effectively been dismissed from service:

At last accounts, Pemberton had but 4,000 left with him, and they were no doubt men whose homes are in the states east of here, and are only waiting to get near them to desert, too. The country is full of these paroled prisoners, all of them swearing that they will not take up arms again if they are exchanged. Thousands have crossed the Mississippi river and gone west; many buy passages north, and quite a number expressed a strong anxiety to enlist in our service. This of course I would not permit.[12]

In Mississippi the Confederacy was helpless. By the middle of July Johnston evacuated Jackson and retreated to the East. Sherman reflected on Grant's orders that he "damage the enemy as much as possible," and undertook to carry them out: a task for which he was admirably fitted. Railroad tracks, bridges, cars, roundhouses and every installation which might conceivably be of use to a struggling Confederacy were destroyed with grim effectiveness. Sherman reported to Grant that "Jackson cannot again become a place for the assemblage of men and material with which to threaten the Mississippi river," private soldiers looked at the wreckage and gave Jackson the descriptive name of "Chimneyville," and on July 23 Sherman pulled his army back and prepared to give all hands a rest.[13] He left a desert behind him. Vicksburg was secure.

Meanwhile, the Federals had gone flocking into Vicksburg. It was an odd sort of occupation. There was no cheering, and nobody turned any handsprings. Grant noted that "the men of the two armies fraternized as if they had been fighting for the same cause," and an officer who guided a wagon train of rations into the city wrote that the sight of the first Confederate brigade he passed, "every man of which looked so gaunt and hungry," moved him so deeply that he simply stopped and broke open his barrels and boxes of hardtack, sugar and coffee and dealt out a liberal allowance to everybody within sight. He was rewarded, he said, by "the heartfelt thanks and cheers" of the Confederates, and that night when his own men complained that their rations were deficient "I swore by all the saints in the calendar that the wagons had broken down and the Johnnie Rebs had stolen all of the grub." One Confederate staff officer who rode a white pony, on which he had daily made the circuit of the Confederate lines, was brightly accosted by a Unionist, who sang out: "See here, Mister — you man on the little white horse. Danged if you ain't the hardest feller to hit I ever saw; I've shot at you more'n a hundred times!" He remembered, too, that the only cheer he heard on the day of Federal occupation was a cheer which one Federal outfit raised for "the gallant defenders of Vicksburg." A reporter for Greeley's *New York Tribune* saw soldiers from each army standing together talking good-humoredly about the ins and outs of the siege, and wrote: "There is no jeering or tormenting from our men. . . . We have even refrained from cheering, and nothing — absolutely nothing — has been done to add humiliation to the cup of sorrows which the Rebels have been compelled to drink." Grant said that he believed that "there was a feeling of sadness among the Union soldiers at seeing the dejection of their late antagonists." [14]

And here, shining out from under the dissolving smoke of battle, was the mysterious, haunting leitmotiv of the Civil War.

Strangest of all the strange sides of this war was the inexplicable feeling of understanding and half-suppressed sympathy that grew up between the rival armies. In battle, these men fought without reservations. Fury descended on them, and they gave way to fire-born anger in the desperate attempt to kill and maim. Yet there was a queer, inexpressible bond between them. They were brothers, or cousins, or at the very least men of the same blood and tradition, and in the long run they probably understood their enemies better than they understood the patriots back home who were waving flags and pushing them forward. War was the one real enemy — war, and much of the time officers; and the desperate killing that took place was accomplished by men who had a working but unvoiced knowledge of the real inwardness of the brotherhood of man.

Of all men, Grant himself had a deep knowledge of this. He could not put it into words, except that he could spare 29,491 men a trip to Northern prison camps with the remark that he did not want to humiliate them and that in time to come they would be better fellow citizens if they were decently treated; and the same General who could urge Sherman to "do the enemy all the harm possible" could also see the enemy as men with whom he and his own folk would some day be good friends. This was not a conscious, carefully-worked-out attitude; it was something born in him, something that had blossomed in the Mexican War, when he had developed a deep respect and liking for the brown-skinned men against whom he had had to fight. He had never jeered at the Mexicans as poor fighters; he always had thought that they did pretty well, considering what they had to fight for, and with, and under; and fighting them had somehow made him feel closer to them. It was the same here at Vicksburg. He shared with the soldiers he commanded a deep, overriding respect, something finally resembling affection, for the men who had been enemies — the logical corollary to which was the ingrained belief that something worth winning, keeping and dying for lay behind the fearful tumult of battle. Victory was something to be won, but final fellowship between victors and vanquished was something that would come afterward, justifying victory. Grant could be very military, on occasion, but he could never be warlike — in which points he was the precise opposite of his great lieutenant, Sherman.

Grant took up quarters in Vicksburg, in a comfortable house on the heights overlooking the river. He had his chief engineer lay out a new line of works which could be held by a garrison of five thousand men, he sent the Ninth Corps back to Burnside, and he shipped other troops up the river to help repel a Rebel thrust into Arkansas. Sending troops to Banks, he let his intense pride in his army find brief expression, telling Banks that the men going downstream were "as good troops as ever trod American soil: no better are found on any other." He tried to get rest and a breathing spell for the rest of the army, and he warned Halleck that the men were too exhausted for much immediate duty that involved extensive marching. He took time, too, to return to the thorny old subject of cotton-trading. Secretary of the Treasury Chase wanted to see the trade expanded, and Grant warned him against being in a hurry about it:

> The people in the Mississippi valley are now nearly subjugated. Keep trade out but for a few months, and I doubt not but that the work of subjugation will be so complete that trade can be opened freely with the states of Arkansas, Louisiana and Mississippi. . . . My position has given me an opportunity of seeing what could not be known by persons away from the scene of the war, and I venture, therefore, a great caution in opening trade with Rebels.[15]

Grant wanted the corrupting influence of the cotton trade held away for a time; and it seemed to him equally important to hold the whole valley area free from the presence of Confederate armies, so that the people could adjust themselves to the developing fact of reunion. To Halleck he sent a statement of his views:

> This state and Louisiana would be more easily governed now than Kentucky or Missouri if armed Rebels from other states

could be kept out. In fact the people are ready to accept anything. The troops from these states too will desert and return
as soon as they find that they cannot be hunted down. I am informed that movements are being made through many parts of
Mississippi to unite the people in an effort to bring this state
into the Union. I receive letters and delegations on this subject
myself, and believe the people are sincere.[16]

Meanwhile, if it mattered to him — and beyond any question it
did matter, in some area of the spirit buried far down inside —
Grant had become famous. A Grant legend was developing, and
the bits and pieces of it were no longer pinned to the ancient tale
of too much whisky; men were telling, instead, little stories illus-
trating his capacity for handling men, his ability to remain relaxed
and unperturbed under pressure, his general goodness and humanity — very different, all of this, from the network of tales that made
the rounds after Shiloh. One officer recorded that Grant had a great
knack for getting his subordinates to work harmoniously together;
when rows and bitterness developed, Grant could somehow get
things adjusted without fuss, so that there was never (now that Mc-
Clernand was gone, at any rate) any backbiting or hard rivalry
around the headquarters tents. "None of his officers," said this man,
"ever quarreled or ever showed any heat of discussion in his presence. . . . In the presence of Grant or in the face of an order issued by him all of them were submissive, unresentful and quiet.
They never attempted to explain this."

A staff officer told a story which would be told and retold. Grant
was walking the lines one day and saw a mule driver beating his
team in profane fury; he ordered the man to stop, and since the
General was wearing nothing much in the way of uniform the man
failed to recognize him and turned to swear at him. Grant ordered
the staff man to arrest the driver and punish him. The staff man
went to Grant's tent a bit later and reported that he had the of-
fender strung up by the thumbs. He added that the man was frightened and contrite, because he had just learned that it was the Commanding General whom he had been tangling with. Grant had the
man released and brought before him, and gave him a stiff reprimand; the man apologized and explained that he had never dreamed
he was swearing at a major general. Grant sent him away, explain-

ing that punishment and reprimand had been visited on him not because he had cursed a general officer but simply because he had abused a mule. "I could defend myself," Grant told the driver. "The mule could not." [17]

These and other tales made the rounds, as such things always do when a man suddenly attains great prominence. Meanwhile, more solid evidences of recognition were coming in. From Halleck came word that Grant had been appointed a major general in the Regular Army, and that the appointment had quickly been confirmed by the Senate. It was less than ten years since he had resigned as a captain of infantry, a man under a cloud, his career wrecked; now the Army that had not wanted him was giving him the highest gift in its capacity — permanent tenure, security for old age, the promise that a starred flag would fly over his grave when things came to an end. Grant never said much about this, but an indication of what it meant to him can be found in a letter he wrote a few months later to his old boyhood friend Daniel Ammen, now an officer in the Navy. Always, until now, when he wrote to intimates about postwar plans, Grant had said that he hoped for nothing more than the chance to go back to Galena and live out his days in decent, peaceful obscurity. To Ammen he sounded a new note, writing:

. . . My only desire will be, as it has been, to whip out rebellion in the shortest way possible, and to retain as high a position in the army afterward as the administration then in power may think me suitable for.[18]

He had found himself, finally. He had not chosen a military career, and most of the time he had not liked it — this unobtrusive man with the sensitive eyes and the firm mouth. Now he was at home in it, it was the career he belonged in, and he proposed to stay in it. This was what he could do; this was what, from now on, he would want to do.

Far down inside, perhaps, it was what he had always wanted. No one knew this general as well as his wife Julia, and she saw him as the born fighter. Many years later she summed up his feeling about the army by writing: "He was happy in the fight and the din of battle, but restless in the barracks. . . . He could no more resist the sound of a fife or a drum or a chance to fire a gun than a woman can resist bonnets." [19]

Some of Grant's fame was rubbing off on his associates. Halleck wrote to say that General George Gordon Meade, new commander of the Army of the Potomac, had just been given a Regular Army brigadier's commission in recognition of the victory at Gettysburg. There were three or four other vacancies in brigadier's ranks, and Halleck suggested that if Grant felt like recommending Sherman and McPherson they would promptly be promoted: "The feeling is very strong here in favor of your generals." Grant immediately sent in the recommendations, and was pleased to see the promotions made. He felt that Sherman and McPherson were equipped for almost any command, and when he wrote in praise of them he touched on one point that was always important to him: "The army does not afford an officer superior to either, in my estimation. With such men commanding corps or armies, there will never be any jealousies or lack of hearty co-operation." [20]

Best of all, probably, was the letter that presently came to Grant from Abraham Lincoln.

Lincoln and Grant had never set eyes on one another, but they had been moving together, slowly but surely, from the moment when Grant marched east from Fort Henry with the remark that he would just step over and capture Fort Donelson. Of all the officers in the Army, Grant was the one who best fitted in with what Lincoln was trying to do. He had sent the President no letters of complaint or protest, he had not tried to substitute policies of his own for policies laid down in Washington, and from first to last he had shown a quality of complete dependability Lincoln saw in few other commanders. Now Lincoln sent him this letter:

My dear General:

I do not remember that you and I ever met personally. I write this now as a grateful acknowledgment for the almost inestimable service you have done the country. I wish to say a word further. When you first reached the vicinity of Vicksburg, I thought you should do, what you finally did — march the troops across the neck, run the batteries with the transports, and thus go below; and I never had any faith, except a general hope that you knew better than I, that the Yazoo Pass expedition, and the like, could succeed. When you got below, and took Port Gibson, Grand Gulf and vicinity, I thought you should go down the river and join Gen. Banks; and when you turned Northward East of the Big Black, I feared it was a mistake. I now wish to make the personal acknowledgment that you were right, and I was wrong.

Yours very truly,

A. LINCOLN[21]

The summer was moving on. In the East, Lee had taken a beaten army back into Virginia, and he and Meade were sparring cautiously. In Tennessee, Rosecrans was at last on the move, coming down to maneuver Bragg out of Tennessee. West of the great river were isolated Confederate armies that would never quite be able to make their strength felt on any major strategic issue. And in the Deep South itself there was wreckage and a sense of disaster, with no solid nucleus of force to oppose any advance the Federals might choose to make. It was no time for Grant's army to remain idle in the camps around Vicksburg. An invisible door had swung open; somewhere, far ahead, no matter how thick the haze of gun smoke, victory was in sight.

Grant was ready, at last. The time of testing was over, and he had reached his full stature. He had developed — through mistakes, through trial and error, through steady endurance, through difficult lessons painfully learned, through the unbroken development of his own capacities — into the man who could finally lead the way through that open door. Better than any other Northern soldier, better than any other man save Lincoln himself, he understood the necessity for bringing the infinite power of the growing nation to bear on the desperate weakness of the brave, romantic and tragically archaic little nation that opposed it; understood, too, that although Rebellion must be crushed with the utmost rigor, the Rebels themselves were men who would again be friends and fellow citizens. Now it was time to go on. Sherman had said it: *Sling the knapsack for new fields.*

Notes

CHAPTER ONE

"Tomorrow I Move South"

1. James L. Crane, "Grant as a Colonel," in *McClure's Magazine*, Vol. VII, pp. 40–45; Dr. John A. Meskiwen in the *St. Louis Globe-Democrat* of August 6, 1885; Aaron Elliott in the *Missouri Republican* of August 22, 1885; ex-Governor Richard Yates of Illinois in the *Army and Navy Journal* for August 11, 1866.
2. Aaron Elliott, as Note 1; Regimental Order Book of the 21st Illinois, in the National Archives, entry for June 16, 1861; J. L. Ringwalt, *Anecdotes of Gen. Ulysses S. Grant*, pp. 27–29; interview with Major J. W. Wham, in the *New York Tribune* of September 27, 1885.
3. Regimental Order Book, Orders Nos. 1, 4, 5 and 6.
4. Regimental Order Book, Order No. 7, dated June 18, 1861.
5. *Personal Memoirs of U. S. Grant*, Vol. 1, p. 243. (Cited hereafter as Grant's Memoirs.)
6. Regimental Order Book, Order No. 8, dated June 19; James H. Wilson, *Under the Old Flag*, Vol. I, p. 206. (Hereafter cited as *Under the Old Flag*.)
7. Major Wham, as cited in Note No. 2.
8. Regimental Order Book, Order No. 14, June 21.
9. Hamlin Garland, *Ulysses S. Grant: His Life and Character*, p. 175. (Cited hereafter as Garland.)
10. Regimental Order Book, Order No. 9; also entry dated June 26.
11. *Galena Weekly Northwestern Gazette* for July 8, 1861; ex-Governor Yates, as Note 1, p. 807; Grant's Memoirs, Vol. I, pp. 246–247; Aaron Elliott, as Note 1.
12. Colonel John W. Emerson, "Grant's Life in the West," in the *Midland Monthly* for January, 1898, p. 50. (Cited hereafter as Emerson.)
13. Regimental Order Book, entry for July 6, 1861; William Conant Church, *Ulysses S. Grant and the Period of National Preservation and Reconstruction*, p. 76. (Cited hereafter as Church.)
14. Emerson, pp. 51–52.
15. Regimental Order Book, Orders No. 23 and 24, both dated July 9.
16. Grant's Memoirs, Vol. I, pp. 247–248; Jesse Grant Cramer, *Letters of Ulysses S. Grant*, p. 42 (cited hereafter as Cramer); Memoir written by Julia Dent Grant.
17. Grant's Memoirs, Vol. I, pp. 248–250.

18. Regimental Order Book, list of deserters, also Order No. 29; Emerson, p. 51.
19. Cramer, pp. 43–45.
20. Crane, *Grant as a Colonel*, p. 42.
21. Crane, as Note 20, p. 44; Emerson, p. 52.
22. Letter of U. S. Grant to Colonel Dent, printed in *St. Louis Globe Democrat* of December 3, 1916; letter to Jesse Grant, in Cramer, p. 36.
23. Washington correspondence of the *Cincinnati Commercial* for November 16, 1868; Henry Coppee, *Life and Services of General U. S. Grant*, p. 29; Louis A. Coolidge, *Ulysses S. Grant*, p. 59.
24. Crane, p. 43; letter of U. S. Grant to Jesse Grant, dated August 3, 1861, in the U. S. Grant Papers at the Missouri Historical Society.
25. Letter of U. S. Grant to Julia Dent Grant, dated August 15, 1861, in the Missouri Historical Society collection; Church, p. 84.
26. Emerson, p. 52; Grant's Memoirs, Vol. I, p. 253.
27. Grant to Frémont, August 9, 1862, in the Official Records, Vol. III, p. 432 (these volumes will be cited hereafter as O. R.); Grant's Memoirs, Vol. I, pp. 256–257.
28. Emerson, in the *Midland Monthly* for February, 1898; S. W. Thompson, "Recollections with the 3rd Iowa Regiment."
29. Grant's letter to Julia, cited in Note 25; Grant to Frémont, August 10, O. R., Vol. III, pp. 432–433; Grant to J. C. Kelton, August 12, p. 437.
30. Grant to Major W. E. McMackin, August 12, O. R., Vol. III, pp. 438–439; Grant to Kelton, August 13, pp. 440–441; Grant to commanding officer of 6th Missouri, August 16, p. 445.
31. Frémont to Lincoln, O. R., Vol. III, p. 441; to Prentiss, p. 443; Grant's August 15 letter to Julia Grant, previously cited.

CHAPTER TWO

Assignment in Missouri

1. Grant to Frémont, O. R., Vol. III, p. 444.
2. Roy Basler, *The Collected Works of Abraham Lincoln*, Vol. IV, pp. 457–458 (cited hereafter as Basler); Lincoln's "Memorandum of Military Policy Suggested by the Bull Run Defeat."
3. Colonel Emerson gives an extremely detailed account of this in the installment of "Grant's Life in the West" which appears in the February, 1898, issue of the *Midland Monthly*. For Grant's prewar acquaintance with him, see Lloyd Lewis, *Captain Sam Grant*, p. 365.
4. General John M. Thayer, "Grant at Pilot Knob," in *McClure's Magazine*, Vol. V, pp. 433–434. (Cited hereafter as Thayer.)
5. O. R., Vol. III, p. 443; Grant's Memoirs, Vol. I, pp. 257, 263.
6. Thayer, pp. 434–436.

7. Thayer goes into substantial detail on all of this, pp. 436–437, and quotes an alleged postwar statement by Montgomery Blair in substantiation.

8. Emerson says that Frank Blair told him, after the war, that when Grant proceeded with the campaign that led him through Fort Donelson and Shiloh down toward Vicksburg, Montgomery Blair often said: "That fellow Grant is sticking to his text; that's exactly according to his plan I heard read last summer." Emerson quotes a letter which he says he received from Congressman Washburne in February, 1881, saying: "Referring to our conversation at Jefferson City recently on the subject of General Grant's plan of campaign in August, 1861, I can say that within a few days — not more than a week — after he was appointed Brig. Gen. I received from him a plan of campaign to be submitted to the President. I did so at once, with words of commendation, for it impressed me greatly as the conception of a daring soldier of comprehensive views. Without stating particulars, the plan proposed breaking the Confederate lines on the rivers and advancing through Ky. and Tenn." See Emerson's account in the March, 1898, issue of the *Midland Monthly*. Grant's letter to Washburne, dated March 22, 1862, is in the E. B. Washburne Papers, in the Library of Congress. (These are cited hereafter as Washburne Papers.)

9. Grant's Memoirs, Vol. I, pp. 258–260.

10. For an engaging description of the Confederate levies under Price, see Colonel Thomas L. Snead, "The First Year of the War in Missouri," in *Battles and Leaders of the Civil War*, Vol. I, pp. 269–273. (This work is cited hereafter as *B. & L.*)

11. For a slightly more detailed account of Frémont's career at St. Louis, together with a citation of sources, see Bruce Catton, *This Hallowed Ground*, p. 58 ff.

12. Grant to Frémont, August 22, in O. R., Vol. III, p. 452.

13. Same, pp. 452–454; Grant's report of August 27, p. 463.

14. Grant to Jesse Grant, August 22, 1861, in the Grant Papers at the Missouri Historical Society.

15. Emerson, quoting Washburne's letter of Feb. 7, 1881; General John C. Frémont, "In Command in Missouri," *B. & L.*, Vol. I, p. 284; Grant's Memoirs, Vol. I, pp. 260–261.

16. General Justus McKinstry, in the *Missouri Republican* for July 24, 1885. In his manuscript memoirs Frémont wrote that he had hesitated between Grant and Pope for the new command; that most of the Regular Army men around headquarters favored Pope, having heard of Grant's "habits," but that he himself was very strongly impressed by Grant when McKinstry brought him in, and gave him the place. (Frémont's Ms. Memoirs, in the Bancroft Library of the University of California.)

17. Frémont to W. A. Croffet, in J. L. Ringwalt, *Anecdotes of General*

Grant, p. 34. Emerson, in the *Midland Monthly,* insists that Frémont gave the assignment to Grant because of orders from Washington.

18. O. R., Vol. III, pp. 141–143, 461, 463, 465.
19. Frémont to Grant, O. R., Vol. III, pp. 141–142.
20. Polk to Hardee and to Pillow, orders dated August 26; Pillow to Polk, August 28; in O. R., Vol. III, pp. 683, 684, 686. See also A. L. Conger, "The Rise of U. S. Grant," p. 38. (This work is cited hereafter as Conger.)
21. Polk to Governor Magoffin, September 1, in O. R., Vol. IV, p. 179; Polk's account of his order to Pillow, "in consequence of the armed position of the enemy, who had posted himself with cannon and entrenchments opposite Columbus," is p. 180. See also Frémont to Lorenzo Thomas, O. R., Vol. IV, p. 177.
22. Grant's Memoirs, Vol. I, pp 262–263; O R., Vol. III, pp. 145–146; Vol. IV, pp. 181, 190.
23. O. R., Vol. III, p. 693.

CHAPTER THREE

Time of Preparation

1. Frémont, in *B. & L.,* Vol. I, p. 281; Marion Morrison, "History of the 9th Regiment Illinois Volunteer Infantry"; "Personal Memoirs of John H. Brinton" (cited hereafter as Brinton), p. 68; Thomas W. Knox, in the *New York Herald* for December 28, 1863.
2. George W. Driggs, *Opening of the Mississippi, or Two Years' Campaigning in the Southwest,* p. 63 ff.
3. Grant to Jesse Grant, dated August 31, in Cramer, pp. 54–55; Grant to Washburne, September 3, 1861, in the Grant Papers at the Illinois State Historical Library.
4. Grant's Memoirs, Vol. I, p. 264.
5. A. T. Mahan, *The Gulf and Inland Waters,* pp. 12–13.
6. Brinton, p. 37.
7. Grant's Memoirs, Vol. I, pp. 264–265. Note that Frémont had a really good intelligence system. He maintained a map-compilation room in the basement of his headquarters house, and he used a scout named Charles D'Arnaud to penetrate Kentucky and Tennessee and bring back plans of roads, military installations and so on. In his manuscript memoirs, previously cited (Note 16 Chapter Two) Frémont says that he had D'Arnaud make a second visit to the Tennessee Cumberland area, because he intended to move south along those rivers and the Mississippi. Presumably it was D'Arnaud whom Grant saw in Cairo, but it would be interesting to know more about the encounter.
8. Grant's Memoirs, Vol. I, p. 266; Charles H. Wills, "Army Life of an

Illinois Soldier," p. 29; Grant to E. A. Paine, O. R., Vol. IV, p. 198; Vol. III, p. 149.

9. Grant to Speaker of Kentucky House of Representatives, September 5, O. R., Vol. III, p. 166.

10. Grant to Frémont, September 6, O. R., Vol. IV, p. 197; Frémont to Grant, September 6, O. R., Vol. III, p. 471; Grant's Memoirs, Vol. I, p. 267.

11. Augustus L. Chetlain, "Recollections of U. S. Grant," in Vol. I, *Military Essays and Recollections*, pp. 22–23; Lew Wallace, *An Autobiography*, p. 339; John H. Page, in Vol. V of *Glimpses of the Nation's Struggle*, p. 8.

12. Letter of George B. McClellan to "My Dear General," not otherwise identified, dated January 24, 1885, in the C. F. Smith Papers; Special Orders No. 80 of the Adjutant General's Office (dated March 15, 1861) and No. 222 (dated August 19, 1861), also in the Smith Papers; Grant to Captain Chauncey McKeever, October 9, in O. R., Vol. III, p. 528.

13. Lieutenant Matthew H. Jamison, in *Recollections of Pioneer and Army Life;* Captain Ephraim A. Wilson, in *Memoirs of the War;* George H. Woodruff, in *Fifteen Years Ago; or, the Patriotism of Will County.*

14. Brinton, p. 37.

15. Brinton, pp. 40–44, 67; Manuscript "Reminiscences of Dr. John Cooper," owned by Harley Bronson Cooper of Lynbrook, N. Y.

16. Grant's reports and orders covering these matters are in O. R., Vol. III, pp. 486, 489, 505, 519, 537, 556.

17. O. R., Vol. III, pp. 490, 501, 511, 520, 529, 537.

18. Colonel R. M. Kelly, "Holding Kentucky for the Union," *B. & L.,* Vol. I, p. 373 ff; O. R., Vol. IV, pp. 404–406, 413. For Grant's prewar meeting with Buckner, see Lloyd Lewis, *Captain Sam Grant,* p. 338.

19. The interchange between Polk and the committee is in O. R., Vol. IV, pp. 185–186. Anderson's announcement of his resignation — made, he said, "with less reluctance for that purpose" — is p. 296. For a detailed examination of the problems confronting Johnston, see Stanley Horn, *The Army of Tennessee,* pp. 55–62.

20. Grant to Frémont, September 9 and 10, O. R., Vol. III, pp. 168–169; Grant to Colonel G. Waagner and Colonel Oglesby, September 11, p. 487; Grant to Frémont, September 12, p. 489.

21. Frémont to Grant, September 12, O. R., Vol. III, p. 489. His letter to Lincoln is in *B. & L.,* Vol. I, p. 285.

22. Colonel Mulligan's account of the Lexington disaster is in *B. & L.,* Vol. I, pp. 307–313. Winfield Scott's admonitory message to Frémont, dated September 3, is in O. R., Vol. III, p. 185. For the order detaching two of Grant's regiments, see p. 494.

23. Grant's Memoirs, Vol. I, p. 269; O. R., Vol. III, pp. 199, 556.

24. Frémont's September 15 report to the War Department is in O. R., Vol. III, p. 493. It shows 3057 at Ironton, 650 at Cape Girardeau, 3510 at Bird's Point and Norfolk, 4826 at Cairo, 3595 at Fort Holt and 900 at Mound City. In addition, C. F. Smith had 7021 at Paducah.

25. Frémont to Grant, September 26, O. R., Vol. III, p. 507; same, Grant to Smith, September 20, pp. 501–502; Grant to Oglesby, October 1, p. 511.

26. Grant's Memoirs, Vol. I, p. 269.

27. Brinton, pp. 53, 61–62; John Beatty, *Memoirs of a Volunteer*, p. 95; John K. Duke, *History of the 53rd Regiment Ohio Volunteer Infantry*, p. 5.

28. Unidentified newspaper clipping in the Joseph Kirkland Papers, Newberry Library, Chicago, quoting a speech before the George H. Thomas Post, Grand Army of the Republic, in Chicago on April 23, 1880. See also John Beatty, cited Note 27.

29. Photostatic copy of *The Camp Register*, published in the fall of 1861 by the 37th Illinois Infantry at Otterville, Mo.; in the Lloyd Lewis Papers.

30. Letter of U. S. Grant to Benson J. Lossing, printed in William W. Belknap's *History of the 15th Regiment of Iowa Veteran Volunteer Infantry*, p. 422; A. H. Markland, in the printed *Proceedings of the Society of the Army of the Tennessee* for 1885, p. 162.

31. Robert W. McClaughry, "The Boys of 1861 — and Their Boys," in Vol. III, *Military Essays and Recollections*, p. 404; P. O. Avery, *History of the 4th Illinois Cavalry*.

32. Major Hoyt Sherman, in a speech before the 1897 reunion of the Society of the Army of the Tennessee.

33. Captain John H. Page, "Recollections of 1861 as Seen Through a Boy's Eyes," in *Glimpses of the Nation's Struggle*, Vol. V, p. 10.

34. Interview with J. N. Tyner, printed in the *New York Tribune*, August 23, 1885.

35. Interview with W. S. Hillyer in the *Cincinnati Commercial*, January 27, 1869; Wilbur F. Crummer, *With Grant at Fort Donelson, Shiloh and Vicksburg*, p. 179; interview with J. A. J. Cresswell in the *New York Herald*, April 5, 1885; Samuel H. Beckwith in the *Utica Herald*, reprinted in the *New York Times* for July 25, 1885.

36. A. C. Chetlain to Washburne, October 16, 1861, in the Washburne Papers.

37. Benjamin to Bragg, December 27, 1861, in O. R., Vol. VI, p. 788.

CHAPTER FOUR

"You Looked Like Giants"

1. Article on John Rawlins in the *Chicago Times* for September 7, 1869.

2. James H. Wilson, *The Life of John A. Rawlins,* pp. 57–58; Lloyd Lewis, *Captain Sam Grant,* pp. 380–381, 399; John A. Rawlins interviewed in the *Hartford Post,* reprinted in the *Army and Navy Journal* for September 12, 1868.

3. Captain John M. Shaw, "The Life and Services of General John A. Rawlins," in *Glimpses of the Nation's Struggle,* Vol. III, p. 387; Grant to Washburne, letter dated September 3, 1861, in the Grant Papers, Illinois State Historical Library.

4. Wilson, as Note 2, p. 60.

5. *Cincinnati Commercial,* March 9, 1869, reprinting a *New York Tribune* interview with Colonel Chetlain; Rawlins interview in the *Hartford Post,* cited in Note 2.

6. O. R., Vol. III, p. 209.

7. Report of Colonel G. Waagner, dated September 2, O. R., Vol. III, p. 151.

8. O. R., Vol. III, pp. 267–268.

9. Rawlins, in a speech before the Society of the Army of Tennessee; from the report of the Society's Proceedings published in Cincinnati in 1866.

10. O. R., Vol. III, p. 268.

11. Same, pp. 269–270.

12. O. R., Vol. IV, pp. 513, 517, 522; Vol. III, p. 732.

13. Captain John Seaton, "The Battle of Belmont," in "Sundry Papers" of the Kansas Commandery, Military Order of the Loyal Legion of the United States, Vol. I; Brinton, pp. 72–73; Grant's Memoirs, Vol. I, pp. 272–273.

14. Dr. William L. Polk, "General Polk and the Battle of Belmont," *B. & L.,* Vol. I, pp. 348–349.

15. Both Brinton and Captain Seaton give interesting details about the disorganization in the Federal ranks following the initial triumph and during the subsequent retreat, and their accounts have been used extensively in the preparation of this chapter. In his Memoirs (Vol. I, pp. 273–274) Grant says of his men: "Veterans could not have behaved better than they did up to the moment of reaching the Rebel camp. At this point they became demoralized from their victory."

16. Grant's Memoirs, Vol. I, pp. 274–276.

17. In her old age Julia Dent Grant wrote the story of this strange incident. As it happened, on the day of the battle of Belmont she was going to leave Galena with the children and go to Cairo to visit General Grant; this vision came to her just before she left the Grant home. This enabled her to fix the time of its occurrence, when she told Grant about it after reaching Cairo. Grant mentions the dangerous ride away from the boats — without referring to Julia's strange vision — in his Memoirs, Vol. I, pp. 277–279.

18. Captain John Seaton, as Note 13.

19. Grant's Memoirs, Vol. I, p. 279; Captain John Seaton, as Note 13; Charles Wills, *Army Life of an Illinois Soldier*, p. 43
20. Casualty figures are from *B. & L.*, Vol. I, pp. 355–356.
21. Smith's report in O. R., Vol. III, pp. 299–300.
22. O. R., Vol. III, p. 274.
23. Grant's Memoirs, Vol. I, pp. 280–281.
24. Conger, pp. 99–101. See also Grant's statement to Colonel Oglesby: "The confidence inspired in our troops in the engagement will be of incalculable benefit to us in the future" — in O. R., Vol. III, p. 272.
25. James B. Eads, "Recollections of Foote and the Gunboats," in *B. & L.*, Vol. I, pp. 342, 346; Rear Admiral Henry Walke, "The Gunboats at Belmont and Fort Henry," *B. & L.*, Vol. I, pp. 359–360.
26. Wilson, as Note 2, p. 68.
27. Dr. William L. Polk, as Note 14, pp. 356–357; Grant's Memoirs, Vol. I, p. 281; O. R., Vol. VIII, pp. 369–370.
28. Dr. William L. Polk, as Note 14; letter of Charles M. Scott, pilot in 1861 of the steamer *Belle of Memphis*, to the *St. Louis Republican*, reprinted in the *Chicago Tribune* of February 4, 1887.
29. O. R., Vol. III, pp. 304, 309; Captain John Seaton, as Note 13.

CHAPTER FIVE

General Halleck Takes Over

1. For a good discussion of the circumstances attending Frémont's removal, see K. P. Williams, *Lincoln Finds a General*, Vol. III, pp. 62–66.
2. Original in the C. F. Smith Papers. See also letter of John P. Hawkins (who in the fall of 1861 was on Halleck's staff) in the 1906 *Reunion Book of the Society of the Army of the Tennessee*, pp. 92–93; also "Recollections of the Fallen" in the *Army and Navy Journal* for July 8, 1865. For details on the messy situation in St. Louis, see O. R., Vol. VIII, pp. 389, 409.
3. The documents exchanged between Smith and Halleck and between Smith and Wallace are in the C. F. Smith Papers.
4. Letters of Sherman, dated November 28, 1861, and January 4, 1862, in the Sherman papers, Library of Congress. Sherman to Mrs. Sherman, January 1, 1862, in the possession of Miss E. Sherman Fitch.
5. Halleck to Mrs. Halleck, printed in General James Grant Wilson's "General Halleck: A Memoir," in the *Journal of the Military Service Institution of the United States*, Vol. XXXVI, p. 554.
6. Sherman to John Sherman, dated January 4, 1862, cited in Note 4; Smith's letter of December 31, 1861, in the C. F. Smith papers.
7. Letter to Colonel L. F. Ross of the 17th Illinois, dated January 5, 1862, in the Iowa Historical Record for October, 1888.
8. Grant to Colonel John Cook, O. R., Series Two, Vol. I, p. 794.

9. Grant to General E. A. Paine, O. R., Vol. VIII, pp. 494–495.
10. Grant to Halleck, November 21, 1861, O. R., Vol. VII, p. 442.
11. Halleck to McClellan, November 27, O. R., Vol. VIII, p. 382; Halleck to Mrs. Halleck, December 14, in the Oliver Barrett Collection.
12. Grant discussed this situation in substantial detail in a long letter to Washburne dated November 7, 1862; original in the Grant Papers, Illinois State Historical Library. See also Major Julian Kune, *Reminiscences of an Octogenarian Hungarian Exile*, p. 107.
13. Wilson's *Life of John A. Rawlins*, p. 67; Lew Wallace, *An Autobiography*, Vol. I, pp. 352–353; letter of W. R. Rowley to Elihu Washburne, January 30, 1862, in the Washburne Papers.
14. Rawlins's long letter is printed in full in Wilson's *Life of John A. Rawlins*. See also Albert Richardson, *A Personal History of Ulysses S. Grant*, pp. 195–196.
15. Grant to Halleck, January 12, 1862, O. R., Vol. VII, p. 546. See also John Eaton, *Grant, Lincoln and the Freedmen*, pp. 101–102, and the Rawlins letter cited in Note 14.
16. For the interchange between Grant and Halleck, see O. R., Series Two, Vol. I, pp. 120–122.
17. Grant to Halleck, November 22, 1861, O. R., Vol. VIII, p. 373; Grant's report of November 18, O. R., Vol. III, p. 367; Thompson to Polk, Same, p. 368; Grant to Halleck, November 25, O. R., Series Two, Vol. I, p. 117; Grant's Memoirs, Vol. I, p. 268.
18. For the correspondence mentioned here, see O. R., Vol. III, p. 571; Vol. VII, p. 465; Vol. VIII, p. 404.
19. Grant's Special Orders dated November 26, O. R., Vol. VII, p. 449.
20. Grant to Oglesby, December 21, O. R., Vol. VIII, p. 453; to McClernand, December 22, p. 457.
21. Grant to Halleck, November 21, O. R., Vol. VII, p. 442; dispatch of November 29, p. 460; dispatch to J. C. Kelton, December 1, p. 462.
22. Grant to J. C. Kelton, November 28, O. R., Vol. VII, p. 455. See also *B. & L.*, Vol. I, pp. 338–339.
23. Henry Walke, "The Gunboats at Belmont and Fort Henry," *B. & L.*, Vol. I, pp. 358–359; Grant to Halleck, January 6, 1862, O. R., Vol. VII, p. 534; Charles W. Wills, "Army Life of an Illinois Soldier," p. 62.
24. O. R., Vol. VIII, pp. 430, 432, 433.
25. Hoyt Sherman, "Personal Recollections of General Grant," in the *Midland Monthly* for April, 1898; Fred Grant in *B. & L.*, Vol. I, p. 352; Brinton, pp. 99–100.
26. Cramer, pp. 58, 62–63, 68–69, 72.
27. Memoir of Julia Dent Grant.
28. Brinton, pp. 98–99, 193–194.
29. Hoyt Sherman as Note 25.
30. Leonard Swett, quoted in the *Chicago Tribune* for April 27, 1880; O. R., Vol. VII, p. 7.

CHAPTER SIX

Limited Objectives

1. Basler, *Collected Works*, Vol. IV, pp. 544–545.
2. Late in November McClellan was telling Buell that his own operations in Virginia must be co-ordinated with the projected campaign in East Tennessee: O. R., Vol. VII, p. 458. In January he made the point more emphatically, writing Buell that "my own advance cannot, according to my present views, be made until your troops are soundly established in the eastern portion of Tennessee." O. R., Vol. VII, p. 531.
3. See Buell's letter to McClellan dated December 29, O. R., Vol. VII, pp. 520–521; also Colonel R. M. Kelly, "Holding Kentucky for the Union," *B. & L.*, Vol. I, p. 385.
4. Kelly, *B. & L.*, Vol. I, pp. 377–378; O. R., Series Two, Vol. I: John M. Branner to Judah P. Benjamin, November 9, p. 838; to Jefferson Davis, November 11, p. 839; Colonel W. B. Wood to Samuel Cooper, p. 840; message of Governor Isham Harris, p. 841; A. G. Graham to Davis, p. 841; Branner to Benjamin, p, 843.
5. Report of Colonel D. Leadbetter, O. R., Series Two, Vol. I, pp. 849, 853, 859.
6. McClellan to Buell, November 7, O. R., Series Two, Vol. I, p. 891.
7. Buell to Lorenzo Thomas, December 23, O. R., Vol. VII, p. 511; Buell to McClellan, November 22, pp. 443–444.
8. Buell to McClellan, December 29, O. R., Vol. VII, p. 521.
9. Buell to Halleck, January 3, 1862, O. R., Vol. VII, pp. 528–529.
10. See O. R., Vol. VII: Lincoln to Halleck, December 31, p. 524; Buell to Lincoln, p. 526; Halleck to Lincoln, January 1, p. 526.
11. Same, Halleck to Buell, January 2, p. 527.
12. Same, McClellan to Halleck, January 3, pp. 527–528; Buell to Halleck, January 3, pp. 528–529.
13. Same, Lincoln to Buell, January 4, and Buell's reply of same date, pp. 530–531; McClellan to Buell, January 6, p. 531.
14. Same, Halleck to Lincoln, January 6, pp. 532–533; Lincoln's gloomy endorsement (dated January 10) is p. 533.
15. Same, Halleck to Grant, pp. 533–534.
16. Same, Grant to Halleck, pp. 537–538. Grant's troop return for January 10 is on p. 544.
17. Same, pp. 535, 543, 547.
18. Grant's orders governing the expedition are in O. R., Vol. VII, p. 551. His message regarding Captain Kountz is pp. 551–552. The Kountz affair had a curious aftermath. Kountz sent to the War Department an extensive statement accusing Grant of drunkenness, both at Cairo and on flag-of-truce boats, and asserting that Grant

and his aides went to a Negro ball where much champagne was served. Assistant Secretary of War Thomas A. Scott passed the charges on to Secretary Edwin M. Stanton, pointing out that Kountz drew up his list of charges while in prison and adding that "there seems to be some little personal feeling in this matter between the General and Q. M. Kountz." Scott recommended that Kountz be released from custody and that "the examination of charges against General Grant be suspended for the present." (See Vol. III, Stanton Papers, Library of Congress.) Apparently, the Kountz charges were not taken seriously by the War Department; the court-martial he demanded for Grant was never held.

19. Emerson, "Grant's Life in the West," in the *Midland Monthly* for May, 1898.
20. Halleck to McClellan, O. R., Vol. VIII, p. 503; Grant to J. C. Kelton, O. R., Vol. VII, p. 565; Emerson, as Note 19.
21. C. F. Smith to Grant, O. R., Vol. VII, p. 561; Emerson, as Note 19.
22. Thomas to Buell, January 23, O. R., Vol. VII, pp. 563–564.
23. Grant's Memoirs, Vol. I, pp. 234–235; Emerson, as Note 19.
24. Brinton, p. 110; Garland, p. 185; Memoir of Julia Dent Grant.
25. Galena *Northwestern Gazette* for December 16, 1861, printing a St. Louis dispatch to the *Cincinnati Enquirer;* Colonel Charles Whittlesey to Halleck, November 20, 1861, O. R., Vol. VII, p. 440.
26. Halleck to McClellan, January 20, O. R., Vol. VIII, p. 509.
27. Halleck's orders are in O. R., Vol. VIII, pp. 406, 411, 431.
28. John Russell Young, *Around the World with General Grant,* Vol. II, p. 465; Brinton, p. 110.
29. O. R., Vol. VII, pp. 518–519.
30. In O. R., Vol. VIII: Halleck to T. Ewing, January 1, pp. 475–476; Halleck to McClellan, December 19, 1861, pp. 448–449. For Colonel C. R. Jennison's proclamation, O. R., Series Two, Vol. I, pp. 231–232; editorial in the *Missouri Republican* for October 3, 1861.
31. O. R., Vol. VII: Halleck to Grant, January 22, pp. 561–562; Foote to Halleck, January 28, p. 120; Grant to Halleck, January 28, p. 121; his letter of January 29 is also on p. 121. The rumor about Beauregard is in McClellan's January 29 dispatches to Halleck and Buell, p. 571.
32. The point is made by Conger, pp. 152–154.
33. Halleck to McClellan, January 29 and 30, O. R., Vol. VII, pp. 571–572.
34. O. R., Vol. VII: Halleck to Buell, January 30, p. 574; to Grant, pp. 121–122.
35. The exchange between Halleck and Buell is in O. R., Vol. VII, pp. 574–576.
36. Same, p. 575.
37. *Official Records of the Union and Confederate Navies in the War of the Rebellion,* Vol. XXII, pp. 427–428.

CHAPTER SEVEN

Between the Rivers

1. Emerson, "Grant's Life in the West," *Midland Monthly* for May, 1898.
2. Grant to Smith, Jan. 31, O. R., Vol. VII, p. 575.
3. Same, pp. 577–579. Note that it took just two days to get this expedition moving — as good a record, for speed, as was made in all the war for a major expedition. Obviously, Grant had been anticipating Halleck's orders.
4. O. R., Vol. VII: Halleck to Buell, February 2, pp. 578–579; Buell to Thomas, February 2, p. 580; Buell to Halleck, February 3, p. 580; Grant to Halleck, February 3, p. 581.
5. Same: Halleck to Buell, February 5, and Buell to Halleck, same date, p. 583; McClellan to Buell, February 5, and Buell to McClellan, also February 5, pp. 584–585; Halleck to McClellan, Feb. 6, p. 586; McClellan to Buell and Buell to McClellan, dispatches of Feb. 6, p. 587; Halleck to Buell, Feb. 7, p. 593.
6. Rawlins, quoted in Emerson, as Note 1.
7. *Chicago Tribune*, printing Cairo dispatch dated February 2 and Paducah dispatch dated February 4. One correspondent insisted that the leak occurred because Grant's own staff had been kept in the dark. The officer who passed on press telegrams, he said, had the quaint habit of supressing those which were true and approving those which were false, on the theory that the enemy would best be deceived thereby. Seeing the item about the expedition into Tennessee — written by an alert reporter who had seen the waterfront preparations and had drawn his own conclusions — this officer assumed that the story was completely untrue and let it go. (Richardson, *A Personal History of Ulysses S. Grant*, pp. 214–215.)
8. Colonel Charles Whittlesey, *War Memoranda*, pp. 28–29.
9. Eliot Calendar, "What a Boy Saw on the Mississippi," in *Military Essays and Recollections*, Vol. I, pp. 53–55.
10. *Chicago Tribune*, Paducah dispatch dated February 4.
11. Grant's battle orders are in O. R., Vol. VII, p. 125.
12. Correspondence of the *Memphis Appeal*, dated January 29, quoted in a *Chicago Tribune* dispatch from Louisville dated February 7; Tilghman's report, in O. R., Vol. VII, p. 140; Captain Jesse Taylor, "The Defense of Fort Henry," in *B. & L.*, Vol. I, p. 370.
13. See Lieutenant Col. E. C. Dawes, "The Army of the Tennessee," in Vol. IV, *Papers of the Ohio Commandery, Military Order of the Loyal Legion of the United States.*
14. *Chicago Tribune*, Cairo dispatch dated February 9; H. Allen Gos-

nell, *Guns on the Western Waters,* pp. 49–50; McClernand's report, O. R., Vol. VII, p. 129.

15. Captain Jesse Taylor, as Note 12, pp. 370–371; Flag Officer Foote's report, O. R., Vol. VII, pp. 122–123.
16. Tilghman's report, O. R., Vol. VII, p. 136; Captain Jesse Taylor, as Note 12, p. 372.
17. Grant to Halleck, February 6, O. R., Vol. VII, p. 124.
18. O. R., Vol. VII: Grant to Halleck, p. 125; Halleck to McClellan, p. 120.
19. Grant's letter to his sister, in Cramer, p. 78; Richardson, as in Note 7, p. 217.
20. Albert Sidney Johnston to Judah P. Benjamin, O. R., Vol. VII, p. 131.
21. *Chicago Tribune* dispatch from Cairo dated February 7; dispatch dated Fort Henry, February 9, via Cairo, February 11; Grant's Memoirs, Vol. I, p. 241; Grant's orders of February 9, O. R., Vol. VII, pp. 598–599. Grant's memory seems to have betrayed him; Pillow did not actually reach Fort Donelson until February 9, two days after Grant made his trip. (O. R., Vol. VII, p. 877.)
22. Commander Phelps's report dated February 10, O. R., Vol. VII, pp. 153–156.
23. Cairo dispatch dated February 9, in the *Chicago Tribune;* Cullum to Grant, February 7, O. R., Vol. VII, p. 594; Grant's General Field Orders No. 7 and No. 8, both of February 10, p. 601; Halleck to Cullum, February 14, p. 614.
24. Letter of Cullum to Smith, dated February 1, in the C. F. Smith Papers; Brinton, p. 131. Brinton says McPherson told him: "I have been ordered here and instructed to obtain special information. All sorts of reports are prevalent at St. Louis as to Gen. Grant's habits. It is said he is drinking terribly and in every way is inefficient." It is perhaps worth noting that in a short time McPherson became one of Grant's most faithful supporters.
25. *Chicago Tribune* dispatch dated Fort Henry, February 7; Brinton, p. 112.
26. The messages between Halleck, Grant, Foote and Cullum can be found in O. R., Vol. VII, pp. 595, 600, 601, 603–604.
27. Foote to Halleck, O. R., Vol. VII, p. 604; Grant's Memoirs, Vol. I, p. 298.
28. Grant to Halleck, February 12, O. R., Vol. VI, p. 612.
29. Grant to Halleck, O. R., Vol. VII, p. 609.
30. Lew Wallace, "The Capture of Fort Donelson," in *B. & L.,* Vol. I, p. 410 (hereafter cited as Wallace); Brinton, pp. 115–116.
31. For a sympathetic examination of Johnston's dilemma, see Col. William Preston Johnston, "Albert Sidney Johnston at Shiloh," *B. & L.,* Vol. I, pp. 546–548. See also Stanley Horn, *The Army of*

Tennessee, pp. 83–87, and T. Harry Williams, *Beauregard: Napoleon in Gray*, pp. 116–119. Beauregard's memorandum on the course to be followed after the fall of Fort Henry, dated February 7, is in O. R., Vol. VII, pp. 861–862.

32. Henry Walke, "The Western Flotilla at Fort Donelson, Island Number Ten, Fort Pillow and Memphis," *B. & L.*, Vol. I, pp. 430–431. Hereafter cited as Walke.
33. O. R., Vol. VII, pp. 205, 212–213; Wallace, pp. 408–409.
34. McClernand's report, O. R., Vol. VII, p. 174; Oglesby's report, p. 185.

CHAPTER EIGHT

Unconditional Surrender

1. Major David Reed, *Campaigns and Battles of the 12th Iowa Volunteer Infantry*, p. 18 ff. For regimental reports on the night and the activities at dawn, see O. R., Vol. VII, pp. 188, 190, 194, 201, 215.
2. Colonel John W. Emerson, "Grant's Life in the West," in the *Midland Monthly* for June, 1898.
3. Brinton, pp. 144–145; Grant to Halleck, February 14, O. R., Vol. VII, p. 613; Grant to Cullum, pp. 613–614.
4. Grant to Halleck, February 14, O. R., Vol. VII, p. 613.
5. Wallace, pp. 413–414; Walke, *B. & L.*, Vol. I, pp. 433–436; Foote's report, O. R., Vol. VII, p. 166.
6. For a discussion of Grant's dispositions, see Conger, p. 169. In his report to Halleck, dated February 16, Grant says: "I concluded to make the investment of Fort Donelson as perfect as possible, and partially fortify and await repairs to the gunboats." (O. R., Vol. VII, p. 159.) See also Grant's Memoirs, Vol. I, pp. 303–305.
7. Colonel Charles Whittlesey, *War Memoranda*, pp. 30–31.
8. Whittlesey, as Note 7, p. 31; Grant's Memoirs, Vol. I, p. 304; M. F. Force, *From Fort Henry to Corinth*, p. 48. (Hereafter cited as Force.)
9. McPherson's report, O. R., Vol. VII, p. 163; Grant's Memoirs, Vol. I, p. 305.
10. Wallace, pp. 415–418.
11. Force, p. 50; Wallace, pp. 419–421; Whittlesey, *War Memoranda*, pp. 34–35.
12. *Chicago Tribune* for September 23, 1865, reprinting a September 18 article in the *Galena Northwestern Gazette*.
13. Wallace, pp. 421–422.
14. Grant's Memoirs, Vol. I, p. 307; *Galena Northwestern Gazette*, as Note 12; Grant in O. R., Vol. VII, pp. 159–160.
15. Grant to Foote, O. R., Vol. VII, p. 618.
16. This paragraph is based on a manuscript draft signed by Thomas J. Newsham, in the C. F. Smith Papers. The reference to Grant's ride

along the lines with McClernand is from the previously quoted article in the *Galena Northwestern Gazette*. For an account very similar to Newsham's, see John G. Greenwalt, War Papers No. 87, District of Columbia Commandery of the Loyal Legion.

17. Brinton, pp. 120–121; Newsham, in the C. F. Smith Papers.
18. There is a good discussion of the Confederate command situation in Stanley Horn, pp. 93–96. The dreary explanations by Floyd and Pillow are in O. R., Vol. VII, pp. 269–275, 283–284, 287–289, *et seq.* Forrest's report is pp. 383–387.
19. Whittlesey, as Note 7, pp. 36–37; letter of Private William H. Tebbetts of the 45th Illinois, in the Journal of the Illinois State Historical Society for June, 1940, p. 232; A. H. Markland, interviewed in the *Washington Star* for August 1, 1885, quoted in the *New York Times* of August 4, 1885.
20. Emerson, "Grant's Life in the West," in the *Midland Monthly* for June, 1898.
21. Whittlesey, as Note 7, p. 37.
22. Newsham, in the C. F. Smith Papers; Brinton, p. 129; Richardson, p. 225.
23. For the odd sequence of events at Confederate headquarters, see Wallace, pp. 425–426; Robert Selph Henry, *First with the Most: Forrest*, pp. 58–61.
24. Whittlesey, as Note 7, pp. 37–38; unidentified clipping, apparently from the *Chicago Tribune*, bearing a Fort Donelson dispatch dated February 18, in the Lloyd Lewis Papers; Wallace, p. 428.
25. *New York Tribune* dispatch reprinted in an undated clipping from the *Chicago Tribune*, in the Lloyd Lewis Papers; Arndt M. Stickles, *Simon Bolivar Buckner*, p. 173.
26. Grant to Halleck, Feb. 16, O. R., Vol. VII, p. 625.

CHAPTER NINE

Aftermath of Victory

1. Newspaper clippings give details about the public response to news of Fort Donelson in Chicago, St. Louis, Cincinnati and Washington; stories cited here are from the *Chicago Tribune, Cincinnati Commercial, New York Herald* and *St. Louis Republican*, all of Feb. 18, 1862.
2. Whittlesey's *"War Memoranda,"* pp. 38–39 (hereafter cited as Whittlesey); Brinton, p. 142; O. R., Vol. X, Part Two, p. 62.
3. O. R., Vol. VII, p. 626; Whittlesey, p. 39.
4. Brinton, pp. 125–126, 133.
5. O. R., Vol. VII, p. 629.
6. Same, p. 629; Vol. VIII, p. 555.
7. O. R., Vol. VII, pp. 422–423.

8. Same, pp. 423–424, 648.

9. On November 27, 1861, Grant wrote to his father: "I am somewhat troubled lest I lose my command here, though I believe my administration has given general satisfaction not only to those over me but to all concerned. This is the most important command within the Department however, and will probably be given to the senior officer next to General Halleck himself." Three weeks later, however, Grant wrote to his sister Mary: "I do not now see that the probabilities are so strong that I will likely be removed. A full disposition seems to have been made of all my seniors." (Cramer, pp. 71, 75.) For Halleck's letter of February 8 about Hitchcock, see O. R., Vol. VII, p. 594.

10. O. R., Vol. III, p. 208: Stanton to Halleck, February 8, Halleck to Sherman, February 9. For Halleck's proposed Western Division and its three Departments, see his February 8 dispatch to McClellan in O. R., Vol. VII, p. 595. Long afterward, Grant wrote that the fall of Fort Donelson opened the Southwest to Federal conquest: "If one general who would have taken the responsibility had been in command of all the troops west of the Alleghanies, he could have marched to Chattanooga, Corinth, Memphis and Vicksburg with the troops we then had." (Grant's Memoirs, Vol. I, p. 317.)

11. In his diary, Hitchcock wrote that he declined the appointment partly because of his delicate health and partly because he felt that it would be unfair for him to take a field command which he had not earned: "As soon as Donelson surrendered to Grant I felt it a positive duty to decline the commission & did so." (Ethan Allen Hitchcock Diaries; original in the Gilcrease Museum, Tulsa, Oklahoma; copies in possession of Harvey Snitiker.) There is a good brief sketch of Hitchcock's career in the *Dictionary of American Biography*.

12. O. R., Vol. VII: Halleck to McClellan, February 17, pp. 627, 628; Halleck to Buell, February 18, p. 632; to McClellan on Smith, February 19, p. 637.

13. Same, Halleck to McClellan, February 20, p. 641; Halleck to Scott, February 21, p. 648; to Stanton, p. 655.

14. The replies of McClellan and Stanton are in O. R., Vol. VII, pp. 645, 652.

15. Confederate losses at Fort Donelson have been in dispute for years, but it seems clear from an examination of Federal Reports in the Official Records (O. R.) that Grant captured somewhere between 14,000 and 16,000 men. On February 19 General Cullum at Cairo wrote that he had sent 9,000 prisoners to St. Louis and 1,000 to Chicago, with 500 more ready to leave the next day; on the same day, Rawlins notified General Buckner that transportation was available to send 6,000 men north "this evening" from Fort Donelson. (O. R., Series Two, Vol. III, pp. 282–283). On Feb. 24, Assistant Quarter-

master J. A. Potter notified Washington that "at least 10,000 prisoners" were being held in Chicago and Springfield, Illinois, and on February 27 the adjutant general of Indiana reported 4000 prisoners at Indianapolis, 500 at Terre Haute and 800 at Lafayette. (O. R., Series Two, Vol. III, pp. 317, 333.)

16. Grant's order to Nelson is printed in a message he sent to Cullum on February 24, O. R., Vol. VII, pp. 662–663.
17. Grant to Julia Dent Grant, in the U. S. Grant Papers, Missouri Historical Society.
18. Grant to Sherman, February 25, O. R., Vol. VII, p. 667.
19. O. R., Vol. VII: Grant to Cullum, February 25, p. 666. As noted, February 21 Grant had written Cullum: "It is my impression that by following up our success Nashville would be an easy conquest" (p. 424), and on the same date Foote wrote Cullum that "General Grant and myself consider this a good time to move on Nashville." For Buell's state of mind, see pp. 659, 668, 944–945.
20. Grant's Memoirs, Vol. I, pp. 320–321.
21. Grant to Buell, February 27, O. R., Vol. VII, p. 670.
22. Grant's Memoirs, Vol. I, p. 321.
23. For an excellent study of this strange administrative arrangement, and some of its damaging consequences, see Roscoe Pound, *The Military Telegraph in the Civil War*, in Vol. 66 of the Proceedings of the Massachusetts Historical Society.
24. Halleck to Sherman, with a message for Grant, February 24, O. R., Vol. VII, p. 655; Halleck to Cullum and Sherman, February 25, p. 667; Halleck to McClellan, February 27, O. R., Vol. LII, Part One, p. 217.
25. Halleck to Cullum and Halleck to Grant, dispatches dated March 1, O. R., Vol. VII, p. 674.
26. O. R., Vol. VII, p. 674. Grant to J. C. Kelton, March 1, and Buell to Halleck, also March 1, pp. 674–675.
27. For McClellan's rebukes to Halleck, see O. R., Vol. VII, pp. 645, 646.
28. Halleck to McClellan, in a message whose date, March 3, is apparently the date of its receipt; O. R., Vol. VII, pp. 679–680.
29. McClellan to Halleck, March 3, O. R., Vol. VII, p. 680; Halleck to McClellan, March 4, p. 682; Halleck to Grant, March 4, O. R., Vol. X, Part Two, p. 3.

CHAPTER TEN

"What Command Have I Now?"

1. Grant to Halleck, March 5, O. R., Vol. X, Part Two, pp. 4–5.
2. Grant to Smith, in the C. F. Smith Papers; Grant to Halleck, March 10, O. R., Vol. X, Part Two, p. 25.

3. This note, in Grant's handwriting, is in the C. F. Smith Papers.
4. Gwin to Foote, March 5, O. R., Vol. X, Part Two, p. 8; A. T. Mahan, *The Gulf and Inland Waters*, p. 28; Grant to Smith, March 5, in the C. F. Smith Papers; Smith's letter dated March 9 to Wm. L. Martin, also in the Smith Papers.
5. Halleck to Grant, March 5, O. R., Vol. X, Part Two, p. 7.
6. O. R., Vol. X, Part Two: Halleck to Grant, March 6, and Grant to Halleck, March 7, p. 15.
7. Same, Halleck's retort, and Grant's reply with the troop returns, p. 21.
8. Same, Halleck to Grant, March 9, p. 22.
9. Same, Halleck to Grant, March 6, p. 13. The unsigned letter to David Davis is p. 14; Grant's reply, dated March 11, is p. 30; Halleck's answer to this is p. 32.
10. Thomas's March 10 dispatch to Halleck, and Halleck's reply dated March 15, are in O. R., Vol. VII, pp. 683–684.
11. Grant to Halleck, O. R., Vol. X, Part 2, pp. 36, 63: Grant's Memoirs, Vol. I, pp. 327–328.
12. Brinton, p. 147; Rowley to Washburne, March 14, and Chetlain to Washburne, March 16, in the Washburne Papers. General John M. Schofield, who insisted that "I knew personally at the time the exact truth" about the matter, believed that Halleck simply wanted to replace Grant with C. F. Smith and that he was checkmated by "Grant's soldierly action" in asking to be relieved. (Lieutenant Gen. John M. Schofield, *Forty-six Years in the Army*, p. 361.)
13. Garland, p. 198.
14. It must be remembered Grant's final bitterness against Halleck did not develop until after the war, when he saw the dispatches Halleck sent to McClellan and realized that Halleck had been playing a double game with him.
15. Grant to Washburne, March 22, in the Washburne Papers.
16. Brinton, p. 148; Rowley to Washburne, November 20, 1862, and December 16, 1862, in the Washburne Papers; *History of Alexander, Union and Pulaski Counties, Illinois*, p. 60; W. T. Sherman to Dr. W. G. Eliot, Sept. 12, 1885, in the W. T. Sherman Papers, Library of Congress; *Cincinnati Commercial* for March 11, 1862.
17. M. F. Force, *From Fort Henry to Corinth*, pp. 96–97.
18. Grant to Smith, March 11, O. R., Vol. X, Part Two, p. 29.
19. Halleck to Grant, March 13, and March 16; O. R., Vol. X, Part One, pp. 32, 41.
20. O. R., Vol. X, Part Two: Halleck to Grant, March 18, p. 46; Grant to Smith and Wallace, March 20, p. 52; Grant to Halleck, March 19, p. 49.
21. Same, Halleck to Grant, March 20, p. 51; Grant to Capt. N. H. McLean at St. Louis, March 20, p. 51; Grant to Halleck, March 21, p. 55; Grant to Smith, March 23, p. 62.

22. Letter dated Pittsburg Landing, March 26, addressed to "My Dear William," in the C. F. Smith Papers.
23. Confederate numbers, expedients and troop movements are admirably detailed in Horn, pp. 107–115. See also T. Harry Williams, *Beauregard; Napoleon in Gray*, p. 119 ff. For Beauregard's estimate of his numbers, and his desperate efforts to increase them, see O. R., Vol. VII, pp. 899–900. On February 24, Secretary of War Judah P. Benjamin was notifying Robert E. Lee, then in charge of Confederate defenses along the southeast coast, that "the recent disaster to our arms in Tennessee" made it necessary to send all possible troops to the Tennessee front. (O. R., Vol. VI, p. 398.) Horn (p. 115) remarks of this crisis that "fortunately for the Confederate plans, the Federals had been behaving with inexplicable deliberation and want of enterprise."
24. Halleck to Assistant Secretary of War Thomas Scott, March 6, O. R., Vol. X, Part Two, p. 10.
25. Colonel William Preston Johnston, *Albert Sidney Johnston at Shiloh*, in *B. & L.*, Vol. I, p. 555.
26. Captain C. L. Sumbardo, "Some Facts about the Battle of Shiloh," in *Glimpses of the Nation's Struggle*, Vol. III, pp. 31–32.
27. *New York Herald* for April 3, quoting a *St. Louis Republican* dispatch of March 29; Grant to Julia Dent Grant, letter of March 29, in the Grant Papers, Illinois State Historical Society; Lieutenant S. D. Thompson, *Recollections with the Third Iowa*.
28. Grant to Sherman, April 4, O. R., Vol. X, Part Two, pp. 90–91; Captain Charles Morton, "A Boy at Shiloh," in the *Papers of the New York Commandery of the Loyal Legion*, Vol. III; statement of Captain I. P. Rumsey, from the printed Proceedings of the Reunion of Taylor's Battery in Chicago, 1890, p. 46; Lieutenant Colonel E. C. Dawes in *The History of the 53rd Ohio*.
29. Grant's April 5 dispatch to St. Louis, O. R., Vol. X, Part One, p. 89; Grant's letter to the Cincinnati *Commercial*, reprinted in the *New York Herald*, May 3, 1862.
30. Ammen's account of the conversation is in O. R., Vol. X, Part One, pp. 330–331.
31. Lieutenant S. D. Thompson, *Recollections with the Third Iowa*; J. F. C. Fuller, *The Generalship of Ulysses S. Grant*, p. 104.

CHAPTER ELEVEN

The Guns on the Bluff

1. O. R., Vol. X, Part One: Report of John A. Rawlins, p. 184; General Buell's report, p. 291; Halleck's telegram to Grant, April 5, O. R., Vol. X, Part Two, p. 94; statement of William I. Cherry to Lloyd Lewis, June 29, 1939, in the Lloyd Lewis Papers; Ms. letter,

Mrs. William H. Cherry to the Reverend T. M. Hurst of Arnot, Pa., dated Dec. 6, 1892, also in the Lloyd Lewis Papers.

2. O. R., Vol. X, Part Two, p. 95; Vol. LII, Part One, p. 232.

3. O. R., Vol. X, Part One, McPherson's report, p. 181; Grant to Halleck, Vol. X, Part Two, p. 94.

4. O. R., Vol. X, Part One, Rawlins's report. p. 185; Grant's Memoirs, Vol. I, p. 336. In 1896, in a letter to James Grant Wilson, Wallace described the meeting, saying that Grant seemed mildly puzzled and that Grant's last word to him was to "hold yourself in readiness to move in any direction." (Letter in the Palmer Collection, Western Reserve Historical Society, Cleveland.)

5. Badeau, Vol. I, p. 79; John K. Duke, *History of the 53rd Regiment Ohio Volunteer Infantry*, p. 49; O. R., Vol. X, Part One, p. 185.

6. William W. Belknap, *History of the 15th Iowa Veteran Infantry*, pp. 189–190.

7. O. R., Vol. X, Part One, pp. 181, 568; M. F. Force, *From Fort Henry to Corinth*, pp. 122–124.

8. *History of the 53rd Regiment Ohio Volunteer Infantry*, as Note 5, pp. 27, 46; T. J. Lindsey, *Ohio at Shiloh: Report of the Commission*, pp. 37–38; O. R., Vol. X, Part One, pp. 264–265; Henry H. Wright, *History of the Sixth Iowa Infantry*, p. 80; *History of the 15th Iowa*, p. 83.

9. O. R., Vol. X, Part One, p. 133.

10. Lieutenant S. D. Thompson, *Recollections with the Third Iowa*, p. 214; Warren Olney, *Shiloh as Seen by a Common Soldier*, in War Paper No. 5, California Commandery, Military Order of the Loyal Legion of the United States, p. 6 ff.

11. Richard Miller Devens, *The Pictorial Book of Anecdotes and Incidents of the War of the Rebellion*, p. 253; Badeau, Vol. I, p. 79; Grant's account of Shiloh in *B. & L.*, Vol. I, p. 473.

12. O. R., Vol. X, Part One, p. 278; *Sketches of War History: Papers prepared for the Ohio Commandery, Military Order of the Loyal Legion of the United States*, Vol. V, pp. 431–432.

13. Samuel H. Fletcher, *History of Company A, Second Illinois Cavalry*, pp. 49–52.

14. O. R., Vol. LII, Part One, pp. 232–233.

15. Lieutenant Colonel Douglas Putnam, in *Sketches of War History*, Vol. III, p. 199; Sergeant Alexander Downing, *Downing's Civil War Diary*, pp. 41–42.

16. Interview with Hillyer, *Chicago Tribune*, January 27, 1869.

17. O. R., Vol. X, Part One, p. 119.

18. O. R., Vol. X, Part One, p. 288; F. Y. Hedley, *Marching Through Georgia*; Gen. Edward Bouton, *Events of the Civil War*, p. 31; *The Story of the 55th Regiment Illinois Volunteer Infantry*, by a committee.

19. John R. Rerick, *The 44th Indiana Volunteers in the Rebellion*, p. 231.

20. Chaplain Marion Morrison, *History of the 9th Regiment Illinois Volunteer Infantry;* O. R., Vol. X, Part One, pp. 203, 245; pamphlet, *Ninth Reunion of Iowa Hornets' Nest Brigade,* held at Pittsburg Landing, April 6 and 7, 1912, p. 13; Warren Olney, *Shiloh as Seen by a Common Soldier,* as Note 10.

21. Grant's Memoirs, Vol. I, p. 340; A. L. Chetlain, quoted in *Chicago Inter-Ocean,* May 10, 1881; Chetlain, *Recollections of Seventy Years,* pp. 88–89.

22. O. R., Vol. X, Part One, pp. 186, 259, 263.

23. In his coldly savage criticism of Grant's actions at Shiloh (*B. & L.,* Vol. I, pp. 486–536), General Buell remarks that Grant is very seldom seen in reports of the April 6 fight, and implies broadly that the army commander was very inert. Actually, there are few Civil War battles in which one gets so many glimpses of a commanding general going about his business energetically and competently. Colonel J. F. C. Fuller has cited 18 separate movements and actions which Grant carried out in a space of nine hours, and concludes that "during the turmoil, his activity and generalship appear to me, in the circumstances which surrounded him, to have been quite wonderful." (*The Generalship of Ulysses S. Grant,* pp. 111–113.) For another discussion of Grant's activities on April 6, reaching a similar conclusion, see Conger, pp. 243–251.

24. O. R., Vol. X, Part One, pp. 130-131, 161–162, 226–227; Belknap, pp. 189–190.

25. Rawlins's original account of the meeting is given in his Shiloh report, O. R., Vol. X, Part One, p. 186. A slightly more elaborate version, probably derived from Rawlins himself, is given in Wilson's "Life of John A. Rawlins," p. 88. In his account of Shiloh printed in *B. & L.,* Buell flatly asserts that nothing whatever was said about surrender, and depicts Grant as a rather frightened and stupid man. (Vol. I, pp. 492–493.) Grant refers to the meeting in his Memoirs, Vol. I, pp. 344–345.

26. John K. Duke, *History of the 53rd Regiment Ohio Volunteer Infantry,* pp. 39–55; Lieutenant Colonel Douglas Putnam in Vol. III, *Sketches of War History,* p. 202.

27. O. R., Vol. X, Part One, p. 149; John T. Bell, *Tramps and Triumphs of the Second Iowa Infantry,* p. 8.

28. O. R., Vol. X, Part One, pp. 277–278, 562.

29. *B. & L.,* Vol. I, pp. 590, 599–601; O. R., Vol. X, Part One, p. 464.

30. Lieutenant Colonel Douglas Putnam, as Note 26; Whitelaw Reid, *Ohio in the War,* Vol. I, p. 375.

31. Whitelaw Reid, in an address at a testimonial dinner to Grant at the Lotus Club, New York, reported in the *Chicago Tribune,* Nov. 21, 1880. When he copied this report for future use, Lloyd Lewis added his own caustic comment: "Reid lies like a dog, for it was he who spread blame on Grant for Shiloh's massacre." A slightly dif-

ferent version is given by Reid in *Ohio in the War*, Vol. I, p. 375.

32. Wilbur F. Hinman, *The Story of the Sherman Brigade;* Sergt. N. V. Brower, *The Battle of Shiloh,* at the 5th annual reunion of the 9th Illinois Regiment Veteran Volunteer Association, 1888, p. 58; William R. Hartpence, *History of the 51st Indiana Veteran Volunteer Infantry,* pp. 36–37; O. R., Vol. X, Part One, p. 331.

33. O. R., Vol. X, Part One, p. 333.

34. John Beatty, *The Citizen Soldier,* p. 161; *History of the 51st Indiana Veteran Volunteer Infantry,* p. 38.

35. G. T. Beauregard, "The Shiloh Campaign," in the *North American Review* for February, 1886.

36. Colonel William H. Heath, "Hours with Grant," in the *National Tribune,* June 29, 1916; O. R., Vol. X, Part One, p. 339.

37. Edwin Witherby Brown, "Reminiscences of an Ohio Volunteer," in *Ohio Archaeological and Historical Quarterly,* Vol. 48, p. 311; Henry H. Wright, *History of the Sixth Iowa Infantry,* p. 86, 89–90; Captain James G. Day. *The 15th Iowa at Shiloh,* in Vol. II, *War Sketches and Incidents,* published by the Iowa Commandery, Military Order of the Loyal Legion of the United States, p. 186.

38. Charles F. Hubert, *History of the 50th Regiment Illinois Volunteer Infantry,* p. 93; Lieutenant Colonel Douglas Putnam, in Vol. III, *Sketches of War History,* p. 205.

39. Grant voiced sharp criticism of Wallace when he wrote of Shiloh, but modified his criticism materially in his Memoirs, Vol. I, pp. 351–352. Accounts by Rowley, McPherson and Rawlins of the various efforts to get Wallace's division to the battlefield are in O. R., Vol. X, Part One, pp. 178–182, 185–188. Wallace's own report on Shiloh is in that volume, beginning p. 169. Wallace gives a detailed and convincing justification of his course of action in his letter to James Grant Wilson, Western Reserve Historical Society, as Note 4.

40. O. R., Vol. X, Part One, p. 159; Grant's Memoirs, Vol. I, p. 349.

41. Interview with Sherman in the *Washington Post,* quoted in the *Army and Navy Journal* for December 30, 1893.

CHAPTER TWELVE

The Question of Surprise

1. George W. Cable, in *B. & L.,* Vol. II, p. 18; Charles Wright, *A Corporal's Story;* Beauregard, "The Campaign of Shiloh," in *B. & L.,* Vol. I, p. 592.

2. Beauregard, as Note 1; C. C. Briant, *History of the Sixth Indiana Infantry,* pp. 102–103; Grant's Memoirs, Vol. I, p. 350.

3. *Lew Wallace: An Autobiography,* Vol. II, pp. 544–545.

4. Wallace, *Autobiography,* p. 524

5. Brigadier General Thomas Jordan, "Notes of a Confederate Staff

Officer at Shiloh," in *B. & L.*, Vol. I, p. 603; Grant's Memoirs, Vol. I, pp. 350–351. This is probably the basis for the totally false legend that Grant in person led a final victorious charge at Shiloh.

6. O. R., Vol. X, Part Two, pp. 94, 96–97. See also Grant's remarks in his Memoirs, Vol. I, pp. 354–355.

7. O. R., Vol. X, Part Two, pp. 97–98.

8. Bragg to Beauregard, O. R., Vol. X, Part Two, pp. 398, 400.

9. O. R., Vol. X, Part Two, p. 97.

10. The point is well made by Thomas B. Van Horne in his *History of the Army of the Cumberland*, Vol. I, p. 119; "Perhaps no battle of the war was projected with greater objects than that of Shiloh. The aims were to crush, first, Grant, then Buell, and then take the offensive throughout the west. But the magnitude of the interests involved did not find correspondence in the strength of the army gathered at Corinth, and the initial movement of the grand scheme was undertaken too late to succeed. . . . A grand plan there failed through inadequate resources and comparative feebleness of execution."

11. Badeau, Vol. I, pp. 597–598. Beauregard's note to Grant is most curiously worded. It begins: "At the close of the conflict yesterday, my forces being exhausted by the extraordinary length of time during which they were engaged with yours . . . and it being apparent that you had received and were still receiving reinforcements, I felt it my duty to remove my troops." It almost sounds as if Beauregard were offering Grant the explanation which was due to Jefferson Davis; according to a newspaperman who was then at Federal headquarters, Grant chuckled over it, and said he was tempted to reply that no apologies were necessary. (Richardson, p. 255.)

12. *Downing's Civil War Diary*, p. 43; *History of the 51st Indiana Veteran Volunteer Infantry*, p. 43.

13. AGATE (Whitelaw Reid) in the *Cincinnati Commercial*, April 15; O. R., Vol. X, Part Two: Grant's Order, p. 100; Halleck to Grant, p. 99.

14. O. R., Vol. X, Part Two, pp. 109, 130.

15. The original of this letter is in the De Coppet Collection at the Princeton University Library.

16. O. R., Vol. X, Part Two: Halleck to Stanton, p. 98; to Pope, pp. 107–108.

17. O. R., Vol. X, Part Two, p. 99.

18. O. R., Vol. X, Part Two: General Orders No. 16, p. 105; Halleck to Grant, April 13, pp. 105–106.

19. Letter of W. C. Carroll to Congressman Washburne, dated December 24, 1862, in the Washburne Papers. Carroll had been invited that spring to serve on the staff of John A. Logan, had gone upstream to Savannah to wait for Logan, and while waiting had formed a temporary connection with Grant. When he wrote to Washburne, eight months later, he was asking for help to get an appointment as

an aide to one of the major generals in the Regular Army, and he recited his feat in writing the story about Shiloh to show that his was a deserving case.

20. *New York Herald*, April 10, 1862; Emmet Crozier, *Yankee Reporters*, p. 217.

21. *New York Herald*, April 16, 1862; for Sherman's comment, see his letter to Grant dated Sept. 10, 1884, in the Sherman Letter Book. The Crozier book mentioned in Note 20 (hereafter cited as Crozier) has a very good account of the way Reid got and wrote his story, pp. 210–217.

22. *Sherman, Fighting Prophet*, pp. 233–234; *Chicago Times*, May 6, 1862; *Cincinnati Commercial*, April 25, 1862; *New York Herald*, April 22; F. W. Keil, *The Thirty-fifth Ohio Regiment*, p. 64.

23. Capt. W. Irving Hodgson, C. S. A., of the Washington Artillery, wrote that his battery opened fire at 7:10 A.M. — approximately two hours after the first clash between Prentiss's and Hardee's advance patrols — "on the first camp attacked and taken by our army" — and said that Confederate infantry stormed and occupied this camp only after his guns had silenced two Union batteries. Colonel Daniel W. Adams of the 1st Louisiana Infantry, which was in the column that attacked Prentiss's camp, said Federal resistance was so stiff that he feared for a time his brigade would have to retreat. General Hardee said that his skirmishers were attacked at dawn, that "in half an hour the battle became fierce," and that Cleburne's brigade, "after a series of desperate charges," was driven back, entering "the enemy's encampments" only after a second line came up to its support. For these and other Confederate reports bearing on the fight for the camps, see O. R., Vol. X, Part One, pp. 513, 514, 532, 536, 541, 548, 568 ff., 573, 581. The report of Sherman's 53rd Ohio (same, p. 264) one of the Union regiments most prominently involved in the rout, shows the 53rd in line and ready for action "shortly after daybreak." After some time it was moved to a new position directly in the rear of the camp, at which time Confederate skirmishers appeared on the opposite side of the camp. Still later a Confederate line of battle came up behind the skirmishers, and the Ohioans got off two volleys before their colonel bolted — after which the regiment disintegrated. Major D. W. Reed, historian of the postwar National Shiloh Commission, says the opening shots were fired at 4:55 A.M., and estimates that more than four hours fighting occurred before Prentiss's camp was taken. See *Ohio at Shiloh: Report of the Commission*, by T. J. Lindsay, pp. 79–80.

24. *New York Herald*, May 3, 1862. Grant almost certainly was driven to write this letter by the fact that Julia, then in Covington, Kentucky, was reading the bitter attacks on him which were appearing in the Cincinnati newspapers.

25. *The Sherman Letters: Correspondence between General and Sen-*

ator Sherman from 1837 to 1891, edited by Rachael Sherman Thorndike, pp. 143–145. See also letter of Gen. Sherman to Senator Sherman dated May 12, 1862, in the Sherman Papers. After the war Sherman wrote furiously: "The truth is that Buell took no part in the battle of April 6, 1862, which was the Battle of Shiloh. He came on the field grudgingly and actually held back Nelson's division at Savannah after Grant had ordered it forward. Had Wallace and Nelson come on the Field as they might have done by noon, we could have assumed the offensive and recovered all the ground lost — we lost ground, nothing else — for at night the Rebs were as much beaten as we were." (Letter of April 12, 1886, to "Dear Moulton," in the Sherman Papers at the Huntington Library.)

26. Rowley to E. Hempstead, April 19, 1862; Rowley to Washburne, April 23; J. E. Smith to Washburne, May 16; all in the Washburne papers. Ammen's diary entry, which does not appear in the portion printed in the Official Records, is in his original manuscript in the Illinois State Historical Library. Clyde C. Walton, Illinois State Historian, writes: "We have no reason to assume that the diary was not written at the time of the battle of Shiloh. I suspect that it was written from notes kept day by day from the battle and put in the book possibly beginning April 8." The interesting point here, of course, is that Ammen wrote this testimonial to Grant's sobriety before any accusation of intoxication at Shiloh had been publicly made. On May 20, 1862, General N. J. T. Dana wrote to his brother: "As to Gen. Grant's intemperance, it is pure fiction and slander . . . I hope my testimony on this will be conclusive with those who know me." (Ms. letter in the Huntington Library.)

According to Walter Q. Gresham, then Colonel of the 53rd Indiana, who commanded the post of Savannah before and during the battle, Rawlins asked every officer who had had contact with Grant to write a statement covering every occasion on which he had seen Grant during the 10 days previous to and including the day of the battle. Colonel Gresham said that he himself had seen Grant at all hours of the day and night during that time and never saw the slightest sign that the man had been using intoxicants. (*The Life of Walter Quintin Gresham*, by Matilda Gresham, Vol. I, p. 182.) If Rawlins did make such a collection, it is not in the National Archives today. A search made there in the winter of 1959 revealed only a letter of inquiry written in 1909 by Colonel Gresham's son, Otto Gresham, who sought to find the report which the colonel had made.

27. James Grant Wilson, *The Life and Campaigns of General Grant*, p. 37.

28. Letter of Julia Grant to E. B. Washburne, May 16, 1862, in the Grant Papers, Illinois State Historical Library.

29. Letter of Joseph Medill to Washburne, May 24, 1862, in the Washburne Papers.

30. O. R., Vol. X, Part One, p. 99.
31. Letter of Grant to "E. B. Washburn" May 14, 1862, in the Washburne Papers. This letter, incidentally, shows how Grant's carelessness about spelling extended even to his method of writing Washburne's name in his letters. As often as not Grant would omit the final "e."
32. Col. Chetlain, who was in a position to know the headquarters opinion of the battle, wrote (in *Recollections of Seventy Years*, p. 89) that Grant's staff officers always believed that if Lew Wallace's division had come promptly into action when ordered the battle would have been won by midafternoon of April 6. This belief is of course debatable, but it apparently was the basis for the position Grant took in his letter to Washburne.

CHAPTER THIRTEEN

The Unpronounceable Man

1. *New York World*'s correspondence, printed in the *Chicago Times*, May 19, 1862; letter from Henry Doolittle to Senator James R. Doolittle of Wisconsin, undated, in the Doolittle Papers, State Historical Library, Madison, Wis.
2. On June 4 Halleck made his attitude explicit by writing to Pope: "Our main object now is to get the enemy far enough south to relieve our railroads from danger of an immediate attack. There is no object in bringing on a battle if this object can be obtained without one." (O. R., Vol. X, Part Two, p. 252.) Grant said that in the advance on Corinth Federal commanders were warned not to bring on an engagement "and informed in so many words it would be better to retreat than to fight." (Grant's Memoirs, Vol. I, p. 373.)
3. O. R., Vol. X, Part Two, pp. 138–139, 144.
4. Same, p. 144.
5. William F. G. Shanks, *Personal Recollections of Distinguished Generals*, pp. 80–81. See also a speech by General James H. Wilson before survivors of the Army of the Cumberland at Columbus, Ohio, in 1897, quoted in *History of the 68th Indiana Infantry*, by Edwin W. High. In his Memoirs (Vol. I, p. 372), Grant remarks that none of Buell's Shiloh reports were submitted to him — an irregularity which caused him to refuse to write a full report on the battle himself.
6. Letter of Grant to Halleck dated May 11, 1862, in the Civil War Papers of the Missouri Historical Society.
7. O. R., Vol. X, Part Two, pp. 182–183.
8. Grant's Memoirs, Vol. I, p. 377.
9. O. R., Vol. X, Part Two, pp. 166, 172, 214. On May 22 Governor Oliver P. Morton of Indiana, who was then visiting the army, wrote

Stanton that the Federals appeared to be outnumbered and should be reinforced. (Same, p. 209.)

10. O. R., Vol. X, Part Two, pp. 439–440, 618.
11. Leander Stillwell, *The Story of a Common Soldier;* Robert L. Kimberly and Ephraim S. Holloway, *The 41st Ohio Veteran Volunteer Infantry*, p. 28; *Chicago Times* for June 3, 1862; William Witherby Brown, "Reminiscences of an Ohio Volunteer," in the *Ohio Archaeological and Historical Quarterly*, Vol. 48; Alexis Coupe, *History of the 15th Ohio;* letter of Edward D. Kittoe, dated June 24, and letter of Colonel J. E. Smith, dated June 1, to Congressman Washburne, both in the Washburne Papers; C. C. Briant, *History of the 6th Regiment Indiana Volunteer Infantry*, pp. 130–131; E. W. Keil, *History of the 35th Ohio Regiment Volunteer Infantry;* Charles F. Hubert, *History of the 50th Illinois Infantry*, p. 119; Charles H. Smith, *History of Fuller's Ohio Brigade*, p. 72.
12. *Personal Memoirs of P. H. Sheridan*, Vol. I, pp. 152–153.
13. Stanley Horn, *The Army of Tennessee*, p. 148.
14. Grant's Memoirs, Vol. I, p. 378; interview with Webster in the *New York Times*, reprinted in the *Cincinnati Commercial* October 26, 1867.
15. O. R., Vol. X, Part Two, p. 130; letter of W. T. Sherman to R. W. Scott, dated Sept. 6, 1885, in the Sherman Papers.
16. Richardson, pp. 257–258. See also the same author's *Siege, Dungeon and Escape*, p. 244.
17. Address by Brevet Major General William W. Belknap, printed in *War Sketches and Incidents*, by the Iowa Loyal Legion, pp. 161–162.
18. Correspondence of the *New York World*, reprinted in the *Chicago Times* May 19, 1862.
19. Letter of W. R. Rowley to Washburne, May 24, 1862; note of same date, Rowley to Washburne; letter from Colonel Clark B. Lagow to Washburne, also dated May 24; from the Washburne Papers.
20. Letter of U. S. Grant to the Reverend J. M. Vincent, dated May 25, 1862, loaned by Mrs. George Vincent of Westport, Connecticut: in the Lloyd Lewis papers.
21. Memoirs of General W. T. Sherman, Vol. I, p. 255. The manuscript of Sherman's work, in the Library of Congress, differs slightly from the published version.
22. Grant to Washburne, letter dated June 1, 1862, from the Grant Papers in the Illinois State Historical Library. Grant's Memoirs give his brief reference to Sherman's visits in Vol. I, p. 385.
23. Grant to Washburne, June 19, 1862, from the Washburne Papers.
24. Grant to Washburne, July 22, 1862, from the Washburne Papers.
25. Halleck to Mrs. Halleck, letter dated Aug. 13, 1862, in the Oliver Barrett Collection.
26. See also Badeau, Vol. I, pp. 120–121.

27. O. R., Vol. X, Part Two, pp. 225–226.
28. Lieutenant S. D. Thompson, *Recollections with the 3rd Iowa*, p. 275; letter of John E. Smith to Washburne, dated June 17, 1862, in the Washburne Papers; Grant's Memoirs, Vol. I, p. 381; *B. & L.*, Vol. II, p. 720.
29. O. R., Vol. X, Part Two, p. 235; Vol. X, Part One, pp. 774–86.
30. O. R., Vol. X, Part One, p. 671; Vol. XVI, Part Two, pp. 14, 63; letter of Grant to Washburne dated July 22, 1863, in the Washburne Papers.
31. O. R., Vol. XVI, Part Two, p. 14; Vol. XVII, Part Two, p. 5; Vol. X, Part Two, p. 254.
32. O. R., Vol. XVII, Part Two, p. 9.
33. O. R., Vol. X, Part Two, pp. 111, 114–118, 124–125, 236, 243–244, 264–265; Vol. XVI, Part Two, pp. 9, 46.
34. For the use which Bragg made of the breathing spell granted by the Federals after Corinth, see Stanley Horn, *Army of Tennessee*, pp. 157–159.
35. In this paragraph I am following a suggestion advanced by Major General U. S. Grant III, grandson of the Civil War General, who wrote a lucid summary of the argument for Lloyd Lewis.
36. O. R., Vol. XVI, Part Two, p. 3.
37. O. R., Vol. XVII, Part Two, pp. 29–30.
38. Grant's letter to Washburne, dated June 19, 1862, in the Washburne Papers.
39. Grant's Memoirs, Vol. I, pp. 368–369.

CHAPTER FOURTEEN

"To Be Terrible on the Enemy"

1. O. R., Vol. XVI, Part Two, p. 8.
2. O. R., Vol. XVII, Part Two, pp. 17, 20; Vol. XII, Part Three, p. 435.
3. O. R., Vol. XVI, Part Two, pp. 69–70. It is a matter of no importance but of some interest that while Stanton was sending this dispatch — which proposed to cripple the entire campaign in the West in order to restore the campaign in Virginia — McClellan was writing his famous dispatch to Stanton demanding immediate reinforcements of from ten to twenty thousand men, and was saying bitterly: "If I save this army now, I tell you plainly that I owe no thanks to you, or any other persons in Washington." (*McClellan's Own Story*, pp. 424–425.)
4. O. R., Vol. XVII, Part Two, pp. 55–56; Vol. XVI, Part Two, pp. 60, 74–76.
5. O. R., Vol. XVI, Part Two, p. 75.
6. O. R., Vol. XVI, Part Two, pp. 82, 88, 100, 117.
7. Halleck to Farragut, O. R., Vol. XV, p. 517. The message from

Stanton announcing Halleck's appointment to the top command is Vol. XVII, Part Two, p. 90.

8. O. R., Vol. XVII, Part Two, pp. 90, 101; Grant's Memoirs, Vol. I, p. 393.

9. O. R., Vol. XVII, Part Two, pp. 90–91; Badeau, Vol. I, pp. 107–108.

10. O. R., Vol. XVII, Part Two, pp. 46–47, 68. It should be remarked that there was a good deal of substance to Halleck's complaint that at Memphis Grant was too remote from most of the troops in his district to exercise effective day-to-day direction of them.

11. Grant's Memoirs, Vol. I, pp. 394–395.

12. O. R., Vol. XVII, Part Two, pp. 78, 84.

13. Correspondence of the *Chicago Times,* dispatch from Memphis dated June 7, printed June 10, 1862.

14. Grant to Halleck, O. R., Vol. XVII, Part Two, p. 88; Grant's Memoirs, Vol. I, p. 390.

15. General Orders No. 60, O. R., Vol. XVII, Part Two, p. 69.

16. O. R., Vol. XVI, Part Two, p. 14.

17. Testimony of Gen. Lovell H. Rousseau at the Buell Court of Inquiry, O. R., Vol. XVI, Part One, p. 355.

18. Matilda Gresham, *Life of Walter Quintin Gresham,* Vol. I, p. 178; Albion W. Tourgee, *The Story of a Thousand,* p. 72; the Rev. J. B. Rogers, "War Pictures"; Captain S. S. Canfield, "History of the 21st Regiment Ohio Volunteer Infantry"; the Rev. W. W. Lyle, *Lights and Shadows of Army Life,* pp. 341–343; memoir of Meade Holmes, Jr., *A Soldier of the Cumberland,* pp. 104, 116; letter of Dr. Edward Kittoe to E. B. Washburne, dated June 24, 1862, in the Washburne Papers.

19. Halleck to Grant, O. R., Vol. XVII, Part Two, p. 150.

20. Grant to Halleck, O. R., Vol. XVII, Part Two, p. 82; Papers of Grenville Dodge, Vol. II, p. 72, letter dated July 22, 1862; Lieut. S. D. Thompson, *Recollections with the Third Iowa,* p. 275 ff.; O. R., Vol. XVII, Part Two, p. 15; Theodore Clarke Smith, *The Life and Letters of James A. Garfield,* Vol. I, p. 373.

21. Clipping from the *Cincinnati Commercial,* March 25, 1862; testimony of Colonel James Fry at the Buell Court of Inquiry, O. R., Vol. XVI, Part One, p. 714; the Rev. Thomas M. Stevenson, *History of the 78th Ohio.*

22. Beauregard to Bragg, O. R., Vol. XVI, Part One, p. 711.

23. Cramer, p. 69; letter of W. R. Rowley to Washburne, dated March 24, 1862, in the Washburne Papers; letter of Grant to Washburne, dated March 22, 1862, in *General Grant's Letters to a Friend,* p. 7.

24. Cramer, pp. 85, 88.

25. *Chicago Tribune,* Aug. 30, 1880; Grant's Memoirs, Vol. I, p. 398; Cramer, p. 84.

26. "War Memoirs" in the *Iowa Historical Record* for October, 1892.

27. Letter of Mrs. William H. Cherry to the Rev. T. M. Hurst, in the

possession of William I. Cherry of St. Louis; Memphis dispatch in the *Chicago Tribune* of July 11, 1862.

28. J. L. Ringwalt, *Anecdotes of General Ulysses S. Grant*, p. 98.
29. Cramer, pp. 87–89.
30. O. R., Vol. XVII, Part Two, pp. 132, 139.
31. Grant's Memoirs, Vol. I, pp. 396–397; returns for the District of West Tennessee, O. R., Vol. XVII, Part Two, pp. 143–144. For messages from Sheridan and Rosecrans, and for Grant's exchange with Halleck, see the same volume, pp. 114, 136, 139, 142. It was this period Grant called "the most anxious period of the war to me" (Memoirs, Vol. I, p. 395).
32. O. R., Vol. XVII, Part Two: Grant to Halleck, p. 155; Halleck to Sherman, p. 186.
33. Sherman to Grant, O. R., Vol. XVII, Part Two, pp. 178–179; correspondence of the *Chicago Times*, June 27, 1862.
34. The Isham affair is described in Sylvanus Cadwallader, *Three Years with Grant*, pp. 3–14. See also the *Chicago Times*, July 31 and Aug. 4, 1862, and the *Chicago Tribune*, Aug. 22, 23 and 30, 1862.

CHAPTER FIFTEEN

Victory, and a New Plan

1. See Grant's reports to Halleck, O. R., Vol. XVII, Part Two, pp. 182, 197, 209–210.
2. For the various reports on the Clarksville debacle, see O. R., Vol. XVI, Part One, pp. 862–863, 865, 868–869. After the war, the cashiered officers got the Presidential orders revoked, so that they finally appear in the records simply as having been mustered out of service. Grant discusses the affair in his Memoirs, Vol. I, pp. 398–399.
3. The best summary of Confederate plans, numbers and movements for this campaign is in Stanley Horn, *Army of Tennessee*, beginning at p. 159.
4. For the interchange of messages between Buell and Grant, see O. R., Vol. XVI, Part Two, pp. 302, 315–316, 325, 333, 337, 344–345. See also the Grant-Halleck messages in O. R., Vol. XVII, Part Two, pp. 209–210, 214, 220, 222, 227.
5. Horn, as Note 3, pp. 172–174; Grant to Halleck, O. R., Vol. XVI, Part Two, p. 333.
6. Sheridan's Memoirs, Vol. I, pp. 181–182; Grant's Memoirs, Vol. I, p. 402.
7. Halleck to Wright, O. R., Vol. XVI, Part Two, p. 421. For the exchange of messages involving Buell and Thomas, see pp. 539–549, 554–555, 619–622.
8. O. R., Vol. XVII, Part Two, pp. 194, 206.

9. Charles W. Wright, *Experiences in the Ranks of Company C, 81st Ohio Volunteer Infantry*, p. 54.
10. Grant's Memoirs, Vol. I, p. 412; C. S. Hamilton, "The Battle of Iuka," *B. & L.*, Vol. II, pp. 734–736; Lieut. Colonel Cyrus Sears, "The Eleventh Ohio Battery at Iuka," in the "Sundry Papers" of the Loyal Legion, Chicago Historical Society; Lyman B. Pierce, *History of the Second Iowa Cavalry*.
11. *History of the 41st Ohio Veteran Volunteer Infantry*, by Robert L. Kimberly and Ephraim S. Holloway, p. 43; John Beatty, *The Citizen Soldier*, p. 229 ff.; *History of the 85th Illinois*, p. 61; *Army Life of an Illinois Soldier*, p. 144.
12. In his report to Halleck on Iuka, Grant gave Rosecrans good marks: "I cannot speak too highly of the energy and skill displayed by General Rosecrans in this attack." (O. R., Vol. XVII, Part One, p. 64.)
13. Rosecrans gives a good description of this fight in *B. & L.*, Vol. II, pp. 737–757. See also *The History of Fuller's Ohio Brigade* by Charles H. Smith, p. 410; D. Leib Ambrose, "*History of the Seventh Illinois Infantry*," p. 112; Capt. Henry M. Neil, pamphlet, *A Battery at Close Quarters;* Charles F. Hubert, *History of the 50th Illinois Infantry*, pp. 147–148.
14. Rosecrans, as Note 13, p. 753; *History of Fuller's Ohio Brigade*, p. 89.
15. Grant to Halleck, October 5, in O. R., Vol. XVII, Part One, p. 155.
16. Grant to Halleck, October 8, O. R., Vol. XVII, Part One, p. 156. Grant discusses the pursuit at length in his Memoirs, Vol. I, pp. 417–419. To Halleck, on October 30, he wrote: "Two days hard fighting without rest had probably so fatigued the troops as to make hard earlier pursuit impossible. I regretted this, as the enemy would have been compelled to abandon most of his artillery and transportation in the difficult roads of the Hatchie crossing had the pursuit commenced then." (O. R., Vol. XVII, Part One, p. 158.) Rosecrans's protest at his recall is in the same volume, pp. 163–164. There is a good summary of the campaign in Greene, pp. 51–53.
17. Horn, p. 168.
18. Rosecrans to Halleck, Oct. 22, O. R., Vol. XVII, Part Two, p. 286. Rosecrans's message to Grant is in the same volume, p. 283.
19. "Personal Biography of Maj. Gen. Grenville M. Dodge," typewritten copy in the Iowa State Department of History and Archives, Vol. I, pp. 78–79; O. R., Vol. XVII, Part Two, p. 307; speech by Dodge before the New York Commandery of the Loyal Legion.
20. Thomas to Halleck, O. R., Vol. XVI, Part Two, p. 657; Halleck's reply, and Thomas's final note, are in the same volume, p. 663. What is of primary interest here is Thomas's considered opinion that East Tennessee could have been taken and held in the fall of 1861. Most other Union officers felt otherwise, and critics since then have often assumed that Lincoln's insistence on such a move simply shows that

the President did not know what he was asking. It is illuminating to
realize that an officer of Thomas's stature felt that Lincoln was entirely right.
21. O. R., Vol. XVII, Part Two, p. 278.
22. Same, pp. 225, 240–241.
23. Same, Sherman to Grant, Oct. 4, pp. 260–261. For the business of
    sending new regiments to Grant, see O. R., Vol. XVI, Part Two,
    pp. 574–575, 588–589, 656.
24. Grant to Halleck, October 26, O. R., Vol. XVII, Part Two, p. 296.

CHAPTER SIXTEEN

Forrest, Van Dorn and McClernand

1. McClernand set forth his views in detail in a long memorandum to
   Secretary Stanton dated November 10, 1862, in O. R., Vol. XVII,
   Part Two, pp. 332–334. See also the unpublished manuscript biogra-
   phy written by his son, General Edward J. McClernand, in the Illi-
   nois State Historical Library. According to this manuscript, Mc-
   Clernand presented his argument to President Lincoln verbally in
   September, 1862.
2. For the early cabinet discussions of this Mississippi project, see David
   Donald, ed., *Inside Lincoln's Cabinet: the Civil War Diaries of
   Salmon P. Chase*, pp. 107–108. Lincoln's note is in Basler, *Collected
   Works*, Vol. V, p. 484.
3. Chase's diary entries, in Donald, as Note 2, pp. 162–163; John E.
   Smith to E. B. Washburne, letter dated June 17, 1862, in the Wash-
   burne Papers; Grant to Halleck, December 13, 1862, O. R., Vol. LII,
   Part One, p. 314; Grant's Memoirs, Vol. I, p. 426; Halleck to
   Gamble, O. R., Series Three, Vol. II, pp. 703–704. See also Badeau,
   Vol. I, p. 129.
4. The order to McClernand is in O. R., Vol. XVII, Part Two, p. 282.
   for Lincoln's endorsement, see Basler, *Collected Works*, Vol. V,
   p. 468. Although Stanton's order was marked "Confidential," Lincoln's endorsement authorized McClernand to show it to the Midwestern governors with whom he would be dealing.
5. Halleck to Banks, O. R., Series Three, Vol. II, pp. 736–737.
6. O. R., Vol. XVII, Part One, pp. 466–467; Vol. XVII, Part Two, pp.
   315, 320, 322–323.
7. For the Grant-Halleck exchange, see O. R., Vol. XVII, Part One,
   p. 469.
8. Grant to Sherman, O. R., Vol. XVII, Part Two, pp. 347–348.
9. Editorial in the *Chicago Tribune* for November 25, 1862.
10. O. R., Vol. XVII, Part Two: Grant to Sherman, pp. 336, 366–367;
    to General Allen, p. 355; Grant to Halleck and Halleck to Grant,

O. R., Vol. XVII, Part One, p. 470. For Allen, see Garland, pp. 128–129.

11. O. R., Vol. XVII, Part One, p. 471.
12. Grant outlines his plans in dispatches to Halleck, O. R., Vol. XVII, Part One, p. 472, and in his orders to Colonel Dickey, Vol. XVII, Part Two, p. 388. Sherman's understanding of the program is set forth in a long dispatch to Admiral Porter in Vol. XVII, Part Two, p. 392.
13. O. R., Vol. XVII, Part One, pp. 472–474.
14. McClernand to Stanton, O. R., Vol. XVII, Part Two, pp. 371–372; to Lincoln, p. 401; Halleck to Curtis, p. 402.
15. O. R., Vol. XVII, Part Two, pp. 402–403, 408, 410.
16. Cramer, pp. 96–97.
17. O. R., Vol. XVII, Part Two, pp. 326–327, 350; *Army Memoirs of Lucius W. Barber*, p. 91; *Downing's War Diary*, pp. 56, 92.
18. The telegrams regarding Forrest's move, and the measures taken to meet it, are in O. R., Vol. XVII, Part Two, pp. 399, 400, 404, 415, 426–427, 428, 430, 435. An admirable account of Forrest's raid is to be found in Robert Selph Henry, pp. 108–121.
19. O. R., Vol. XVII, Part Two, pp. 415, 420.
20. Same, pp. 425, 432–433. Regarding the division of his command into four army corps, Grant's postwar comment is significant: "This interfered with my plans but probably resulted in my ultimately taking the command in person." (Grant's Memoirs, Vol. I, p. 432.)
21. Same, pp. 461–462.
22. Grant's Memoirs, Vol. I, pp. 430–431. See also the manuscript biography of McClernand, previously cited Note 1.
23. Grant to "Commanding Officer Expedition Down the Mississippi," and Grant to "Commanding Officer Memphis," O. R., Vol. XVII, Part Two, pp. 463, 480. Grant describes the Holly Springs debacle in Vol. XVII, Part One, pp. 477–478. At least one contemporary report blamed the loss of Holly Springs on excessive drinking by officers at that post. Major John J. Mudd of the 2nd Illinois Cavalry, reporting to Rawlins on December 27, insisted: "This disaster is another added to the long list occasioned by the drunkenness or inefficiency of commanding officers. I cannot doubt but that the place could have been successfully defended by even half the force here had suitable precautions been taken and the infantry been concentrated, their officers in camp with them and prepared to fight." (O. R., Vol. XVII, Part One, p. 513.)
24. Sherman's account of the battle is in his Memoirs, Vol. I, pp. 290–292. For a strikingly different narrative by Brigadier General George W. Morgan, see *B. & L.*, Vol. III, pp. 462–470. See also Francis Vinton Greene, *The Mississippi*, pp. 75–79. (Hereafter cited as Greene.)

25. O. R., Vol. XVII, Part Two, pp. 528–530, 534–535; Sherman's Memoirs, Vol. I, p. 296.
26. Sherman's Memoirs, Vol. I, p. 296 ff.
27. Halleck to Grant, O. R., Vol. XVII, Part Two, p. 542.
28. O. R., Vol. XVII, Part Two, pp. 546–547, 553–554, 555, 559. Note that Grant presently reversed himself, after learning that it was Sherman who had originally suggested the move on Arkansas Post, and commended the venture; and this is usually taken as an indication that he was simply playing favorites, praising in Sherman what he had denounced in McClernand. Actually, there was a little more to it than that. When he first heard of the move, he knew only that McClernand, who was hard to control and who seemed to want independence of command above all other things, had taken the army off into Arkansas for what might well be an extended tour just when it was essential to keep the troops in the vicinity of Vicksburg because of the prospective arrival of Banks. When he changed his tune the situation itself had changed materially.
29. O. R., Vol. XVII, Part Two: Halleck to Grant, p. 555; Grant to McPherson, pp. 545, 557.

CHAPTER SEVENTEEN

A Noun Is the Name of a Thing

1. Cramer, p. 97. The story of the attempted bribe was printed in the *Missouri Republican*, July 25, 1885. Excellent accounts of the pressures generated by the re-opened cotton trade can be found in M. B. Hammond, *The Cotton Industry: an Essay in American Economic History*, pp. 103, 261; Charles W. Ramsdell, *Behind the Lines in the Southern Confederacy*, pp. 57–59; Joseph H. Parks, "A Confederate Trade Center under Federal Occupation," in the *Journal of Southern History*, Vol. VII, No. 3, p. 292. See also O. R., Series Four, Vol. II, p. 151, and Series One, Vol. XVII, Part Two, pp. 839–840.
2. *Chicago Tribune*, Oct. 6, 1862; *New York Times*, Dec. 24, 1862.
3. Grant's General Orders No. 64, dated July 25, 1862, are in O. R., Vol. XVII, Part Two, p. 123. See also O. R., Series Three, Vol. II: Sherman to Grant, p. 353; Sherman to Chase, p. 349.
4. Grant's General Orders No. 8, dated Nov. 19, 1862, in O. R., Vol. LII, Part One, pp. 302–303.
5. Sherman's Memoirs, Vol. I, pp. 266–268; M. A. DeWolfe Howe, ed., *Home Letters of General Sherman*, p. 232.
6. O. R., Vol. XXIV, Part Three, p. 631; O. R., Series Four, Vol. III, pp. 645–648; Ramsdell, as Note 1, p. 107; Charles A. Dana, *Recollections of the Civil War*, pp. 17–20; Grant to Chase, July 31, 1863, in O. R., Vol. XXIV, Part 3, p. 538; Edmund Newsome, *Experiences in the War*, p. 22.

7. Letters from J. Russell Jones to Washburne, dated January 28, February 5 and February 15, 1863, in the Washburne Papers.

8. The deal between Jesse Grant and the Mack brothers is set forth in detail in a lawsuit which Jesse filed against the brothers in the Cincinnati courts early in 1863 — a bit of litigation which the judge nonsuited, and which is described in the *New York Tribune*, September 19, 1872. See also Nelson Cross, *The Modern Ulysses, LL.D.: His Political Record*, p. 76; and William B. Hesseltine, *Ulysses S. Grant, Politician*, pp. 30–31. There is an extensive discussion of the rather singular relationship between Grant and his father in *Captain Sam Grant*.

9. Grant's General Orders No. 11, dated December 17, 1862, in O. R., Vol. XVII, Part Two, p. 424. The visit of Jesse and the Macks, and Grant's response to it, is described in Cadwallader, pp. 45–50.

10. O. R., Vol. XVII, Part Two, pp. 330, 337, 421–422.

11. Dana, *Recollections*, p. 18; Hovey to Brig. Gen. Fred F. Steele, December 5, 1862, in O. R., Vol. XVII, Part One, p. 532. Sherman's correspondence, and that of other Army officers for this period, bristles with references to the activities of "Jewish traders."

12. *Chicago Tribune* for April 9, 1885, an interview with Rabbi Browne, who quoted his own diary entry for an interview with Grant on Aug. 27, 1875.

13. The details as to Colonel Dubois are in the *Chicago Tribune* for December 18, 1862, in a dispatch from Oxford, Mississippi. See also J. R. Grant's letter to Washburne dated Jan. 20, 1863, in the Washburne Papers; undated clipping from the *Cincinnati Commercial*, apparently for early January, 1863, in the Lloyd Lewis Papers; *New York World*, August 18, 1863; Otto Eisenschiml, "Anti-Semitism in Lincoln's Times," in the *Chicago Forum*, Vol. I, No. I, p. 11.

14. O. R., Vol. XVII, Part Two, pp. 530, 544; Vol. XIV, Part One, p. 9.

15. Washburne to Lincoln, dated January 6, 1863, in the R. T. Lincoln Collection, Library of Congress.

16. John Eaton, *Grant, Lincoln and the Freedmen* (cited hereafter as Eaton), pp. 2–3; *Chicago Times*, June 3, 1863; John Beatty, *The Citizen Soldier*.

17. O. R., Vol. XVII, Part One, p. 481; Vol. LII, Part One, p. 323; O. R., Series Three, Vol. II, pp. 569, 663.

18. Eaton, pp. 5–6.

19. The whole of this account of the work for the contrabands is taken from Eaton, pp. 18–39. The book is recommended as an absorbing narrative by a conscientious and thoughtful observer. For a sample of the average soldier's reaction, see *Army Life of an Illinois Soldier*, p. 83: "I don't care a damn for the darkies, and you know that they are better off with their masters 50 times over than with us, but of course you know I couldn't help to send a runaway nigger back."

20. Benjamin A. Quarles, *The Negro in the Civil War*, pp. 108–119, 166;

Dudley Taylor Cornish, *The Sable Arm: Negro Troops in the Union Army, 1861–1865*, pp. 46–47, 50.

CHAPTER EIGHTEEN

Winter of Discontent

1. Oran Perry, pamphlet, *Recollections of the Civil War*, p. 17; letter of J. Russell Jones to Washburne, dated January 28, 1863, in the Washburne Papers.
2. *Army Memoirs of Lucius W. Barber*, p. 74; Lieutenant W. H. Bentley, *History of the 77th Illinois Volunteer Infantry*; Joseph Grecian, *History of the 83rd Regiment Indiana Volunteer Infantry*, p. 22; H. Allen Gosnell, *Guns on the Western Waters*, p. 146; Charles Beneulyn Johnson, *Muskets and Medicine; or, Army Life in the Sixties*, pp. 60–61; Ms. letter of George L. Lang of the 12th Wisconsin, dated January 1, 1863; B. F. Stevenson, *Letters from the Army*, pp. 178, 184.
3. Ms. letter of Isaac Jackson, of the 83rd Ohio, dated March 23, 1863; *Reminiscences of the Civil War: from Diaries of Members of the 103rd Illinois Volunteer Infantry*, p. 18.
4. *New York World*, issues dated January 14, January 15, January 20 and January 26, 1863; *New York Times*, issue dated February 23, 1863.
5. Letter of Joseph Medill to E. H. Washburne, dated January 16, 1863, in the Washburne Papers.
6. Shortly after Grant's arrival on the Mississippi, Russ Jones saw him "out on the point with 1½ miles of the city" and reported, "with a glass everything is perfectly distinct." Letter of Jones to Washburne, dated January 29, 1863, in the Washburne Papers.
7. Grant's Memoirs, Vol. I, p. 435; Badeau, Vol. I, pp. 140–141; Charles A. Dana and James H. Wilson, *The Life of Ulysses S. Grant*, pp. 98–99.
8. O. R., Vol. XVII, Part Two, p. 542.
9. Department of Tennessee returns for January 31, 1863, O. R., Vol. XXIV, Part Three, p. 20.
10. *Chicago Journal* for February 23, 1863, printing a Vicksburg dispatch dated February 15.
11. Letter of General Washburn to Congressman Washburne, dated January 28, 1863, from Gaillard Hunt, *Israel, Elihu and Cadwallader Washburne: a Chapter in American Biography*, p. 340; O. R., Vol. XVII, Part Two: Sherman to Grant, January 17, pp. 570–571; Grant to Halleck, January 18, p. 573.
12. Grant's order, and the exchange between Grant and McClernand, are in O. R., Vol. XXIV, Part One, pp. 11–13; and Part Three, p. 19.

For a slightly earlier note in which Lincoln warned McClernand, "I have too many *family* controversies (so to speak) already on my hands, to voluntarily, or so long as I can avoid it, take up another," see Basler, *Collected Works*, Vol. VI, p. 155.

13. Badeau, Vol. I, pp. 163–165; Greene, pp. 21–23. Oddly enough, the Mississippi did break through the peninsula some years after the war, although it did not precisely follow the canal on which Grant's soldiers worked so hard. The hairpin bend no longer exists, and the main channel of the river no longer flows by the Vicksburg waterfront.

14. Grant to Porter, O. R., Vol. XXIV, Part Three, p. 17; Greene, pp. 95–96. Grant's geography was hazy. In going from Lake Providence to the Red River, one would not navigate the Ouachita River.

15. O. R., Vol. XXIV, Part Three: Grant to McPherson, p. 33; Sherman to Grant, p. 32.

16. James H. Wilson, *Under the Old Flag*, Vol. I, pp. 133 ff.; Greene, p. 97. Grant's attitude toward this venture is expressed in a letter he wrote to Sherman on March 27, in which he said he had banked so heavily on the Yazoo project "that I have made really but little calculation upon reaching Vicksburg by any other than Haynes Bluff." (O. R., Vol. XXIV, Part Three, p. 127.) Grant's note to McClernand is in the same volume, p. 7. Throughout the campaign, Federal officers uniformly confused Snyder's Bluff, the site of the Confederate strongpoint, with Haynes Bluff, which lay three miles further upstream and was only lightly fortified.

17. Letters of W. T. Sherman to Mrs. Sherman, dated January 28 and February 15, in the Sherman Papers; Badeau, Vol. I, p. 165.

18. Edmund Newsome, *Experiences in the War*, diary entry for February 23; William W. Belknap, ed., *History of the 15th Regiment Iowa Veteran Volunteer Infantry*, pp. 245–247; Badeau, Vol. I, pp. 167–168. For Grant's unavailing effort to get enough small boats to carry his army through the Lake Providence route, see O. R., Vol. XXIV, Part Three, pp. 102–103, 115, 117, 131.

19. Wilson, *Under the Old Flag*, Vol. I, pp. 15–52; O. R., Vol. XXIV, Part One, p. 374; letter of J. Russell Jones to Washburne, dated February 5, in the Washburne Papers.

20. Badeau, Vol. I, pp. 169–171; O. R., Vol. XXIV, Part Three, pp. 35–36.

21. O. R., Vol. XXIV, Part One, pp. 379–381; Badeau, Vol. I, p. 172; A. T. Mahan, "The Gulf and Inland Waters," pp. 141–146. For Porter's account, see his *Incidents and Anecdotes of the Civil War*, pp. 139–141. (Hereafter cited as Porter.)

22. Porter, pp. 145–171; Badeau, Vol. I, pp. 173–178.

23. Grant to Washburne, letter dated March 10, 1863, in the Grant Papers, Illinois State Historical Library; Grant to Banks, letter dated

March 22, in O. R., Vol. XXIV, Part Three, p. 126; C. C. Washburn to E. H. Washburne, letter dated April 11, in Gaillard Hunt, pp. 341–342.

CHAPTER NINETEEN

The Man on the River

1. Charles A. Dana, *Recollections of the Civil War*, pp. 20–30; *Three Years with Grant*, p. 61. There is a good sketch of Dana by Allan Nevins in the Dictionary of American Biography, Vol. V. Grant's shift of his headquarters to Milliken's Bend is noted in a dispatch to the *Chicago Times*, printed on April 13, 1863.
2. Dana, pp. 61–62.
3. *New York World* of February 20, 1863, printing a dispatch dated February 13; *New York Times* for June 21, with a dispatch dated June 4.
4. Interview with Dr. E. A. Duncan, McPherson's former medical officer, printed in the *National Republican*, August 9, 1886; A. O. Marshall, *Army Life*, pp. 274–276.
5. Interview with W. T. Sherman in the *New York Tribune* for August 2, 1885; Marshall, *Army Life*, p. 275.
6. There is no way to document this, yet I think that anyone who plows through the endless pages of dispatches and reports in the Official Records (O. R.) will find that early in the winter of 1863 Grant's dispatches become recognizable. The reader can identify them without looking for the signature; suddenly, Grant's writings become unmistakably Grant. Here, in the midst of barren acres of official jargon, are things written by a man who knows exactly what he is doing and exactly what he wants to say.
7. Mary Livermore, *My Story of the War*, p. 310 ff.
8. *Chicago Tribune* for September 28, 1885, printing a letter from Halstead to Chase dated February 19, 1863.
9. Letters of C. S. Hamilton to Senator Doolittle, dated October 22, 1862, January 30, 1863, and February 11, 1863; in the Doolittle Papers. Hamilton's friendly letter to Grant is in O. R., Vol. XXIV, Part Three, p. 41; for Grant's letter to Halleck, and additional correspondence on the matter, see the same volume, pp. 137–151.
10. Eaton, pp. 64, 89–90. Lincoln's remark about Grant's whisky has come to be regarded as myth, apparently because similar stories have been told about other soldiers in earlier wars. Eaton, however, is accepted as a reliable source on other matters; the story is precisely the sort of story Lincoln would tell; and this writer can see no good reason for doubting its authenticity.
11. Emmet Crozier, pp. 292–305, gives an extended account of the Knox affair. The documents in the case are in O. R., Vol. XVII, Part Two,

p. 890 ff. See also Sylvanus Cadwallader, *Three Years with Grant*, pp. 45–46.

12. Sylvanus Cadwallader, *Three Years with Grant*, pp. 19–22.
13. *New York World* for March 12, April 10, 1863; *Chicago Journal* dated March 20; *New York Times* for April 4 and April 13.
14. Richardson, p. 295. McPherson was a man of character, deeply devoted to Grant. If he could casually invite the General to stop working and have a drink, the old legend that the inner circle at headquarters conspired tirelessly to keep Grant away from the bottle must have a flaw in it. Rawlins was a dedicated teetotaler, to be sure — and his unremitting campaign to protect Grant left a lasting stain on Grant's name by making it appear that if left to himself Grant would give way to an appetite he could not control. McPherson appears not to have had this feeling; the obvious implication is that he found Grant to be like most other generals — a man who could occasionally enjoy a drink without immediately lapsing into drunkenness.
15. Grant to Hurlbut, January 3, 1863; O. R., Vol. XVII, Part Two, p. 525.
16. Grant's Special Field Orders No. 2, dated February 12, in O. R., Vol. XXIV, Part Three, pp. 46–47; also Grant to McPherson, p. 105; Halleck to Grant, p. 157.
17. O. R., Vol. XXIV, Part Three, pp. 186–187.
18. George W. Williams, *A History of the Negro Troops in the War of the Rebellion*, p. 110.
19. *History of the 53rd Regiment Ohio Volunteer Infantry*, p. 103; *Army Life of an Illinois Soldier*, pp. 166–167, 183–184.
20. Grant's General Orders No. 25, dated April 22, in O. R., Vol. XXIV, Part Three, p. 220.
21. O.R., Series Two, Vol. IV, pp. 857, 916; Series Four, Vol. II, p. 345.

CHAPTER TWENTY

An End to Worry

1. On April 2 Halleck notified Grant that President Lincoln "seems to be rather impatient" about the Vicksburg campaign, and asked if Grant could not co-operate with Banks in an assault on Port Hudson. (Badeau, Vol. I, p. 181.)
2. O. R. Vol. XXIV, Part Three: Grant to Banks, dated March 22, p. 125; Grant to Farragut, March 23, p. 131. See also the report of Col. L. B. Parsons, p. 115.
3. There is an engaging account of this advance in Oran Perry's pamphlet, *Recollections of the Civil War*, pp. 20–23.
4. O. R., Vol. XXIV, Part Three: McClernand to Grant, April 4, pp. 170–71; Grant to Porter, March 29, pp. 151–152.

5. O. R., Vol. XXIV, Part Three: Porter to Grant, March 29, p. 152; Grant to Porter, April 2, p. 168. Grant continues to refer to Snyder's Bluff as "Haynes'."

6. J. D. Ringwalt, "Anecdotes of General Grant," pp. 63–64; Dana, pp. 32–33; Sherman to Grant, April 8, O. R., Vol. XXIV, Part Three, p. 180; Badeau, Vol. I, pp. 183, 616–618. Sherman's profound distrust of McClernand caused him to urge Rawlins that corps commanders should be required to go on record, in writing, before the new campaign began. "There are men," wrote Sherman, most certainly thinking of McClernand, "who will, in any result falling below the popular standard, claim that their advice was unheeded and that fatal consequences resulted therefrom."

    It is interesting to note that Frank Blair had just written to his brother Montgomery that Sherman "is the only man of brains in this army," adding that Grant usually did as Sherman advised. He went on to say that Grant "is surrounded by a bunch of fools" who tried to undercut Sherman's good ideas. (Blair Family Papers, Library of Congress: letter of Frank Blair to "Dear Judge" dated March 10, 1863.)

7. General John B. Sanborn, "The Campaign Against Vicksburg," in Vol. II, *Glimpses of the Nation's Struggle*, p. 122.

8. A. T. Mahan, *The Gulf and Inland Waters*, pp. 154–156; Porter, pp. 175–177; *Pen and Powder*, by Franc B. Wilkie; Dana, pp. 36–37; Wilson, *Under the Old Flag*, Vol. I, pp. 163–164; Brevet Brigadier General Joseph Stockton, War Diary, pamphlet; Sherman's Memoirs, Vol. I, p. 318; Badeau, Vol. I, pp. 190–191.

9. Wilson, *Under the Old Flag*, Vol. I, p. 164; O. R., Vol. XXIV, Part Three, p. 190; Grant's Memoirs, Vol. I, pp. 466, 471.

10. Greene, pp. 110–112; O. R., Vol. XXIV, Part Three, pp. 188, 201, 205, 211, 212–213; *Confidential Correspondence of Gustavus V. Fox*, Vol. I, p. 170.

11. William Conant Church, "*U. S. Grant and the Period of National Preservation and Reconstruction*," p. 160.

12. General John B. Sanborn, p. 126; *Muskets and Medicine*, pp. 73–74; *Downing's War Diary*, p. 113; *History of the 16th Battery of Ohio Volunteer Light Infantry*, compiled by a committee, p. 30; manuscript letters of Abram S. Funk of the 35th Iowa Volunteers.

13. Wilson, *Under the Old Flag*, Vol. I, pp. 168–169; *History of the 16th Battery of Ohio Volunteer Light Artillery*, p. 33; "*Story of the Service of Company E and of the 12th Wisconsin Regiment*, written by One of the Boys," p. 179; O. R., Vol. XXIV, Part One, p. 47.

14. S. H. M. Byers, "Some Recollections of Grant," in *The Annals of the War Written by Leading Participants*, pp. 342–343.

15. Sanborn, p. 125; Dana, pp. 43–44.

16. O. R., Vol. XXIV, Part Three, p. 231.

17. On February 13, Grant notified Hurlbut at Memphis to give some thought to this project, and he specified Grierson as a good man to lead the expedition. (O. R., Vol. XXIV, Part Three, pp. 50, 95.) For a detailed account of the raid, see D. Alexander Brown, *Grierson's Raid*.

18. O. R., Vol. XXIV, Part Three: Grant to Sherman, p. 240; Sherman to Grant, pp. 242–244; W. L. B. Jenney, "Personal Recollections of Vicksburg," in *Military Essays and Recollections*, Vol. III, p. 258.

19. Apparently no Federal soldier in the war was ever able to transcribe Negro speech accurately. Invariably, the scribe has the Negro saying "dese" and "dar" in one sentence, and "these" and "there" in the next; and no writer felt that he was presenting the slave properly unless he reduced at least part of his speech to a gumbo. The account followed here is from General Isaac H. Elliott, *History of the 33rd Illinois Veteran Volunteer Infantry,* p. 236. In his Memoirs, Vol. I, p. 478, Grant tells of the help given him by this Negro. For the bombardment at Grand Gulf, see *B. & L.*, Vol. III, pp. 567–568.

20. Grant's Memoirs, Vol. I, pp. 480–481.

CHAPTER TWENTY-ONE

"Hardtack! Hardtack!"

1. For the early exchange of messages between Pemberton and Major Gen. C. L. Stevenson, see O. R., Vol. XXIV, Part Three, p. 800.

2. Grant to Halleck, O. R., Vol. XXIV, Part One, pp. 32–33; Greene, pp. 125–133; interview with S. H. M. Byers in the *Washington Post*, July 26, 1885; Jenkin Lloyd Jones, *An Artilleryman's Diary*, entry for May 2, 1863; Grant's Memoirs, Vol. I, pp. 482–484; Grant to McClernand, O. R., Vol. XXIV, Part Three, p. 260.

3. Grant to Halleck, as cited in the preceding footnote. See also Grant to Sherman, O. R., Vol. XXIV, Part Three, pp. 268–269.

4. O. R., Vol. XXIV, Part Three, Pemberton to Davis, pp. 807, 821. Pemberton's wire to Governor Pettus is on p. 821.

5. Same, pp. 248, 268–269.

6. Dana to Stanton, May 4, O. R., Vol. XXIV, Part One, p. 84.

7. O. R., Vol. XXIV, Part Three, pp. 275, 278, 288, 827; Badeau, Vol. I, pp. 224–226.

8. *New York Times* for May 23, 1863, carrying a dispatch dated Bruinsburg, May 1; *Memoir of George Boardman Boomer*, by Amelia M. Stone, letter dated May 6; "Army Life in an Illinois Regiment," pp. 197–199; Brevet Major Henry G. Hicks, "The Campaign and Capture of Vicksburg," in Vol. VI, *Glimpses of the Nation's Struggle*, p. 96; Brevet Major General M. F. Force, "Personal Recollections of the Vicksburg Campaign," in Vol. I, *Sketches of War History*, p. 298.

9. It is interesting to note how precisely the same compulsion rested on the Army of Northern Virginia when Lee took it into Pennsylvania in the campaign which culminated at Gettysburg.

10. O. R., Vol. XV: Gardner to Pemberton, April 29, p. 1059; Pemberton to Gardner, May 4, p. 1071.

11. On May 23 Halleck wrote Banks that the administration had planned to get united action "by authorizing you to assume the entire command as soon as you and General Grant could unite." Opening the river, said Halleck, was the biggest end in view; "I have continually urged these views upon General Grant, and I hope there will be no further delay in adopting them." (O. R., Vol. XXVI, Part One, p. 500.) Grant's commission as major general dated from February 16, 1862; Banks's, from May 16, 1861.

12. Greene, pp. 219–222; 259; Badeau, Vol. I, p. 218; Grant's Memoirs, Vol. I, pp. 491–492; O. R., Vol. XXIV, Part Three, p. 192.

13. Halleck to Banks, April 9 and April 18, O. R., Vol. XV, pp. 700, 702.

14. T. S. Bowers to Maj. Gen. Stephen Hurlbut, May 5, O. R., Vol. XXIV, Part Three, p. 275; Grant, in B. & L., Vol. III, p. 499.

15. O. R., Vol. XXIV, Part Three, pp. 284–285. The estimate of Grant's numbers comes from Badeau, Vol. I, p. 232.

16. Pemberton's state of mind is clear from his dispatches; see O.R., Vol. XXIV, Part Three, pp. 834, 843, 846, 854, 856. His dispatch to Davis is p. 859.

17. Dana, p. 45; Grant's Memoirs, Vol. I, pp. 486–487.

18. Speech of General Frederick Dent Grant, in the printed Proceedings of the Reunion of the Society of the Army of the Tennessee, 1905.

19. O. R., Vol. XXIV, Part Three, pp. 288–289, 297; Grant to McPherson, May 11: original autograph letter in the Rutgers University Library.

20. O. R., Vol. XXIV, Part One, p. 36; B. & L., Vol. III, pp. 503–504.

21. Brevet Major General M. F. Force, p. 300; O. R., Vol. XXIV, Part Three, pp. 873, 876; B. & L., Vol. III, pp. 478–479, 505–506; Gilbert Govan and James W. Livingood, "A Different Valor," pp. 198–201.

22. General Fred Grant, as Note 18. In Three Years with Grant, pp. 73–74, the newspaperman Sylvanus Cadwallader gives a slightly different version of this incident.

23. An Artilleryman's Diary, entry for May 14; Marshall, Army Life, pp. 208–209.

24. Badeau, Vol. I, pp. 252, 654.

25. O. R., Vol. XXIV, Part One, pp. 84, 87.

26. O. R., Vol. XXIV, Part Two, pp. 125–126; A Different Valor, pp. 201–202.

27. Dana, p. 64; Force, p. 302; O. R., Vol. XXIV, Part Two, pp. 41–42, 49, 55–56.

28. B. & L., Vol. III, pp. 503, 510–511; O. R., Vol. XXIV, Part Two, pp. 55, 73, 78, 80, 85.

29. B. & L., Vol. III, p. 513.

30. O. R., Vol. XXIV, Part Three, p. 888.

31. O. R., Vol. XXIV, Part Two, p. 44.

32. Wilson, *Under the Old Flag*, Vol. I, pp. 177–178; Sylvanus Cadwallader, *Three Years with Grant*, p. 83; Badeau, Vol. I, pp. 277–278; O. R., Vol. XXIV, Part Two, p. 138; Marshall, *Army Life*, p. 220 ff.

33. O. R., Vol. XXIV, Part Three, p. 322; Sherman's Memoirs, Vol. I, p. 324.

34. Grant's Memoirs, Vol. I, pp. 524–526. In the account which appears in *B. & L.*, Vol. III, p. 515, an editor's footnote identifies the officer as General Dwight.

35. The whole episode is hazy, and it is hard to feel that one knows precisely what happened. In his Memoirs, Grant was quite definite about it: the message came from Halleck, it was a flat order, and it reached Grant by way of New Orleans, to be forwarded by Banks. This version is given by Badeau, Vol. I, p. 228; Horace Porter got it from Rawlins at City Point in 1865 (*Campaigning with Grant*, p. 364) and Grant gave much the same story to John Russell Young during the world cruise he took after leaving the White House. (Young, *Around the World with General Grant*, Vol. II, pp. 622–623.)

But the sort of order Grant describes simply does not exist. The only thing in the Official Records that is anything like it is the dispatch quoted in the text, which appears in Vol. XXIV, Part One, p. 36; and it is not an order at all. Furthermore, it is marked "Via Memphis, Tenn.," which as a matter of fact is the only route anyone at the War Department would have used at that time to get a message to Grant. A search of the material in the National Archives at Washington fails to bring up the message Grant describes. It is not to be found in the files of the Office of the Secretary of War, in the Halleck papers or in the Records of the Department of the Tennessee.

On top of all of this, Halleck in mid-May, 1863, appears to have blamed Banks rather than Grant for the fact that the two had not joined forces. On May 19, he wrote to Banks; "I learn from the newspapers that you are in possession of Alexandria, and General Grant of Jackson. This may be well enough, so far, but these operations are too eccentric to be pursued. I must again urge that you co-operate as soon as possible with General Grant east of the Mississippi river. Your forces must be united at the earliest possible moment. Otherwise the enemy will concentrate on Grant and crush him. Do all you can to prevent this. . . . I have urged him to keep his forces concentrated as much as possible and not to move east until he gets control of the Mississippi river." (O. R., Vol. XXVI, Part One, pp. 494–495.)

Four days later, on May 23, Halleck wrote Banks that he was sorry Banks continued to pursue a divergent course instead of concentrating with Grant east of the Mississippi river. Halleck feared that the result might be disastrous, and he concluded: "I have urged these views on General Grant and I hope there will be no further delay in adopting them." (O. R., Vol. XXVI, Part One, p. 500.) Between "urging these views" on Grant and sending him an order to go back to the river and help take Port Hudson there is, of course, a world of difference. Banks, naturally, was indignant when he found out what Grant was doing. He forwarded Grant's May 10 dispatch to Halleck on May 12, complaining bitterly and saying that he could do nothing now but go back to Baton Rouge and move against Port Hudson unaided. (O. R., Vol XV, pp. 314–315.) Meanwhile, Banks sent General Dwight to Grand Gulf, and on May 16 Dwight wrote to Banks saying that Grant had taken Jackson and that he, Dwight, would do his best to get from Grant the desired co-operation. He did not, however, feel that Banks should count very heavily on it. (O. R., Vol. XXVI, Part One, p. 489.)

Finally, when Halleck wrote his report on the army's doings during the spring and summer, dated Nov. 15, 1863, he dealt specifically with the story: "It has been alleged, and the allegation has been widely circulated by the press, that General Grant, in the conduct of his campaign, positively disobeyed the instructions of his superiors. It is hardly necessary to remark that General Grant never disobeyed an order or instruction, but always carried out to the best of his ability every wish or suggestion made to him by the government." (O. R., Vol. XXIV, Part One, p. 6.)

In the face of all of this, the biographer can do little more than speculate mildly. It occurs to this writer that General Dwight probably did ride inland from Grand Gulf, encountering Grant on May 17, and that — as one of Bank's loyal subordinates — he strongly urged Grant to return to the river and join Banks in the move against Port Hudson. It is possible that Halleck's May 13 message to Grant reached Grand Gulf while Dwight was there, and that Dwight took it with him and gave it to Grant when he saw him. Grant, in his turn, may have got Halleck's dispatch confused with the verbal protest which Dwight made. All of this, of course, is supposition, but it is the best guess this writer can make.

36. William E. Strong, "The Campaign Against Vicksburg," in Vol. II, *Military Essays and Recollections*, p. 328; Badeau, Vol. I, p. 281; Grant's Memoirs, Vol. I, p. 530; O. R., Vol. XXIV, Part Two, p. 252.

CHAPTER TWENTY-TWO

The Core of Iron

1. William E. Strong, "The Campaign Against Vicksburg," p. 328.
2. O. R., Vol. XXIV, Part Two, pp. 160–165, 206–207, 244, 273, 298.
3. U. S. Grant, "The Vicksburg Campaign," in *B. & L.*, Vol. III, p.

518; O. R., Vol. XXIV, Part One, p. 37; Vol. XXIV, Part Two, p. 170.

4. Report of Grant's engineer officers on the Vicksburg Campaign, O. R., Vol. XXIV, Part Two, p. 177.

5. Johnston to Seddon, O. R., Vol. XXIV, Part One, p. 222.

6. Grant to Banks, May 31, in O. R., Vol. XXVI, Part One, pp. 525–526.

7. *New York Times* for June 2, 1863, printing a dispatch dated "In Rear of Vicksburg," May 24; *New York World* of June 22, with a dispatch dated at Walnut Hills, June 14.

8. Wilson, *Under the Old Flag*, Vol. I, pp. 182–183.

9. Winchester Hall, *The Story of the 26th Louisiana Infantry*, citing a report by Brigadier General Francis L. Shoup. For Pemberton's numbers, see O. R., Vol. XXIV, Part Three, pp. 929–930, 978, 1000.

10. Ord's corps: *Army Life*, June 22; O. R., Vol. XXIV, Part Two, p. 175.

11. George Cooke, *The 21st Iowa Volunteer Infantry*; Isaac H. Elliott and Virgil G. Way, *History of the 33rd Regiment Illinois Veteran Volunteer Infantry*, p. 45; *Story of the Service of Company E. and of the 12th Wisconsin Regiment, written by One of the Boys*, p. 196; Ms. letters of Abram S. Funk, of the 35th Iowa; Ms. letter of Richard Puffer of the 8th Illinois, in the Chicago Historical Society; Newsome, *Experience in the War*, p. 63.

12. Alonzo L. Brown, *History of the 4th Regiment of Minnesota Infantry Volunteers*, p. 230; J. T. Woods, *Services of the 96th Ohio*, p. 30; *Anecdotes of General Grant*, quoting a writer for the *Indianapolis News*. Like the Army of Northern Virginia, which on occasion shouted "Lee to the rear!" the Army of the Tennessee had protective instincts concerning its commanding general; it just took a different way of showing them.

13. Grant's "The Vicksburg Campaign," pp. 524–526; Captain Jacob S. Wilken, in *Military Essays and Recollections*, Vol. IV, p. 234; Ms. letter of Richard Puffer, as cited in Note 11.

14. Sherman to Grant, O. R., Vol. XXIV, Part Two, p. 247; Grant to Sherman, Vol. XXIV, Part Three, p. 449.

15. The Cadwallader story, which is found in his *Three Years with Grant*, pp. 103–109, has stirred up much controversy. A vigorous discussion of the story's credibility, or lack of it, carried on by Benjamin P. Thomas and Kenneth P. Williams, can be found in *American Heritage*, Vol. VII, No. 5, pp. 106–111. Dana, in his *Recollections*, refers to Grant's trip up the river, says that he himself went with him, and mentions that Grant was ill; the reference to the illness may or may not have been a polite euphemism, but Dana's account of other details of the trip is different from Cadwallader's. To this writer the decisive point is the Rawlins letter, and its endorsement; if Cadwallader is to be believed, Rawlins could not possibly have written that letter. This letter and its endorsement appear in an address given on December 8, 1891, before the Minnesota Commandery, Military

Order of the Loyal Legion of the United States, by Captain John M. Shaw, printed in *Glimpses of the Nation's Struggle,* Vol. III, pp. 393–394.

16. The story is found in John B. McMaster's *The Life, Memoirs, Military Career and Death of General Grant.*

17. *B. & L.,* Vol. III, p. 522, 524–545.

18. O. R., Vol. XXIV, Part Three, Pemberton to Johnston, June 23, p. 974; Johnston to Pemberton, June 27, p. 980.

19. Letter of U. S. Grant to George G. Pride, dated June 15, 1863, in the George G. Pride Collection at the Missouri Historical Society. In mid-June, Frank Blair noted that the lines were so close that "I pitched a clod of dirt into one of their bastions from a point which we can reach without exposure." (Letter of June 16 to Montgomery Blair, in the Blair Papers, Library of Congress.)

20. Dana to Stanton, May 24, O. R., Vol. XXIV, Part One, p. 87.

21. Wilson, *Under the Old Flag,* Vol. I, pp. 184–186; Wilson's *Life of John A. Rawlins,* pp. 133–134. The order of dismissal appears in O. R., Vol. XXIV, Part One, pp. 164–165.

22. O. R., Vol. XXIV, Part One, p. 169 ff.

23. Grant's Memoirs, Vol. I, p. 541.

24. *Sherman, Fighting Prophet,* p. 288. For instances of fraternization, see *This Hallowed Ground,* pp. 262–263.

25. Greene, pp. 197–198; Grant's Memoirs, Vol. I, pp. 551–553.

26. O. R., Vol. XXIV, Part Two, pp. 190–192.

27. A useful summary of Johnston's moves and plans at this time is to be found in *A Different Valor,* pp. 213–214. For graphic reports on the conditions of Pemberton's troops, see O. R., Vol. XXIV, Part Two, pp. 347–349, 368, 377–378, 382–383.

28. Grant's Memoirs, Vol. I, pp. 556–557. It might be remarked that General Bowen had done much of the fighting at Champion's Hill and had been very active in the defense of Vicksburg itself.

CHAPTER TWENTY-THREE

Sling the Knapsack for New Fields

1. This account of the meeting follows Grant's version in *B. & L.,* Vol. III, pp. 530–532. See also Dana, *Recollections,* pp. 95–97. Pemberton's account of the meeting, differing somewhat from Grant's, is in *B. & L.,* Vol. III, pp. 543–545. In the John Page Nicholson Collection at the Huntington Library, there is a letter which Pemberton wrote to Col. Nicholson on June 12, 1875, in which Pemberton said that it was Grant, rather than Bowen, who kept the conference alive when Pemberton turned to go away. At Grant's suggestion, said Pemberton, two Union and two Confederate officers informally worked out terms while Grant and Pemberton stood aside, "con-

versing only upon topics which had no relation to the important
subject that brought us together." Pemberton added that "there was
no display of indifference by General Grant as to the result of this
interview — nor did he feel indifferent."

2. Letter of Richard Puffer, of the 8th Illinois.
3. For Northern references to the parole problem, see O.R., Series
   Three, Vol. IV, pp. 570, 576, 596, 644; Vol. V, p. 374.
4. Grant's account of the conference is in *B. & L.*, Vol. III, p. 532. See
   also O. R., Vol. XXIV, Part Three, p. 460; Dana, *Recollections,* p. 97.
5. Grant in *B. & L.*, Vol. III, pp. 532–533.
6. Grant, *B. & L.*, Vol. III, p. 533; letter from Grant to an unidentified
   correspondent, undated but written during the summer of 1863, in
   the Chicago Historical Society Collection.
7. Sherman to Grant, July 4, O. R., Vol. XXIV, Part Three, p. 472.
   Grant's messages to Sherman are in the same volume, pp. 460–461.
   The account of his exchange with Pemberton, regarding modifica-
   tion of the terms, follows Grant, *B. & L.*, Vol. III, p. 533. His orders
   regarding the occupation of Vicksburg are in O. R., Vol. XXIV, Part
   Three, pp. 479, 483, 484.
8. O. R., Vol. XXIV, Part Two, pp. 190–192.
9. *Under the Old Flag,* Vol. I, pp. 222–223; Porter to Grant, O. R.,
   Vol. XXIV, Part Three, p. 470; Badeau, Vol. I, p. 387.
10. Badeau, Vol. I, p. 388; *New York Times* for June 1, 1863, reprinting
    a dispatch in the *St. Louis Republican.*
11. The exchange of messages in respect to slaves is in O. R., Vol. XXIV,
    Part Three, pp. 479, 483, 484.
12. *A Different Valor,* p. 126; O. R., Vol. XXIV, Part Three, pp. 546,
    1010.
13. O. R., Vol. XXIV, Part Three, p. 534; *A Different Valor,* pp. 220–
    221.
14. *B. & L.*, Vol. III, pp. 492, 536; Major George H. Heafford, "The
    Army of the Tennessee," in Vol. I, *War Papers* of the Wisconsin
    Commandery, Loyal Legion, p. 313; *New York Tribune* for July
    15, 1863, printing a Vicksburg dispatch dated July 4.
15. Badeau, Vol. I, pp. 388, 409–410; O. R., Vol. XXIV, Part Three, pp.
    546–547.
16. O. R., Vol. XXIV, Part Three, p. 587.
17. *Anecdotes of General Grant,* pp. 42–43; Captain Jacob S. Wilken,
    in *Military Essays and Recollections,* Vol. IV, p. 223.
18. Rear Admiral Daniel Ammen, *The Old Navy and the New,* p. 383.
19. Excerpt from a sketch written by Julia Dent Grant, printed in the
    Chicago Sunday Tribune of December 14, 1902.
20. O. R., Vol. XXIV, Part Three, pp. 498, 547. Promotion in the Regu-
    lar service was of enormous importance to all Regular Army officers
    in the Civil War. Commissions in the Volunteer service would of
    course lapse when the war ended, and a major general might go back

to captain's rank, overnight — a thing which finally happened to several soldiers of real distinction. A man who won a general's commission in the Regular service could go his way knowing that his professional career was assured. To put the matter on an extremely practical basis, he would not need to look on the coming of peace as a disaster to his own personal fortunes.

21. Basler, *Collected Works*, Vol. VI, p. 326. The letter is dated July 13, 1863.

Bibliography

Manuscript Sources

U. S. Grant Papers in the Missouri Historical Society.
U. S. Grant Papers in the Illinois State Historical Library.
Letters of U. S. Grant to General James B. McPherson, in the Rutgers University Library.
Memoirs written by Julia Dent Grant, in the possession of a descendant.
Elihu B. Washburne Papers, in the Library of Congress.
William T. Sherman Papers, in the Library of Congress.
Letter of General Sherman to Mrs. Sherman, loaned by Miss E. Sherman Fitch; in the Lloyd Lewis Papers.
W. T. Sherman Papers, in the Huntington Library.
The R. T. Lincoln Collection, in the Library of Congress.
Manuscript Memoir of General John C. Frémont, in the Bancroft Library, University of California.
The George G. Pride Collection, in the Missouri Historical Society.
Papers of General Charles F. Smith, loaned by W. Terry Oliver, of Glenbrook, Connecticut.
Joseph Kirkland Papers, in the Newberry Library, Chicago.
Edwin M. Stanton Papers, in the Library of Congress.
The DeCoppett Collection, Princeton University Library.
Ethan Allen Hitchcock Diaries, in the Gilcrease Museum, Tulsa, Oklahoma.
Ms. Diary of General Jacob Ammen, in the Illinois State Historical Library.
Papers of Senator James R. Doolittle, in the State Historical Library, Madison, Wisconsin.
Ms. Biography of General John A. McClernand, by General Edward J. McClernand, in the Illinois State Historical Library.
The John Page Nicholson Collection, at the Huntington Library.
Blair Family Papers, in the Library of Congress.
Letters of General Lew Wallace, in the Palmer Collection, Western Reserve Historical Society.
Regimental Order Book of the 21st Illinois, in the National Archives.
Letter of General N. J. T. Dana, in the Huntington Library.
Ms. Letter of Richard Puffer of the 8th Illinois, in the Chicago Historical Society.
Biography of Major General Grenville M. Dodge: typescript in the Iowa State Department of History and Archives.

The Oliver Barrett Collection.
Civil War Reminiscences of Dr. John Cooper; manuscript loaned by Harley Bronson Cooper of Lynbrook, New York.
Letters of George L. Lang, of the 12th Wisconsin; loaned by Stanley Barnett of Cleveland.
Letters of Isaac Jackson of the 83rd Ohio; loaned by J. O. Jackson of Detroit.
Letters of Abram S. Funk of the 35th Iowa; loaned by Mrs. Erie M. Funk of Long Beach, California.

NEWSPAPERS AND MAGAZINES

Use was made of numerous newspaper and magazine files. Many of these were in the immense set of newspaper clippings collected by Lloyd Lewis; others were consulted in various libraries. Newspapers and magazines quoted in the text include:

St. Louis Globe-Democrat, Missouri Republican, New York Tribune, New York Herald, New York Times, New York World, Washington Post, Galena Northwestern Gazette, Cincinnati Commercial, Chicago Times, Chicago Tribune, Chicago Journal, National Tribune and *National Republican.*

Also *McClure's Magazine, Army and Navy Journal, Midland Monthly, Journal of the Military Service Institution of the United States, Iowa Historical Record, Journal of the Illinois State Historical Society, Proceedings of the Massachusetts Historical Society, North American Review, Ohio Archaeological and Historical Quarterly, Journal of Southern History, Chicago Forum* and *American Heritage.*

BOOKS

A principal reliance in any study of the Civil War is of course the massive War Department compendium, "The War of the Rebellion: A Compilation of the Official Records of the Union and Confederate Armies." This is cited in the footnotes simply as O.R.; unless otherwise specified, the volumes used are from Series One. Use has also been made of the companion "Official Records of the Union and Confederate Navies during the War of the Rebellion."
Other books consulted include the following:

BOOKS RELATING DIRECTLY TO GRANT

Adam Badeau, *Military History of Ulysses S. Grant.* 3 vols. New York, 1868.
Sylvanus Cadwallader, *Three Years with Grant,* edited by Benjamin P. Thomas. New York, 1955.
William Conant Church, *Ulysses S. Grant and the Period of National Preservation and Reconstruction.* New York, 1897.

A. L. Conger, *The Rise of U. S. Grant.* New York, 1931.
Louis A. Coolidge, *Ulysses S. Grant.* Boston and New York, 1917.
Henry Coppee, *Life and Services of General U. S. Grant.* Chicago, 1868.
Jesse Grant Cramer, ed., *Letters of Ulysses S. Grant to his Father and his Youngest Sister.* New York, 1912.
Nelson Cross, *The Modern Ulysses, LL.D.; His Political Record.* New York, 1872.
Wilbur F. Crummer, *With Grant at Fort Donelson, Shiloh and Vicksburg.* Oak Park, Ill., 1915.
Charles A. Dana and James H. Wilson, *The Life of Ulysses S. Grant.* Springfield, 1868.
John Eaton, *Grant, Lincoln and the Freedmen.* New York, 1907.
J. F. C. Fuller, *The Generalship of Ulysses S. Grant.* London, 1929.
Hamlin Garland, *Ulysses S. Grant; his Life and Character.* New York, 1898.
U. S. Grant, *Personal Memoirs of U. S. Grant.* 2 vols. New York, 1885.
William B. Hesseltine, *Ulysses S. Grant, Politician.* New York, 1935.
Lloyd Lewis, *Captain Sam Grant.* Boston, 1950.
John B. McMaster, *The Life, Memoirs, Military Career and Death of General Grant.* Philadelphia, 1885.
General Horace Porter, *Campaigning with Grant.* New York, 1897.
Albert D. Richardson, *A Personal History of Ulysses S. Grant.* Hartford, 1868.
J. L. Ringwalt, *Anecdotes of General Grant.* Philadelphia, 1886.
James Grant Wilson, *The Life and Campaigns of General Grant.* New York, 1897.
——, ed., *General Grant's Letters to a Friend, 1861–1880.* New York, 1897.
John Russell Young, *Around the World with General Grant.* 2 vols. New York, 1879.

GENERAL WORKS

Rear Admiral Daniel Ammen, *The Old Navy and the New.* Philadelphia, 1891.
Roy Basler, ed., *The Collected Works of Abraham Lincoln.* 8 vols. Rutgers, New Jersey, 1953.
D. Alexander Brown, *Grierson's Raid.* Urbana, Illinois, 1954.
Bruce Catton, *This Hallowed Ground.* New York, 1956.
Augustus L. Chetlain, *Recollections of Seventy Years.* Galena, Illinois, 1899.
Dudley Taylor Cornish, *The Sable Arm: Negro Troops in the Union Army, 1861–1865.* New York, 1956.
Jacob D. Cox, *Military Reminiscences of the Civil War.* 2 vols. New York, 1900.
Emmet Crozier, *Yankee Reporters, 1861–65.* New York, 1956.
Charles A. Dana, *Recollections of the Civil War.* New York, 1902.

Major General Grenville Dodge, *Personal Recollections*. Council Bluffs, Iowa, 1914.

David Donald, ed., *Inside Lincoln's Cabinet: The Civil War Diaries of Salmon P. Chase*. New York and London, 1954.

Clement Eaton, *A History of the Southern Confederacy*. New York, 1954.

M. F. Force, *From Fort Henry to Corinth*. New York, 1882.

Gustavus V. Fox, *Confidential Correspondence of G. V. Fox, 1861–65*. 2 vols. New York, 1920.

Jessie Benton Frémont, *The Story of the Guard; a Chronicle of the War*. Boston, 1863.

H. Allen Gosnell, *Guns on the Western Waters: The Story of River Gunboats in the Civil War*. Baton Rouge, 1949.

Gilbert Govan and James W. Livingood, *A Different Valor: The Story of General Joseph E. Johnston, C.S.A.* Indianapolis, 1956.

Francis Vinton Greene, *The Mississippi*. New York, 1884.

Matilda Gresham, *The Life of Walter Quintin Gresham*. 2 vols. Chicago, 1919.

M. B. Hammond, *The Cotton Industry: An Essay in American Economic History*. New York, 1892.

Francis B. Heitman, *Historical Register and Dictionary of the United States Army*. 2 vols. Washington, 1903.

Robert Selph Henry, *First with the Most: Forrest*. Indianapolis, 1944.

———, *The Story of the Confederacy*. Indianapolis, 1931.

Stanley Horn, *The Army of Tennessee*. Indianapolis, 1941.

M. A. DeWolfe Howe, ed., *Home Letters of General Sherman*. New York, 1909.

Gaillard Hunt, *Israel, Elihu and Cadwallader Washburne: A Chapter in American Biography*. New York, 1925.

R. U. Johnson and C. C. Buel, eds., *Battles and Leaders of the Civil War*. 4 vols. New York, 1884–1887.

Lloyd Lewis, *Sherman, Fighting Prophet*. New York, 1932.

T. J. Lindsay, *Ohio at Shiloh: Report of the Commission*. Cincinnati, 1903.

T. L. Livermore, *Numbers and Losses in the Civil War*. Boston and New York, 1900.

A. T. Mahan, *The Gulf and Inland Waters*. New York, 1883.

George B. McClellan, *McClellan's Own Story*. New York, 1887.

Alexander K. McClure, *Recollections of Half a Century*. Philadelphia, 1892.

———, *Abraham Lincoln and Men of War Time*. Philadelphia, 1892.

A. Howard Meneely, *The War Department, 1861: A Study in Mobilization and Administration*. New York, 1928.

Allan Nevins, *Frémont: Pathmarker of the West*. New York and London, 1939.

John C. Pemberton, *Pemberton, Defender of Vicksburg*. Chapel Hill, 1944.

Admiral David Porter, *Incidents and Anecdotes of the Civil War*. New York, 1885.

Benjamin A. Quarles, *The Negro in the Civil War*. Boston, 1953.

Charles W. Ramsdell, *Behind the Lines in the Southern Confederacy*. Baton Rouge, 1944.

Whitelaw Reid, *Ohio in the War; her Statesmen, her Generals and Soldiers*. 2 vols. Cincinnati, 1868.

Carl Sandburg, *Abraham Lincoln: The War Years*. 4 vols. New York, 1939.

Lieutenant General John M. Schofield, *Forty-six Years in the Army*. New York, 1897.

William F. G. Shanks, *Personal Recollections of Distinguished Generals*. New York, 1866.

Fred A. Shannon, *The Organization and Administration of the Union Army, 1861–1865*. 2 vols. Cleveland, 1928.

General Philip Sheridan, *Personal Memoirs of P. H. Sheridan*. 2 vols. New York, 1891.

General W. T. Sherman, *The Memoirs of Gen. William T. Sherman*. 2 vols. New York, 1893.

Theodore Clarke Smith, *The Life and Letters of James A. Garfield*. 2 vols. New Haven, 1925.

Arndt M. Stickles, *Simon Bolivar Buckner*. Chapel Hill, 1940.

Benjamin P. Thomas, *Abraham Lincoln*. New York, 1952.

Rachel Sherman Thorndike, ed., *The Sherman Letters; Correspondence between General and Senator Sherman from 1837 to 1891*. New York, 1894.

Thomas B. Van Horne, *History of the Army of the Cumberland*. 2 vols. Cincinnati, 1875.

Lew Wallace, *An Autobiography*. 2 vols. New York and London, 1906.

George W. Williams, *A History of the Negro Troops in the War of the Rebellion*. New York, 1888.

Kenneth P. Williams, *Lincoln Finds a General*. 4 vols. New York, 1950–1956.

T. Harry Williams, *P. G. T. Beauregard: Napoleon in Gray*. Baton Rouge, 1954.

James H. Wilson, *Under the Old Flag*. 2 vols. New York, 1912.

——, *The Life of John A. Rawlins*. New York, 1916.

REGIMENTAL HISTORIES, SOLDIERS' MEMOIRS, PERSONAL REMINISCENCES, etc.

In an attempt to simplify the reader's search for the account of a given unit, these are listed by titles rather than by the names of the authors.

The Annals of the War, written by Leading Participants. Philadelphia, 1879.

Army Life of an Illinois Soldier: Letters and Diaries of the late Charles H. Wills, compiled and published by his Sister. Washington, 1906.

Army Life: from a Soldier's Journal, by A. O. Marshall. Joliet, Illinois, 1884.

Army Memoirs of Lucius W. Barber, Company D, 15th Illinois Infantry. Chicago, 1894.

An Artilleryman's Diary, by Jenkin Lloyd Jones. Madison, Wisconsin, 1914.

A Battery at Close Quarters, by Captain Henry Neil; pamphlet of paper read before the Ohio Commandery, Military Order of the Loyal Legion of the United States. N.p.,n.d.

Campaigns and Battles of the 12th Iowa Infantry, by Major David Reed. Evanston, Illinois, 1903.

Civil War Papers, read before the Commandery of the State of Massachusetts, Military Order of the Loyal Legion of the United States. 2 vols. Boston, 1900.

A Corporal's Story: Experiences in the Ranks of Company C, 81st Ohio Volunteer Infantry, by Charles W. Wright. Philadelphia, 1887.

Downing's War Diary, by Sergeant Alexander Downing, edited by Olynthus B. Clark. Des Moines, 1916.

Events of the Civil War, by General Edward Bouton. Los Angeles, 1906.

Experiences in the War of the Great Rebellion, by Edmund Newsome. Carbondale, Illinois, 1876.

Fifteen Years Ago: or, the Patriotism of Will County, by George H. Woodruff. Joliet, 1876.

Fifth Annual Reunion of the Ninth Illinois Regiment Veteran Volunteer Association. Pamphlet. 1885.

The 15th Ohio Volunteers and its Campaigns, War of 1861–65, by Alexis Coupe. Columbus, Ohio, 1916.

The 41st Ohio Veteran Volunteer Infantry, by R. L. Kimberly and Ephraim S. Holloway. Cleveland, 1897.

The 44th Indiana Volunteers in the Rebellion, by J. H. Rerick. Lagrange, Indiana, 1880.

Glimpses of the Nation's Struggle: a series of Papers read before the Minnesota Commandery, Military Order of the Loyal Legion of the United States. 6 vols. St. Paul and Minneapolis, 1887–1909.

History of Alexander, Union and Pulaski Counties, Illinois, edited by William Henry Perrin. Chicago, 1883.

History of the 15th Regiment Iowa Veteran Volunteer Infantry, by William W. Belknap. Keokuk, Iowa, 1887.

History of Company A, Second Illinois Cavalry, by Samuel Fletcher. N.p.,n.d.

History of the 4th Illinois Cavalry Regiment, by P. O. Avery. Humboldt, Nebraska, 1903.

History of the 53rd Regiment Ohio Volunteer Infantry, by John K. Duke. Portsmouth, Ohio, 1900.

A History of the Ninth Regiment Illinois Volunteer Infantry, by Marion Morrison. Monmouth, Illinois, 1864.

History of the Sixth Iowa Infantry, by Henry H. Wright. Iowa City, 1923.

History of the 51st Indiana Veteran Volunteer Infantry, by William R. Hartpence. Cincinnati, 1894.

History of the Sixth Regiment Indiana Veteran Volunteer Infantry, by C. C. Briant. Indianapolis, 1891.

History of the 68th Regiment Indiana Volunteer Infantry, by Edwin W. High. Metamora, Ind., 1902.

History of the 50th Regiment Illinois Volunteer Infantry, by Charles F. Hubert. Kansas City, 1894.

History of Fuller's Ohio Brigade, by Charles H. Smith. Cleveland, 1909.

History of the 21st Regiment Ohio Volunteer Infantry, by Captain S. S. Canfield, Toledo, 1893.

History of the 78th Regiment Ohio Veteran Volunteer Infantry, by the Rev. Thomas M. Stevenson. Zanesville, Ohio, 1865.

History of the Second Iowa Cavalry, by Lyman B. Pierce. Burlington, Iowa, 1865.

History of the Seventh Regiment Illinois Volunteer Infantry, by D. Lieb Ambrose. Springfield, Illinois, 1868.

History of the 77th Illinois Volunteer Infantry, by Lieutenant W. H. Bentley. Peoria, Illinois, 1883.

History of the 83rd Regiment Indiana Volunteer Infantry, by Joseph Grecian. Cincinnati, 1865.

History of the 16th Battery of Ohio Volunteer Light Artillery, compiled by a committee. N.p., 1906.

History of the 33rd Regiment Illinois Veteran Volunteer Infantry, by Isaac H. Elliott and Virgil G. Way. Gibson City, Illinois, 1902.

History of the Fourth Regiment of Minnesota Infantry Volunteers, by Alonzo H. Brown. St. Paul, 1892.

Letters from the Army, by B. F. Stevenson. Cincinnati, 1884.

Lights and Shadows of Army Life, by the Rev. W. W. Lyle. Cincinnati, 1865.

Marching Through Georgia, by F. Y. Hedley. Chicago, 1890.

Memoir of George Boardman Boomer, by Amelia M. Stone. Boston, 1864.

Memoirs of the War, by Captain Ephraim A. Wilson. Cleveland, 1893.

Memoirs of a Volunteer, by John Beatty, edited by Henry S. Ford. New York, 1946.

Military Essays and Recollections: Papers read before the Commandery of the State of Illinois, Military Order of the Loyal Legion of the United States. 4 vols. Chicago, 1894–1907.

Muskets and Medicine; or, Army Life in the Sixties, by Charles Beneulyn Johnson, M.D. Philadelphia, 1917.

Opening of the Mississippi; or, Two Years Campaigning in the Southwest, by George W. Driggs. Madison, Wisconsin, 1864.

Papers of the Kansas Commandery, Military Order of the Loyal Legion of the United States. Leavenworth, 1894.

Pen and Powder, by Franc B. Wilkie. Boston, 1888.

Personal Memoirs of John H. Brinton, Major and Surgeon, U.S.V., 1861–1865. New York, 1914.

Personal Recollections of the War of the Rebellion: Addresses delivered before the New York Commandery, Military Order of the Loyal Legion of the United States. 3 vols. New York, 1891.

The Pictorial Book of Anecdotes and Incidents of the War of the Rebellion, by Richard Miller Devens. Hartford and Philadelphia, 1867.

Printed Proceedings of the Society of the Army of the Tennessee; pamphlets covering meetings in the years 1866, 1885, 1897, 1906, 1907.

Proceedings of the Reunion of Taylor's Battery. Chicago, 1890.

Recollections with the Third Iowa Regiment, by S. W. Thompson. Cincinnati, 1864.

Recollections of Pioneer and Army Life, by Lieutenant Matthew H. Jamison. Kansas City, 1911.

Recollections of the Civil War, by Oran Perry. Pamphlet in the Lloyd Lewis papers.

Reminiscences of the Civil War; from the Diaries of Members of the 103rd Illinois Volunteer Infantry, compiled by a committee. Chicago, 1904.

Reminiscences of an Octogenarian Hungarian Refugee, by Major Julian Kune. Chicago, 1911.

Ninth Reunion of Iowa Hornet's Nest Brigade. N.p., 1912.

Services of the 96th Ohio Volunteers, by J. T. Woods. Toledo, 1874.

Sketches of War History, 1861–1865: Papers read before the Ohio Commandery, Military Order of the Loyal Legion of the United States. 5 vols. Cincinnati, 1888–1903.

The Story of a Common Soldier of Army Life in the Civil War, by Leander Stillwell. Erie, Kansas, 1920.

The Story of the Sherman Brigade, by Wilbur F. Hinman. Alliance, Ohio, 1897.

The Story of a Thousand: being a History of the Service of the 105th Ohio Volunteer Infantry, by Albion W. Tourgee. Buffalo, 1896.

The Story of the 55th Regiment Illinois Volunteer Infantry, by a committee. Clinton, Massachusetts, 1887.

Story of the Service of Company E and of the 12th Wisconsin Regiment, written by One of the Boys. Milton, Wisconsin, 1893.

The Story of the 26th Louisiana Infantry, by Winchester Hall. N.p., 1890.

My Story of the Civil War, by Mary Livermore. Hartford, 1888.

The Secret Service, the Field, the Dungeon and the Escape, by Albert D. Richardson. Hartford, 1865.

A Soldier of the Cumberland, by Mead Holmes, Jr. Boston, c.1864.

The Thirty-fifth Ohio Regiment: A Narrative of Service, by F. W. Keil. Fort Wayne, 1894.

The Twenty-first Iowa Volunteer Infantry, compiled by George Cooke. Milwaukee, 1891.

Tramps and Triumphs of the Second Iowa Infantry, by John T. Bell. Omaha, 1866.

War Diary of Brevet Brigadier General Joseph Stockton. Pamphlet. Chicago, 1910.

War Pictures, by the Rev. J. B. Rogers. Chicago, 1863.

War Papers read before the Commandery of the State of Wisconsin, Military Order of the Loyal Legion of the United States. Milwaukee, 1891.

War Papers and Personal Reminiscences, 1861–1865: Papers read before the Commandery of the State of Missouri, Military Order of the Loyal Legion of the United States. St. Louis, 1892.

War Papers read before the Commandery of the State of Maine, Military Order of the Loyal Legion of the United States. Portland, 1898.

War Papers read before the Indiana Commandery, Military Order of the Loyal Legion of the United States. Indianapolis, 1898.

War Memoranda, by Colonel Charles Whittlesey. Cleveland, 1884.

War Sketches and Incidents: Papers of the Iowa Commandery, Military Order of the Loyal Legion of the United States. 2 vols. Des Moines, 1898.

Acknowledgments

In making proper acknowledgment of the help which was so generously given to me by so many people while this book was in preparation, I must mention first of all Mrs. Kathryn Lewis, who made available the invaluable files of notes collected over many years by her husband, the late Lloyd Lewis. These files provided the foundation on which the book was written, and to work with them was a most rewarding experience. I am profoundly grateful to Mrs. Lewis.

In the course of his researches, Lewis interviewed many people and was given access to private letters and documents. An attempt has been made to give proper credit to these people in the various footnote citations, and if any have been omitted the fault is my own and an all-inclusive apology is hereby offered.

A writer of a book of this kind usually does not realize the extent of his indebtedness to others until he begins to make a list of those who have helped him. Those who are named here have been uncommonly generous with their time and with their knowledge, and I thank all of them.

Allan Nevins read the manuscript and made many suggestions which were of much value to me. He also made available much material bearing on the Missouri command of Major General John C. Frémont.

E. B. Long also read the manuscript and provided help in ways too numerous to specify. I am especially indebted to him and to his wife Barbara for supplying material for the maps which are printed with the text.

Ralph Newman of Chicago was still another who undertook the task of reading the manuscript. There were times when his Abraham Lincoln Book Shop was a sort of task force headquarters for my labors.

Paul Angle of the Chicago Historical Society helped me to find material which I needed.

Clyde Walton of the Illinois State Historical Library was similarly helpful in respect to the resources of that institution.

Colonel Willard Webb of the Library of Congress directed me to certain books which I would not have found unaided.

Edwin C. Bearss, research historian at the Vicksburg National Military Park, read the portion of the manuscript which deals with the Vicksburg campaign and saved me from the commission of a great number of errors.

Harvey Snitiker of Brooklyn was an exceptionally able and industrious research assistant.

Victor Gondos of the National Archives conducted many searches through the files for material bearing on Grant, on Halleck and on the 21st Illinois Infantry.

Stanley Horn of Nashville, from the depth of his knowledge of the Confederate Army of Tennessee, saved me (I trust) from making an egregious misappraisal of the qualities of that gallant army.

W. Terry Oliver of Glenbrook, Connecticut, made available to me the valuable papers left by Major General Charles F. Smith.

Earl Schenck Miers of Edison, New Jersey, helped me arrive at a better understanding of Grant and of the Mississippi Valley campaign.

Harley Bronson Cooper of Lynbrook, New York, let me borrow and use the manuscript memoirs of Dr. John Cooper.

Major General U. S. Grant III shared with me his reminiscences and the family traditions regarding his distinguished grandfather.

Miss Louise Lewis of Chicago gave up a day of her time to make a last-minute search for material in the newspaper files of the Newberry Library.

Stanley Barnett of Cleveland loaned me the Civil War letters of George L. Lang of the 12th Wisconsin.

J. O. Jackson of Detroit permitted me to borrow the letters of Isaac Jackson of the 83rd Ohio.

Mrs. Erie M. Funk of Long Beach, California, loaned me the letters of Abram S. Funk of the 35th Iowa.

B.C.

Index